Introduction

Welcome to 'Today's The Day', a unique book which takes an in-depth look into Birmingham City Football Club on each particular day. The book lists the playing record of the club on each day including all the goal times for and against the Blues since 2 January 1950. Every competitive game is listed, including wartime League games and all the various cup competitions the Blues have been involved in over their 12_ year history. On each day where Birmingham have played at least five games (267 in all), statistics have been compiled to show the total matches and that day's success rate. The 267 days have then been ranked from the best day at number 1 – 1 March at 80.77%, to the worst day at 267 – 30 December at 17.86%. Where the success rates were the same for more than one day goal difference and then, if needed, the number of goals scored were taken into account. On six days; 1 January, 10 April, 3 September, 25 December, 26 December and 27 December, the number of games played exceeds 30, and therefore goal times have not been included in order to keep the lists to a reasonable size.

The book includes birth and death dates of many of the players which Blues have used over the years, as well as any other news relating to the club and players, including international appearances. The records of players contained in the book are correct up until the start of the 2002-03 season, as is all other information in the book.

There is a selected 'Match of the Day' for 266 days (with two on Boxing Day). At least one report comes from every decade from Birmingham's first Football League match in 1892 to the present day. Also, at least one report is from every year from 1950 to the present day. Therefore whatever the age of the supporter there will be a match report in this book recounting a memory that should be familiar, culminating, of course, with that dramatic penalty shoot-out win in Cardiff's Millennium Stadium on 12 May 2002.

Hope you enjoy the book 'Today's The Day - Birmingham City Football Club'.

THIS BOOK IS DEDICATED TO
Morgan and Evelyn Henry

AND IN MEMORY OF
Richard Brettle and Craig Beesley

Acknowledgements

First of all I would like to thank Roger Marshall, Paul Burns, Linda Perkins, Steve Parry, Chris Russell and all at Britespot Publishing Solutions Ltd for their confidence and help in making this book possible. I would also like to thank Ian Nannestad, Jim Cadman, Roy Smiljanic and Jen at Empics. It's the first time I have undertaken the writing of any publication and I will be forever grateful for the opportunity of producing this book on the team I have supported fanatically since boyhood.

Support for Birmingham City was instilled in me before I could even walk, so in the next group of people I would like to thank my father Kevin for dragging me down St Andrews to stand on the often cold, wet and usually overcrowded terraces on the Kop in the early 1970s, first and foremost. He knew then what I know now, that the experience would be treasured forever, thanks to his perseverance. During the course of writing the book I have been given fantastic support from all my family and friends namely Josie, Margaret, Robert, Emma, Danny, Francesca, Alan, Clare, Anthony, Carol, Darren, Marcus, Samantha, Cate, Ken, Jack, Daniel, Lennie, Roy, Steve, Pete, Janet, Jess Hardman, Steve Jinks, Mike Lees and Ross Collins. I would also like to thank the teachers and staff at St Thomas' CE Primary School, Great Colmore St, Birmingham.

The idea of writing about the Blues in this format was initiated via a fans' website message board two and a half years ago. Thanks to the kind messages of appreciation from the regular members on the forum, I decided to take their advice and put this into print. I would therefore like to thank the regulars, Graham (Pudsey), Blacksmith, Boise in Idaho, Leigh (In Leeds), Jani, Charles (the postman), Taz, Colin, Emma, Janet (In Tamworth), Chris, Phil Blue, Grant, Neil, Bulldog, Kirsty, Keith Wrighton, Ray Nolan and Stuart Wallington.

During the last year I worked tirelessly in writing out a synopsis and draft copy of the book, as well as spending many hours in researching the finished product once it was agreed the work would be published. Over the course of a busy year, and hectic summer I have had a tremendous amount of encouragement and well wishes from the management, staff and customers of The Raven public house, Weoley Castle, Birmingham. I would therefore like to thank my boss and colleagues, Jim, Trudy, James, Joanne, Sean and Christopher Leach, Angela Parry, Sue Dunn, Sue Bird, and Liz White. To the regular customers I would like to thank Brian Callaghan, Dave Howell and little Sophie, Paddy and Sheila Boyle, Peter Roberts, Martin and Jean Waller, Sue Melville, Kim and Tony Hamilton, Mick Daly, Dave Pollar, Tony and Sue Parsons, Andy, Lynn and Zoe Moore, Paul and Nicky Roberts, Wendy and Andy Parsons, Pauline, Ursula, Mick, Karen Franklin and Graham and Cale, Eric, George, Colleen, Suzie, Paul Ollie and Jack (and Grandpa John R.I.P.), Lee and Paul Beesley. Also to my friends and collegues at St Andrews many thanks go to fellow match day programme sellers John Hill, Chris, Sarah, Stuart, Bobby, Geoff, Andy, Ken, stadium announcer Keith Laurent and Ivan Barnsley of the club's historical society. My final thanks and go to three people who have helped over and beyond the above and, indeed, made the book possible. Firstly Steve Keating for his support. It must be said that if the club's owners continue to finance the team in the same manner Steve has helped me over the years, then we will not only be competing in the Premier League but actually winning it very soon.

Secondly my mother-in-law Carolyn Brettle who has helped from the outset, first finding potential publishers, to then sifting through my countless spelling errors in the "Match-of-the-Day" reports, the latter whilst trying to enjoy her well-earned summer holiday.

Finally the person who has made it all possible. I had a busy year, then this lady has surely done it all. Moving house in March, giving birth to our gorgeous daughter Evelyn in April, and playing sole parent, due to my many hours spent at the library, to our son Morgan. Add to this the stats she has meticulously compiled which have been the basis of the book, and the fact she has helped write many of the reports herself. Still finding time to sift through my notorious spelling and grammar errors, and yet still remain the perfect wife I am so very forunate to have, a conclusion I came to long before this publication got off the ground. She has been inspirational, and without Jennifer this book could not have been published. My love and thanks go to Jen, and hopefully now I can get back to being a half decent husband and father again.

Foreword

It gives me pleasure to be associated with this book, '*Today's The Day - Birmingham City FC*', recapturing the many memorable days over this great clubs 127 year history.

Over the years that I have been with this club, I have enjoyed many fantastic days which are featured in the book, Auto Windscreens Shield win at Wembley in 1995, our promotion to the 1st Division and the great Worthington Cup victories on our way to that classic final with Liverpool in 2001 and of course the magnificent penalty shoot out win which put the club back in English footballs elite league for the first time in over 16 years. These treasured and unforgettable days are highlighted in the book through the match of the day report.

The club has had many thrilling triumphs in its history and all are covered in this 366 day diary which has plotted every game since the first major league encounter back in 1892.

As Chairman of Birmingham City Football Club, my Board and I will continue to support the club as it embarks on its biggest challenge to date, the first season in the Premier League. With continued support from all connected with the club it is hoped that many more memorable days are just around the corner in Birmingham City Football Club's future.

The Blues are on their way...

David Gold

Chairman of Birmingham City Football Club

Playing record for this day

Playing record for this day...32 games,Won 7, Drawn 8, Lost 17, GF 39, GA 57.

Todays success rate 34.38% Year Ranking....252nd

January 1

Match of the Day

FROM 1985

BLADES SHAVED BY BLUES

A Happy New Year as Blues claim first Bramall Lane win in 12 years

The New Year got off to a very happy and thrilling start for the Blues after some high drama in Sheffield. Seven goals, plenty of incident, and two welcome points away from home, and in fabulous style too. Blues came back from 2-0 down to make clear their intentions for promotion. Four second half goals in 16 minutes for Blues gave them a well deserved victory, four days after United beat Portsmouth 4-1 at the same ground. It was Blues ninth away win of the season, and showed without a doubt that they have the ability and determination to succeed.

Ron Saunders' side were battling against a tight Blades defence, and it took a scoreless first half to bring about the rewards for their efforts. However at the other end, Sheffield winger Colin Morris won a free kick in the 54th minute, and Tom Heffernan converted it into a goal with a perfectly measured header.

Just three minutes later it looked as if Blues would have to admit defeat, when ex-Villa captain Dennis Mortimer produced a smashing through ball to Morris, who passed on to Keith Edwards who swept it into the goal for number two.

In the 62nd minute, Blues staged an amazing comeback, with Robert Hopkins beginning the fight back with a superb volley which flew into the net from 15 yards. Then just four minutes later Hopkins turned provider, touching the ball down for Nicky Platnauer, and on to David Geddis, who turned in his fourth goal in as many games.

Sheffield United were now understandably shell shocked and worried. From being comfortably in the lead, they were now level, and Blues were in total control. The pressure was on, and they just couldn't live up to the expectations of their fans. Hopkins was again responsible for providing the last two goals as Blues continued to dominate the game. Firstly his inch-perfect cross floated over to Wayne Clarke on 73 minutes, was headed home with ease. Then five minutes later Gary West could do nothing to prevent an unfortunate deflection on another Hopkins cross, which resulted in an own goal past his despairing keeper and former Villa player John Burridge.

There was yet more incident in this action-packed thriller when Brian Roberts felled Morris in the penalty area. The referee duly awarded the spotkick, and the winger quickly got up to take it himself to give Sheffield some late hope with the score now 4-3. It wasn't enough, however, and the win desevedly went to Blues, the side who had given by far the better performance in a truly classic game.

BIRMINGHAM CITY   **REFEREE**

Seaman, Ranson, Roberts, Wright, Armstrong (Hagan), Daly, Platnauer, Clarke, Bremner, Geddis, Hopkins.   Mr Joe Worrall (Warrington)

SHEFFIELD UNITED

Burridge, Heffernan, Atkins, Mortimer, West, Thompson, Morris, Cockerill, Edwards, Eves, Arnott.

Robert Hopkins

Sadly Missed

Jack Badham died today in1992, aged 72

The Matches played on this day		
1897, Division 2		
Manchester City 3	Blues 0	Att. 16,000
1906, Division 1		
Bury 1	Blues 0	Att. 10,000
1907, Division 1		
Middlesbrough 1	Blues 0	Att. 10,000
1909, Division 2		
Bolton Wanderers 2	Blues 1	Att. 25,000
	Beer	
1910, Division 2		
Blues 0	WBA 1	Att. 15,500
1913, Division 2		
Bury 3	Blues 0	Att. 10,000
1914, Division 2		
Stockport County 2	Blues 0	Att. 6,000
1921, Division 2		
Leeds United 1	Blues 0	Att. 24,000
1924, Division 1		
Bolton Wanderers 1	Blues 1	Att. 30,000
	Cringan	
1925, Division 1		
Bolton Wanderers 3	Blues 0	Att.20,000
1926, Division 1		
Bolton Wanderers 5	Blues 3	Att.25,000
	Bradford(2),Harris	
1927, Division 1		
Blues 2	Leicester City 1	Att. 34,500
Bradford(2)		
1938, Division 1		
Blues 1	Stoke City 1	Att. 25,000
Jones		
1944, Wartime		
Blues 4	WBA 0	
Bright(2),Trigg		
Mulraney		
1949, Division 1		
Chelsea 2	Blues 0	Att. 28,850
1955, Division 2		
Rotherham United 0	Blues 2	Att. 17,000
	Kinsey, Govan	
1957, Division 1		
Newcastle United 3	Blues 2	Att. 29,383
	Brown, Govan	
1966, Division 2		
Norwich City 2	Blues 2	Att. 15,829
	Vowden, Fenton	

January 1

The Matches played on this day

1972, Division 2
Bristol City 1   Blues 0   Att. 17,457
A Goal from Galley three minutes before half time condems Blues to their last league defeat of the 1971/72 promotion season

1974, Division 1
Derby County 1   Blues 1   Att. 31,189
    Hatton

1980, Division 2
Blues 2   QPR 1   Att. 25,983
Ainscow, Gemmill

1983, Division 1
Blues 2   Manchester City 2   Att. 16,362
Fergusson(2)

1985, Division 2
Sheffield United 3   Blues 4   Att. 16,571
    Hopkins, Geddis, Clarke, West(og)

1986, Division 1
Manchester United 1   Blues 0   Att. 43,095

1987, Division 2
Blues 3   Plymouth Argyle 2   Att. 8,696
Kuhl, Clarke, Mortimer
Paul Hart on his debut, collided accidently with team-mate Tommy Williams. Hart broke his leg and never played for Blues again

1988, Division 2
Bournemouth 4   Blues 2   Att. 8,500
    Dicks, Wigley
1st league meeting against Bournemouth

1990, Division 3
Blues 1   Fulham 1   Att. 8,932
Gleghorn

1991, Division 3
Mansfield Town 1   Blues 2   Att. 3,652
    Gayle(2)

1992, Division 3
Blues 2   Hull City 2   Att. 12,983
Paskin, Gleghorn

1994, Division 1
Southend United 3   Blues 1   Att. 10,729
    Peschisolido

2001, Division 1
Blues 0   Nottingham Forest 2   Att. 20,034
Dave Beasant saves Martin Graingers early penalty with the score at 0-0

2002, Division 1
Blues 1   Nottingham Forest 1   Att. 19,770
Mooney

Jack Badham died today in 1992, aged 72. He was born in Birmingham and joined Blues from the Muntz St youth club as an amateur in July 1934. He turned professional in May 1946 after his service in the armed forces finished. He made 190 appearances for Blues as a full back however he was used in eight different position in his 23 year career at Blues. He scored four goals for the club.

Birthdays

Jon Bass born today in 1976

Playing record for this day

Playing record for this day is... 23 games, Won 6, Drawn 10, Lost 7, GF 33, GA 32.

Today's success rate....47.83%, Year Ranking....173rd

Match of the Day

FROM 1978

BLUES STUN THE REDS

Old Trafford silenced by Dillon and Francis goals

Blues' Kevin Dillon scored his first league goal for the club today against Manchester United, in front of a huge Old Trafford crowd of 53,501. United were hoping not to repeat Saturday's performance where they lost 3-0 to Coventry. Blues were hoping for their first away win since October in the local derby against Villa.

An early goal was what Blues were after as they came out and immediately put United under pressure. Their efforts were quickly rewarded with an early strike on12 minutes, after Manchester United's hopelessly timed offside trap had failed. Terry Hibbitt took advantage and raced from the halfway line down the right wing, his cross to Keith Bertschin was knocked down into the path of England international Trevor Francis, his shot was brilliantly parried by Roche, but the unfortunate United goalkeeper was unable to stop Dillon's follow up from close in tapping the ball into the back of the net.

Just seconds later and Blues had the opportunity to increase their lead, again thanks to Dillon, but his shot from inside the penalty area was rushed, and Roche was able to gather the ball cleanly on this occasion.

United's attempts came intermittently, with the most dangerous threat coming from Steve Coppell, but in truth they never really looked like scoring. Blues in contrast always looking likely to gain a second goal and held their 1-0 advantage comfortably. Typically then it was Birmingham who handed their hosts a generous lifeline when a mistake by defender Joe Gallagher who had until then played extremely well, led to the equaliser in the 19th minute. He sent a weak back-pass to goalkeeper Jim Montgomery, which lost pace in the deep mud allowing Jimmy Greenhoff to seize the golden opportunity and push the ball past the stranded Blues keeper.

Just three minutes later Francis regained Blues' lead with a top class strike which proved to be a worthy winner. Collecting a pass from Tony Towers, the Blues striker rushed through the United defence beating first Arthur Albiston, then Brian Greenhoff and Martin Buchan, before hitting a fierce right-footed shot which flew past Roche who stood no chance of stopping the ball.

Despite a slight rally from United their fight back consisted of Jimmy Greenhoff's five-yard shot which sailed harmlessly over the crossbar, and a much better looking Gordon Hill volley which caused Montgomery to pull off a quick diving save.Then in the closing minutes Hibbitt was forced to clear off the goaline from another Greenhoff snap shot from within the penalty area.

This was never enough though, and try as they might the Red Devils just could not break through a solid Blues defence intent on holding on to their precious away lead. At the final whistle the Blues players celebrated by paying tribute to the travelling Blues fans who had sung their hearts out in encouragement throughout the game, despite being severely outnumbered. Blues had thoroughly deserved their win and thus avenged their opening day defeat by Utd by 4-1 at St Andrews.

BIRMINGHAM CITY

Montgomery, Calderwood, Styles, Towers, Howard, Gallagher, Connolly, Francis, Bertschin, Hibbitt, Dillon.

MANCHESTER UNITED

Roche, Nicholl, Albiston, McIlroy, B Greenhoff, Buchan, Coppell, J Greenhoff, Ritchie, Macari, Hill.

Kevin Dillon

Birthdays

Mark Smalley born today in 1965

The Matches played on this day

1892, Football Alliance		
Ardwick 2	Blues 2	Att.3,000
	Harrison(2)	
1897, Division 2		
Gainsborough Tr. 1	Blues 3	Att. 1,500
	Hodgetts(2),Izon	
1904, Division 1		
Sheffield United 1	Blues 1	Att. 15,000
	Jones	
1905, Division 1		
Bury 1	Blues 1	Att. 10,000
	Green	
1909, Division 2		
Blues 2	Gainsborough Trinity 1	Att. 5,000
King,Beer		
1915, Division 2		
Blues 2	Leicester Fosse 2	Att. 15,000
Gibson,Windridge		
1926, Division 1		
Blues 2	Sunderland 1	Att. 20,000
Briggs,Russell		
1928, Division 1		
Newcastle United 1	Blues 1	Att. 40,000
	Briggs	
1932, Division 1		
Blues 4	Everton 0	Att. 30,000
Haywood(2),		
Curtis, Bradford		
1934, Division 1		
Sheffield Wed. 2	Blues 1	Att. 12,754
	McGurk	
1937, Division 1		
Blues 0	Chelsea 0	Att. 16,000
1943, Wartime		
Blues 2	Northampton Town 4	
Dearson,Jones		
1954, Division 2		
Blues 2	Rotherham United 3	Att. 17,000
Purdon 41, 83	Grainger 59	
	Wilson 78	
	Burke 80	
1960, Division 1		
Blues 0	Tottenham Hotspur 1	Att. 27,525
	Allen 57	

Tottenham's 700th league win

1965, Division 1		
Blues 1	Tottenham Hotspur 0	Att.33,833
Beard 25		
1971, FA Cup 3rd round		
Huddersfield Town 1	Blues 1	Att. 24,486
Hoy 19	Summerill(pen) 68	
1978, Division 1		
Manchester United 1	Blues 2	Att. 53,501
J.Greenhoff 49	Dillon 12	
	Francis 52	
1982, FA Cup 3rd round		
Blues 2	Ipswich Town 3	Att. 17,236
Worthington 43(pen)	Brazil 35, 79	
Curbishley 50	Wark 72	
1984, Division 1		
Blues 0	Everton 2	Att. 10,004
	Stevens 67	
	King 71	
1988, Division 2		
Blues 1	Swindon Town 1	Att. 7,829
Childs 54	Barnes 74	
1989, Division 2		
Blues 0	Oldham Athletic 0	Att. 5,998
1995, Division 2		
Bradford City 1	Blues 1	Att. 10,539
Taylor 24	Cooper 90	

Blues extended their undefeated run to 23 games they also created a new club record of 20 Football League matches without defeat

1999, FA Cup 3rd round		
Leicester City 4	Blues 2	Att. 19,846
Sinclair 21	Robinson 36	
Ullathorne 27	Adebola 89	
Cottee 51		
Guppy 70		

January 3

Playing record for this day
Playing record for this day is... 17 games, Won 6, Drawn 7, Lost 4, GF 23, GA 25.
Today's success rate.... 55.88% Year Ranking....94th

The Matches played on this day

1891, Football Alliance

Darwen 5	Blues 3	Att. 3,000
	W.Devey,Hallam	
	Wheldon	

1903, Division 2

Blues 4	Leicester Fosse 3	Att. 6,000
Leonard(2), Field,		
McRoberts		

1914, Division 2

Blues 2	Notts County 1	Att. 10,000
Morgan,Pointon		

1920, Division 2

Blues 1	Bristol City 1	Att. 14,000
Millard		

1925, Division 1

Blues 2	Sunderland 1	Att. 25,000
Crosbie,Barton		

1931, Division 1

Blues 1	Derby County 1	Att. 15,000
Curtis		

1948, Division 2

Blues 1	Plymouth Argyle 1	Att. 36,000
Goodwin		

1953, Division 2

Fulham 3	Blues 1	Att. 20,000
Robson 10	Purdon 60	
Jezzard 44, 87		

1959, Division 1

Luton Town 0	Blues 1	Att. 15,538
	Neal 4	

1970, FA Cup 3rd round

Chelsea 3	Blues 0	Att. 45,088
Osgood 40		
Hutchinson 77, 90		

1976, FA Cup 3rd round

Portsmouth 1	Blues 1	Att. 19,414
Eames 14	Francis 3	

1981, FA Cup 3rd round

Blues 1	Sunderland 1	Att. 23,098
Bertschin 43	Chisholm 81	

1983, Division 1

Stoke City 1	Blues 1	Att. 15,428
Painter 68	Phillips 17	

Blues' Dave Langan sent off after 87 minutes

1987, Division 2

Bradford City 0	Blues 0	Att. 8,679

1994, Division 1

Blues 1	Oxford United 1	Att. 15,142
Donowa 60	Dyer 33	

1998, FA Cup 3rd round

Crewe Alexandra 1	Blues 2	Att. 4,607
Rivers 31	Furlong 22(pen), 56	

2000, Division 1

Blues 1	Huddersfield Town 0	Att. 19,958
Hughes 3		

Blues first game of the new millennium.

Match of the Day

FROM 1903
LEICESTER ARE OUT FOXED

Blues edge seven goal thriller at Muntz Street

Blues had beaten Leicester 3-1 on the opening day of the seaon in perfect sunshine. In complete contrast, an early morning hailstorm had left the ground wet and slippy as the Blues kicked off this first fixture of 1903, looking to extend their nine game, 100 percent home league record against Leicester City.

It didn't take long for the Blues to settle, and Athersmith had soon sprinted forward after a long clearance gave him some space. His swerving shot was partially saved by a surprised Ling, and as the ball bobbled through the muddy goal-mouth Leonard charged in to easily tap the ball over the goal line, and Blues had a 1-0 lead after just two minutes. As Leicester struggled in the mud, Blues excelled, boosted by their early breakthrough, they continued in relentless attacking style. After ten minutes Wharton's inch-perfect corner was met by Field who headed Blues' second goal to the delight of the 1,000 crowd, now bathed in mid-afternoon sunshine.

Arthur Leonard was proving to be a handful for Leicester. Already on the scoresheet, he also won the corner which led to the second goal, and within a further four minutes he was hauled down by Atterbury after he had beaten Mills and Collins with some more skilful trickery just outside the area. A free kick was awarded which was rolled to Leonard, and from his shot, Ling pulled off one of the best saves seen at Small Heath for years. This perked up the Leicester side, and Simpson had the chance to charge clean through on Blues' goal, but he opted for a long range shot which Robinson saved comfortably. His next effort a minute later was closer and much more firmly struck, and Robinson this time was fortunate to block the shot for a corner. From the clearance the ball fell to Leonard who slipped it past Atterbury and was clear. He drew Ling from the goalline and tucked the ball into the corner of the net. It was 3-0 with half an hour gone.

With half-time approaching, a quick passing movement by the Blues got McRoberts away on goal. Leicester players appealed desperately for offside, but play was waved on and McRoberts rolled in number four after taking the ball past Ling. Leicester were upset by the goal, and Bolton protested by kicking the ball some 25 yards away from the centre spot.

Leicester resumed the second half in style. Simpson ran and centred the ball for the unmarked Lewis, who controlled and shot past Robinson in the same movement to reduce the score to 4-1. Ling then made saves from Leonard, Field and Beer, whilst Dougherty's shot found the back of the net but was deemed offside. On 52 minutes, Simpson got free again and ran clear of the Blues defence to score with a low drive into the corner of the net, and give his side some hope of an unlikely comeback.

Blues were still creating chances, and Beer struck the crossbar before Ling saved a stinging shot from Field. With 18 minutes to go Lewis beat Robinson with a volley inside the penalty area to reduce the score to 4-3. Within a minute, the Leicester fightback should have been completed. Robinson charged out to catch a swirling cross, but missed the ball completely, leaving an open goal for Brown.He hurried his shot, not realising he had more time, and the ball rolled wide from just four yards. This proved costly as it was the last chance Leicester had of saving the game, the Blues defence closed out the visitors late rally and held on without further addition to the score.

BIRMINGHAM CITY

Robinson, Goldie, Wassell, Beer, Wigmore, Dougherty, Athersmith, Leonard, McRoberts, Field, Wharton.

LEICESTER FOSSE

Ling, Atterbury, Robinson, Mills, Collins, Roulston, Pollock, Lewis, Brown, Belton, Simpson.

REFEREE

Mr Ashcroft (Bolton)

Jim Dougherty

Walter Wigmore

Birthday

Chris Marsden born 1969

Playing record for this day
Playing record for this day is... 14 games, Won 4, Drawn 4, Lost 6, GF 18, GA 21.
Today's success rate...42.86% Year ranking....216rd

Match of the Day

FROM 1969

CUP CHEER FOR BLUES

But only just as lowly Lincoln put up brave fight

Blues' FA Cup run got on its way with a win over Lincoln City at St Andrews, but the Fourth Division side made Blues fight all the way before going down 2-1. Blues looked to have made the game safe when Robinson converted a 59th minute penalty, however the Imps came back and gave their hosts a traumatic last 20 minutes.

The game started typically with Blues well on top looking for an early goal to unsettle the opposition who from a lower league had nothing to lose, Lincoln in turn pulled men back to defend stoutly the Blues onslaught. It wasn't long before the Imps had a seven-man wall at the back as Blues threw everything forward. Blues best chance fell to Greenhoff who was put clear from a great through ball from Pickering, but after beating Hubbard on the left he moved in on goal, steadied himself but then cleared the bar with a casual sidefoot shot from inside the penalty area. The Blues problem was despite their dominance they clearly needed a goal now before panic set in. On 29 minutes they did just that when Fred Pickering scored what many thought would be the goal to open up the flood gates, but this wasn't to be. It was Blues full back Green who came storming through before hitting a cracking drive from the edge of the area, his shot was charged down by a defender and the ball fell to Pickering. After taking the ball round the keeper McClelland he calmly swept the ball into the roof of the net to ease the tension amongst the 31,429 crowd, as well as his team-mates. The game was far from won though and evidence that Blues were still not safe came just before half time when a free kick lofted into the Blues penalty area was just fractionally high for the unmarked Hughes who had nipped in to sneak his header past Herriott's punched clearance.

It was the visitors who started the second half the more keener and they forced an early corner when Smith's piledriver was expertly turned round the post by Herriott. The corner came to nothing but it was an early wake up call to the Blues who seemed to content with their one goal lead and were now getting lethargic as the game went on. The change in Lincoln's play helped Blues find their own form however and during their first real spell of pressure Blues managed to bag a second goal. Pickering who had started a run outside the box beat two men before finding himself in the area, Lincoln's centre half Harford realised the danger but could only mount a desperate lunge to stop the big centre forward, his challenge was penalised by a penalty kick. Dave Robinson stepped up and made no mistake with the 12-yard kick to put Blues surely now safe at 2-0 up, with just half an hour left. This wasn't to be and just ten minutes later Jim Smith (later to become Blues manager) beat Herriott with a snap shot only for Martin to scramble away off the line, however an alert linesman immediatley flagged that the ball had crossed the line significantly without protest from the Blues defender. A nervy 20 minutes ensued and in the closing stages Robinson almost put through his own net when trying to head away a corner and moments later Martin cleared, this time successfully, from the goal line again. There was still time for Pickering to miss an open goal at the other end, from close in he somehow scooped his shot over the bar with the goal at his mercy.

BIRMINGHAM CITY
Herriot, Martin, Green, Wylie, Robinson, Page, Hockey, Greenhoff, Pickering, Darrell, Summerill.
LINCOLN CITY
McClelland, Hubbard, Peden, Jim Smith, Harford, Grummett, Hughes, Kearns, Corner, Svarc, Dave Smith.

REFEREE
Mr L Callaghan (Merthyr Tydfil)

Jim Smith

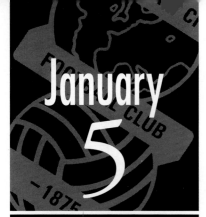

January 5

Playing record for this day
Playing record for this day is... 17 games, Won 4, Drawn 6, Lost 7, GF 24, GA 36
Today's success rate....41.18% Year ranking....230th

Matches Played on this day

1895, Division 1
Blackburn R. 9   Blues 1   Att. 4,000
   Walton
Blues first league meeting v Blackburn Rovers.
A disastrous debut for keeper Tilson Pritchard as Blues crash to their joint worst heaviest defeat to date. Both Kilean and Chippendale score hat-tricks for Blackburn

1901, Division 2
Leicester Fosse 1   Blues 1   Att. 6,000
   Aston
Leicester Fosse became Leicester City

1907, Division 1
Newcastle United 2   Blues 0   Att. 26,000

1918, Wartime
Notts County 3   Blues 3
   Shea,Roulson,Butler

1924, Division 1
Blues 3   Tottenham Hotspur 2   Att. 19,500
Bradford, Cringan, Lane

1929, Division 1
Blues 1   Huddersfield Town 2   Att. 20,000
Barkass(pen)

1935, Division 1
Blues 0   Stoke City 0   Att. 20,000

1946, FA Cup 3rd round, 1st leg
Blues 1   Portsmouth 0   Att. 33,845
Flewin(og)

1952, Division 2
Blues 1   Brentford 2   Att. 28,500
Wardle 40   Dare 30
   Badham(og) 90

1957, FA Cup 3rd round
Carlisle 3   Blues 3   Att. 27,500
Ackerman 46, 84, 88   Murphy 22, 54
   Astall 51
Carlisle's record home attendance to date produces gate receipts of £3,350.

1971, FA Cup 3rd round, replay
Blues 0   Huddersfield Town 2   Att. 26,558
   Krzywicki 9
   Worthington 90

1974, FA Cup 3rd round
Blues 5   Cardiff City 2   Att. 22,435
Francis 3   Impey 59
B.Latchford 35, 65   McCulloch 60
Hatton 75, 88

1980, FA Cup 3rd round
Blues 2   Southampton 1   Att. 24,648
Bertschin 7   Channon 36(pen)
Gallagher 74
This game screened by BBC's, Match of the Day

1982, Division 1
Blues 2   Ipswich Town 3   Att. 19,188
Van Mierlo 69   Mariner 29, 40
Broadhurst 78   Brazil 68

1985, FA Cup 3rd round
Blues 0   Norwich City 0   Att.12,941

1991, Division 3
Blues 1   Bradford City 1   Att. 6,315
Frain 4(pen)   Adcock 73

2002, FA Cup 3rd round
Liverpool 3   Blues 0   Att. 40,875
Owen 16,25.
Anelka 86.

Match of the Day
FROM 1974
EASY FOR 5 STAR BLUES
Cardiff no match for Hatton, Francis & Latchford

A super performance by the Blues today puts them into the fourth round of the FA Cup when they beat Cardiff in a true battle. Vincent was back playing for Cardiff after a seven-week injury absence, and was desperate to put on a good show against his former club mates. However, an early opportunist goal from the brilliant Trevor Francis gave the 22,435 fans a taste of what was to come, and Blues, after a sustained nervy period of play, eventually went on to produce a five-star show of their own.

The lead was further increased on 35 minutes with a superb volley into the net from Bob Latchford, and this paved the way for the goalfest. However, it was not to come just yet, and the rest of the first half was filled with half chances which were not made the most of.

The second half was a completely different story, but Blues in their eagerness to get forward had started to let their defences slip, being 2-0 up had given them the over confidence that they would win easily, but they were in for a shock. Cardiff had shown throughout the match so far that they were more than capable of scoring, they just hadn't had the right opportunity to turn their skill into goals.

It was a mistake in the Birmingham defence which led to the first Cardiff goal being scored on 59 minutes. They had an opportunity to put in a challenge to John Impey's remarkable run with the ball, weaving all the way through he went on to finish a lovely solo run with a crisp low shot past Sprake to renew the visiting team's hope, which now was still very much alive.

Blues were taken aback by this sudden burst of success from Cardiff, and were left completely shell-shocked when, just a minute later, Andy McCulloch scored and brought the scores level. This was not what Blues had expected, and they needed a jump start to get them back to the job in hand. Cardiff's equaliser had clearly rattled the entire side. Gary Sprake in the Blues goal was poised to accept a simple back-pass from Roger Hynd, but the ball came with more force than expected, and the Welsh international had to make a quick save, which he only just managed.

Blues were clearly up against it now and were in desperate need of inspiration from somewhere to regain their composure and control back on the game, which seemed easy not so long ago. On 65 minutes the spark Blues required arrived via a superb shot by Bob Latchford and there was a huge collective sigh of relief amongst the fans, and a huge roar greeted the goal that put Blues back in the lead. The relief was tangible from the fans, who were more than disappointed at Blues' ability to have lost a two goal lead in the first place. Farrington then had two attempts energetically saved by Sprake as Cardiff decided to play the remainder of the game with a risky all out attack.

This tactic was soon manipulated in Bimingham's favour and they soon increased their lead when Bob Hatton headed the ball into the back of the net on 75 minutes, and all hope was abandoned when Hatton again sent a fine header sailing into the net on 88 minutes to finish the scoring.

BIRMINGHAM CITY
Sprake, Martin, Gallagher, Pendrey, Roberts, Hynd, Campbell, Francis, Latchford, Hatton, Taylor.
CARDIFF CITY
Irwin, Dwyer, Bell, Impey, Murray, Phillips (Reece 45), Farrington, McCulloch, Vincent, Villars, Anderson.

REFEREE
Mr Gordon Hill (Leicester)

Trevor Francis

Blues news extra   Blues v Bury, FA Cup 3rd round 1963

After a pitch inspection the game was postponed, the first of 14 postponements and one abandoned game. When the tie eventually got under way the game inevitably finished a draw 3-3. A replay was required at Bury and the tie was eventually settled by the home side 2-0 on March 7th. Blues however gained some revenge when they met Bury in the League Cup semi-finals over two legs also in March, winning the tie 4-3 on aggregate to reach the final.

Birthdays
Gary Jones born 1951   **Steve Barnes born 1976**   **Dean Williams born 1972**

Playing record for this day

Playing record for this day is... 16 games, Won 5, Drawn 4, Lost 7, GF 42, GA 24.
Today's success rate...43.75% Year ranking....210th

Match of the Day

FROM 1962
ALL SQUARE IN SIX GOAL THRILLER

Blues robbed of late winner after fantastic three goal fightback

FA Cup holders Tottenham remained in the FA Cup after an amazing blunder by the officials who denied Ken Leek a match-winning fourth goal for Blues.

When the draw was made many gave Blues little chance against the north London cup experts and after just seven minutes those people were being proved correct. A long clearance from Maurice Norman was chased by Greaves who got a half-decent shot in, but was blocked by keeper Schofield. However, the rebound kindly went straight back to Greaves who this time made no mistake. The cup favourites had got what they wanted, an early goal.

This relaxed Spurs into playing some wonderful football and Schofield was busy again, saving spectacular efforts from Cliff Jones and goal scorer Jimmy Greaves. Tottenham, well on top, went 2-0 up on 29 minutes through their Welsh international Jones. He finished off Terry Medwin's cross with a fierce shot which gave the battered Blue's keeper no chance. Three minutes later Spurs had a third when some neat, one-touch passing left Jimmy Greaves a simple headed goal. Now many in the ground were wondering not who was going to win, but by how many Spurs would win by?

Birmingham needed some inspiration fast and got it within a minute, a Stan Lynn free kick was blocked and the loose ball ran towards Jimmy Harris who belted it first time, it flew past a shell-shocked Brown who up to then had only been a spectator, now he was picking the ball out of the net. Blues had a consolation goal at least. At half time the score remained Blues 1 Tottenham 3.

Blues came out fired up and clearly encouraged by the goal from Harris and had a real belief they could save the tie, if not win it. They desperately needed an early goal and got it after just four minutes of the re-start. Mike Hellawell broke free and his cross was met again by an unmarked Jimmy Harris who this time planted a firm header past Brown and into the corner of the net to reduce the score to 3-2. As the fans settled after invading the pitch, Ken Leek sensationally equalised on 54 minutes, and St Andrews erupted with fans again rushing on to the field, this was becoming the best cup tie seen at the ground ever. What an amazing turn around.

Blues were now by far the better of the two sides and Terry Hennessey was running the game in the midfield, with Spurs unable to break out of their own half. It was under this pressure and with minutes to go that the incident many will never forgive or forget came. With Blues throwing everything forward Ken Leek's shot went in with Spurs defender Norman standing on his goal line, but no one in the 46,096 crowd could believe it, Blues had been denied the greatest cup comeback by a linesman's offside flag. The game finished all square, Malcolm Beard said afterwards, "Our fourth 'goal' was the best of the lot-I saw nothing wrong with it". The replay at White Hart Lane was won by Tottenham 4-2 in another entertaining game between these two sides. Spurs then went on to retain the cup beating Burnley in the final at Wembley 3-1.

BIRMINGHAM CITY
Schofield, Lynn, Sissons, Hennessey, Smith, Beard, Hellawell, Orritt, Harris, Leek, Auld.
TOTTENHAM HOTSPUR
Brown, Baker, Henry, Blanchflower, Norman, Mackay, Medwin, White, Allen, Greaves, Jones.

REFEREE
Mr. K.Howley (Middlesbrough)

Ken Leek

Blues news extra   1983...6-a-side success for Blues

Blues made the final of the Soccer 6 tournament at the NEC in Birmingham by beating Nottingham Forest in a tense semi final penalty shoot out. Earlier in the night the holders of the trophy thrashed Ipswich Town by 8-0. Blues went on to win the final and retain the cup.

Birthdays

Dave Madden born in 1963   **Phil Robinson born 1967**

The Matches played on this day
1894, Division 2		
Northwich Victoria 0	Blues 7	Att. 500
	Walton,Mobley(3)	
	Hands(2),Wheldon.	

Blues record away win in the Football League, equalled 104 years later at Stoke City's Britannia Stadium(see Jan 10)

1900, Division 2		
Blues 5	Middlesbrough 1	Att. 1,000
McRoberts(2), Scrivens,		
Bennett, Bayley		
1906, Division 1		
Blues 0	Newcastle United 1	Att. 8,000
1912, Division 2		
Blues 1	Fulham 3	Att. 7,000
Tinkler		
1915, Division 2		
Blues 11	Glossop 1	Att. 8,000
AW.Smith(4),		
Windridge(5,1pen),		
Eyre ,Hodges		
1917, Wartime		
Blues 2	Chesterfield 2	
Arrowsmith(og),		
Whitehouse(pen)		
1923, Division 1		
Blues 1	Sunderland 2	Att. 25,000
Barratt		
1934, Division 1		
Everton 2	Blues 0	Att. 18,000
1945, Wartime		
Blues 5	Coventry City 1	
Hilkins, Tigg(3), White		
1951, FA Cup 3rd round		
Blues 2	Manchester City 0	Att. 30,057
Stewart 30		
Higgins 70		
Gate receipts £2,300		
1962, FA Cup 3rd round		
Blues 3	Tottenham 3	Att. 46,096
Harris 33, 49	Greaves 7, 32	
Leek 54	Jones 29	
1968, Division 2		
Ipswich Town 2	Blues 1	Att. 16,681
Wigg 22, 87	Vowden 25	
1976, FA Cup 3rd round, replay		
Blues 0	Portsmouth 1	Att. 26,106
	McGuinness 45	

Trevor Francis had a 2nd half goal disallowed

1990, FA Cup 3rd round		
Blues 1	Oldham Athletic 1	Att. 13,131
Gleghorn 53	Bunn 65	
1996, FA Cup 3rd round		
Blues 1	Wolverhampton W. 1	Att. 21,349
Poole 72	Bull 25	
2001, FA Cup 3rd round		
Manchester City 3	Blues 2	Att. 19,380
Morrison 18,	Grainger 57	
Huckerby 31	Adebola 60	
Goater 42(pen)		

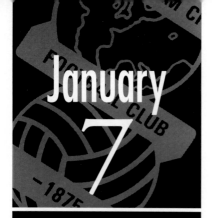

January 7

Playing record for this day
Playing record for this day is... 17 games, Won 7, Drawn 6, Lost 4, GF 30, GA 16.
Today's success rate....58.82% Year ranking....63rd

The Matches played on this day

1893, Division 2		
Lincoln City 3	Blues 4	Att. 1,500
	Wheldon(3),Hands	
1899, Division 2		
Burslem Port Vale 1	Blues 0	Att. 4,000
1905, Division 1		
Notts County 0	Blues 0	Att. 6,000
1911, Division 2		
Blues 2	Bradford PA 2	Att. 10,000
Firth,Hall		
1928, Division 1		
Manchester United 1	Blues 1	Att. 16,853
	Briggs	
1933, Division 1		
Blues 4	Everton 0	Att.. 20,000
Haywood(3),Grosvenor		
1939, FA Cup 3rd round		
Blues 2	Halifax Town 0	Att. 23,522
Jennings,Phillips		
First meeting between the two sides at any level.		
1950, FACup 3rd round		
Swansea 3	Blues 0	Att. 10,000
Allchurch 11		
Burns 44		
Scrine 49		
1956, FA Cup 3rd round		
Torquay United 1	Blues 7	Att. 18,730
Shaw 51	Astall 22,	
	Brown 26, 29, 47	
	Kinsey 34	
	Murphy 48, 73	
Crowd includes 2,000 Blues fans and the record attendance for Torquay produces receipts of £2,270		
1961, FA Cup 3rd round		
Nottingham Forest 0 Blues 2....Att. 29,905		
	Singer 11, 84	
1967, Division 2		
Blues 1	Coventry City 1	Att. 36,316
Curtis(og) 23	Machin 62	
1978, FA Cup 3rd round		
Blues 4	Wigan Athletic 0	Att. 29,202
Francis 4, 16		
Bertschin 21, 79		
First, and only win, against Wigan to date		
1981, FA Cup 3rd round, replay		
Sunderland 1	Blues 2 (A.E.T)	Att. 27,793
Rowell 5	Bertschin 88	
	Evans 91	
Tony Evans goal came 15 seconds into extra time		
1984, FA Cup 3rd round		
Sheffield United 1	Blues 1	Att. 17,202
Brazil 55	Wright 17(pen)	
1989, FA Cup 3rd round		
Blues 0	Wimbledon 1	Att. 10,431
	Gibson 28	
1992, Auto Glass Trophy, preliminary round		
Blues 0	Walsall 1	Att. 5,239
	Ntamark 74	
1995, FA Cup 3rd round		
Blues 0	Liverpool 0	Att. 25,326

Match of the Day

FROM 1956
CUP RUN STARTS IN STYLE

Brown bags hat-trick as super Blues march on to round four

Blues got their 1956 FA Cup run off to a magnificent start with a crushing 7-1 victory over Third Division Torquay at Plainmoor. On a tricky bumpy pitch they quickly adapted after a shaky start to totally destroy the poor Devon side, scoring four goals in the first half alone. Shaw gained a mere consolation goal for the home side with a 51st minute strike, but by then Blues were already in a commanding 6-0 lead.

A crowd of 18,730 gathered at the tiny but picturesque Plainmoor Ground at kick off with almost 2,000 travelling from Birmingham, and in foggy conditions the game got under way with Torquay starting the better. Shaw dribbling his way down the right flank centred for Mills who mistimed his running header thus spurning a glorious chance within the first couple of minutes. Moments later Shaw narrowly missed the target with a shot from the edge of the area as the lower league side continued to exert pressure on their First Division opponents. Blues were having difficulty measuring their passes on such a narrow pitch and the uneven bumpy surface was a clear disadvantage, but when they finally made the necessary adjustments the effects were devasting for their hosts. Astall had already brought a great save out of Kirk when heading down a cross from Lane after 16 minutes play, his next chance six minutes later started the Blues goal rout. Kinsey and Murphy had worked the opening which put Lane in the clear. From his centre Astall was lurking in the box and smashed a fierce volley past Kirk who had absolutely no chance of saving this one. Brown then added a second goal four minutes later, shooting through a crowd of players from a partially cleared corner. He then grabbed a second goal within three minutes, again from a corner which he knocked in easily from barely two yards out. Then from another corner kick just after the half hour mark Kinsey headed in Blues fourth goal to effectively settle the tie by half time.

Nothing changed after the break and Blues were scored not once but twice in the space of three minutes. A fine 40-yard pass from Boyd was helped on its way by Lane into the path of Brown who completed his hat-trick with a first-time right-foot shot, this the pick of the Blues goals during the whole afternoon. A minute later Astall after a fine run crossed for Murphy who blasted in a sixth Birmingham goal which went in off the upright. Torquay supporters were then treated to a goal of their own to cheer, albeit a freak one by their best player Shaw. He chased what seemed a lost cause with the ball wide on the right rolling out of play, however he caught it and crossed it in one movement from right on the byline which Merrick seemed to gather cleanly from under the cross bar. After an appeal from the Torquay players the referee awarded the goal, not even consulting his linesman who must have had a better view of whether or not the keeper had landed over the line whilst holding the ball. Blues responded with a strange goal of their own 17 minutes from the end. After several well-placed cross-field passes went unconverted by the men in the middle, Murphy wide on the right finally mishit one and his pass although not intended, went towards goal. Then in a farcical finish Torquay keeper Kirk dived late and over the top of the ball as it bobbled over the goal line. Blues saw out the remainder of the game content with their seven-goal haul and went on to meet Orient in the fourth round of the FA Cup.

BIRMINGHAM CITY
Merrick, Hall, Green, Boyd, Smith, Warhurst, Astall, Kinsey, Brown, Lane, Murphy.
TORQUAY UNITED
Kirk, John Smith, Anderson, Lewis, Norman, Lloyd, Shaw, Sammy Collins, Jack Smith, Mills, Tony Collins.

REFEREE
Mr A Bond (Fulham)

Gordon Astall

Blues news extra   1922...Blues 5 Corinthians 0

A friendly against the top amateur side at St Andrews, saw the professionals turn on the style with an emphatic win.Henry Deacon and Maker both scored twice, with the other goal coming from George Getgood.

Birthdays

Les Phillips born 1963   Kevin Summerfield born 1959

Playing record for this day

Playing record for this day is... 14 games, Won 5, Drawn 4, Lost 5, GF 22, GA 19.

Today's success rate...50% Year ranking....153rd

Match of the Day

FROM 1972
PLAIN SAILING, BLUES

Blues cruise through Pompey in St Andrews nine goal feast

Yet another wet and rainy day, in possibly the wettest season to date saw Bob Latchford kick off this crucial match towards the Railway End. Support was plentiful, despite the bad weather, and Blues began the match confidently, gaining control almost immediately. Unfortunately this promising start didn't last, and Portsmouth defied the odds by taking a shock lead. Then amazingly the unthinkable happened when the visitors on their very next attack managed to put the ball in the back of the net for a second time within 20 minutes. It would be understandable for Blues to have lost some of their confidence, being two goals down already, but they fought on, and shortly afterwards Bob Hatton belted the ball past Milkins bringing the score to 2-1.

It wasn't long until another goal arrived for Blues, when Trevor Francis was brought down in the penalty area. Alan Campbell was the man to do the honours, and never looked like missing, sending Milkins the wrong way to place the ball neatly in the corner. Relief was felt all around as Blues had now drawn level. The crowd even began to stop noticing the rain, and when Latchford came soaring down the right wing, crossing the ball into the path of Hatton, who forced the ball home, the fans went wild, the tension, frustration and aggression all out in one huge roar which lasted well past the time Portsmouth had restarted from the kick off.

Blues went into the half-time interval still in the lead, and there was even more excitement to look forward to in the second 45 minutes. Although Blues started the second period in control again, it wasn't long before Portsmouth created more worry for the rain-drenched Blues fans by hitting them on the break again with another sharp shot from distance past the unfortunate Cooper, and the scores were level once more at 3-3. This brought a short period of quiet play, making the crowd wonder if Blues would settle for a draw in this nail-biting game. Little did they know what was in store for the last ten minutes!

The pace picked up, and as time began to run out, Francis crossed a perfect ball to Latchford, who had no trouble heading it into the net on 83 minutes. Blues were now in the lead, and the advantage certainly picked up the spirits of both players and fans. On 88 minutes, Francis scored another blinding goal, and the bombardment was completed by Latchford who finished the scoring in the 90th minute.

The 6-3 score was the beginning of an 18-match unbeaten run and meant that Blues moved up to fifth position in the table, bringing them one step closer to promotion.

BIRMINGHAM CITY

Cooper, Carroll, Pendrey, Page, Hynd, Harrison, Campbell, Francis, Bob Latchford, Hatton, Taylor

PORTSMOUTH

Milkins, Smith, Collins, Piper, Hand, Blant, Jennings, Trebilcock, Hiron, Ley, McCann

REFEREE

Mr G Jones (Lancaster)

Bob Latchford

Birthdays

Joe Mallett born 1916.

January
9
-1875-

The Matches played on this day

1904, Division 1
| Blues 3 | Newcastle United 0 | Att. 8,000 |
Beer(2), Jones

1909, Division 2
| Grimsby Town 0 | Blues 3 | Att. 5,000 |
Williams(2) ,Chapple

1915, FA Cup 1st round
| Blues 2 | Crystal Palace 2 | Att. 18,000 |
AW Smith(pen), Eyre

1926, FA Cup 3rd round
| Blues 2 | Grimsby Town 0 | Att. 36,000 |
Russell, Briggs

1932, FA Cup 3rd round
| Blues 1 | Bradford City 0 | Att. 37,749 |
Bradford

1937, Division 1
| Stoke City 2 | Blues 0 | Att. 15,000 |

1943, Wartime
| Blues 5 | Leicester City 0 |
McCormick, Howe(og),
Jones(2), Craven

1946, FA Cup 3rd round, 2nd leg
| Portsmouth 0 | Blues 0 | Att. 23,716 |
Blues won 1-0 on aggregate

1954, FA Cup 3rd round
| Wolverhampton W. 1 | Blues 2 | Att. 36,784 |
Wilshaw 14 | Rowley 16
| | Murphy 68
Champions-elect Wolves suffered rare home defeat. Wolves hit the post twice in the last minute of the first half

1957, FA Cup 3rd round, replay
| Blues 4 | Carlisle United 0 | Att. 56,500 |
Astall 3
Brown 64, 80
Kinsey 76
Birmingham's first cup tie under floodlights
Gate receipts £6,930

1960, FA Cup 3rd round
| Watford 2 | Blues 1 | Att. 31,500 |
Uphill 6 | Hooper 83
Holton 66

1965, FA Cup 3rd round
| West Ham United 4 | Blues 2 | Att. 31,056 |
Byrne 42 | Thwaites 7
Hurst 51, 68 | Jackson 27
Sissons 89

1971, Division 2
| Blues 2 | Bristol City 0 | Att. 15,292 |
Taylor 16
B.Latchford 44

1979, FA Cup 3rd round
| Blues 0 | Burnley 2 | Att. 19,034 |
| | Morley 1
| | James 85
Morley's goal timed at 56 seconds

1982, Division 1
| Nottingham Forest 2 Blues 1 | Att. 15,906 |
Ward 61 | Worthington 73
Wallace 67

1988, FA Cup 3rd round
| Gillingham 0 | Blues 3 | Att. 9,267 |
| | Greenall(og) 3
| | Williams 31
| | Handysides 87

1993, Division 1
| Blues 2 | Luton Town 1 | Att. 9,601 |
Frain 13(pen) | Dreyer 30
Gayle 87

1999, Division 1
| Blues 1 | Port Vale 0 | Att. 18,632 |
Furlong 25

2001, League Cup Semi Final, 1st leg
| Ipswich Town 1 | Blues 0 | Att 21,684 |
Stewart 44(pen)

Playing record for this day
Playing record for this day is... 19 games, Won 11, Drawn 2, Lost 6, GF 34, GA 17.
Today's success rate....63.16% Year ranking....35th

Match of the Day
FROM 1957
BLUES CUP CRACKER

Carlisle hammered by Brown & Co, at packed St Andrews

A huge crowd of 56,500 turned out at St Andrews for the Blues' first FA Cup tie at home for two years. The gates were closed shortly after this third round replay against Carlisle kicked off, with many thousands still locked outside. Greeted by the club's cup anthem of 'Keep Right On to the End of the Road', Birmingham eventually won 4-0. Despite leading 1-0 with just 26 minutes remaining, this tie was anybody's game for over an hour's play, and not as easily won as the scoreline suggests.

Blues settled well under the St Andrews floodlights, and when Govan sent over a beautifully flighted corner in the ninth minute, Astall rose well in the middle to head past Fairley. Many expected this to open the goal floodgates against third Division opponents, but Carlisle were undaunted. They tightened their defence, and confidently passed the ball around with the patience to wait for an opening to level the tie. Indeed, for much of the first half it was difficult to tell which side was from the First Division.

The tie became even more intense from the start of the second half, as Blues went in search of a killer second goal. Astall thought he'd won just that a minute into the half when he sprinted in from the right to hit Kinsey's low pass past Fairley. Sadly he was judged offside, and Carlisle were still in the tie.

Blues kept on attacking, and a Murphy shot just cleared the bar. Fairley magnificently denied Astall with a great reflex save moments later. However, at the other end Blues were fortunate to escape when Bond "scored" from Broadis' cross. Only he, too, was ruled offside, but there was very little in this decision. In the 64th minute Blues' nerves relaxed again when another piece of luck went their way. A corner by Govan entered the net after it struck Brown on the back after an awkward bounce. This luck was balanced out a moment later as Fletcher, in trying to clear a cross by Astall, headed against his own cross bar. Blues' football improved now they were relaxed, and they put the game safe in the 76th minute when Brown scored the third. Just four minutes later Kinsey added another, which was tough on Carlisle as they put up a much harder fight than the final score showed.

BIRMINGHAM CITY
Merrick, Hall, Allen, Linnecor, Smith, Warhurst, Astall, Kinsey, Brown, Murphy, Govan.

CARLISLE UNITED
Fairley, Fletcher, Kenny, Johnston, Waters, Thompson, Mooney, Broadis, Ackerman, Garvie, Bond.

Noel Kinsey (r) in action against Fulham

Birthdays
Danny Sonner born 1972.

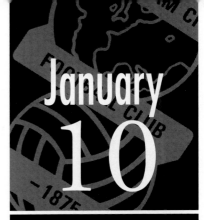

Playing record for this day
Playing record for this day is... 19, Won 11, Drawn 2, Lost 6, GF 38, GA 16.
Today's success rate....63.18% Year ranking....34th

Match of the Day
FROM 1998
THE MAGNIFICENT SEVEN

"Just like watching Brazil" As Blues crush Stoke

Birmingham equalled the best away win in the club's history today when Stoke were blitzed 7-0 at the Britannia Stadium.

Goals started to fly in after every attack, starting as early as the forth minute when Hughes headed in from close range. Hughes again made it two after nine minutes as he curled in a great strike from 20 yards, and on 29 minutes Forster turning sharply hit a first time shot which crept in the bottom corner of the shell-shocked Muggleton in Stoke's goal. Somehow the scoring dried up and at half time with the game surely lost Stoke were glad to get a break.

Birmingham were back on the attack soon after the break showing relentless pressure on the Stoke defence and within five minutes Furlong, unmarked in the penalty area fired home the fourth, and the first of his second half hat-trick. McCarthy cutting in from the right wing smashed a shot into the roof of the net to make it 5-0 on 57 minutes. It was becoming all too much for the angry Stoke fans and at this point several ran on to the pitch.

Birmingham now took complete control and a pass from Bass sent Forster clear again and his neat lay-off found Furlong who in one movement side-stepped and shot home to make it 6-0 . With two minutes remaining and riot police surrounding the gathering hordes of Stoke fans surrounding the pitch, Furlong got his third and Blue's record-breaking seventh, after a throw in found him on the edge of the box he turned and lobbed the ball over a beleaguered Muggleton and the rout was complete.

At the final whistle Stoke fans invaded the pitch calling for chairman Peter Coates to stand down, but police with riot gear and horses kept the crowd reasonably orderly.

BIRMINGHAM CITY
Bennett, Bass, Charlton, Bruce (Johnson 51), Ablett, O'Connor, Marsden, Hughes, McCarthy, Furlong, Forster (Ndlovu 80).

STOKE CITY
Muggleton, Griffin, Nyamah(Wallace h/t), Sigurdsson, Tweed, Keen, Forsyth, MacKenzie, Thorne, Stewart (Gabbiadini h/t), Kavanagh.

REFEREE
Mr T Heilbron (Co Durham)

Paul Furlong

Blues news extra   Manchester City v Blues, 1903.
This Division Two game was abandoned after 83 minutes when fog made it impossible for the officials to see clearly. Blues were 1-0 up when play was suspended and lost the re-scheduled game on Feb 23, 4-0.

Middlesbrough v Blues, 1959
With the scores level at 1-1, this FA Cup third round tie was abandoned due to snow after 60 minutes play. In the re-arranged game played two weeks later Blues won 1-0.

Birthdays
Martin Kuhl born in 1965.

The Matches played on this day
1891, Football Alliance
Blues 7   Sheffield W. 1   Att. 500
Wheldon, Short(2),
Jenkyns(2), W.Devey(2)
1914, FA Cup 1st round
Blues 2   Southend United 0   Att. 18,000
Duncan(2)
1920, FA Cup 1st round
Blues 2   Everton 0   Att. 44,000
Burkinshaw, Whitehouse
1925, FA Cup 1st round
Blues 2   Chelsea 0   Att. 32,000
Briggs(2)
1931, FA Cup 3rd round
Blues 2   Liverpool 0   Att. 43,907
Curtis, Bradford
Birmingham went all the way to the 1931 FA Cup final being beaten by WBA 2-1 at Wembley
1948, FA Cup 3rd round
Blues o   Notts County 2   Att. 53,000
1953, FA Cup 3rd round
Oldham Athletic 1   Blues 3   Att. 26,580
McKennan 78   Murphy 12, 81, 86
1962, FA Cup 3rd round, replay
Tottenham Hotspur 4 Blues 2   Att. 62,917
Medwin 29, 70   Harris 1
Greaves 57   Leek 78
Allen 88
Ken Leek scored in his sixth consecutive game. Spurs went on to retain the FA Cup. Gate receipts £12,420
1970, League Division 2
Blues 3   Charlton Athletic 0   Att. 18,031
Vincent 23
Beard 39
Johnston 77
1976, League Division 1
Blues 0   Wolverhampton W. 1   Att. 28,552
                 Carr 54(pen)
1981, League Division 1
Totenham Hotspur 1 Blues 0   Att. 24,909
Crooks 63
1984, FA Cup 3rd round, replay
Blues 2   Sheffield United 0   Att. 10,888
Harford 80
Wright 85(pen)
1987, FA Cup 3rd round
Ipswich Town 0   Blues 1   Att. 11,616
                 Mortimer 54
1990, FA Cup 3rd round, replay
Oldham Athletic 1   Blues 0   Att. 9,982
Holden 75
1995, Auto Windscreens Shield 4th round
Blues 3   Hereford United 1   Att. 22,351
Claridge 6   Lyne 42
Ward(pen) 68
Otto 72
Birmingham went all the way to the final at Wembley beating Carlisle, to win the trophy in a double-winning season. This game attracted a bigger gate than the FA Cup tie between Sheff Utd and Man Utd on the same night.
1996, Coca Cola League Cup 5th round
Norwich City 1   Blues 1   Att. 13,028
Fleck 69 Francis 64
Bryan Gunn saved Blues Jonathon Hunt's 21st minute penalty
1997, League Division 1
Stoke City 1   Blues 0   Att. 10,009
Wallace 18
1998, League Division 1
Stoke City 0   Blues 7   Att. 14,240
                 Hughes 4, 9
                 Forster 29
                 Furlong 50, 69, 87
                 McCarthy 56
Blues joint biggest Football League away win, the other war 104 years ago v Northwich Victoria
2002, League Division 1
Millwall 1   Blues 1   Att. 11,856
Dyche 69   Mooney 45
Curtis Woodhouse sent off .

January 11

Playing record for this day
Playing record for this day is... 16 games, Won 7, Drawn 4, Lost 5, GF 19, GA 27.
Today's success rate....56.25% Year ranking....91st

The Matches played on this day

1902, Division 1
| Blues 1 | Manchester City 0 | Att. 12,000 |
McRoberts(pen)

1904, FA Cup 1st round, 3rd replay
| Manchester United 3 | Blues 1 | Att. 10,000 |
| | Athersmith | |
Played at neutral ground, Hyde Park, Manchester

1908, FA Cup 1st round
| WBA 1 | Blues 1 | Att. 36,727 |
| | WH Jones | |

1913, FA Cup 1st round
| Manchester City 4 | Blues 0 | Att. 17,442 |

1919, Wartime
| Blues 0 | Notts County 7 | |

1930, FA Cup 3rd round
| Blues 1 | Bolton Wanderers 0 | Att. 35,000 |
Morrall

1936, FA Cup 3rd round
| Barnsley 3 | Blues 3 | Att. 29,330 |
| | White ,Jones, Harris | |

1947, FA Cup 3rd round
| Fulham 1 | Blues 2 | Att. 30,000 |
| | Jones,Dorman | |

1958, Division 1
Newcastle United 1	Blues 2	Att. 34,825
White 65	Kinsey 67	
	Brown 78	
Newcastle defender Bob Stokoe forced to leave the field injured after 55 minutes

1964, Division 1
Manchester United 1	Blues 2	Att. 44,695
Sadler 27	Harley 3	
	M.Bullock 47	
18-year-old Ray Martin makes his debut for Blues.

1969, Division 2
Oxford United 1	Blues 2	Att. 11,492
G.Atkinson 60	Pickering 17	
	Summerill 24	

1975, Division 1
| Stoke City 0 | Blues 0 | Att. 26,157 |
Screened on BBC's Match of the Day

1983, FA Cup 3rd round
| Blues 1 | Walsall 0 | Att. 14,774 |
Summerfield 92
After extra time, 90 mins. 0-0.
Kevin Summerfield was recalled from his loan spell at Walsall and came on as a subsitute to net the winner in extra time. Summerfield resumed his loan period after the game and signed for Walsall a month later.

1986, Division 1
| Blues 0 | Ipswich Town 1 | Att. 6,856 |
| | Wilson 35 | |

1992, Division 3
Blues 2	Leyton Orient 2	Att. 10,445
Cooper 51	Nugent 37	
Paskin 68	Castle 88	

1994, Division 1
Notts County 2	Blues 1	Att. 7,212
Devlin 30	Cooper 86	
McSwegan 85		

Match of the Day
FROM 1936
TEN MAN BLUES BATTLE FOR A REPLAY

After a lapse of 24 years Blues set about beating Barnsley for the first time in the FA Cup. Last time the two sides met, Barnsley won a replay at Oakwell by 3-0, and then went on to beat West Brom in the final and lift the cup.

It was only Frank Clack's second appearance in goal that season, due to Hibbs suffering from a neck infection, and pulling out at the last minute. Blues started sensationally and took the lead inside a minute when White's shot found the top corner from inside the penalty area. This was Blues' first goal in three games against Barnsley.

Blues almost doubled their lead just three minutes later when Guest broke free, but his shot only hit the side netting. On seven minutes Barnsley equalised when Hine converted an Ashton cross low into the corner. Blues were stung into action immediately when White's good work on the wing ended with a hard low centre ball which Jones fired past Ellis to give Blues the lead again within a minute. After quarter of an hour Ashton put Hine clear to level the scores yet again, now it was 2-2.

For the third time it took a minute for Blues to gain the lead as, straight from the kick-off, Harris shot the ball past Ellis. The game's turning point came on half an hour when Devine was brought down by Waring, who was given a stern warning. Devine was taken off and, as there were no substitutes in those days, Blues were down to ten men.

Blues started the second half, still without Devine, who rejoined the game after a few more minutes. From another corner Ashton shot wide, then on 53 minutes Barnsley's pressure paid off after a goalmouth melee. The ball ran clear to Ashton who crashed his shot into the roof of the net making the score 3-3.

Clack made several good saves, and Devine was still struggling with his injury. Blues were constantly bombarded by Barnsley, but they held out well and earned a replay.

BIRMINGHAM CITY
Clack, Barkas, Steel, Stoker, Fillingham, Loughran, White, Devine, Jones, Harris, Guest.
BARNSLEY
Ellis, Shotton, Topping, Holley, Henderson, Crawford, Thomas, Gallacher, Waring, Hine, Ashton.

REFEREE
Mr S Slater (West Riding)

Frank Clack

Birthdays
Joe Gallagher born in 1955   Tony Evans born in 1954   Bunny Larkin born in 1936

Playing record for this day

Playing record for this day is... 13 games, Won 5, Drawn 3, Lost 5, GF 26, GA 15.

Today's success rate...50% Year ranking....141st

January 12

Match of the Day

FROM 1935

BLUES IN FIVE GOAL FIGHTBACK

Early penalty lead then Coventry blitzed in second half burst

The first FA Cup tie between these two midland blues was won by the Royal Blues after a surprise third minute lead by the Sky Blues, roared on by thousands of their visiting fans at St Andrews. The game, just deemed playable despite a covering of snow which froze as the game went on and resembled an ice rink towards the finish, had been eagerly anticipated since the draw was made and a crowd of 40,349 witnessed a great game under difficult conditions.

Coventry's first attack led to a goal, through a penalty from Jones. A swirling cross from Birtley forced Booton to scramble the ball clear with a combination of arm and head, the ball dropped to Liddell who tapped in from two yards but, the referee had already penalised the defender for handball awarding the spot kick, which Jones converted. Blues immediately stormed back but could not find the finish required to equalise with Morgan in the Coventry goal and his defenders playing well above themselves. However Blues pressure eventually paid off after 22 minutes with the best goal of the game. White broke free after collecting the ball in his own half and squared to Harris, his first time ball to Mangnall allowed him to run into the area to collect a return pass which he drove first time across Morgan and low into the corner.

With the pitch becoming increasingly difficult to stand up on let alone play football a drawn game looked likely, however a devastating six-minute period by Birmingham won the tie after an hour had passed. Goals from Mangnall(60 mins), Guest(63 mins), and a second goal for Harris(66 mins) finished a brave fight by Coventry and completed a thrilling comeback for Birmingham. With eight minutes remaining Harris completed his hat-trick with another precise finish within the penalty area to set Blues up for a fourth round tie with Southampton at the Dell.

BIRMINGHAM CITY

Hibbs, Booton, Barkas, Stoker, Fillingham, Calladine, White, Harris, Mangnall, Bradford, Guest.

REFEREE

Mr AE Fogg (Bolton)

COVENTRY CITY

Morgan, Brown, Bisby, Frith, Mason, Boileau, Birtley, Wilson, Bouton, Jones, Liddle.

Harold Booton

Birthdays

John Cheesewright born today 1973
Noel Blake born today in 1962

Carl Richards born today 1960
Harry Roberts born today 1920

Sadly Missed

Arthur Turner died today in 1994, aged 84

January 13
-1875-

Playing record for this day
Playing record for this day is... 17 games, Won 8, Drawn 3, Lost 6, GF 25, GA 28.
Today's success rate...55.88% Year ranking....95th

Match of the Day
FROM 2001
TRUE BRAZILIAN BLEND
Marcelo lucky run and Aussie magic combine to beat Tykes

Marcelo a late replacement for toothache victim Dele Adebola made his mark in the 15th minute when he stooped to nod in a low Grainger cross. Blues never looked back after this despite a late rally by the home side which was far too late to deny Blues their fifth away win in the league this season. Blues should have won by a bigger margin and when Lazaridis was bundled over in the area shortly after the opening goal, O'Connor marred a great performance with a softly hit penalty which Miller saved diving low to his left. Blues quickly put the disappointment out of their minds and six minutes before the interval they eventually got their deserved second goal. Michael Johnson heading in from close range from Eaden's corner to the far post sending Blues into the break with the game effectively won.

Any doubts about the result were quickly ended within three second half minutes. Lazaridis deciding not to burden his team mates picked up a loose ball on the half way line and proceeded to run straight down the middle on his own leaving four Barnsley defenders in his wake, as Miller came,out to close him down the Aussie winger deftly chipped the ball over him and then hurdled the keeper to watch the ball roll over the line. With Blues coasting they collectively switched off during a crazy last ten minutes as Barnsley pinched not one but two consolation goals. The first was harsh on Poole who had made a great save from Jones only to see the rebound bobble past him on the opposite side to his dive seconds earlier. The other goal four minutes into stoppage time was O'Connor's second glaring error as he made a hash of a simple pass back to Jenkins which sent Jones running free to finish well with a low cross shot which went in off the post. Blues had done more than enough to record an impressive win but in the end had to settle for a score line of 3-2, but a convincing one nonetheless.

BIRMINGHAM CITY
Poole, Jenkins, Grainger, Sonner, Purse, Michael Johnson, Eaden, O'Connor, Marcelo (Horsfield 87), Ndlovu (Andrew Johnson 71), Lazaridis (Hughes 89).
BARNSLEY
Miller, Morgan, Chettle, Barker, O'Callaghan, McClare (Thomas 73), Neil, Corbo (Jones h/t), Sheron (Ripley h/t), Shipperley, Dyer.

REFEREE
Mr M Pike (Barrow)

Marcelo

Playing record for this day

Playing record for this day is... 19 games, Won 7, Drawn 2, Lost 10, GF 36, GA 40.
Today's success rate...42.11% Year ranking....219th

Match of the Day

FROM 1928
POSH SPICE UP BLUES

Peterborough so close to upset, but Bradford is the hero

Non league Peterborough & Fletton United had never before reached the FA Cup third round, so many of the 38,128 were expecting a comfortable home win, indeed many of the 4,000 stong contingent from Peterborough wouldn't have given their side much of a chance against First Division Birmingham. It took just seven minutes for Blues to execute a chance their dominance had created, Benny Bond laying on the cross for Welsh international Stan Davies to fire home. Blues were one up and looked comfortable, many at this point would have anticipated a landslide win. With 19 minutes gone however a rare shot by Peterborough's Willis was badly fumbled by the usually reliable Dan Tremelling and Bruton scrambled the loose ball over the goal line for a shock equaliser, now it was a real cup tie. With Blues under pressure Peterborough took the lead five minutes later when another mistake from Tremelling left Brown a simple tap in. With Blues clearly rankled and Peterborough players and their masses of fans jubilant they continued to press forward, not happy to sit back on their 2-1 advantage. Blues counter attacked and Davies had a great opportunity but like so many of his team-mates his nerves got the better of him to and he blasted over the bar from five yards out. With just two minutes to half time, Peterborough broke away again through Willis's fine solo run, his cross was inch perfect and found McGuigan who fired in Posh's third past a bemused Dan Tremelling.

A more determined and clearly shaken Blues team emerged from the dressing room after the break, and straight away they were bearing down on the Peterborough goal desperate to get back into the game. Whitehead saved well from Ellis and followed it up with two wonderful saves from Davies. After an hour Johnny Crosbie finally found some space to feed Bradford an inch-perfect pass and the deadly Blues forward pulled a goal back at last, 3-2.

With just 15 minutes remaining Crosbie again found Bradford sending him clear on goal with a superb pass, Bradford raced on and very coolly tucked in the equaliser. It was now non-stop Blues pressure with Whitehead and his defenders performing heroics to keep them out. Time ticked away and just when Peterborough had thought they had achieved a moral victory by holding the Blues to a famous draw they were dealt a cruel blow. Crosbie again he won the ball deep in his own half and in one movement beat his man and found Joe Bradford with a breathtaking 30-yard pass. Bradford rounded the keeper and tapped in his third of the game and Blues now led 4-3 after 86 minutes. There was no further score and Blues progressed to round four, Peterborough were given a rousing ovation from the thrilled St Andrews crowd and their supporters would have returned home very proud of their team's incredible performance.

BIRMINGHAM CITY

Tremelling, Womack, Randle, Morrall, Cringan, Leslie, Bond, Crosbie, Bradford, Davies, Ellis.

PETERBOROUGH & FLETTON UNITED

Whitehead, Hutchinson, Betteridge, Dickinson, Forrester, Irving, McGuigan, MacNaughton, Bruton, Lowson, Willis.

REFEREE

Mr I Stouther (Nottingham)

Johnny Crosbie

Birthdays

Micky Darrell born in 1947 .

January 15

Playing record for this day
Playing record for this day is... 12 games, Won 4, Drawn 2, Lost 6, GF 19, GA 21.
Today's success rate...41.67% Year ranking....222nd

The Matches played on this day

1898, Division 2
| Lincoln City 1 | Blues 2 | Att. 2,500 |
| | Abbott,Lewis | |

1908, FA Cup 1st round, replay
| Blues 1 | WBA 2 | Att. 24,895 |
| Eyre | | |

The first FA Cup tie to be played at St Andrews involving the Blues, previously a tie between Arsenal and Sheff Wed was played in March 1907

1910, FA Cup 1st round
| Blues 1 | Leicester City 4 | Att. 15,119 |
| Lappin | | |

1921, Division 2
Stockport County 0	Blues 3	Att. 10,000
	Crosbie, Lane,	
	Whitehouse	

1927, Division 1
| Blackburn Rovers 3 | Blues 2 | Att. 9,000 |
| | Islip, Scriven | |

1936, FA Cup 3rd round, replay
| Blues 0 | Barnsley 2 | Att. 34,000 |

1938, Division 1
| Portsmouth 1 | Blues 1 | Att. 20,000 |
| | Beattie | |

1949, FA Cup 3rd round, replay
| Leicester City 1 | Blues 1 After extra time | Att. 37,000 |
| | Bodle | |

1972, FA Cup 3rd round
Blues 3	Port Vale 0	Att. 32,937
Hynd 9		
Francis 40, 57		

1983, Division 1
Blues 1	Manchester United 2	Att. 19,333
Dillon 54(pen)	Whiteside 50	
	Robson 55	

This match screened by Centrals 'The Big Match'

1994, Division 1
Watford 5	Blues 2	Att. 7,636
Porter 7	Willis 69	
Hessenthaler 30	McGavin 74	
Furlong 40, 51(pen), 56		

Blues had Gary Cooper sent off in the 51st minute, then Steve Claridge sent off in the 73rd minute. Hat-trick scorer Paul Furlong later became a Blues player. This was Blues heaviest defeat by Watford to date

2000, Division 1
| Blues 2 | Norwich City 0 | Att. 21,007 |
| Grainger 17, 31 | | |

Norwich keeper Andy Marshall sent off for deliberate hand ball outside of his penalty area.

Match of the Day
FROM 1972
EASY CUP BONUS FOR BLUES
Third Division Vale comfortably swept aside

When the third round FA Cup draw was made in December there was something of a sigh of relief when Blues were given a home tie against lower league opposition. Blues aim was promotion and with injury worries already mounting the last thing they wanted was a prolonged cup battle, Port Vale at St Andrews was an ideal draw. However Vale, managed by former Villa full back Gordon Lee, genuinely fancied their chances and made it known to the media in pre-match interviews. Blues went into the game with a goalkeeper crisis,both first choice Dave Latchford and reserve Mike Kelly were out again forcing Freddie Goodwin to stick with youth 'keeper Paul Cooper who made his debut the previous week in a 6-3 win over Portsmouth. Blues only other change was Harland returning to the side at the expense of Harrison. Port Vale went into the game unchanged. Port Vale were a very physical side and within a minute they had set out their intentions for the game when their defence sent Francis flying, for the first of many free kicks that afternoon. As Blues pressed forward in the opening minutes they left a gap which brought about the game's best chance for the visitors. A long ball out released Morgan as the Blues defence appealed hopefully for offside Cooper rushed out just in time to knock the ball clear. With nine minutes gone however Blues got their lead and eased any worries of an upset. The goal was a perfect set piece move from Taylor's corner Roger Hynd headed in his first goal for the Blues since his move from Crystal Palace. This opened up the game for Port Vale and after Sharratt had saved well from Latchford, his opposite number Cooper made important blocks to efforts from Flowers and Morgan, the former after a dreadful error by Pendrey. With just five minutes to go before half time Blues effectively finished the game off with a well taken second goal. Yet another foul on Francis led to a free kick which Hynd played into
Latchford, his flick across the penalty area was finished by a crisp Francis cross shot into the corner. Blues almost scored again moments later when a lovely through ball from Campbell put Francis clean through, as the 'keeper came out Francis produced a deft lob which just cleared the bar. At half time Blues were well worth their 2-0 lead.

Blues lost no momentum in the second half and should have been three up within minutes, Hatton this time clean through but missed with just keeper Sharratt to beat. Another chance was soon forthcoming and from a set piece Taylor's free kick was headed just wide by Latchford. Blues second half dominance eventually paid of on 57 minutes when good play from Pendrey on the left wing allowed Taylor to cross into the box and Francis scored a rare headed goal to put his team 3-0 up and into the fourth round of the Cup.

Blues continued their fine form in all competitions by beating Ipswich in round four. They then beat Portsmouth and Huddersfield to reach the semi-final where a very strong Leeds side eventually put an end to their cup run winning 3-0 at Hillsborough. The main priority, however, was promotion and just two weeks after the cup defeat they achieved their goal by beating Orient to join the First Division.

BIRMINGHAM CITY
Cooper, Carroll, Pendrey, Page, Hynd, Harland, Campbell, Francis, Latchford, Hatton, Taylor.
PORT VALE
Sharratt, Brodie, Loska, Summerscales, Cross, Flowers, Gough, Lacey, McLaren, Morgan, Horton.

REFEREE
Mr P Baldwin (Redcar)

Paul Cooper

Playing record for this day

Playing record for this day is... 14 games, Won 4, Drawn 3, Lost 7, GF 26, GA 32.

Today's success rate...39.29% Year ranking....236th

Match of the Day
FROM 1954
FOXES JUST PIPPED IN GOAL RACE

Blues win seven-goal thriller at Filbert street

Two quick goals on the quarter hour mark helped Blues win a cracking tussle with Leicester City by the odd goal in seven. Blues in their change strip of red were strengthened by the return of Roy Warhurst from injury and had Peter Murphy playing at centre forward for the first time, and were well worth their 4-3 win, Murphy scored the all-important forth goal. Leicester made one change to their line up which saw off Middlesbrough in a cup replay in midweek, Fincham obtaining Army leave to replace Warner at centre half.

Leicester were the brighter starters and Merrick had to be alert on two occasions in the opening ten minutes with important but regulation saves. However it was Birmingham who took a surprise lead on fourteen minutes with a well worked goal for Ken Rowley. Murphy chased a loose ball on the right wing sent over a low cross which Astall cleverly ran and jumped over, the ball ran free to Rowley to finish with a well placed left-foot shot into the corner. Before Leicester could retaliate Blues stormed back with a second goal just a minute later. Govan picking up the ball midway in the Leicester half, tricked Lever with some neat footwork and ran on to finish easilly with only Anderson in the Leicester goal to beat. An unfortunate error allowed Leicester back into the game when Green hesitated with his clearance and Hines nipped in to rob him of the ball, his shot went through a ruck of players and an unsighted Merrick could only parry the ball which went in off the post. On the stroke of half time Merrick made a magnificent save to deny Rowley an equaliser. The former Albion striker hit a rocket like right-foot shot from the angle of the penalty area which Merrick dived full length to finger-tip over the bar for an unproductive corner. Leicester started the second half the better side and they were rewarded with a goal after just five minutes. An inswinging corner from the right was uncharacteristically fumbled by Merrick and Hines punished the error by stabbing the ball in from barely two yards out to put Leicester back on level terms. Blues restored their lead after 65 minutes when Govan converted a mis-hit shot from Murphy and four minutes later Blues scored a matchwinning fourth goal. Kinsey was put away down the wing off a quickly taken throw in and played the ball into the middle for Murphy. The newly appointed centre forward out paced two Leicester defenders before slamming the ball in to the top corner of the net with a rasping 16-yard shot. The Blues were well on top now and soon after a Baldwin miskick allowed Astall to fire in a shot from distance which skimmed the crossbar. However Blues gave themselves a nervy final four minutes when the ever dangerous Arthur Rowley scored to reduce the score to 4-3, however they saw out the final minutes without any further problems and in the end deservedly avenged the 2-1 defeat by Leicester earlier in the season.

BIRMINGHAM CITY

Merrick, Hall, Green, Warhurst, Newman, Boyd, Astall, Ken Rowley, Murphy, Kinsey, Govan.

LEICESTER CITY

Anderson, Lever, Jackson, Russell, Fincham, Baldwin, Griffiths, Morris, Hines, Arthur Rowley, Small.

REFEREE

Mr FH Gerrard (Preston)

Peter Murphy outjumps Arsenal's Cliff Holton

Birthdays

Stuart Storer born today 1967.   Ian Atkins born today 1957.

The Matches played on this day

1886, FA Cup 5th round

| Blues 2 | Davenham 1 | Att. 6,000 |

Figures, Davenport

1892, FA Cup 1st round

| Blues 5 | Woolwich Arsenal 1 | Att. 4,000 |

Hallam(2),
Wheldon(2),
Walton

First competitive game v Arsenal. Game kicked off 25 minutes late due to the late arrival of the referee. Blue's keeper Charsley saved a penalty from Arsenal's Shaw. Blue's record their biggest win over the Gunners to date.

1904, Division 1

| Aston Villa 1 | Blues 1 | Att. 20,000 |
| | Green | |

1909, FA Cup 1st round

| Blues 2 | Portsmouth 5 | Att. 18,813 |

Chapple(pen),
King

A shock defeat for Blues by Southern League Portsmouth

1926, Division 1

| Blackburn Rovers 4 | Blues 4 | Att. 20,000 |
| | Bradford(3), Harris | |

1932, Division 1

| Arsenal 3 | Blues 0 | Att. 37,843 |

1937, FA Cup 3rd round

| Stoke City 4 | Blues 1 | Att. 26,155 |
| | Morris | |

Freddie Steele scored a hat-trick for Stoke

1943, Wartime

| Leicester City 2 | Blues 1 | |
| | Acquaroff | |

1954, Division 2

Leicester City 3	Blues 4	Att. 34,604
Hines 23, 50	K.Rowley 14	
A.Rowley 86	Govan 15, 65	
	Murphy 69	

1960, Division 1

Manchester United 2	Blues 1	Att. 47,361
Quixall 38(pen)	Larkin 59	
Violett 51		

1965, Division 1

Burnley 2	Blues 0	Att. 9,959
Harris 42		
Irvine 68		

1971, Division 2

Leicester City 1	Blues 4	Att. 25,657
Sjoberg 72	B.Latchford 5, 54	
	Bowker 13	
	Summerill 43	

1988, Division 2

Stoke City 3	Blues 1	Att. 10,076
Talbot 8	Kennedy 10	
Henry 82, 86		

1999, Division 1

| Barnsley 0 | Blues 0 | Att. 17,114 |

January 17

The Matches played on this day

1903, Division 2

| Blues 3 | Burnley 0 | Att. 6,000 |

Leonard, Field,
Athersmith

1911, FA Cup 1st round, replay

| Oldham Athletic 2 | Blues 0 | Att. 6,400 |

1914, Division 2

| Leicester Fosse 0 | Blues 0 | Att. 6,000 |

1920, Division 2

| Blues 1 | Bristol City 0 | Att. 29,500 |

Davies

1925, Division 1

| Cardiff City 1 | Blues 0 | Att. 10,000 |

1931, Division 1

| Manchester City 4 | Blues 2 | Att. 18,000 |
| | Briggs, Gregg | |

1948, Division 2

| Luton Town 0 | Blues 1 | Att. 20,000 |
| | Bodle | |

1949, FA Cup 3rd round, 2nd replay

| Blues 1 | Leicester City 2 | Att. 31,609 |

Dorman

1953, Division 2

| Blues 2 | West Ham United 0 | Att. 22,000 |

Purdon 1
Trigg 75

1967, League Cup Semi Final, 1st leg

Blues 1	QPR 4	Att. 34,295
Bridges 4	Marsh 56	
	Morgan 65	
	Lazarus 75	
	Allen 89	

1970, Division 2

Carlisle United 4	Blues 3	Att. 7,912
Barton 17, 68	Summerill 6, 70, 72	
Peddelty 29		
Murray 39		

1976, Division 2

| QPR 2 | Blues 1 | Att. 16,759 |
| Masson 20, 33 | Francis 62 | |

1981, Division 1

Blues 0	Southampton 3	Att. 16,491
	Moran 18	
	Channon 71	
	Keegan 78	

Ian Handysides made his Blues debut, coming on as a sub for
Archie Gemmill

1993, Division 1

Wolverhampton W. 2	Blues 1	Att. 13,560
Burke 84	Tait 31	
Mutch 88		

This match shown live on Central TV's 'The Big Match'

1996, FA Cup 3rd round, replay

Wolverhampton W. 2	Blues 1	Att. 28,088
Ferguson 17	Hunt 50	
Bull 62		

Wolves keeper Mike Stowell saved Jonathon Hunt's penalty in
the second half, with the score 1-1.

1998, Division 1

| Blues 0 | Huddersfield Town 0 | Att. 17,850 |

Playing record for this day

Playing record for this day is... 16 games, Won 4, Drawn 2, Lost 10, GF 17, GA 26.

Today's success rate....31.25% Year ranking....262nd

Match of the Day

FROM 1953

BLUES SPURRED ON BY PURDON

Early goal sets up fine 2-0 victory over the Hammers

Blues claimed their first double of the season following up their win at Upton Park in September with a comfortable victory at St Andrews. Roared on by their 22,000 partizan supporters Blues thoroughly deserved the maximum points, often playing the more direct football. Although West Ham had their chances, they were in contrast often timid and hesitant throughout the game.

Blues were given a fantastic start by Ted Purdon when he scored after just 75 seconds. In the first attack of the game the ball was played out to Wardle on the left, his centre evaded Trigg in the centre and O'Farrell miscued his clearance. The ball fell to Purdon who had time to stop and control the ball before carefully slotting in a low right-foot drive past Gregory. Their perfect start Blues relaxed and played some delightful football, only once being troubled when John Gregory had a chance inside the area, but shot wide with only Merrick to beat. The remainder of the half was fairly evan and despite countless opportunities from corners the score remained the same at half time.

It was a different story after the break when Blues immediately took total control. Gregory was soon having shots raining in on his goal from all angles and distances, the closest to a goal came from the boot of Murphy which the West Ham keeper fortuitously stopped with his outstetched leg. The spell of total Blues pressure was momentarilly broken when John Gregory missed another glorious chance for the visitors. Blues then wrapped up the game with 15 minutes to play when Trigg doubled their lead. A long ball from defence by Green fell between two West Ham defenders who both waited for the other to take control and clear. Whilst they dallied Trigg nipped in between them to take the ball on and beat Gregory with a crisp low shot from just inside the penalty area. The goal was just reward for the Blues perseverance with attacking football, although most of it coming from the route one, long ball tactic. Blues however were indeed good value for their first league win since Christmas Day.

BIRMINGHAM CITY

Merrick, Hall, Green, Bannister, Ferris, Boyd, Stewart, Purdon, Trigg, Murphy, Wardle.

WEST HAM UNITED

Ernie Gregory, Wright, Bond, Parker, Allison, O'Farrell, Woodgate, John Gregory, Kearns, Gazzard, Andrews.

Ted Purdon

Blues news extra   1921...Blues and Villa share the Cup

The Lord Mayor of Birmingham's charity game for the unemployment fund ended in stalemate and the specially commisioned cup shared between the clubs. Although a 'friendly' it was as fiercely contested as any other games between these two rivals.

1982... Blues win the Cup!

Guernsey was the pleasant setting for this Sports Argus Artic Cup match between local rivals WBA and Blues. Blues won the game and took the cup with goals from Tony Van Mierlo and Frank Worthington. The final at Corbet Field, Guernsey was watched by 2,658.

Birthdays

Colin Gordon born today 1963.   **Steve Robinson born today 1975.**

Playing record for this day
Playing record for this day is... 18 games, Won 8, Drawn 3, Lost 7, GF 33, GA 28.
Today's success rate...52.78% Year ranking....130th

January 18

Match of the Day

FROM 1977

SUPER MAC 3, SUPER MAN 3

Francis and Macdonald create Football League history in six goal draw

An outstanding performance from both sides saw Blues take a two-goal lead, only to lose it in this classic clash with Arsenal at St Andrews. The Gunners were currently unbeaten in nine Football League games.

It was Blues' lowest crowd of the season, with just 23,247 filing in to see this piece of history being played. Kenny Burns was out of the team for Blues, and Welsh youngster Gary Emmanuel started in the side. Blues opted to use the successful 4-2-4 formation, whilst Arsenal played with a four-man midfield. Their new signing Alan Hudson, a £220,000 buy from Stoke, was included in the line-up, and was to make his presence felt. After half an hour of the game, the fans were looking for something exciting to cheer them up. Both teams were not to disappoint, and it was Blues who began. Trevor Francis opened the scoring on 31 minutes when the ball was presented to him by Emmanuel and he had the easy job of slamming it past Arsenal goalkeeper Rimmer who stood no chance.

Just six minutes later it was Francis again with a goal. Jones evaded the Arsenal defence to pass the ball onto him, and he calmly slotted it past the goalkeeper. However, this joy didn't last for long as it took only four minutes for Arsenal to pull one goal back. A neat little back heel pass from Hudson went to Nelson, who passed to Stapleton. Gallagher moved out to try and deter the shot, but it was passed to Macdonald who headed it into the net. The third goal for Blues again came from Francis. He set himself up in the Arsenal area with a sly flick of the ball over O'Leary's head, only for the centre half to handle it. The spot kick was taken on 51 minutes by Francis, who never looked like failing to score his tenth goal of the season, and his first hat-trick for three years.

Arsenal were determined not to end their unbeaten run, and their perseverance paid off in the 75th minute when Macdonald added another to his tally with a super left-footed strike into the net. Despite the fact that Blues still attacked, and did not give up their belief that they could win, the equalising goal was destined to come for Arsenal. It arrived with just five minutes of the game left, giving Macdonald a hat trick to equal Francis's. It came from a clever pass from Ross outside the area which deflected off Gallagher to fall for Macdonald on the six-yard line. He wasted no time in ensuring its passage over the goal line, and earned Arsenal the point they deserved.

BIRMINGHAM CITY
Latchford, Page, Rathbone, Kendall, Gallagher, Want, Jones, Francis, Emmanuel, Hibbitt, Connolly.
ARSENAL
Rimmer, Rice, Nelson, Ross, O'Leary, Simpson, Hudson, Brady, Macdonald, Stapleton, Armstrong.

Trevor Francis

Blues news extra   1961..Blues players will not be on strike.

The PFA led by chairman Jimmy Hill have today reached an agreement with the Football League and FA thus averting the threatened strike action called earlier. Under scrutiny was the contract binding players to their clubs for life known as the 'slavery contract' this has been agreed to be scrapped. In the meeting with league officials the maximum wage of £20 was also scrapped and it was confirmed that strike action by players would not go ahead.

Birthdays

Dennis Clarke born today 1948.   Eric Barber born today in 1942.   Bob Latchford born today 1951.

The Matches played on this day		
1890, FA Cup 1st round		
Blues 3	Clapton 1	Att. 2,000
W.Devey, Stanley(2)		
1896, Division 1		
Blues 3	Wolverhampton W. 2	Att. 6,000
Adlington,		
Bruce, Ollis		
1902, Division 1		
Wolverhampton W. 2	Blues 1	Att. 9,000
	McRoberts	
1908, Division 1		
Aston Villa 2	Blues 3	Att. 39,500
	Eyre, Green, Drake	
1913, Division 2		
Blues 5	Leicester Fosse 1	Att. 12,000
AR.Smith, Hall(2),		
Jones, King(og)		
1919, Wartime		
Notts County 2	Blues 0	
1930, Division 1		
Blues 2	Sheffield United 1	Att. 25,000
Curtis, Bradford		
1936, Division 1		
Blues 0	Manchester City 1	Att. 20,000
1947, Division 2		
Blues 1	Barnsley 2	Att. 35,000
Duckhouse		
1958, Division 1		
Blues 2	Burnley 3	Att. 22,281
Murphy 12	White 25, 79	
Hooper 70	Pilkington 58	
1964, Division 1		
Blues 0	Burnley 0	Att. 15,871
1969, Division 2		
Blues 3	Blackburn Rovers 1	Att. 27,160
Coddington(og) 24	Fryatt 6	
Robinson 27(pen)		
Pickering 78		
1975, Division 1		
Blues 0	Everton 3	Att. 32,284
	Styles(og) 66	
	Latchford 71, 75	
1977, Division 1		
Blues 3	Arsenal 3	Att. 23,247
Francis 31,	Macdonald 41,	
37, 51(pen)	75, 83	
1986, Division 1		
Blues 0	Everton 2	Att. 10,502
	Lineker 35, 46	
Blues 17th consecutive Football League match without a win, a record to date.		
1992, Division 3		
Swansea city 0	Blues 2	Att. 4,147
	Rodgerson 26	
	Rowbotham 87	
1995, FA Cup 3rd round, replay		
Liverpool 1	Blues 1	Att. 36,275
Redknapp 21	Otto 69	
Liverpool win 2-0 on penalties.		
1997, Division 1		
Blues 4	Reading 1	Att. 15,363
Furlong 33	Holsgrove 51	
Devlin 56(pen), 75		
Gilkes(og) 89		

January 19

The Matches played on this day

1901, Division 2
Gainsborough Trinity 1 Blues 2   Att. 2,000
                          Aston, McRoberts

1907, Division 1
Blues 3   Aston Villa 2   Att. 50,000
Glover,
Mounteney, Green
John Glover's goal was a tremendous effort hit on the volley from 30 yards out. Blues conceded their first goals at St Andrews, opend in December 1906

1918, Wartime
Huddersfield Town 4   Blues 2
                          Whitehouse(2)

1924, Division 1
Nottingham Forest 2   Blues 0   Att. 15,000

1929, Division 1
Everton 0   Blues 2   Att. 20,000
                  Hicks(2)

1935, Division 1
Manchester City 0   Blues 0   Att. 25,000

1946, Wartime
Blues 3   Aston Villa 1
Jones(2), Mulraney
Blues went on to claim the League South Championship, just edging out Aston Villa by 0.206 of a goal.

1952, Division 2
Doncaster Rovers 0   Blues 5   Att. 20,000
                  Murphy 11, 39, 70
                  Stewart 67
                  Briggs 79
Peter Murphy netted a hat-trick on his debut, only two players have achieved this feat for Blues the other was Charlie Izon in 1893

1957, Division 1
Blues 0   Chelsea 1   Att. 30,157
                  McNichol 68
Gordon Astall missed a 46th minute penalty for Blues

1974, Division 1
Blues 1   Manchester City 1   Att. 31,401
B.Latchford 4   Law 62
This match was screened by ATV's Star Soccer

1991, Division 3
Blues 0   Cambridge United 3   Att. 5,859
                  Wilkins 12
                  Taylor 31
                  Dublin 47(pen)

2002, Division 1
Blues 0   Wimbledon 2   Att. 17,766
                  Hughes 80
                  Agyemang 90
Tommy Mooney hit the bar with a penalty, with the score at 0-0. Wimbledon completed the double over Blues for the second season in succession.

Playing record for this day

Playing record for this day is... 12 games, Won 5, Drawn 2, Lost 5, GF 18, GA 17.

Today's success rate....50% Year ranking....160th

Match of the Day

FROM 1952

INSTANT HERO

Debutant Murphy bags hat-trick in Blues' five-star win

For this Second Division game at Doncaster's Belle Vue ground South African Ted Purdon made way for new signing Peter Murphy, a £20,000 midweek buy from Tottenham Hotspur. Huddersfield were boosted by the return of player-manager Peter Doherty. A win would put Blues top of the table, and they started well, taking just 11 minutes to prize open Rovers' defence. Murphy played an intelligent one-two with Wardle before clipping the ball over Hardwick to score.

With six minutes to go before the half-time break Blues doubled their lead, Badham winning the ball with another telling challenge in the centre circle releasing Warhurst, who chased forward before slipping the ball inside for Murphy to hit first time, giving Hardwick little chance to move. The ball struck the back of the net, and Blues went into half time 2-0 up, with Murphy on a hat-trick.

In the second half, Doncaster played well, forcing Merrick to pull off a great save from Harrison. Further chances from Tindall and Miller were also saved by the newly appointed England international 'keeper. Blues added a third goal on 67 minutes, courtesy of a Jackie Stewart 20-yard thunderbolt, supplied by Smith.

Three minutes later Blues went 4-0 up, goal-scorer Stewart turning provider for Murphy's hat-trick. With 11 minutes remaining Blues completed only their second five-goal haul away from home since the war, with Briggs squeezing in a tight-angled shot between 'keeper and post.

Blues deserved their top spot, having won 5-0, and registered a post-war record of four successive away league wins.

BIRMINGHAM CITY

Merrick, Green, Martin, Badham, Atkins, Warhurst Stewart, Smith, Briggs, Murphy, Wardle.

DONCASTER ROVERS

Hardwick, Makepeace, Graham, Jones, Patterson, Miller, Martin, Doherty, Harrison, Lawler, Tindall.

REFEREE

Mr F Jerrard (Preston)

Jackie Stewart

Blues news extra   1981...Blues hammer Poole 5-0

In a friendly today Blues comfortably beat non-league side Poole Town 5-0 with goals coming from Tony Evans(2), Frank Worthington, Keith Bertschin and Kevin Dillon.

Birthdays

Fred Pickering born today 1941   **Keith Neale born today 1935**

Playing record for this day

Playing record for this day is... 12 games, Won 6, Drawn 2, Lost 4, GF 23, GA 16.

Today's success rate....58.33% Year ranking...72nd.

Match of the Day

FROM 1990

CREWE DERAILED

Sturridge & Bailey earn Blues first win of the 90's

Blues needed a win to raise their spirits after they were hammered 4-0 by Bristol City the previous week, and they did it with style, securing the first double of the season. Blues manager Dave Mackay kept Ian Atkins as sweeper, moved Trevor Matthewson out to left-back, with John Frain in midfield. Robert Hopkins was brought into attack after a three and a half month injury break, and Dennis Bailey was placed wide on the right to counter Crewe's talented left-back Paul Edwards.

Hopkins' presence proved to be most valuable as he worked constantly to increase problems for the Crewe defence. However the referee was not so impressed with his enthusiasm, and cautioned him halfway through the first period for his over-eager efforts. The play from Blues was superb, and passing was exceptional, but for most of the game it seemed that it would come to nothing. Then after 65 minutes Vince Overson created the first real goal opportunity. It was seized upon by Sturridge, who took the ball and slid into the area to nudge the ball into the net. Sturridge was also involved in the second goal, when six minutes before the end, he ran half the length of the pitch to centre, and Bailey was on hand to help the ball over the goal line. There was some disagreement over whose goal it actually was, with both players claiming responsibility, but it was eventually accepted that Bailey was the scorer.

BIRMINGHAM CITY

Thomas, Clarkson, Frain, Atkins, Overson, Peer, Hopkins, Bailey, Sturridge, Gleghorn, Langley.

CREWE ALEXANDRA

Greygoose, Swan, Edwards, Smart, Dyson, Callaghan, Joseph (Hignett), Murphy, Clayton, Cutler, Walters.

REFEREE

Mr E Parker (Preston)

John Frain

Blues news extra   1905...Blues 7 West Bromich Albion 2

Birmingham Senior Cup final A crowd of 8,500 saw Blues lift the Birmingham Senior Cup today at Muntz Street. Birmingham dominated from the first minute, and could have, and indeed should have scored more. Thomas Jones opened the scoring for Blues and finished with a hat-trick. His feat was matched by James Windridge who also got three goals, the seventh for Blues was scored by Charles Field.

1982...Friendly v Torquay

Blues won their friendly against Torquay by 2-1 in Devon. The goals come from Kevin Dillon and Frank Worthington and the game was watched by 1,423 at Plainmoor.

Birthdays

Dennis Isherwood born today 1947.   Marco Gabbiadini born today 1968.

The Matches played on this day

1900, Division 2		
Blues 8	Gainsborough Trinity 0	Att.4,000
Wharton, McRoberts(3),		
Layton(2), Bennett, Main		
1906, Division 1		
Aston Villa 1	Blues 3	Att. 40,000
	Mounteney,	
	Jones, Dougherty	
1917, Wartime		
Blues 1	Nottingham Forest 0	
Buckley		
1923, Division 1		
Blues 0	WBA 2	Att. 32,180
1934, Division 1		
Blues 0	Middlesbrough 0	Att. 20,000
1940, Wartime		
Northampton Town 3	Blues 0	
1945, Wartime		
Aston Villa 3	Blues 1	
	Harris	
1951, Division 2		
Blues 3	Bury 3	Att. 26,000
Stewart 44	Bodle 27	
Trigg 55(pen), 66	B.Giffiths 48	
	Hazlett 70	
1962, Division 1		
Blues 3	Ipswich Town 1	Att. 26,968
Leek 11, 26	Crawford 53	
Baker(og) 50		
1968, Division 2		
Blackburn Rovers 1	Blues 2	Att. 17,934
Darling 47	Pickering 53	
	Vowden 70	

Trevor Hockey sent off after 74 minutes. Blackburn's Mike Ferguson missed an 84th minute penalty

1990, Division 3		
Crewe Alexandra 0	Blues 2	Att. 4,681
	Sturridge 65	
	Bailey 84	
1996, Division 1		
Ipswich Town 2	Blues 0	Att. 12,540
Milton 23, 57		

January 21

Playing record for this day
Playing record for this day is... 15 games, Won 9, Drawn 2, Lost 4, GF 31, GA 20.
Today's success rate....66.67% Year ranking....18th

The Matches played on this day

1893, FA Cup 1st round		
Burnley 2	Blues 0	Att. 6,500
1899, Division 2		
Blues 6	Loughborough Town 0	Att. 3,000
Abbott(3),		
Wharton(2), Wilcox		
1905, Division 1		
Newcastle United 0	Blues 1	Att. 24,000
	Tickle	
1911, Division 2		
Blues 1	Burnley 1	Att. 6,000
Jones		
1922, Division 1		
Blues 0	Newcastle United 4	Att. 20,000
1928, Division 1		
Blues 2	Everton 2	Att. 30,000
Ellis,Briggs		
1933, Division 1		
Blackpool 0	Blues 1	Att. 10,000
	Calladine	

With 8 draws and 12 defeats away from home this was the Blues only victory on their travels this season

1939, FA Cup round 4		
Blues 6	Chelmsford City 0	Att. 44,494
Harris(2), Brown,		
Jennings, Madden(2)		
1950, Division 1		
Liverpool 2	Blues 0	Att. 37,668
Payne 23		
Stubbins 69		
1956, Division 1		
Luton Town 0	Blues 1	Att. 20,000
	Brown 65	
1961, Division 1		
Preston North End 2	Blues 3	Att. 7,644
Farmer(og) 44	Singer 43	
Alston 50	Bloomfield 52	
	Hellawell 70	

Blues first win at Deepdale for over 25 years

1967, Division 2		
Blues 3	Preston North End 1	Att. 18,486
Vowden 22	Lawton 68	
Bridges 47, 69		
1978, Division 1		
Liverpool 2	Blues 3	Att. 48,401
Thompson 74	Emmanuel 54	
Dalglish 87	Bertschin 57	
	Francis 67(pen)	
1984, Division 1		
Ipswich Town 1	Blues 2	Att. 12,900
D 'Avray 16	Harford 19	
	Butcher(og) 54	
1989, Division 2		
Blues 2	Watford 3	Att. 6,396
Whitton 28, 37(pen)	Wilkinson 11	
	Thompson 19, 59	

Match of the Day
FROM 1978
KOP SILENCED AS BLUES RIP POOL APART
Liverpool stunned by 13 minute, three goal Blues riot

An irresistible second half purple patch from the Blues made a complete mockery of the league's meanest defence on their own soil. Before the Blues blitz, Liverpool had conceded just three goals at Anfield all season, however Gary Emmanuel in the 54th minute got the first of three goals in 13 minutes, and two further efforts from Trevor Francis struck the woodwork as Blues plundered away in front of a deathly silent Anfield Kop. All seemed to be going to plan although after the first half the mighty Reds had nothing to show for their better play, good goalkeeping from the reliable Jim Montgomery and sound defensive play from the other ten in blue shirts being the major reason. However Blues, with the quality of Francis, were a danger on the break and when Hibbitt sprang a well disciplined offside trap midway through the first half, Francis from his cross planted a brave header which stuck the base of the post. Liverpool soon retaliated and just before the interval Souness struck a fabulous free kick which smacked the Blues crossbar. The other incident of note from the first 45 minutes was when Blues centre half Pat Howard was booked for a reckless challenge on Alan Hanson.

It was Liverpool who started the brighter in the second period, however the more they attacked the more susceptible to a dangerous break they became. The home team were prepared to gamble despite the likely cost and so it was from a Liverpool attack which Towers broke down that Blues scored, nine minutes into the restart. Towers collected a loose ball and the move ended with Emmanuel who found space to shoot just inside the penalty area. His effort flew past a bemused Clemence, who by now could barely remember what the feeling was like to pick the ball out of the Kop side goal. Just three minutes later Towers again manoeuvred the ball expertly from the middle of the field out to Francis, his precise pass put Bertschin clean through and as he raced forward he struck the ball sending it whistling past the England 'keeper. At this point a visitor would have sworn both sides had merely swapped jerseys such was Blues total dominance, with Liverpool unable to do anything to stop them. The inevitable third goal spoke volumes for Blues superiority when Francis raced past Thompson only to be felled by the defender's outstretched leg, A penalty was awarded immediately Francis picked himself up and swept the ball into the corner Clemence dived but the ball passed him without a touch. Blues fans behind the goal at the other end were almost as stunned, but after pinching themselves, still managed a chorus of "Easy, Easy" to taunt the eerily silent Anfield. The atmosphere was positively strange, football researchers and learned historians scampered around trying to find out when last, a band of visiting supporters to Anfield had sincerely sang out "City 3 Scousers 0 All-el-u-ia" the answer is still not known. With 16 minutes to go Liverpool at last got a consolation goal when substitute Jimmy Case slung the ball across the Blues box and Thompson, who had come up for a corner, took advantage of the fact he'd been to slow in getting back into position by sliding the ball past Montgomery. Still Blues were undaunted by the rejuvenated home side, and on another break Dillon fed Francis who weaved his way to an acute angle before letting fly with a low shot, which for the second time struck the post. In the final few minutes Liverpool scored a second through Dalglish to ensure a nervous for the visitors, and the referee seemed to play forever before eventually calling time. Blues had won a memorable. and monumental game at Anfield.

BIRMINGHAM CITY
Montgomery, Calderwood, Pendrey, Towers, Gallagher, Howard, Emmanuel, Francis, Bertschin, Hibbitt, Dillon.
LIVERPOOL
Clemence, Neal, Hansen, Thompson, Kennedy, Hughes, Dalglish, McDermott, Johnson, Souness, Callaghan (Case).

Jim Montgomery

Blues news extra 1942...Fire destroys St Andrews Main Stand.

A fire caused total havoc today and resulted in extensive damage to the Main Stand at St Andrews. The seemingly harmless incident was spotted by an alert fireman who in trying to help extinguish the smoking bin, picked up a container of petrol thinking it was water, the flames rapidly spread and when the fire service finally got the blaze under control the damage had destroyed virtually all the official player registrations and records from the nearby main office. Other artefacts and programmes were destroyed in the fire which in the end took several hours to control.

Birthdays

Alan Campbell born today 1948.   Danny Wallace born today 1964.

Playing record for this day
Playing record for this day is...14 games, Won 6, Drawn 3, Lost 5, GF 22, GA 18.
Today's success rate....53.57% Year ranking....120th

Match of the Day

FROM 1966
JUST ENOUGH

Vowden at the double, Blues through to round four

After missing out on a match the previous week due to bad weather the Blues squad were more than ready to face Bristol City on a pitch covered with a layer of sand. It was Bristol who kicked off, but they only succeeded in losing possession of the ball to Blues who welcomed the opportunity and started their attacking moves early. Hockey's pass to Thomson was sent back but amounted to nothing when the ball trickled off the field. Fraser worried the defenders in the Bristol area, and then a super cross from Hockey saw the crowd waiting with baited breath as Vowden came lurching in to get a touch. He was too late however, and the ball was nodded out for a corner. Hockey took the kick, and his cross went to Thomson, but the ball was headed over the bar by the Blues striker. Thomson soon won a corner for Blues himself, and hopes were high. The ball fell to Vowden, and again the ball was headed out.

Peters made a super effort with a long run down half the length of the pitch. He evaded the Blues defence and won a corner for his efforts, but the ball was punched away by Blues goalkeeper Herriot. Blues went into the lead on 23 minutes thanks to a slip-up from Connor. The ball ran loose and was picked up by Thomson who presented it for Vowden to send straight past Gibson in the Bristol goal. Herriot soon had to dive for a save from Bristol's comeback, and managed to keep the ball safe. Another corner won by Hockey proved fruitless, and then Bristol pulled out all the stops to equalise in the 35th minute. It was a mix-up within the Blues defence which led to the goal after Fraser and Martin both expected the other to clear the ball. Bush took advantage of the static defenders and slipped through to nudge the ball over the line and bring the scores level.

The restart was delayed due to a pitch invasion from the Bristol fans and when play resumed it was Blues on the attack again. Vowden's attempt on goal was cleared by Drury, and the game paused for Briggs to receive treatment for a knee injury just before the half-time break. The second period saw the attacks increase from Blues. Just two minutes in the lead was restored for the home side when Vowden smashed the ball into the net from a pass by Thomson. Then Jackson's try went just wide of the post, and more attempts were made at both ends. A corner for Bristol came after 54 minutes, and Peters took the kick which he sent to Low, whose header entered the top corner of the net to once again bring the scores level.

A counter-attack was mounted by Blues, and as time went by the home team were beginning to think that a draw was all they would get from the match. Thomson took a free kick, but the ball was lacking in direction and pace and didn't pose any threat to Bristol. The attacks continued, and the only relief from the barrage for Bristol was when Blues won a corner. The kick came to nothing but it inspired Blues, encouraging them to keep up the pace. It paid off when Thomson finally scored the winning goal after 73 minutes when Jackson made a lovely move through the Bristol defence and passed the ball to the Blues striker. The crowd invaded the pitch to congratulate him, and play was delayed again. After the restart there was no more action, and Blues fully deserved their win.

BIRMINGHAM CITY
Herriot, Fraser, Martin, Wylie, Foster, Beard, Hockey, Jackson, Thomson, Vowden, Thwaites.
BRISTOL CITY
Gibson, Ford, Briggs, Drury, Connor, Low, Derrick, Atyeo, Bush, Clark, Peters.

REFEREE
Mr E Crawford (Nottingham)

Season 1949-50

January 23

Playing record for this day
Playing record for this day is... 10 games, Won 3, Drawn 4, Lost 3, GF 15, GA 15.
Today's success rate....50% Year ranking....163rd

Match of the Day
FROM 1960
WINTER BLUES FOR PRESTON

Preston's bad run continues, Blues gain first win of 1960

Blues needed the uplift that a win would provide, and fortunately they managed it, scoring for the first time since beating West Ham on Boxing Day. The game at St Andrews was played in the worst conditions of the winter so far, and the home team were determined that they would not lose in front of a crowd of 24,137. This showed throughout with their hard work dominating the game right from the start. The scoreline does not reflect the performance given by Blues, all that was missing was a little bit of luck and the winning margin would have been greater.

Despite the muddy, worn pitch, Blues began attacking from the beginning. On three minutes Rudd was brought down in the penalty area, and the spot-kick was taken by Astall. The winger shot the ball straight towards Preston goalkeeper Else, who tipped it over the crossbar.

The first goal was not far away however, arriving just two minutes later. Larkin took a quick shot and made up for the penalty miss by hitting the ball home to the surprise of Else.

Astall, just recovered from a lengthy injury, was not having a good game. After missing the spot kick, he then pulled a muscle in his thigh. He gallantly played on, but was obviously suffering, and his play was hampered.

The first half hour was dominated by Blues, but in the 37th minute Preston equalised. Finney sped up, despite being slowed until now with the mud, and passed the ball with force. It landed for Sneddon who avoided a tackle and shot the ball into the net.

After half time Preston kept up the fight despite also having an injured and limping player on the field.

Blues, on the other hand, persisted in the attack, sensing that the visitors were struggling and believing they could win. The constant pressure on goal tired the Preston defence, and Blues seized the advantage on 71 minutes they took the lead once again. Neal netted the perfect long-shot from a centre from Astall, and Preston did not have the willpower or ability to make a comeback.

BIRMINGHAM CITY
Schofield, Farmer, Allen, Watts, Smith, Neal, Astall, Larkin, Weston, Hume, Rudd.
PRESTON NORTH END
Else, Wilson, Walton, Milne, Dunn, Smith, Mayers, Thompson, Finney, Sneddon, Taylor.

Dick Neal

Birthdays
Ray Martin born today 1945.   **Steve Lynex born today 1958.**   **George Allen born today 1932.**

Playing record for this day

Playing record for this day is... 11 games, Won 7, Drawn 2, Lost 2, GF 22, GA 12.

Today's success rate....72.73% Year ranking....7th

Match of the Day

FROM 1996

CANARIES NOT SINGING ANYMORE

Ten man Blues stun Norwich with last gasp win

On another big night of cup football roared on by 21,097 fans at St Andrews, Birmingham City played Norwich for a place in the two-legged semi-final of the Coca-Cola Cup against Leeds United, a chance to avenge that 1972 semi-final defeat in the FA Cup, when Blues lost 3-0 at Hillsborough.

This was Blues tenth Coca Cola Cup tie of the season, and their 42nd match, their tired players struggled to match a Norwich side which betrayed few signs of a team that had only won once in 13 outings. Blues were playing Doherty after an absence of 13 months, and with Steve Castle and Louie Donowa making only their fourth start between them in eight matches, the midfield was at sixes and sevens. Norwich had two good openings early on, and ended the first half with another flurry as Ashley Ward burst clear of Frain and Daish before being apparently brought down just inside the area. Referee Roger Milford waved away all appeals.

Manager Barry Fry removed Doherty at half-time, replacing him with Jason Bowen. The change worked wonders, with the Welshman scoring his second goal of the competition. On 54 minutes he finished emphatically in yards of space at the far post, volleying Castle's cross over Gunn from 12 yards. At last Blues were one goal up. But as time went on, that appeared to have been their last chance to score. Norwich increasingly pinned back the Blues attack, pressurising them until Poole, already booked for a foul in the first half, was left exposed in the 69th minute on the half-way line by Donowa's hesitancy and handled the ball. His sending off put Birmingham's hopes of a resounding victory on the line, as Norwich continued to pile on the pressure and within 10 minutes Molby was able to push the Norwich advantage home. He was allowed to advance before curling a left-footed shot from 20 yards which disected Griemink's right hand and the upright. With the scoreline one goal all, neither side seemed likely to break through, and the prospect of a sapping 30 minutes extra-time and penalties loomed ever larger, until the 89th minute, when a pass to John Frain from Richard Forsyth produced desperate cover and a rare Blues corner. It was Birmingham's last throw of the dice. Frain swung his kick in deep and to the edge of the area, where captain Liam Daish rose majestically to loop his header in at the far corner. Daish had headed Blues into their first semi-fnal for 21 years, and himself into Blues folklore.

BIRMINGHAM CITY

Griemink, Poole, Edwards, Daish, Frain, Donowa, Castle (Tait 66), Forsyth, Doherty (Jason Bowen h/t), Francis (Bull 80), Claridge

NORWICH CITY

Gunn, Bradshaw, Polston, Prior, Mark Bowen, Eadie (Johnson 63), Adams, Molby, O'Neill, Ward, Fleck.

REFEREE

Mr R Gifford (Llanbradach)

The Matches played on this day

1903, Division 2
| Preston North End 2 | Blues 1 | Att. 5,000 |
Beer

1914, Division 2
| Blues 4 | Wolverhampton W. 1 | Att. 25,000 |
Reed, Duncan, Ballantyne, Morgan

1920, Division 2
| Blues 1 | Stockport County 1 | Att. 30,000 |
Elkes

1925, Division 1
| Blues 3 | Preston North End 0 | Att. 15,000 |
Linley, Briggs(2)

1931, FA Cup 4th round
| Blues 2 | Port Vale 0 | Att. 39,885 |
Bradford(2)

1953, Division 2
| Leicester City 3 | Blues 4 | Att. 27,478 |
Hines 26 | Murphy 17, 38, 74
Rowley 55(pen) | Trigg 52
Griffiths 86

1959, FA Cup 3rd round
| Middlesbrough 0 | Blues 1 | Att. 36,587 |
| | Harris(og) 17 |

1981, FA Cup 4th round
| Coventry City 3 | Blues 2 | Att. 29,492 |
Daly 29, 63(pen) | Worthington 52(pen)
Blair 44 | Ainscow 61

1987, Division 2
| Blues 0 | Stoke City 0 | Att. 10,641 |

1996, Coca Cola League Cup 5th round, replay
| Blues 2 | Norwich City 1 | Att. 21,097 |
Bowen 53 | Molby 78
Daish 88
Blues have Gary Poole sent off after 69 minutes

1998, FA Cup 4th round
| Blues 2 | Stockport County 1 | Att. 18,882 |
Hughes 32, 84 | Armstrong 67
Brett Angell(25 mins) and Martin McIntosh(53 mins) sent off

Barry Fry

Birthdays

Mark Yates born today 1970.   **Steve McGavin born today 1969.**

January 25

The Matches played on this day

1896, Division 1
Blues 2 | Wolverhampton W. 7 | Att. 4,000
Wheldon, Mobley

1908, Division 1
Blues 1 | Liverpool 1 | Att. 15,000
Mounteney

1913, Division 2
Stockport County 0 | Blues 1 | Att. 4,000
Jones

1919, Wartime
Blues 1 | Huddersfield Town 0
Davies

1930, FA Cup 4th round
Arsenal 2 | Blues 2 | Att. 50,000
| Briggs(2)

1947, FA Cup 4th round
Blues 1 | Portsmouth 0 | Att. 30,000
Harris

Blues keeper Gil Merrick pulled off a magnificent penalty save to deny Pompey's Duggie Reid

1969, FA Cup 4th round
Sheffield W. 2 | Blues 2 | Att. 52,062
McCalliog 59 | Pickering 20
Young 75 | Thwaites 71

1975, FA Cup 4th round
Chelsea 0 | Blues 1 | Att. 35,450
| Burns 43

1997, FA Cup 4th round
Blues 3 | Stockport County 1 | Att. 18,487
Furlong 29 | Angell 82
Devlin 48
Francis 69

Playing record for this day
Playing record for this day is... 9 games, Won 5, Drawn 3, Lost 1, GF 14, GA 13.
Today's success rate....72.22% Year ranking....8th

Match of the Day
FROM 1975
BATTLE OF THE BLUES

Brummie Blues see off the London Blues thanks to a Scot.

This match, in the fourth round of the FA Cup took place at Stamford Bridge against Chelsea in front of a crowd of 35,450. Blues celebrated their 100th birthday later on in the year, and they fully intended to make sure of their success, going into this game with the determination and enthusiasm needed to bring about a win. Weather conditions could have been a lot better. A piercing wind threatened to hamper the game as it swept through the crowd and the pitch, and the players had to work harder to control the ball. Trevor Fancis was still not back in the squad, and also missing was Bob Hatton. This, combined with a pudding pitch away from home, should have put the Birmingham side at a disadvantage right from the outset. Blues refused to accept that, and despite all the odds stacked against them came out battling for a win.

Free-flowing play was also hampered by the fickle tendencies of the referee. Birmingham played with skill and passion, and the referee punished them for it. Some bookings were justified, some were not. Some incidents from Chelsea deserved a booking, but didn't get one, and all in all the cautions seemed randomly given.

Blues took the lead with what was the only goal of the game when Kenny Burns found the back of the net in the 43rd minute. Howard Kendall picked up the ball from the right and, taking into account the strength and direction of the wind, he sent a curling pass to land perfectly for Burns. The Scot slammed in his first goal in ten games to snub the taunting fans who had troubled him recently. Styles, Pendrey, Burns and Hendrie all found their way into the referee's notebook for varying reasons, some of which were questionable, and then the ref did himself no favours when he ignored a knee-high kick on Malcolm Page right in front of him. Frustrated gasps were heard from the away fans when shortly after this he decided that Dave Latchford deserved a mention in his book for the petty offence of delaying a goal clearance. All in all Blues were not only relieved to have won this game, but they were clearly the happier to hear the final whistle. They thoroughly earned their victory, totally outplaying the home side despite the referee's attempts to ruin their game.

BIRMINGHAM CITY
Latchford, Page, Styles, Kendall, Gallagher, Pendrey, Emmanuel, Taylor, Burns, Hynd, Hendrie.
CHELSEA
Phillips, Locke, Harris, Hollins, Droy, Hay, Kember, Ray Wilkins, Garland, Hutchinson, Sissons.

REFEREE
Mr Tom Reynolds (Swansea)

Kenny Burns

Playing record for this day

Playing record for this day is... 14 games, Won 6, Drawn 3, Lost 5, GF 25, GA 17

Today's success rate....53.57%   Year ranking....119th

Match of the Day
FROM 1957
SOUTHEND'S SIX AND OUT
Blues into round five after seaside romp at Southend

The previous season in the FA Cup it was Torquay in Devon, this time the Blues goal-scoring machine rolled over Southend in similar emphatic style. Make no mistake this also could have been seven, or even more. On a difficult pitch where the players were ankle deep in mud in parts of the centre circle and penalty area, Blues ran the ball on the relatively untouched flanks where they pulverised Southend's full backs from the first to last kick.

Blues were in front from the fourth minute after a raid on the right wing by Brown who received a pass from Kinsey. From the forward's low cross Murphy dashed in to hit a shot across Threadgold and into the corner. A minute later Blues produced an identical move but Duthie made a well timed sliding tackle on Murphy as he was about to shoot. The second goal was always just minutes away and eventually arrived after ten minutes, a Southend break was stopped and cleared by Hall and the ball found Govan on the left wing from his low hit cross Lawler got in a tangle trying desperately to clear and only succeeded in hooking the ball into his own net. Just five minutes later it was 3-0, again Kinsey and Brown started the move with quick passing on the right as Brown cut in both full back and 'keeper were chipped by the Blues centre forward and Govan, alone in the centre, headed a simple goal into the empty net. After a couple of rare goalbound shots from Southend's Thompson and McCrory both of which went harmlessly wide, Blues got a fourth goal after 24 minutes. This time it was Cox who broke down the right flank and from his cross shot toe poked the ball in from four yards. A minute later Govan almost completed his hat-trick after a repeat of his first goal, this time however Williamson was well placed to head clear from on the goal line.

The second half started with Southend scoring just five minutes into the half much to the delight of the home crowd of 30,000. Hollis turned sharply in the penalty area after Blues had failed to clear a corner, and scored from within the six yard box. The goal brought about Southend's best period of play and for 20 minutes they appeared confident but without further troubling Merrick or the Blues goal. With 20 minutes remaining Blues made it 5-1 with a well deserved goal for Cox. He had put Brown away on the right and after the forward had tricked Anderson he waited for Cox before chipping an inch perfect return pass which the winger hammered in first time on the volley. Govan then completed his hat-trick with a goal on 78 minutes, when a cross field ball was just missed by the sliding Williamson leaving the winger in the clear just inside the Southend half. His run took him to within 18 yards of goal before unleashing a glorious left footer to leave the score and the final result 6-1.

BIRMINGHAM CITY

Merrick, Hall, G.Allen, Newman, Smith, Warhurst, Cox, Kinsey, Brown, Murphy, Govan.

SOUTHEND UNITED

Threadgold, Williamson, Anderson, Duthie, Stirling, Lawler, Barker, McCrory, Hollis, Thompson, McGuigan.

REFEREE

Mr RJ Leafe (Nottingham)

Alex Govan (l) heads a goal past Millwall goalkeeper Billy Lloyd (r)

Birthdays

Gil Merrick born today 1922.   **Roger Hansbury born today 1955.**

January 27

Playing record for this day

Playing record for this day is... 15 games, Won 8, Drawn 0, Lost 7, GF 22, GA 19
Today's success rate....53.33% Year ranking....123rd

Match of the Day
FROM 1951
RAMS RAIDED

Attendance record smashed, Cup win grabbed by Blues

On their home ground a much fancied Derby County started this FA Cup tie expecting to walk away with a win. A crowd of 38,384, an all-time record attendance in both league and cup games, had piled in to see the clash. The gates were closed 20 minutes before kick off, with hundreds left outside. 10,000 Blues fans had travelled to the game after an overnight frost. The pitch was bare in the middle, but a covering of sand had been applied to give a firm footing.

Team changes consisted of Badham playing at right back for Blues, in place of an unfit Green, and Parr on at full back in place of Savin for Derby. Blues kicked off toward the Normanton End, and with Trigg putting the ball to Higgins they had an early chance. Unfortunately the inside forward hung on to the ball too long, and it ran loose. Blues continued in control, and therefore it was no shock when, in the tenth minute, they scored a text book goal. A free kick from Trigg, two yards outside the penalty area, went out to the left where Brown rushed in to nod the ball into the net. There were plenty more chances, but none of them successful, and the game went into half time with Blues still in the lead. Both sides began the second half enthusiastically, and it was Derby who broke away to level the score on 60 minutes. Morris' corner kick came to Atkins' head, and then to Stamps, and on to McLaren. He was tackled by Atkins, but managed a left-footed flick to Lee, who simply tapped it with his right foot into the net.

Blues were now hampered by a limping Smith, in effect bringing them down to ten men. It wasn't long, however, before they put themselves into the lead again on 70 minutes. A weak pass from Parr to Brown enabled Stewart to slip in, avoiding Brown's attempt to cover the ball. With a quick flick, he had the ball planted firmly in the back of the net, and his momentum carried him straight over the prone goalkeeper.

Blues became assertive and even more determined to win, and as a result the winning goal came from Trigg on 80 minutes. A free kick against Mozley allowed Berry to swing the ball into the goalmouth. Trigg simply had to jump up and head the ball home, and this he did with ease. With a few last ditch attempts from Derby, causing Merrick to bring about some energetic saves, the game was brought to a close with the result Derby County 1, Birmingham City 3.

BIRMINGHAM CITY
Merrick, Badham, Martin, Boyd, Atkins, Ferris, Stewart, Higgins, Trigg, Smith, Berry
DERBY COUNTY
Brown, Mozley, Parr, Ward, Oliver, Musson, Morris, Stamps, Lee, Powell, McLaren

REFEREE
Mr JW Bowers (Huddersfield)

Len Boyd (r) runs out before a match, followed by goalkeeper Gil Merrick (l)

Birthdays
Mike Newell born today 1965

Playing record for this day

Playing record for this day is... 14 games, Won 10, Drawn 1, Lost 3, GF 28, GA 15.

Today's success rate....75% Year ranking....3rd

Match of the Day

FROM 1984

LATE BLUES ROAR AT ROKER

Blues snatch cup tie win after late drama at Roker

Blues took on Sunderland away from home in this FA Cup tie. The team which did so well against Ipswich was kept for this game, so Mark McCarrick was playing his second game. Welsh international Byron Stevenson, although passing a fitness test, was put on the subs' bench. For Sunderland Leighton James was back in the team bringing the side to full strength. Sunderland were raring to go after missing out the previous week because of bad weather. There was no problem with the Roker Park surface, and at kick-off the pitch was in perfect condition.

Blues were made to defend early on when an attempt from Rowell, latching onto a loose ball, was sent to Bracewell, who was then tackled by McCarrick, nudging the ball to safety. Harford then had to leap into the air to nod away a corner kick which was threatening the goal, and then it was Blues' turn. A corner was awarded when clever play forced Elliott to head the ball out. McCarrick took the kick and passed to Blake, but his header went wide of the post. Seven minutes into the game and Sunderland were attacking again. The first attempt was cleared but came back on the rebound to be cleared eventually the second time around.

This about summed up the action of the first half, with play passing from one end of the pitch to the other. Each side pushed for a goal, but the ball was not keen to go over the line. A clash of heads after 15 minutes between Noel Blake and Ian Atkins resulted in Blake wearing a plaster on his forehead and Atkins suffering from concussion. He lasted another eight minutes before he had to be helped off the pitch. His substitute West did not come onto the field straight away as Durban wanted to see if Atkins could carry on before sending on West. When he finally joined the field he took up position up front as partner to Chapman.

The first goal came just before the half-time break, with an own goal from Wright putting Sunderland into the lead. West's header was no threat for Coton, that was until Wright decided to help it along and his header saw the ball hit the back of the net on 40 minutes.

The embarrassment was turned into determination, and there were more attempts for Blues before the break.

The second half began with Blues searching for an equaliser to ease the pain of that first goal. Play remained on the same level for a long while, and they were beginning to accept that they may not score. Coton had to make a good save on 60 minutes from Chapman who nearly added to Sunderland's lead. Blues decided to step up their efforts and the pace of the game increased. The visitors proved it wasn't too late to stage a comeback when they were rewarded for their work with an equaliser on 85 minutes. A superb shot from Martin Kuhl found its way eventually into the net via a deflection, and the Blues fans, were jubilant. Just a minute later Blues surprised Sunderland again when a quick-fire shot from Harford also found the net to put them into the lead for the first time. It was a tough battle, but in the end they deserved their win.

BIRMINGHAM CITY

Coton, McCarrick, Van den Hauwe, Blake, Wright, Broadhurst, Gayle, Kuhl, Harford, Halsall, Hopkins.

SUNDERLAND

Turner, Venison, Pickering, Atkins (West), Chisholm, Elliott, Bracewell, Rowell, Chapman, Proctor, James.

REFEREE

Mr D Richardson (Great Harwood)

Pat Van den Hauwe

January 29

Playing record for this day
Playing record for this day is... 15 games, Won 3, Drawn 2, Lost 10, GF 15, GA 25.
Today's success rate....26.67% Year ranking....265th

The Matches played on this day

1898, Division 2		
Blues 2	Blackpool 3	Att. 6,000
Lewis, Robertson		
1910, Division 2		
Fulham 0	Blues 0	Att. 10,000
1927, FA Cup 4th round		
Southampton 4	Blues 1	Att. 15,804
	Briggs	
1930, FA Cup 4th round, replay		
Blues 0	Arsenal 1	Att. 47,521
1934, Division 1		
Blackburn Rovers 3	Blues 1	Att. 20,000
	McGurk	
1938, Division 1		
Charlton Athletic 2	Blues 0	Att. 20,000
1944, Wartime		
Blues 1	Stoke City 4	
Trigg		
1955, FA Cup 4th round		
Blues 2	Bolton Wanderers 1	Att. 56,800
Wheeler(og) 7	Moir 11	
Govan 88		
1966, Division 2		
Crystal Palace 1	Blues 0	Att. 14,190
Whitehouse 25		

Whitehouse also had a goal disallowed after 8 mins

1972, Division 2		
Blues 4 Swindon Town 1....Att. 27,824		
Francis 32	Horsfield 83	
Hatton 41		
B.Latchford 45, 49		
1977, FA Cup 4th round		
Blues 1	Leeds United 2	Att. 38,663
Burns 81	Jordan 57	
	Clarke 72	

This game screened on ATV's Star Soccer

1983, FA Cup 4th round		
Crystal Palace 1	Blues 0	Att. 12,327
Edwards 50		

Palace's Henry Hughton sent off after 69 mins

1997, Division 1		
QPR 1	Blues 1	Att. 12,138
Spencer 60	Devlin 37	
2000, Division 1		
Blues 2	Stockport County 1	Att. 17,150
Holdsworth 63	Johnson.M 20(og)	
Hughes 73		
2002, Division 1		
WBA 1	Blues 0	Att. 25,266
Roberts 43		

Match of the Day

FROM 1972

LATCHFORD SWOOPS TO SWAT SWINDON

Blues unbeaten record goes on as Swindon swept aside

Blues extended their unbeaten home league record to 28 games with this latest 4-1 win over Swindon. The game kicked off in brilliant sunshine and even the fleeting snow didn't dampen the day, or the team's spirits. Blues were in control right from the outset, as though the pitch was still solid from the overnight frost, and beginning to cause problems for both sides. A right wing corner in the opening seconds for Blues produced no reward, but it was a sign of the frenetic action to come. This was welcomed by the 27,804 in attendance.

There were attempts at goal from both sides as they endeavoured to keep the game flowing at a fast pace. Harland then earned himself a stern lecture from the referee after 'hiding' the ball behind his back during a rare stoppage in the game. Although it amused the crowd the ref didn't see anything funny and the name Harland was fortunate not to go into his notebook.

The first goal of the game came on 32 minutes and it was Birmingham who were celebrating. It was another trademark wonder strike by none other than Trevor Francis who almost burst the roof of the net with a terrific volley, this his sixth goal in as many games. This fired up the Blues performance even more and with four minutes of the half remaining they scored again to go 2-0 up. Latchford aimed a perfect cross towards the far post where Taylor glanced it on for Hatton to finish of a great move with a simple header.

Right on the stroke of half time Blues effectively wrapped up the game with a third, and killer goal. Page this time doing most of the legwork on the right expertly picked out Latchford with a glorious sweeping pass into the area, after the centre forward's first effort had smashed against the post, he hit the rebound with an equally emphatic whallop and the ball this time soared into the roof of the net.

Although comfortably in the lead, Blues began the second half showing no signs of easing up on the attack. This commendable approach was further encouraged by the home crowd who were appreciating their efforts with a huge roar every time Blues got within striking distance of the Swindon goal. It took just four minutes for Birmingham to reap further reward with a fourth goal.

Swindon keeper Downsborough, impeded by a team mate, only partially cleared a cross from Pendrey and the loose ball fell to Campbell lurking on the edge of the penalty area. He tapped a short pass into the path of Taylor who centred again, this time with Swindon in total disarray Latchford fired in his second goal of the game bringing his seasonal goals tally to 18.

Piece by piece the Swindon defence was dismantled by Birmingham's forwards. It almost seemed like they were deliberately teasing them with a threat of a goal during every attack. Swindon were becoming increasingly frustrated and Taylor became the first victim of some nasty tackling by the visitors when sent sprawling on the turf by Peterson in the 56th minute. This led to one irate Blues fan jumping the fence and running onto the pitch to protest to the referee.

With seven minutes of the game left Swindon got a late consolation goal through good work and a neat finish from their centre forward Horsfield. This did little to ease the disappointment of the visiting fans, Birmingham's supporters in contrast left with huge smiles all round, and oblivious to the bitter cold wind which had blown up by the time the final whistle sounded.

BIRMINGHAM CITY
Cooper, Carroll, Pendrey, Page(Martin), Hynd, Harland, Campbell, Francis, Latchford, Hatton, Taylor.
SWINDON TOWN
Downsborough, Peterson, Trollope, Bunkell, Burrows, Butler, Hubbard, Smart, Horsfield, Noble, Rogers.

REFEREE
Mr S J Kayley (Preston)

Bob Hatton

Gordon Taylor

Blues news extra   1949...Friendly in London
Leyton Orient 1 Birmingham 2 ... Att.8,000

Birthdays
Simon Marsh born today in 1977   Trevor Dark born today in 1961

Playing record for this day

Playing record for this day is... 15 games, Won 3, Drawn 2, Lost 10, GF 15, GA 25.

Today's success rate.....36.67% Year ranking....245th

Match of the Day
FROM 1988
REES ENDS DROUGHT WITH A CRACKER
Blues into round five after storming win at Oakwell

Blues stormed through the strong wind at Barnsley's Oakwell ground to secure a fine 2-0 win and march on to round five of the FA Cup. For one Blues player in particular it was an even sweeter return to form, striker Tony Rees ended his barren scoring record by hitting a magnificent strike, his first goal since September which proved to be the winner.

The first half of this typical cup tie was anything but a classic, as two honest and hard-working sides battled with 100 per cent endeavour. But with silky skills at a premium, things were not helped by the Oakwell mud and the heavy South Yorkshire high wind. There was little in the way of goalmouth action but plenty of commitment all this changed on 11 minutes when Rees conjured up a magical strike to put Blues 1-0 up. Barnsley looked to have soaked up another Blues attack when the ball fell to Dobbin, however he made a total mess of his pass and Rees nipped in to steal the ball away just inside his own half. With yards of clear space Rees streaked forward on a determined run with the ball, as he neared the penalty area and just before the Barnsley defence sent men out to close him down, the pint-sized Welshman looked up, pulled back his right boot and let fly with a belting shot which went in off the upright. It had taken five months for this fifth goal of the season and it was greeted with total joy from the 3,000 Blues fans amongst the 13,219 crowd. With the advantage now established, Blues set about their next task of being disciplined in defence as Barnsley sought a quick equaliser, the backline didn't disappoint.

Barnsley came out for the second half determined to up the pace and within minutes the Blues goal suffered its first real threat. A header from Lowndes, who had evaded Overson for once, was placed wide of Hansbury's reach but the ball bobbled against the post before going wide. Seconds later, in the next Barnsley assault, Broddle's low pass rolled across the face of the Blues goal as at least four pairs of feet failed to make contact in front of the open net. It was almost three full minutes before Blues managed to take the ball into the opposition half. Then a mistake by Williams almost proved fatal, his back pass was sent without consideration of the mud and never looked likely to make its way safely back to its intended target, Blues keeper Hansbury. Broddle realised this immediately and a two-man race for the ball started, Hansbury coming out and Broddle sprinting in. Fortunately the Blues man won by a split second, his kicked clearance deflecting off the Barnsley forward and out for a throw in. Grateful of the let-off, it was Blues who then surprisingly almost increased their lead soon after, Wigley missing twice in the same attack both from within ten yards, one from his right boot, the other a follow up header which went inches wide. Now the play was a little more end-to-end and Rees and Handysides were both making progress for the Blues. With the game coming to an end it was these two who played a significant part in laying on the chance for Wigley to make amends for his earlier misses, with a goal in the 89th minute. The goal, a simple but effective finish from inside the area came right in front of the travelling fans and put Blues into the FA Cup fifth round for the first time in four years.

BIRMINGHAM CITY
Hansbury, Ranson, Dicks, Williams, Overson, Trewick, Bremner, Childs, Rees, Handysides, Wigley.
BARNSLEY
Baker, Joyce, Cross, Thomas, McGugan, Futcher, Foreman (McDonald 71), Agnew, Lowndes, Dobbin, Broddle.

REFEREE
Mr Joe Worrall (Warrington)

Gary Breen celebrates scoring against Wolves

Blues news extra Breen breaks Blues transfer record

Coventry manager Gordon Strachan today snapped up Irish international defensive prospect Gary Breen for a cool £2.5 million pounds. Breen became Blues highest transfer sale, ironically Trevor Francis who sanctioned the sale previously set the record in 1979 when he became the first £1 million sale in the country.

Birthdays
Rui Esteves born today in 1967

January 31

Playing record for this day
Playing record for this day is... 16 games, Won 8, Drawn 4, Lost 4, GF 26, GA 17.
Today's success rate....62.50% Year ranking....37th

The Matches played on this day

1903, Division 2
Blues 5   Burslem Port Vale 1   Att. 6,000
McRoberts, Jones,
Beer, Windridge(2)

1914, FA Cup 2nd round
Blues 1   Huddersfield Town 0   Att. 45,000
Morgan

1920, FA Cup 2nd round
Blues 4   Darlington 0   Att. 47,000
Millard, Whitehouse(3)

1925, FA Cup 2nd round
Blues 1   Stockport County 0   Att. 36,000
Harris

1931, Division 1
Arsenal 1   Blues 1   Att. 30,913
          Bradford

1948, Division 2
Blues 0   Brentford 0   Att. 37,000

1953, FA Cup 4th round
Sheffield United 1   Blues 1   Att. 43,104
Hagan 39   Purdon 73

1959, Division 1
Burnley 0   Blues 1   Att. 22,151
         Gordon 55

1970, Division 2
Blues 2   Bristol City 2   Att. 20,421
Summerill 32   Bush 32
Vincent 66   Skirton 83
Vincent's goal scored direct from a corner Hately goal
disallowed in 31st minute for Blues

1976, Division 1
Manchester United 3   Blues 1   Att. 50,724
Forsyth 36   Withe 60
Macari 45
McIlroy 89

1981, Division 1
Manchester United 2   Blues 0   Att. 39,081
Jordan 5
Macari 85

1987, FA Cup 4th round
Walsall 1   Blues 0   Att. 14,810
Cross 81

1995, Auto Windscreens Shield, southern area,
Semi Final
Blues 3   Swansea City 2   Att. 20,326
Claridge 14   Pascoe 3
Francis 65   Lowe(og) 41
Tait 97
Blues first encounter with the sudden death 'golden goal' rule
it was a successful outcome when Tait ended the tie seven
minutes into extra time. £800,000 striker Kevin Francis
scored on his debut for Blues.At 6 foot 7 inches he is the
football League's tallest player. Blues have Chris Whyte sent
off

1998, Division 1
Reading 2   Blues 0   Att. 10,315
Hodges 75
Asaba 84
Blues finished the game with nine men, Paul Furlong and
Chris Marsden were both sent off during the second half.
Blues centre half, Steve Bruce plays his 900th game as a
professional player.

1999, Division 1
Blues 2   Bradford City 1   Att. 19,290
Furlong 45, 90(pen)   Lawrence 27

2001, Worthington Cup Semi Final, 2nd leg
Blues 4   Ipswich Town 1   Att. 28,624
Grainger 42   Scowcroft 56
Horsfield 55, 103
Johnson.A 116
A.E.T scores level on aggregate 2-2 after 90 mins

Match of the Day

FROM 2001
THE CARDIFF DANCE

Millennium Stadium next stop for Blues first major final in 45 years

A thrilling game, a fantastic night, a dream of a major final reward. All witnessed by the highest St Andrews attendance of the season at 28,624, many of whom would be queueing for their first tickets to a showpiece final ever. Although Blues won this very competition in 1963, back then it was a cup competition shunned by the top clubs as a distraction to the big domestic titles - the championship and FA Cup, the latter because of a prestigious final at Wembley Stadium. The competition was now a major honour carrying a European qualification, and in 2002 was the added bonus of a new stadium holding the event for the first time. With Wembley padlocked up and waiting for the bulldozers, the stage had now been moved to Cardiff's impressive and aptly named Millennium Stadium.

Blues set about the deficit from the first leg against a Premiership team with the second best away record with an all-out attack. However, despite their efforts on a poor pitch better suited for the Tractor Boys, they didn't level the tie until the 42nd minute. Adebola swung the ball across as Lazaridis and Croft challenged for it, the defender sliced his clearance, which swung over his head and bounced invitingly for Grainger to nod in from underneath the crossbar, from barely a yard out. The teams went in at half time with the tie equal at 1-1.

The policy of attacking Ipswich didn't stop after the break, and within ten minutes Blues deservedly took the lead. A long, high ball from Gill in the centre circle dropped between Adebola and Ipswich defender Mowbray. The luck of the bounce went the tall striker's way, and he neatly clipped the ball to his right to Horsfield. Although his first shot was well saved by Wright, Horsfield quickly pounced on the rebound and smashed it in. Blues were now in front for the first time in the tie. All that was needed was to hold on without conceding a costly away goal, but whilst Blues fans were still celebrating, Ipswich, through Scowcroft, levelled again. The goal was almost a replica of the one scored a minute earlier. Scowcroft's shot from close range was blocked well by Bennett, but again the rebound only went back to the striker, who made no mistake the second time. So the tie went into a nailbiting period of extra time, but with Ipswich holding the important away goal, Blues would be out unless they won the tie outright.

Extra time was played at the same tempo as the previous 90 minutes. As the first period drew to a close, Blues were rewarded with a priceless goal. O'Connor fed the ball to Sonner, who threaded a superb pass to Horsfield, he got round the back of the entire Ipswich defence and taking the ball in his stride, coolly placed his low shot into the corner. The second period of extra time was a little more difficult as Blues were content to hold on to their slender advantage and wait for an Ipswich mistake. With just four minutes remaining, a long goal kick from Bennett was headed down by an Ipswich defender to team-mate Armstrong, who knocked a regulation back pass to keeper Wright. On the edge of his area the England goalkeeper inexplicably miskicked, allowing Andrew Johnson the chance every supporter dreams of, rolling the ball into an empty net in front of the Tilton. Blues had won the game 4-1, the tie 4-2, and at the end we were all doing 'The Cardiff Dance.'

BIRMINGHAM CITY
Bennett, Gill, Grainger, Sonner, Purse,Michael Johnson, Eaden(Hughes), Adebola(Andrew Johnson), Horsfield, O'Connor, Lazaridis(Burrows).

IPSWICH TOWN
Richard Wright, Croft (Reuser 106), McGreal, Venus, Hreidarsson, Jermaine Wright, Holland, Magilton, Clapham (Karic 108), Stewart, Naylor (Scowcroft 56).

REFEREE
Mr J Winter (Stockton-on-Tees)

Dele Adebola

Playing record for this day

Playing record for this day is... 14 games, Won 4, Drawn 1, Lost 9, GF 20, GA 32.

Today's success rate....32.14.% Year ranking....261st

Match of the Day

FROM 1986
AT LAST!!!

Clarke's strike ends 17 game sequence without a win

Under constant pressure and against the run of play, a solitary strike from master goal poacher Wayne Clarke ended Blues worst-ever sequence of league results. Blues, without a league victory since 21 September had to weather the Oxford storm on a muddy Manor Ground pitch before Clarke's late strike at last brought home the win for Blues and newly appointed manager John Bond.

Blues had keeper David Seaman as much to thank for the rare victory as the goal-scorer, after a first half almost entirely dominated by the home side Oxford. As early as the second minute he had dashed out bravely to thwart the on-rushing John Aldridge who had left the slow reacting Blues defence for dead. Soon after a clumsy collision between Armstrong and Hebbard brought more danger as the loose ball fell fortunately for Aldridge again, this time he was stopped by a strong challenge from Hagan which on another day may have been punished by the award of a penalty, Blues had escaped again. The strong wind around the open Manor Ground didn't help the Blues defence and aided the goalkicking of Judge, all his kicks were being defended from the edge of the Blues penalty area with varying degrees of difficulty. From one huge kick by the Oxford 'keeper, Shotton back headed towards the Blues goal and only another fantastic leap and catch from Seaman prevented the game's opening goal. With almost 20 minutes of the game gone Blues finally managed to bring the Oxford keeper into defensive action when he did well to keep out a header from Armstrong, but this was the only chance Blues had as they soon found themselves back in the position of clinging on to the 0-0 scoreline. This was the successful outcome at the half way point, from John Bond's point of view.

Blues started the second half with an early blow, when Armstrong limped off to be replaced by Andy Kennedy, Bremner was forced to drop back from midfield to cover for the influential central defender. But with an added forward it was hoped this may take some of the pressure away from the over worked Blues defence. Indeed it was Kennedy who created Blues first chance of the half, and best chance of the game, within minutes of his introduction. Receiving a pass from Hopkins he went forward to send over a great cross for Geddis, however his disappointing first-time shot sailed high and wide landing deep into the terracing behing the goal. Oxford responded through Slatter whose fiercely hit shot from 30 yards took a deflection of Hagan, and it seemed destined to hit the back of the net. The shot was somehow stopped by an athletic two-handed save from Seaman at the last second, pushing the ball round the post for a corner. The Blues 'keeper was soon called on again to prevent another chance from Slatter moments later from Hagan's underhit backpass. As the half wore on Oxford, whether through tiredness or sympathy, eased off the gas, which allowed Blues a lengthy period of attacking play. This improved after Geddis almost broke the stalemate with a left-foot shot which curled just wide of the post. With just 12 minutes of the game remaining the unthinkable happened when the closely marked, and Clarke put Blues ahead with his first strike at goal. Again a ball from Kennedy which was intended for Geddis, was blocked and Clarke picking up the scraps inside the area chipped the ball across Judge and into the corner. A simple but devastating finish which stunned the majority of the 9,086 crowd bar the 1,800 or so travelling Blues fans behind the goal the ball nestled in. A delighted John Bond was off and running with his first win as Blues' boss.

BIRMINGHAM CITY

Seaman, Ranson, Roberts, Hagan, Armstrong (Kennedy 47), Kuhl, Bremner, Clarke, Whitton, Geddis, Hopkins.

OXFORD UNITED

Judge, Trewick, Slatter, Phillips (Thomas 50), Briggs, Shotton, Houghton, Aldridge, Leworthy, Hebbard, Brock.

REFEREE

Mr MJ Heath (Stoke)

The Matches played on this day

1890, FA Cup 2nd round
Wolverhampton W. 2   Blues 1   Att. 3,000
                          W.Devey

1896, FA Cup 1st round
Blues 1   Bury 4   Att. 15,000
Lewis

1902, Division 1
Newcastle United 2   Blues 0   Att. 13,000

1930, Division 1
Blues 1   Blackburn Rovers 2   Att. 20,000
Bradford

1933, Division 1
Blues 3   Derby County 1   Att. 19,687
Gregg,
Haywood, Curtis

1936, Division 1
Blues 4   Blackburn Rovers 2   Att. 25,000
Guest,
Harris(2), Jennings
Blues equalled their best win over Blackburn set in 1931

1947, Division 2
Blues 3   Southampton 1   Att. 32,878
Trigg(2), Mulraney

1958, Division 1
Preston North End 8   Blues 0   Att. 21,373
Finney 4, 12
Thompson 54, 71, 73
Taylor 61, 70, 81
Blues heaviest league defeat for 28 years

1964, Division 1
Ipswich Town 3   Blues 2   Att. 13,349
Hegan 6   Regan 11
Blackwood 59, 61   Farmer 60

1969, Division 2
Blackpool 2   Blues 1   Att. 11,294
Brown 23   James(og) 59
Suddick 69

1975, Division 1
Blues 1   Burnley 1   Att. 24,990
Emmanuel 22   Hankin 44
Gary Emmanuel scored on his St Andrews debut, on his 21st birthday

1978, FA Cup 4th round
Derby County 2   Blues 1   Att. 31,955
Daly 2   Bertschin 44
Masson 12

1986, Division 1
Oxford United 0   Blues 1   Att. 20,326
                     Clarke 78
Blues end their worst ever sequence of winless matches.
First game in charge for new Blues manager John Bond

1997, Division 1
Bolton Wanderers 2   Blues 1   Att. 16,737
McGinlay 78(pen)   Devlin 46
Pollock 29
Blues had Martin Grainger sent off after 78 minutes

Sadly Missed

Walter Abbott died today in 1941, aged 63

Birthdays

Gary Emmanuel born today in 1954   **John Paskin born today in 1962**

February 2

Playing record for this day

Playing record for this day is... 16 games, Won 6, Drawn 2, Lost 8, GF 21, GA 21.

Today's success rate.....43.75% Year ranking....214th

Match of the Day
FROM 1991
EXETER BLOWN AWAY BY GAYLE

Two goal hero seals an impressive winning performance

Blues today travelled to the snow covered West Country under caretaker-manager Bill Coldwell, looking to maintain their improved performances of late. They won last week at Bury, and were hoping that today's pitch would not hamper their game. The referee had inspected the field early on and decided that, despite the mix of snow, slush and mud, the game could go ahead. This decision was backed up by Exeter manager Terry Cooper, and the stage was set for a battle.

In front of the 5,154 crowd, Exeter were eager to increase their unbeaten home run, which stood at nine games, and Blues were looking to ensure that no goals were conceded for the second successive week. Defenders Ian Clarkson and Robert Hopkins were brought into the Blues squad in place of Vince Overson and John Frain.

Blues' much criticised striker John Gayle became both hero and villain today, stealing much of the action. He was booked in the 20th minute for his third foul on Exeter skipper Shaun Taylor, and was given his last warning just 12 minutes later after yet another challenge on Taylor.

The first half ended with no goals.

The first goal came on 56 minutes with a stunning header from Gayle. He was also the scorer of the second goal after Aylott's shot had been blocked and rebounded out.

Gayle again caused uproar when he brought down Peter Cawley in the penalty area. The referee awarded the spot kick, and Tom Kelly stepped up to try his luck. However, he miscued his shot completely as Martin Thomas stretched out to his left to save his second consecutive penalty. The save was one of only three that the Blues goalkeeper had to make in this match, the others coming from Gordon Hobson and Murray Jones.

BIRMINGHAM CITY

Thomas, Rodgerson, Clarkson, Matthewson, Hopkins, Bailey, Sturridge, Peer, Gleghorn, Aylott, Gayle.

EXETER CITY

Miller, Hiley, Cawley, Taylor, Kelly, Eshelby (Morgan), Hobson, O'Toole, Marshall, Neville, Jones.

REFEREE

Mr M Pierce (Portsmouth)

John Gayle

Blues news extra   2001...Blues £1 million swoop

Blues today completed the signing of midfielder Curtis Woodhouse for £1 million from Sheffield United. 2002...Blues v Crewe This first Division fixture was abandoned after 58 minutes play due to a waterlogged pitch with the score 0-0.

Birthdays

Jim Blyth born today in 1955

Playing record for this day

Playing record for this day is... 13 games, Won 3, Drawn 2, Lost 8, GF 14, GA 27.

Today's success rate.....30.77% Year ranking....263rd

Match of the Day

FROM 2001

BLUES DO IT THE WOODHOUSE WAY

Curtis joins the double-seeking Blues who are still on course

New £1million signing Curtis Woodhouse settled into a winning debut as Blues continue their dream of promotion and League Cup success. Before the game more than a few of the 18,551 attending St Andrews for this bread-and-butter clash with Norwich would have already been rehearsing their cliches, this was the party hangover, the banana skin around the corner, the proverbial 'one' after the Lord Mayor's show, how wrong they proved to be. It was just three days since that illustrious cup semi final win over Ipswich, now it was the turn of their neighbours Norwich City to become the latest victims of the all-conquering Blues bandwagon now in top gear.

The game started with the pitch surface the only lasting memory of that great night, large sanded areas had blotted the scars of the thrilling two hour victorious battle. Particular attention had been paid to the Tilton Road end penalty area, which Blues, who had won the toss, decided to defend first. Blues, still on an obvious high started the brighter and it took just nine minutes for a chance to come along which Hughes put away with confident ease. Grainger started the move by putting Lazaridis away down the left wing. Running to the by line he sent over a difficult low outswinging cross which deflected off Andy Johnson at the near post into the path of Hughes following closely behind to volley into the corner from eight yards. Blues held their lead to the half-time interval thanks mainly to the tigerish enthusiasm of Woodhouse in midfield and the the commanding defence led by man-of-the-match Darren Purse.

Blues had to wait 17 minutes to double their lead and they did courtesy of a penalty. Geoff Horsfield shielded the ball well from Grainger's throw in and as he turned to cross the ball caught defender Lee Marshall on the arm preventing Woodhouse from capitalising on the pass. Darren Purse ran up and hammered the 12-yard kick into the top corner with Marshall well beaten depite guessing correctly diving to his left. With tired limbs on a pudding pitch the Blues naturally tired and with 11 minutes remaining they concede to a quick Norwich counter attack. A teasing cross from the right wing from Nedergaard evaded Michael Johnson and Llewellyn nipped in between McCarthy and Purse to head in from close range. Although Bennett got both hands to it the the ball squirmed through his grip and into the net. Blues held out and at the end the score remained 2-1.

BIRMINGHAM CITY

Bennett, Gill, Grainger, Woodhouse, Purse, Michael Johnson, Eaden (McCarthy 76 mins), Andrew Johnson (Adebola 54), Horsfield, Hughes, Lazaridis (O'Connor 76).

NORWICH CITY

Andy Marshall, Kenton (De Blasiis 67), Mackay, Jackson, Sutch, Lee Marshall (Coote 64), Nedergaard (Dalglish 83), Russell, Llewellyn, Abbey, Roberts.

REFEREE

Mr L Cable (Surrey)

Norwich City's Phil Mulryne (l) tackles Birmingham City's Curtis Woodhouse (r)

Birthdays

James Higgins born today in 1926

February 4

Playing record for this day

Playing record for this day is... 18 games, Won 10, Drawn 1, Lost 7, GF 32, GA 28.
Today's success rate.....58.33% Year ranking....73rd

Match of the Day

FROM 1956

ICE MAN BROWN THE HERO

Super cool Eddie Brown is hat-trick hero on ice

Bristol-based referee Mr Pullin arrived at St Andrews early before finally giving the game's go ahead at lunchtime, after a thorough inspection of a snow bound pitch which in his opinion was playable and safe for the players.

Charlton started with problems coming into the game on the back of a run of six away defeats and without two of their regular players, centre half Upton, and the influential midfielder Gauld. Blues kept to the same side which knocked out Orient from the FA cup by an emphatic 4-0 scoreline.

It was Birmingham who quickly adapted to the tricky conditions and Kinsey almost capitalised on Bartram's fumble within a minute, before the ball scrambled away for a corner. On six minutes Blues got in front when Brown volleyed in from close range after Astall's cross was twice left uncleared by the visitors. Straight from the restart Charlton should have levelled the score from an identical move, but Ayre's final shot was rushed and it sailed high and wide. Charlton then spurned two more efforts within a minute both of which should have been put away. Still Charlton pressed and Merrick brilliantly smothered the ball from Ryan's feet as he was about to shoot from just six yards. The 24,611 crowd were being treated to some great football, totally vindicating the ref's decision to play the game on such a surface. A shot by Astall was well saved but the ball only fell to Finney who fired it back first time with a fierce drive, once again Bartram blocked the effort superbly and a defender cleared the loose ball off the goal line.

Blues were the better starters to the second half. Straight from the kick-off Murphy went through the middle on a fantastic dribble which was only stopped by an equally brilliant tackle from Hewie. However from the resultant corner Blues increased their lead, Murphy's outswinger slipped out of Bartram's grip and Brown stabbed the ball in from on the goal line. Astall should have made the game safe soon after when he anticipated well to intercept Townsend's free kick which put him in the clear but with just the 'keeper to beat he finished with a dreadful shot which rolled harmlessly wide. Then from Astall's free kick on 56 minutes Brown just failed to score with a spectacular diving header, however the ball floated into the arms of Bartram who then dropped it and Murphy accepted the simple tap in. The goal ended Charlton's fight and Blues took total command of the remaining half hour, there just remained the question of whether Brown would cap a great game with a three goal reward. This was duly answered when he completed his hat-trick with 20 minutes remaining, and Blues had completed impressive back-to-back 4-0 victories. Brown left the field firmly clutching his match ball.

BIRMINGHAM CITY
Merrick, Hall, Green, Boyd, Smith, Warhurst, Astall, Finney, Brown, Kinsey, Murphy.
CHARLTON ATHLETIC
Bartram, Campbell, Townsend, O'Linn, Hewie, Hammond, Ayre, Ryan, Leary, White, Kiernan.

REFEREE
Mr GW Pullin (Bristol)

(R-L) Charlton Athletic goalkeeper Sam Bartram punches clear from teammate Ken Chamberlain and Birmingham City's Eddie Brown, watched by teammate Cyril Hammond

Birthdays

Mark McCarrick born today in 1962   Peter Shearer born today in 1967

Playing record for this day

Playing record for this day is... 14 games, Won 6, Drawn 5, Lost 3, GF 18, GA 17.

Today's success rate.....60.71% Year ranking....46th

Match of the Day
FROM 1983

BLUES 3
WEST HAM-MERED 0

Harford and co hand out sweet revenge to the Hammers

Blues set off at an electrifying pace eager to put the record straight against West Ham. They had been waiting five months for this and it was clear the blow to their professional pride was still hurting from that game at Upton Park. It was back on 11 September when Blues arrived back from the capital having been truly walloped by 5-0, now it was pay-back time. Before the kick-off the 12,539 crowd stood in perfect silence in respect of the recent death of Blues long serving secretary Alan Instone, a fitting tribute to a fine club servant.

Blues started with tremendous enthusiasm, clearly this was a game they had to win to end a disappointing five game winless sequence, and exact revenge for the humiliating defeat earlier in the season. The only thing going against Blues was their over-exuberance and Dennis fell foul of the ref when he recklessly clattered into Goddard earning him a booking on 18 minutes. Blues dominance had to reap reward and after 30 minutes they had the goal they dearly wanted. Curbishley more than anyone was up for this game and he suddenly burst forward on the right, centred for Harford who crashed it in. Astonishingly this was his first of the season in his 'lucky' 13th game. Curbishley continued to be a thorn in his old team-mates' side with a wonderful and determined game in the heart of the midfield, where Blues were clearly now on top and controlling the game.

With Blues feeble current form a second goal was always going to be vital and the crowd didn't have to wait too long in the second half for the killer goal to arrive. It was precisely nine minutes, before Ferguson netted and thus received justice for his effort two minutes earlier when he finished of a brilliant five man move with a header which struck the bar. This time he rose to plant a cross from Dillon firmly past Parkes into the bottom corner of the goal. Blues were now rampant but try as they might they couldn't add to the score until Gayle's last-minute strike.

BIRMINGHAM CITY

Coton, Langan, Dennis, Stevenson, Blake, Broadhurst, Gayle, Ferguson, Harford, Curbishley, Dillon.

WEST HAM UNITED

Parkes, Lampard, Gallagher, Bonds, Martin, Devonshire, Van Der Elst, Goddard, Clark, Allen, Cowie.

REFEREE

Mr Tom Fitzharris (Bolton)

Malcolm Page

Blues news extra   1936...Hibbs wins 25th and final cap for England.

Harry Hibbs, Blues goalkeeper played his last international today at Molineux, Wolverhampton against Wales. He is Birmingham's most capped player. England lost the game 2-1 but no fault was attached to Hibbs who was as sound as ever between the posts. Hibbs kept ten clean sheets from his 25 games a record at the time for England.

Birthdays

Malcom Page born today in 1947   **Jae Martin born today in 1976**

The Matches played on this day

1898, Division 2.
Burnley 4 | Blues 1 | Att. 4,000
Oakes

1921, Division 2.
Blues 2 | Notts County 0 | Att. 35,000
Burkinshaw(2)

1927, Division 1.
Blues 1 | WBA 0 | Att. 34,000
Bradford

1938, Division 1.
Blues 0 | Preston North End 0 | Att. 25,000

1944, Wartime
Wolverhampton W. 0 | Blues 2
Trigg(2)

1949, Division 1.
Blues 0 | Burnley 0 | Att. 35,000

1955, Division 2.
Blues 3 | Lincoln City 3 | Att. 20,500
Kinsey 8 | Gibson 7
Murphy 50, 89 | Garvie 14
Finch 76

1966, Division 2.
Blues 1 | Preston North End 1 | Att. 14,600
Jackson 79 | Lee 18

1972, FA Cup 4th round.
Blues 1 | Ipswich Town 0 | Att. 40,709
B.Latchford 1
This match was shown on ATV's Star Soccer

1977, Division 1.
Liverpool 4 | Blues 1 | Att. 41,073
Neal 37(pen) | Burns 1
Toshack 42, 72
Heighway 78
Match screened by ATV's, Star Soccer

1983, Division 1.
Blues 3 | West Ham United 0 | Att. 12,539
Harford 35
Ferguson 54
Gayle 90

1991, Division 3.
Blues 0 | Wigan Athletic 0 | .Att. 5,319

1994, Division 1.
Blues 0 | Peterborough U. 0 | Att. 15,140
Posh's Dave McDonald was sent off after 56 minutes.

2000, Division 1.
Crewe Alexandra 2 | Blues 3 | Att. 6,289
Macauley 20, 90 | O' Connor 45(pen)
Hughes 54
Adebola 71

February 6

Playing record for this day

Playing record for this day is... 16 games, Won 6, Drawn 3, Lost 7, GF 29, GA 31.

Today's success rate.....46.88% Year ranking....191st

Match of the Day
FROM 1971
VINTAGE BLUES

After early set back Blues storm from behing to beat the Lions

Blues welcomed back their teenage super star Trevor Francis who was making his first league appearance since the Boxing Day draw at Blackburn, as they embarked on their belated promotion surge. Blues were still ten points behind leaders Hull despite taking ten points from a possible 12 since their last defeat, this was against their opponents this afternoon, who were also above Birmingham in the Second Division table.

Blues started the better in a slow and cautious game, the midfield being the most contentious area of the field in the opening minutes. Goal chances were rare but this was to change on 11 minutes when three goals were scored in as many minutes. Millwall grabbed the first goal taking the lead after a fantastic four man move set Neil up with a chance to shoot from the edge of the penalty area, his fierce drive hurtled past Latchford who could only watch the ball crash into the net behind him. The visitors however enjoyed their lead for less than 60 seconds. When Taylor's run was stopped by a crunching tackle from Cripps, Campbell flicked the in-direct free kick up just off the ground for Page who slammed the ball into the top corner. The 21,893 crowd had barely finished celebrating when Blues through Francis surged forward again, picking up the ball from the half way line he weaved his way through the middle of the Millwall defence on an amazing solo run, as the last man Dunphy came across to stop him, the teenager showed his growing strength by holding off the challenge to place a low angled drive into the bottom far corner of the net. The St Andrews crowd had witnessed one of the all time great goals from the wonder boy, Trevor Francis. This completed a staggering three minutes play, the sort you don't want to find you have missed whilst going for a pie and ... loo break. There was no further addition to the score and Blues went into the break with the crowd still humming after that quite exceptional piece of individual skill which separated the two teams. The second half went almost as most of the first half had, with both sides cautiously respectful of making any error to hand their opponents an advantage, and this ensured a tight midfield battle for a large proportion of the remaining 45 minutes. Not untill the last 15 minutes did the pattern change when Millwall decided to gamble in search of a much needed equaliser, this was when play opened up, to Birmingham's liking. Blues always had the perfect weapon in this situation , with Francis they had the deadly pace to counter attack any side in the country, and Millwall soon found this to their cost when both points slipped away for sure after 80 minutes. From an attack by Millwall the ball broke to Taylor who quickly looked for Francis realising the visitors were now stretched out in defence. His ball seemed to be over hit but the Blues number 8 made up the ground with breath taking acceleration, as he was about to make contact with the ball Brown clipped his back leg and a penalty was immediately awarded. Summerill took the ball, chose power over placement with his 12-yard spot kick, and put the game safe at 3-1 to Birmingham City.

BIRMINGHAM CITY

Dave Latchford, Martin, Pendrey, Page, Hynd, Robinson, Campbell, Francis, Bob Latchford, Summerill, Taylor.

MILLWALL

King, Brown, Cripps, Durney, Kitchener, Burnett, Possee, Dunphy, Bridges, Bolland, Neil (Holmes).

Phil Summerill

Birthdays

Paul Jones born today in 1974   Bill Steel born today in 1908

Playing record for this day

Playing record for this day is... 15 games, Won 6, Drawn 6, Lost 3, GF 28, GA 21.

Today's success rate.....60% Year ranking....55th

Match of the Day

FROM 1931

BRADFORD 4 ROVERS 0

Joe Bradford scores a staggering 13th hat-trick

Blues went into this important game without flu' victim George Briggs. In desperate need for points to aid their First Division survival, Harry Lane was introduced as a late replacement. They were up against a Blackburn side fresh from an 8-2 hammering at Sunderland a week earlier. The visitors won the toss, and kicked off towards the Railway End. They had the better of the opening chances with Hibbs having to block a Cunliffe shot. Jones and Gorman put up a safe defence against the Blues' attack, and when the home team did get through, Curtis' half chance sailed over the bar without troubling Binns.

It was no surprise when the opening goal came from Blackburn on 21 minutes with a swerving kick into the right-hand corner from McLean. Blackburn were in charge of the game, when a long-range snap shot from Leslie called on Binns to make his first save of any note, clutching the ball on his second attempt. With half time approaching, Bradford equalised for Blues with a narrow angled shot on 41 minutes.

The second half started welll for Blues when Bradford scored again after just 30 seconds without a Blackburn player having touched the ball. Blues continued on the attack, leaving Blackburn chasing an equaliser. As the game entered the final five minutes, many of the 30,000 crowd turned to leave, confident that Blues would hold out for the valuable two points. Blackburn's penalty appeal was ignored when McLean went down in the area, and Blues needed a killer third goal to keep them safe. It came with just three minutes left to play when Curtis broke free and passed to Bradford, who again hit a swift low shot past Binns to complete his 13th hat-trick - his fourth against Blackburn, and his last for Blues. Just a minute later a beaten Blackburn allowed their concentration to lapse, letting Bradford pounce and score a fourth from close range. Blues improved their league position with this 4-1 win, and avoided the drop by one place, finishing 19th in Division One.

BIRMINGHAM CITY

Hibbs, Liddell, Barkas, Cringan, Morrall, Leslie, Lane, Crosbie, Bradford, Gregg, Curtis.

BLACKBURN ROVERS

Binns, Gorman, Jones, Imrie, Healless, Roscamp, John Bruton, Puddefoot, Leslie Bruton, McLean, Cunliffe.

REFEREE

Mr E Wood (Sheffield)

Joe Bradford

February 8

Playing record for this day
Playing record for this day is... 13 games, Won 3, Drawn 3, Lost 7, GF 11, GA 18.
Today's success rate.....34.62% Year ranking....251st

Match of the Day
FROM 1947
BRUM WIN BATTLE OF CITIES
Liverpool next after Man City thumped by five

On a bitterly cold day, with snow cleared from the pitch which was heavily scattered with sawdust and sand, this eagerly awaited fifth round FA Cup tie got under away between Second Division leaders Manchester City and fourth placed Birmingham City. The teams were greeted by bell ringing, rattle swinging, hooter blowers, and trumpeters in the 50,000 crowd, which included the Lord Mayor of Birmingham and 5,000 Mancunians all making up a terrific atmosphere inside a packed St Andrews. Both sides made one change from their previous line ups. Dougall returned from a one-week absence through injury for McIntosh, whilst Manchester City had regular centre forward Constantine sidelined through injury so in stepped Scottish international forward Andy Black to their line up.

Despite the treacherous suface, play got off at fast pace, the Blues of Birmingham having slightly the better of the early stages against their oppenents in their change strip of red shirts and white shorts. Despite good approach play by Blues it was the visitors who had the best chance of an early lead through Black's header, only a superb diving save by Merrick preventing a goal. The opening goal however came on nine minutes and it was the Blues who took first blood with a fantastic three-man move. Harris eluded the challenge of Emptage to race through the middle of the park, he passed to Mulraney who rolled the ball into the path of Bodle, who whacked a shot on the run hard and low. Although Swift got a hand to it he could not prevent the ball rolling agonisingly over the line despite scrambling back after it. The next scoring chance also fell to the Blues only this time Swift saved well from Harris. When Man City mounted sporadic counter attacks most were easily cleared up by centre half Turner who was having his best game for the club.

Blues resumed the second half with Trigg coming close with a shot following a neatly chipped cross from Mulraney. The visitors' best effort came from a free kick given just outside the area when Jennings handled. Westwood's direct free kick however sailed over the bar. Blues then conceded a corner which Dunkley curled in, hitting the crossbar. Blues doubled their lead when a dreadful miskick from McDowall allowed Trigg in on goal and as Swift advanced to narrow the angles, he drove the ball into the top corner, well out of the keeper's reach. It was all Blues pressure at this stage and two quick corners in succession bought a chance for Mulraney which was only averted by a well-timed sliding tackle by Barkas. Blues wrapped up the game eventually with a third goal on 79 minutes which summed up their confidence and classy performance. It was started by Harris and finished by Trigg and Mulraney who after a quick interchange of passes, both went clear on goal in a two-on-one with the 'keeper. Unselfishly Mulraney pushed the ball to his left for Trigg to finish into an empty net, as Swift was left with no alternative but to commit himself and was left stranded. Blues added further goals through Mitchell's penalty awarded after Sproston's handball with five minutes remaining, and with just two minutes left Edwards added a fifth to complete a commanding and well deserved win.

BIRMINGHAM CITY
Merrick, Duckhouse, Jennings, Harris, Turner, Mitchell, Mulraney, Dougall, Trigg, Bodle, Edwards.
MANCHESTER CITY
Swift, Sproston, Barkas, Fagan, McDowall, Emptage, Dunkley, Smith, Black, Capel, Westwood.

REFEREE
Mr WF Daly (Essex)

Arthur Turner

Birthdays
John Schofield born today in 1931   John Vincent born today in 1947

Playing record for this day

Playing record for this day is... 14 games, Won 6, Drawn 5, Lost 3, GF 19, GA 16.

Today's success rate.....60.71% Year ranking....45th

Match of the Day

FROM 1980

BERTSCHIN'S FINEST HOUR

Nine minute hat-trick puts Blues in promotion driving seat

Blues, and Keith Bertschin in particular, stepped up a gear to destroy a good Orient side within nine spectacular first half minutes. Despite periods when they tried to fritter away their lead the Blues defence then held on to win another important two points towards their on course promotion goal. Blues had the most uneasy start, but fortunately 'keeper Wealands was alert when he saved from Chiedozie and Mayo within the opening 15 minutes. Blues eventually settled and began to look positive, but for the first half hour the game remained uneventful. Then out of the blue came Bertschin, and he transformed the whole game within nine minutes. From a surging run and sweetly hit shot by Ainscow, Day in the Orient goal did extremely well to parry the ball away. As the Orient defenders stood momentarily admiring the save, Bertschin pounced to smash the loose ball into the top corner of the net. The next goal eight minutes later was simply stunning. A chipped free kick from Gemmill towards Bertschin, had the tall striker turning in a split second to unleash a fizzing right-foot volley which flew into the top right-hand corner, Day rooted to the ground without enough time to move. Whilst the 17,474 crowd were still celebrating that speciality Blues came forward again and Bertschin completed his quick-fire hat-trick. A clever pass from strike partner Frank Worthington went right across the face of Orient's goal eluding everyone, Dennis collected the ball from the other side of the penalty area, he looked up and delivered a beautifully weighted chipped cross to the unmarked Bertschin who placed his header wide of Day and into the corner. With Blues on fire at this point it is hard to believe that they didn't really turn the screw and look for an even bigger margin of victory, at this point they had Orient dead and buried. Keith Bertschin had completed his second hat-trick of the season bringing his seasonal goal tally to ten, he should in all honesty have got more in this game.

Blues however dropped the pace, content with the three goal lead, and almost declared, such was the lack of desire after the third goal. Orient soon woke them up and on 52 minutes they punished a sloppy piece of defending when Mayo unmarked, unchallenged and completly unnoticed headed in a corner from barely two yards out. This was just what was needed to pep the Blues up, and they came storming back as if to make up for the time spent in the wilderness since their last goal. A great chance fell to Bertschin again and only a despairing header by Fisher from just underneath the cross bar prevented Blues from re-establishing their three goal lead. But the game soon dwindled back into a midfield struggle and ended up in the same pattern as the opening 30 minutes.

BIRMINGHAM CITY

Wealands, Broadhurst, Dennis, Curbishley, Gallagher, Towers, Ainscow, Worthington, Bertschin, Gemmill, Johnston (Lynex 80).

ORIENT

Day, Fisher, Roffey, Taylor, Gray, Hughton, Chiedozie, Jennings, Mayo, Margerrison, Coates.

Keith Bertschin

Blues news extra 1963...Friendly Swindon Town 4 Blues 2

Due to bad weather and seven weeks without a game Blues played a friendly at Swindon, one of the few places in the country where play was possible, in front of 5,494. Ken Leek got both the Blues goals.

1977...Francis for England

Birmingham City's 'wonder boy' Trevor Francis finally made his international debut. He lined up for England against a strong Dutch team who dominated from the start although Francis overall had a good first game for the national side.

1979...The First Million Pound Footballer

At 2.40pm this afternoon, Birmingham's Trevor Francis ended his lengthy association with the club. He signed for Brian Clough's Nottingham Forest, becoming the first footballer in Britain to be transfered for a £1 million pound fee.

Birthdays

Garry Pendrey born today in 1949

The Matches played on this day

1895, Division 1.
Blues 1 — Sunderland 1 — Att. 15,000
Hands

1901, FA Cup 1st round.
Stoke 1 — Blues 1 — Att. 13,000
Main

1907, Division 1.
Notts County 2 — Blues 2 — Att. 8,000
Jones(2)

1918, Wartime.
Sheffield W. 0 — Blues 2
Bowser, Whitehouse

1924, Division 1.
Burnley 1 — Blues 2 — Att. 8,000
Cringan, Bradford

1929, Division 1.
Blues 1 — Sunderland 0 — Att. 16,000
Pike

1935, Division 1.
Blues 3 — Arsenal 0 — Att. 50,188
Jones, Bradford, Harris

1946, FA Cup 5th round, 1st leg.
Sunderland 1 — Blues 0 — Att. 45,000

1952, Division 2.
Southampton 2 — Blues 0 — Att. 18,688
McGowan 15
Daly 47
Players and spectators observed a minutes' silence for King George VI who died on 6 February.

1957, Division 1.
Blues 2 — Wolverhampton W. 2
Astall 29 — Hooper 74
Govan 32 — Murray 87

1980, Division 2.
Blues 3 — Orient 1 — .Att. 17,474
Bertschin 30, 38, 39 — Mayo 52

1988, Division 2.
Blues 1 — Millwall 0 — Att. 5,819
Whitton 72

1990, Division 3.
Tranmere Rovers 5 — Blues 1 — Att. 6,033
McNab 28 — Bailey 78(pen)
Steel 63
Malkin 70
Hughes 72
Muir 81

1993, Division 1.
Blues 0 — Millwall 0 — Att. 8,504

February 10

Playing record for this day
Playing record for this day is... 11 games, Won 6, Drawn 1, Lost 4, GF 22, GA 12.
Today's success rate.....59.09% Year ranking....59th

The Matches played on this day

1900, Division 1.
Blues 6   Loughborough Town 0 Att. 2,000
Aston(3),
Leake(2), Adey
1906, Division 1.
Blues 4   Notts County 2   Att. 6,500
Mounteney,
Green, Jones(2)
1912, Division 2.
Blues 3   Wolverhampton W. 1   Att. 25,000
Hall(3, 1pen)
1923, Division 1.
Blues 2   Oldham Athlectic 3   Att. 8,542
Bradford(2)
1934, Division 1.
Leeds United 1   Blues 0   .Att. 14,753
1951, FA Cup 5th round.
Blues 2   Bristol City 0   Att. 47,831
Stewart 28
Trigg 82
1962, Division 1.
Blues 1   Arsenal 0   Att. 27,797
Harris 21
Arsenal's keeper Kelsey saved Jimmy Harris's penalty on
43 minutes. Jimmy Harris goal disallowed for Blues on
54 minutes
1968, Division 2.
Millwall 1   Blues 1   Att. 13,961
Possee 55   Vowden 71
1973, Division 1.
Blues 2   Derby County 0   Att. 38,096
B.Latchford 29
Francis 48
Blues beat reigning champions Derby in a game screeened by
ATV's Star Soccer.
1979, Division 1.
Blues 0   Leeds United 1   Att. 17,620
                 Gray 22(pen)
This match screened by ATV's Star Soccer
2001, Division 1.
Sheffield United 3 Blues 1   Att. 19,313
Murphy 31   Horsfield 89
Devlin 41(pen)
Peschisolido 64

Match of the Day
FROM 1973
SUPER BOB BATTERS RAMS

Deadly duo Latchford & Francis again earn the points

Blues manager Freddie Goodwin was very happy with this performance which saw off Brian Clough's Derby County at St Andrews in front of a crowd of 38,096. Clough was also impressed with the home team's game, but not with his 22-year-old centre forward Roger Davies. He was, however, pleased with the performance of debut players, Tony Parry and John Sims. Out of the Derby team through injury were Alan Hinton, Colin Todd and John O'Hare.

For Blues, new captain John Roberts and Roger Hynd in midfield were marking Davies and Kevin Hector, and did a very good job of it too. Goalkeeper Dave Latchford had to make three cracking saves from shots by Archie Gemmill, Alan Durban and David Nish. An injury-hit Derby side were given more problems when England centre half Roy McFarland had to come off the field for 11 minutes when he suffered a nasty clash of heads with Bob Latchford. He later returned to the game, and played on despite the blood still flowing from his wound.

After 29 minutes a miskick from Ron Webster resulted in Bob Latchford scoring the first goal for Blues, and that was the end of the action for the first half.

The second half began, and in the 49th minute Francis converted Gordon Taylor's left-wing centre into Blues' second goal, the ball missing keeper Colin Boulton's fingertips as he dived to his left. This wrapped up the scoring for the match and, in fact, wrapped up the action.

Blues played with determination and skill, and were never really at threat of conceding goals from the opportunities created by Derby.

BIRMINGHAM CITY
Dave Latchford, Martin, Pendrey, Page, Hynd, Roberts, Campbell (Burns), Francis, Bob Latchford, Hatton, Taylor.
DERBY COUNTY
Boulton, Webster, Nish, Durban, McFarland, Parry, McGovern, Sims, Davies, Hector, Gemmill.

John Roberts

Birthdays
Andrew Johnson born today in 1981   Colin Green born today in 1942

Playing record for this day
Playing record for this day is... 15 games, Won 5, Drawn 4, Lost 6, GF 21, GA 19.
Today's success rate.....46.67% Year ranking....193rd

February 11

Match of the Day

FROM 1939

FULL HOUSE AT ST. ANDREWS

Cup tie thriller ends 2-2 in front of bumper Brum crowd

Since the draw was made the Birmingham public had eagerly waited for this attractive tie to come around, and that expectation was properly measured by the crowd size. 67,341 crammed into St Andrews the biggest ever, producing record gate receipts of £4,556 and the game lived up to its anticipated 'thriller' bill.

Everton were still on course for League and Cup success whilst Blues were looking likely candidates for relegation. The perfect tie for a shock and with this the crowds flocked to witness a potential upset. Birmingham were quickly defying league form though and were soon on the attack and had pegged Everton back with Jackie Brown looking a constant threat. After 15 minutes Dennis Jennings almost opened the scoring but his shot struck the post, then Craven headed over from six yards out with the goal at his mercy. Everton sensed that luck was on their side and began to attack themselves. Tommy Lawton came close with two efforts within a minutes but Frank Clack the Blues keeper saved well both times. In an end-to-end tussle it was Birmingham through Jennings again who came close this time hitting the side netting from just ten yards, then Sagar saved brilliantly from Owen Madden. As half time approached it was Everton who looked likely to score with Blues holding out for the break. However on 44 minutes a quick counter attack and fine 25-yard shot by Madden and the Blues took the lead, Sagar was unlucky as the ball took a deflection on the way into the net. Everton however found an equaliser within seconds of the restart, Irish international Alex Stevenson netting with a speculative shot which went past the unsighted Clack. So at half time the scores were level at 1-1.

In the second half both teams began with a more cautious approach in contrast to the first 45 minutes. After an hour Everton won a corner which was only half cleared by Clack who punched the ball out to Boyes who shot first time and althought the effort appeared to be going wide it hit Lawton and went in. Everton now led for the first time in the game and looked favourites to win comfortably.

Birmingham, to their credit, pushed forwards and Sagar was called on to keep Everton's lead on several occasions. With just ten minutes remaining a superb run from Craven found Owen Madden again unmarked and he powered his header in for a deserved equaliser. Birmingham continued to press forward encouraged by the excited crowd and came close in the dying minutes but again Sagar and the Everton defence kept them out. The game ended 2-2, Birmingham having come so close to the biggest surprise result of the round and in the replay it was indeed Everton who won 2-1. Everton advanced to round six to play Wolves who ended their hopes of the double by beating them 2-0, Everton settled for the championship instead. As for Birmingham, they were relegated at the season's end after 18 years in the First Division.

BIRMINGHAM CITY
Clack, Trigg, Hughes, Dearson, Halsall, Richards, Jennings, Craven, Harris, Madden, Brown.
EVERTON
Sagar, Cook, Greenhalgh, Mercer, Jones, Thomson, Gillick, Bootham, Lawton, Stevenson, Boyes.

REFEREE
Mr. WF Daly (Orpington)

Cyril Trigg

Birthdays

Thomas Robinson born today in 1909   Juan Miquel De Souza born today in 1970

The Matches played on this day

1899, FA Cup 2nd round.

Stoke 2	Blues 2	Att. 16,000
	Robertson,	
	Wharton	

1905, Division 1.

| Wolverhampton W. 1 | Blues 4 | Att. 15,500 |
| | Wilcox(3), Green | |

1922, Division 2.

| Liverpool 1 | Blues 0 | Att. 30,000 |

1928, Division 1.

| Bolton Wanderers 3 | Blues 2 | Att. 10,000 |
| Bradford, Crosbie | | |

1933, Division 1.

Blues 2	Leeds United 1	Att. 22,157
Haywood,		
Curtis(pen)		

1939, FA Cup 5th round.

| Blues 2 | Everton 2 | Att. 67,341 |
| Madden(2) | | |

Biggest St Andrews crowd to date, gate receipts of £4,556.

1956, Division 1.

| Tottenham Hotspur 0 | Blues 1 | Att. 26,160 |
| | Astall 68 | |

Gill Merrick saved a penalty from Brooks

1961, Division 1.

| Nottingham Forest 1 | Blues 0 | Att. 23,407 |
| Booth 42 | | |

1967, Division 2.

Blues 2	Millwall 0	Att. 18,008
Bullock 50		
Bridges 62		

1969, FA Cup 5th round.

Blues 2	Manchester United 2	Att. 51,685
Beard 66	Law 61	
Robinson 84(pen)	Best 75	

1984, Division 1.

| Blues 0 | Wolverhampton W. 0 | Att. 14,319 |

1989, Division 2.

| Blues 0 | Bournemouth 1 | Att. 6,444 |
| | Newson 46 | |

1992, Division 3.

Bradford City 1	Blues 2	Att. 7,008
Reid 90	Gleghorn 9	
	Sturridge 53	

1995, Division 2.

Crewe Alexandra 2	Blues 1	Att. 6,359
Clarkson 31	Donowa 90	
Murphy 63		

Barry Fry said after this defeat "I paid £800,000 each for Ricky Otto and Kevin Francis, on this display I wouldn't have paid £8 for both of them."

1996, Coca Cola Cup Semi Final, 1st leg.

Blues 1	Leeds United 2	Att. 24,781
Francis 27	Yeboah 54	
	Whyte(og) 73	

A cracking 25-yard strike by Kevin Francis gave Blues an early lead in this semi final against the Premiership side.

February 12

The Matches played on this day

1898, Division 2.		
Blues 4	Luton Town 2	Att. 4,000
Oakes,		
Abbott(2, 1pen),		
McEwan(og)		
1900, Division 2.		
Blues 0	Grimsby Town 1	Att. 2,000
1910, Division 2.		
Leeds City 2	Blues 1	Att. 10,000
	Freeman	
1921, Division 2.		
Clapton Orient 1	Blues 1	Att. 15,000
	Burkinshaw	
1927, Division 1.		
Bury 3	Blues 1	Att. 12,000
	Islip	
1938, Division 1.		
Grimsby Town 4	Blues 0	Att. 10,000
1944, Wartime.		
Blues 2	Wolverhampton W. 1	
Trigg(pen),		
Bright		
1949, Division 1.		
Blues 0	Everton 0	Att. 35,000
1955, Division 2.		
Bury 0	Blues 1	Att. 12,547
	Brown 5	
1966, FA Cup 4th round.		
Blues 1	Leicester City 2	Att. 46,680
Thwaites 26	Sinclair 39	
	Goodfellow 60	
1972, Division 2.		
Preston North End 0	Blues 0	Att. 17,794
1977, Division 1.		
Blues 3	Norwich City 2	Att. 21,809
Burns 2, 49	Steele 5	
Broadhurst 70	Reeves 25	
1994, Division 1.		
Millwall 2	Blues 1	Att. 9,438
Verveer 39, 59	Saville 63	
2000, Division 1.		
Blues 2	Bolton Wanderers 1	Att. 18,426
Rankin 50	Johnston 20	
Adebola 65		

Bolton had Gudjohnsen sent off in the last minute following a late tackle.

Playing record for this day

Playing record for this day is... 14 games, Won 5, Drawn 3, Lost 6, GF 17, GA 21.

Today's success rate.....46.43% Year ranking....196th

Match of the Day

FROM 1977

TEENAGER IN DREAM DEBUT

Broadhurst grabs the late winner in five goal thriller

The St Andrews crowd of 21,809 acclaimed a new hero at this match, a teenager on his Football League debut by the name of Kevan Broadhurst. He stepped in for Blues £110,000 signing from Everton, winger Gary Jones, who was left out for the first time since his arrival in September, and took his chance with a sensational late winning goal. Blues having led the game early on through man of the match Kenny Burns, were pegged back by goals from Steele and Reeves. Blues levelled again though Burns early in the second half which set up Broadhurst's super strike which won the game in the 70th minute.

Blues made one other team change before the game started with Tony Want in defence in place of Mick Rathbone who was suffering from a heavy cold. Norwich made one change to their side with youngster Doug Evans making his debut in place of the experienced ex-Albion player Colin Suggett. It was Blues who made a sensational start to the game, when after just 80 seconds Burns put them 1-0 up. From Hibbitt's corner Joe Gallagher rose at the far post to knock down and Burns reacted quickest turning on the ball and hitting a low close-range shot into the corner. The goal was just two seconds slower than the one he scored the previous week. Blues continued to press forward and moments later Keelan saved well from Burns again, tipping a rising shot over the bar. It was from Norwich's first attack that they gained an equaliser after five minutes, against the run of play. A cross from Ryan should have been cut out , but for once the ball evaded Kendall and fell to Steele who hit his right-foot shot past Latchford from the edge of the penalty area. The two early goals setled both sides into a more cautious approach. The next goal-scoring chance fell to Blues when Connolly's shot across Keelan was brilliantly blocked by the Norwich 'keeper after 20 minutes. Blues eagerness to push forward ultimately led to their undoing however, as they slipped again to trail 2-1. A sudden counter attack by Norwich left the Blues defence caught too far forward and too stretched. An unmarked Reeves chased onto a through ball on his own and with just Latchford to beat he smashed a long low drive into the net. Blues luck was out and this was perfectly highlighted in the 33rd minute. Keelan's push sent Connolly flying inside the box, and it seemed a certain penalty. Amazingly, the ref gave an indirect free kick which came to nothing, Francis hitting the ball straight into the wall and Norwich clearing comfortably.

Blues almost started the second half like the first with a goal. A free kick by Hibbitt was perfectly met by Gallagher and his header was thumped towards the top corner. However, Keelan somehow managed to twist in the air and touch it over, a breath-taking save. Blues were soon back and from another free kick in almost the identical position they equalised in the 49th minute. The kick this time was taken by Styles, his outswinging cross to the far post found Burns rushing in to crash his header into the roof of the net. Blues again started to dominate and Burns was close to gaining a hat-trick when a shot deflected off Peters and Keelan did well to touch the ball round the post. Moments later from Hibbitt's corner Jones just beat Burns to head clear when the Scot again had a perfect chance to record his third goal. From this corner, again sent over from Hibbitt, the ball was only partially cleared by the defence to the edge of the penalty area, where Broadhurst nipped in, controlled first time, and struck the ball firmly through a crowd of players into the bottom corner. Moments later another cracking long ball by Hibbitt found the newly-capped England international Trevor Francis clean through but his end shot was magnificently saved by Keelan again. With Blues for the first time in total control the game was safe, and in the closing moments they could have added a fourth but for great defending. Francis croosed hard and low for Burns and his first-time shot beat Keelan for once, but Sullivan had got back to clear from the goal line.

BIRMINGHAM CITY

Latchford, Page, Styles, Kendall, Gallagher, Want, Broadhurst, Francis, Burns, Hibbitt, Connolly.

NORWICH CITY

Keelan, Ryan, Sullivan, Steele, Dave Jones, Powell, Neighbour, Reeves, Gibbins, Evans, Peters.

REFEREE

Mr HP Hackney (Barnsley)

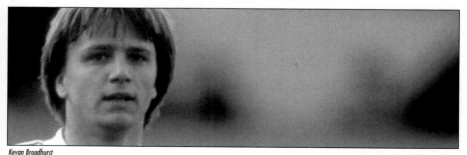

Kevan Broadhurst

Birthdays

Trevor Matthewson born today in 1963   Mick Harford born today in 1959

Playing record for this day

Playing record for this day is... 21 games, Won 7, Drawn 5, Lost 9, GF 32, GA 30.

Today's success rate.....45.24% Year ranking....200th

Match of the Day

FROM 1971

A CLASSIC AT HILLSBOROUGH

Blues and the Owls share six goals in super show

At Hillsborough today Blues took the lead and then came from 3-1 down to level the scores thanks to the efforts of Trevor Francis and Bob Latchford. Sheffield Wednesday's Sissons set up a chance in the 12th minute, but his hard work came to nothing when Prendergast volleyed the ball high over the bar. Blues also had chances when firstly Taylor drove the ball into the side netting, and then Summerill shot inches wide after taking a sharp chance with his weaker foot.

In the 26th minute Blues were rewarded with a goal when Francis performed a great solo effort. He collected an awkwardly bouncing ball midway in Wednesday's half and lobbed it over Thompson's head, rushing onto the dropping ball to complete the move with a super left-footed shot into the far corner of the net. However the Blues fans were not cheering for long. In the 32nd minute Prendergast fortuitously deflected a hopeful shot from Sunley straight which crept past Latchford to level the scores at 1-1.

Just two minutes later Wednesday went ahead thanks to a penalty kick from Sunley who had been floored in the area by a clumsy challenge from Pendrey, despite Blues protests. Sunley picked himself up and coolly sent Latchford the wrong way to make the score 2-1 to the home side. There was still no respite for Blues as in the 38th minute Sinclair increased the lead with a fine opportunist goal to leave the score at 3-1. Sinclair picking the ball up some 30 yards from goal let fly with a superb shot which left Latchford helpless as the ball sped past him with arrow-like speed and accuracy into the roof of the net.

The second half began with a series of free kicks for both sides but none of them yielded a goal. However there were plenty of near misses and opportunities fell to Blues to raise their hopes of a comeback. One of these attempts paid dividends in the 70th minute when Francis executed a spectacular scissors kick from a cross by Campbell, to give them real hope now just one goal in arrears.

Just four minutes later Blues achieved parity when Thompson then Prophet failed to cut out a cross from Martin, leaving Bob Latchford a simple tap in from five yards to the absolute delight of the relieved and jubilant travelling Blues fans.

BIRMINGHAM CITY

Dave Latchford, Martin, Pendrey, Page, Hynd, Robinson, Campbell, Francis, Bob Latchford, Summerill, Taylor.

SHEFFIELD WEDNESDAY

Grummitt, Rodrigues, Burton, Thompson, Prophett, Pugh, Sinclair, Craig, Prendergast, Sunley, Sissons (Todd).

Hillsborough, home of Sheffield Wednesday

Blues news extra   1986...Unlucky Armstrong calls it a day.

Ken Armstrong the former Blues centre half who recently transferred to Walsall broke his ankle today during a training session with his new team mates. The injury effectively ended his nine year professional career. He never played again and formally retired from the game in November 1986.

The Matches played on this day

1886, FA Cup 6th round.
| Blues 2 | Redcar 0 | Att. 6,000 |
| Davenport(2) | | |

1892, Football Alliance.
| Lincoln City 1 | Blues 1 | Att. 2,000 |
| | Wheldon | |

1897, Division 2.
Burton Wanderers 2	Blues 6	Att. 2,000
	Gadsby(2), Inglis,	
	Hare, Hodgetts, Walton	

1901, FA Cup 1st round, replay.
Blues 2	Stoke 1	Att. 10,000
Bennett, Wharton		
After extra time		

1904, Division 1.
| Blackburn Rovers 1 | Blues 1 | Att. 2,000 |
| | Jones | |

1909, Division 2.
| Wolverhampton W. 2 | Blues 0 | Att. 10,000 |

1911, Division 2.
| Stockport County 3 | Blues 1 | Att. 2,000 |
| | Buckley | |

1915, Division 2.
| Stockport County 3 | Blues 1 | Att. 3,000 |
| | A.W. Smith | |

1926, Division 1.
| Blues 2 | Sheffield United 0 | Att. 18,000 |
| Linley, Briggs | | |

1937, Division 1.
| Leeds United 0 | Blues 2 | Att. 13,674 |
| | Beattie, Morris | |

1943, Wartime.
| WBA 2 | Blues 1 | |
| | McEwan | |

1946, FA Cup 5th round, 2nd leg.
Blues 3	Sunderland 1	Att. 40,000
Jones(2), Mulraney		
Blues won 3-2 on aggregate		

1954, Division 2.
Blues 2	West Ham United 0	Att. 22,704
Astall 5		
Cochrane 41		

1965, Division 1.
| Blues 0 | Aston Villa 1 | Att. 32,491 |
| | Stobart 44 | |

1971, Division 2.
Sheffield W. 3	Blues 3	Att. 13,138
Prendergast 32	Francis 26, 70	
Craig 34(pen)	B.Latchford 74	
Sinclair 38		

1979, Division 1.
| Liverpool 1 | Blues 0 | Att. 35,207 |
| Souness 37 | | |

Blues eighth consecutive league defeat, equalling the record for the worst losing sequence.

1982, Division 1.
West Ham United 2	Blues 2	Att. 22,512
Orr 46	Whatmore 35	
Stewart 89(pen)	Van Mierlo 54	

Van Mierlo put Blues ahead with an absolutely stunning 30-yard volley

1990, Division 3.
| Swansea City 1 | Blues 1 | Att. 3,603 |
| Kelly 16 | Madden 61 | |

1991, Division 3.
| Bradford City 2 | Blues 0 | Att. 4,776 |
| McCarthy 52, 74 | | |

This was the first game in charge for new Blues boss Lou Macari

1993, Division 1.
Blues 2	Portsmouth 3	Att. 10,935
Sturridge 50	Whittingham 51, 84	
Peschisolido 81	McLoughlin 26	

1999, Division 1.
| Stockport County 1 | Blues 0 | Att. 9,056 |
| Angell 12 | | |

A Darren Purse header in the 54th minute appeared to go well over the line as 'keeper Nash pushed it away from inside the net, however both referee and linesman failed to award the goal.

February 14

Playing record for this day

Playing record for this day is... 13 games, Won 7, Drawn 3, Lost 3, GF 27, GA 10.

Today's success rate.....65.38% Year ranking....21st

Match of the Day

FROM 1953

VALENTINE'S DAY MASSACRE

Blues in mean mood at Stamford Bridge

Blues arrived at Stamford Bridge for this clash against Chelsea to be greeted by a crowd of 45,872 happy fans looking forward greatly to this match. The sun was shining and Blues kicked off. Play was determined from both teams, and the first corner of the game was awarded after 12 minutes. It was Blues shot, and although taken well it came to nothing. The second corner also fell to Birmingham and Murphy got onto the ball and just headed it wide of the post. This seemed to spell out the plan for the game. Both teams attacking, both winning corners, and both failing to score. Birmingham always seemed more fortunate than Chelsea, but even so they didn't have enough luck to produce anything from their efforts.

After a goalless first half, the teams entered the field after the break both wanting to break the deadlock. The pitch was now suffering badly due to the hard play, and the weather was getting worse too. Chelsea goalkeeper Thomson was hurt for the second time in the game whilst making a save and had to receive treatment.

Murphy's shot was deflected in the area causing him to call for a penalty. The referee decided instead to award a corner which was taken quickly, but proved as fruitless as all the others. Chelsea had another corner within a minute, but nothing came from that either. Both sides were beginning to become disheartened by their ill luck, so it was a surprise all round when Birmingham took the lead on 57 minutes from yet another corner. Stewart sent the ball goalwards where it was perfectly placed for young South African Purdon to get his head to it and nod it into the net past the stationary Chelsea defence. Bentley then brought down Boyd, and another free kick was awarded. Following on from this came Blues' second goal. Trigg crossed the ball and Boyd carried it on for Purdon again to send it over the line with his head on 70 minutes. Birmingham were now eventually reaping the rewards for all their hard work on a difficult pitch, and against a battling team.

12 minutes from the end of the game the lead was increased once again. Stewart provided the ball for Murphy to send it into the net for Blues' third. Chelsea had by now given up hope of a comeback, but weren't finished yet. The 80th minute saw the fourth goal arrive for the visiting team when Stewart's corner was sent to Bannister who slipped it past an unsuspecting Thomson in the Chelsea goal. Triggs almost made it five for Birmingham with a great solo effort, but his shot went just wide of the post. It didn't matter too much though, as the game had been well and truly won already.

BIRMINGHAM CITY

Merrick, Hall, Green, Boyd, Ferris, Bannister, Stewart, Purdon, Murphy, Trigg, Warhurst.

CHELSEA

Thomson, Willemse, Tickridge, Armstrong, Saunders, Dickson, Spector, McNichol, Bentley, Gray, Parsons.

REFEREE

Mr JH Clough (Bolton)

Roy Warhurst

Birthdays

Jason Beckford born today in 1970   **Darren Purse born today in 1977**

Playing record for this day
Playing record for this day is... 15 games, Won 8, Drawn 2, Lost 5, GF 30, GA 22.
Today's success rate.....60% Year ranking....54th

February 15

Match of the Day
FROM 1975

WALSALL'S DREAM UP IN SMOKE AFTER BURNS FIRES BLUES

Giant killers are slain by Burns and Hatton strikes

Brave Walsall, whose giant killing exploits in this year's FA Cup which had already accounted for Manchester United and Newcastle United, had their hopes ended by neighbours Birmingham. Their dream ended in something of an anti-climax here at St Andrews as Blues cruised to a comfortable win by 2-1.

Blues win was largely down to their captain Howard Kendall, his midfield leadership thwarted the early surge form the Third Division side and he not only kept Walsall at bay, but found time to get forward in devastating form to set up both goals which eventually laid the Saddlers impressive cup run to rest in this fifth round tie. They now return to their more important priority of gaining promotion from the Third Division. Blues were handed the perfect start against their lower league neighbours when Walsall fell behind after just nine minutes. Walsall slipped behind when Blues capitalised on their first error from the game's first set piece. Walsall's defence only partially cleared a free kick and the ball fell to Kendall, opting not to shoot first time from the edge of the box he instead threaded the ball through a tight gap in the melee of players in front of him. The lethal Bob Hatton was quickly on the ball and in confident mood he turned to sweep it wide of Kearns and into the corner of the net. For once there was a clear dispirited look on the Walsall players' faces and this transferred to their mass ranks of travelling support.

Blues striker Kenny Burns took advantage, winning almost every ball played to him, and with better finishing could well have walked off with a hat-trick. Instead Burns finished the game with one solitary strike, after 46 minutes. Taylor and Page together delayed taking a free kick which confused the visitors and of all the players to choose from, it was Kendall who unmarked floated his cross from inside the area to Burns who, unchallenged couldn't really miss the chance from close in. The goal signalled the end of the tense atmosphere as everyone amongst the 45,881 crowd now knew the inevitable result. The tie therefore pettered out in a sad anti-climax and Walsall's late consolation goal poached by Taylor from close range was hardly noticed. Blues had won with ease and now faced Middlesbrough in the sixth round at St Andrews.

BIRMINGHAM CITY
Latchford, Clarke, Bryant, Kendall, Gallagher, Pendrey, Page, Taylor, Burns, Hatton, Emmanuel.
WALSALL
Kearns, Saunders, Harrison, Robinson, Bennett, Atthey, Taylor, Andrews, Wright, Buckley, Birch.

Kenny Burns (r) in typically aggressive action

Blues news extra   1958...Fog the only winner at Maine Road

Blues First Division fixture at Maine Road ended after 40 minutes when the referee abandoned the game due to the thick fog which had fallen throughout the afternoon and made vision almost impossible. Manchester City had taken the lead early on but Blues equalised soon after, at the time the match was halted the score remained 1-1.

Birthdays

Seymour Morris born today in 1908   **David Langan born today in 1957**

The Matches played on this day

1890, Football Alliance.
Blues 6   Darwen 2   Att. 500
Jenkyns, Hallam,
W.Devey, Wheldon(2),
Wilcox
1899, FA Cup 2nd round, replay.
Blues 1   Stoke 2   Att. 14,279
Inglis
1902, Division 1.
Sheffield United 1   Blues 4   Att. 8,000
                 McRoberts, Field,
                 Leonard, Wharton
1908, Division 1.
Chelsea 2   Blues 2   Att. 30,000
                 Jones, Eyre
1913, Division 2.
Barnsley 3   Blues 0   Att. 2,000
1919, Wartime.
Blues 4   Sheffield W. 2
A.W.Smith,
Whitehouse(2),
Davies
1930, Division 1.
Blues 1   Liverpool 0   Att. 20,000
Haywood
1936, Division 1.
Blues 2   Liverpool 0   Att. 18,000
Jones, Harris
1939, FA Cup 5th round, replay.
Everton 2   Blues 1   Att. 64,796
                 Harris
1941, Wartime.
Leicester City 3   Blues 3
                 Dearson, Shaw, Gardner.
1947, Division 2.
Blues 2   Coventry City 0   Att. 30,000
Trigg(2)
1975, FA Cup 5th round.
Blues 2   Walsall 1   Att. 45,881
Hatton 9 T   Taylor 89
Burns 46
This match screened by ATV's Star Soccer
1992, Division 3.
Blues 0   Bournemouth 1   Att. 10,898
                 Quinn 69
1997, FA Cup 5th round.
Blues 1   Wrexham 3   Att. 21,511
Bruce 38   Hughes 51
                 Humes 67
                 Connolly 90
Blues had Paul Devlin sent off after 57 minutes
2000, Division 1.
Blues 1   Blackburn Rovers 0   Att. 20,719
O'Connor 33

February 16

-1875

The Matches played on this day

1901, Division 2.		
Blues 3	Barnsley 1	Att. 5,000
McRoberts,		
Aston, Tebbs		
1907, Division 1.		
Blues 0	Sheffield United 0	Att. 10,000
1918, Wartime.		
Blues 2	Rotherham County 0	
Bell, Whitehouse		
1921, Division 2.		
Notts County 0	Blues 0	Att. 14,000
1924, Division 1.		
Blues 2	Middlesbrough 1	Att. 11,000
Bradford(2)		
1927, Division 1.		
Sunderland 4	Blues 1	Att. 8,000
	Briggs	
1929, Division 1.		
Derby County 2	Blues 2	Att. 15,000
	Bond, Mills	
1946, Wartime.		
Blues 1	Charlton Athletic 0	Att. 56,615
Jones		

Blues biggest home crowd during World War Two
Charlton keeper Sam Bartram hit the bar with a penalty.

1952, Division 2.		
Swansea Town 4	Blues 0	Att. 22,000
Scrine 7		
Bellis 18, 53		
Allchurch 85		
1957, FA Cup 5th round.		
Millwall 1	Blues 4	Att. 41,000
Shepherd 70	Kinsey 13, 46	
	Govan 36	
	Brown 58	
1974, Division 1.		
Wolverhampton W. 1	Blues 0	Att. 33,821
Munro 13		

Howard Kendall made his Blues debut

1980, FA Cup 5th round.		
Tottenham Hotspur 3	Blues 1	Att. 49,936
Armstrong 11	Bertschin 27	
Hoddle 35(pen), 43		
1982, Division 1.		
Blues 2	Sunderland 0	Att. 10,776
Van Mierlo 31		
Worthington 90		
1986, Division 1.		
Coventry City 4	Blues 4	Att. 14,271
Bennett 51, 73	Kennedy 2, 83	
Kilcline 58, 88	Whitton 18	
(2,pens)	Kuhl 60	

Blues first competitive game on a Sunday

1991, Division 3.		
Bournemouth 1	Blues 2	Att. 6,330
Watson 68	Sturridge 43	
	Peer 81	

Blues best win over Bournemouth.

2002, Division 1.		
Blues 1	Barnsley 0	Att. 19,208
John 51		

Stern John scored the winner on his debut for Blues.

Playing record for this day
Playing record for this day is... 16 games, Won 8, Drawn 4, Lost 4, GF 24, GA 22.
Today's success rate.....62.50% Year ranking....39th

Match of the Day
FROM 1986
SUNDAY BEST FOR BLUES

Sky and Royal Blues share eight goals in first Sunday treat

On a Sunday morning first, in front of a crowd of an encouraging 14,271 crowd, Birmingham and Coventry shared the goals and the points in a thrilling game, which Birmingham by rights should have won.

Andy Kennedy put the Royal Blues ahead after just two minutes, and 16 minutes later the visitors were leading by two goals when Steve Whitton scored after Kennedy's second attempt had been blocked by Ogrizovic.

It was beginning to look like Coventry would be well beaten, but an attempt by David Geddis hit the post and Clarke's header also bounced off the woodwork. After the half-time interval Coventry took the field stronger and more determined. Their efforts paid off quickly with Dave Bennett opening the scoring for the home side on 51 minutes, slotting in a headed cross from Brazil. Just seven minutes later Coventry were awarded a penalty after Roberts was judged to have fouled Bennett in the area. Kilcline took the kick and put it away with ease.

Birmingham climbed back into the lead on 60 minutes with a goal from Martin Kuhl, forcing its way into the top of the net, but shortly afterwards Coventry drew level again. Brazil managed to get Hagan out of position, and passed the ball to Bennett who shot in a superb 20-yard drive. The visitors again took the lead seven minutes from the end when Kennedy grabbed his second goal of the game, but their lead wasn't to last. The first penalty awarded to Coventry had been questionable, but it was nothing compared to their 88 minute gift. The referee ruled that Ray Ranson had fouled Nick Pickering in the area, when it seemed Pickering had tripped over Ranson's leg after he nudged the ball away. Wayne Clarke was booked for dissent in the ensuing row, and Kilcline stepped up to slot the ball home from the resultant spot kick.

BIRMINGHAM CITY
Seaman, Ranson, Roberts, Hagan, Whitton, Kuhl, Bremner, Clarke, Kennedy, Geddis, Hopkins.
COVENTRY CITY
Ogrizovic, Borrows, Downs, Bowman, Kilcline, Peake, Bennett, Turner, Regis, Brazil, Pickering.

REFEREE
Mr K. Lupton (Stockton-on-Tees)

Jamie Pollock in action against Wolves

Birthdays
Jose Dominguez born today in 1974.

Playing record for this day
Playing record for this day is... 17 games, Won 5, Drawn 4, Lost 8, GF 23, GA 32.
Today's success rate.....41.18% Year ranking....228th

Match of the Day
FROM 1968
VOWDEN SEES BLUES HOME

Into round five via Geoff's two goal Orient express

Blues continued their FA Cup run with another dominant performance over lower league opposition. Blues went into the game making just one change to the side that earned a draw at the Den. Page came off the bench to cover for Bert Murray who had failed a fitness test in the morning. Orient went into the game unchanged and at full strength. An expectant crowd of 29,320 greeted the sides at St Andrews before the start, many hoping Blues could emulate last year's cup run.

Blues were given an early scare from their plucky Third Division opponents who started eagerly relishing the big crowd and tense atmosphere. From an early free kick delivered by Wood, Mancini managed to avoid any attention by the Blues defence to sneak in and plant a free header past Herriott only for it to come back off the post. Blues stung into action by the let off were soon making amends and on 18 minutes their sustained period of pressure on the Orient goal paid off when Vowden got the first of his two goals to put Blues in front. A good build up from the back four arrived on the right flank to Wylie who swung over a great cross for the Blues striker to head home his 18th goal of the season. Despite continuous free-flowing attacking football Blues could not add to the score and at half time it was still 1-0.

Blues were quickly back into their stride in the early moments of the second half and it took ten minutes for Blues to effectively kill the tie when going 2-0 up. Page was the provider, having collected a loose ball in midfield he threaded it through to Bridges who skillfully allowed the ball to bounce once before lobbing over 'keeper Goddard as he charged out to cover the danger within his penalty area. This goal however inspired the away side into their best period of the game as they threw caution to the wind in search of a goal to get back into the game. Blues found this tactic to their liking as they found inviting spaces in which to quickly counter. An ideal opportunity arrived with just 15 minutes left Vincent catching the Orient defence hopelessly out of position with a superb through ball to Vowden in the clear. As Goddard again raced out to cover Vowden slipped the ball under his dive to complete an impressive 3-0 win.

BIRMINGHAM CITY
Herriott, Martin, Green, Wylie, Foster, Beard, Bridges, Vincent, Pickering, Vowden, Page.
ORIENT
Goddard, Jones, Howe, Allan, Mancini, Wood, Slater, Harper, Massey, Halom, Simpson.

St Andrews

Blues news extra 1979...A friendly in Guernsey Blues 1 West Bromwich Albion 1

In a desperate bid to get some much needed practice during the severe weather in England the midland rivals flew to scenic and unfrozen Guernsey. Cyril Regis put the Baggies 1-0 up after 37 mins. Blues equalised through Don Givens five minutes into the second half.

1994...Blues hit with £55,000 fine for poaching Fry

Blues today found the punishment meted out by the Football League for illegally approaching manager Barry Fry from Southend was a fine of £55,000, a League record. Fry quit the Southend manager's post suddenly in December 1993 joining Blues almost immediately, a move which angered the board and fans at Roots Hall.

Birthdays

Steve Fox born today in 1958.

The Matches played on this day

1900, Division 2.
Newton Heath 3   Blues 2   Att. 6,000
                   Aston, Wharton
1902, Division 1.
Blues 1   Stoke 1   Att. 8,000
Athersmith
1906, Division 1.
Stoke 2   Blues 2   Att. 5,000
                   Jones(2)
1912, Division 2.
Leicester Fosse 5 Blues 2   Att. 10,000
                   Conlin, Jones(pen)
1917, Wartime.
Blues 1   Bradford City 1
Whitehouse
1923, Division 1.
Sheffield United 7 Blues 1   Att. 10,000
                   Rawson
Harry Johnson nets four times against the Blues defence who are soundly thrashed. Albert Rawson joined Blues from Sheffield Utd just three days ago, scored on his debut against his former team mates.
Blues 8th consecutive league defeat, a new club record.
1932, Division 1.
Portsmouth 2   Blues 1   Att. 10,000
                   Haywood
1934, FA Cup 5th round.
Blues 1   Leicester City 2 Att. 48,561
Haywood
1945, Wartime.
WBA 4   Blues 0
1951, Division 2.
Blues 2   Chesterfield 1   Att. 34,980
Trigg 53   Massart 85
Harris 56
1962, Division 1.
Bolton W. 3   Blues 2   Att. 13,308
Hennessey (og) 14 Auld 38
Hill 43   Leek 78
Stevens 44
1968, FA Cup 4th round.
Blues 3   Orient 0   Att. 29,320
Vowden 18, 70
Bridges 56
1973, Division 1.
Sheffield United 0 Blues 1   Att. 22,220
                   Francis 26
Blues' Bob Hatton sent off after 85 minutes after an incident involving Speight of Sheff Utd.
1990, Division 3.
Blues 0   Wigan Athletic 0 Att. 5,473
1996, Division 1.
Stoke City 1   Blues 0   Att. 12,612
Sturridge 25
1998, Division 1.
Crewe Alexandra 0 Blues 2   Att. 6,334
                   Adebola 42
                   Hughes 44
Darren Purse made his debut as a substitute replacing Steve Bruce on 84 minutes.
2001, Division 1.
Blues 2   WBA 1   Att. 25,025
Adebola 36   Butler 38
O'Connor 57

February 18

Playing record for this day
Playing record for this day is... 19 games, Won 9, Drawn 5, Lost 5, GF 24, GA 16.
Today's success rate.....60.53% Year ranking....48th

Match of the Day

FROM 1995

HEADS!! BLUES WIN

Four headed goals earn the points against York

Blues kept up their promotion push, and recorded their first-ever win against York City thanks to under-fire Kevin Francis and Ricky Otto. Severely criticised by manager Barry Fry after the Crewe defeat the previous week, and dropped to Blues reserve team in midweek, Francis and Otto were inspirational today.

Blues were dominant from the kick off and Francis almost scored as early as the first minute. With only nine minutes gone Otto raced clear down the wing sent over a deep cross to the far post where Francis this time made no mistake by heading home Birmingham's first goal. Just a minute later he caused more panic in the York defence, and from Gary Cooper's corner he rose again to head in his second goal. With Blues two up and clearly on top the crowd sat back and waited for the expected avalanche, but despite pressure on Dean Kiely's goal York made it to half time without further conceding.

After the break the ever influential Jon McCarthy started to threaten the Blues defence for the first time in the game. Rather than a whitewash York were now making more of a game of things. From a McCarthy cross and mistake from Blues centre back Mick Bodley came sub Paul Baker's easily taken goal after 57 minutes, York were back in the game. Blues however settled well after the goal and began to reassert their earlier dominance. On 62 minutes Louis Donowa skipped clear of full back Wilson and his cross was met by fellow winger Otto who headed goal number three past Kiely and regained Blues two goal lead.

Fry immediately brought on Peter Shearer for Mark Ward in an attempt to keep up the attacking momentum and win the game. However another defensive error from Bodley let in McCarthy and his shot on the run beat 'keeper Bennett to bring York back within a goal again at 3-2. It was, however, York's last real threat and in the last 20 minutes only Birmingham looked like adding to the score. With 13 minutes remaining another pin-point cross from man-of-the-match Otto was met by Shearer who headed in Blues fourth goal of the afternoon to settle the game 4-2.

BIRMINGHAM CITY
Bennett, Poole, Cooper, Ward (Shearer 62), Barnett, Bodley, Donowa, McGavin (Saville 81), Francis, Otto, Tait.

YORK CITY
Kiely, McMillan, Wilson, Pepper, Tutill, Atkin, McCarthy, Naylor, Barnes (Baker 36), Jordan (Hall 53), Canham.

REFEREE
Mr E Wolstenholme (Blackburn)

Kevin Francis

Birthdays
Paul Holmes born today in 1968.

Playing record for this day

Playing record for this day is... 11 games, Won 5, Drawn 3, Lost 3, GF 17, GA 12.

Today's success rate.....59.09% Year ranking....61st

February 19

Match of the Day

FROM 2000

A FOUR GOAL CONCLUSION

Blues continue to climb, poor Swindon rooted to the bottom

A super three goal blitz inside 26 minutes helped Blues to fourth in the table, whilst Swindon fell to their 18th league defeat and were now eight points adrift at the First Division basement.

Blues were on top from the kick-off as the form book suggested this was the perfect away banker and it took just 11 minutes for the first goal. A Lazaridis run ended with a finger tip save from former Blues keeper Bart Griemink, but from Grainger's corner Rankin got in a shot which was blocked and his return shot was nudged over the line by centre half Darren Purse from two yards out. This was surely the start Blues needed to go all the way and run riot, however Swindon got an equaliser two minutes later. A hopeful long ball from Davis went over the flat-footed Blues defence for Hay who ran on and from wide of the 18-yard box lobbed Bennett who had come off his line to cover the danger. Rather than unnerve the promotion hopefuls the equaliser produced more determination from the Blues who quickly countered Griemink this time making a good save from a Bryan Hughes effort. After 21 minutes Blues regained their lead when a long goal kick from Bennett was flicked on by Adebola to Grainger, and his neat header steered the ball into Rankin's path. Running in he coolly placed his shot into the corner from 12 yards. This was his second goal in three games since his arrival on loan from Bradford City in January and he was clearly getting better by every game. Blues were in no mood to give away the lead a second time and continued to defend well by attacking Swindon relentlessly. A move started by Grainger in midfield and ending with an inch perfect Rowett cross fed Adebola who controlled with one touch and smashed the ball into the roof of the net with the next and Blues had the game won on 26 minutes. Indeed they should have gone in at half time 4-1 up when Adebola, again controlling the ball well, spun his marker and hit a first-time effort which struck Griemink's right-hand post just five minutes before the interval.

The second half was played out almost under exihbition mode by Blues who now had total control. Poor finishing from captain Martin O'Connor should have put Blues three goals clear in the 67th minute. With 17 minutes remaining Martin Grainger edged out a Hey effort. Awarded a direct free kick some 35 yards out Grainger strolled up and curled a low but blistering shot which beat Griemink comfortably into the left hand corner. At 4-1 the beleaguered Swindon fans started exiting the County Ground having witnessed just three wins all season, relegation was surely a certainty come May. Blues meanwhile continued to pressurise the top half and in particular those automatic places, they were now fourth just six points behind second placed Ipswich Town.

BIRMINGHAM CITY

Bennett, Rowett, Purse, Holdsworth, Charlton, Grainger, O'Connor, Hughes (Hyde 77), Lazaridis (Andrew Johnson 77), Adebola (Marcelo 77), Rankin

SWINDON TOWN

Griemink, Robinson, Hall, Leitch, Davies, Hay, Reeves (Willis 77), Davis, Andy Williams, James Williams (Griffin h/t, McHugh 77), Cowe.

REFEREE

Mr. MJ Jones (Chester)

The Matches played on this day

1898, Division 2.		
Gainsborough T. 0	Blues 0	Att. 2,000
1910, Division 2.		
Blues 1	Wolverhampton W. 0	Att. 2,000
Freeman		
1921, Division 2.		
Blues 0	Clapton Orient 0	Att. 20,000
1938, Division 1.		
Blues 3	Leeds United 2	Att. 20,403
Dearson(2),		
White(pen)		
1944, Wartime.		
Blues 1	Aston Villa 1	
Trigg		
1949, Division 1.		
Stoke City 2	Blues 1	Att. 28,000
	Harris	
1955, FA Cup 5th round.		
Blues 2	Doncaster Rovers 1	Att. 57,800
Brown 42, 53	Mooney 48	
Eddie Brown's opening goal came direct from a corner kick		
1966, Division 2.		
Charlton Athletic 2	Blues 1	Att. 13,722
Burridge 26	Thwaites 9	
Peacock 31		
1972, Division 2.		
Blues 2	Burnley 0	Att. 32,035
Taylor 32		
Hatton 86		
This match shown on ATV's Star Soccer		
1994, Division 1.		
Blues 2	Notts County 3	Att. 12,913
Frain 59(pen)	McSwegan 24	
Saville 61	Wilson 67	
	Legg 81	
2000, Division 1.		
Swindon Town 1	Blues 4	Att. 7,591
Hay 13	Purse 11	
	Rankin 21	
	Adebola 26	
	Grainger 73	

Stan Lazaridis

Birthdays

Jimmy James born today in 1934.

February 20

Playing record for this day

Playing record for this day is...17 games, Won 5, Drawn 6, Lost 6, GF 23, GA 15.
Today's success rate.....47.06% Year ranking....184th

Match of the Day
FROM 1971
OH BOY, WHAT A PERFORMANCE
16-year-old comes of age with a four goal blitz against Bolton

What a performance, what a player, what a game!! Blues unbeaten run in the Second Division was increased to nine matches, with this their fifth successive home league win, all due to the unbelievable exploits of a 16-year-old boy by the name of Trevor Francis. His incredible performance set a personal league record, the youngest scorer of four goals in a Football League match, and took his tally to 16 goals from just ten games. It also sank the unfortunate Bolton who like most teams struggled to stop the talented youngster who came of age at St Andrews in front of 25,600 spectators.

The game started with Summerill sending a shot over the bar within seconds of the kick off. This was quickly followed by a header from Francis which was a fraction too high of the crossbar. Frequent free kicks were breaking up the flow of the game and, more annoyingly for the Blues defence, these were creating Bolton's best chances of taking the lead. From one deeply-hit set piece McAllister nudged the ball on for the unmarked Fletcher who drove in a first-time shot and only a desperate stop from Dave Latchford's outstretched leg kept it out.

Bolton were spurred on by this and for a brief spell had the upper hand, but it wasn't for long. After 16 minutes a free kick in Birmingham's favour taken by Martin, was floated towards the far post. Taylor was there to nod the ball back for Francis who bravely lunged forward to shoot at goal, the ball ballooned over the head of Boswell and Francis ran round the keeper to finish off the unintentional shot with a simple header into the unguarded goal.

Just three minutes later Francis had the crowd wild with delight again with a second goal. Former Bolton winger Gordon Taylor started the move with an inch-perfect centre to Summerill, his intelligent knock-down was pounced on by Francis to fire in from close range. Blues kept up the fast pace throughout the remainder of the half creating many more chances in which to increase their lead still further. The best of these came to the unfortunate Robinson who had a goal disallowed ten minutes before the break for a minor infringement on the 'keeper when heading in almost from on the goal line.

The second half began with Bolton making a substitution and Manning replaced Phillips who was still troubled by a first-half knock. Blues were still the dominant side and attacked with the same regularity as before. All the fans wanted to round off a great afternoon was to witness the history making hat-trick goal from the schoolboy, thier patient support was rewarded in the 78th minute. The leg work was done by Summerill who charged through the middle splitting Bolton's defence wide apart, his cracking low drive was only parried by Boswell and this allowed Francis the split-second required to race in and smash the loose ball past the unfortunate keeper before he could recover.

With seven minutes of the game remaining Francis then created history with a magical and record breaking fourth goal. It was another simple but devastating finish. When Foster broke on the right centred and Francis charged in bravely to head past the on-rushing 'keeper, Francis was clearly hurt in the prossess which spoilt the goal celebration and deprived the fans of any more entertainment from their new found hero. Bowker replaced the injured star giving the Blues fans an opportunity to give him a resounding ovation when he was helped off the field.

In the dying minutes of the game Taylor was desperately unlucky not to put Blues 5-0 up when his curling shot from distance struck the bar.

BIRMINGHAM CITY

Dave Latchford, Martin, Pendrey, Page, Hynd, Robinson, Campbell, Francis (Bowker 84), Bob Latchford, Summerill, Taylor.

BOLTON WANDERERS

Boswell, Ritson, McAllister, Williams, Hurley, Rimmer, Waldron, Greaves, Fletcher, Jones, Phillips (Manning 47).

REFEREE

Mr BH Daniels (Rainham)

Trevor Francis (r) in action against Sheffield United

Playing record for this day
Playing record for this day is...17 games, Won 6, Drawn 2, Lost 9, GF 16, GA 26.
Today's success rate.....41.18% Year ranking....229th

February 21

Match of the Day

FROM 1967

BLUES GRIND MILLERS DOWN AND OUT OF THE CUP

Hockey and Bridges see Blues through to FA Cup fifth round

Birmingham were left the only side from the West Midlands still in the FA Cup after this latest fourth round victory over Rotherham. It was the first time in six years Blues had progressed to the fifth round. A crucial goal on the stroke of half time, and another soon after the restart should have put them on the road to a comfortable and convincing win against their lower league opponents. However the well timed goals failed to inspire the Blues on, and worse, it brought the best out of Rotherham who scored on 59 minutes. Then they produced two excellent chances to win the game, or at least save it. Blues held out and went on to play the victors of the Arsenal-Bolton tie at St Andrews. Blues eagerness to take full advantage of a 35,482 partisan home crowd was soon evident. Thomson was battling tigerishly in midfield, and the Vowden-Barber front pairing were soon showing they were prepared to run for anything played to them. Blues peppered the Rotherham goal, Barber went close with an effort which hit the side netting. Then moments later Hill saved bravely at his feet when Barber had gone clear again and was about to shoot, this time from a closer and much more central position to goal. Rotherham's chances were rare, their two best both fell to former Wolves player John Galley. First with a header which went narrowly wide, then an effort from the boot of Galley which also beat Herriott, but came back off the post. In between these a header from Vowden shaved the cross bar from one of Birmingham's numerous corners. Just as the opening half seemed likely to end goalless, Blues pressure was finally rewarded. A free kick was floated into the Rotherham area where Vowden headed down for Hockey who stabbed the ball in from six yards out.

With the second half barely a minute old Blues increased their lead with a spectacular effort from Bridges. A corner by Hockey was headed clear by the Millers defence, but only as far as Bridges who hooked the ball on the volley over his shoulder, and it sailed over everyone in the middle, including the keeper Hill, and went in off the far post.

Now Rotherham were desperate for a goal and this brought about their first sustained period of pressure on Jim Herriott's goal. Still Birmingham looked comfortable and Hill remained the busier keeper, saving from Vowden then Murray. Blues fans now sensed victory and started their celebrations with a loud burst of "Keep Right On", but before the first verse had been sung, St Andrews was suddenly silenced by a goal from Rotherham. A simple ball from the right wing should have been dealt with by Brum's defence but twice they made a complete mess of the clearance, Galley took over to score with a simple tap in from three yards. Soon after this Rotherham almost equalised when Chambers came close from Rabjohn's chip from the byline, the ball just running wide of the post before the right winger could properly bring it under control. Chambers, the visitors most influential player, then had to leave the field with an injury after 69 minutes. Immediately after the substitution his replacement Casper was involved in a push-and-shove clash with Thomson, the ref halted play to consult a linesman but took no further action than to speak to both players. Within a minute Casper was again in the thick of the action, this time almost supplying the equaliser with a superb 25-yard strike which went inches wide.

With time almost up and Rotherham still pressing forward, another mistake in the Blues defence allowed Chappell a shot at goal, which unfortunatley hit team mate Galley on the back, and bounced wide of the unguarded goal. Blues held on by the skin of their teeth, and at the final whistle a huge collective sigh of relief from the crowd was almost matched by that of the Blues players.

BIRMINGHAM CITY
Herriott, Murray, Martin, Thomson, Sharples, Beard, Hockey, Vincent, Barber, Vowden, Bridges.
ROTHERHAM UNITED
Hill, Wilcockson, Clish, Harrity, Tiler, Rabjohn, Chambers (Casper 69), Galley, Chappell, Pring.

Trevor Hockey

Birthdays
Terry Twell born today in 1947   **Neil Doherty born today in 1969**

February 22

Playing record for this day
Playing record for this day is...18 games, Won 6, Drawn 2, Lost 10, GF 29, GA 35.
Today's success rate.....38.89% Year ranking....238th

Match of the Day
FROM 1998
MAGIC JOHNSON, AT LAST
First goal for defender Michael Johnson wins it for Blues

It took eight seasons, 249 games and 66 minutes before Michael Johnson finely had a goal to celebrate as a senior professional. Some celebration too wheeling away like a headless chicken not knowing what to do or where to sprint off, but as they say they all count.

Blues, looking to keep the pressure on the play-off places, needed to win this televised Sunday afternoon game against a Sheffield United side already occupying fourth place. Birmingham started well and were kept out by two fine saves from 'keeper Kelly within the opening 20 minutes, the first from a Bruce header after McCarthy corner, then from an Adebola effort. However it was through Kelly Birmingham managed to open the scoring after 31 minutes. Steve Bruce broke down a United counter attack, found McCarthy who chased right down the middle of the park. His through ball down the centre found Martin Grainger who from 25 yards slotted in first time past Kelly who was stranded after rushing out beyond his penalty area to cover. At half time the Blues looked comfortable at 1-0 and their defence solid and in control.

The second half went almost as the first with the Blades' forwards unable to make any headway, Blues continued to dominate the game. Finally after some intense pressure they were rewarded with another goal they deserved for their continued hard work. A Simon Charlton cross was only half-cleared to Steve Bruce. His clever threaded pass gave Martin O' Connor space to run in and pass the ball into the area hard and low where Michael Johnson's outstretched leg beat both Adebola and Ndlovu to steer the ball high into the corner of Kelly's goal. Johnson already celebrating his 250th professional appearance reeled away first to his team mates then the crowd, before coming to a complete halt probably now in shock. It was a special moment for the central defender who had done enough in the game already to earn the man-of-the-match award. His achievement was acknowledged by the St Andrews crowd who gave him a standing ovation when he was substituted for Darren Purse in the last minute of the game. A delighted manager Trevor Francis awarded him the match ball saying, "If he carries on like that he'll get more pressies because I thought he was outstanding."

The win moved Blues above the Baggies and into eight place just a point away from sixth placed Wolves who Blues were due to face at Molineux the following weekend.

BIRMINGHAM CITY

Bennett, Bass, Bruce, Johnson (Purse 90), Charlton, McCarthy O'Connor, Hughes (Robinson 88), Grainger, Ndlovu (Forster 89), Adebola.

SHEFFIELD UNITED

Kelly, Borbokis (Derry h/t), Quinn (Marcelo 70), Barrett, Sandford, Holdsworth, Saunders, Marker, Taylor (Katchouro 70), Ford, Stuart.

REFEREE

Mr. B Knight (Kent)

Michael Johnson and Andy Johnson

Blues news extra   1908...The day the roof came off

High winds caused havoc at St Andrews and resulted in the game against Nottingham Forest being abandoned after the main stand roof was blown off. The game was evenly poised at 1-1 but with safety in mind the ref had no alternative but to cease play in the second half.

1936...Snow halts the Blues

Just 36 minutes play was possible against Sheffield Wednesday today when an already snow bound St Andrews was battered by a blizzard. At the time Blues were already a goal up but any further play was impossible with visibility almost nil.

Birthdays

Bryan Orritt born today in 1937.

Playing record for this day

Playing record for this day is...16 games, Won 8, Drawn 0, Lost 8, GF 21, GA 24.

Today's success rate.....50% Year ranking....168th

Match of the Day

FROM 1974

QUICK FIRE FROM BLUES OUT GUNS ARSENAL

Super ten minute second half burst turns the whole game round

An expectant crowd of 29,828 were at St Andrews today for the home debut of £180,000 rated midfielder Howard Kendall, who arrived at Birmingham as part of the deal which saw Blues striker Bob Latchford sign for Everton. Blues fans left the ground with no doubts to his abillity after watching Kendall impose his quiet authority on the game. His quick intelligence and accuracy in passing the ball stood out, making him the best player on the field. The St Andrews faithful had a new hero and in the 86th minute when Kendall received a knee injury requiring his substitution, he left the field to a prolonged and sympathetic ovation from the Blues fans, many of whom were aware that it was a similar knee injury that kept him out of action for four months earlier in the season.

After having only dropped two points in their last six home games, Blues were expected to extend the sequence against Arsenal. However, a lack lustre performance during the first half with little attacking football from either side, and an Arsenal goal from Ray Kennedy left the home crowd in despondent mood by half time.

The interval gave manager Freddie Goodwin the chance to reshape the side, and Gordon Taylor was switched to the right flank and given the freedom to push further forward. The change proved inspirational and brought about a rapid improvement to the Blues performance in the second half. In the 55th minute Kenny Burns' huge leap enabled him to head Taylor's deep corner back across goal for Joe Gallagher, and the 18-year-old centre half claimed his first senior goal for the club, with a simple shot close in. This was just the beginning of a ten minute period of sustained aggression from Blues which left Arsenal reeling. Within two minutes of the equaliser Bob Hatton evaded Peter Storey's sliding challenge and fed the ball to Kendall on the overlap. The midfielder wasted no time chipping a pass sraight into the path of Burns who took the ball on, as 'keeper Bob Wilson came out he squared to Hatton who tapped into the empty net at the far post. Now there was no stopping Blues, and within a few minutes Trevor Francis put the ball away for a third goal, and they were in total control.

With confidence at a high there were plenty chances to increase the lead still further, with little response from a shell-shocked Arsenal side. The visitors soon became frustrated and this was highlighted by Alan Ball's lunge at Jimmy Calderwood which earned the Arsenal midfielder a booking. This after Nelson had floored the unfortunate Kendall resulting in Calderwood's introduction. An even later challenge by Charlie George left Burns in agony in the game's closing minute as Arsenal's discipline fell apart.

BIRMINGHAM CITY

Latchford, Martin, Pendrey, Kendall (Calderwood 86), Gallagher, Hynd, Campbell, Francis, Burns, Hatton, Taylor.

ARSENAL

Wilson, Rice, Nelson, Storey, Simpson, Kelly, Ball, George, Radford, Kennedy, Brady.

Howard Kendall

Blues news extra   1957..Weather hits Second City derby

Heavy rain caused the postponement of the eagerly awaited Blues-Villa game at St Andrews. The match was eventually played on 10 April when Villa won 2-1.

Birthdays

Bertie Mills born today in 1900.

The Matches played on this day

1895, Division 1.
Blues 1   WBA 2   .Att. 8,100
Mobley
1901, FA Cup 2nd round.
Blues 1   Burnley 0   Att. 11,000
McMillan
1903, Division 2.
Manchester City 4   Blues 0   Att. 20,000
1914, FA Cup 3rd round.
Blues 1   QPR 2   Att. 35,000
Duncan
1918, Wartime.
Rotherham County 1   Blues 0
1924, Division 1.
Middlesbrough 0   Blues 1   Att. 10,000
                  Islip

1929, Division 1.
Blues 4   Sheffield W. 1   Att. 28,599
Bond, Mills,
Hicks, Bradford
1935, Division 1.
Blues 1   Liverpool 3   Att. 25,000
Harris
1946, Wartime.
Blues 2   Fulham 0
Laing, White
1959, FA Cup 5th round, 2nd replay.
Blues 0   Nottingham Forest 5   Att. 34,458
                 Dwight 17, 58, 59
                 Gray 35, 64(pen)
Played at Filbert Street, Leicester.
1974, Division 1.
Blues 3   Arsenal 1   Att. 29,828
Gallagher 55   Kennedy 29
Hatton 57
Francis 65
1980, Division 2.
Blues 2   Wrexham 0   Att. 19,306
Dillon 8
Evans 89
This match screened by ATV's Star Soccer
1985, Division 2.
Shrewsbury Town 1   Blues 0   Att. 7,177
Tester 40
1991, Division 3.
Blues 1   Chester City 0   Att. 6,702
Dolan 50
1997, Division 1.
Blues 1   Port Vale 2   Att. 13,192
Devlin(pen) 8   Porter 16
                 Glover 54

2002, Division 1.
Blues 3   Watford 2   Att. 18,059
Purse 21   Pennant 59
Mooney 42,   M.Johnson(og) 90
53(pen)

February 24

Playing record for this day

Playing record for this day is...15 games, Won 6, Drawn 3, Lost 6, GF 24, GA 30.
Today's success rate.....50% Year ranking....172nd

Match of the Day

FROM 1968
BRIDGES DOUBLE SINKS VILLA

Blues rule Second City derby

This home win for Blues increased hopes of promotion, with 36 points out of 30 games. The match began furiously when Geoff Vowden's pass rolled perfectly into the path of Barry Bridges, who outpaced the Villa full back Charlie Aitken and shot the ball into the net past Colin Withers after just 17 seconds play. This was close to the League record for the fastest goal, which stood at four seconds by Bradford's Jim Fryatt in 1964. After this flying start for Blues, Villa gradually fought themselves back into the game, performances from midfielders Bobby Park and Tommy Mitchinson helping along their efforts.

For a good while there were no more real thrills, aside from those expected from this local derby, and it was not until the 43rd minute that another goal came along. Brian Godfrey equalised for Villa after a long cross from Keith Bradley, touched down by John Woodward.

The second half began and just seven minutes later Bridges was brought down in the penalty area by Aitken, but to the amazement of the huge 45,283 crowd the referee ignored the appeals from Birmingham for the clear cut penalty. After this the game was incident-free until justice was done on 83 minutes. Johnny Vincent mis-hit a shot, but Bridges was on hand to sweep the ball into the net from a narrow angle.

An attempt from Park in the final minute was saved by Jim Herriot, and the game ended with a win for Blues. It was only their third `double' over Villa, over some 36 league campaigns, but few were more sweeter than this one.

The goals for Bridges brought his tally up to 20 in the league, nine short of Joe Bradford's club record, with a dozen games to go.

The other bright spot of the game was off-the-field where officials reported no trouble between the two sets of fans before, during or after the game.

BIRMINGHAM CITY

Herriot, Martin, Foster, Beard, Green, Wylie, Page, Vincent, Bridges, Pickering, Vowden.

ASTON VILLA

Withers, Bradley, Deakin, Chatterley, Aitken, Park, Mitchinson, Roberts, Godfrey, Woodward, Anderson.

REFEREE
Mr Norman Burtenshaw

Barry Bridges

Playing record for this day

Playing record for this day...19 games, Won 8, Drawn 6, Lost 5, GF 34, GA 30.

Today's success rate....57.89% Year ranking....78th

Match of the Day

FROM 2001

HEROES OF THE MILLENNIUM

Battling Birmingham beaten on penalties

What a magnificent start for the new temporary home of English cup finals. With Wembley closed for refurbishment Cardiff's Millennium Stadium hosted the Worthington Cup final of 2001.

Premiership Liverpool were hot favourites and quickly took control. It took them just 29 minutes before Heskey flicked on Westerveldt 's deep goal kick, for Fowler to volley home from 25 yards. At 1-0 it seemed the Nationwide team would fold, however it only inspired Birmingham to fight back and in the end they came so very close to a major upset.

England manager Sven-Goran Ericksson, in attendance as guest of honour, must have been impressed by the solid defensive display from the Blues centre back Darren Purse. After being beaten by Heskey for the opening goal he rarely put a foot wrong, this gave Birmingham the opportunity to attack more. In the second half the first real chance fell to substitute Andrew Johnson who might have made more of his snap shot from a fired in cross by Eaden.

With normal time almost up Birmingham threw everything forward looking for an equaliser and eventually a neat move ended with a loose ball in the Reds' area, O'Connor chased it and as he was about to control the ball Hamann's outstretched leg brought him down, referee Elleray immediately awarding a penalty. After a long nervous pause whilst O'Connor recieved treatment for the knock, Darren Purse, with 35,000 Blues fans congregated behind the goal he was facing, strode up striking his penalty to Westeveldt's left firmly into the corner, the 'keeper had no chance. During extra time the pressure from Birmingham was relentless, a superb 35-yard chip from Hughes almost caught out the Reds' 'keeper, a solitary hand just pushing the ball wide of the post. Then came the moment Birmingham will never forget, on a breakaway, Hughes played the ball to Eaden and he knocked it into the on-rushing Andrew Johnson, as he was about to collect the ball he was clearly tripped by his marker, but amazingly Elleray who seemed to have a perfect view of the foul waved play on.

In the last minute of extra time a quick Liverpool free-kick found Hamann who hit a fierce shot which came back off the Birmingham post to safety. So at 1-1 the match was to be decided on a penalty shoot out, Liverpool's fortune held and they took the cup, their first of a superb treble winning season, 5-4 on penalties.

BIRMINGHAM CITY

Bennett, Eaden, Grainger, Sonner (Hughes), Purse, Michael Johnson, McCarthy, Adebola (Andrew Johnson), Horsfield (Marcelo), O'Connor, Lazaridis.

LIVERPOOL

Westerveld, Babbel, Henchoz, Hyypia, Carragher, Gerrard (McCallister 78), Hamann, Biscan (Ziege 96), Smicer (Barmby 83), Heskey, Fowler.

REFEREE

Mr D Elleray (Harrow)

Darren Purse

Blues news extra   1893..England 6 Ireland 1

Blues' keeper Chris Charsley won his first cap becoming the first Blues player to gain England recognition. He performed well in a game dominated by the home forwards who scored six at the Perry Barr Stadium in Birmingham. The Irish goal came as a result of a defensive error and no blame could be attached to the debutant keeper. Charsley, however, was never selected for his country again.

1963..Blues v Bury, FA Cup 3rd round chaos continues.

After 14 previous postponements, this long awaited FA Cup third round finally got under way at St Andrews. After an hour's play and Blues leading 1-0 the conditions worsened and the referee had no alternative but to abandon play due to the falling snow and freezing conditions, much to the disappointment of the 19,287 fans in the ground. When the game was eventually played in March, it ended all square at 3-3 creating further fixture problems. The replay was won by Bury.

Birthdays

Peter Ndlovu born today 1973.

February 26

Playing record for this day

Playing record for this day is...14 games, Won 9, Drawn 3, Lost 2, GF 22, GA 14.

Today's success rate.....75% Year ranking...4th

Match of the Day
FROM 1991
BLUES ON THEIR WAY

Just two rounds away from Wembley after Mansfield win

Blues moved on into the area semi-final of the Leyland Daf cup with this trouble-free win over Mansfield. Lou Macari's team were now nearing their first trip to Wembley since their FA Cup defeat by Manchester City in 1956, something which most of the 5,365 crowd at this match would not have been around to see.

Blues rapidly took control over struggling Mansfield. In the 25th minute, Jason Pearcey in the stags' goal could do nothing to prevent Blues going ahead. Trevor Aylott and Ian Rodgerson produced a lovely quick move which brought about a corner. Dean Peer took the kick, crossing into the goal area, where Trevor Matthewson made sure the ball hit the back of the net with a superbly hit volley.

Mansfield now decided not to defend so much, but to take their chances and attack. It wasn't to be, however, and their only action in the first 25 minutes was when Chris Fairclough received a fully deserved booking for a mistimed tackle. After that they had a couple of good chances. Steve Charles' shot went wide of the post, and the man who had scored four goals against Blues last April, Steve Wilkinson, shot straight into the arms of goalkeeper Thomas. During the second half Blues had ample chance to increase their lead, but found it difficult to reach the back of the net. Sturridge had a go, and Overson tried twice, but their efforts were fruitless.

John Gayle was brought on as substitute in the 78th minute, and just two minutes later he put the game beyond Mansfield's reach when he rammed home a header, won from a free kick.

Blues now faced Cambridge United, who had beaten them 3-0 at St Andrews in the previous seaon. Blues' confidence was high, though, after a fourth win in five games under Lou Macari, and they were becoming a force to be reckoned with.

BIRMINGHAM CITY

Thomas, Clarkson, Matthewson, Overson, Frain, Rodgerson, Peer, Sturridge, Gleghorn (Bailey), Dolan (Gayle), Aylott.

MANSFIELD

Pearcey, Chambers, Fairclough, Foster, Gray, Lowery (Hathaway), Charles, Prindiville, Wilkinson, Kent, Christie.

REFEREE

Mr D B Allison (Lancaster)

Lou Macari (Birmingham City manager)

Birthdays

Anthony Blake born today 1927

Playing record for this day

Playing record for this day is...20 games, Won 9, Drawn 4, Lost 7, GF 32, GA 30.

Today's success rate.....55% Year ranking....110th

Match of the Day

FROM 1999

BLUES ARE BACK IN STYLE

After three games without a win, Blues are back to hammer Grimsby

Blues sent out a clear message to their promotion rivals today, the recent slump over. Without a win in three games, facing a Grimsby side who had not been beaten by any other First Division side this season at Blundell Park, and hampered by their recent lack of goal-scoring power they travelled to Cleethorpes needing to find some winning form.

After half an hour of this game it looked increasingly likely yet again Blues nice football would go unrewarded, and something special was needed to break Grimsby's well organised resistance. Blues got that something special on 36 minutes when a five-man move involving Charlton, Grainger, Hyde, Bass and then Hughes put Peter Ndlovu through goal. He dummied Gallimore with a quick side step and curled his 25-yard shot wide of Davison into the corner. This was all Blues needed and the relaxed control they now had on the game was delightful, at half time there was no further addition to the one goal lead.

Blues continued to dominate the game in the second half, but with time running out only had Ndlovu's earlier wonder strike to show on the scoreboard. With five minutes remaining however they added two quick goals. First a Davison goal kick was headed back by Hughes on the half way line to Adebola and after controlling well with his first touch he turned perfectly disecting the Grimsby defence. With 'keeper Davison stranded he rolled the ball into the corner. At 2-0 and the game won Blues went all-out for the final kill and in stoppage time a Grainger corner was powerfully headed in by Gary Rowett at the near post.

Blues had bought an end to their mini drought, ruined Grimsby's unbeaten home record, and strikers Ndlovu and Adebola had their first goals since December. Things were looking brighter at last and Blues now occupied fifth place in the table just four points from second placed Bradford City with 13 games remaining. It was going to be a close and exciting run in.

BIRMINGHAM CITY

Poole, Bass, Rowett, Johnson, Charlton (McCarthy 78), Hughes, Hyde, O'Connor, Grainger, Ndlovu (Adebola 72), Furlong (Forster 89)

GRIMSBY TOWN

Davison, McDermott, Lever (Burnett 45), Richard Smith, Gallimore, Donovan, Coldicott (Widdrington 64), Groves, Black, Nogan (Clare 45), Ashcroft.

REFEREE

Mr. D Laws (Whitley Bay)

Blues news extra   1892...Welsh honour for Jenkyns

Ceasar Jenkyns became the first Blues player to be capped at international level when he lined up for Wales against Ireland at Bangor. Jenkyns had a good debut in a closely fought 1-1 draw.

Birthdays

Martin Hicks born today 1957   Mark Sale born today 1972

Sadly Missed

Bob McRoberts died today in1959, aged 84

Pat Beasley died today in1986, aged 72

The Matches played on this day

1892, Football Alliance.

Blues 3	Newton Heath 2	Att. 3,000
Walton,		
Hallam, Wheldon		

1897, Division 2.

Blues 3	Burton Wanderers 2	Att. 6,000
Hodgetts,		
Hare, Oakes		

1904, Division 1.

Sheffield W. 3	Blues 2	Att. 6,000
	Jones(2)	

1909, Division 2.

Clapton Orient 3	Blues 2	Att. 7,000
	King, Bumphrey	

1915, Division 2.

Leeds City 2	Blues 0	Att. 7,000

Blues last ever competitive match against the now defunct Leeds City.

1924, Division 1.

Blues 2	Burnley 1	Att. 14,500
Bradford(2)		

1926, Division 1.

Blues 2	Aston Villa 1	Att. 45,000
Briggs(2)		

1932, Division 1.

Grimsby Town 1	Blues 1	Att. 7,000
	Horsman	

1937, Division 1.

Blues 2	Everton 0	Att. 21,150
Beatie, White		

1943, Wartime.

Blues 3	Coventry City 1	
Craven,		
Watton,		
McEwan		

1954, Division 1.

Lincoln City 0	Blues 1	Att. 13,853
	Lane 78	

1960, Division 1.

Manchester City 3	Blues 0	Att. 23,479
Hayes 26, 50		
Barlow 40		

1965, Division 1.

Blues 0	Sheffield Wed. 0	Att. 12,138

1971, Division 2.

Swindon Town 1	Blues 2	Att. 19,860
Porter 46	Francis 25, 73	

1973, Division 1.

Blues 0	Wolverhampton W. 1	Att. 43,759
	Dougan 53	

1982, Division 1.

Southampton 3	Blues 1	Att. 20,620
Keegan 18(pen)	Worthington 41(pen)	
Baker 56, 61		

This match screened by Central TV's The Big Match

1988, Division 2.

Huddersfield Town 2	Blues 2	Att. 5,441
Banks 33	Robinson 25	
Barham 63	Whitton 26	

1996, Division 1.

Crystal Palace 3	Blues 2	Att. 12,965
Dyer 7, 55, 83	Bowen 30, 77	

1999, Division 1.

Grimsby Town 0	Blues 3	Att. 7,807
	Ndlovu 36	
	Adebola 85	
	Rowett 90	

2000, Division 1.

Blues 1	Ipswich Town 1	Att. 20,493
Mowbray(og) 17	D.Johnson 45	

February 28-9

Playing record for this day
Playing record for this day is...29 games, Won 14, Drawn 7, Lost 8, GF 42, GA 30.
Today's success rate.....60.34% Year ranking....51st

Match of the Day
FROM 1998
LITTLE AND LARGE SINK WOLVES
Adebola and Ndlovu set up win and play-off push

Brilliant Blues overcame falling a goal behind to their local rivals, and stormed back to comfortably beat the Wolves at Molineux by 3-1. It was a magnificent display from Ndlovu and a great winner from Adebola which set up Blues victory. The win enabled Blues to leapfrog their rivals in the table putting them into the top six with just 12 games left of the season.

After a closely fought opening ten minutes it was Wolves who surged into the lead after a wonderful strike from Dougie Freedman on 14 minutes. Waiting for the ball to drop over his shoulder from a Lee Naylor cross, he smashed a beautiful volley past Bennett who was given no chance. This brought about a sustained period of pressure for the home side and Blues found themselves under the cosh. However they fought back well and the Little and Large strike partnership of Adebola and Ndlovu proved too much for the Wolves. Adebola turned Richards inside out to lay on Ndlovu's blistering strike from 20 yards, the equaliser coming ten minutes before half time.

Blues controlled the second half and the winning goal inevitably came along after 71 minutes. Again it was Adebola who spun Richards to sprint clear down the left-hand side of the penalty area. The new £1million striker then showed his precise shooting skills with a super goal accurately hit from an acute angled shot. Dean Richards must have wished he'd marked someone else, his afternoon's woe was complete when he was penalised for a trip on O'Connor which gave away the 77th minute penalty. Ndlovu planted the kick low and into the left-hand corner to cap another fine win for this promotion-seeking, impressive Blues side.

BIRMINGHAM CITY
Bennett, Johnson, Charlton, Marsden, Bruce, Ablett, McCarthy, O'Connor (Grainger 80), Adebola, Hughes (Robinson 61), Ndlovu (Forster 90)

WOLVERHAMPTON WANDERERS
Stowell, Muscat (Simpson 76), Naylor, Carl Robinson, Curle, Richards, Atkins, Keane (Bull 78), Paatelainen, Osborn, Freedman.

REFEREE
Mr G Cain (Bootle)

Chris Marsden challenges Wolverhampton Wanderers' Simon Osborne

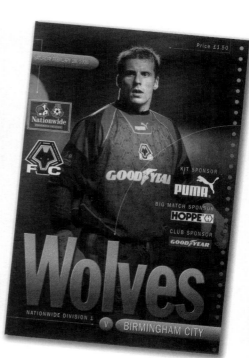

Birthdays
Syd Owen born today 1922   Eddie Brown born today 1926

Sadly Missed
Stan Cullis died today in 2001 aged 85

Steve Bruce

1980*, Division 2.

Swansea City 0	Blues 1	Att. 16,363
	Lynex 55	

Blues keeper Jeff Wealands saved Tommy Craig's 40th minute penalty

1981, Division 1.

WBA 2	Blues 2	Att. 24,853
Moses 5	Worthington 32	
Brown 71	Ainscow 38	

1984, Division 1.

Blues 2	WBA 1	Att. 16,780
Rees 22	Mackenzie 84	
Broadhurst 28		

1987, Division 2.

Blues 0	Hull City 0	Att. 6,858

1989, Division 2.

Stoke City 1	Blues 0	Att. 7,904
Berry 33		

1992, Division 3.

Blues 1	Stoke City 1	Att. 22,162
Frain 21(pen)	Barnes 89	

1993, Division 1.

Leicester City 2	Blues 1	Att. 10,284
Walsh 43	Matthewson 44	
Lowe 50		

This game shown live on Central TV's, The Big Match

1995, Auto Windscreens Shield, Southern Area Final, 1st leg.

Blues 1	Leyton Orient 0	Att. 24,002
Shearer 4		

1998, Division 1.

Wolverhampton W. 1	Blues 3	Att. 25,591
Freedman 14	Ndlovu 35, 77 pen	
	Adebola 71	

March 1

Playing record for this day
Playing record for this day is...13 games, Won 10, Drawn 1, Lost 2, GF 28, GA 12.
Today's success rate.....80.77% Year ranking....1st

The Matches played on this day

1902, Division 1.		
Bury 2	Blues 0	Att. 5,000
1913, Division 2.		
Glossop 0	Blues 2	Att. 3,000
	Jones, Robertson	
1915, Division 2.		
Blues 1	Fulham 0	Att. 5,000
Barton		
1919, Wartime.		
Blues 4	Grimsby Town 0	
Whitehouse(2),		
A.W.Smith(2)		
1924, Division 1.		
Blues 2	Preston North End 0	Att. 12,000
Bradford(2)		
1941, Wartime.		
Luton Town 2	Blues 5	
	Dearson(3),	
	Gill, Forsyth(og)	
1947, FA Cup 6th round.		
Liverpool 4	Blues 1	Att. 51,911
	Mitchell(pen)	
1952, Division 2.		
Blues 3	Coventry City 1	Att. 33,000
Stewart 47	Jamieson 81	
Briggs 56		
Murphy 68		
1958, Division 1.		
Blues 4	Arsenal 1	.Att. 26,824
Hooper 1	Bloomfield 50	
Murphy 42		
Brown 47, 85		
1969, Division 2.		
Norwich City 1	Blues 1	Att. 16,429
Manning 47	Vowden 46	
1975, Division 1.		
Wolverhampton W. 0	Blues 1	Att. 28,256
	Hendrie 68	

Garry Pendrey broke his nose in the first minute and was forced out of the game.

1986, Division 1.		
Blues 2	QPR 0	Att. 7,093
Clarke 52(pen)		
Hopkins 85		

This ended a run of 12 home games without a win, stretching back to September (10 league,1 LC,1 FAC)

1997, Division 1.		
Grimsby Town 1	Blues 2	Att. 5,166
Southall 8	O'Connor 60	
	Forster 61	

Match of the Day
FROM 1958
HOOPER RUNS RINGS ROUND THE GUNNERS

Harry scores one assists two, and shows his £20,000 class

Harry Hooper began to repay some of that £20,000 transfer fee paid to Wolves, having a fantastic game capped by a great goal within seconds of the kick off to earn Blues their first home league win since October. Blues, who had conceded 13 goals in their previous two games, were also tighter in defence, but they needed more of the same in their final 12 games to make sure of avoiding the drop. Blues made three changes from the previous week's devastating 5-1 defeat by Wolves. Ken Green returned to left back in place of Farmer, Dick Neal replaced Watts at number six, and although Govan missed out through injury they were boosted by the return of Gordon Astall.

Blues made a sensational start to the game, taking the lead before many of the crowd of 26,824 had arrived on the terraces. Straight from the kick off a crossfield pass by Astall found Hooper on the left wing, collecting the ball he began a 40-yard run and finished with a shot from the edge of the penalty area which flew past Kelsey in the Arsenal goal. Arsenal kicked off with over half their side still to touch the ball, yet they soon forced a corner which Merrick came out and took confidently. Confidence was running high against a lethargic looking Arsenal side such that even right back Hall got forward to take a snap shot at Kelsey which was saved at the second attempt. Then Hooper was brought down by Fotherington and depite huge appeals for a penalty the referee waved play on. Blues dominance brought about a second goal just three minutes before half time and again it was Hooper who paved the way. After receiving the ball from Astall he slipped it perfectly into the path of the on-rushing Murphy who whacked it in first time from 20 yards, again giving Kelsey no chance of saving.

Blues started the second half as they did the first, with another quick goal to put the game well beyond Arsenal. This was a simple tap in for Brown. After good wing work by Astall produced a low centre right across the goalmouth, Brown sidefooted in from three yards. At 3-0 it was a case of how many could Blues rattle up in the final 43 minutes. However whilst they were calculating the possibilities Bloomfield popped up at the other end to reduced the arrears for Arsenal. It looked very much like a cross but Bloomfield will point to Merrick being well off his line as he looped the ball high from wide on the left and it dropped into the net after clearing the 'keeper's head. This seemed to subdue Blues back into their shell and the game went into a dull period of midfield scraps. Blues eventually came strong again during the closing ten minutes when Charlton cleared off the line from Murphy and then they added a fourth goal on 85 minutes. Again it was clever play from man-of-the-match Hooper who cut in from the right to shoot and although Kelsey blocked the effort he was close enough in to nudge it forward again, Brown then nipped in to make sure as the ball rolled over the goal line.

BIRMINGHAM CITY
Merrick, Hall, Green, Larkin, Smith, Neal, Astall, Orritt, Brown, Murphy, Hooper.
ARSENAL
Kelsey, Charlton, Evans, Ward, Fotherington, Petts, Clapton, Groves, Herd, Bloomfield, Nutt.

REFEREE
Mr E.J Meaden (Trowbridge)

Harry Hooper

Birthdays
Ted Purdon born today 1930.

Playing record for this day
Playing record for this day is...20 games, Won 8, Drawn 6, Lost 6, GF 36, GA 17.
Today's success rate.....55% Year ranking....104th

March 2

Match of the Day

FROM 1985

BLUES RULE THE MANOR

Blues edge closer to promotion and the championship

Blues promotion dream was still alive after an impressive win against Oxford managed by former Blues boss Jim Smith. Two opportunist strikes from rebounds within the penalty area from Clark then Geddis, both in the space of seven first-half minutes, put Blues well on their way to maximum points, and now looking for the added bonus of the Division Two championship.

Blues began the game under extreme early pressure and within the first minute were defending the home side's second corner. Then a through ball from Charles had Aldridge breaking into the box but he was thwarted by a well-timed dive at his feet from the alert David Seaman in the Blues goal. Birmingham finally won a free kick to put the ball into the Oxford penalty area and this produced the opening goal on seven minutes. Ranson played a short kick to Kuhl to launch it forward, Hardwick then under pressure from Geddis could only manage a tame looking pat away, and the ball fell to Clarke who could hardly wait to smash a low drive into the corner from just eight yards out. Another bad back pass this time from Jones had Seaman dashing out again from his goal to kick clear almost giving Oxford a quick equaliser. Blues seemed to have weathered the early storm and were now attacking with just as much frequency as their hosts, as they pressed for an all-important second goal. This duly arrived on 28 minutes from another free kick driven in by Kuhl, this time a full blooded shot hit team mate Clarke on the back and fell perfectly for Geddis, who simply tapped the ball wide of the unfortunate Hardwick who had no chance. Play continued with end to end attacking and both sides coming close , the best chance came the way of former Blues full back Dave Langan whose shot from within the area came back off the post straight into Seaman's arms. Oxford then lost the services of their influential skipper Malcolm Shotton through injury just three minutes from half time, Rhoades-Brown came on as the substitute.

The second half started at an incredible pace and again Oxford stormed forward but were kept at bay by the coolness of Jim Hagan in defence. Within five minutes Aldridge became the first player booked after a wild challenge on Geddis. With Blues content to play the ball around denying Oxford opportunities to get forward, the home side began to get increasingly frustrated and this led to a third Blues goal on the hour mark. A lovely exchange of passing by Roberts and Jones on the left resulted in a fine cross for an unmarked Clarke who rose to plant a precise header past Hardwick and into the top corner of the net. The goal ended any realistic hope Oxford had of a recovery, and despite two late chances from Aldridge which Seaman dealt with easily, Blues held out for a comfortable 3-0 win, much to the delight of the celebrating fans in the visitors enclosure.

BIRMINGHAM CITY
Seaman, Ranson, Roberts, Wright, Hagan, Kuhl, Jones, Clarke, Bremner, Geddis, Hopkins.

OXFORD UNITED
Hardwick, Langan, Spearing, Trewick, Briggs, Shotton(Rhoades-Brown 42), McDermott, Aldridge, Charles, Hebbard, Brock.

REFEREE
Mr L. Sharpe (Torquay)

Billy Wright

Birthdays

John Kelly born today 1913.

March 3

-1875-

The Matches played on this day

1894, Division 2.		
Grimsby Town 2	Blues 1	Att. 5,000
	Mobley	
1906, Division 1.		
Woolwich Arsenal 5	Blues 0	Att. 25,000
1917, Wartime.		
Blues 3	Grimsby Town 0	
Bowser(2),		
Whitehouse		
1923, Division 1.		
Preston North End 2	Blues 3	Att. 14,000
Rawson,		
Bradford,		
Crosbie		
1926, Division 1.		
Notts County 3	Blues 0	Att. 15,000
1928, Division 1.		
Bury 2	Blues 3	Att. 10,000
	Bradford(2), Briggs	
1934, Division 1.		
Wolverhampton W. 2	Blues 0	Att. 30,000
1945, Wartime.		
Walsall 0	Blues 2	
	Kernick(2)	
1951, Division 2.		
Barnsley 0	Blues 2	Att. 15,381
	Dailey 57	
	Stewart 77	
1956, FA Cup 6th round.		
Arsenal 1	Blues 3	Att. 67,872
Charlton 72	Astall 30	
	Murphy 41	
	Brown 68	
1962, Division 1.		
Blues 1	Manchester United 1	Att. 25,777
Leek 52	Herd 88	
1973, Division 1.		
Chelsea 0	Blues 0	Att. 26,259
1979, Division 1.		
Aston Villa 1	Blues 0	Att. 42,419
Cowans 80		
1984, Division 1.		
Coventry City 0	Blues 1	Att. 13,705
	Gayle 28	
1987, Division 2.		
Huddersfield Town 2	Blues 2	Att. 5,177
Overson(og) 50	Whitton 26	
Cork 86	Rees 45	
1990, Division 3.		
Blues 4	Mansfield Town 1	Att. 5,746
Sturridge 12	Christie 58	
Bailey 44, 59		
Ashley 50		
Blues 1st league meeting v Mansfield		
1992, Division 3.		
Blues 1	Swansea City 1	Att. 9,475
Rowbotham 26	Williams 52	

Playing record for this day

Playing record for this day is...17 games, Won 8, Drawn 4, Lost 5, GF 26, GA 23.

Today's success rate.....58.82% Year ranking....67th

Match of the Day

FROM 1956

BLUES AWAY DAY
CUP RECORD BREAKERS

Another round, another ground and yet another great victory

Blues record breaking cup run continued with a memorable win at Highbury in the sixth round. Starting with Torquay they had added Orient, WBA and now Arsenal to an impressive array of cup victims and all away from home. Never before in the FA Cup's history had a side reached the final at Wembley having played all their ties away from home, so Blues had a chance of creating history.

It was Arsenal who dominated the early stages with the better passing and quicker movement. However, Blues excelled in the important areas and produced the match winning goals. It was against the run of play when Birmingham swept into the lead in the 30th minute, when Astall scored an almost identical goal to the one he netted in a league game between the sides at St Andrews back in December. A great 40-yard pass into the area was chased by Astall who headed the ball over the advancing Kelsey who watched it roll into the net behind him. The goal transformed both teams, Arsenal were now having difficulty holding the ball and Birmingham, in contrast, were finding men with ease and free space. Blues had progressed in the competition mainly due to their tremendous fighting spirit and this was perfectly highlighted with the second goal just before half time. Brown's cross from the by line appeared to be rolling harmlessly out of play for a goal kick, Kinsey however ran in like a greyhound to keep the ball in aided by the corner flag. He then centred and in trying to clear the ball hit an Arsenal defender and fell nicely to Murphy who smashed it home. This gave Peter Murphy his own personal FA Cup record of scoring in every round in the Blues impressive run. On the stroke of half time Kelsey pulled off a brilliant save to deny Murphy a second goal when tipping a long-range shot over the bar.

Birmingham kept up their momentum in the second half starting very well but at 2-0 Arsenal were still not out of the game. Encouraged by this the home side, urged on by a 67,107 crowd, soon got back into their stride to take over as the dominant side. Their best chance came on the hour mark when Merrick just kept out Clapton's shot with his knees. The England 'keeper then sensationally saved a close range pile driver from Groves. The save inspired the Birmingham players and they broke away to score a match winning third goal on 68 minutes. The move started with Astall passing to Murphy ten yards within his own half, he took the ball on beating man after man in a a great run to the byline, cutting it back for Brown who picked his spot precisely past a stranded Kelsey. Arsenal were given slight hope with a quick-reply goal just four minutes later but it proved a false dawn, Smith got the consolation and Blues held on to win the tie and earn a semi-final showdown with Sunderland, away again at Hillsborough.

BIRMINGHAM CITY

Merrick, Hall, Green, Boyd, Smith, Warhurst, Astall, Murphy, Brown, Kinsey, Govan.

ARSENAL

Kelsey, Charlton, Evans, Goring, Dodgin, Bowen, Clapton, Tapscott, Groves, Bloomfield, Nutt.

Len Boyd

Blues news extra   1920...Blues break the bank for Lane

Blues smashed their transfer fee record when signing Blackpool's highly rated centre forward Joe Lane. Blues paid £3,600 for the 27-year-old who went straight into Saturday's team for the game at Lincoln City.

Birthdays

David Regis born today 1964.

Playing record for this day

Playing record for this day is...20 games, Won 8, Drawn 6, Lost 6, GF 36, GA 31.

Today's success rate.....55% Year ranking....105th

Match of the Day

FROM 2000

WHAM BAM THANK YOU YAM

Dele the Yam buster in seven minute burst

Dele Adebola did it again only this time without the aid of Peter Ndlovu how he would have loved the little Zimbabwean winger along with him. The two had haunted the Albion three times now and every time with a goal blitz which had the game won early on. The latest humiliation however likely to prove costly for the Baggies as they slipped into the relegation zone, dropping below neighbours Walsall. Albion went into the game having won just one game in 17 and without leading scorer Lee Hughes and influential midfielder Richard Sneekes. Blues on the flip side were slowly welcoming their wounded players back after a horrid winter which often reduced Trevor Francis to a skeleton squad. They were now seven games unbeaten and this latest win took them to fifth, just seven points behind a top-two place, a position unthinkable just 2 months previously.

The game got off to a sensational start for the visitors but it was Albion who could have pinched an early lead from their first attack when Quinn hit the post with a shot within the Blues penalty area, the let off was to prove devastatingly costly. Blues had yet to threaten the before Bennett's long goal kick dropped 25 yards from the Albion goal. The ball bounced first, which should have made for a simple header back to the keeper for Carbon, but he somehow managed to hold the ball up by nudging his header upwards, this allowed Adebola to nip round the defender and in front of Sigurdsson to head over him and the hopelessly stranded Albion 'keeper to give Blues a 1-0 lead in five minutes. Just two minutes later the game was effectively over when Adebola beat the Baggies woeful offside trap to latch onto Charlton's long ball 40 yards out in acres of free space. The Blues striker had enough time to play a neat one-two with the post before prodding the ball over the line as he left Adamson in the Albion goal helplessly stranded for the second time in almost as many minutes. That was that as a contest and both sides seemed content, Albion purely for damage limitation, Blues happy to secure the three points which would stabilise their top six and play-off position. Blues through Adebola almost went 3-0 up on the stroke of half time with a narrowly missed shot from an acute angle.

The second half was a little less dramatic and the first incident of note was Sigurdsson's dismissal with 15 minutes left after receiving a second yellow card. With four minutes to play a Lazaridis corner which drifted over everyone in the area found Andrew Johnson who squared the ball to Grainger, his cross from the left hand flank found Albion's marking desperately inadequate again as Marcelo just beat team mate Rowett to head in from five yards with both Blues men unmarked. Another Albion hammering had been completed in front of a fast emptying Brummie Road stand, Albion faced an almighty difficult job in avoiding relegation this season, but they escaped ... just!!!

BIRMINGHAM CITY

Bennett, Rowett, Charlton, Grainger, Purse, Holdsworth, Hyde, Adebola, Rankin (Andrew Johnson), Hughes, Lazaridis.

WEST BROMWICH ALBION

Adamson, Chambers, Sigurdsson, Van Blerk, Carbon, Hall, Flynn, (De Freitas), Evans,Townsend, Fredgaard

REFEREE

Mr M Dean (Heswall, Wirral)

David Holdsworth

Vol 91: Issue 22 £2   04.03.2000   Birmingham City Issue Kick Off 1pm   Nationwide

The Matches played on this day

1899, Division 2.		
Blues 4	Woolwich Arsenal 1	Att. 3,000
Abbott(3), Wharton		
1905, Division 1.		
Blackburn Rovers 1	Blues 4	Att. 5,000
	Jones(2,1 pen),	
	Field, Beer	
1911, Division 2.		
Blues 1	Leicester Fosse 0	Att. 8,000
Buckley		
1931, FA Cup 6th round, replay.		
Chelsea 0	Blues 3	Att. 74,365
	Firth, Bradford(2)	
This was the largest attendance Blues had played in front of to date.		
1933, FA Cup 6th round.		
West Ham United 4	Blues 0	Att. 44,233
1939, Division 1.		
Aston Villa 5	Blues 1	Att. 40,874
	Dearson	
1944, Wartime.		
Blues 3	Leicester City 1	
Mulraney, Trigg(2)		
1950, Division 1.		
Blues 2	Huddersfield Town 1	Att. 27,000
Brennan 1	Nightingale 24	
Dailey 59		
1953, FA Cup 6th round, replay.		
Tottenham Hotspur 2	Blues 2	Att. 59,543
Duquemin 16	Boyd 59	
Bennett 64	Ferris 85	
1961, Division 1.		
Chelsea 3	Blues 2	Att. 27,727
Tindall 12	Gordon 3	
Tambling 24	Astall 21	
Greaves 86		
1967, Division 2.		
Blackburn Rovers 1	Blues 0	Att. 14,908
Harrison 85		
1969, Division 2.		
Blues 2	Sheffield United 2	Att. 25,123
Beard 14	Badger 67	
Pickering 29	Woodward 75	
1970, Division 2.		
Blackburn Rovers 1	Blues 1	Att. 8,639
Darling 70	Mulvaney(og) 25	
Blues' Dave Latchford saved Martin's 67th minute penalty		
1972, Division 1.		
Blues 4	Norwich City 0	Att. 40,899
Hatton 19, 79		
B.Latchford 25		
Hynd 50		
Half time substitute Mike O'Grady became the first on loan player to appear for the Blues		
1978, Division 1.		
Coventry City 4	Blues 0	Att. 22,925
Ferguson 1, 35, 77		
Beck 44		
Mick Ferguson's first goal timed at 30 seconds. This game screened by ATV's Star Soccer		
1989, Division 2.		
Blues 0	Oxford United 0	Att. 4,954
1995, Division 2.		
Hull City 0	Blues 0	Att. 9,845
Hull City's Gary Hobson sent off after 61 minutes. Steve Robinson makes his debut coming on as a sub for Louis Donowa		
1997, Division 1.		
Blues 1	Wolverhampton W. 2	Att. 19,838
Forster 70	Bull 1	
	Goodman 23	
The 100th league meeting v Wolves		
1998, Division 1.		
Norwich City 3	Blues 3	Att. 9,819
Bellamy 47, 68	Ndlovu 13, 88	
Llewellyn 58	Adebola 44.	
2000, Division 1.		
WBA 0	Blues 3	Att. 17,029
	Adebola 5, 7	
	Marcelo 86	

March 5

Playing record for this day

Playing record for this day is...21 games, Won 9, Drawn 5, Lost 7, GF 37, GA 29.

Today's success rate.....54.76% Year ranking....111th

Match of the Day

FROM 1991

WEMBLEY BOUND

Brentford next for glory hunting Blues

In front of a crowd of 9,429 Blues came through their Southern Area semi-final tie in the Leyland Daf Cup, with the resounding anthem "Keep Right On to the End of the Road" ringing in their ears. Lou Macari's men were hoping to gain their sixth straight win and move another step closer to that elusive Wembley appearance, the first since 1956. They were facing Cambridge United who were fresh from their 3-1 defeat in the FA Cup quarter final with Crewe. Prior to this Cambridge had been on their own impressive unbeaten sequence of matches totalling 17. On their last visit to St Andrews, Cambridge won 3-0, and this led to the resignation of then Blues boss Dave Mackay. U's were again expecting success, but a resurgent Blues gave them an almighty shock.

Blues stated their attacking intent right from the kick off. Cambridge keeper John Vaughan was given an early work out when he had to make a diving save from a crisply hit John Gayle effort. He was just recovering from this when Blues midfielder Dean Peer picked up a loose ball in the area and shot straight past him into the net for the game's opening goal. A great start for Birmingham after just two minutes with a rare goal from Peer, this just his second of the season.

Birmingham fans were still celebrating 20 minutes later when Gleghorn increased the lead. Rodgerson crossed the ball from the right to Gayle. Although his shot was blocked, the rebound fell perfectly for Gleghorn who smashed it high into the roof of the net.

Cambridge tried desperately to get back into the game but lacked any sort of accuracy when playing the ball up to their forwards Dion Dublin and John Taylor. This was due to the excellent cover supplied by the Blues defence who kept the visitors at bay with an exceptional display. After just one save from keeper Martin Thomas in the first half, Dublin then fired Cambridge into the game with an unexpected goal on 64 minutes. Dublin put through, went on to beat Thomas easily with the Blues back four still frantically appealing for offside.

Just one goal ahead, Blues decided to centre all their attentions on attack. It took just seven minutes to restore their two goal lead, with central defender Vince Overson slotting the ball home to make the score now 3-1. The goal came from a corner kick taken by Simon Sturridge, when the ball was only partially punched clear from Vaughan, it fell to Overson who placed his crisply hit right-foot shot into the net to put the result beyond any doubt for Birmingham. Blues now faced Brentford, conquerers of Southend by 3-0, in the Southern Area final over two legs.

BIRMINGHAM CITY

Thomas, Clarkson, Overson, Matthewson, Frain, Rodgerson, Sturridge, Peer, Gleghorn, Aylott, Gayle.

CAMBRIDGE UNITED

Vaughan, Fensome, Chapple, O'Shea, Kimble, Cheetham, Wilkins, Leadbitter, Philpott, Taylor, Dublin.

REFEREE

Mr DJ Axcell (Southend)

Trevor Matthewson

Blues news extra   1993...New regime starts at Blues

Blues new owner was announced as David Sullivan a multi-millionaire publisher who had bought the club for a reported £1.7 million. One of his first acts was to employ Karren Brady as managing director.

The Matches played on this day

1898, Division 2.
Woolwich Arsenal 4   Blues 2   Att. 8,000
                        Hare, Oakes

1904, Division 1.
Blues 2   Sunderland 1   Att. 12,000
Beer(2)

1910, Division 2.
Blues 2   Grimsby Town 4   Att. 14,000
Needham, Chapple

1921, Division 2.
Blues 4   Bury 0   Att. 35,000
Crosbie(2),
Linley, Barton

1927, Division 1.
Derby County 4   Blues 1   Att. 12,000
                        Crosbie

1932, Division 1.
Blues 3   Middlesbrough 0   Att. 22,000
Curtis(2 pens),
Crosbie

1938, Division 1.
Derby County 0   Blues 0   Att. 14,533

1949, Division 1.
Blues 0   Bolton Wanderers 0   Att. 35,000

1955, Division 2.
Swansea City 0   Blues 3   Att. 25,000
                        Boyd 44
                        Kinsey 63
                        Lane 84

1958, Division 1.
Manchester City 1   Blues 1   Att. 27,812
Barlow 54   Murphy 61

1960, Division 1.
Blues 4   Nottingham Forest 1   Att. 24,820
Neal 24   Wilson 11
Hooper 27
Gordon 31, 73

1963, FA Cup 3rd round.
Blues 3   Bury 3   Att. 11,361
Lynn 45   Griffin 30, 32
Leek 46   Eastham 81
Harris 50
Finally after 13 postponements and one abandoned game the match wascompleted. However the tie remaind unsettled and required a replay.

1966, Division 2.
Southampton 0   Blues 1   Att. 18,295
                        Thwaites 30

1977, Division 1.
Blues 3   Coventry City 1   Att. 22,607
Francis 15   Powell 50
Connolly 64
Emmanuel 89

1983, Division 1.
Ipswich Town 3   Blues 1   Att. 16,436
Putney 46   Dennis 67
Osman 53
Brazil 56

1985, Division 2.
Blues 0   Oldham Athletic 1   Att. 10,489
                        Palmer 60

1988, Division 2.
Blues 1   Bradford City 1   Att. 8,101
Whitton 2   Hendrie 39
17-year-old Mark Yates made his Blues debut

1991, Leyland Daf Cup, Southern Area Semi Final.
Blues 3   Cambridge United 1   Att. 9,429
Peer 2   Dublin 64
Gleghorn 22
Overson 71
Blues biggest win over Cambridge to date.

1994, Division 1.
Blues 0   Barnsley 2   Att. 15,382
                        O'Connell 51
                        Rammell 89

1996, Division 1.
Blues 2   Wolverhampton W. 0   Att. 22,051
Devlin 28(pen), 40
Blues' Griemink saved Andy Thompson's penalty on 85 minutes

2002, Division 1.
Blues 1   Manchester City 2   Att. 24,160
Johnson 4   Jensen 45
                        Horlock 67

Playing record for this day

Playing record for this day is...20 games, Won 9, Drawn 5, Lost 6, GF 27, GA 24.

Today's success rate.....57.50% Year ranking....81st

Match of the Day
FROM 1999

PREMIER DREAM STILL ON

Blues come from a goal down to hammer poor Pompey

Blues game-by-game on-off automatic promotion hopes were back on again. But only just, after another uneasy start coming from a goal behind, but come back they did, in emphatic style. After Tuesday's disappointing 0-0 draw with Norwich a top two slot looked unlikely. Despite the disappointment Trevor Francis made just one change to that team, Jon McCarthy swapping with Dele Adebola on the subs' bench, an astute tactical change as the big striker was insrtumental in the impressive comeback.

The 20,617 crowd were quickly stunned into silence by a simple yet well worked goal for the visitors just four minutes into the game. Durnin carved his way through the Blues defence before cutting the ball back from the byline for ex-Villa forward Guy Whittingham to head in from two yards. To their credit Blues took the knock on the chin and carried on in a determined all-out attack, gaining their just reward within 21 minutes. A sloppy knock back by scorer Whittingham on the half-way line was intercepted by Adebola who easily shrugged of the first challenge and bustled forward leaving the Pompey back four hopelessly behind. Approaching the edge of the penalty area he hit a fierce cross shot which Knight got a hand to but failed to keep out and Blues were level. Then in the five minutes prior to half time both sides had chances to take an advantage into the break with them. Charlton blocked a Durnin effort from the line for Blues, and at the other end Ndlovu cleared the crossbar when heading under pressure from four yards out.

During the break Francis made another slight but effective team change and when the sides reappeared Nicky Forster was on in place of Paul Furlong. It took just four minutes for the benefit of that switch to show reward. O'Connor and Hughes combined well on the right and from the latter's cross, Forster got across his man to head in from close range. Then moments later Forster left a chance for Adebola but he scuffed his shot wide with the goal at his mercy. Blues were now in total control. On the hour mark a great long ball pass from Charlton found Forster who turned brilliantly to skip clear of Awford, as the Pompey defence converged on Forster who had advanced to just inside the penalty area, he neatly tapped the ball square to Adebola who hit a sweetly-timed left-foot shot past Knight. With 12 minutes remaining Grainger, who had replaced Ndlovu in the second half, struck the post with a long-range effort as Blues kept up their relentless pressure on a tired Portsmouth side. Blues completed a convincing win on 84 minutes when Hughes weaved his way through the middle of the Pompey defence and stroked the ball into the bottom corner of the net, to make the final score 4-1.

BIRMINGHAM CITY

Poole, Bass, Charlton, Hyde (McCarthy 72), Johnson, Rowett, Hughes, Adebola, Furlong (Forster h/t), O'Connor, Ndlovu (Grainger 57).

PORTSMOUTH

Knight, Robinson, Simpson, McLoughlin, Whitbread, Awford, Whittingham, Peron, Vlachos (Perrett 68), Durnin (Nightingale 62) Igoe (Thogerson 62).

REFEREE

Mr G Laws (Whitley Bay)

Nicky Forster

The Matches played on this day

1886, FA Cup Semi Final.			
WBA 4	Blues 0		Att. 4,100
Played at Aston Lower Grounds.			
Blues introduced their new strip of chocolate and white coloured halves. They never used the colours again following their defeat			
1897, Division 2.			
Blues 1	Blackpool 3		Att. 5,000
Hodgetts			
1915, Division 2.			
Blues 1	Clapton Orient 0		Att. 10,000
A.W.Smith			
1920, Division 2.			
Lincoln City 2	Blues 2		Att. 8,000
	Hampton, Lane		
Record signing Joe Lane scored on his debut			
1926, Division 1.			
Leicester City 1	Blues 0		Att. 20,000
1935, Division 1.			
Chelsea 2	Blues 2		Att. 18,000
	Guest, Harris		
1937, Division 1.			
Bolton Wanderers 0	Blues 0		Att. 15,000
1943, Wartime.			
Walsall 1	Blues 2		
	Watton, Trickett		
1948, Division 2.			
Blues 0	West Ham United 1		Att. 44,000
1954, Division 2.			
Blues 1	Bristol Rovers 1		Att. 25,300
Boyd 21	Leonard 5		
1965, Division 1.			
Blackpool 3	Blues 1		Att. 11,464
Armfield 37	Vowden 24		
Rowe 80			
Moir 88			
1971, Division 2.			
Blues 2	Watford 0		Att. 27,605
Summerill 1			
Francis 5			
Summerill goal timed at 12 seconds			
1973, Division 1.			
Crystal Palace 0	Blues 0		Att. 26,014
1976, Division 1.			
West Ham United 1	Blues 2		Att. 19,868
Page(og) 76	Withe 35		
	Emmanuel 48		

March
6

1979, Division 1.
Blues 3   QPR 1   Att. 12,605
Buckley 67   Busby 66
Towers 77(pen)
Broadhurst 88
Alan Buckley's seventh minute penalty saved by QPR
keeper Derek Richardson. Unlucky Blues striker Keith
Bertschin broke his leg for the second time in the season.
The first time since 21 November that Blues had scored
more than once in a game.
1982, Division 1.
Blues 0   Manchester United 1 Att. 19,637
                     Birtles 18
Byron Stevenson made his Blues debut
1990, Division 3.
Blues 3   Blackpool 1   Att. 7,085
Peer 29   Richards 89
Sturridge 31
Bailey 76(pen)
1993, Division 2..
Blues 1   Oxford United 0   Att. 11,104
Peschisolido 29
Chairman Jack Wiseman introduced the new owners of the
club to the the crowd before kick off. They were
represented by the new managing director Karen Brady
1999, Division 1.
Blues 4   Portsmouth 1   Att. 20,617
Adebola 25, 60   Whittingham 4
Forster 49
Hughes 84
2001, Division 1.
Crystal Palace 1   Blues 2   Att. 13,987
Austin 61   Upson(og) 48
                     Adebola 59

Martin O'Connor

Blues news extra   1982...Reserves suffer freak own goal
Stuart Gibson netted a bizarre own goal playing for the Blues reserves in a Football Combination game. From Tony Coton's goal kick he headed back
towards his own goal from 50 yards the ball going in off a post leaving Coton stunned.

Birthdays
Gary Rowett born today 1974.   **Don Weston born today 1936**   **Paul Harding born today 1964**

Playing record for this day

Playing record for this day is...16 games, Won 8, Drawn 6, Lost 2, GF 20, GA 13.

Today's success rate.....68.75% Year ranking....14th

Match of the Day

FROM 1959

BLUES IN SEVENTH HEAVEN

Forest cut down to size in sweet revenge win

Blues gained sweet revenge for their dismal 5-0 hammering by Nottingham Forest in the FA Cup two weeks previously by handing them their heaviest home defeat in years, Blues cruised to easily their best win of the season, and maintained their unbeaten run at the City Ground going back to 1914. Incredibly this was almost the same side that played in the FA cup second replay at Filbert Street, Leicester, Robin Stubbs in for Bryan Orritt being the only change. 17-year-old former grammar school boy Stubbs proved his worth in this game, his second in senior football, scoring two goals. Indeed this win was even more remarkable for the fact Blues were down 1-0 thanks to a 19th minute strike from Dwight. The teams kicked off in horrible conditions, with a strong cross wind and driving rain, this had much to do with the low attendance of only 18,827. Both sides made a decent start playing some good football despite the weather. In the opening few minutes Merrick saved well from Wilson and Gray. At the other end Fraser fumbled a shot from Hooper and Larkin pounced but only to concede a foul on the Forest 'keeper. Understandably errors started to occur as the wet greasy pitch started taking effect. From one such slip Forest capitalised and opened the scoring. Morley started the move in midfield, passing the ball on to Gray. His pass to Dwight deflected off Blues centre half Smith and, in trying to clear up the loose ball, Hall slipped. This put Dwight clear and he moved in to drive the ball across Merrick and into the far corner of the net. Forest almost made it 2-0 moments later when Imlach missed the target when close in following a free kick. This was to be Forest's last real chance, Blues went on to equalise through Stubbs on 32 minutes, and then lead 2-1 after 43 minutes. Stubbs' first goal came after a defensive error in the penalty area, and he pounced to claim his first senior goal for the club. His second was a beautifully executed half-volley, following a well timed run to meet Astall's cross. Blues still had time to net a third time when Fraser missed his punch from Gordon's lobbed cross, the ball fell to Astall who, faced with an empty net, didn't miss with his tap in.

There was only one team in the second half as Blues dominated from the first kick, and they quickly went 4-1 ahead just two minutes after the restart. The goal came from Hooper who scored at the second attempt after his first effort was blocked on the line by Whare. It was Hooper who was running the Forest defence ragged, and after another devastating run he squared the ball across the open goalmouth where Astall knocked back to Gordon to smash the ball in from close range. That fifth goal for Blues came after an hour, two minutes later it was 6-1. Again Hooper was involved, shaping to cross a free kick into the box, he instead squared the ball to Watts who hit an unstoppable first-time shot from 15 yards. Blues wrapped up their scoring exhibition after 84 minutes, Astall's speculative shot from 20 yards took Fraser by surprise and he watched as it sailed over his head and into the net behind him. This was the last goal of the game but not the last incident. Right at the death Forest were granted a free hit from the penalty spot. Smith brought down Dwight, and Forest's cup of woe was filled to the brim when Gray shot the spot-kick wide.

BIRMINGHAM CITY

Merrick, Hall, Allen, Watts, Smith, Neal, Astall, Gordon, Stubbs, Larkin, Hooper.

NOTTINGHAM FOREST

Fraser, Whare, McDonald, Whitefoot, Watson, Morley, Dwight, Younger, Wilson, Gray, Imlach.

REFEREE

Mr JH Clough (Bolton)

Robin Stubbs

Blues news extra 1981...Friendly at Boston

Goals from Tony Evans and Joe Gallagher gave Blues a comfortable win over Norwich City in a friendly attended by 2,420 at Boston United's York Street ground.

March 8

Playing record for this day
Playing record for this day is...17 games, Won 7, Drawn 2, Lost 8, GF 27, GA 18.
Today's success rate.....47.06% Year ranking....183rd

The Matches played on this day

1890, Football Alliance.
Blues 12   Nottingham Forest 0   Att. 1,000
W.Devey(6),
G.Short(3),
Hallam,
E.Devey(2)
Will Devey became Blues first hat-trick hero in the Football Alliance. He also set a new club record for most individual goals scored in a game.

1899, Division 2.
Blackpool 1   Blues 1   Att. 2,000
   Devey

1902, Division 1.
Blues 2   Blackburn Rovers 0   Att. 15,000
Wharton(2)

1913, Division 2.
Blues 1   Clapton Orient 1   Att. 14,000
Duncan

1915, Division 2.
Barnsley 2   Blues 1   Att. 10,000
   Roulson(pen)

1919, Wartime.
Lincoln City 1   Blues 0

1924, Division 1.
Preston North End 1   Blues 0   Att. 15,000

1930, Division 1.
Blues 2   Burnley 0   Att. 20,000
Bradford, Cringan

1933, Division 1.
Blues 3   Aston Villa 2   Att. 50,000
Briggs, Bradford,
Grosvenor

1952, Division 2.
West Ham United 0   Blues 1   Att. 24,000
   Briggs 75

1958, Division 1.
Bolton Wanderers 1   Blues 0   Att. 18,309
Lofthouse 66
Trevor Smith failed a late fitness test and so Graham Sissons made his senior debut for blues.

1969, Division 2.
Blues 0   Crystal Palace 1   Att. 25,298
   Kember 16

1975, FA Cup 6th round.
Blues 1   Middlesbrough 0   Att. 47,260
Hatton 46
This game screened by BBC's Match of the Day

1980, Division 2.
Shrewsbury Town 1   Blues 0   Att. 14,801
Maguire 43

1986, Division 1.
Sheffield W. 5   Blues 1   Att. 17,491
Shutt 9, 27, 65   Geddis 81
Chapman 40
Chamberlain 64

1988, Division 2.
Blues 0   WBA 1   Att. 12,331
   Hopkins 80

1997, Division 1.
Blues 2   Southend United 1   Att. 13,189
Forster 6   Marsh 69
O'Connor 37(pen)

Match of the Day

FROM 1933
BLUES NICK IT AGAINST THE VILLAINS

Five goal derby thriller at packed St Andrews

Blues received an early boost to this long awaited derby clash against Villa with the return to the side of striker Joe Bradford out since the game against Newcastle on 27 December, and it was Bradford who kicked off against an unchanged and full-strength Villa side.

Birmingham soon got into their stride and looked the better of the two sides in the opening 15 minutes. Two efforts from Gregg came close to opening the scoring but Villa's goal attempts were restricted to long-range efforts. The best of these was a 20-yard free kick which was acrobatically tipped over the bar by Hibbs. The Villa 'keeper then saved brilliantly to deny Briggs from a point-blank shot with his chest. The Blues pressure continued and Morton saved expertly again from Morrall. Hibbs at the other end was enjoying the game in virtual spectator mode, but he had to be alert soon after the half-hour mark when he twice made vital contributions to keep the Blues goal intact. In an end-to-end game Briggs was presented with the best chance so far by a great pass from Grosvenor, however with just Morton in front of him he sliced his shot horribly wide. Briggs soon made amends when he grabbed a dramatic goal just before half time much to the delight of the 50,000 St Andrews crowd. Another teasing chipped centre from Grosvenor was headed on by Bradford for Curtis to hit on the volley, Morton flung himself to the right to pull off yet another magnificent save, but Briggs reacted quickly to knock in the rebound to give Blues' a 1-0 interval lead.

There was a sensational start to the second half when Bradford conjured up a moment of magic to put Blues 2-0 up. A long ball out of defence from Stoker found Grosvenor. Taking the ball wide he crossed for Bradford in the centre, taking the ball in his stride the centre forward placed the ball into the far corner of the net beyong the despaering dive of Morton. Bradford was back with a trademark finish and Blues scented victory. Now it was all Birmingham pressure and only desperate defending was preventing their forwards from running riot. But from a break away Villa got themselves back in the game against the run of play. A superb ball from Houghton set up the chance for Brown who rushed through a non-existent defence to easily put past Hibbs. What a change this had on the game, as suddenly it was Villa who threatened to score with every forward pass. Twice Hibbs came to the rescue as Villa piled men forward seeking an equaliser. But in similar circumstances to Villa's goal, it was Birmingham who restored their two goal advantage after 62 minutes. Curtis this time set up the chance by squaring the ball to Grosvenor who hammered a first time shot which gave Morton no chance of stopping. Blues almost increased their lead soon after with close efforts from Briggs then Bradford as the Villa goal fell under siege. Villa to their credit continued to battle away and earned a consolation reward with five minutes remaining when the Blues defence faltered a second time. After a strange bout of head tennis within the penalty area Mandley nipped in to win the ball and head past Hibbs. Villa pressed right up to the final whistle, but Blues held on to claim victory in this the 40th Second City derby. Blues now had 11 wins to Villa's 18.

BIRMINGHAM CITY
Hibbs, Booton, Barkas, Stoker, Morrall, Calladine, Briggs, Grosvenor, Bradford, Gregg, Curtis.

ASTON VILLA
Morton, Blair, Mort, Gibson, Callaghan, Simpson, Mandley, Astley, Brown, Walker, Houghton.

REFEREE
Mr E Carnwell (Lichfield)

George Briggs

Playing record for this day

Playing record for this day is...21 games, Won 6, Drawn 9, Lost 6, GF 38, GA 36.
Today's success rate.....50% Year ranking....155th

Match of the Day
FROM 1960
LATE FORTUNE GAINS A POINT

Twice behind by two, Blues fight back, to draw

Blues battled from 3-1 down with 13 minutes remaining of this crucial relegation battle to earn a valuable point against fellow strugglers Leeds. Leeds who threw away a two goal lead twice also lost two much-needed points, and this left them almost doomed to relegation. Watched by Elland Road's lowest crowd since the war of 8,557, the stay-aways missed a cracking game in the mud, both sides showing a determination and fight which had been lacking all season. Indeed had these two teams played like this earlier in the season this might have been a battle for points for places at the opposite end of the table.

Despite hours of work by the groundstaff to get the pitch playable, pools of rain lay across the field as Leeds kicked off, and within minutes the pitch was a mud bath. It was no surprise then that the players took some time to adapt to the conditions as passes were held up in the mud and defenders over slid when making a tackle for the ball. Practice in the conditions was impossible for 'keeper Schofield and before he had handled the ball Blues were behind. Leeds opened the scoring in the 13th minute from Smith's mishit free kick. The Blues centre half slipped as he was about to launch the ball forward from 20 yards inside his own half, the sliced kick put Revie away on the left wing and he cut inside to hammer the ball past Schofield. He soon became the hero, as moments later an encouraged Leeds side broke again, Schofield doing well to block McCole's shot from close range with his knees. Blues attacks were limited to set pieces as the Leeds defence executed a frustrating but effective off-side trap which Weston fell for on numerous occasions. Just after Leeds had scrambled away a free kick from Hooper, they broke away to double their lead on 34 minutes. From a long ball out of defence Revie was away again, as the Blues defence stood waiting for a linesman's flag which never came. He advanced on goal and as Schofield came out to cover he struck a shot which went in off the post. Mr Callaghan the Rochdale official was surrounded by Blues players still complaining and they were only removed by the appearance of the ref's notebook, and at least two names were taken. Blues then scored a goal out of nothing, perfectly timed just two minutes before the break. Gordon put over an innocuous cross which only became a danger after Ashall's complete miskick. As the ball rolled across the face of the Leeds goal Hume stuck a foot out to deflect it in. After a bright start in which Hume almost equalised a minute after the restart, Blues were kept out by a solid Leeds defence and the game became a midfield battle. Blues seemed doomed to defeat when Bremner struck another blow on 73 minutes to restore Leeds two-goal advantage. Neal was at fault as the pint-sized young Scot dispossesed him to run clear and beat Schofield from an acute angle within the penalty area. Blues stormed back though and four minutes later had reduced the arrears to 3-2. A fine individual goal from Hooper who beat three defenders before sliding his shot under the advancing Humphreys in the Leeds goal. From being dead and buried, Blues incredibly equalised just two minutes later, albeit fortunately. From a harmless looking cross from Gordon, McConnell panicked into making contact when he should have let the ball sail over him, the result was a header which gave Humphreys no chance of saving. It was harsh on the Leeds man who had played so well, but overall Blues have shown enough fight in the second half to justify a share of the points, the game finishing without further incident, 3-3.

BIRMINGHAM CITY

Schofield, Farmer, Allen, Watts, Smith, Neal, Astall, Gordon, Weston, Hume, Hooper.

LEEDS UNITED

Humphreys, Ashall, Kerfoot, McConnell, Cush, Gibson, Bremner, Revie, McCole, Peyton, Meek.

REFEREE

Mr H Callaghan (Rochdale)

Trevor Smith

Blues news extra   1998...Francis returns

Blues manager Trevor Francis decided to return to first team duties today after his shock resignation two days previously.

The Matches played on this day

1901, Division 2.		
Stockport County 0	Blues 0	Att. 2,000
1907, Division 1.		
Stoke 3	Blues 0	Att. 10,000
1912, Division 2.		
Blues 4	Nottingham Forest 2	Att. 8,000
Jones(2),		
Hastings, Hall		
1918, Wartime.		
Lincoln City 3	Blues 3	
	Smith, Lees, Bell	
1929, Division 1.		
Aston Villa 1	Blues 2	Att. 59,322
	Mills, Crosbie	
1935, Division 1.		
Blues 1	Wolverhampton W. 1	Att. 25,000
Jones		
1940, Wartime.		
Northampton Town 1	Blues 3	
	Turner(pen),	
	Brown, Bodle	
1946, FA Cup 6th round, 2nd leg.		
Blues 6	Bradford Park Avenue 0	Att. 49,858
Dougall(2),		
Bodle(2),		
Mulraney(2)		
Blues won 8-2 on aggregate		
1953, FA Cup 6th round, 2nd replay.		
Blues 0	Tottenham Hotspur 1	Att. 50,801
	Walters 78	
Played at Molineux, Wolverhampton. Gate receipts £7, 071		
1957, Division 1.		
Blues 1	Everton 3	Att. 23,781
Brown 3	Thomas 42, 55	
	Williams 72	
1960, Division 1.		
Leeds United 3	Blues 3	Att. 8,557
Revie 13, 34	Hume 43	
Bremner 73	Hooper 77	
	McConnell 79(og)	
1962, Division 1.		
Chelsea 1	Blues 1	Att. 23,959
Murray 10	Leek 38	
1963, Division 1.		
Blues 3	Wolverhampton W. 4	Att. 18,217
Lynn(2 pens) 15, 74	Wharton 6	
Auld 46	Stobbart 66	
	Kirkham 71	
	Broadbent 78	
1968, FA Cup 5th round.		
Arsenal 1	Blues 1	Att. 45,526
Radford 23	Vowden 88	
Gate receipts of £15,027		
1974, Division 1.		
Everton 4	Blues 1	Att. 33,944
Lyons 46, 88	Hatton 70	
Latchford 64, 77		
Former Blues striker Bob Latchford scored twice for Everton, past his brother Dave, in goal for the Blues.		
1985, Division 2.		
Blues 2	Notts County 1	Att. 9,046
Clarke 4	Sims 76	
Hopkins 16		
Blues David Seaman saved Harkouk's penalty after 90 mins		
1991, Division 3.		
Rotherham United 1	Blues 1	Att. 5,015
Mendonca 43	Frain 79(pen)	
1993, Division 1.		
Peterborough U. 2	Blues 1	Att. 7,600
Holmes(og) 27	Peschisolido 6	
Barnes 75		
1996, Division 1.		
Tranmere Rovers 2	Blues 2	Att. 8,696
Aldridge 40	Legg 39	
Rogers 70	Hunt 62	
1999, Division 1.		
Tranmere Rovers 0	Blues 1	Att. 7,184
	M.Johnson 46	
Tranmere's Dave Challinor records a thow in of 45 metres breaking ex-Blues player Andy Legg's previous record(41 metres) for the longest throw-in in a match.		
2002, Division 1.		
Blues 2	Wolverhampton W. 2	Att. 22,104
John 36	Lescott 8	
Devlin 45	Butler 20	
Heavy winds of up to 70 mph causd structual damage to the Main Stand roof at St Andrews.		

March 10

The Matches played on this day

1900, Division 2.
Blues 2   Burton Swifts 0   Att. 5,000
Leake, Aston

1906, FA Cup 4th round.
Blues 2   Newcastle United 2   Att. 27,000
Green, W.H.Jones

1917, Wartime.
Notts County 1   Blues 1
    Whitehouse

1920, Division 2.
Blues 8   Nottingham Forest 0   Att. 15,000
Hampton(4),
Lane(2),
Burkinshaw(2)
Joe Hampton and Joe Lane both made their St Andrews debuts for the Blues

1923, Division 1.
Blues 1   Preston North End 0   Att. 20,000
Rawson

1928, Division 1.
Blues 4   Sheffield United 1   Att. 20,000
Briggs(3), Bond

1934, Division 1.
Blues 0   Stoke City 1   Att. 25,000

1945, Wartime.
Aston Villa 5   Blues 0

1951, FA Cup Semi Final.
Blackpool 0   Blues 0   Att. 70,000
Played at Maine Road, Manchester
Jackie Stewart hit the post with the last kick of the game

1956, Division 1.
Blues 0   Wolverhampton W. 0   Att. 45,161

1973, Division 1.
Blues 3   Manchester United 1   Att. 51,278
B.Latchford 30   Macari 83
Hatton 62
Campbell 90(pen)
Match screened by BBC's Match of the Day.

1979, Division 1.
Blues 0   Coventry City 0   Att. 17,311

1984, FA Cup 6th round.
Blues 1   Watford 3   Att. 40,220
Terry 60(og)   Barnes 23, 80
    Taylor 78
This was the last attendance of 40,000 plus for a game at St Andrews. This match screened by BBC's Match of the Day

1990, Division 3.
Walsall 0   Blues 1   Att. 6,036
    Gleghorn 3

1992, Division 3.
Blues 1   Brentford 0   Att. 13,290
Matthewson 34

1998, Division 1.
Sunderland 1   Blues 1   Att. 18,298
Johnston 90   Adebola 50

2001, Division 1.
Blues 2   Crewe Alexandra 0   Att. 28,042
Purse 61(pen)
A.Johnson 79

Playing record for this day
Playing record for this day is...17 games, Won 8, Drawn 6, Lost 3, GF 27, GA 15.
Today's success rate.....64.71% Year ranking....26th

Match of the Day
FROM 1920
NEW BOYS ARE SIMPLY GR-EIGHT!
Hampton and Lane greet St Andrews with super show

Recent signings Joe Lane a record £3,600 buy from Blackpool and Harry Hampton who arrived from across the city from arch rivals Aston Villa were on show for the first time at St Andrews and any doubts to their ability were emphatically dispelled after a wonderful display of clinical finishing against a sorry looking Nottingham Forest.

Forest started well and the game flowed from end to end with Blues eager to involve the burly Hampton and test the pace of fellow forward Lane, while Forest countered with good efforts from Shearman and Lythgoe. However it was Blues who opened the scoring after 20 minutes when a Davies cross was headed over the on-rushing 'keeper Johnson and went in off the underside of the crossbar. With Forest desperate to get the equaliser Blues extended their lead just six minutes later when Lane's shot was only parried by Johnson and Hampton was left with a simple tap in. With the game looking lost Forest still tried gamely to attack at every opportunity and from a desperate goalmouth scramble the visiting centre forward Hart fractured his leg just four minutes from half time, having to leave the field at 2-0 down. The ten men had an virtual impossible task now.

After the half-time break Blues took full control and turned their superiority into goals as early as the 48th minute. Another Davies cross this time was met by Lane's volley and the ball flew past a motionless Johnson in the Forest goal. Blues were simply overwhelming the visitors with play constantly in the Forest half and after 63 minutes Blues added a fourth. In an almost replica of goal two this time Lane's shot smashed off the crossbar to an unmarked Hampton who headed in a simple goal to complete his hat-trick. Laurie Burkinshaw got the fifth just five minutes later with the goal of the game. Collecting the ball in midfield he advanced to within 30 yards and slammed the ball past a helpless Johnson. Then man of the match George Davies who had mesmerised the Forest defence with his sparkling wing play again put over a pin point centre to Burkinshaw who finished with a simple side foot at the far post. Keeper Johnson had now conceded six but was entirely blameless and with 15 minutes remaining he saved brilliantly from a Jackie Whitehouse thunderbolt but again to his dismay the rebounding ball went to Hampton who knocked in his fourth and Blues seventh. In the last minute the brilliant Davies sent over another fantastic cross which eluded both Barrett and Lowe for Joe Lane to net his second and the Blues had thoroughly destroyed Forest by 8-0.

BIRMINGHAM CITY
Tremelling, White, Womack, Evans, Millard, Roulson, Burkinshaw, Hampton, Lane, Whitehouse, Davies.
NOTTINGHAM FOREST
Johnson, Barratt, Jones, Belton, Lowe, Armstrong, Davis, Spaven, Hart, Lythgoe, Shearman.

REFEREE
Mr E Pullan (Leeds)

Dan Tremelling

Blues news extra   1983...Friendly
AP Leamington 1 Blues 4 Blues scorers, Mick Harford(3), Pat Van Den Hauwe

Playing record for this day
Playing record for this day is...19 games, Won 6, Drawn 5, Lost 8, GF 28, GA 32.
Today's success rate.....44.74% Year ranking....202nd

March 11

Match of the Day

FROM 1980

FIVE STAR SHOW PUTS BLUES ON TOP

Chelsea hammered by championship seeking Blues

Birmingham City sat proudly at the top of the Division Two table after whacking their promotion rivals Chelsea by 5-1 in a memorable night in front of 27,297 delighted fans at St Andrews. After a lacklustre and disappointing defeat at Shrewsbury just three days before, Blues bounced back in sensational style to record their biggest win of the season. Playing fast flowing and high quality football Chelsea were simply outclassed, and although the total included two of the most bizarre goals seen at St Andrews in years the Blues of London can be grateful the scoreline was not even greater than the final tally of five.

Indeed before Chelsea had broken into the opposition half of the field they were already 1-0 down in a fantastic opening for the Blues. Frank Worthington, who was recalled to the side in place of Steve Lynex, started the move and from his right wing cross Gemmill fired in a scorching shot which was blocked by a defender. The loose ball was seized on by Broadhurst on the edge of the penalty area and his first-time shot, which appeared to be going wide, took a fortunate deflection of Hales and looped over Barota as he came out to narrow the angle. The Blues barrage continued and soon after Barota saved well from Worthington after a corner from Dillon and then a superbly hit drive from 25 yards by Curbishley grazed the crossbar in the 19th minute. However a minute later Blues doubled their lead with a most peculiar goal, a real freak. Blues full back Mark Dennis crossed from the left where Curbishley rushed in to meet the ball on the volley, which started a penalty area pantomime. The ball struck Nutton and balloooned high into the air. As the Chelsea defence stood stood watching, Bertschin challenged Barota as the ball dropped on the goal line. The challenge put the Chelsea 'keeper off and he missed the ball completely, it bounced on the line and as the Blues forward moved in to challenge again, Barota lept high and punched it into his own net. This had a brief effect on both sides and it brought about a nice little spell from Chelsea which ended with a goal from Langley on 35 minutes. A neat move from Harris to Walker who quickly slipped the ball through to Langley, the Chelsea striker out paced Gallagher and beat Wealands with a firmly stuck low cross shot from the edge of the penalty area. The pace of the game then slowed and Blues took their 2-1 advantage into the half-time interval.

It took just seven second half minutes for Blues to find the goal which proved to wrap the game up at 3-1. A great through ball from Colin Todd put Ainscow away in acres of space, the winger cut inside and left Barota scrambling at thin air as his angled drive from 15 yards raced past him and into the bottom corner. 20 minutes later Blues responded to manager Jim Smith's complaint that they did not score enough goals when dominating games, with a fourth goal from Ainscow again. Once more it was Worthington the instigator of the chance and his clever ball to the right gave Ainscow ample opportunity to rush in on goal again. He rounded his full back, cut inside to beat another defender before bending in a delightful shot from 18 yards wide on the right-hand edge of the box. The Chelsea 'keeper then adequately made up for his earlier error by making two wonderful saves from Dillon but could do little to help prevent a fifth Blues goal a minute from time. Blues saved their best goal for the last when Dillon finally beat Barota with a spectacular 20 yard shot after a run from the half way line by the Blues attacking midfielder. He beat the entire Chelsea defence as he cut through the middle and the end shot whistled past the keeper who had no chance. A great finish to a super night for the Birmingham Blues.

BIRMINGHAM CITY
Wealands, Broadhurst, Dennis, Curbishley, Gallagher, Todd, Ainscow, Worthington, Bertschin, Gemmill, Dillon.

CHELSEA
Barota, Wilkins, Rofe, Hales (Johnson 55), Droy, Nutton, Britton, Fillery, Langley, Walker, Harris.

REFEREE
Mr K Hackett (Sheffield)

Frank Worthington

Blues news extra   1888...Blues crash in Long Eaton friendly

Long Eaton Rangers thrashed a strong looking Blues side in a friendly on this day in 1888. Blues were second best all over the park as Rangers ran out winners by 7-3.

The Matches played on this day

1899, Division 2.
| Luton Town 2 | Blues 3 | Att. 1,000 |
| | Abbott(3, 1pen) | |

1905, Division 1.
| Blues 1 | Nottingham Forest 2 | Att. 8,500 |
| Field | | |

1907, Division 1.
| Bolton Wanderers 2 | Blues 3 | Att. 10,000 |
| | Tickle, Green, Anderson | |

1911, Division 2.
| Wolverhampton W. 3 | Blues 1 | Att. 8,000 |
| | Hall | |

1922, Division 1.
| Aston Villa 1 | Blues 1 | Att. 52,000 |
| | Liddell | |

1933, Division 1.
| Middlesbrough 2 | Blues 2 | Att. 12,000 |
| | Bradford, Curtis | |

1939, Division 1.
| Blues 3 | Wolverhampton W. 2 | Att. 45,000 |
| Harris, Morris, Jones | | |

1944, Wartime.
| Leicester City 2 | Blues 1 | |
| | Bright | |
A.E.T.

1950, Division 1.
| Fulham 0 | Blues 0 | Att. 25,000 |

1953, Division 2.
Blues 1	Swansea Town 4	Att. 8,820
Purdon 60	Beech 29, 77	
	Medwin 66, 86	

1961, Division 1.
| Blues 1 | Aston Villa 1 | Att. 41,645 |
| Singer 86 | Hitchens 7 | |

1967, FA Cup 5th round.
| Blues 1 | Arsenal 0 | Att. 40,665 |
| Vowden 83 | | |

1970, Division 2.
Millwall 6	Blues 2	Att. 7,825
Bolland 21, 47, 58	Murray 37(pen)	
Possee 26	Hockey 41	
Weller 74		
Dumphy 84		

1972, Division 2.
| Blues 0 | QPR 0 | Att. 35,557 |

1980, Division 2.
Blues 5	Chelsea 1	Att. 27,297
Broadhurst 2	Langley 35	
Borota(og) 20		
Ainscow 52, 72		
Dillon 89		

1989, Division 2.
| Portsmouth 1 | Blues 0 | Att. 8,078 |
| Chamberlain 86 | | |

1995, Division 2.
| Blues 0 | Swansea City 1 | Att. 16,191 |
| | Hodge 38(pen) | |

Swansea had full back Mark Clode sent off late in the first half. This defeat ended Blues 22 match unbeaten home record in all competitions.

1997, Division 1.
Blues 2	Manchester City 0	Att. 20,084
Furlong 61(pen)		
Francis 70		

2000, Division 1.
Tranmere Rovers 2	Blues 1	Att. 9,232
Koumas 4	Rowett 45	
G.Jones 83		

March 12

Playing record for this day
Playing record for this day is...22 games, Won 10, Drawn 4, Lost 8, GF 30, GA 28.
Today's success rate.....54.55% Year ranking....112th

The Matches played on this day

1898, Division 2.
Grimsby Town 2   Blues 0   Att. 6,500
1904, Division 1.
WBA 0   Blues 1   Att. 22,760
   Green
Blues record their first league win over the Baggies
1910, Division 2.
Manchester City 3   Blues 0   Att. 15,000
1921, Division 2.
Bristol City 0   Blues 1   Att. 26,000
   Lane
1923, Division 1.
Blues 4   Sheffield United 2   Att. 15,000
Rawson(2),
Daws, Bradford
Blues gain revenge for a 7-1 defeat by United suffered just three weeks ago.
1927, Division 1.
Blues 4   Manchester United 0   Att. 14,392
Bradford(2),
Crosbie, Scriven
1932, Division 1.
Bolton Wanderers 5   Blues 1   Att. 8,000
   Keating
1938, Division 1.
Blues 2   Manchester City 2   Att. 25,000
Harris(2).
1949, Division 1.
Liverpool 1   Blues 0   Att. 43,763
1955, FA Cup 6th round.
Blues 0   Manchester City 1   Att. 58,000
   Hart 88
The winner was a real freak piece of luck. Roy Clarke's sliced free kick struck a startled Johnny Hart. The ball bobbled up keeper Merrick's arm hit him on the cheek and dropped over the line with just two minutes of the game remaining. Blues skipper Roy Warhurst described the goal as "The biggest fluke in football I ever saw."
1958, Division 1.
Blues 1   Sheffield Wednesday 0 Att. 15,939
Orritt 5
1960, Division 1.
Fulham 2   Blues 2   Att. 25,100
Leggatt 38, 48   Gordon 3
   Hooper 31
1966, Division 2.
Portsmouth 0   Blues 1   Att. 12,367
   Vowden 59
1968, FA Cup 5th round.
Blues 2   Arsenal 1   Att. 51,586
Bridges 65, 71   Gould 68
1977, Division 1.
Derby County 0   Blues 0   Att. 24,523
Jim Montgomery saved Charlie George's 87th minute penalty on his Blues debut.
1985, Division 2.
Carlisle United 2   Blues 1   Att. 4,099
Shoulder 61   Clarke 2
O'Riordan 78
1986, Division 1.
Leicester City 4   Blues 2   Att. 8,458
McAllister 6   Clarke 2
A.Sealey 15   Whitton 13
Smith 28
Lynex 80(pen)
Billy Garton made his Blues debut. David Seaman saved, Steve Lynex's 62nd minute penalty
1988, Division 2.
Reading 1   Blues 1   Att. 6,285
Whitehurst 27   Handysides 11
Ian Handysides last goal for the club, before he was forced to quit through illness.

Match of the Day

FROM 1968

BRILLIANT BRACE BY BRIDGES

Blues pull off shock cup win thanks to wonder goal

Three days before with Arsenal 1-0 up playing against Second Division Birmingham and into the 90th minute many could be forgiven thinking Blues were out of this year's FA Cup competition, however as a result of a last gasp Geoff Vowden header they were given a surprise chance in a replay, a chance they took thanks to a piece of Barry Bridges brilliance.

Arsenal were desperate to prove the form guide correct and advance to the quarter-finals, the added incentive of a London derby was at stake against Chelsea in round six. They started well and were the dominant side throughout the first 45 minutes, but Birmingham matched them defensively and looking confident themselves towards the end of the first half.

This tie came to life however in a six minute spell just after the hour mark when Blues were awarded a free kick on 65 minutes. Bert Murray floated the ball in to Wylie who headed across the penalty area to the far post where Bridges with his back to goal rose to meet the dropping ball with a thunderous scissors kick which whistled past 'keeper Furnell in the Arsenal goal and went in off the underside of the crossbar. It was a truly magnificent goal and worthy winner, however shortly after restarting Arsenal broke and within two minutes had equalised through Bobby Gould. Blues were not to be denied though and with the 51,586 mainly partisan Birmingham crowd still buzzing from the first Bridges goal, they inspired Blues to go forward and get a second. That second goal came sooner than expected as Bridges again found space and fired home his second this time in more conventional style.

With the crowd now at fever pitch egging on the Blues to a famous cup win, Arsenal pressed in desperation to find another equaliser and as the clock ticked away the last few minutes they came close with a George Graham effort which was well saved from Herriot who had a superb game in the Blues goal. This was the last salvo from the Gunners and soon after referee Smith blew the final whistle signalling some amazing scenes of celebration by Blues players and supporters. It was they who were advancing into the sixth round to meet Barry Bridges former club Chelsea and another giantkilling opportunity was on the cards.

BIRMINGHAM CITY
Herriott, Murray, Martin, Wylie, Foster, Beard, Bridges, Vincent, Pickering, Vowden, Hockey.
ARSENAL
Furnell, Storey, McNab, McLintock, Simpson, Neil, Radford, Gould, Graham, Sammels, Armstrong.

Bobby Gould - Arsenal

1991, Division 3.
Blues 2   Fulham 0   Att. 8,083
Peer 26
Gleghorn 55
Fulham hit the woodwork three times during the game
including Milton's 59th minute penalty which struck the bar
1994, Division 1.
Grimsby Town 1   Blues 0   Att. 5,405
Croft 87
Jose Dominguez made his Blues debut, at just 5 foot 3 inches
tall he was the smallest player in the club's history.
1996, Division 1.
Blues 2   Huddersfield Town 0   Att. 15,296
Devlin 12
P.Barnes 63
2002, Division 1.
Bradford City 1   Blues 3   Att. 13,105
Jess 45 Purse 6
John 31
Horsfield 82

Bert Murray

Birthdays

David Geddis born today in 1958

March 13

Playing record for this day
Playing record for this day is...19 games, Won 7, Drawn 4, Lost 8, GF 30, GA 19.
Today's success rate.....47.37% Year ranking....177th

The Matches played on this day

1897, Division 2.		
Lincoln City 1	Blues 3	Att. 2,000
	Inglis, Oakes, Jones	
1909, Division 2.		
Barnsley 3	Blues 1	Att. 4,000
	King	
1915, Division 2.		
Arsenal 1	Blues 0	Att. 19,067
1920, Division 2.		
Blues 7	Lincoln City 0	Att. 28,000
Davies, Lane(3),		
Atkin(og), Hampton,		
Whitehouse		
1926, Division 1.		
Blues 1	Newcastle United 1	Att. 30,000
Crosbie		
1929, Division 1.		
Blues 1	Arsenal 1	Att. 11,001
Hicks		
1937, Division 1.		
Blues 4	Brentford 0	Att. 25,000
Morris(2),		
White, Harris		

Seymour Morris put Blues ahead after just 45 seconds

1943, Wartime.		
Blues 2	Walsall 1	
Romp, Turner		
1946, Wartime.		
Blues 0	Arsenal 1	
1948, Division 2.		
Bury 1	Blues 1	Att. 23,420
	Edwards	
1954, Division 2.		
Brentford 2	Blues 0	Att. 12,600
Dudley 65, 67		
1964, Division 1.		
Blues 2	Blackburn Rovers 2	Att. 15,780
Auld 37	Ferguson 25	
Leek 58	Jones 78	

17-year-old Johnny Vincent made his Blues debut.

1965, Division 1.		
Blues 0	Wolverhampton W. 1	Att. 18,860
	Wharton 51	
1971, Division 2.		
Orient 0	Blues 2	Att. 11,167
	Francis 8	
	Summerill 58	

Francis' goal was the first Orient had conceded for 563 minutes

1976, Division 1.		
Blues 0	Liverpool 1	Att. 31,797
	Neal 87(pen)	

Blues keeper Steve Smith made his debut

1982, Division 1.		
Blues 2	Stoke City 1	Att. 12,018
Curbishley 18	Chapman 79	
Hawker 62		

Dave Linney made his only appearance for the Blues as a sub replacing Neil Whatmore after 85 minutes.

1990, Division 3.		
Blues 0	Brentford 1	Att. 8,169
	Holdsworth 73	
1993, Division 1.		
Blues 0	Bristol City 1	Att. 15,611
	Morgan 45	
1999, Division 1.		
Blues 4	WBA 0	Att. 29,060
Adebola 24, 62		
Ndlovu 50		
Grainger 88		

Blues equalled their best ever win against WBA, the other 4-0 victory came in 1948.

Match of the Day
FROM 1999
DELE' IGHTFUL

Adebola destroys the Baggies in demolition derby

This was Blues biggest defeat of West Bromwich Albion for 51 years in front of St Andrews largest attendance since the fifth round FA cup tie with Nottingham Forest in 1988. The result put Blues within a win of second place and dumped Albion out of the top six and into eighth place. Blues almost total domination bought about their first goal on 24 minutes after a few half chances had narrowly missed being converted. A typical Ndlovu run took him wide and level on the penalty area where he knocked the ball in low to Adebola, his control and quick turn beat both Carbon and Burgess allowing a 15-yard left-foot shot past Whitehead. Despite the constant menace of Blues 'little and large' front runners Blues failed to add to the score again before the break, but it wasnt long before the goals started rattling in at will.

Just five minutes after the restart a long over the top ball from Charlton set Ndlovu away with Carbon hopelessly trying to cover. As the Zimbabwean took the ball into the area he easily side-stepped the Albion defender and crashed his shot across a helpless Whitehead in the West Brom goal. Blues third was by far the best of the afternoon and came just after an hour's play. Adebola picked up a loose ball just inside the Albion half and looked to play a one-two with Ndlovu, it was the perfect foil as the ball instead was pushed into the gap and depite a despairing lunge by Potter, Adebola skipped the challenge and left him and McDermott well beaten for pace. As he raced clear the Blues forward waited for Whitehead to commit and when he did he merely slipped the ball past him into the corner. Blues immediately swapped McCarthy for O'Connor, sensing a possible cricket score, later on a double substitution Forster and Furlong replaced the tormenting Adebola and Ndlovu. Whilst Albion were collectively letting out a huge sigh of relief they conceded a fourth just two minutes from time. McCarthy started the move slipping the ball to Hyde who had made a clever diagonal run to the right of Albion's penalty area. From his low cross from the byline Whitehead was forced to partially push out the ball under pressure from Furlong, it ran to Grainger who rifled it into the roof of the net from six yards, the rout was complete.

BIRMINGHAM CITY
Poole, Bass, Charlton, Grainger, Johnson, Rowett, Hughes, Adebola (Furlong 82), Ndlovu (Forster 82), O'Connor (McCarthy 62), Hyde.
WEST BROMWICH ALBION
Whitehead, McDermott, Burgess, Carbon, Potter (Murphy 72), Flynn, Sneekes, Maresca (Bortolazzi 72), Kilbane, De Freitas, Quinn (Angel 67).

REFEREE
Mr T Heilbron (County Durham)

Martin Grainger

Birthdays
Ryan Price born today in 1970.

Playing record for this day

Playing record for this day is...14 games, Won 3, Drawn 4, Lost 7, GF 11, GA 22.

Today's success rate.....35.71% Year ranking....246th

Match of the Day
FROM 1931
WE'RE ON OUR WAY

Curtis double earns first Wembley final for Brum

Although Blues had beaten both Liverpool and Chelsea in reaching the semi-final they lined up as the under dogs in this Elland Road clash against the mighty Wearsiders from Sunderland. However 15,000 Brummies had descended on Yorkshire for the showdown to roar on their heroes every move in the near capacity crowd of 43,570.

Sunderland came the closest to opening the scoring in the early stages and Hibbs in the Birmingham goal saved well from Gurney, Leonard and Eden. Birmingham, though, were still holding firm and grew in confidence from Hibbs heroics coming close themselves with an effort from Bradford, then a snap shot from Jack Firth which was well saved by Sunderland keeper Middleton. With half an hour gone it was the Blues who took a surprise lead with a tremendous strike from Welshman Ernie Curtis. Jimmy Cringan started the move finding Briggs with a pass which allowed him the space to move forward and attack the Sunderland goal, after beating full back Murray his quick pass found Curtis. Evading a desperate challenge from Hastings and a lunge from Andrews he fired in a stinging right-foot shot from inside the penalty area which flew past a diving Middleton and went in off the post. Sunderland were stung into action and immediately hit back trying to find the equaliser. First Gurney shaved the crossbar with a tremendously fierce 20-yard drive. Then Brum defender Ned Barkas slipped and fell trying to cover another Sunderland attack this allowed O'Connor to head agonisingly wide of the Blues goal, despite being left in the centre totally unmarked. Brave defending, some superb goalkeeping and a little luck helped Blues to half time still holding a slender but hugely important lead by 1-0.

The respite over Sunderland started the second half as they had finished the first. They dominated the Blues all over the park and attacked at every opportunity. Within five minutes Leonard twice went through one-on-one with Hibbs in the Blues goal only for the latter to smother the ball with brave dives at the on-rushing forwards' feet. The Blues goal was under constant siege for the first quarter of this tense second period but Blues were slowly finding the opportunity to move forward themselves. On one such occasion Bradford went close and from a better chance Crosbie had a fine shot saved by Middleton. With time running out and Sunderland still surging forward a rare Blues counter attack put the tie safe in the 87th minute. Blues cleared a dangerous looking cross from Eden and Bradford collected the ball, inside his own half. He chased forward and as the Sunderland defence closed in he slipped the ball to his forward partner. Curtis side-stepped Shaw easily before shooting at Middleton. Evan though he got both hands to the ball the rebound only went back to Curtis who chased in to thump in the loose ball. Blues were safe now at 2-0, and Wembley bound.

BIRMINGHAM CITY

Hibbs, Liddell, Barkas, Cringan, Morrall, Leslie, Briggs, Crosbie, Bradford, Firth, Curtis

SUNDERLAND

Middleton, Murray, Shaw, Hastings, McDougall, Andrews, Eden, Devine, Gurney, Leonard, O'Connor

REFEREE

Mr AE Fogg (Bolton)

George Liddell

Blues news extra 1942...Villa take honours in friendly

The long awaited friendly between the big city rivals Blues and Villa finished disappointingly for the Blues when they were handsomely beaten by 4-0 at Villa Park.

Birthdays

Bobby Brennan born today in 1925.

The Matches played on this day

1906, FA Cup 4th round, replay.
Newcastle United 3   Blues 0   Att. 39,059
1908, Division 1.
Bolton Wanderers 1   Blues 0   Att. 5,000
1914, Division 2.
Blues 0   Blackpool 0   Att. 7,000
1925, Division 1.
Blues 1   West Ham United 1 Att. 20,000
Crosbie
1931, FA Cup Semi Final.
Sunderland 0   Blues 2   Att. 43,570
                       Curtis(2)
Played at Elland Road, Leeds. Gate receipts of £3,930
1936, Division 1.
Portsmouth 0   Blues 3   Att. 15,000
                       Harris, Morris(2)
1951, FA Cup Semi Final, replay.
Blackpool 2   Blues 1   Att. 70,114
Mortensen 4   Smith 64
Perry 63
Played at Goodison Park, Liverpool. Gate receipts £15,000
1953, Division 2.
Blues 1   Sheffield United 2 Att. 22,500
Cox 47   Green(og) 36
                       Ringstead 78
1959, Division 1.
Blues 0   Wolverhampton W. 3 Att. 37,222
                       Broadbent 28
                       Murray 38, 64
1970, Division 2.
Blues 0   Middlesbrough 0   Att. 17,984
1987, Division 2.
Crystal Palace 6   Blues 0   Att. 6,201
Wright 41, 42
Gray 46
Taylor 52
Cannon 64
Finnigan 76
Blues keeper Roger Hansbury saved Kevin Taylor's penalty after just nine minutes. Blues defender Tommy Williams was sent off after 25 minutes
1995, Auto Windscreens Shield, Southern Area Final, 2nd leg.
Leyton Orient 2   Blues 3   Att. 10,830
Purse 65   Claridge 42, 47
McGleish 84   Williams 57
Blues won 4-2 on aggregate and went on to meet Carlisle in the final at Wembley.
For the second time this season future Blues centre half Darren Purse scored for Orient against Blues
1998, Division 1.
Blues 0   Bradford City 0   Att. 16,492
2001, Division 1.
Blues 0   Blackburn Rovers 2 Att. 29,150
                       Bent 41
                       Duff 53

March 15

The Matches played on this day

1890, Football Alliance.
Blues 1　　　　Newton Heath 1　　Att. 2,000
Wilcox
First competitive meeting v Newton Heath
1902, Division 1.
Stoke 1　　　　Blues 0　　　　　Att. 4,000
1913, Division 2.
Lincoln City 0　　Blues 1　　　　　Att. 5,000
　　　　　　　Duncan
1919, Wartime.
Blues 3　　　　Lincoln City 0
Short, McClure,
Whitehouse
1920, Division 2.
Stockport County 2　Blues 1　　　　Att. 4,000
　　　　　　　Robson(og)
1922, Division 1.
Blues 1　　　　Aston Villa 0　　　Att. 34,190
Crosbie
1924, Division 1.
Chelsea 1　　　Blues 1　　　　　Att. 25,000
　　　　　　　Ashurst
1930, Division 1.
Arsenal 1　　　Blues 0　　　　　Att. 32,174
1947, Division 2.
Manchester City 1　Blues 0　　　　Att. 59,535
1952, Division 2.
Blues 3　　　　Sheffield United 0　Att. 28,000
Murphy 23, 88
Trigg 49
1958, Division 1.
Blues 1　　　　Luton Town 1　　　Att. 25,225
Orritt 8　　　　Turner 59(pen)
Luton reduced to ten men after 47 minutes when Groves was
stretchered off
1966, Division 2.
Huddersfield Town 2 Blues 0　　　　Att. 19,156
Gilliver 9, 86
1969, Division 2.
Portsmouth 0　　Blues 0　　　　　Att. 15,556
1975, Division 1.
Arsenal 1　　　Blues 1　　　　　Att. 17,845
Kidd 60　　　　Burns 51
1978, Division 1.
Newcastle United 1　Blues 1　　　　Att. 18,146
Nattrass 86　　　Francis 7
1980, Division 2.
Blues 2　　　　Preston North End 2　Att. 19,548
Gemmill 41(pen)　Elliott 72
Worthington 62　McGee 83
Archie Gemmill played his 500th professional match.
1983, Division 1.
Blues 2　　　　Arsenal 1　　　　Att. 11,276
Van Den Hauwe 80 Sunderland 85
Dillon 90
1986, Division 1.
Blues 1　　　　Tottenham Hotspur 2 Att. 9,394
Kennedy 53　　　Stevens 4
　　　　　　　Waddle 34
1994, Division 1.
Blues 0　　　　Leicester City 3　Att. 14,681
　　　　　　　Joachim 9
　　　　　　　Ormondroyd 29
　　　　　　　Roberts 82
2002, Division 1.
Norwich City 0　　Blues 1　　　　　Att. 18,258
　　　　　　　John 22
Blues Nico Vaesen saved Gary Holt's second half penalty.

Playing record for this day
Playing record for this day is...20 games, Won 6, Drawn 7, Lost 7, GF 20, GA 20.
Today's success rate.....47.50% Year ranking....176th

Match of the Day
FROM 1983
CAPITAL GOLD

Blues continue to show liking for London's finest.

Blues earned their victory against FA Cup semi-finalists Arsenal, raising them from the bottom of the First Division table. The match at St Andrews was played in front of Blues' second lowest crowd of the season, 11,276, and plenty of chances went begging. Blues were not going to give in without a fight, and the struggle they put up was enough to win the game.

Pat van den Hauwe scored his first goal of the season, putting Blues into the lead, but it didn't last long. Arsenal took just five minutes to draw level thanks to a goal from Alan Sunderland.

The majority of the match was devoid of action, and almost dipped into a sea of boredom. Then Gayle moved over from the left to the right wing and the pace changed. Attempts from both sides amounted to nothing, however. Mick Harford struck the bar twice, Howard Gayle was over cautious in front of an open goal, and Ian Handysides and Noel Blake also missed close-range shots. Vladi Petrovic had struggled to get free of his marker for the entire game, and after 66 minutes was replaced by Brian Talbot. Arsenal had three good chances, one of which brought about a splendid fingertip save from Tony Coton.

In the last ten minutes Arsenal came under fire from the entire Blues side. Blake's shot went just wide of the nearside post, and Harford missed the perfect opportunity when he headed the ball with Jennings seemingly stuck to the goal line, only to see his effort hit the bar.

Injury time was added and it proved to be a valuable gift for Blues. Dillon delivered a right-footed drive from just outside the area and it shot straight past the Irish international goalkeeper into the net.

BIRMINGHAM CITY
Coton, Hagan, Dennis, Stevenson, Blake, Van den Hauwe, Gayle, Handysides, Harford, Curbishley, Dillon.

ARSENAL
Jennings, Hollins, Sansom, Robson, Whyte, Nicholas, Petrovic (Talbot), Davis, Sunderland, Woodcock, Rix.

REFEREE
Mr Trevor Jones.

Kevin Dillon

Blues news extra　1888...Blues edge it in Macclesfield friendly
The friendly game arranged between Blues and Macclesfield at Muntz Street ended in favour of the Small Heath club by 3-2.

Birthdays
Kevin Miller born today in 1969

Playing record for this day

Playing record for this day is...22 games, Won 6, Drawn 5, Lost 11, GF 21, GA 33.

Today's success rate.....38.64% Year ranking....240th

Match of the Day
FROM 1955
BLUES STILL IN PROMOTION RACE

After a terrific start Blues scored vital early goals through Warhurst and Kinsey to gain two valuable promotion points against Doncaster. Indeed the only disappointment at St Andrews was the pathetic attendance, for the game was watched by just 5,621. Blues perfomances were certainly worthy of more and with just six more league games to play at home they had more than an outside chance of winning the championship. Blues were forced to make just one change to the side that had beaten Swansea 11 days before, Alex Govan was missing with an injured toe and Jack Lane was drafted into the side, Murphy swapped wings to play on the left with Lane on the right. The Doncaster side included three players named Walker in their forward line.

Blues were soon a goal up, taking advantage of their first chance. The build-up in midfield seemed pretty standard and cautious when suddenly a through ball sent Warhurst away down the middle. From his finishing shot hit with considerable power Hardwick managed to partially save on the line but the ball bobbled out of his grip to roll into the net. Blues then nearly gifted Rovers a soft equaliser. Newman woefully underhit a backpass to Merrick which forced the keeper to charge out and bravely dive at Tindill's feet. The ball wasn't taken cleanly and broke instead to the path of Jimmy Walker again Merrick had to drop at the forward's feet only this time he safely clutched the ball. The Blues then went further ahead after some fine quick passing left Kinsey inside the area with a glorious shooting chance and when the ball arrived he whipped his shot into the top corner first time. However in a thrilling end-to-end game sadly lacking in atmosphere, Rovers stormed back and only a fortunate block by Warhust prevented a goal for the visitors as the ball narrowly passed the angle of post and crossbar.

Blues failed to properly clear the resulting corner and a neat pass found Jimmy Walker who hammered the ball past Merrick from just eight yards out. At least the goal settled the Blues defence and from that moment they seemed much more steady. Blues started the second half in as dramatic style as the first and should have been rewarded within minutes with a penalty. Lane's close-range shot was blocked by a defender's arm and despite the loud appeals the ref quickly waved play on. The rebound fell to Astall who then dragged his shot wide. Soon after a shot by Murphy was dropped by Hardwick and the 'keeper had to scurry back and claw the ball gratefully away for a corner. At the other end Merrick chased well outside his area to clear then suddenly found the ball coming back towards goal from an effort near the half-way line. The 'keeper got back just in time to drop on the ball. Blues then hit their opponents with two goals in a minute to kill their chances of any success. The first on 68 minutes came from a corner delivered by Murphy, again a defender handled in the area but this time the official awarded a penalty. Astall with a short run up blasted the ball into the corner of the net and the rebounding ball ended up almost 20 yards away near the penalty area arc, such was the power of his shot. Within seconds of the restart Lane Kinsey and Murphy combined to leave the latter with a simple chance which he converted with a low left-foot drive. As the game neared the end Blues could, and really should have had a fifth goal. Brown slipped the ball round his man to sprint clear and he crossed the perfect ball to Kinsey who with just the keeper to beat slipped and fell over as he ran in to shoot. At the end the score remained 4-1.

BIRMINGHAM CITY

Merrick, Hall, Green, Boyd, Newman, Warhurst, Astall, Kinsey, Brown, Lane, Murphy.

DONCASTER ROVERS

Hardwick, Makepeace, Graham, Gavin, Williams, Herbert, Ron Walker, Jeffrey, Jimmy Walker, Tindill, Geoff Walker.

REFEREE

Mr FL Overton (Derby)

Geoff Hall

The Matches played on this day

1891, Football Alliance.		
Blues 1	Birmingham	Att. 1,000
Hands	St George's 4	
1895, Division 1.		
Blues 3	Derby County 5	Att. 6,000
Jenkyns,		
Hallam, Walton		
First league meeting against Derby. Blues had skipper Caesar Jenkyns sent off .		
1901, Division 2.		
Chesterfield 1	Blues 1	Att. 3,000
	McMillan	
1907, Division 1.		
Blues 2	Blackburn Rovers 0	Att. 10,000
Jones, Tickle		
1912, Division 2.		
Chelsea 0	Blues 2	Att. 27,000
	Hall, Robertson	
1918, Wartime.		
Blues 0	Nottingham Forest 0	
1925, Division 1.		
Blues 0	WBA 0	Att. 30,000
1929, Division 1.		
Blues 0	Liverpool 0	Att. 20,000
1931, Division 1.		
West Ham United 1	Blues 2	Att. 12,000
	Firth, Bradford	
1935, Division 1.		
Leicester City 2	Blues 1	Att. 20,000
	Stoker	
1940, Wartime.		
Wolverhampton W. 3	Blues 1	
	Bodle	
1946, Wartime.		
Plymouth Argyle 1	Blues 0	
1955, Division 2.		
Blues 4	Doncaster Rovers 1	Att. 5,621
Warhurst 4	J.Walker 12	
Kinsey 8		
Astall 68(pen)		
Murphy 69		
1957, Division 1.		
Blackpool 3	Blues 1	Att. 17,610
Perry 12	Brown 57	
Taylor 53		
Mudie 78		
1963, Division 1.		
Aston Villa 4	Blues 0	Att. 46,680
Woosnam 23		
Deakin 27		
Baker 31		
Burrows (pen) 51		
1968, Division 2.		
Blues 0	Norwich City 0	Att. 28,951
1974, Division 1.		
Blues 1	Manchester United 0	Att. 37,768
Gallagher 81		
Joe Gallagher on as sub for Garry Pendrey, scored a freak winner. A clearance only reached the edge of the penalty area where Gallagher made a tackle and the block caused the ball to balloon up and over the head of 'keeper Stepney. This match was screened by ATV's Star Soccer.		
1985, Division 2.		
Blackburn Rovers 2	Blues 1	Att. 10,596
Lowey 23	Rees 15	
Barker 64		
1991, Division 3.		
Preston North End 2	Blues 0	Att. 5,334
Cartwright 46		
Joyce 48		
Blues Vince Overson and Dennis Bailey both had goals disallowed		
1993, Division 1.		
Blues 1	Sunderland 0	Att. 10,934
Peschisolido 86		
1997, Division 1.		
WBA 2	Blues 0	Att. 16,125
Sneekes 16		
Hamilton 49		
Bryan Hughes debut for Blues		
2001, Division 1.		
Stockport County 2	Blues 0	Att. 7,166
Kuqi 40, 83		

March 17

The Matches played on this day

1894, Division 2.
Blues 10   Ardwick 2   Att. 2,500
Wheldon(2), Hallam(2), Hands, Jenkyns, Walton, Mobley(3)

1900, Division 2.
Blues 2   New Brighton Tower 0   Att. 5,000
Scriven(2)

1906, Division 1.
Sunderland 3   Blues 1   Att. 15,000
       Anderson

1923, Division 1.
Blues 1   Aston Villa 0   Att. 50,000
Rawson

1928, Division 1.
Aston Villa 1   Blues 1   Att. 60,000
       Bradford

1934, Division 1.
Liverpool 4   Blues 1   Att. 40,000
       Moffatt

1945, Wartime.
Blues 0   Aston Villa 3

1951, Division 2.
Blackburn Rovers 2   Blues 3   Att. 25,000
Fenton 25   Dailey 24, 85
Todd 89   Higgins 44

1956, FA Cup Semi Final.
Sunderland 0   Blues 3   Att. 65,107
       Kinsey 11
       Astall 65
       Brown 83
Played at Hillsborough, Sheffield

1962, Division 1.
Blues 0   Aston Villa 2   Att. 45,885
       Burrows 14
       Wylie 36
Both sides finish with ten men after clash of heads between Auld and Dugdale

1965, Division 1.
Stoke City 2   Blues 1   Att. 12,899
Bebbington 12   Vowden 10
Ritchie 75

1973, Division 1.
Southampton 2   Blues 0   Att. 14,674
Channon 1, 57(pen)
Mike Channon's first goal timed at 48 seconds

1981, Division 1.
Blues 1   Wolverhampton W. 0   Att. 20,005
Worthington 73

1984, Division 1.
Stoke City 2   Blues 1   Att. 13,506
Dyson 20   Gayle 89
Bould 55
Blues Tony Coton saved Robbie James's 62nd minute penalty
Blues had Mick Harford sent off after 78 minutes

1990, Division 3.
Blues 4   Rotherham United 1   Att. 6,985
Tait 28   Mendonca 83
Atkins 48
Gordon 57
Sturridge 79

1992, Division 3.
Bolton Wanderers 1   Blues 1   Att. 7,329
Brown 90   Rodgerson 43

1996, Division 1.
Blues 0   Sunderland 2   Att. 23,251
       Agnew 16
       Melville 65
Shown live on Sky Sports TV.

Playing record for this day
Playing record for this day is...17 games, Won 7, Drawn 2, Lost 8, GF 30, GA 27.
Today's success rate.....47.06% Year ranking....185th

Match of the Day
FROM 1956
BLUES KEEP RIGHT ON TO WEMBLEY

Man City next after Blues cruise past Sunderland

The anthem 'Keep Right On to the End of the Road' was first introduced to the the Blues fans by the players when arriving at Arsenal for their sixth round FA Cup tie. As the players descended from the team bus the team were still singing the song started by Scottish winger Alex Govan, this was quickly picked up by the fans and collectively they sang out together which spurred the Blues on to a tremendous 3-1 win to reach this semi final berth. It was a most appropriate song too, as the Blues had kept right on to the end of the road and had played every round of their FA Cup campaign on their travels. Torquay became the first victims, then came Blues first trip to the capital depositing Orient from the competition 4-0. A short trip to West Brom then followed before that incredible win over the mighty Gunners in front of 67,000 at Highbury, and thus 'Keep Right On to the End of the Road' was forever to remain the Blues battle hymn.

So next to Hillsborough, Sheffield, went the anthem with 30,000 Blues fans who joined an equal number of Wearsiders following Sunderland for this FA Cup semi final. Straight from the kick off Blues ripped into the red and white stripes of their opponents who had no answer to the constant pressure. It took 11 minutes for the inevitable goal with Sunderland still waiting to put a single pass of any note together. Govan had teased Hedley and McDonald with two runs at them already and when he beat the latter again he sent over a beautifully flighted cross which Kinsey lashed past Fraser in the Sunderland goal. Blues continued to control the game for the remainder of the half. They easily dealt with anything Sunderland threw at them, and even the great Len Shackleton and Billy Bingham were too well marshalled by Trevor Smith and Len Boyd to cause any danger to a well disciplined Blues side.

Blues started the second half eager to finish the game off by adding a killer goal, and eventually it came 20 minutes after the restart. A fantastic six man move from defence started by Jeff Hall ended with Gordon Astall coolly slotting the ball home from six yards out, all this without a Sunderland player getting the slightest touch of the ball. The Blues team of 1956 were masters of possesion football, and this was one of their better days, poor Sunderland therefore had no chance. With just seven minutes remaining Peter Murphy slipped a superb through ball for Eddie Brown to run on to, with everyone expecting a firmly hit shot he stopped suddenly checked back inside which caused his marker to fall over, taking one look up he then arrogantly chipped the ball over Fraser who was on his way out to narrow the acute angle. It was a truly magnificent goal and it gave the crowd ample time to start rehearsing the Blues anthem. At the final whistle the Blues fans belted out the loudest 'Keep Right On' ever heard, the song continuing to resound round Hillsborough as they made their way home. A fitting tribute to the Blues who had earned their first trip to Wembley to contest an FA Cup final in 25 years.

BIRMINGHAM CITY
Merrick, Hall, Green, Boyd, Smith, Badham, Astall, Kinsey, Brown, Murphy, Govan.
SUNDERLAND
Fraser, Hedley, McDonald, Anderson, Daniel, Aitken, Bingham, Fleming, Holden, Elliott, Shackleton.

Alex Govan rises for a back post header

Birthdays
Lee Jenkins born today in 1961.

Playing record for this day

Playing record for this day is...19 games, Won 9, Drawn 3, Lost 7, GF 32, GA 32.

Today's success rate.....55.26% Year ranking....103rd

March 18

Match of the Day

FROM 1959
SUPER STUBBS THE HERO

Blues in control at Filbert Street

Blues today returned to the ground where they had crashed 5-0 to Nottingham Forest the previous month, thus ending their interest in the FA Cup. This time however, in front of a crowd of 15,413, it was league action at Filbert Street. Not Nottingham Forest, but Leicester, and Blues put the record straight against their labouring and often ragged looking hosts.

Leicester didn't take long in going a goal behind when Stubbs began the scoring on three minutes. Anderson, the home goalkeeper, was at fault with the clearance, allowing Allen to get on to the ball. He returned it to Larkin, who pushed a pass through the middle. Stubbs was there straight away, and although the keeper got his hand to the ball, it's driving force carried it over the line.

Leicester drew level on six minutes when Kelly made a fine 40-yard pass to Stephenson. The shot was deflected by Merrick, but Walsh moved in to score. The home side then took the lead after just 14 minutes after Stephenson centred low. Thanks to Merrick's mistimed dive, Walsh was able to force the ball home.

It wasn't long before Blues got back into the scoring, drawing level in the 20th minute. Another error by Anderson, failing to get the ball to a team mate, resulted in Stubbs being presented with a golden opportunity on the edge of the penalty area. His shot brought the score to 2-2, and began a relatively quiet period, with not many chances for either side. It was during this time that Blues took advantage of the dip in Leicester's morale, steadily gaining control with their strong defence. With 11 minutes remaining Stephenson needed treatment, and Blues saw this as another invitation to score. During his absence Gordon collected a pass from the wing, and buried the ball in the back of the net on 82 minutes. With the scoreline now 3-2 to Blues, Hooper went all out to ensure victory in the dying moments of the game, gifting the ball to Stubbs. With the shot glancing in off the post, Stubbs had got his hat-trick, and in doing so, secured 4-2 win.

BIRMINGHAM CITY

Merrick, Hall, Allen, Watts, Smith, Hume, Astall, Gordon, Stubbs, Larkin, Hooper

LEICESTER CITY

Anderson, Cunningham, Ogilvie, Newman, King, Appleton, McDonald, Kelly, Walsh, Stephenson, Leek

Robin Stubbs

March 19

Playing record for this day

Playing record for this day is...15 games, Won 3, Drawn 4, Lost 8, GF 15, GA 22.
Today's success rate....33.33% Year ranking....257th

Match of the Day
FROM 1949
BLUES BUOYED BY BOYD

Brave Len battles through pain barrier to net the winner

Len Boyd who carried a knee injury throughout the second half was pushed up into a forward position as a virtual passenger as he limped bravely through the final 45 minutes. However he still managed to score the all important goal which earned Blues the points over FA Cup holders Manchester United. Blues started the game with new signing Johnny Jordan from Italian giants Juventus making his debut, replacing Berry on the right wing. Blues also recalled Fred Slater to the forward line in place of the injured Dorman. Meanwhile Ray Ferris who started in the 1-0 defeat at Liverpool made his St Andrews debut. A huge crowd, many having queued hours before the gates opened at 1pm, greeted the teams at the start. 46,819 were crammed into St Andrews on a sweltering day and busy St John's ambulance men scurried round the kop treating many with sun stroke and exhaustion.

Blues started the game with an all out attack and soon had United pegged back unable to get out of their own half. A move from defence started by Badham ended with a cross from Ferris which Slater bundled into the net with a diving header, but he had been flagged offside as the cross came over to him. Blues by this time were swarming forward taking full advantage of the United defenders facing the bright sun which hampered their vision. A wonderful opportunity fell to Roberts but he hesitated too long on the ball allowing Carey to come across to block his eventual shot. Moments later Slater hit a first time shot which took United 'keeper Crompton by surprise, but somehow he managed to block with his chest and clear with his left leg, the ball broke to Jordan whose return shot from distance shaved the crossbar. United at last broke and forced their first corner on 39 minutes which was greeted by ironic cheers. From the kick however Anderson flicked on to Pearson whose header was just fractionally wide of the post with Merrick well beaten.

Blues resumed the second half with Len Boyd limping ominously and his right knee heavily bandaged. Slater dropped back to cover his defensive duties whilst Boyd hovered up front where he could be best used without further handicapping the team. However it was Boyd who incredibly got the opening goal just four minutes into the half. Birmingham attacked through Stewart whose shot was charged down by some desperate defending. The ball then broke to Jordan but his effort was scrambled off the line by Chilton but only as far as Boyd who placed it into the opposite corner. Boyed accepted his team mates hand shakes as he celebrated by limping all the way back to his own half for the restart. United were soon handicapped by injury themselves when Rowley came off the worst in an accidental head clash with McDonnell. The Blues defender walked away within seconds although clearly dazed, Rowley however left the field with blood running down his face and neck from a gashed cheek. He resumed 16 minutes later and was soon creating United's best chance all afternoon. After beating two men, Rowley got in a lovely position to shoot on goal but sliced his shot right across the penalty area. He inadvertently found Anderson who snatched at his chance and scooped the ball high over the bar. This was the game's last clear cut chance and Blues held out for the remaining five minutes to secure a well deserved one goal victory.

BIRMINGHAM CITY
Merrick, Badham, Green, Boyd, McDonnell, Ferris, Stewart, Jordan, Slater, Harris, Roberts.
MANCHESTER UNITED
Crompton, Carey, Aston, Cockburn, Chilton, McGlen, Delaney, Anderson, Rowley, Pearson, Mitten.

REFEREE
Mr JG Williams (Nottinghamshire)

Johnny Jordan narrowly fails to connect with a header against Charlton Athletic

Birthdays
Greg Farrell born today in 1944.

Playing record for this day
Playing record for this day is...20 games, Won 4, Drawn 10, Lost 6, GF 26, GA 26.
Today's success rate.....45% Year ranking....201st

March 20

Match of the Day

FROM 1993

PESCHI STINGS THE BEES

Blues bag the points thanks to Canadian's brace

Paul Peschisolido finished this game with style before leaving for World Cup duty. Both his goals came in a four-minute period in the second half, and earned Blues only their second away win of the season, moving them out of the relegation zone and above Brentford. Peschisolido and Blues defender Paul Fenwick left for Canada after the game, with Blues destined to miss his presence in the side, with seven goals in his last ten games. Blues began well in front of the 7,532 crowd, and Dave Smith's attempt in the fifth minute was blocked by Benstead, then just a minute later Gary Blissett made it clear to Blues why none of the Brentford team had scored in the last 650 minutes of play when he fluffed his 12-yard shot completely.

Peschisolido tried to make his way through the Brentford defence when Mickey Bennett brought him to the ground. Blues fans were calling for him to be sent off, but the referee disagreed and didn't even give a warning. Billy Manuel slipped through in the 25th minute, but Bob Catlin saved the shot. The Blues goalkeeper also kept out a try from Bennett, then Benstead denied Moulden before Peschisolido was booked for a foul on the Brentford goalkeeper.

The second half began with one change to the Blues team. Dean Peer, who had been injured in a clash of heads before half time, was replaced by Fenwick. Brentford went all-out for a goal early on, and captain Keith Millen had three good chances to score, but was denied on all of them. On 71 minutes Peschisolido struck his first goal with a header after Scott Hiley sent a deep cross over from the right. Just four minutes later Peschisolido again cut in on the left and managed to beat Benstead from 18 yards out to get the second goal. The final whistle brought huge cheers from the Blues fans who felt that this result avenged Brentford's 3-1 win at St Andrews.

BIRMINGHAM CITY

Catlin, Hiley, Frain, Parris, Dryden, Matthewson, Moulden (Clarkson), Rodgerson, Peschisolido, Peer (Fenwick), Smith.

BRENTFORD

Benstead, Statham, Bennett, Millen, Bates, Ratcliffe, Stephenson, Dickens, Allon (Jones), Blissett, Manuel (Gayle).

REFEREE

Mr IJ Borrett (Norfolk)

Paul Peschisolido

March 21

Playing record for this day

Playing record for this day is...20 games, Won 8, Drawn 4, Lost 8, GF 38, GA 29.
Today's success rate.....50% Year ranking....143rd

Match of the Day
FROM 1995
BATTLE WON BY BLUES
Blues close in on the title after Oxford scrap

Oxford arrived at fortress St Andrews unbeaten in eight previous league games and holding firmly on to third place in the league. Blues were fresh from a three goal weekend away win at Wycombe and looking to close in on the top two and take third spot from their visitors. A battle was promised and the crowd was urged to get behind the team to ensure the three points.

The early exchanges however seemed to favour Oxford and they played with the confidence their eight match record had given them, Blues however matched them in the physical stakes never giving them time to settle and Gary Poole was in particular lucky not to have been booked as early as the third minute. Blues weathered the early Oxford storm, Bennett pulling off a spectacular save from Matt Murphy before starting to move forward themselves. After Lewis was adjudged to have fouled Claridge, Ward floated in a high free kick to the far post where Kevin Francis rose to plant his header past Whitehead for the opening goal, slightly against the run of play. At half time Blues still had the advantage but had got hold of a better balance of possession and were looking comfortable in defending. Within minutes of the restart there was more danger in the Blues penalty area and Shearer was unlucky to handle a bobbling ball. Although the linesman flagged immediately referee Barry was happy to allow play to go on, the persistence of the Oxford players eventually led the two officials to consult and Blues fears were realised soon after when the penalty was given. Dave Rush who had had a great game stepped up but his shot was superbly blocked by a full stretch Bennett and an alert Gary Cooper hacked away the rebound before Rush could get to it. The incident seemed to spur Blues and after 57 minutes Shearer was again involved in penalty area action, this time his flicked header found Claridge who tucked the ball in from a near post shot. With Blues now buzzing it was Oxford under siege and just four minutes later a perfect Otto corner was met by a determined and powerful Daish header for Blues third and final goal.

The win took Blues into third place just six points behind the league leaders Huddersfield Town but with four games in hand. Oxford's fine eight game run was crushed and they had swapped their third place with Birmingham.

BIRMINGHAM CITY
Bennett, Poole, Cooper, Ward, Barnett, Daish, Robinson (Otto 45), Claridge, Francis, Williams (Doherty 72), Shearer

OXFORD UNITED
Whitehead, Robinson, Rogan, Lewis, Elliott, Gilchrist Murphy, Smith (Dyer 67), Druce (Moody 55), Rush, Allen

REFEREE
Mr N Barry (Scunthorpe)

Steve Claridge

Blues news extra   1942..Friendly match
Blues 2 Derby County 2

Birthdays
George Johnston born today in 1947   Bobby Thomson (inside forward and wing half) born today in 1937   Colin Withers born today in 1940

Playing record for this day

Playing record for this day is...16 games, Won 9, Drawn 2, Lost 5, GF 31, GA 19.

Today's success rate.....62.50% Year ranking....36th

Match of the Day

FROM 1986

BLUES OUT WITH A BANG

Villa crushed by defiant Brum in three goal blitz

Birmingham's hopes of survival were given another boost by their easy win over local rivals Aston Villa. It had been nearly nine years since Blues had even scored a goal at this ground, but they made up for it this time.

John Bond brought former skipper Billy Wright into a five-man defence, Des Bremner and Martin Kuhl were in midfield, with Robert Hopkins, Steve Whitton and Wayne Clarke up front. Chances for Blues started on 14 minutes with Clarke picking up a free kick by Roberts and heading it goalwards, just hitting the bar. Clarke had his name entered in the referee's notebook after 30 minutes for constantly chipping away at Allan Evans and Paul Elliott , but within a minute had compensated for his booking with a lovely goal. It began with a long kick from David Seaman which should have been cleared by Elliott.

Amazingly he misjudged it completely, presenting Clarke with the perfect opportunity to drive the ball past Villa goalkeeper Nigel Spink.

Just seven minutes later Blues were two goals in front, thanks to another goal from Clarke coming from a miskick by Evans. Clarke could have got a hat trick when he justifiably claimed for a penalty, but his appeals fell on deaf ears and the game continued.

The third goal for Blues came due to more poor defending by the home team. Tony Dorigo tried to clear the ball to Mark Walters, but his volley lacked pace and Ray Ranson headed it towards the penalty area. It was Williams' turn to misjudge the ball, and Spink left it too late to move off his line. Whitton took full advantage of the mistakes and had an unguarded net to nod in his simple header. Seaman had to make only three saves in the entire match, none of which were memorable, and Blues thoroughly deserved their victory.

BIRMINGHAM CITY

Seaman, Ranson, Roberts, Hagan, Garton, Kuhl, Bremner, Clarke, Wright, Whitton, Hopkins.

ASTON VILLA

Spink, Williams, Dorigo, Evans, Elliott, Hunt, Blair, Shaw, Gray, Hodge, Walters.

David Seaman

March 23

Playing record for this day
Playing record for this day is...20 games, Won 7, Drawn 7, Lost 6, GF 26, GA 22.
Today's success rate.....52.50% Year ranking....136th

Match of the Day
FROM 1993
BLAZING SAVILLE

Easy for Blues as Barnsley are burnt by hot Saville double

Blues' new signing Andy Saville, a £155,000 buy from Hartlepool, took no time in getting used to higher grade football, helping his new team to victory with his first two goals for the club. Also scoring his first goal for Blues since his £150,000 signing from Oldham was Paul Moulden. This was Blues third victory in a row, and the 12,664 crowd saw a contender for the best performance of the season.

After just three minutes Trevor Matthewson was booked for a challenge on Biggins, but it wasn't long before the home team won a corner. They were close to scoring from it as the kick, taken by Smith, was flicked goalwards by Peer at the near post. Whitehead instinctively reached up and saved, with Blues disappointed not to score.

The opening goal came on 15 minutes when Frain passed wide to Moulden, whose cross was so perfect that Saville had the easy job of volleying the ball past Whitehead from eight yards. Hendon almost equalised minutes later, but his clever dipping volley was not destined for the back of the net. Another booking for Blues arrived on 27 minutes when Hiley made a nasty challenge on Graham and was cautioned for the offence. Then it was Barnsley's turn when Brendan O'Connell tackled Frain and was duly given a yellow card. Blues were looking for a second goal to ease the pressure a bit, and their efforts in attack were beginning to pay off as Barnsley were beginning to flail. The last attempt before half time came from Moulden's crisp header, but the score remained 1-0 going into the break.

The second half began with a shot on target from Saville, but it was collected by Whitehead. However, the elusive goal soon arrived for the home side on 55 minutes. Hiley threaded his pass and Saville fooled the Barnsley defence. Moulden let the ball roll before seizing his chance and knocking the ball into the net from 14 yards out.

Saville suffered a knock in the 60th minute when he collided with Whitehead after his shot was saved. He made it 3-0 in the final minute of the game, sliding in a centre from Hiley. The home team performed brilliantly, and the win could have been far greater.

BIRMINGHAM CITY
Catlin, Hiley, Frain, Parris, Dryden, Matthewson, Moulden, Rodgerson, Saville, Peer, Smith.
BARNSLEY
Whitehead, Bishop, Fleming, Davis (Bullimore), Taggart, O'Connell, Biggins, Hendon, Currie (Godfrey), Redfearn, Graham.

REFEREE
Mr G Poll (Berkhamsted)

Andy Saville

Birthdays
Bertie Auld born today in 1938.

Playing record for this day

Playing record for this day is...20 games, Won 8, Drawn 5, Lost 7, GF 38, GA 25.

Today's success rate.....52.50% Year ranking....134th

Match of the Day

FROM 1973

ROYAL BLUES RULE

Sky Blues well beaten by super Royal Blues display

Blues kicked off towards the Tilton, and the action began. Campbell and Francis started in earnest with a clever one-two almost giving a goal-scoring opportunity at the outset. Glazier saved an early try from Francis, and the momentum picked up. It took 30 minutes for Blues to gain the lead thanks to a typical winning run down the left side by Bob Hatton, crossing the ball to Francis who passed it back, allowing a great header from Hatton to hit the back of the net.

Straight away Coventry woke up and tried to come back into the game, but this was easier said than done with a strong Blues defence consisting of Hynd and Roberts standing in their way. Two minutes before half time saw another Blues goal headed in. Hatton had a shot on goal saved by Glazier, who lost his hold of the ball. Fortunately Bob Latchford was in a perfect position to head the ball home, bringing the scoreline to 2-0. Blues started the second half seemingly content with the current score, and Coventry appeared more defensive, not wanting Blues to increase their lead. 20 minutes into the second half, and Hatton created the third goal for Blues. Taylor blasted the ball from 20 yards, and it effortlessly entered the top corner of the net.

A convincing 3-0 win for Blues, towards the end of their first season back in top flight football. They finished the campaign in a respectable tenth position, winning five and drawing one of their last six games.

BIRMINGHAM CITY

Dave Latchford, Martin, Pendrey, Page, Hynd, Roberts, Campbell, Francis, Bob Latchford, Hatton, Taylor

COVENTRY:

Glazier, Coop, Cattlin, Smith, Barry, Parker, Mortimer, Alderson, Stein, Carr, Hutchison

Bob Hatton

Birthdays

Archie Gemmill born today in 1947.   Brian Taylor born today in 1937.

March 24

The Matches played on this day

1894, Division 2.		
Blues 6	Burslem Port Vale 0	Att. 4,000
Hands, Walton(2), Mobley(2), Wheldon		

Blues completed a remarkable goal-scoring week, netting 19 in three games and nine in two days.

1900, Division 2.		
Grimsby Town 2	Blues 0	Att. 5,000

1906, Division 1.		
Blues 3	Wolverhampton W. 3	Att. 5,000
Mounteney, Jones(2)		

1913, Division 2.		
Fulham 3	Blues 2	Att. 8,000
	Robertson, Duncan	

1915, Division 2.		
Blues 2	Hull City 2	Att. 10,000
Reed, A.W.Smith		

1917, Wartime.		
Blues 5	Leicester City 1	
Bowser, Moore, Bell, McClure, Whitehouse		

1923, Division 1.		
Aston Villa 3	Blues 0	Att. 40,000

Blues conceded two penalties, both converted by Billy Walker.

1928, Division 1.		
Blues 4	Burnley 0	Att. 20,000
Bradford(3), Crosbie		

1934, Division 1.		
Blues 3	Portsmouth 1	Att. 12,000
Barkas(pen), Guest, Mangnall		

1945, Wartime.		
Northampton Town 0	Blues 2	
	Mulraney, Massart	

1951, Division 2.		
Blues 2	Hull City 1	Att. 28,000
Boyd 25	Harrison 60	
Dailey 58		

1956, Division 1.		
Blues 1	Blackpool 2	Att. 47,933
Murphy 26	Durie 15 Perry 86	

1962, Division 1.		
Blackpool 1	Blues 0	Att. 11,584
Hauser 7		

1973, Division 1.		
Blues 3	Coventry City 0	Att. 34,775
Hatton 30		
B.Latchford 43		
Taylor 65		

Match shown on ATV's Star Soccer

1979, Division 1.		
Middlesbrough 2	Blues 1	Att. 15,013
Burns 16	Givens 36	
Ashcroft 25		

1984, Division 1.		
Blues 0	Notts County 0	Att. 9,040

1990, Division 3.		
Blues 0	Chester City 0	Att. 7,584

1992, Division 3.		
Torquay United 1	Blues 2	Att. 2,446
Myers 32	Rowbotham 63 Matthewson 82	

2001, Division 2.		
Blues 1	Sheffield W. 2	Att. 19,733
Horsfield 60	De Bilde 24 Di Piedi 87	

Horsfield scored after latching on to the rebound from Purse's penalty miss

2002, Division 1.		
Coventry City 1	Blues 1	Att. 17,945
Healy 61	Horsfield 81	

March 25

Playing record for this day

Playing record for this day is...20 games, Won 7, Drawn 7, Lost 6, GF 27, GA 23.

Today's success rate.....52.50% Year ranking....135th

Match of the Day
FROM 1969
FIVE STAR SHOW BLUES

Phil Summerill the hero in Bolton massacre

After an exciting and highly entertaining evening at St Andrews, Blues' victory over Bolton Wanderers moved them above local rivals Aston Villa in the Second Division. Bolton were overwhelmed by illness and injury, while skipper Ron Wylie was absent for Blues. This meant that the home side's driving force was Malcolm Beard. Wylie's place was taken by Garry Pendrey on his debut, who showed astuteness and skill, and went a long way to ensuring his place in the team in the future.

Phil Summerill earned his second hat-trick of the season, and goals from Johnny Vincent and Malcolm Beard completed the scoring. Chances began straight away for Blues with four shots on goal in the first eight minutes. Pickering's three minute volley went into the net, only to be disallowed due to Summerill being offside. Cooper managed to clear a header off the line before Summerill's attempt at a header failed.

A bungle by the Blues defence gifted Bolton with a corner after a series of fruitless goal attempts by both sides. On 29 minutes a lapse from Bolton was seized upon by Blues, and the first goal was scored. Bromilow was dribbling the ball, seemingly out of danger, and Vincent made the steal and fired in an unstoppable shot.

There were even more chances before the next goal came after 53 minutes. Greenhoff hit a shot which was pushed aside by the Bolton goalkeeper Hopkinson. Summerill was on hand to tap the ball into the net.

Seven minutes later Beard hit a superb shot from 35 yards which flew past Hopkinson into the top corner of the net. Then just two minutes later Beard turned provider, crossing the ball for Summerill to head home. The game was well and truly over when, on 89 minutes, Summerill headed another goal straight past the confused Bolton defence.

BIRMINGHAM CITY
Herriot, Green, Thomson, Beard, Robinson, Pendrey, Greenhoff, Vincent, Pickering, Hockey, Summerill.

BOLTON WANDERERS
Hopkinson, Hallows, Cooper, Williams, Marsh, Bromilow, Phillips, Hill, Jones, Byrom, Taylor.

Jimmy Greenhoff

Blues news extra   1905..Birmingham not Small anymore

After a lengthy meeting between senior club officials Small Heath decided to change their name to Birmingham FC. A move not entirely to everyone's liking got the vote in the end and was due to take effect for the start of the 1905-06 season.

Birthdays

Bill Robertson born today in 1923.   Mark Rutherford born today in 1972.

Playing record for this day
Playing record for this day is...19 games, Won 6, Drawn 4, Lost 9, GF 29, GA 37.
Today's success rate.....42.11% Year ranking....220th

March 26

Match of the Day

FROM 1983

FERGIE GOAL LIVENS UP THE COUNTY SHOW

Blues romp to impressive 3-0 win after wonder goal start

An uninspiring, often drab opening 29 minutes at St Andrews was brought to life by a fantastic individual piece of skill by Blues striker Mick Ferguson. His goal, a cracker, helped put the team on their way to a fine 3-0 win. The 11,744 who had patiently supported the Blues' efforts were then further rewarded with a second goal from Ferguson just six minutes later from the penalty spot. Fellow striker Mick Harford completed the scoring early in the second half.

A slow start to the game brightened slightly when the first reasonable chance of a goal fell to Harford after ten minutes. A cross from Van Den Hauwe was neatly controlled by the Blues striker who then turned and shot first time, the ball looked to be beating the 'keeper but struck the outstretched boot of Richards who bravely lunged across to block the effort for a corner. This one chance remained the only highlight of a disappointing game in which the two midfields dominated, but the entertainment value was at a very low level. This all changed at the half hour mark when Ferguson brought the sparse crowd to life. Collecting a pass from Hopkins on the edge of the penalty area, he swivelled round lobbing the ball over a defender and ran round before meeting the dropping ball on the volley. His shot looped over 'keeper Avramovic and dropped into the far corner, a quite breathtaking finish easily the best seen all season at St Andrews. With play now open, as County had to come forward for an equaliser, Blues midfield found space and Hopkins who had been almost non-existent became inspirational after the goal. After another cracking through ball by Hopkins, Ferguson ran free into the area again only to be upended by Hunt. Picking himself up, Ferguson took the penalty himself sending Avramovic the wrong way to put Blues into a comfortable 2-0 lead.

The second half started in sensational style for the Blues when they added a third goal within 90 seconds of the restart. A lovely combination of passes between Van Den Hauwe and man-of-the-match Robert Hopkins allowed the latter a firmly hit shot from within the penalty area, this was exceptionally well saved by Avramovic who was unlucky to see the ball roll out to the waiting Harford who tapped in from two yards out. With Blues now streaming forward Gayle was inches away from from adding a fourth goal moments later, but his 20-yard effort was just too high. Although several more half chances were presented to the Blues forwards during the latter stages of the game, Blues failed to add to their three goals.

BIRMINGHAM CITY
Coton, Hagan, Dennis, Stevenson, Blake, Van Den Hauwe, Gayle, Ferguson, Harford, Halsall, Hopkins.

NOTTS COUNTY
Avramovic, Benjamin, Worthington, Hunt, Kilcline, Richards, Harkouk, Goodwin, McCullough, Christie, O'Brien.

REFEREE
Mr Brian Daniels (Brentwood)

Mick Ferguson

The Matches played on this day

1892, Football Alliance.		
Blues 4	Bootle 1	Att. 2,000
Walton(2), Wheldon(2)		
1898, Division 2.		
Leicester Fosse 2	Blues 0	Att. 2,000
1904, Division 1.		
Blues 1	Everton 1	Att. 10,000
Beer		
1906, Division 1.		
Blues 2	Bolton 5	Att. 10,000
Mounteney, Tickle		
1910, Division 2.		
Lincoln City 3	Blues 2	Att. 5,000
	Burton, Millington	
1921, Division 2.		
Blues 1	Barnsley 3	Att. 40,000
Hampton		
1932, Division 1.		
Leicester City 3	Blues 1	Att. 20,000
	Smith	
1937, Division 1.		
Middlesbrough 3	Blues 1	Att. 10,000
	Clarke	
1938, Division 1.		
Blues 1	Blackpool 1	Att. 9,440
Harris		
1940, Wartime.		
Blues 5	Luton Town 4	
Bodle(2), Jones(2), Gordon		
1949, Division 1.		
Sheffield United 4	Blues 0	Att. 26,000
1951, Division 2.		
Cardiff City 2	Blues 1	Att. 20,000
McLaughlin 3, 11	Rowley 75	
1955, Division 2.		
Blues 1	West Ham United 2	Att. 8,600
Brown 19	Dick 57	
	Musgrove 67	

Gordon Astall took over in goal for ten minutes due to an injury to Johnny Schofield.

1960, Division 1.		
Luton Town 1	Blues 1	Att. 19,620
McBride 55(pen)	Weston 20	
1966, Division 2.		
Ipswich Town 0	Blues 1	Att. 9,375
	Beard 14	
1983, Division 1.		
Blues 3	Notts County 0	Att. 11,744
Ferguson 29(pen), 35		
Harford 47		
1988, Division 2.		
Middlesbrough 1	Blues 1	Att. 15,465
Pallister 77	Atkins 50	

Blues keeper Martin Thomas suffered a fractured cheek, Andy Kennedy took over in goal. Ian Atkins made his Blues debut

1991, Leyland Daf Cup, Southern Area Final, 1st leg.		
Blues 2	Brentford 1	Att. 16,219
Rodgerson 31	Gayle 66	
Gayle 52		
1994, Division 1.		
Blues 1	Middlesbrough 0	Att. 12,409
Saville 90		

Blues finally broke the sequence of 14 league games without a win. Mark Ward made his Blues debut

March 27

Playing record for this day
Playing record for this day is...17 games, Won 8, Drawn 2, Lost 7, GF 18, GA 23.
Today's success rate.....52.94% Year ranking....129th

Match of the Day

FROM 1963
ALMOST THERE
Advantage Brum but everything to play for in second leg

This was the third cup tie against Bury in March of 1963 and Blues were hoping for their first win, having been dumped out of the FA Cup third round by 2-0 in a replay at Bury after a 3-3 draw at St Andrews. Blues went into the game with problems, they had lost both full backs Stan Lynn and Colin Green to injury and brought in Rushton to cover at right back, whilst Malcolm Beard continued to cover at left back. Forward Jimmy Harris was also unavailable but the good news was the return of the inspirational Jimmy Bloomfield.

The game quickly became a real cagey affair with Bury content to take a stalemate to Gigg Lane in the second leg, a policy that had worked well in the FA Cup ties. Blues, conscious of Bury's devastating counter attacks were playing cautiously with a priority not to concede anything. The 11,266 crowd had very little to cheer in the first 20 minutes until Blues first real chance, which fell to Peter Bullock who was replacing the injured Harris. After being put in the clear he spent far too much time bringing the ball under control when faced with a great chance to shoot, the opportunity disappeared when he chose to pass inside to Auld and Eastham nipped into clear. Blues were left to rue this chance as Bury soon took the lead on 30 minutes. Griffin finished off a fine run down the left wing cutting in to beat Beard and slam the ball into the roof of the net past Schofield in the Blues goal. Blues found it difficult to mount any retaliation to the strike as Bury defended well up to the break more than happy now with a one goal lead.

There was a much better start to the second half as Blues discarded the cautious approach and went in search of goals. Twice Bury 'keeper Harker was called on to block efforts from Bloomfield and Auld. On 60 minutes Blues had their just reward when Watts and Hellawell combined to put Bullock in on goal again. This time the striker's first touch was clinical as he strode forward to clip the ball over the advancing keeper and into the corner of the net. Then just three minutes later Blues took the lead. This time some great first time passing between Hellawell, Bloomfield and Auld finished with the latter nodding in the former's short cross. Blues continued to dominate, Leek this time went on a dangerous run into the box only to be tripped by Stokoe. The penalty was taken by Auld who could have put the tie safe but he sent his spot kick just wide. Blues did get a third goal, however, just ten minutes later when Leek powerfully headed in another perfect Hellawell cross. With Blues coasting now at 3-1 they briefly lost concentration defensively allowing Bury to get right back in the tie. In the last minute Calder ran through the middle of a static Blues defence to shoot past a stranded Schofield and give them hope for the second leg at Gigg Lane.

BIRMINGHAM CITY
Schofield, Rushton, Beard, Watts, Smith, Hennessey, Hellawell, Bloomfield, Bullock, Leek, Auld.
BURY
Harker, Threlfall, Eastham, Turner, Stokoe, Atherton, Griffin, Jones, Calder, Beaumont, Bartley.

Johnny Schofield

Blues news extra   1926..No luck for the Irish against Blues.
Top Irish side Glentoran were torn apart today at St Andrews in a friendly won by the Blues 8-2. Joe Bradford led the scoring with four goals and strike partner George Briggs finished with two.

1961..FA Cup Semi Final at St Andrews.
Leicester City finally overcame Sheffield United in the second semi-final replay staged at Birmingham's St Andrews ground by 2-0. Both goals were scored by Ken Leek a future Blues star. Leicester went on to lose the final against Tottenham 3-1 at Wembley.

Birthdays
Paul Hendrie born today in 1954.

The Matches played on this day

1897, Division 2.
Leicester Fosse 0 — Blues 1 — Att. 5,500
Hodgetts
First league meeting v Leicester Fosse.

1901, FA Cup 3rd round, replay.
Aston Villa 1 — Blues 0 — Att. 15,000

1909, Division 2.
Hull City 4 — Blues 1 — Att. 8,000
Bumphrey

1915, Division 2.
Lincoln City 0 — Blues 1 — .Att. 3,000
Morgan

1920, Division 2.
Blues 0 — Bury 2 — Att. 25,000

1937, Division 1.
Blues 1 — Preston North End 0 — Att. 33,828
Harris

1943, Wartime.
Coventry City 2 — Blues 1
Acquaroff

1946, FA Cup Semi Final, replay.
Derby County 4 — Blues 0 — Att. 80,407
After extra time
Played at Maine Road, Manchester

1948, Division 2.
Doncaster Rovers 0 — Blues 0 — Att. 25,000

1954, Division 2.
Bury 1 — Blues 1 — Att. 11,293
Pearson 46 — Stewart 63

1963, League Cup Semi Final, 1st leg.
Blues 3 — Bury 2 — Att. 11,266
Bullock 61 — Griffin 29
Auld 64 — Calder 87
Leek 79
Auld missed a penalty, after 66 mins.

1967, Division 2.
Blues 2 — Hull City 1 — Att. 17,506
Isherwood 65 — Wilinson 3
Beard 75
Blues right back Dennis Isherwood marked his St Andrews debut with a superb 25-yard equaliser.

1971, Division 2.
Blues 2 — Cardiff City 0 — Att. 49,025
Francis 3
Summerill 75

1976, Division 1.
Derby County 4 — Blues 2 — Att. 28,161
James 7 — Francis 65
Rioch 32 — Needham 87
Davies 60
Nish 62

1979, Division 1.
Blues 1 — Norwich City 0 — Att. 12,168
Givens 20
Doug Evans of Norwich sent off after 49 minutes
Norwich 'keeper Roger Hansbury saved a penalty from Tony Towers in the 88th minute

1982, Division 1.
Blues 1 — Brighton & Hove A. 0 — Att. 13,234
Harford 72
Mick Harford netted the winner on his debut

1989, Division 2.
Blues 1 — Shrewsbury Town 2 — Att. 4,964
Sturridge 22 — Thomas (og) 49
Kelly 74

Playing record for this day

Playing record for this day is...20 games, Won 8, Drawn 6, Lost 6, GF 33, GA 28.

Today's success rate.....55% Year ranking....106th

March 28

Match of the Day

FROM 1978

BLUES LOOKING GOOD

Francis double, and Blues look for their best league finish

Blues maintained their fine current form with a fifth unbeaten game in succession, their third win since manager Jim Smith took over the team from Alf Ramsay earlier in the month. Blues again looked impressive as they overcame West Ham by 3-0 with goals from Francis(2) and Bertschin. Blues with the two points had now assured their place in English football's elite league for another campaign with seven games still left to play. This despite the fact that they were now under the leadership of their third manager of the season.

Blues started cautiously against a good West Ham side who monopolised the attacking play in the opening 30 minutes. But the new look Blues remained defiant in defence patiently soaking up the pressure and refusing to yield. When the Hammers rested the home side broke with devastating ability, if only the start of the season had been like this! The 23,554 crowd at St Andrews could expect to have a few more comrades the next time they congregate on the terraces as once again the goals flowed after the initial breakthrough inspired by young winger Steve Fox just after the half hour mark. From his magical piece of wing play and acceleration to cross from the right Hibbitt found a shooting chance but amazingly hit the post from seven yards out. Fortunately for him the ball fell to Francis who made no mistake inside the six yard box. West Ham then never looked troublesome and the Blues took control of the game. Jimmy Calderwood excelled in midfield with some exceptionally high class passing, he combined with the tireless Terry Hibbitt and with striker Keith Bertschin willing

to run himself almost dizzy Blues looked irresistable. Francis's second goal of the game, his 24th of the season, came from the penalty spot just two minutes before half time. A fine through ball from Gallagher put Bertschin away and as he cleverly rounded the 'keeper Ferguson pulled him down. A clear cut penalty, and the keeper was lucky not to have been sent off as a further punishment.

Blues continued to punish a beaten and demoralised West Ham side after the break. Francis having the best of the chances and he will feel disappointed he didn't complete a hat-trick over the 90 minutes. Ferguson helped as well with a fine goalkeeping display to keep the scoreline somewhat respectable. However despite the pressure a third Blues goal did not arrive until a minute before time. Another reflex save from Ferguson from Francis popped up for Bertschin who simply headed the dropping ball into the empty net to complete the 3-0 victory.

BIRMINGHAM CITY

Montgomery, Calderwood, Pendrey, Towers, Gallagher, Howard, Page, Francis, Bertschin, Hibbitt, Fox.

WEST HAM UNITED

Ferguson, Bond, Lampard, Curbishley, Taylor, Green, Pike, Holland, Cross, Brooking, Robson.

Trevor Brooking - West Ham United

Blues news extra   1942..Friendly at Molineux.

Wolverhampton Wanderers 0 Blues 3

The Matches played on this day

1890, Football Alliance.
Blues 1   Sunderland Albion 3   Att. 2,000
W.Devey
1897, Division 2.
Woolwich Arsenal 2 Blues 3   Att. 3,000
                 Hodgetts(2), Hare
1902, Division 1.
Sunderland 1   Blues 1   Att. 8,600
                 Athersmith
1907, Division 1.
Blues 4   Manchester City 0   Att. 10,000
Green, Gooch,
Anderson, Jones
1913, Division 2.
Bristol City 0   Blues 3   Att. 6,000
                 Reed(2), Robertson
1919, Wartime.
Blues 1   Nottingham Forest 0
Walker
1921, Division 2.
Blues 1   Fulham 0   Att. 25,000
Booth
1929, Division 1.
Portsmouth 3   Blues 1   Att. 30,000
                 Ellis
1930, Division 1.
Everton 2   Blues 4   Att. 25,000
                 Crosbie, Bradford,
                 Blyth, Briggs
1932, Division 1.
Blues 1   Manchester City 5   Att. 12,000
Bradford
1937, Division 1.
Blues 0   Middlesbrough 0   Att. 15,000
1939, Division 1.
Blues 1   Huddersfield Town 1   Att. 12,000
Jones

Playing record for this day

Playing record for this day is...24 games, Won 10, Drawn 8, Lost 6, GF 34, GA 26.

Today's success rate.....58.33% Year ranking....71st

Match of the Day
FROM 1948

BLUES SHOW TRUE LEADERSHIP QUALITIES

Blues remain in top spot after neighbours take an emphatic beating

The Second Division of the 1947-48 season had almost been entirely dominated by these two midland clubs. West Brom had led the division since September, and were only deposed of top spot by Birmingham in December. Blues showed true leadership quality by winning this all important four-pointer clash against Albion who were still in contention for promotion.

Blues went into the game unchanged and at full strength. Albion, in a change strip of white shirts and blue shorts, made one change with ex-Arsenal forward Drury in place of Hodgetts. It quickly became apparent that the morning's heavy rainfall had badly affected the pitch, making it difficult for defenders. Birmingham took advantage of this by taking the lead after seven minutes. Following a corner taken by Edwards, two Albion players slipped in a goalmouth skirmish, allowing Stewart to score from two yards. In Albion's response, Merrick moved swiftly to save a ground shot from Drury, however in the build up, the referee had already blown for a foul on Harris by Drury, for which he was given a stern warning.

After 17 minutes the slippy pitch was again prominent in Blues' second goal. Vernon, under no pressure, hit a back pass to Heath, which skidded off the pitch. Despite a desperate sliding dive by Heath, the ball went out for a corner. From Stewart's flag kick Bodle rose at the far post to head in. Desperate to get back in the game Albion attacked relentlessly, but found Birmingham's defence, led by Jennings, in superb form. It was Birmingham who could have taken the lead again just before half time through another Albion error, this time by their skipper Vernon. The corner by Stewart again caused confusion and a scramble in the Albion goalmouth, but this time Pemberton managed to get the ball clear.

Blues continued the second half in the same vein, dominating all the way. A goal from Trigg, and another for Stewart brought the scoreline to 4-0. A resounding and well deserved victory for Blues.

BIRMINGHAM CITY

Merrick, Green, Jennings, Harris, Duckhouse, Mitchell, Stewart, Dorman, Trigg, Bodle, Edwards.

WEST BROMWICH ALBION

Heath, Pemberton, Kinsell, Millard, Vernon, Evans A.J, Elliot, Drury, Walsh, Haines, Rowley.

REFEREE

Mr A Baker (Crewe)

Dennis Jennings

Birthdays

Bart Griemink born today in 1972

Alan Miller born today in 1970

David Smith born today in 1968

Wally Halsall born today in 1912

Terry Duckhouse

1947, Division 2.

Sheffield W. 1	Blues 0	Att. 27,500

1948, Division 2.

Blues 4	WBA 0	Att. 43,168
Stewart(2),		
Bodle, Trigg		

1952, Division 2.

Blues 2	Hull City 2	Att. 15,000
Briggs 13	Harris 19	
Smith 88	Carter 26	

1958, Division 1.

Blues 2	Everton 1	Att. 21,628
Hooper 35, 40	Thomas 60	

1960, Inter Cities Fairs Cup Final, 1st leg.

Blues 0	Barcelona 0	Att. 40,524

1969, Division 2.

Huddersfield Town 0	Blues 0	Att. 8,105

1975, Division 1.

Liverpool 1	Blues 0	Att. 49,454
Keegan 63(pen)		

Match screened by BBC's Match of the Day.

1980, Division 2.

Blues 2	Watford 0	Att. 16,582
Bertschin 16		
Gemmill 64(pen)		

1986, Division 1.

Blues 1	Manchester United 1	Att. 22,551
Handysides 66	Robson 85	

1994, Division 1.

Oxford United 2	Blues 0	Att. 8,344
Moody 13(pen)		
Byrne 41		

1995, Division 2.

Bristol Rovers 1	Blues 1	Att. 8,010
Whyte(og) 43	Claridge 72	

1997, Divsion 1.

Crystal Palace 0	Blues 1	Att. 16,331
	Grainger 40	

Blues were refused permission to use their change strip as it would cause a colour clash. Instead they borrowed Palace's change strip for this game. Birmingham's Martin O'Connor was sent off on 58 minutes

March 30

The Matches played on this day

1895, Division 1.
Derby County 4   Blues 1   Att. 1,500
                 Mobley
Caesar Jenkyns was sent off.

1901, Division 2.
Lincoln City 3   Blues 1   Att. 3,000
                 McMillan

1907, Division 1.
Derby County 1   Blues 1   Att. 5,000
                 Wigmore

1908, Division 1.
Blues 1   Nottingham Forest 0   Att. 10,000
Jones

1912, Division 2.
Bristol City 2   Blues 1   Att. 8,000
                 Hastings

1918, Wartime.
Notts County 5   Blues 1
                 Tinsley

1929, Division 1.
Blues 0   Newcastle United 0   Att. 30,000

1935, Division 1.
Grimsby Town 4   Blues 3   Att. 10,000
                 White(2,1pen),
                 Bradford
Joe Bradford's last goal for the Blues, his 267th in total from his 15 year career at the club. A club goal scoring record to date.

1940, Wartime.
Blues 4   Luton Town 1
Jones, Trigg(2),
Bodle

Playing record for this day

Playing record for this day is...24 games, Won 10, Drawn 5, Lost 9, GF 38, GA 38.

Today's success rate.....52.08% Year ranking....139th

Match of the Day
FROM 2002
HERE WE COME!!

Four goal blast sends clear messages to play-off rivals

A new look Blues team sent out a new message to the division's play-off hopefuls today that they fear no one. Looking slick, quick, hungry and lethal in front of goal they destroyed a Grimsby team who had arrived at St Andrews as the form team of Division One. The previous week they put six past Wimbledon, the week before they had stunned Molineux with a comfortable away win. However Grimsby were beaten within half an hour after a couple of Bryan Hughes goals, his first since September.

Blues were in total control and from the first minute were laying siege to the Grimsby goal. From one such attack the ball ran to man-of-the-match Hughes who coolly controlled and planted a composed shot into the roof of Coyne's goal giving him no chance from 15 yards. Blues 1-0 up as early as 22 minutes put the game totally out of reach just ten minutes later when a surging run and dragged low cross from Lazaridis eluded Stern John and the Grimsby defence but not by Hughes who swept his shot easily beating Coyne again. Blues could now relax and the home debutants Michael Hughes, Olivier Tebily, Tom Williams and Damien Johnson settled to almost a training exercise the three points and a top six league position now guaranteed, their first occasion since October.

Blues came out for the second half as they did the first and within five minutes Stern John had found acres of space inside the Grimsby six-yard area to steer his header in from Williams cross for 3-0. Grimsby, struggling to keep Blues at bay, could find no respite anywhere on the pitch and when Gallimore failed to control a loose ball instantly he was pressurised then robbed by the diminutive winger Damien Johnson who charged forward toward the Grimsby goal, Coyne reacted came to meet him but Johnson merely poked the ball between his legs and watched it ball trundle over the line to complete the sinking of the Mariners. Despite a few efforts from Mooney, Grimsby made it to 90 minutes without further mishaps. Blues now occupied that sixth place and with a game in hand were just one point away from fourth placed Burnley.

BIRMINGHAM CITY
Vaesen, Kenna, Tebily, Michael Johnson, Williams, Damien Johnson (Eden 74), Michael Hughes (Carter 78), Lazaridis, John (Horsfield 66), Bryan Hughes, Mooney

GRIMSBY TOWN
Coyne, Groves, McDermott, Gallimore, Todd, Butterfield, Pouton, Coldicott (Burnett 69), Campbell, Allen (Falconer 56), Boulding (Robinson 80)

REFEREE
Mr P Taylor (Herts)

Stern John

Birthdays
Frank Clack born today in 1912.

Steve Bruce (Birmingham City Manager)

Blues news extra 1977..TF off the mark for England.

Birmingham City's Trevor Francis helped England to a 5-0 win at Wembley over Luxembourg with his first international goal in only his second appearance for England.

1946, Wartime.

Portsmouth 3	Blues 4	
	Mulraney, Jones,	
	Dougall, Bodle	

1948, Division 2.

WBA 1	Blues 1	Att. 51,945
	Bodle	

1955, Division 2.

Blues 3	Fulham 2	Att. 9,686
Astall 48, 63(pen)	Robson 40	
Lane 66	Dwight 55	

1957, Division 1.

Charlton Athletic 1	Blues 0	Att. 17,839
Hewie 42		

1962, Division 1.

Blues 2	Blackburn Rovers 1	Att. 17,430
Hellawell 11	Lawther 90	
Leek 14		

1963, Division 1.

Blues 1	Sheffield Wednesday 1	Att. 12,272
Auld(pen) 77	Fantham 63	

1964, Division 1.

Aston Villa 0	Blues 3	Att. 25,890
	Hellawell 32	
	Harris 46	
	Lynn 63(pen)	

1968, FA Cup 6th round.

Blues 1	Chelsea 0	Att. 51,556
Pickering 63		

A capacity crowd bringing record gate receipts of £14,400

1970, Division 2.

Blues 0	Aston Villa 2	Att. 41,696
	Rioch 14	
	McMahon 81	

1974, Division 1.

Blues 1	Sheffield United 0	Att. 27,877
Hatton 41		

1982, Division 1.

Liverpool 3	Blues 1	Att. 24,224
Rush 22, 72	Harford 82	
McDermott 74		

1985, Division 2.

Blues 1	Wolverhampton W. 0	Att. 10,230
Geddis 78		

1991, Division 3.

Brentford 2	Blues 2	Att. 6,757
Ratcliffe 6	Frain 41	
Blissett 43	Gleghorn 86	

1996, Division 1.

Grimsby Town 2	Blues 1	Att. 5,475
Groves 35	Barnes 5	
Livingstone 40		

Martin Grainger made his debut for the Blues.

2002, Division 1.

Blues 4	Grimsby Town 0	Att. 23,249
Hughes 22, 32		
John 50		
D.Johnson 64		

March 31

Playing record for this day
Playing record for this day is...25 games, Won 10, Drawn 8, Lost 7, GF 37, GA 38.
Today's success rate.....56% Year ranking....92nd

The Matches played on this day

1891, Football Alliance.
| Sunderland Albion 4 | Blues 0 | Att. 3,000 |

1894, Division 2.
Woolwich Arsenal 1	Blues 4	Att. 6,000
	Jenkyns, Wheldon,	
	Mobley, Hallam	

Blues fourth goal scored by John Hallam was their 100th of the season a record. Blues became the first team to score 100 league goals in one season in Football League history.

1899, Division 2.
| Lincoln City 2 | Blues 2 | Att. 5,000 |
| | Wigmore, Bennett | |

1900, Division 2.
Blues 3	Woolwich Arsenal 1	Att. 3,000
Leake,		
McRoberts, Aston		

1902, Division 1.
| Derby County 0 | Blues 0 | Att. 6,000 |

1917, Wartime.
| Blues 1 | Notts County 1 | |
| Edwards | | |

1923, Division 1.
| Blues 0 | Liverpool 1 | Att. 30,000 |

1928, Division 1.
| Arsenal 2 | Blues 2 | Att. 13,990 |
| | Crosbie, Ellis | |

1934, Division 1.
| Sunderland 4 | Blues 1 | Att. 18,000 |
| | Booton(pen) | |

1945, Wartime.
| Blues 2 | Northampton Town 2 | |
| Massart, Mulraney | | |

1951, Division 2.
| Doncaster Rovers 0 | Blues 1 | Att. 17,000 |
| | Trigg 29 | |

Doncaster's Miller missed a 27th minute penalty

1956, Division 1.
| Manchester City 1 | Blues 1 | Att. 44,799 |
| Hayes 70 | Murphy 21 | |

1961, Division 1.
Cardiff City 0	Blues 2	Att. 23,122
	Orritt 35	
	Harris 79(pen)	

1964, Division 1.
Blues 3	Aston Villa 3	Att. 28,048
Lynn 16(pen), 23	Chatterley 2, 30	
Bloomfield 90	Tindall 13	

1970, Division 2.
Swindon Town 4	Blues 1	Att. 20,835
Butler 7	Summerill 34(pen)	
Rogers 23(pen), 73		
Horsfield 60		

1972, Division 2.
| Oxford United 0 | Blues 1 | Att. 18,740 |
| | Hatton 17 | |

1973, Division 1.
| Norwich City 1 | Blues 2 | Att. 24,209 |
| Stringer 61 | B.Latchford 14, 30 | |

1979, Division 1.
Bristol City 2	Blues 1	Att. 15,584
Meyers 5	Gallagher 47	
Garland 89		

1981, Division 1.
Arsenal 2	Blues 1	Att. 17,431
Stapleton 25	Worthington 65	
O'Leary 83		

1984, Division 1.
Blues 2	Aston Villa 1	Att. 23,993
Stevenson 8	Withe 29	
Gayle 46		

This match screened by BBC's Match of the Day

1986, Division 1.
Nottingham Forest 3	Blues 0	Att. 13,134
Clough 27(pen)		
Metgod 48		
Webb 87		

1987, Division 2.
Blues 2	Sunderland 0	Att. 5,563
North 23		
Whitton 53		

1990, Division 3.
Huddersfield Town 1	Blues 2	Att. 5,837
Withe 14	Bailey 50	
	Gleghorn 84	

Blues' Dennis Bailey hit the post with a 67th minute penalty.

1992, Division 3.
Peterborough United 2	Blues 3	Att. 12,081
Barnes 5, 67	Frain 27(pen)	
	Sturridge 60	
	Matthewson 70	

1997, Division 1.
| Blues 0 | Charlton Athletic 0 | Att. 14,525 |

Match of the Day
FROM 1992
UPPER CLASS BLUES
BEAT THE POSH IN THRILLER

Matthewson strike aids Blues promotion push at London Road

Blues long awaited promotion clash with rivals Peterborough ended with a 70th minute Trevor Matthewson header which claimed the points in a five goal thriller. A real see-saw scoring game was a delight to watch for the 12,081 crowd and left Blues boss Terry Cooper with a smile as long as his lanky match winner's legs. Unable to contain his excitement Cooper beamed, "We played with style tonight, flowing football, it was great. We hit some great crossfield balls and when we play like that I love it, because we are exciting."

The game started with the home side applying all the goalmouth pressure and they deservedly opened the scoring after just five minutes. Posh full back Gary Cooper got round the Blues defence on a left wing overlap to send his cross in for Tony Adcock, he rose well to flick a header into the path of Bobby Barnes who slammed the ball past Dearden from six yards. Blues then found themselves pegged back by a confident Peterborough side, who only allowed them the occasional counter attack. From one such raid 22 minutes later Blues equalised with a controversially awarded penalty. Mark Cooper was adjudged to have been fouled in the area by 'keeper Fred Barber and referee Willard had no hesitation pointing to the spot, Frain took the kick and hammered it straight down the middle of the goal to put Blues back in the game. This galvanised them and within two minutes a shot from Hicks looked on its way in after deflecting off Welsh, only a desperate lunge by Noel Luke scrambled the ball away from off the goal line. Blues continued to hold the upper hand for the remainder of the half and further efforts from Rowbotham and Rodgerson almost gave them an interval lead. Peterborough, however weathered the storm and right at the death came the closest to scoring a second goal when Adcock's header struck the post.

Blues started the second half the better side and their sustained pressure eventually put them into the lead for the first time on the hour. The goal was fittingly scored by man-of-the-match Simon Sturridge after a horrendous mistake from Robinson. Posh's big centre half was guilty of being too casual and his intended back header to his keeper was seized on by the nippy Sturridge who raced in to lob the ball over the stranded Barber. However it wasn't long before Blues returned the gift and handed Peterborough an equaliser on a plate. Just seven minutes after taking the lead, Sterling hit a hopeful and innocuous looking shot across the face of the Blues goal which Hicks decided to shepherd it back to his 'keeper Dearden. The quick thinking Barnes, however, ran in to take full advantage of this defensive casualness nipping in to steal the ball and steer it calmly into goal while the red-faced Blues defender looked on. Blues responded well and three minutes later they won the corner from which Matthewson strode forward to thump in a powerful header past Barber and claim the victory and most importantly those crucial promotion points. Blues were now looking good in third place in the Division Three table.

BIRMINGHAM CITY

Dearden, Clarkson, Frain, Rennie, Hicks, Matthewson, Rodgerson (Sale 78), Mark Cooper, Rowbotham, Gleghorn, Sturridge.

PETERBOROUGH UNITED

Barber, Luke, Ronnie Robinson, Halsall, Dave Robinson, Welsh, Sterling, Gary Cooper, Adcock, Steve Cooper (Charlery 73), Barnes.

REFEREE

Mr G Willard (Worthing)

Peterborough United's London Road stadium

Playing record for this day

Playing record for this day is...23 games, Won 11, Drawn 5, Lost 7, GF 34, GA 26.

Today's success rate.....58.70% Year ranking....69th

Match of the Day

FROM 2000
NEVER A DULL MOMENT

Concede a penalty, finish with nine men, but Blues win a thriller

A penalty save, two sent off, a confrontation in the dugout, a controversial referee, this game had the lot. Oh and yes it also had a goal to decide the contest just to keep the football connoisseur genuinely pleased. The catalogue of incidents started in the 24th minute when match winner Holdsworth was adjudged to have fouled Akinbiyi and when that round of modest protests subsided Keith Curle stepped up only to see his well-placed penalty pushed away by a brilliant save from Thomas Myhre. Myhre, who arrived just days before from Premiership Everton on loan became an instant hero and cries of "Sign him up!" were quickly ringing round the ground. Myhre had matched the feat of Tony Coton against Sunderland in 1980, saving a penalty on his debut only this time in front of the Tilton Road. Spurred on by the new 'keeper's heroics Blues started to get the upper hand and that's when incidents of note became less and less football related. A Martin O'Connor challenge soon had the Wolves dug out rushing towards the touchline. Blues began the second half better and within nine minutes had the all important first goal. From a deep Gary Rowett corner Holdsworth found space at the far post to plant a solid header which crashed into the roof of the net before anyone in gold and black could move.

Blues looked comfortable and seemed to be handling all Wolves had to offer with ease, then came a crazy last ten minutes. Firstly skipper Martin O'Conner was sent off following an incident with the visitors' Kevin Muscat and then Bryan Hughes received a second yellow card for an innocuous offence. However, despite being down to ten men Blues hung on for a victory.

BIRMINGHAM CITY

Myhre, Rowett, Purse, Holdsworth, Michael Johnson, Grainger, Hughes, O'Connor, Lazaridis (Campbell 64), Furlong (Adebola 74) , Rankin (Marcelo 30).

WOLVERHAMPTON WANDERERS

Oakes, Emblen, Pollet, Curle, Muscat, Bazeley, Robinson (Branch 74), Sedgley, Nielsen, Sinton (Ndah h/t), Akinbiyi.

REFEREE

Mr E Wolstenholme (Blackburn)

David Holdsworth

Birthdays

Paul Ivey born today 1961

The Matches played on this day

1892, Football Alliance.		
Blues 3	Grimsby Town 0	Att. 2,000
Hallam, Wheldon(2)		
1898, Division 2.		
Luton Town 1	Blues 2	.Att. 3,000
	Dunlop, Inglis	
1904, Division 1.		
Stoke 1	Blues 0	Att. 6,000
1910, Division 2.		
Blues 1	Clapton Orient 2	Att. 8,000
Burton		
1915, Division 2 .		
Preston North End 2	Blues 0	Att. 10,000
1921, Division 2.		
Barnsley 1	Blues 1	.Att. 20,000
	Davies(pen)	
1923, Division 1.		
Stoke 0	Blues 0	Att. 20,000
1925, Division 1.		
Blackburn Rovers 7	Blues 1	Att. 3,000
	Islip	
1926, Division 1.		
Manchester City 2	Blues 4	Att. 60,000
	Briggs(2), Linley, Crosbie	
1927, Division 1.		
Burnley 0	Blues 2	Att. 8,000
	Bradford, Crosbie	
1930, Division 1.		
Newcastle United 1	Blues 1	Att. 10,000
	Morrall	
1932, Division 1.		
Blues 1	Aston Villa 1	Att. 48,000
Smith		
1938, Division 1.		
Wolverhampton W. 3	Blues 2	Att. 30,000
	Jones, Phillips	
1945, Wartime.		
Wolverhampton W. 2	Blues 1	
	Turner(pen)	
1949, Division 1.		
Arsenal 1	Blues 1	Att. 38,503
	Jordan	

Playing record for this day

Playing record for this day is...27 games, Won 10, Drawn 10, Lost 7, GF 42, GA 36.

Today's success rate.....55.56% Year ranking....96th

Match of the Day
FROM 1968
SUPER BLUES BLIZZARD

Blues stayed in the Second Division promotion race with a win over Derby County in a game with very diverse weather conditions. The first half was played on firm green turf, the second in a raging blizzard, so bad that firstly the referee had to halt play to swap the white football for an orange one, and then he called for sweepers to come on and clear the lines. Almost 30,000 poured into St Andrews to watch the clash, and were rewarded with plenty of action. Early danger from Derby came thanks to ex-Wolves winger Alan Hinton, but Jim Herriot saved all three attempts, including a smashing low 25-yard drive. Barry Bridges' overhead kick was saved by Colin Boulton, and on 22 minutes Malcolm Page shot straight over the crossbar. On 27 minutes Trevor Hockey left the field limping, and was replaced by Ray Martin. It was the third time Hockey had left the field with the same injury, coming back into play on the first two occasions. He was obviously hurt quite badly and incapable of playing with any speed, so it was only a matter of time before he was substituted. It was 32 minutes before the first goal was scored. Malcolm Beard passed the ball to Geoff Vowden, who raced down the right wing and fired an accurate shot which left Boulton with no chance. The second goal came just three minutes later, with John Richardson misjudging a cross from Page and heading it down into his own net. There were more chances in the second half as the snow came down more furiously. The orange ball came into play on 66 minutes, and just a few minutes later play was halted while the snow was swept from the lines. Derby's goal came on 75 minutes when John O'Hare beat two players and ran around Herriot, who had slipped over, to push the ball into the net. Five minutes later Blues regained their two goal lead when Wylie sent Vowden away on the right, and the winger nudged the ball into the goalmouth. Bridges was there to tap the ball into the net and finish the scoring in an enjoyable and eventful game.

BIRMINGHAM CITY

Herriot, Murray, Green, Wylie, Foster, Beard, Vowden, Hockey (Martin), Pickering, Page, Bridges.

DERBY COUNTY

Boulton, Webster, Richardson, Stewart, McFarland, Hopkinson, O'Hare, Durban, Hector, Barker, Hinton.

REFEREE

Mr Vernon Batty

Chelsea goalkeeper Peter Bonetti (r) saves under pressure from Birmingham City's Barry Bridges (l)

Birthdays

Gary Jones born 1951.

Winston Foster

The Matches played on this day

1955, Division 2.
Blackburn Rovers 3	Blues 3	Att. 27,800
Langton 63	Kinsey 17	
Quigley 76	Murphy 21(pen)	
Briggs 85	Lane 73	

1956, Division 1.
Blues 2	WBA 0	Att. 38,892
Murphy 18		
Brown 73		

1960, Division 1.
Blues 2	Everton 2	Att. 24,872
Astall 25	Vernon 19	
Gordon 76	J.Harris 39	

1966, Division 2.
Cardiff City 1	Blues 3	Att. 8,290
Hole 54	Vowden 17, 44	
	Carver(og) 52	

1968, Division 2.
Blues 3	Derby County 1	Att. 29,327
Vowden 32	O'Hare 75	
Richardson 35(og)		
Bridges 80		

1977, Division 1.
Blues 1	Newcastle United 2	Att. 20,283
Fox 73	Craig 11(pen)	
	Barrowclough 89	

1983, Division 1.
| Blues 1 | Swansea City 1 | Att. 13,591 |
| Stevenson 87(pen) | Latchford 80 | |

1988, Division 2.
| Blues 1 | Hull City 1 | Att. 7,059 |
| Williams 65 | Heard 28 | |

1991, Division 3.
| Blues 1 | Tranmere Rovers 0 | Att. 7,675 |
| Yates 61 | | |

1994, Division 1.
Blues 3	Stoke City 1	Att. 13,568
Claridge 35	Carruthers 33	
Ward 55		
Willis 57		

1996, Division 1.
Blues 2	Portsmouth 0	Att. 14,886
P.Barnes 18		
Devlin 79(pen)		

1999, Division 1.
| Crewe Alexandra 0 | Blues 0 | Att. 5,582 |

April 3

Playing record for this day
Playing record for this day is...22 games, Won 10, Drawn 6, Lost 6, GF 40, GA 32.
Today's success rate.....59.09% Year ranking....60th

The Matches played on this day

1896, Division 1.
Burnley 1   Blues 1   Att. 8,000
                   Robertson

1897, Division 1.
Notts County 1   Blues 2   Att. 4,000
                   Abbott(2)

1909, Division 2.
Blues 1   Derby County 1   Att. 5,000
King

1920, Division 2.
Port Vale 1   Blues 3   Att. 15,000
                   Hampton,
                   Lane, Elkes

1926, Division 1.
Liverpool 2   Blues 2   Att. 35,000
                   Bradford(2, 1pen)

1931, Division 1.
Sunderland 1   Blues 0   Att. 15,000
1934, Division 1.
Blues 3   Sheffield W. 0   Att. 24,021
Catlin(og),
Roberts, Guest
1937, Division 1.
Sheffield W. 0   Blues 3   Att. 20,804
                   Morris(2),
                   Richards
Blues keeper Harry Hibbs saved a penalty with the score 1-0.
Dai Richards goal was a cracker from 50 yards out!!
1943, Wartime.
Blues 5   WBA 3
Ottewell(3),
Walton, Dearson
1948, Division 2.
Blues 2   Nottingham Forest 1   Att. 40,000
Stewart,
Mitchell(pen)
1953, Division 2.
Doncaster Rovers 1 Blues 0   Att. 20,000
Lawlor 22(pen)
McMorran was sent off for Doncaster after 17 minutes
1954, Division 2.
Blues 2   Oldham Athletic 1   Att. 15,848
Murphy 70   Green(og) 23
Boyd 88
1956, Division 1.
WBA 0   Blues 2   Att. 35,780
                   Murphy 29, 60

Match of the Day
FROM 1976
BLUES, BY A SHORT HEAD
Derby thriller at St Andrews is settled by rare Francis header

A crowd of 46,251 packed into St Andrews to see this local clash, accompanied by the resounding anthem of "Keep Right On to the End of the Road" and a sea of blue and white in the stands. Skipper Kenny Burns returned to the squad as a third striker, despite his number 4 shirt, playing alongside Trevor Francis and Andy Needham. His presence was enough to ensure a skilful and penetrative front line. It also secured him the opportunity to score a very valuable goal, one which threatened for quite a while to be the winner. The action began with plenty of hard tackles, the inevitable complaints and lots of knocks and bruises, and it was young Needham who had the first goal opportunity. His six-yard shot missed, but Terry Hibbitt followed up on the 18th minute with his first goal for Blues, slotting home a left-foot volley. Villa worked hard, pushing forward, trying to give their away supporters something to cheer about. They were desperate to reward themselves and their fans with their first away win of the season at the ground of their tradional rivals. Their determination paid off five minutes before half time when the equaliser came. Ray Graydon made an impressive cross over from the right and Chris Nicholl leapt high to head down for Gray to swoop in and push it over the line. The crowd began to think that Blues were the ones who would fall first in this battle, adding to their relegation worries. Thankfully, that thought never occurred to the home team who fought on with pride and confidence. There were near misses at both ends of the field before Francis pushed the ball forward on 57 minutes, presenting it to Burns who slotted it between the left-hand upright and John Burridge. Villa's efforts increased, and it wasn't long before a challenge on Graydon from Joe Gallagher in the area resulted in a penalty being awarded. The referee was swamped with home players, arguing against the decision, but he was unmoved. Graydon duly obliged, and his shot went into the net, high over Dave Latchford's left. The frenetic action continued, and a substitution by Blues seemed to help the home team. Bob Hatton came on in place of Gallagher, a decision which had some of the fans annoyed as they hadn't seen the defender holding his back in pain. Just six minutes before the end the game was won with a splendid header from Trevor Francis, weaving its way into the net inside the near post. A few fans managed to evade the police presence and race onto the pitch to congratulate the scorer, and for everyone it was a moment of complete triumph, one to savour for a long time to come.

BIRMINGHAM CITY
Latchford, Calderwood, Want, Kendall, Gallagher (Hatton), Burns, Emmanuel, Francis, Needham, Styles, Hibbitt.
ASTON VILLA
Burridge, Gidman, Robson, Ross, Nicholl, Mortimer, Graydon, Little, Gary, Hamilton, Carrodus.

Archie Styles attempts a tackle on Arsenal's George Armstrong

Birthdays
Gary Sprake born today 1945   Bill Bradbury born today 1933

Sadly Missed
Jimmy Bloomfield died today in 1983, aged 49

Jim Calderwood

The Matches played on this day

1957, Division 1.
| Luton Town 0 | Blues 0 | Att. 15,000 |

1961, Division 1.
Blues 2	Cardiff City 1	Att. 20,047
Harris 60	Moore 90	
Orritt 86		

1963, Division 1.
Blues 2	Bolton Wanderers 2	Att. 13,190
Leek 17, 51	Birch 32	
	Hill 43	

1965, Division 1.
Chelsea 3	Blues 1	Att. 28,975
Tambling 13	Lynn 26(pen)	
Lynn(og) 67		
Bridges 83		

1971, Division 2.
Luton Town 3	Blues 2	Att. 25,172
Busby 36, 43	B.Latchford 5	
Slough 48	Summerill 22	

1976, Division 1.
Blues 3	Aston Villa 2	Att. 46,251
Hibbitt 18	Gray 40	
Burns 57	Graydon 68(pen)	
Francis 84		

1979, Division 1.
| Blues 1 | Ipswich Town 1 | Att. 12,499 |
| Gallagher 64 | Muhren 36 | |

Kevin Dillon had a goal disallowed for the Blues after 25 minutes

1990, Division 3.
Mansfield Town 5	Blues 2	Att. 4,163
Wilkinson 2, 12,	Gleghorn 5	
40, 42, 83	Bailey 88	

1993, Division 1.
Blues 1	West Ham United 2	Att. 19,053
Saville 12	Brown 87	
	Bishop 89	

April 4

Playing record for this day

Playing record for this day is...23 games, Won 6, Drawn 6, Lost 11, GF 28, GA 45.

Today's success rate.....39.13% Year ranking....237th

Match of the Day
FROM 1927
BLUES BLITZ BOLTON
Wanderers left wandering what hit' em at St Andrews

With two valuable points gained in this emphatic win over Bolton, Blues took a substantial step towards First Division safety and re-established themselves as a capable team worthy of gracing the League's elite division for 1927-28. Their 6-1 win was the best of the season beating the previous best of 4-0 set in their previous home game against Manchester City. Although Bolton were without regulars Pym, Nuttall, Seddon and Vizard this was still a great performance and it was a pity that a paltry 8,000 crowd were at St Andrews to witness by far Blues best performance of the season. Bradford had never had better service from his midfield and wingers, nor finer support from his fellow striking partner Briggs. Scriven played his best game in a Blues shirt and Bond on the other flank created enough chances for Birmingham to have won by a bigger margin than they did. Despite a strong cross wind that occasionally caused misjudgement between the Blues back line, their defence led by Liddell handled things soundly. Blues took the lead after just six minutes the right wing pair of Womack and Bond worked cleverly to hand Bradford the opening and he converted with ease. But a minute later a high swirling ball allowed the Bolton forwards to score a 'rush' goal (a goal scored by charging the goalkeeper over the line, allowed only if the ball was in contact with the goalkeeper at the time) Gibson it was who claimed the equaliser. However midway through the first half Blues regained the lead, which they held on to and increased as the game went on. Crosbie and Womack combining well to tee up a Briggs header past Gill in the Bolton goal. Blues took total control of the game after the interval and scored further goals from Cringan, Crosbie, Bradford and Crosbie again to make the final score 6-1.

BIRMINGHAM CITY

Tremelling, Womack, Barton, Liddell, Cringan, Dale, Bond, Crosbie, Bradford, Briggs, Scriven.

BOLTON WANDERERS

Gill, Greehalgh, Finney, Cope, Round, Thornborough, Butler, Jack, Roberts, Gibson, Wright.

Frank Womack

Blues news extra   1942..Friendly RAF XI 1 Blues 1

played at Villa Park.

Sadly Missed

Jeff Hall died today in 1959, aged 29

Playing record for this day

Playing record for this day is...20 games, Won 7, Drawn 6, Lost 7, GF 32, GA 28.

Today's success rate.....50% Year ranking....149th

Match of the Day

FROM 1958

SORRY SUNDERLAND HIT FOR SIX

Blues put final nail to Wearsiders season with super show

Blues repaired some of their away day reputation which had already seen them thrashed by Spurs 7-1, Chelsea 5-1, and Preston 8-0, by handing out a hammering of their own at Roker Park. Blues had earlier shown a liking for the north east with a win at Newcastle in January, their previous away success. Sunderland, needing to win to help in their forlorn fight against relegation, must have seen Birmingham as a good bet for some points and a very beatable side especially having to play them fresh from another away set back at Portsmouth just 24 hours before. The Birmingham team decided to fly the 350-mile trip to Roker Park, but were further burdened when their flight was delayed by 40 minutes due to fog, the team arriving at the ground just in time for kick-off.

The Blues were quick to settle into an attacking stride once the whistle went and straight away they had Sunderland defending desperately. With barely two minutes gone another Birmingham corner taken by Hooper this time landed perfectly on the head of Bryan Orritt who powered in the header which although cleared on the goal line by defender and 'keeper was signalled over the line before Brown blasted in the loose ball. Brown then fluffed a simple looking chance soon after. In another Blues attack Murphy and Hooper combined well, with the latter's shot smashing back off the crossbar, the ball came to Hooper however, who belted the rebound past a grounded Fraser in the Sunderland goal. Blues now were 2-0 up with just nine minutes gone they waited just two more minutes before centre half Trevor Smith tried his luck with a hopeful long range effort, his powerful but slightly misdirected shot deflected off his Sunderland counter part Aitken and ran free to Murphy who had enough space to fire home number three. Blues relentless pressure continued and this caused the hapless Aitken to mistime a simple back pass to his 'keeper, Hooper took full advantage, rushing in to pinch the ball from a stranded Fraser and slot in the Blues fourth. Sunderland down and out of the game, their goal under constant siege, were then reduced to ten men when Anderson had to leave the field to have a head wound treated. They defended admirably with Elliott clearing from his own goal line from an Eddie Brown effort and then Murphy saw his follow up shot also blocked on the line by Sunderland's desperate defending. The Wearsiders also rode their luck, Eddie Brown's first-time volley hitting a post as they made it to half time without further goals.

After the break the first half pattern continued with play almost continually in the Sunderland half. In their best move of the game, superb one touch passing between Hooper, Brown and Murphy set up Astall who made it 5-0 with just five second half minutes gone. This seemed to mark the beginning of a less frantic Blues attack and Sunderland began to have the odd pass or two in previously unknown Blues territory. Indeed it was beginning to look like they might even score themselves and they did on 74 minutes when a Don Revie shot crept in past Schofield. Just as Blues fifth goal seemed to turn Blues off, this consolation effort from Revie quickly revived the machine into overdrive and the game went back into its previous routine of Blues dominating play in every area, and Sunderland deperate to keep them out. With just three minutes remaining man-of-the-match Brown finally got his deserved goal, when he put away another pin-point cross from Hooper. The game finished with one final Blues attack which ended when a 20-yard shot from Brown again thundered back off the woodwork.

SUNDERLAND

Fraser, Hedley, Elliott, Anderson, Aitken, Pearce, Fogarty, Revie, Kichenbrand, O'Neill, Goodchild

BIRMINGHAM CITY

Schofield, Hall, Green, Larkin, Smith, Neal, Hooper, Orritt, Brown, Murphy, Astall

REFEREE

Mr. WR Tuck (Chesterfield)

Bryan Orritt

Birthdays

Dennis Mortimer born today 1952

1890, Football Alliance.		
Darwen 4	Blues 2	Att. 1,000
	Hallam, Morris	
1902, Division 1.		
Blues 1	Nottingham Forest 1	Att. 8,600
Athersmith		
1912, Division 2.		
Leeds City 0	Blues 0	Att. 5,000
1913, Division 2.		
Blackpool 2	Blues 0	Att. 5,000
1915, Division 2.		
Blues 1	Preston North End 1	Att. 10,000
Hodges		
1919, Wartime.		
Blues 0	Notts County 3	
1920, Division 2.		
Fulham 1	Blues 2	Att. 18,000
	Russell(og), Short	
1924, Division 1.		
Blues 4	Newcastle United 1	Att. 20,000
Linley,		
Bradford(2), Crosbie		
1930, Division 1.		
Blues 2	Derby County 4	Att. 20,000
Briggs, Robinson		
1933, Division 1.		
Sheffield W. 1	Blues 1	Att. 6,088
	Curtis	
1947, Division 2.		
Blues 2	Fulham 1	Att. 30,000
Hall, Goodwin		
1952, Division 2.		
Blackburn Rovers 1	Blues 4	Att. 19,000
Warhurst(og) 71	Smith 15	
	Briggs 31, 47	
	Dailey 83	

Blues equalled their best win against Blackburn set in 1931.

1958, Division 1.		
Sunderland 1	Blues 6	Att. 34,184
Revie 74	Orritt 2, 14	
	Hooper 9	
	Murphy 11	
	Astall 54	
	Brown 87	

Future England manager Don Revie hit Sunderland's consolation goal

1969, Division 2.		
Blues 3	Carlisle United 0	Att. 22,397
Hockey 4		
Greenhoff 45, 62		
1975, FA Cup Semi Final.		
Blues 1	Fulham 1	Att. 54,166
Gallagher 57	Mitchell 50	

Played at Hillsborough, Sheffield.
Match screened by ATV's Star Soccer

1980, Division 1.		
QPR 1	Blues 1	Att. 45,181
Burke 90	Dillon 35	
1985, Division 2.		
Grimsby Town 1	Blues 0	Att. 6,926
Henshaw 29(pen)		
1988, Division 2.		
Leicester City 2	Blues 0	Att. 13,541
Osman 12, 20		
1997, Division 1.		
Barnsley 0	Blues 1	Att. 13,092
	Grainger 11	
1999, Division 1.		
Blues 1	Watford 2	Att. 24,877
Holdsworth 88	Mooney 25	
	Daley 57	

April 6

Playing record for this day

Playing record for this day is...24 games, Won 10, Drawn 6, Lost 8, GF 34, GA 31.

Today's success rate.....54.17% Year ranking....114th

The Matches played on this day

1896, Division 1.		
WBA 0	Blues 0	Att. 3,750
1901, Division 2.		
Blues 1	Newton Heath 0	Att. 6,000
McMillan		
1907, Division 1.		
Blues 1	Everton 0	Att. 11,000
Green		
1912, Division 2.		
Blues 4	Burnley 0	Att. 35,000
Hall, Reed(2),		
Hastings		

Arthur Reed making his debut for Blues scored two, and has another disallowed for offside.

1917, Wartime.		
Nottingham Forest 3	Blues 3	
	Bowser(2),	
	Montgomery	
1918, Wartime.		
Blues 3	Notts County 2	
Bowser,		
Wooton, Butler		
1920, Division 2.		
Blues 2	Fulham 0	Att. 20,000
Jones(2)		
1929, Division 1.		
Burnley 4	Blues 0	Att. 12,000
1931, Division 1.		
Blues 1	Sunderland 0	Att. 18,000
Gregg		
1935, Division 1.		
Blues 3	Preston North End 0	Att. 18,000
White(3, 1pen)		
1938, Division 1.		
Liverpool 3	Blues 2	Att. 15,000
	Harris, Jennings	
1940, Wartime.		
Blues 2	Coventry City 0	
Trigg(2)		
1946, Wartime.		
Nottingham Forest 1	Blues 0	
1953, Division 2.		
Blues 2	Doncaster Rovers 1	Att. 12,500
Lane 72	Walker 31	
Boyd 83		
1957, Division 1.		
Blues 1	Sunderland 2	Att. 24,548
Brown 44	Fleming 43	
	Anderson 79	
1962, Division 1.		
West Ham United 2	Blues 2	Att. 22,568
Musgrove 55, 75	Bloomfield 59	
	Lynn 60	

Johnny Schofield saved Bond's penalty on 65 minutes

1963, Division 1.		
Blues 0	Ipswich Town 1	Att. 16, 745
	Stephenson 68	
1965, Division 1.		
Arsenal 3	Blues 0	Att. 16,048
Baker 44		
Skirton 70		
McLintock 71		
1968, Division 2.		
Preston North End 0	Blues 0	Att. 16,872
1974, Division 1.		
Leicester City 3	Blues 3	Att. 28,486
Cross 2	Burns 21, 40, 49	
Glover 19, 65		

This match screened by ATV's Star Soccer

1982, Division 1.		
Blues 0	Everton 2	Att. 12,273
	Heath 1	
	Ainscow 53	

Adrian Heath's goal timed at 37 seconds. Blues; Tony Evans's 85th minute penalty hit the bar.

1986, Division 1.		
Blues 0	Luton Town 2	Att. 8,836
	Harford 49, 90	
1993, Division 1.		
Blues 1	Derby County 1	Att. 15,424
Moulden 81	Johnson 9	

Blues have Darren Rogers sent off after 86 minutes

1996, Division 1.		
Blues 3	Port Vale 1	Att. 17,469
Barnes 6	Porter 67	
Peschisolido 44		
Tait 58		

Match of the Day

FROM 1972

BLUES SPOIL BURNLEY HOPES

League leaders get St Andrews thrashing from new boy Reed

League leaders Burnley who many had admired for their fine and dominant football during the 1911-12 season sat proudly and deservedly on top of the table with just five games of their promotion campaign left to play. Blues on the other hand were settling for a mid-table finish and looking forward to their end of season break with only professional pride to play for.

Blues went into the game with new signing Arthur Reed, an experienced striker from Doncaster Rovers, making his debut. Burnley made no changes and were at full strength. At kick off the only problem for the expectant Division Two champions was the bright sun, a hazard many teams had suffered with at St Andrews during the season. Blues started confidently and the Burnley 'keeper saved well from Hall and Robertson before they had launched any attack of their own. Within the first 15 minutes Gibson too had a snap shot well saved by the visiting 'keeper and Reed was unlucky when he scored only to have the effort disallowed after being caught fractionally offside. It was the Blues who deservedly went ahead on 20 minutes though, their pressure eventually paying off. Robertson and Gardner exchanged a couple of quick passes which left Hall with a clear opening and he duly planted a crisp right foot shot past a stranded Dawson. Just six minutes later Blues further stunned the leaders with another goal. This time Hall was the provider, after good work from Hastings he fed Reed who fired home from the edge of the penalty area for his first goal for the Blues to make it 2-0. Blues were by far the better side and only some inspired saves from Dawson prevented a huge score for the rampant Blues strikers three of which had efforts blocked by the keeper inside a frantic four minute barrage. At half time Blues were given a resounding cheer from the delighted crowd of 35,000.

Blues continued their relentless pressure at the start of the second period and were 3-0 up on 61 minutes. They broke down the right wing through Gibson who sent over a high swirling cross which everyone in the centre missed, the ball ran to Hastings who had chased in from the opposite flank to hit an unstoppable first-time shot past Dawson. They then made the score an incredible 4-0 with just 15 minutes remaining when Reed grabbed a second goal with a simple header. Burnley had been torn apart and looked dejected at the final whistle as they left the field, the result clearly affected them for the remainder of the season as they blew their championship hopes and worse they were pipped at the post for promotion too. A game at St Andrews should never be taken lightly!!

BIRMINGHAM CITY

Bailey, Ball, Womack, Gardner, Tinkler, Bumphrey, Gibson, Hall, Reed, Robertson, Hastings.

BURNLEY

Dawson, Reid, Taylor, McClaren, Boyle, Watson, Nesbitt, Hodgson, Freeman, Weightman, Harris.

REFEREE

Mr T Kirkham (Burslem)

Blues news extra   1942...Blues 2 Aston Villa 1

Nothing was at stake today apart from city pride as Blues edged out their neighbours by 2-1 in this 'friendly' played at St Andrews.

1957...Jeff Hall's 14th cap for England

England 2 Scotland 1

Duncan Edwards hit the winner with a 20 yard shot seven minutes from time. Blues full back Jeff Hall also had a good game after a shaky start.

Birthdays

Peter Atherton born today 1970   Lindley Jenkins born today 1954

April 7

Playing record for this day

Playing record for this day is...25 games, Won 9, Drawn 9, Lost 7, GF 29, GA 35.

Today's success rate.....54% Year ranking....116th

Match of the Day

FROM 1958

POOR POMPEY PUMMELLED

St Andrews crowd enjoy the goal blitz as Blues make it ten in two

Two wins over the Easter Bank Holiday finally lifted the threat of relegation that had loomed over St Andrews for almost the entire 1957-58 season. Blues, continued their good form which saw them beat Sunderland on Good Friday, and moved safely from the bottom three with an important, if not entirely convincing, display against Portsmouth. For long periods they looked shaky, and when visiting centre half Rutter injured an ankle early in the first half they should have made more of this misfortune, but not until the last half hour did they really look comfortable. It was Blues, however, who had the better start, but it quickly became apparent their problem was to convert good-looking approach play into goals. It was Portsmouth who had the game's first real opportunity when Crawford, deputising for Blues' old boy Govan, got clear but shot straight at Schofield. Soon after this Rutter fell awkwardly at the other end, twisting his ankle. He had to leave the field and, although he returned within ten minutes, he spent the remainder of the game hobbling in the centre-forward position. Dickinson dropped back into the vacancy he had left, and despite this disadvantage it was Portsmouth again who came closest to scoring when Harris shot against the post from Crawford's corner kick. Blues finally had an effort on goal shortly afterwards, and Uprichard only kept out Murphy's shot with his legs. Encouraged by this, the 23,380 crowd lifted the home team. This brought relief all round when Hooper scrambled in a much needed, but scrappy, goal. A deep centre by Murphy was caught by the keeper, but Hooper clattered into him, and as the ball dropped from Uprichard's grip, Hooper prodded it over the line. Blues eased the tension quickly in the second half when Murphy headed in Brown's cross from close range in the 48th minute. Blues then allowed Pompey back into the game 11 minutes later when Smith miskicked a clearance completely in front of goal and Crawford took full advantage. However just a minute later, following a free kick, Uprichard saved Astall's shot, only for the ball to land at Orritt's feet. He swept it into the net from just inside the six-yard box. This third goal signalled the end for Portsmouth, and they rarely encroached into the Blues' half from then on. This allowed Blues the attacking freedom they had strived for all afternoon.

Blues got a fourth goal to wrap up the points in the 76th minute. Hooper broke free from inside the Pompey half, and from his shot, which probably would have gone in anyway, Brown raced through just to make sure. The goal stood despite offside appeals, and the game finished Birmingham City 4, Portsmouth 1.

BIRMINGHAM CITY
Schofield, Hall, Green, Larkin, Smith, Neal, Hooper, Orritt, Brown, Murphy, Astall.
PORTSMOUTH
Uprichard, McGee, Wilson, Phillips, Rutter, Dickinson, Harris, Gordon, Dougan, Barnard, Crawford.

(L-R) Dick Neal and Harry Hooper

Blues news extra   1981...Friendly at St Andrews.

Blues 0 Kuwait National XI 2

Birthdays

Barry Fry born today in 1945

Sadly Missed

Peter Murphy died today in 1975, aged 53

The Matches played on this day

1890, Football Alliance.		
Newton Heath 9	Blues 1	Att. 4,000
	W.Devey	
This equalled Blues record defeat		
1894, Division 2.		
Blues 3	Notts County 0	Att. 8,500
Hands(2), Walton		
1896, Division 1.		
Blues 2	Sheffield United 1	Att. 6,000
Mobley(2)		
1900, Division 2.		
Barnsley 1	Blues 1	Att. 2,000
	Leake	
1906, Division 1.		
Derby County 0	Blues 0	Att. 5,000
1923, Division 1.		
Liverpool 0	Blues 0	Att. 30,000
1928, Division 1.		
Blues 2	Portsmouth 0	Att. 30,000
Bond, Ellis		
1934, Division 1.		
Blues 0	Chelsea 3	Att. 30,000
1939, Division 1.		
Liverpool 4	Blues 0	Att. 30,000
1945, Wartime.		
Blues 0	Wolverhampton W. 0	
1947, Division 2.		
Blues 2	Newcastle United 0	Att. 43,000
Bodle, Trigg		
1950, Division 1.		
Manchester United 0	Blues 2	Att. 47,170
	Stewart 30	
	Berry 70	
Blues recorded their only away win of the 1949-50 season.		
1951, Division 1.		
Blues 3	Sheffield United 0	Att. 22,000
Rowley 18		
Higgins 30		
Warhurst 36		
1956, Division 1.		
Blues 2	Cardiff City 1	Att. 37,154
Baker(og) 14	Hitchens 55	
Brown 42		
The win put Blues third in the Division One table		
1958, Division 1.		
Blues 4	Portsmouth 1	Att. 23,380
Hooper 31	Crawford 59	
Murphy 48		
Orritt 60		
Brown 76		
1969, Division 2.		
Blues 0	Charlton Athletic 0	Att. 25,894
1973, Division 1.		
Blues 2	Liverpool 1	Att. 48,114
B.Latchford 44	Smith 60	
Hatton 57		
Liverpool defender Emlyn Hughes sent off in the 90th minute.		
1976, Division 1.		
Newcastle United 4	Blues 0	Att. 18,547
Burns 37		
Gowling 41		
Macdonald 72, 80		
1979, Division 1.		
Blues 2	Southampton 2	Att. 12,125
Barrowclough 38,	Baker 47	
84(pen)	Hayes 74	
1980, Division 2.		
Blues 0	West Ham United 0	Att. 28,377
1984, Division 1.		
Manchester United 1	Blues 0	Att. 39,891
Robson 27		
Blues 'keeper Tony Coton saved a twice taken Ray Wilkins penalty in the 90th minute.		
1990, Division 3.		
Blues 0	Bury 0	Att. 6,808
1991, Division 3.		
Bolton Wanderers 3	Blues 1	Att. 11,280
Philliskirk 33	Gayle 44	
Darby 38		
Cunningham 64		
2001, Division 1.		
Wimbledon 3	Blues 1	Att. 6,619
Neilson 15	Marcelo 85	
Hughes 70		
Williams 72		
2002, Division 1.		
Blues 1	Portsmouth 1	Att. 25,030
John 2	Pitt 84	

April 8

1875

Blues won 4-3 on aggregate. Blues keeper Schofield suffered a cut eye after a stone thrown from the crowd hit him.

19-year-old Blues 'keeper Dave Latchford made his debut

This match shown on ATV's Star Soccer

Jim Montgomery saved, Pop Robson's 48th minute penalty

Playing record for this day

Playing record for this day is...23 games, Won 7, Drawn 7, Lost 9, GF 30, GA 29.
Today's success rate.....45.65% Year ranking....198th

Match of the Day

FROM 1985
BLUES BRIGHTEN
BANK HOLIDAY GLOOM

On a typically wet Easter Monday Blues ended their mini-crisis with a resounding win over Sheffield United to rekindle their promotion hopes. They went into the game with three changes from the side which had lost to Grimsby. Out went Byron Stevenson, Mark Prudhoe was bought in to make his debut, whilst Martin Kuhl returned to the side to replace Stevenson. Blues third change was to introduce a young Scot, Andy Kennedy, for the suspended David Geddis. United too had selection problems and were without regular first teamers Kenworthy, Edwards, Eves, Stancliffe and Morris.

Blues were the first to adapt to the wet conditions. After some confident passing football they took the lead on 30 minutes when Daly controlled a super crossfield pass from Kuhl in his stride to side-foot past ex-Villa 'keeper Burridge. Despite a couple of half chances Blues went into the break 1-0 up and new keeper Prudhoe had hardly been troubled the entire 45 minutes.

Blues increased their lead just two minutes after the break. The lively Kennedy latched on to a weak backpass from West and although his first shot was blocked by Burridge, he followed up with a header which proved unstoppable. The striker was having a great debut and 15 minutes later his enterprise and threat led to Blues third goal. After Kennedy had controlled well to give himself space his shot was held up in the mud, Clarke reacted to the stationary ball first to crack it past a wrong-footed Burridge. This led to United's best period of the game and within three minutes they reduced the score to 3-1 when Cockerill got free of the Blues defence to head home from close range. With the game almost over Daly collected a loose ball in midfield to send Clarke through on goal. Clarke made no mistake with the one-on-one with the 'keeper and Blues finished up 4-1 winners.

BIRMINGHAM CITY
Prudhoe, Ranson, Roberts, Wright, Hagan, Kuhl, Daly, Clarke, Bremner, Kennedy, Hopkins.
SHEFFIELD UNITED
Burridge, Heffernan, Eckhardt, McGeeney, Amott, West, Smith, Cockerill, Philliskirk (Cooper), Black, Bolton.

John Roberts (r) beats Manchester United's Jim Holton (l) to a header

Birthdays

Peter Warmington born today in 1934

Playing record for this day

Playing record for this day is...24 games, Won 13, Drawn 3, Lost 8, GF 39, GA 32.
Today's success rate.....60.42% Year ranking....50th

Match of the Day
FROM 1966
10/10 FOR TEN GOAL THRILLER

No one in the 13,083 crowd would have predicted the outcome of this pulsating game at St Andrews when the sides kicked off. In fact the scoreline remained undecided right up to the 84th minute when the last of ten goals hit the back of the net.

It was Blues who netted first in the 15th minute through Trevor Hockey, he smartly controlled a teasing right wing cross from Jackson to hit a crisp, low cross shot past Matthews in the Derby goal. Derby roared back and it took them six minutes to equalise through a simple goal from Durban. From a corner taken by Hughes, Thomas headed the ball against Herriott and it fell kindly to the Derby forward who prodded the ball into the empty net from a yard out. Now goals began to flow in quick succession and within three minutes Derby turned the whole game round when Durban netted a second goal. This time he sprang free through the middle of the Blues defence to collect a long ball from Daniel, drew Herriott out of goal before hitting a cracking shot across the Blues 'keeper into the far corner. Before the the man with the plastic-coated number 2 had slid the panel into the Kop scoreboard he was already making his way for another as Blues swarmed forward to earn a penalty after Saxton brought down Jackson. Beard scored from the spot-kick and the overworked scoreboard attendant was off again in search of a replacement panel. A classic match was already taking shape when Blues took the lead for a second time after 33 minutes. With Blues piling men forward in an all-out attack, right back Fraser got to the byline to whip in a centre which Saxton instinctively knocked into his own goal. Amazingly the score didn't change again for the next 12 minutes and both sides left the field for half time to a rousing ovation from the excited crowd.

The play resumed after the restart when Derby's determination to fight Blues blitz brought them another equalising goal within two minutes. Hughes laid on a great ball for Buxton to chase down the right wing. Cutting back into the area, Buxton finished by hitting the ball under Herriott's dive and into the back of the net. The goals still kept on coming and just three minutes later Blues were ahead for the third time in the game. A corner taken by Hockey just evaded the diving Jackson and the ball ran to Beard who blasted it in via the underside off the crossbar.

At the other end there was a real piece of drama, when Herriott pulled of a magnificent save to deny Durban his hat-trick, yes for once a goal was prevented much to the relief of Mr Scoreboard attendant. The save became more significant in the 67th minute when Blues increased their lead to 5-3. Vowden became the latest scorer when he converted a pin-point cross from Hockey with a beautifully timed header. With six minutes to play Derby gave themselves a chance of saving the game when they reduced the score to 5-4. A high, swirling cross had Blues substitute Thomson in trouble and he ended up deflecting the ball past Herriott for the game's second own goal. A rejuvenated Derby then equalised for the third time a minute later. Durban finished off some great work by Buxton to complete his hat-trick.

BIRMINGHAM CITY
Herriott, Fraser, Martin, Wylie, Foster, Beard, Jackson, Vincent, Fenton (Thomson 64), Vowden, Hockey.
DERBY COUNTY
Matthews, Richardson, Daniel, Webster, Saxton, Upton, Hughes, Thomas, Buxton, Durban, Hopkinson.

(l-r) Winston Foster, Trevor Hockey, Ray Martin, Ron Wylie

The Matches played on this day

1892, Football Alliance.		
Walsall 3	Blues 4	Att. 4,000
	Hallam,	
	Wheldon(2), Hands	
1898, Division 2.		
Newton Heath 3	Blues 1	Att. 3,000
	Higgins	
1904, Division 1.		
Blues 1	Derby County 0	Att. 7,000
Jones		
1906, Division 1.		
Blues 1	Everton 0	.Att. 10,000
Mounteney		
1909, Division 2.		
Stockport County 3	Blues 2	Att. 6,000
	Chapple, Lowe	
1910, Division 2.		
Blackpool 2	Blues 0	Att. 6,000
1917, Wartime.		
Blues 4	Nottingham Forest 3	
Whitehouse(3), Bell		
1921, Division 2.		
Blues 3	Nottingham Forest 0	Att. 30,000
Crosbie, Lane(2)		
1924, Division 1.		
Newcastle United 2	Blues 1	Att. 8,000
	Bradford	
1927, Division 1.		
Blues 2	Newcastle United 0	Att. 30,000
Bradford, Bond		
1928, Division 1.		
Huddersfield Town 2	Blues 0	Att. 15,000
1932, Division 1.		
Huddersfield Town 1	Blues 1	Att. 7,000
	Briggs	

In an accidental collision, Blues keeper Hibbs suffered a serious facial injury which caused him to lose six teeth.

1938, Division 1.		
Blues 2	Bolton Wanderers 0	Att. 20,000
Harris, Phillips		
1949, Division 1.		
Huddersfield Town 0	Blues 0	Att. 18,856
1955, Division 2.		
Blues 3	Plymouth Argyle 1	Att. 25,078
Lane 32	McJarrow 87	
Kinsey 57		
Govan 62		

Jackie Lane scored a fantastic solo effort, receiving the ball on the half way line he took on and beat the entire Plymouth defence before slotting the ball in the net.

1960, Division 1.		
Blackpool 0	Blues 1	Att. 13,595
	Gordon 75	

Birthdays
David Jones born today in 1940

Ian Rodgerson born today in 1966

Darren Rogers born today in 1970

Sadly Missed
Cyril Trigg died today in 1993 aged 76

April
9
1875

The Matches played on this day

1966, Division 2.
Blues 5	Derby County 5	Att. 13,083
Hockey 13	Durban 21, 24, 85	
Beard 25(pen) 50	Buxton 47	
Saxton(og) 33	Thomson(og) 84	
Vowden 67		

1971, Division 2.
Oxford United 1	Blues 0	Att. 16,196
Cassidy 90		

Blues failed to score in a League game for the first time since November 21 1970, 19 matches ago.

1975, FA Cup Semi Final, replay.
Blues 0	Fulham 1	Att. 35,205
	Mitchell 120	

After extra time. Played at Maine Road, Manchester

1977, Division 1.
Blues 3	Bristol City 0	Att. 19,626
Francis 10(pen), 28, 89(pen)		

1983, Division 1.
Blues 0	Norwich City 4	Att. 11,733
	Bertschin 25, 56	
	Deehan 41, 74	

1988, Division 2.
Blues 1	Sheffield United 0	Att. 7,046
Kennedy 39		

1991, Leyland Daf Cup, Southern Area Final, 2nd leg.
Brentford 0	Blues 1	Att. 8,745
	Sturridge 76	

Blues won 3-1 on aggregate

1994, Division 1.
Blues 3	Southend United 1	Att. 14,307
Doherty 23	Bressington 61(pen)	
Saville 47		
Willis 58		

Jim Herriot

Birthdays
Dave Latchford born today in 1949

Playing record for this day
Playing record for this day is...31 games, Won 16, Drawn 3, Lost 12, GF 39, GA 32.
Today's success rate.....56.45% Year ranking....89th

April 10

Match of the Day

FROM 2002

BLUES CREWES TO PLAY-OFFS

Another good home win as Blues aim for fourth time lucky

Blues' game in hand ended with an emphatic win which put them into fourth spot and barring an unthinkable catastrophe should have ensured their fourth play-off berth in successive seasons. With ticket prices just £5 for this resheduled game, Blues were urged on in a great atmosphere. From a corner after just 20 seconds Mooney brought a finger-tip save from Bankole in the Crewe goal with a fierce header. Crewe had come to St Andrews without a win in nine games and were in deep relegation trouble, Blues were unbeaten in seven and looking like a side on a promotion mission. However this could have just as easily been the banana skin Blues had thus far avoided. This looked evident when Crewe who had weathered the early storm moved forward confidently passing the ball about and defying their precarious league position. From one such move Ashton's final header was cleared of the goal line by Grainger. Blues needed a goal to settle the crowd and their own nerves and its arrival was as perfectly timed as Blues own surge up the table in recent weeks. Paul Devlin always had the better of his full back and when given the opportunity to do so again from a long Grainger pass he made the break through. Chesting the ball down and chasing forward he sent over a pacy curling cross which Bankole had to dive full stretch to palm away, unfortunately for him the ball fell to Stern John who belted the ball back into the net from 15 yards. Another flowing move ended with John flicking the outside of a post and moments later a brilliant Bryan Hughes run ended with a shot which just curled wide. On the stroke of half time Blues doubled their lead when Horsfield powered into the box and as he looked for options he was bundled over by Shaun Smith. Darren Carter passed the ball cooly into the corner of the net from penalty spot range. This was Carter's first goal for the club and the smile was still beaming on his face as he proudly made his way to the dressing rooms at the half time break.

Blues resumed in superb form and within four minutes had settled the game after Crewe had just hit a post win a bad miss just seconds earlier. Hughes again running from midfield sent over a delicate cross which reached Mooney at the far post. He cleverly lobbed his header over Bankole who followed the ball as it dropped into the bottom corner of the net. The game was safe Blues relaxed and as time ticked away a rare defensive error from Tebily left substitute Rodney Jack with a clear path to rifle in a consolation goal in the 85th minute.

BIRMINGHAM CITY
Vaesen, Kenna, Grainger, Tebily, Purse, Devlin, Hughes, Horsfield (Damien Johnson 71), John, Mooney (Lazaridis 80), Carter.
CREWE ALEXANDRA
Bankole, Wright, Walton, Sodje, Smith, Lunt, Whalley (Rix h/t), Sorvel, Vaughan, Ashton (Jack 79), Hulse (Tait 52).

REFEREE
Mr A Butler (Sutton-in-Ashfield)

Nico Vaesen

Birthdays
Robert Hatton born today in 1947   **Stephen Claridge born today in 1966**

April 10

The Matches played on this day

1948, Division 2.
Blues 2   Bradford Park Ave 1   Att. 16,782
Mitchell (pen)
Stewart

1950, Division 2.
Blues 0   Manchester United 0   Att. 35,863

1954, Division 2.
Blues 0   Blackburn Rovers 3   Att. 32,100

1957, Division 1.
Aston Villa 2   Blues 1   Att. 29,893
                 Murphy

1965, Division 1.
Blues 0   Leicester City 2   Att. 12,460
                 Vowden, Jackson

1971, Division 2.
Blues 1   Blackburn Rovers 0   Att. 25,572
Campbell

1976, Division 1.
Burnley 1   Blues 0   Att. 13,668

1982, Division 1.
Blues 0   Leeds United 1   Att. 14,497

1990, Division 3.
Cardiff City 0   Blues 1   Att. 3,322
                 Hopkins

1993, Division 1.
Sunderland 1   Blues 2   Att. 16,382
                 Moulden, Saville

1996, Division 1.
Millwall 2   Blues 0   Att. 9,271

1999, Division 1.
Swindon Town 0   Blues 1   Att. 8,896
                 Rowett

2001, Division 1.
Tranmere Rovers 1 Blues 0   Att. 8,084

2002, Division 1.
Blues 3   Crewe Alexandra 1   Att. 28,615
John, Carter,
Mooney

Tommy Mooney

Playing record for this day
Playing record for this day is...22 games, Won 7, Drawn 5, Lost 10, GF 42, GA 30.
Today's success rate.....43.18% Year ranking....215th

April 11

Match of the Day

FROM 1903
THE SCOREBOARD STRIKES 12!

The Blues run riot at Muntz Street

Any chance of Blues having the end-of-season promotion jitters was quickly dispelled at Muntz Street as they blazed to their biggest win for over ten years. Blues needed the win to keep hold of their hopes of promotion and faced a tough Doncaster side who had already beaten them 2-0 earlier in the season. Shortly before kick-off Bob McRoberts, passed himself fit to play although suffering from a heavy cold.

Blues battered the Rovers goal from the the kick off and Eggett in goal for the visitors saved from Wilcox, Field and Leonard before the Blues finally converted their overwhelming pressure into the opening goal on 18 minutes. Arthur Leonard tucked away a loose ball that the Rovers defence had twice failed to clear adequately. On 29 minutes Freddie Wilcox was put through by McRoberts to fire in the second. Wilcox then produced a magnificent opportunity for Field to score just five minutes before half time. A rare Rovers break had barely got over the half way line when inside left Wilcox intercepted the ball and ran 40 yards, beating player after player in a superb dribble, then he calmly laid the ball off to Field ten yards out who smashed it in with a first-time shot. Just before the break McRoberts tried an effort from distance and his 30-yard pile driver was deflected onto the cross bar from Eggett's oustretched leg in yet another remarkable reflex save.

After the short break Doncaster emerged keen to prise away some consolation in the second period. However it wasn't to be, Blues were if anything more rampant and determined to add to their three goal first-half tally. The suffering Bob McRoberts was in sharp form and at every opportunity was egging his team on to press forward. Leonard reached his hat-trick, his third goal a beauty from 40 yards out which Eggett didn't even see before it bulged the net behind him.

Wilcox then notched his third, and then a fourth when McRoberts again set him up with a clean opportunity. Wilcox then returned the favour but amazingly McRoberts who had a hand in eight of the second half goals miskicked and the ball rolled wide of the open goal. Leonard then matched Wilcox's goalscoring feat by shooting home his fourth goal and Blues ninth. Blues had opportunities to score almost every minute and Field was soon guilty of fluffing an easy chance. Athersmith then made it double figures, Jack Dougherty headed in a corner for number 11, and the brilliant Bob McRoberts created another piece of history for the club when he completed a dozen up for the Blues.

This win kept up the pressure at the top of the table and strengthened Blues position in second place.

BIRMINGHAM CITY
Dorrington, Goldie, Wassell, Beer, Dougherty, Howard, Athersmith, Leonard, McRoberts, Wilcox, Field.

DONCASTER ROVERS
Eggett, Simpson, Langton, Murphy, Aston, Wright, Langham, Richards, Price, Ratcliffe, Robinson.

REFEREE
Mr D Hammond (Heywood, Lancashire)

Terry Hennessey (see below)

Blues news extra   2000...Hennessey stars in great Welsh win.

Wales 4 Northern Ireland 0
Terry Hennessey won his first cap as a Blues
player at Ninian Park, Cardiff. The win was inspired by
John Charles who scored all four of the Welsh goals.

The Matches played on this day

1898, Division 2.

Blues 1	Newcastle United 0	Att. 5,000
Higgins		

1902, Division 1.

Blues 5	Derby County 1	Att. 5,000
Leonard(2),		
McMillan,		
McRoberts, Wharton		

1909, Division 2.

Blues 1	Leeds City 0	Att. 3,000
Bumphrey		

1913, Division 2.

Blues 3	Huddersfield Town 2	Att. 10,000
Jones(2), Robertson		

1919, Wartime.

Notts County 1	Blues 2	
	Gardner, Elkes	

1924, Division 1.

Sheffield United 0	Blues 2	Att. 8,000
	Bradford, Linley	

1930, Division 1.

Manchester City 1	Blues 4	Att. 25,000
	Fillingham(2),	
	Hicks, Briggs	

Tom Fillingham scored twice on his debut.

1947, Division 2.

Bury 2	Blues 0	Att. 18,882

1952, Division 2.

Blues 1	QPR 0	Att. 28,000
Trigg 75		

Ken Green missed a penalty on 31 minutes.

1958, Division 1.

Blues 1	Leeds United 1	Att. 23,102
Orritt 63	O'Brien 62	

1965, Division 1.

Aston Villa 3	Blues 0	Att. 37,003
Woosnam 11		
Chatterley 16		
Hateley 67		

1966, Division 2.

Wolverhampton W. 2	Blues 0	Att. 27,500
McIlmoyle 28		
Hunt 67		

Playing record for this day

Playing record for this day is...23 games, Won 9, Drawn 1, Lost 13, GF 29, GA 41.

Today's success rate.....41.30% Year ranking....227th

Match of the Day
FROM 1993

WOULD YOU BELIEVE IT!!
4-1 and Blues serve up even more 'fun 'n games'

The Blues went into this game still in search of points to safely avoid the drop into the relegation zone, with just two home games after this a win would ease the tension around St Andrews. Instead Swindon and Glen Hoddle had Blues manager Terry Cooper and the home crowd completely stunned, and left the team hanging on to their First Division survival.

The game started tentatively with neither side creating anything to suggest a ten-goal thriller, at this point that scenario looked as likely as a snowstorm at half time. Then in a rare moment of brilliance Andy Saville threaded an inch-perfect pass to Dean Peer who placed his shot neatly into the net and the Blues had a one goal lead on 25 minutes. This brought a tame game to life and immediately Blues keeper Gosney was involved in the action as Swindon looked to cancel out the Blues advantage. Blues held off the mini-onslaught and after breaking down a Swindon corner counter attacked with full back John Frain. He raced clear to pick up Moulden's through ball and lashed home a fine low shot which beat Digby and put Blues 2-0 up on 29 minutes. As half time approached with a deserved two goal cushion Swindon pulled one back through Shaun Taylor, the big centre half heading in a Micky Hazard free kick just two minutes before the interval.

Blues caught Swindon two minutes after the resumption through Moulden, his low cross shot eluding the unsighted Digby as the ball past the covering Calderwood and Hoddle and fizzed into the corner of the net. Blues had regained their two goal advantage. With confidence now flowing through the whole team Blues put the game 'safe' on 51 minutes when a neat move involving Peer, Rodgerson and Smith set up Saville who smashed his shot into the roof of the net. Swindon were down, out and beaten they needed to change their approach and a miracle, Hoddle moved forward into a more attacking midfield role and left a three man defence and a transformation started to take shape. With half an hour remaining Craig Maskell latched onto to another fabulous pass by man-of-the-match Hazard and as Gosney came to meet him he clipped the ball to reduce the lead to 4-2.

Now it was all Swindon pressure and the Blues midfield seemed to have evaporated within five minutes another dangerous looking cross from Taylor was only partially clawed away by Gosney at full stretch, the ball landing perfectly on Mitchell's head close in and Swindon now were just one goal behind. The pressure on the Blues defence was relentless there was no stopping Hoddle and Hazard and survival was the sole objective. With 14 minutes remaining Swindon equalised in style when a superb moved started by Hoddle and Ling allowed Mitchell to net his second goal with a neat finish. Two minutes later Swindon completed an incredible comeback when Paul Bodin's corner was hammered in by Maskell to give his side a 5-4 lead and still time to add more. In the last minute Mitchell completed his hat-trick when he outpaced Matthewson to collect a long ball from Ling, nicked it away from Gosney, who had come out to cover, and slotted easily into the empty net. The final whistle went moments later to a chorus of booing from a very disappointed home crowd who only 30 minutes before were enjoying their team's 4-1 lead.

BIRMINGHAM CITY

Gosney, Clarkson (Mardon), Frain, Parris, Dryden, Matthewson, Moulden, Rodgerson, Saville, Peer, Smith.

SWINDON TOWN

Digby, Summerbee, Bodin, Hoddle, Calderwood, Taylor, Hazard, MacLaren, Mitchell, Ling, Maskell.

REFEREE

Mr J Lloyd (Wrexham)

Blues news extra   1890...Kiddy fall Short.

Blues beat Kidderminster 4-1 in a friendly played at Muntz Street helped by centre forward Charlie Short's brace. Both his goals came early in the first half.

Blues news extra   1924...Percy Barton the first..

Blues full back Percy Barton played in the first international at the newly opened Wembley Stadium against Scotland. This was Barton's sixth cap for England and the game finished 1-1.

Blues news extra   1926...Cup shared after stalemate

The Lord Mayor of Coventry Cup final ended in a 2-2 draw between Blues and Coventry, both sides held the trophy for six months each.

Paul Moulden

April 12

The Matches played on this day

1967, FA Cup 6th round, replay.

Tottenham Hotspur 6	Blues 0	Att. 52,304
Venables 2, 21		
Gilzean 23		
Greaves 50, 75		
Saul 86		

1969, Division 2.

Aston Villa 1	Blues 0	Att. 53,584
Simmons 55		

1974, Division 1.

Burnley 2	Blues 1	Att. 16,991
Hankin 15, 49	Campbell 24	

1975, Division 1.

Coventry City 1	Blues 0	Att. 24,180
Green 28		

1980, Division 1.

Leicester City 2	Blues 1	Att. 26,075
Wilson 11	Gemmill 79(pen)	
Young 27		

1982, Division 1.

Sunderland 2	Blues 0	Att. 14,821
West 22, 43		

1983, Division 1.

Luton Town 3	Blues 1	Att. 12,868
Hill 5, 26	Hopkins 68	
Horton 8(pen)		

1986, Division 1.

Newcastle United 4	Blues 1	Att. 19,981
Beardsley 14, 64	Hopkins 78	
Anderson 79		
Whitehurst 88		

Newcastle's Paul Gascoigne sent off in the 2nd half.

1993, Division 1.

Blues 4	Swindon Town 6	Att. 17,903
Peer 25	Taylor 43	
Frain 29	Maskell 60, 78	
Moulden 47	Mitchell 65, 76, 89	
Saville 51		

1987, Division 2.

Blues 0	WBA 1	Att. 11,158
	Reilly 5	

Blues defender Brian Roberts played on despite suffering a broken leg for the last 30 minutes of the game.

1997, Division 1.

Blues 1	Huddersfield Town 0	Att. 14,394
Jenkins(og) 90		

Immediately after his stoppage time own goal, Steve Jenkins was sent off. Blues already had Paul Furlong sent off in the 40th minute.

Playing record for this day

Playing record for this day is...24 games, Won 8, Drawn 11, Lost 5, GF 31, GA 29.

Today's success rate.....56.25% Year ranking....90th

Match of the Day

FROM 1985

GEDDIS FIRES THE BLUES

Promotion party starts early with super hat-trick

A large and vocal crowd saw an exciting and hard fought battle at Fratton Park which resulted in a well-deserved hat trick for Geddis and a goal for ex-Blues player Kevin Dillon. The game began with an impetuous tackle from Hopkins resulting in a free kick being awarded to Portsmouth. However a long high shot down the middle was turned aside by Roberts. Only two minutes in and Birmingham conceded another free kick at the corner of their area. Hopkins, kicked the ball away and was booked for dissent. Birmingham fans could only watch in trepidation as former Blues player Dillon, with plenty to prove to Ron Saunders, rolled his shot down onto Seaman's near side. The 'keeper was helpless to prevent it from striking the inside of the post, and then from rolling alarmingly across the face of the six yard area. thus denying Pompey. But after seven minutes it was Geddis, taking a diagonal pass from Daly, who was able to slip the ball inside Knight's near post, giving Blues that vital early goal advantage. Poor defending resulted in Blues losing the lead after only two minutes.

With only Daly there to block a Gilbert free-kick, he hesitated enabling Dillon to turn and beat the oncoming Seaman. But Blues were not about to give up, Daly immediately issuing the challenge with an excellent 60-yard pass to Hopkins, whose cross caused havoc amongst the Portsmouth defenders. Despite plenty of attacking football from both teams, another goal was not forthcoming, and by the 30th minute the game had settled into a struggle for possession, often between the the half-way line and Blues' penalty area. Referee Butler was quick to use the whistle throughout, which resulted in a great deal of endeavour on both sides, but little to show for it.

The second half began with a curling shot from Bremner connecting with Knight, who just managed to flick it over the bar. This was quickly followed by three corners in two minutes from Kuhl which repeatedly teased the Pompey defence. An injured Bremner was replaced by Andy Kennedy who provided some fine stylish running during Blues forays into the Portsmouth area. In the 63rd minute a corner from Daly was headed down to Geddis who pushed the ball against Hardyman's legs before bundling the rebound inside the near post. Blues were ahead. Portsmouth had to fight hard during the next few minutes when a swerving centre from Kuhl was repulsed only by a full bodied lunge from Knight. And at 72 minutes, Blake, misjudging a corner from Daly, headed the ball onto Knight and he rebounded Geddis's foot, and from there into the empty goal. There was no coming back from that and Blues took the points, 3-1.

PORTSMOUTH

Knight, Stanley, Hardyman, Dillon, Blake, Gilbert, O'Callaghan, Doyle, Morgan, Webb, Hilaire (Waldron).

BIRMINGHAM CITY

Seaman, Ranson, Roberts, Wright, Armstrong, Kuhl, Daly, Clarke, Bremner, Geddis, Hopkins (Kennedy).

REFEREE

Mr Noel Butler (East Molesey)

The Matches played on this day

1895, Division 1.		
Sheffield United 0	Blues 2	Att. 5,000
	Mobley, Hill(og)	
1900, Division 2.		
Lincoln City 0	Blues 0	Att. 5,000
1901, Division 2.		
Glossop 2	Blues 0	.Att. 2,000
1903, Division 2.		
Barnsley 3	Blues 0	Att. 5,000
1907, Division 1.		
Woolwich Arsenal 2	Blues 1	Att. 18,000
	Glover	
1912, Division 2.		
Blues 1	Huddersfield Town 0	Att. 10,000
Hall		
1914, Division 1.		
Clapton Orient 2	Blues 2	Att. 10,000
	Walker, Hall	
1918, Wartime.		
Leicester Fosse 1	Blues 1	
	Butler	
1929, Division 1.		
Blues 0	Cardiff City 0	Att. 15,000
1935, Division 1.		
Tottenham Hotspur 1	Blues 1	Att. 27,190
	Jones	
1936, Division 1.		
Sunderland 7	Blues 2	Att. 15,000
	Loughran, Clarke	

Sunderland striker Bobby Gurney netted four times.

1946, Wartime.		
Blues 3	Nottingham Forest 1	
Bodle, Jones,		
Harris		
1957, Division 1.		
Tottenham Hotspur 5	Blues 1	Att. 33,512
Dunmore 3, 65	Astall 42	
Harmer 30(pen)		
Dyson 71		
Medwin 76		

Ron Saunders (Birmingham City Manager)

Blues news extra   1940...15,000 turn up for Harry Hibbs benefit.

Blues and Villa finished all square at 1-1 in a match to bid Harry Hibbs farewell. The match a first wartime benefit game raised £650 for the Blues and England goalkeeper.

Gary Charles (on loan from West Ham United, September 2000 also see below)

Birthdays

Gary Charles born today in 1970

Tony Towers born today in 1952

Trevor Smith born today in 1936

Johnny Watts born today in 1931

The Matches played on this day

1963, Division 1.
| Nottingham Forest 0 | Blues 2 | Att. 15,575 |
| | Leek 36, 84 | |

1968, Division 2.
| Blues 0 | Cardiff City 0 | Att. 29,044 |

1971, Division 2.
| Blues 0 | Hull City 0 | Att. 33,109 |

1974, Division 1.
| Blues 0 | Stoke City 0 | Att. 20,467 |

1976, Division 1.
Blues 3	Ipswich Town 0	Att. 20,497
Francis 10(pen)		
Hibbitt 66		
Burns 88		

1985, Division 2.
| Portsmouth 1 | Blues 3 | Att. 23,983 |
| Dillon 8 | Geddis 6, 63, 72 | |

1991, Division 3.
| Blues 0 | Mansfield Town 0 | Att. 7,635 |

1996, Division 1.
Blues 4	Luton Town 0	Att. 17,469
Devlin 1		
Francis 76		
Barnes 77, 90		

Paul Devlin's goal was timed at 16 seconds.

1998, Division 1.
| Manchester City 0 | Blues 1 | Att. 29,569 |
| | Adebola 90 | |

For the second time this season Blues beat Man City in stoppage time. Dele Adebola's strike won 'goal of the season' at the club's annual awards dinner. This defeat by Blues virtually condemned Man City to relegation into Division Two.

2001, Division 1.
Bolton Wanderers 2	Blues 2	Att. 15,025
Bergsson 53	O'Connor 15	
Holdsworth 55	Marcelo 57	

2002, Division 1.
Rotherham United 2	Blues 2	Att. 10,336
Byfield 36	Grainger 38	
McIntosh 59	Beech(og) 66	

April 14

-1875

The Matches played on this day

1900, Division 2.
Blues 4   Leicester Fosse 1   Att. 6,000
McRoberts,
Wharton, Main,
Wragg(og)

1906, Division 1.
Blues 5   Sheffield W. 1   Att. 7,000
Tickle(3), Jones(2)

1911, Division 2.
Blues 1   Hull City 0   Att. 10,000
Hall

1915, Division 2.
Blackpool 3   Blues 1   Att. 5,000
     W.Smith

1917, Wartime.
Leicester Fosse 4   Blues 2
     Whitehouse, Bell

1922, Division 1.
Manchester City 1   Blues 0   Att. 35,000

1923, Division 1.
Blues 2   Tottenham Hotspur 1   Att. 15,000
Rawson, McClure
Blues 1st league win over Spurs.

1928, Division 1.
Leicester City 3   Blues 0   Att. 15,000

1933, Division 1.
Sunderland 1   Blues 0   Att. 15,000

1934, Division 1.
Aston Villa 1   Blues 1   Att. 40,000
     Calladine

1945, Wartime.
Wolverhampton W. 1   Blues 0
An experiment into the modern day golden goal
rule. Both managers agreed that the game should end
when a winner was scored. The goal eventually came in
the 63rd minute of extra time. After starting at 3pm the
game then finished at 5.45pm.

1951, Division 2.
Luton Town 1   Blues 1   Att. 16,324
Pemberton 6   Warhurst 22

1952, Division 2.
Cardiff City 3   Blues 1   Att. 30,000
Chisholm 18, 29   Briggs 47
Sherwood 34
Chisholm also missed a penalty for Cardiff.

1956, Division 1.
Arsenal 1   Blues 0   Att. 31,733
Tapscott 70

1959, Division 1.
Blues 4   Arsenal 1.   Att. 25,791
Astall 9, 46   Clapton 47
Larkin 26, 88

1962, Division 1.
Blues 3   Sheffield United 0   Att. 19,476
Harris 7(pen), 58
Hellawell 34

1973, Division 1.
Leicester City 0   Blues 1   Att. 27,652
     Campbell 53

1979, Division 1.
Blues 1   Wolverhampton W. 1   Att. 20,556
Ainscow 23   Richards 7
Mark Dennis became the first Blues player to be sent off
twice in a season against the same opposition.

1984, Division 1.
Blues 0   QPR 2   Att. 10,255
     Gregory 11
     Fenwick 53

1990, Division 3.
Fulham 1   Blues 2   Att. 4,568
Milton 61   Hopkins 26
     Gleghorn 60

1992, Division 3.
Blues 2   Bolton Wanderers 1   Att. 14,440
Frain 32(pen)   Walker 16
Rennie 38

Playing record for this day

Playing record for this day is...21 games, Won 9, Drawn 3, Lost 9, GF 31, GA 28.
Today's success rate.....50% Year ranking....151st

Match of the Day

FROM 1959

GUNNERS SHOT TO PIECES

Larkin double is Blues perfect weapon against London's Arsenal

For the second time in three days Blues struck a blow to the capital's finest football clubs, this time dismantling Arsenal in a rearranged game. Three days before Blues had destroyed the Gunners local rivals Spurs by 5-1, this game was also a magnificent team display, with devastating finishing by the home forwards.

Blues got off to a lucky start when straight from the kick off Barnwell took advantage of a gap in the centre of the home defence and charged forward, his end shot beat Merrick but came back off the post. Taking full advantage of this escape Blues went on the attack and within nine minutes scored the game's opening goal. From a free kick which sailed over the entire defence Astall calmly turned up at the far post to volley the ball past Standen. Moments later the Arsenal 'keeper was at fault dropping the ball from a harmless shot, which McCullough just managed to scramble back and clear before Larkin pounced on the loose ball.

Blues were well on top at this point and it was no surprise when Astall raced clear again down the right to cross for Larkin who headed the ball past Standen. Although Arsenal rallied a little in the period leading up to half time the Blues goal was only once threatened, Merrick saving at the second attempt from Clapton.

Blues started the second half in sensational style adding a third goal through Stubbs within a minute, this his eighth in as many games. Again it was Astall who assisted the strike, feeding off a great through ball from Gordon he centred for Stubbs who converted wiith his first touch close in. Then came a momentary lapse of concentration by the Blues defence, which allowed Barnwell a free header. He unselfishly nodded down for the better placed Clapton to blast past Merrick. However Blues continued to dominate overall, they went close to scoring again when Neal's shot just flashed past the post after Hooper had once again left the Arsenal defence in tatters. The elusive fourth goal came with just two minutes of the game remaining, Larkin finishing off a superb through ball from Hooper by rounding the 'keeper and sliding the ball into the empty net to cap a fantastic team performance by the Blues.

BIRMINGHAM CITY

Merrick, Farmer, Allen, Watts, Smith, Neal, Astall, Gordon, Stubbs, Larkin, Hooper.

ARSENAL

Standen, Evans, McCullough, Ward, Dodgin, Docherty, Clapton, Groves, Herd, Barnwell, Henderson.

Robin Stubbs

Blues news extra   1956...Scotland 1 England 1

Blues full back Jeff Hall won his fifth cap for England in the Home International at Glasgow.

Birthdays

Alex McIntosh born today in 1916   Paul Devlin born today in 1972

Playing record for this day

Playing record for this day is...26 games, Won 10, Drawn 8, Lost 8, GF 32, GA 36.

Today's success rate.....53.85% Year ranking....118th

April 15

Match of the Day

FROM 1978

LEICESTER FEEL BLUES FOUR-CE

Filbert Street treated to top quality finishing by Blues

A splendid second half resulted in another win for Blues, giving them 15 points out of 18 since Jim Smith took over as manager. Malcolm Page failed a late fitness test, giving Kevin Dillon the chance to play his first game under the new boss. Meanwhile, playing without a manager, Leicester brought in Roger Davies in place of the unfit Dean Smith.

The pitch looked uneven, but it didn't stop the pressure from Blues. Calderwood made an early through pass, which was poorly missed by Williams and then by Bertschin.

Francis chipped the ball to Dillon, who delivered a great 25-yard volley which was tipped over the bar by the Leicester goalkeeper Wallington. Leicester were awarded a free kick when Davies ran around Gallagher and was pulled down. Whitworth took the kick, but swerved it straight into the arms of Montgomery. Bertschin knocked the ball to Dillon, who made a weak attempt at a goal but shot wide. Blues were hoping for a penalty when Francis was brought down in the area, but the referee refused to oblige. Finally Leicester's perseverance looked like it might pay off when they pieced together a string of attacks. Goodwin's shot went just inches wide of the post, and White almost managed a shot when he beat Pendrey on the right. Whitworth's attempt passed close to the post, and Hughes was given plenty of room in the centre, but shot poorly.

Francis, who had scored eight goals in eight games, was blocked by the referee who couldn't get out of the way as he geared up to take his shot. As Blues' game gathered momentum, Sims conceded another foul on Francis resulting in a free kick, which came to nothing.

Half time arrived with no score, and the second half began. Jim Smith's words to the team during the break had a major effect. Blues almost took the lead within a minute of returning. Fox knocked the ball to Francis, who left Hibbitt with an easy chance, but he slammed the ball against the legs of Webb. Dillon then missed his chance from the penalty spot and then finally, in the 52nd minute, the first goal came.

Francis fell over taking a pass from Towers, but managed to wrong-foot the defence and cross the ball for Hibbitt to knock into the net. The extra ingredient which was needed to spice up play had, at last, been added. Leicester were getting tired, and it was on 56 minutes when Blues increased their lead. Hibbitt supplied a great reverse pass to Pendrey, who drove past Wallington from just over six yards out. It was Bertschin who scored the next goal, a classic shot on 74 minutes, and Leicester pulled back some hope with a goal on 85 minutes. The game was wrapped up in the final minute with a fine shot by Francis. Blues' success ensured Leicester City's relegation to the Second Division.

LEICESTER CITY

Wallington, Whitworth, Williams, Woollett, Sims, Webb, White, Hughes, Davies, Salmons, Goodwin.

BIRMINGHAM CITY

Montgomery, Calderwood, Pendrey, Towers, Gallagher, Howard, Dillon, Francis, Bertschin, Hibbitt, Fox.

Filbert Street, home of Leicester City

April 16

Playing record for this day
Playing record for this day is...27 games, Won 7, Drawn 10, Lost 10, GF 36, GA 40.
Today's success rate.....44.44% Year ranking....206th

The Matches played on this day

1892, Football Alliance.		
Blues 1	Nottingham Forest 1	Att. 3,500
Walton		
1897, Division 2.		
Blues 2	Leicester Fosse 2	Att. 2,000
Hare, Inglis		
1898, Division 2.		
Blues 4	Lincoln City 0	Att. 4,000
Oakes, Abbott(2),		
Higgins		
1904, Division 1.		
Manchester City 4	Blues 0	Att. 15,000
1906, Division 1.		
Blues 0	Bury 3	Att. 10,000
1910, Division 2.		
Blues 0	Hull City 2	Att. 8,000
1921, Division 2.		
Nottingham Forest 1	Blues 1	Att. 8,000
	Crosbie	
1927, Division 1.		
Leeds United 2	Blues 1	Att. 18,703
	Bradford	
1932, Division 1.		
Blues 3	Liverpool 1	Att. 9,848
Bradford(2),		
Grosvenor		
1938, Division 1.		
Arsenal 0	Blues 0	Att. 35,161
1949, Division 1.		
Blues 1	Blackpool 1	Att. 35,000
Jordan		
1954, Division 2.		
Nottingham Forest 1	Blues 1	Att. 25,135
Gager 14(pen)	Kinsey 10	
1955, Division 2.		
Port Vale 2	Blues 0	Att. 35,000
Askey 18		
Done 43		
1960, Division 1.		
Blues 3	Arsenal 0	Att. 27,216
Gordon 34		
Astall 41, 51		
1963, Division 1.		
Blues 0	Everton 1	Att. 29,668
	Vernon 80	

Blues Johnny Watts left the field after 46 minutes of play.

Match of the Day
FROM 1994
FAREWELL TO THE TERRACES
Blues last stand at the Kop ends in a 2-2 draw

20,316 crowded into St Andrews to witness the last home game of the 1993-94 season and the last game to be played before the Kop, which was due to be rebuilt during the break. Blues went into the game hoping desperately to avoid defeat and boost their fight against relegation. It was an emotion-filled occasion for everyone present. Louie Donowa's presence in Blues' line up was crucial, and the game would have been a totally different story without him. He was only included in the squad due to fact that Paul Harding was out with an injury. It was his first start in the team since the FA Cup tie against Kidderminster in January, and he intended to make up for lost time.

In a game totally dominated by Blues there were only two slip-ups. Unfortunately both of them provided chances for Bristol City, who jumped on them to full effect. The visiting team's first chance came on six minutes when youngster Scott Partridge, on just his second start, evaded the Blues defence and fired a low shot past Ian Bennett in the goal for the visitors' first.

The only other opportunity given to Bristol City was in the 20th minute, and again it was welcomed with open arms. The Blues defence seemed to be repelled by the presence of Wayne Allison as they parted to let him through. With Liam Daish and Barnett deciding too late to try and stop him, Ian Bennett came off his line. Allison slotted the ball to Partridge who slipped it over the line. Blues were 2-0 down, and they didn't deserve to be at all.

Bristol City goalkeeper Keith Welch was on top form, and this was mainly the reason why Blues were not as successful as they should have been. Constant attacking from Blues was rewarded when they won a penalty in the 59th minute.

Steve Claridge took the kick, and the ball was in the net. After a sensational game by Blues the final stages were drawing in and they were still a goal behind. Then Louie Donowa got hold of the ball, and all hopes were pinned on him as he fired a right footed shot - but it went far too wide of the post.

With just two minutes of the game remaining another chance appeared and this time it was different. Mark Ward parted the defence with a fierce shot, and Donowa was waiting for it. As Donowa stood facing the empty Tilton Road stand and the Bristol goalkeeper he struck the ball with the side of his foot. The crowd waited with baited breath, then erupted with cheers as the ball went into the net. A pitch invasion followed, causing a long delay, and after seven minutes of injury time a winning goal had not appeared for either team.

With so many chances created by Blues there really should have been more goals for the home side. The side were playing with the quality expected from a top of the table team, not one fighting against relegation. Unfortunately the points total did not reflect this. Blues now faced an uphill struggle needing at least three wins out of four away games for a secure end to the season.

BIRMINGHAM CITY
Bennett, Hiley, Barnett, Daish, Rogers, Donowa, Ward, Willis, Doherty, Claridge, De Souza (Shutt 89).
BRISTOL CITY
Welch, Herriott, Munro, Scott, McKop, Wyatt, Martin, Edwards, Hewlett, Allison, Partridge.

REFEREE
Mr S Lodge (Barnsley)

Ian Bennett

Birthdays
Dave Barnett born today in 1967   Steve Sutton born today in 1961

Carl Shutt

April 16

The Matches played on this day

1966, Division 2.

Coventry City 4	Blues 3	Att. 27,063
Pointer 6	Jackson 42	
Machin 38	Vowden 47	
Rees 68	Fenton 87	
Curtis 78		

1968, Division 2.

Blues 2	Plymouth Argyle 2	Att. 29,359
Wylie 4	Bickle 23, 32	
Page 50		

1974, Division 1.

Blues 2	Burnley 2	Att. 36,548
Hatton 65, 78	Ingham 30	
	Fletcher 73	

1977, Division 1.

Blues 2	Stoke City 0	Att. 19,554
Francis 79		
Burns 88		

1983, Division 1.

Coventry City 0	Blues 1	Att. 10,420
	Phillips 88	

1985, Division 2.

Blues 3	Crystal Palace 0	Att. 10,721
Geddis 30		
Clarke 74		
Kennedy 86		

1986, Division 1.

Tottenham Hotspur 2	Blues 0	Att. 9,359
Falco 21		
Chiedozie 63		

1990, Division 3.

Blues 2	Bristol Rovers 2	Att. 12,438
Hopkins 14	White 57	
Matthewson 19	Thomas(og) 84	

1991, Division 3.

Blues 2	Stoke City 1	Att. 6,729
Matthewson 6	Ellis 39	
Hopkins 31		

Stoke's Peter Noble saved John Frain's 25th minute penalty

1994, Division 1.

Blues 2	Bristol City 2	Att. 20,316
Claridge 60(pen)	Partridge 5, 19	
Donowa 75		

1996, Division 1.

Sunderland 3	Blues 0	Att. 19,831
Gray 17		
Stewart 21		
Russell 62		

2001, Division 1.

Blues 0	Portsmouth 0	Att. 23,304

April 17

Playing record for this day
Playing record for this day is...22 games, Won 6, Drawn 3, Lost 13, GF 18, GA 30.
Today's success rate.....34.09% Year ranking....255th

Match of the Day
FROM 1957
BLUES WIN INTER THE SEMIS
Alex Govan brace sees off the Italians at St Andrews

Blues made it to the semi-final of the Inter Cities Fairs Cup after beating Italian side Inter Milan in this group decider. Blues topped the group unbeaten with seven points, their opponents finishing second with five, leaving Dinamo Zagreb bottom. However many felt that the competition was not worth the stress after the game quickly deteriorated into a catalogue of fouls.

Blues quickly settled, however it was the Italians who started the better and for the first quarter of an hour their passing controlled the game. Suddenly Blues upped the pace and sent high long balls into the danger area and this changed the whole game, as it was now the Italians who looked likely to concede the first goal. Blues closest effort to goal came from a free kick just before half time, another lobbed high ball from Astall produced an almighty goalmouth scramble and ended when the Italians finally put the ball out for a corner. A minute later another free kick by Astall produced the opening goal. With the defence expecting a high ball, Astall hit low and when two team mates jumped over it creating more confusion, Govan was left with the simple task of sweeping it past Ghezzi to put Blues 1-0 up at half time.

Blues started the second half still the most likely to score and playing the more constructive football if not on the same purist level as the Italians. It took just 11 minutes for Blues and Govan to score a second goal. When once again the Scot was well positioned in the penalty area this time to convert Brown's perfect centre from the right wing. Milan then substituted their 'keeper although he was not at fault with either goals and Matteucci came on to deny Brown and Murphy the chance to wrap the game up. At the other end Blues goal remained relatively untroubled until the very last minute when Lorenzi was left unmarked in the area to grab a late consolation which none of the 34,461 St Andrews crowd would have begrudged him.

BIRMINGHAM CITY
Merrick, Hall, Green, Watts, Smith, Warhurst, Astall, Kinsey, Brown, Murphy, Govan.
INTER MILAN
Ghezzi (Matteucci), Invernizzi, Fongaro, Bearzot, Bernardin, Nesti, Dorigo, Vonlanthen, Lorenzi, Campagnoli, Savioni.

Alex Govan

Birthdays
Curtis Woodhouse born today in 1980

Playing record for this day
Playing record for this day is...22 games, Won 9, Drawn 3, Lost 10, GF 33, GA 34.
Today's success rate.....47.27% Year ranking....180th

Match of the Day

FROM 1998

PROMOTION DREAM STILL ON

Blues keep the pressure on play-off places with emphatic 3-0 win

Blues erased the memory of defeat in their last home game by soundly thrashing a poor Swindon side thanks to two goals from the returning Paul Furlong. They made sure from the start and were handed the bonus of Paul Furlong's return to action and he lost no time in continuing the form that had earned him 15 goals and two hat-tricks from just 27 starts.

Blues needed to win in order to have a chance of a top six place were on their way as early as the ninth minute. Martin O'Connor won a challenge in midfield. His clever pass found Hughes who sent over a curling deep cross which Furlong climbed well above his markers to thump in an unstoppable header. That goal went a long way to easing the nerves. With Blues a goal up and the assured Bruce martialling a tight back four which included debutant Gerry Gill at right back it seemed unlikely Swindon would get anything but a good beating and a second goal was never very far away. That goal came in the 34th minute after Dele Adebola had wriggled free from Kerslake only for the desperate defender to upend him as he was about to shoot. Furlong stepped up with a cool side-footed penalty sending Digby the wrong way for his 17th goal of the season. Blues went into the half-time interval with a two goal cushion after several more attempts had come agonisingly close.

Blues were more intent on quality than quantity in the early exchanges of the second half. Marsden leading the new `keep ball' tactic in midfield and they played at almost exhibition pace. One such move started by Marsden's customary short pass to McCarthy ended with Furlong missing the ball completely when left a glorious chance to net his third hat-trick of the season. Meanwhile at the other end 'keeper Ian Bennett's only problem was how to keep occupied. Blues finally registered a more honest looking scoreline when the majestic Bryan Hughes cut in from a right wing dribble and curled a shot from the edge of the penalty area just inches out of Digby's reach with eight minutes left.

Blues win took them to within three points of sixth placed Sheffield United with just two games to play. United had two games in hand.

BIRMINGHAM CITY
Bennett, Gill, Charlton, Bruce (Purse 88), Johnson, Marsden McCarthy, O'Connor (Robinson 69), Furlong (Forster 88), Adebola, Hughes.

SWINDON TOWN
Digby, Kerslake, Davis, Taylor, Bullock, Borrows, Walters, Collins(Gooden h/t), Hay (Cuervo77), Finney (Crowe 60), Robinson

REFEREE
Mr W Burns (Scarborough)

Chris Marsden

Blues news extra 1942...Friendly at Chester
Chester 3 Blues 3

Birthdays
Keith Bowker born today in 1951

April 19

Playing record for this day

Playing record for this day is...27 games, Won 13, Drawn 6, Lost 8, GF 40, GA 39.
Today's success rate.....59.26% Year ranking....58th

Match of the Day
FROM 1961
SAN SIRO DELIGHT FOR BLUES
Inter's fortress is scaled by Blues in push for the final

Birmingham City were on the brink of another Inter Cities Fairs Cup final after a fantastic win in Inter's San Siro Stadium. They took a one goal advantage into the second leg off the semi final, to be played at St Andrews on 3 May.

The Blues performance, inspired by man-of-the-match Jimmy Bloomfield, was simply awesome and they gave the Italian giants a lesson in the finer arts of football. Although the second half became a scrappy midfield battle, Blues showed their physical and mental toughness was just as good. Roared on by a vociferous crowd of 20,000, Inter pegged Blues back on the defensive for the latter stages of the game, but the defence held firm against their often desperate attack.

Blues started well and within three minutes Bloomfield had forced a great save from 'keeper De Pozzo as Blues poured forward in an all-out assault. It was Bloomfield's perfectly weighted through ball to Harris which led to the first goal after 12 minutes. Harris was the benificiary and was left on his own to race forward with just De Pozzo to beat, when the 'keeper advanced the Blues forward slipped the ball wide of him into the bottom corner of the net. The Italians retaliated and their first real attempt on goal was from Bicicli, but his shot was blocked by Withers who produced a great diving two-fisted punch to clear. Moments later a lapse in the Blues defence allowed Morbello a simple chance but he somehow missed the target completely, when it seemed easier to score. Blues never allowed the Italians another chance throughout the remainder of the game. After this it was all pressure, a Stubbs header going just inches over the bar with the 'keeper well beaten. Then Blues should have been awarded a penalty when Balleri tripped Bloomfield inside the box, but the referee awarded a free kick just outside the area. With five minutes remaining to the break they deservedly went 2-0 up. A beautifully flighted cross from Hellawell drifted dangerously towards Stubbs again, Balleri got there first, but in trying to clear only managed to head past his own 'keeper. Inter eventually got the better of the second half and were rewarded with a 78th minute goal from Firmani, the former Charlton Athletic forward. This came after a great run from midfield by Corso. He split the defence with a super pass, and Firmani had the simple task of finishing from ten yards out. The crowd urged their team on for the equaliser but a tired and frustrated side could not beat the Blues defence again.

INTER MILAN

Da Pozzo, Picchi, Gatti, Bolchi, Guarneri, Balleri, Bicicli, Corso, Firmani, Masiero, Morbello.

BIRMINGHAM CITY

Withers, Farmer, Allen, Hennessey, Smith, Neal, Hellawell, Stubbs, Harris, Bloomfield, Orritt.

Jimmy Bloomfield

Birthdays

Aubrey Powell born today in 1918   Gary Childs born today in 1964   Trevor Francis born today in 1954

Colin Withers

The Matches played on this day

1958, Division 1.

Blues 2	Manchester United 0	Att. 38,991
Hooper 1		
Green 26		

1960, Division 1.

WBA 1	Blues 1	Att. 37,937
Kevan 61	Gordon 11	

1961, Inter Cities Fairs Cup Semi Final, 1st leg.

Inter Milan 1	Blues 2	Att. 20,000
Firmani 78	Harris 12	
	Balleri(og) 40	

1965, Division 1.

Blues 2	Manchester United 4	Att. 28,907
Thwaites 26	Best 12, 64	
Vowden 63	Charlton 66	
	Cantwell 75	

Geoff Vowden had a 53rd minute goal disallowed.
The result left Blues relegated

1969, Division 2.

Blues 3	Middlesbrough 1	Att. 25,899
Summerill 54, 62	McMordie 45	
G.Smith(og) 90		

1975, Division 1.

Blues 1	Luton Town 4	Att. 28,755
Francis 60	J.Ryan 14	
	Alston 44, 48	
	Husband 75	

Trevor Francis scored on his 21st birthday.

1976, Division 1.

Stoke City 1	Blues 0	Att. 19,918
Gallagher(og) 8		

1977, Division 1.

Manchester City 2	Blues 1	Att. 36,203
Kidd 26, 69	Burns 7	

1980, Division 2.

Blues 1	Luton Town 0	Att. 23,662
Bertschin 25		

Luton keeper Jake Findlay saved a penalty from Archie
Gemmill in the 69th minute

1986, Division 1.

Blues 0	Southampton 2	Att. 5,833
	Wallace 47	
	Cockerill 70	

This result finally means relegation for Blues

1995, Division 2.

Plymouth Argyle 1	Blues 3	Att. 8,550
Dalton 90	Whyte 50	
	Claridge 74, 85	

The Blues team coach broke down on the way, and were
delayed for an hour and a half. Chris Whyte scored his only
goal for the club. Plymouth's Peter Swan was sent off

1997, Division 1.

Bradford City 0	Blues 2	Att. 15,123
	Devlin 22	
	Furlong 86	

April 20

Playing record for this day
Playing record for this day is...22 games, Won 8, Drawn 9, Lost 5, GF 34, GA 32.
Today's success rate.....56.82% Year ranking....87th

The Matches played on this day

1892, Football Alliance.
| Crewe Alexandra 0 | Blues 2 | Att. 1,000 |
| | Wheldon(2) | |

This was Blues final game in the Football Alliance, before joining the Football League.

1896, Test Match.
| Blues 0 | Liverpool 0 | Att. 5,000 |

1901, Division 2.
| Blues 2 | Middlesbrough 1 | Att. 8,000 |
| McMillan(2) | | |

1903, Division 2.
| Blues 2 | Manchester United 1 | Att. 4,000 |
| Leonard, Wilcox | | |

Blues finished the 1902-03 season unbeaten at home

1912, Division 2.
| Blackpool 1 | Blues 0 | Att. 2,000 |

A minute's silence was held for the victims of the Titanic which sunk on its maiden voyage on 14 April.

1918, Wartime.
| Blues 1 | Leicester Fosse 0 | |
| Godfrey | | |

1929, Division 1.
| Sheffield United 3 | Blues 2 | Att. 15,000 |
| | Hicks(2) | |

1935, Division 2.
| Blues 2 | Luton Town 1 | Att. 35,790 |
| Murphy(2) | | |

1940, Wartime.
| Newport County 2 | Blues 2 | |
| | Godden(2) | |

1946, Wartime.
| Wolverhampton W. 3 | Blues 3 | |
| | Bodle, Edwards, Harris | |

1955, Division 2.
| Blues 2 | Luton Town 1 | Att. 35,790 |
| Murphy 7, 47(pen) | Turner 36 | |

Blues reduced to ten men for the last 12 minutes due to Noel Kinsey having to leave the field injured.

1957, Division 1.
Blues 6	Leeds United 2	Att. 30,642
Astall 7	Charles 5, 32	
Brown 16, 55		
Govan 24 pen, 25, 67		

1959, Division 1.
Blackpool 2	Blues 0	Att. 12,260
Charnley 40		
Durie 86		

1962, Division 1.
Everton 4	Blues 1	Att. 47,506
Foster 15	Leek 58	
Gabriel 53		
Vernon 66		
Young 75		

1963, Division 1.
Blues 3	Blackpool 6	Att. 15,372
Auld 6	Crawford 7	
Bloomfield 22	Durie 33	
Leek 23	Charnley 38, 56, 65	
	Beard (og) 82	

1968, Division 2.
| Crystal Palace 0 | Blues 0 | Att. 14,949 |

1974, Division 1.
| Newcastle United 1 | Blues 1 | Att. 32,102 |
| Robson 27 | Francis 44 | |

1985, Division 1.
Blues 2	Charlton Athletic 1	Att. 10,697
Kennedy 10	Flanagan 25	
Wright 49(pen)		

1987, Division 2.
| Blues 1 | Reading 1 | Att. 5,427 |
| Frain 72 | Bremner 13 | |

1991, Division 3.
| Grimsby Town 0 | Blues 0 | Att. 8,842 |

1996, Division 1.
| Derby County 1 | Blues 1 | Att. 16,757 |
| Simpson 55 | Breen 74 | |

1999, Division 1.
| Blues 1 | QPR 0 | |
| Forinton 84 | | |

With his first goal for the Blues, Howard Forinton secured the win which guaranteed Blues a play-off place.

Match of the Day
FROM 1957
MATCH BALL NO.5 FOR GOVAN
Leeds the latest victims for Alex's match ball collection

Alex Govan's fifth hat-trick of the season brought his tally to 26 league and cup goals - an impressive record for a winger. Govan was one of three new men from the previous week's disastrous 5-1 defeat at Tottenham. He took over from Murphy, who returned to his regular position at the expense of Bryan Orritt. The other two changes were Brown and Watts in for Finney and Larkin. Meanwhile the 30,642 crowd at St Andrews were to see a Leeds side with John Charles in it for the last time as he was off to join Italian giants Juventus in a high profile transfer to be completed as soon as the season ended.

It was the big centre forward who got the opening goal after five minutes, the Welshman beating Trevor Smith in a race for a long defensive clearance to fire past Merrick. Blues were quickly back and equalised just three minutes later through Astall, A cross from Brown was only half cleared allowing Govan to centre again from the left, Astall met the hard low cross with a diving header from close range. In an end-to-end thriller Merrick saved well from Charles, then Blues took the lead on 16 minutes when Brown came in from the right to brilliantly lob the ball over Leeds 'keeper Wood's head and into the top right-hand corner of the net. Then Blues all but wrapped up the game in the space of a devastating minute as Govan claimed two goals.

The first belting in a penalty after Kerfoot had handled a centre from Astall. Govan's second, straight afterwards was another simple shot after a cracking ball from Murphy left him in the clear and in the centre of the penalty area. He almost stuck his hat-trick goal a minute later, but Wood saved his cross shot at the foot of the post. Back came Leeds, and Charles again scored to reduce the deficit to 4-2 just after the half hour mark. Leeds broke down the wing through Meek and his deep cross was headed in by Charles at the far post. Blues, were terribly unlucky not to go into half time 5-2 up, Brown raced clear from Marsden and once in the area struck a beautiful right-foot shot which came back off the inside of the far post to be cleared by Dunn. Blues had the better of a less exciting second half scoring two more goals through Brown and Govan. The first was a freak goal. Wood charged out to clear the ball from Brown but only succeeded in hitting the striker in the stomach and the ball rebounded back and rolled over the goal line leaving Brown winded but smiling. With 23 minutes of the game remaining in Govan completed another hat-trick when he brilliantly finished off his own created chance, cutting in from the left to smack an unstoppable low drive which flew past Wood's despairing dive and found the far corner of the net.

BIRMINGHAM CITY
Merrick, Hall, Allen, Watts, Smith, Warhurst Astall, Kinsey, Brown, Murphy, Govan
LEEDS UNITED
Wood, Dunn, Hair, Lawson, Marsden, Kerfoot, Meek, Lowe, Charles, O'Brien, Overfield

REFEREE
Mr N N Hough (Macclesfield)

Alex Govan

Birthdays
Alan Buckley born today in 1951   Steve Finnan born today in 1976

Playing record for this day

Playing record for this day is...18 games, Won 7, Drawn 2, Lost 9, GF 27, GA 28.

Today's success rate.....44.44% Year ranking....205th

April 21

Match of the Day

FROM 2002

BLUES ARE ON THEIR WAY

Horsfield and Grainger secure a forth succesive play off showdown

"We're On Our Way" sang Blues biggest crowd of the season. 29,178 had packed into St Andrews waiting for the moment, the goal which would finally seal Blues fourth successive play-off semi-final berth. They needed a win to make sure, a point if at least one other game amongst the five play-off hopefuls went their way.

There was a nervous start by Blues with so much to play for, United in contrast had only their pride to play for and a post season holiday to look forward to. Blues on a ten game unbeaten run almost succumbed to 'old pal' Peter Ndlovu on six minutes. He managed to wriggle his way clear to fire in a shot which Vaesen only managed to claw out with one hand. In a first half dominated by the visitors, Vaesen again saved well to deny Smith from a direct free kick. At half time the radios were turned up to maximum volume as the crowd looked elsewhere for something positive to cheer. However with Millwall clear, Norwich a goal up against ten man Stockport, only Coventry still holding Burnley at Turf Moor were keeping the Blues in the top six. A goal was still desperately needed at St Andrews.

The second half was almost following the familliar pattern as the first, then Blues scored from a chance out of nothing. From a long Kenna throw in, Hughes at full stretch managed to touch the ball on towards the intended target of Horsfield, whilst being pulled and pushed he somehow managed to hook it with enough power past Tracey and Blues were in the driving seat a goal up on 61 minutes, radios were now left as merely a fashion accessory. The noise generated by the goal matched the Ipswich Worthington Cup semi-final, the standard now all celebrations are judged by. Whilst the crowd beloved out the now promotion anthem 'Were On Our Way' there was further joy as Blues doubled their lead. Grainger lined up a 25-yard free kick awarded for a foul on Stern John. He then struck a supreme curling drive which was further aided by Horsfield and Hughes who spun the wall round as the ball whistled past, beating Tracey into his top left-hand corner. Blues were all but safe, thankfully just as news of Burnley's opening goal was being announced. Burnley who were top when Blues boss Steve Bruce took over were to sadly miss out but for the 29,000 at St Andrews, 'they were on their way'. Just one moment of madness marred the perfect 30-minute party from the second goal to final whistle. Darren Purse, pulled Montgomery down when the United player broke free, the ensuring red card meant he would miss the play-off final should Blues see off Millwall in the two legged semi final.

BIRMINGHAM CITY

Vaesen, Kenna, Grainger, Carter, Purse, Tebily, Devlin (Damien Johnson 59), John (Vickers 78), Horsfield (Andrew Johnson 89), Hughes, Mooney.

SHEFFIELD UNITED

Tracey, Doane, Ullathorne, Page (Cryan 74), Murphy, Smith (Montgomery 72), Jagielka, Tonge, D'Jaffo, Javary (Lovell 67), Ndlovu.

REFEREE

Mr P Richards (Darwen)

Martin Grainger (l) congratulates teammate Geoff Horsfield (r) on scoring a goal

The Matches played on this day

1900, Division 2.		
Luton Town 1	Blues 2	Att. 1,000
	Main, McRoberts	
1906, Division 1.		
Nottingham Forest 2	Blues 1	Att. 8,000
	Jones	
1917, Wartime.		
Notts County 0	Blues 2	
	Crowe, Whitehouse	
1923, Division 1.		
Tottenham Hotspur 2	Blues 0	Att. 16,355
1928, Division 1.		
Blues 2	Liverpool 0	Att. 18,000
Bradford(2)		
1934, Division 1.		
Blues 2	Tottenham Hotspur 0	Att. 30,000
Whateley(og),		
Calladine		
1945, Wartime.		
Blues 1	Coventry City 2	
Bright		
1951, Division 2.		
Blues 0	Leeds United 1	Att. 23,809
	Stevenson 24	
1956, Division 1.		
Blues 5	Bolton Wanderers 2	Att. 29,640
Wheeler(og) 36	Stevens 20, 41	
Kinsey 55		
Barras(og) 57		
Astall 65		
Warmington 89		
1962, Division 1.		
Cardiff City 3	Blues 2	Att. 8,800
Tapscott 17, 19, 33	Leek 25, 80	
1973, Division 1.		
Blues 3	Stoke City 1	Att. 32,513
Page 10	Robertson 85	
Francis 42		
Hatton 53		
1979, Division 1.		
Blues 0	Nottingham Forest 2	Att. 22,189
	Birtles 5	
	Robertson 48	

The return of Trevor Francis to St Andrews, as a Forest player. He recieved a mixed reception from the Blues fans. The defeat mathematically relegated Blues to Division Two, despite having five games of the season still to play

1981, Division 1.		
Blues 0	Leeds United 2	Att. 14,505
	Parlane 32	
	Hird 76(pen)	
1984, Division 1.		
Nottingham Forest 5	Blues 1	Att. 15,323
Davenport 2, 89	Harford 88	
Walsh 4		
Wallace 66		
Bowyer 71		
1990, Division 3.		
Preston North End 2	Blues 2	Att. 7,680
Thomas 15	Bailey 6, 24	
Mooney 76		

Blues 'keeper Martin Thomas saved John Thomas's 76th minute penalty, but Mooney scored from the rebound

1992, Division 3.		
Preston North End 3	Blues 2	Att. 7,738
Cartwright 2	Gleghorn 47	
Flynn 34	Rennie 76	
Shaw 55		
2001, Division 1.		
Burnley 0	Blues 0	Att. 17,057
2002, Division 1.		
Blues 2	Sheffield United 0	Att. 29,178
Horsfield 61		
Grainger 63		

Blues secured a play-off place for the fourth season in a row, finishing in fifth place in Division 1. Darren Purse was sent off 13 minutes from time.

April 22

1893, Test Match.		
Newton Heath 1	Blues 1	Att. 4,000
	Wheldon	
Played at the Victoria Ground, Stoke		
1899, Division 2.		
Walsall 2	Blues 0	Att. 4,000
1901, Division 2.		
Woolwich Arsenal 1	Blues 0	Att. 3,500
1905, Division 1.		
Blues 0	Stoke 1	Att. 10,000
1911, Division 2.		
Huddersfield Town 7	Blues 1	Att. 9,000
	Jones	
1922, Division 1.		
Blues 1	Bradford City 0	Att. 20,000
Foxall		
1930, Division 1.		
Blues 0	Grimsby Town 2	Att. 15,000
1933, Division 1.		
Liverpool 1	Blues 0	Att. 15,000
1935, Division 1.		
Blues 3	Leeds United 1	Att. 18,008
Calladine,		
Harris(2)		
1936, Division 1.		
Blues 4	Sheffield W. 1	Att. 9,089
Jones(3), Harris		
1939, Division 1.		
Blues 2	Blackpool 1	Att. 25,000
Craven, Harris		
1944, Wartime.		
Blues 5	Walsall 0	
Jennings, Trigg(4)		
1946, Wartime.		
Newport County 0	Blues 1	
	Massart	
1950, Division 1.		
Charlton Athletic 2	Blues 0	Att. 43,000
Vaughan 5, 48		
1957, Division 1.		
WBA 0	Blues 0	Att. 18,828
1959, Division 1.		
Blues 3	Blackburn Rovers 0	Att. 22,623
Larkin 13, 72		
Taylor 15		
1961, Division 1.		
Blues 0	Blackpool 2	Att. 17,834
	Peterson 9	
	Crawford 70	
1964, Division 1.		
Blues 3	Liverpool 1	Att. 22,623
Lynn 7(pen)	Hunt 80	
Leek 16		
Hellawell 38		
1966, Division 2.		
Blues 1	Bristol City 3	Att. 11,677
Beard(pen) 62	Clark 22	
	Sharp 42, 78	
1967, Division 2.		
Crystal Palace 2	Blues 1	Att. 13,064
Woodruff 10	Bridges 58	
Dyson 52		
Due to a colour clash Blues took the field wearing the Palace change strip of tangerine coloured shirts.		
1972, Division 2.		
Blues 1	Middlesbrough 1	Att. 37,202
Francis 46	Hickton 30	
The game is shown by BBC's Match of the Day		
1978, Division 1.		
Blues 1	Manchester City 4	Att. 25,294
Sbragia 56	Owen 59(pen)	
	Kidd 66, 77	
	Power 88	
1980, Division 2.		
West Ham United 1	Blues 2	Att. 36,167
Martin 51	Ainscow 36	
	Bertschin 69	
Colin Todd of Blues and West Ham's Billy Bonds both sent off in the 53rd minute.		
1989, Division 2.		
Blues 2	Blackburn Rovers 0	Att. 5,813
Robinson 55		
Yates 69		
2000, Division 2.		
Crystal Palace 0	Blues 2	Att. 24,268
	Austin(og) 45	
	Furlong 61	

Playing record for this day

Playing record for this day is...25 games, Won 11, Drawn 3, Lost 11, GF 34, GA 34.

Today's success rate.....50% Year ranking....161st

Match of the Day

FROM 1964

'POOL LEEK GOALS

Blues keep door open on their First Division status

Exhibiting energy and skill throughout, Birmingham City sent Liverpool to a 3-1 defeat at St Andrews, keeping alive their First Division hopes. If Wolves could beat Bolton then Blues would meet Sheffield United on the following Saturday with a chance of retaining their First Division status. A penalty in the seventh minute, the result of handling, gave Lynn Birmingham's first goal.

Fired by this success, Birmingham gave Liverpool no quarter, bombarding the Reds goal. Thomson had two on-target shots charged down, followed by a lob over the crossbar while the goalie was out of range. Thomson and Leek came through the centre with a quick pass. Lawrence saved the shot, at full stretch, and Leek capitalised, shooting the ball in to give Birmingham their second goal. 30 minutes into the game, Withers had still not seen a challenge.

An ecstatic crowd saw Auld side-step a tackle from Byrne which resulted in the right back tangling with the corner flag. Just before the whistle, Thomson made an opening for Hellawell who put a hard cross shot past the Liverpool goalie. The outside right making it 3 - 0 to Birmingham City at the half-time whistle. During the second half, Birmingham defended superbly, whilst still capitalising on any goal-scoring opportunities which arose, Thomson narrowly missed a fourth when he struck the cross-bar. Hunt for Liverpool, also had a chance, hitting the bar, and as the half progressed, Liverpool began to attack, hitting the Birmingham cross-bar again. Smith and Martin both received injuries, and whilst Martin was off the field, Hunt scored a consolation goal for Liverpool.

The game finished 3-1 to Birmingham City, and the jubilant team received the ovation they so richly deserved from the delighted St Andrews crowd.

BIRMINGHAM CITY

Withers, Lynn, Martin, Hennessey, Smith, Foster, Hellawell, Bloomfield, Thomson, Leek, Auld.

LIVERPOOL

Lawrence, Byrne, Moran, Milne, Yeats, Stevenson, Callaghan, Hunt, St John, Arrowsmith, Thompson

Ken Leek

Birthdays

Robin Stubbs born today in 1941

Playing record for this day

Playing record for this day is...19 games, Won 12, Drawn 4, Lost 3, GF 36, GA 18.

Today's success rate.....73.68% Year ranking....5th

Match of the Day

FROM 1995

IT'S BLUES AT THE DEATH

Tait 'Golden Goal' is a Wembley first for the Blues

For the second time in six years the the Blue Army coverged on Wembley's twin towers to roar on their team to another trophy win. An estimated 48,000 were behind the team out of the 73,633 Wembley crowd and although never a spectacular game the day was a memorable one. With Jose Dominguez away on international duty with Portugal, Barry Fry made three changes to the side which beat Orient in the second leg at Brisbane Road in the semi-final. Gary Cooper came in at left back for Chris Whyte, Jonathon Hunt replaced Rui Estevez and Kevin Francis made the starting line-up in place of Steve Robinson.

On the bench was Paul Tait despite his sudden-death winner over Swansea which had set up the Orient tie, and Brummie John Frain was missing from the squad altogether.

Blues soon showed why they were installed as firm favourites as they dominated the early stages, Otto in particular exploiting the huge Wembley pitch, but after Francis picked up an early knock, the crosses he had been winning easily were now dealt with comfortably by a Carlisle back four which included man-of-the-match Derek Mountfield. At the other end Carlisle did little to trouble the Blues defence and Ian Bennett was left to soak up the atmosphere for the majority of the first half. At the break the game remained goalless.

The second half too, was a cagey affair which only opened up after Fry made futher substitution with 13 minutes of normal time remaining. Tait had already been tactically introduced into the game just after the hour mark for Shearer, but the second change saw Donowa replace the struggling Kevin Francis. Within minutes he had two glorious chances to win the game but both were in the air and failed to trouble the 'keeper. As the prospect of the 'sudden death' goal loomed Blues almost snatched the game late on. Gary Poole had surged forward and as people waited for the cross he let fly from outside the area with fiercely hit angled drive which went just wide of the upright.

Extra time got under way with Birmingham stepping up the pace, and the turning point came ten minutes into the first period, when Mountfield, who had been a pillar of strength in the centre of Carlisle's defence, had to leave the field following a cut to his forehead, replaced by Jamie Robinson. Just three minutes later a floated cross by Otto fell into the territory Mountfield had controlled commandingly all afternoon but without his presence Tait rose to flick a header which cleared the outstretched arm of Caig and dropped into the corner of the net. Blues had become the first team to win with a 'golden goal' decider in a final at Wembley.!

BIRMINGHAM CITY

Bennett, Poole, Cooper, Ward, Barnett, Daish,
Hunt, Claridge, Francis (Donowa 77), Otto, Shearer (Tait 63).

CARLISLE UNITED

Caig, Edmondson, Gallimore, Walling, Mountfield (Robinson 100),
Conway, Thomas, Currie, Reeves, Hayward, Prokas (Thorpe 90).

REFEREE

Mr P Foakes (Clacton on Sea)

Paul Tait

April 24

The Matches played on this day

1909, Division 2.
Glossop 3   Blues 1   Att. 500
                 Mounteney
1915, Division 2.
Blues 1   Bristol City 1   Att. 10,000
Windridge
1920, Division 2.
Blues 2   Leyton Orient 1 Att. 20,000
Short, Lane
1926, Division 1.
Blues 1   West Ham United 0 Att. 15,000
Bradford
1937, Division 1.
Blues 1   Wolverhampton W. 0 Att. 30,000
Jennings(pen)
1943, Wartime.
Northampton Town 1 Blues 0
1948, Division 2.
Sheffield W. 0   Blues 0   Att. 25,990
1954, Division 2.
Everton 1   Blues 0   Att. 62,885
Hickson 38
1962, Division 1.
Blues 0   Everton 0   Att. 21,910
1963, Division 1.
Bolton Wanderers 0 Blues 0   Att. 12,860
1965, Division 1.
Blues 5   Blackburn Rovers 5 Att. 8,887
Vowden 30   McEvoy 17
Lynn 40(pen)   Ferguson 20
Beard 54, 71, 78 Hennessey(og) 51
                 Douglas 53, 66
Blues, already mathematically relegated, draw their lowest
crowd of the season. Blues 'keeper Billy Beel made his debut.
1971, Division 2.
Blues 1   Portsmouth 1   Att. 19,440
B.Latchford 8   Hiron 72
1979, Division 1.
Blues 1   WBA 1   Att. 19,897
Gallagher 58   Robson 90
1982, Division 1.
Blues 2   Swansea City 1   Att. 14,973
Broadhurst 31   Walsh 54
Harford 78
This game screened by Central TV's The Big Match
1990, Division 3.
Blues 1   Notts County 2   Att. 10,533
Hopkins 53   Lund 44
                 Palmer 74
1993, Division 1.
Blues 0   Tranmere Rovers 0 Att. 14,600
1999, Division 1.
Bristol City 1   Blues 2   Att. 15,845
Akinbiyi 46   Grainger 49(pen)
                 Ndlovu 71
Brown had a goal disallowed for Bristol City on 26 mins.
2000, Division 1.
Blues 2   Walsall 0   Att. 24,268
Furlong 70, 90(pen)

Playing record for this day
Playing record for this day is...18 games, Won 6, Drawn 8, Lost 4, GF 20, GA 18.
Today's success rate.....55.56% Year ranking....99th

Match of the Day

FROM 1965
BLUES ARE DOWN BUT FIGHTING

Beard the hero in ten goal St Andrews cracker

Blues already mathematically relegated from Division One had an audience of just 8,877 for their penultimate league game against Blackburn at St Andrews. Those who stayed away missed a rare ten-goal score draw in an amazing game of attacking football, one of the best seen at the ground.

After a slow start the scoring started after 17 minutes and never ceased as goals rattled in and time seemed to whizz by, such was the entertainment which unfolded on the pitch. The first goal went to Blackburn, when slack marking allowed McEvoy a simple header past Birmingham debutant 'keeper Beel. From an identical move, Beard should have equalised moments later, but Else in the Blackburn goal escaped when the ball hit his foot after he had dived the wrong way. Blackburn then stormed forward and went 2-0 up seconds later, a quickly taken free kick put Fraser away and after he nutmegged Page he was completely free on goal. Rushing in he slammed the ball into the roof of the net as Beel came out to stop him. At this point Blues looked like receiving yet another defeat. Birmingham, however continued to battle on and got back into the game with a goal on the half-hour mark. A long ball from Hennessey went straight to Jackson who controlled well and sent over the cross which Vowden eventually converted at the second attempt after his initial miskick. Then a minute later Beard missed a glorious chance to level after being presented a gift chance by Vowden's wonderful pass into the area. In a fabulous end-to-end game of non-stop attacking football, Ferguson missed an even better chance at the other end, his shot from closer in this time went horribly wide. With five minutes of the half remaining Blues scored the fourth goal of the game from the penalty spot to level. Lynn blasted home in typical style, the ball hit so ferociously it wedged between the net and back stanchion of the goal and it took the 'keeper some time to prise it clear before play could restart. Blackburn, denied an interval lead, came out the more eager and it took them just eight minutes to regain the advantage by going ahead 3-2. It was tough luck on the new Blues 'keeper who seemed to have Mike England's long-range shot comfortably covered but Hennessey's boot sent the ball into the opposite corner at the last second, and Beel had no chance saving that one.

For the second time in the game Birmingham found themselves two goals behind just two minutes later. A Ferguson cross was met by a crisp downward header by the unmarked Douglas and again there was little Beel could do about it either. Birmingham as they did earlier seemed to play more freely when behind and within no time were looking dangerous, the two-goal deficit not at all daunting. Their first attack ended with a fine save from Else after a real thunderbolt from Vowden, but Beard ran in to sqeeze the rebounding ball in from an acute angle. Blues swarmed forward looking for an equaliser and Vowden had an effort charged down from within the six yard box and then Thwaites was denied from another terrific save from Else. Then on 66 minutes came the game's best goal by far, Douglas collected a loose ball in his own half and weaved his way past four Birmingham men over some 50 yards before finishing with a chip across Beel, who had been forced off his line by the dangerous run. Still Blues refused to give the game up and gave themselves some hope on 71 minutes when reducing the score to 5-4, Beard netting from inside the penalty area. With 12 minutes left Beard completed a 24-minute hat-trick to level the game again for Blues. With both sides still attacking the final whistle brought about a huge ovation, it was a truly remarkable game and well appreciated by an enthralled but small St Andrews crowd.

BIRMINGHAM CITY
Beel, Lynn, Sharples, Hennessey, Foster, Page, Jackson, Martin, Vowden, Beard, Thwaites.
BLACKBURN ROVERS
Else, Newton, Joyce, Clayton, England, Sharples, Ferguson, McEvoy, Byron, Douglas, Harrison.

REFEREE
Mr B Setchell (Luton)

Dennis Thwaites

Playing record for this day
Playing record for this day is...18 games, Won 8, Drawn 3, Lost 7, GF 29, GA 27.
Today's success rate.....52.78% Year ranking....131st

April
25

Match of the Day
FROM 1931

BLUES CLOSE TO GLORY IN FIRST FINAL

Early 'goal' from Gregg is ruled offside

A wet but eager 90,368 crowd packed into Wembley to cheer the first all midland final for 36 years and Birmingham's final for the first time in 50 years of trying. It was Blues from Division One against promotion chasing Second Division West Brom. The rain threatened to spoil the occasion and it was the wettest cup final in years, ensuring both teams would be tested on the huge Wembley pitch in the mud.

Blues settled to the conditions well and on their first real attack had the ball in the Albion net. A free kick from Cringan was floated over towards the running Bob Gregg who steered his header past a flat footed Pearson for a perfect start. However linesman Harold Mee of Nottingham surprised almost everyone in the stadium when he raised his flag to rule it out for offside.

Blues, to their credit, put the disappointment to one side and were soon back attacking. Joe Bradford broke clear but Pearson rushed out to smother the Blues forward, then Curtis sent in a dangerous looking cross which again was clipped away from Bradford this time by centre half Magee. Albion then countered and Barkas just managed to catch and then clear from Glidden who had raced free from a hopeful long-ball clearance. It was now a good end-to-end game with both teams looking likely to score and after 25 minutes Albion went in front. A fiercely hit Glidden cross struck Barkas on the hand and before the Albion players made any appeal Richardson latched on to the loose ball. His first-time shot was blocked by Hibbs but he followed up to smash in the rebound. Blues came close moments later with Bradford and Crosbie, who should have made more of their chances inside the Albion penalty area. Then with half time approaching Bradford should surely have equalised when he stubbed his shot and the ball bobbled past Pearson who scrambled across his line, grateful to see it roll wide of the post.

Albion were the better starters in the second half and Hibbs pulled off a great save from Wood. On their next attack Wood hit the post with a belting shot from 20 yards as Blues held on and tried to settle the game down. As the Albion storm subsided, Blues counter attacked.

A long ball from Crosbie found Bradford, as his fellow forwards looked to make space for a return pass he turned sharply and in the same movement shot past Pearson and Blues were level on 56 minutes at 1-1. But with the Blues fans still celebrating the goal, Albion hit back with a sucker punch. After the ball was thumped forward Liddell failed to clear to any great distance and WG Richardson pounced to slip it past Hibbs from close range. Albion dominated the final moments of the game and only the brilliant Hibbs kept Blues in with a slight chance with some brave diving saves which kept the score down to 2-1. Blues will always rue the early disallowed goal, but Albion had earned their win and made it a promotion double when they won their last two league matches of the season.

BIRMINGHAM CITY

Hibbs, Liddell, Barkas, Cringan, Morrall, Leslie, Briggs, Crosbie, Bradford, Gregg, Curtis
WEST BROMWICH ALBION

Pearson, Shaw, Trentham, Magee, Bill Richardson, Edwards, Glidden, Carter, Billy Richardson, Sandford, Wood.

REFEREE

Mr A. Kingscott (Derby)

Johnny Crosbie

Blues news extra   1942...Friendly
Walsall 0 Blues 0

Birthdays
Jacques Williams born today in 1981

April 26

- 1875

The Matches played on this day

1902, Division 1.
Blues 0   Notts County 0   Att. 20,000
1913, Division 2.
Blues 2   Grimsby Town 1   Att. 3,000
Reed(2)
1919, Wartime.
Leicester Fosse 2   Blues 4
     Crowe, J.Godfrey(3)
1920, Division 2.
Tottenham Hotspur 0   Blues 0   Att. 35,000
1924, Division 1.
Cardiff City 2   Blues 0   Att. 15,000
1930, Division 1.
Sunderland 2   Blues 0   Att. 10,000
1933, Division 1.
Blues 1   WBA 1   Att. 10,000
Briggs
1939, Division 1.
Blues 1   Chelsea 1   Att. 10,000
Brown
1943, Wartime.
Aston Villa 1   Blues 0
1947, Division 2.
Plymouth Argyle 0   Blues 2   Att. 25,000
     Edwards, Bodle
1952, Division 2.
Blues 3   Luton Town 1   Att. 29,000
Purdon 39   Warhurst(og) 89
Stewart 76
Briggs 77
1958, Division 1.
Blues 0   Leicester City 1   Att. 27,614
McNeil 51
Peter Murphy had a goal disallowed after 72 minutes.
The win enabled Leicester to avoid relegation.
1965, Division 1.
Blues 3   Leeds United 3   Att. 16,644
Thwaites 5   Giles 70(pen)
Beard 49   Reaney 80
Vowden 51   Charlton 90
Bottom of the table Blues denied Don Revie's Leeds United of
the title when Manchester United (who beat Arsenal 3-1 at
Old Trafford on the same night) pipped them on goal
average.
1975, Division 1.
Newcastle United 1   Blues 2   Att. 23,471
Macdonald 44   Kendall 12
     Pendrey 22
The win put Blues safe from relegation with one game
left to play.
1980, Division 1.
Burnley 0   Blues 0   Att. 10,314
1986, Division 1.
Liverpool 5   Blues 0   Att. 42,021
Rush 25
Gillespie 46, 58, 83(pen)
Molby 48(pen)
Blues 28th league defeat of the season a new club record
1995, Division 2.
Blues 2   Brentford 0   Att. 25,081
Francis 56
Daish 64
1997, Division 1.
Blues 2   Oxford United 0   Att. 16,109
Devlin 54
Bowen 87

Playing record for this day
Playing record for this day is...18 games, Won 7, Drawn 6, Lost 5, GF 22, GA 21.
Today's success rate.....55.56% Year ranking....100th

Match of the Day
FROM 1995
IT'S TOUGH AT THE TOP
Battered Brum leapfrog Brentford in the table, but at a cost

After a triumphant open top bus ride through Birmingham and a civic reception at the Council House in celebration of the Auto Windscreens Shield win, Blues were back in action for the important one a 'championship and promotion decider' against Brentford. Blues went into the game with the same side that fought out 103 minutes football at Wembley three days earlier. The Brentford team included future Blues stars Martin Grainger and Nicky Forster. There was a record breaking Division Two crowd of 25,081 to greet the teams, knowing a win for either side would eliminate the other from the race for the title.

Despite a frantic start to the game, clear cut chances were rare due to some excellent defending by both sides who had both conceded just 33 goals going into this game. Blues could have broke the deadlock midway through the first half but Daish's header was superbly saved by Dearden in the Brentford goal. This was the closest either side came to scoring in the first 45 minutes.

After the break Brentford were gifted a chance to sneak into the lead through a rare Mark Ward error. He dallied on the ball allowing Taylor to burst through but only to blaze his shot wide when he had time to get closer in. The miss proved expensive as just three minutes later Brentford were a goal down following Blues first corner of the half. Hunt swung the ball in and Daish flicked on for Kevin Francis who controlled well with his back to goal and hooked the ball in as he turned quickly from barely six yards out. As he was mobbed by his team mates in front of the Tilton Road stand, it soon became clear Francis had hurt himself badly in scoring and the shot proved to be his last kick of the season. Louie Donowa replaced him on 56 minutes and it was he who soon got into the game winning another corner just eight minutes later. Hunt sent over another glorious cross and this time Daish's thundering header almost burst the net. The ground erupted, the title seemingly won now with Blues 2-0 ahead. Despite a late rally by Brentford, Blues defence, marshalled well by Daish and Barnett, held firm until disaster struck with just seconds of the game remaining. As Barnett chased back an innocuous long ball which was going safely into the corner he pulled up sharply and dropped to the ground in agony after snapping his achilles tendon. Barnett was stretchered off to a standing ovation and moments later a roar went up to greet the final whistle. Blues had won but at a high cost there influential centre back and forward were to play no further part in the three remaining games.

BIRMINGHAM CITY
Bennett, Poole, Cooper, Ward (Tait 67), Barnett, Daish,
Hunt, Claridge, Francis (Donowa 56), Otto, Shearer.
BRENTFORD
Dearden, Statham, Grainger, Ashby, Bates, Ratcliffe,
Smith, Forster, Taylor, Stephenson (Abrahams 74), Mundee.

REFEREE
Mr M Riley (Leeds)

Ricky Otto

Playing record for this day

Playing record for this day is...21 games, Won 7, Drawn 3, Lost 11, GF 34, GA 37.
Today's success rate.....40.48% Year ranking....232nd

Match of the Day
FROM 1974
BURNS TO THE RESCUE
Blues avoid the drop after wonder goal!

The last game of the 1973-74 season had a very familliar ring to it, Blues had to win to stay in the First Division and a traumatic and exciting game was again anticipated by a large crowd. Both teams went into this game knowing a win would put them safe, the loser hoping that Manchester United would fail to get anything from their game in hand. Southampton, who were bottom, were already doomed. 44,182 packed into St Andrews hoping Blues could add another game to their four game unbeaten run, in fact they had taken 16 points from the last possible 26 losing just three times, one of which was to Norwich 2-1 at Carrow Road. Both sides were unchanged for the game and were at full strength. The atmosphere inside St Andrews was at fever pitch and it must have been intimidating for the visitors as they started the game. The crowd seemed to be affecting the home side more as a nervy Blues were a goal down after just four minutes. Pendrey brought a Steve Grapes run to reckless end and from Suggett's free kick Dave Stringer rose unmarked to nod the ball past a helpless Dave Latchford. Blues restarted in a now silent St Andrews, but determined to get back in the game quickly, and for the first time they managed to create a goal-scoring chance. A nice move between Taylor and Francis allowed Campbell to shoot although his effort hit Steele on the arm but there was no intention to handle despite 44,000 appeals for a penalty. On 20 minutes Blues had a better and more clear cut chance when Taylor cut inside his full back to within range and his fierce cross shot was brilliantly saved by Keelan in the Norwich goal. Moments later Francis tried a long range effort which Keelan saved a little less spectacularly. Blues were now dominating and in their eagerness were leaving the chance for a Norwich break away. Pendrey, who had chased forward, tried his luck from distance but it was blocked by Boyer who collected the rebound and easily outpaced the Blues full back as he broke away, fortunately Hynd was covering well and came across to nip the ball away from the speedy Norwich forward. With half-time approaching Blues finally got back on level terms on 41 minutes. Kendall who had been involved in all of Blues decent play, again collected a loose ball and threaded a lovely weighted through pass to Hatton who just beat Keelan as he rushed out to toe poke the ball in. Blues fans were still celebrating when just two minutes later another great cross from Taylor was met by the full stretch dive of Kenny Burns who planted his header across Keelan and into the top corner. Blues could not have timed their double strike better as moments later they trooped off to half time with a chance to regroup and allow the crowd time to calm down. The job was now half done. The second half was a little less frantic and Blues started to pass more intelligently rather than find their forwards with desperate long balls. The first opportunity to score came through a free kick awarded after Hatton was impeded by Forbes. Kendall hit the direct kick, sweetly the ball narrowly missing the target as it clipped the bar. With the game drawing to a close and victory and survival in sight Norwich produced their best chance of scoring since the fourth minute. Blues failed to clear a right-wing cross and Latchford was called on to pull off a sensational double save from Sissons then McDougall. Blues saw out the final moments of the game without further anxiety and at the final whistle there was mass hysteria from the celebrating Blues fans. A lap of honour was loudly cheered as Blues knew they would be playing First Division football next season.

BIRMINGHAM CITY
Latchford, Martin, Pendrey, Kendall, Hynd, Roberts, Campbell, Francis, Burns, Hatton, Taylor.
NORWICH CITY
Keelan, Butler, Benson, Stringer, Forbes, Grapes(Davies h/t), Steele, MacDougall, Suggett, Boyer, Sissons.

Roger Hynd

Blues news extra 1998...Bruce is tops say fans
Steve Bruce was voted supporters' 'Player of the Year' at the club's annual awards dinner.

Birthdays
Ken Green born today in 1924   **Geoff Vowden born today in 1941**

The Matches played on this day

1893, Test Match.

Newton Heath 5	Blues 2	Att. 6,000
	Walton, Mobley	

Played at Bramall Lane, Sheffield
1896, Test Match.

Blues 8	Manchester City 0	Att. 2,000
Jones(3),		
Wheldon(3),		
Abbott, Hallam		

1901, Division 1.

Burnley 1	Blues 0	Att. 5,000

1907, Division 1.

Bury 1	Blues 0	Att. 10,000

1912, Division 2.

Blues 2	Glossop 0	Att. 6,000
Robertson(2)		

1927, Division 1.

Blues 1	Cardiff City 2	.Att. 20,000
Bradford		

1929, Division 1.

Blues 3	Bury 2	Att. 18,140
Crosbie,		
Bradford(2)		

1935, Division 1.

Huddersfield Town 2	Blues 2	Att. 10,000
	Harris(2)	

1940, Wartime.

Blues 5	Newport County 2	
Trigg(2),		
Bodle(2), Godden		

1946, Wartime.

Blues 0	Wolverhampton W. 1	

1957, Division 1.

Blues 3	Manchester City 3	Att. 23,700
Brown 4	Kirkham 35, 70	
Phoenix(og) 25	Hall(og) 46	
Govan 88		

1960, Division 1.

Blues 0	Burnley 1	Att. 37,014
	Pilkington 72	

1961, Division 1.

Blues 0	Burnley 1	Att. 15,011
	Adamson 56(pen)	

Burnley's team was mainly made up of reserves as they had played a League Cup semi-final replay against Villa 24 hours earlier.
1963, Division 1.

Blackburn Rovers 6	Blues 1	Att. 9,500
England 13	Auld 75	
Ferguson 15		
Pickering 34, 37		
Smith (og) 65		
Douglas 81		

1968, FA Cup Semi Final.

Blues 0	WBA 2	Att. 60,831
	Astle 14	
	Brown 69	

1971, Division 2.

Middlesbrough 0	Blues 0	Att. 12,802

1974, Division 1.

Blues 2	Norwich City 1	Att. 44,182
Hatton 41	Stringer 4	
Burns 43		

1985, Division 2.

Barnsley 0	Blues 1	Att. 6,757
	Geddis 5	

Blues gained their 13th away league win, a club record to date
1991, Division 3.

Blues 0	Crewe Alexandra 2	Att. 6,429
	Edwards 18, 90	

1994, Division 1.

WBA 2	Blues 4	Att. 20,316
Donovan 24	Claridge 38, 90	
Burgess 64	Donowa 50	
	Saville 56	

1996, Division 1.

Leicester City 3	Blues 0	Att. 19,702
Claridge 32		
Heskey 38		
Lennon 89		

Steve Claridge, a former Blues striker scored for Leicester

April 28

Playing record for this day
Playing record for this day is...20 games, Won 8, Drawn 6, Lost 6, GF 33, GA 29.
Today's success rate.....55% Year ranking....108th

The Matches played on this day

1894, Test Match.
Darwen 1	Blues 3	Att. 6,000
	Hallam,	
	Walton, Wheldon.	

Played at the Victoria Ground, Stoke
1906, Division 1.
Blues 3	Manchester City 2	Att. 5,000
Green, Jones,		
Edmondson(og)		

1917, Wartime.
Blues 0	Lincoln City 0

1923, Division 1.
Blues 1	Burnley 0	Att. 19,400
Bradford		

1928, Division 1.
West Ham United 3	Blues 3	Att. 16,000
	Bradford(2), Briggs	

1930, Division 1.
Sheffield W. 1	Blues 1	.Att. 9,310
	Blyth	

1934, Division 1.
Leicester City 3	Blues 7	Att. 18,000
	Moffatt, Guest(3),	
	Mangnall, Roberts, Jones(og)	

1945, Wartime.
Coventry City 2	Blues 2
	Lewis, Bright

1951, Division 2.
West Ham United 1	Blues 2	Att. 16,500
Rowley 56	Kinsell 76 Ferris 4	

1962, Division 1.
Blues 2	Tottenham Hotspur 3	Att. 29,614
Beard 83	Greaves 15, 82	
Leek 87	Mackay 80	

1967, Division 2.
Blues 0	Huddersfield Town 0	Att. 14,385

1973, Division 1.
Blues 3	WBA 2	Att. 36,784
B.Latchford 6	Astle 40	
Hynd 80	Wile 51	
Burns 84		

WBA's 24 year run in Division One came to a close. They finished bottom of the table, and were relegated.
1979, Division 1.
Everton 1	Blues 0	Att. 22,958
King 46		

1982, Division 1.
Tottenham Hotspur 1	Blues 1	Att. 25,470
Villa 60	Harford 44	

Blues 32nd succesive away League match without a win. The sequence stretched back 18 months to November 1980. This is still a club record to date.

Match of the Day

FROM 1934
THE BLUES ARE STAYING UP!!!
First Division status assured after magnificent Filbert Street win

Blues travelled to Filbert Street knowing anything other than victory could condemn them to second Division football for the 1934-35 season. Sheffield United had already lost their fight but Blues were on the brink of relegation Second from bottom with 34 points. Newcastle were only slightly better off also with 34 points whilst Chelsea had 35 and Liverpool and Villa had just 36, together they were all involved in a nail-biting last two games of the season. Blues eased the tension when they took a fourth minute lead through Moffatt who drove in a Billy Guest cross from ten yards out. Hibbs then kept Blues in front with two fantastic saves but could do nothing about Chandler's spectacular shot on 25 minutes to level the score at 1-1. In a nervy end-to-end game Guest then won the ball just inside Leicester's half. He beat Smith then full back Black before cutting in from the wing to blast Blues back in front with 31 minutes of the game gone. Within a minute Moffatt raced forward to send a cross in for Mangnall who overstepped the ball letting it run on to the unmarked Guest who planted his left foot shot firmly in the corner to send the Blues fans wild. Blues were on fire and could have wrapped up the game by half time, McLaren finger-tipped a shot from Roberts over the bar then saved well from Mangnall's header. Then just before the break Guest beat the 'keeper but not the post with a rasping shot from inside the penalty area.

Leicester reduced Blues lead on the hour when Chandler scored after being let in by Morrall's slip, the forward was clean through and beat Hibbs easily. With Blues reeling under the rejuvenated home side Maw capitalised on more slack defending to equalise for Leicester just five minutes later. Straight from the kick off Blues pushed forward and a quick interchange of passing between Bradford and Mangnall left the latter with a clear opening he didn't miss to regain the lead at 4-3. A terrible mix up in the Leicester defence allowed a fifth Blues goal on 70 minutes when centre back Jones put through his own net. Blues wrapped up a remarkable high scoring game just two minutes later when Roberts charged from midfield to smash in Blues sixth goal. With 13 minutes of the game remaining and Blues looking relaxed they opened up the Leicester defence again to allow Billy Guest to score for his hat-trick. Blues had completed an awesome win in difficult circumstances and had avoided the dreaded drop. They leapfrogged Newcastle who joined Sheffield United in Division Two the following season.

LEICESTER CITY
McLaren, Black, Jones, Smith, Heywood, Ritchie, Adcock, Maw, Chandler, Lochhead, Liddle.
BIRMINGHAM CITY
Hibbs, Booton, Barkas, Stoker, Morrall, Calladine, Moffatt, Roberts, Mangnall, Bradford, Guest.

REFEREE
Mr J Brown (Blackburn)

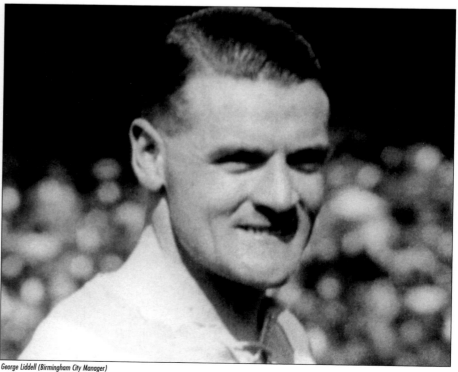
George Liddell (Birmingham City Manager)

Birthdays
Billy Wright born today in 1958

Sadly Missed
Sir Alf Ramsey died today in 1999, aged 79   **Stan Lynn died today in 2002, aged 73**

Billy Guest

1984, Division 1.

Sunderland 2	Blues 1	Att. 13,061
James 42, 49	Wright 55 (pen)	
(2 pens)		

Sunderland had Rob Hindmarsh sent off after 60 minutes. Blues had Mick Harford sent off after 65 minutes. Billy Wright scored on his 26th birthday.

1990, Division 3.

Leyton Orient 1	Blues 2	Att. 5,691
Harvey 33	Hopkins 47	
	Peer 52	

Blues had Kevin Langley sent off after 81 minutes.

1992, Division 3.

Wigan Athletic 3	Blues 0	Att. 5,950
Worthington 22, 74		
Pilling 39		

2000, Division 1.

Manchester City 1	Blues 0	Att. 32,062
Taylor 40		

Jon McCarthy stretchered off after 64 minutes after breaking his leg for a second time this season.

2001, Division 1.

Blues 1	Grimsby Town 0	Att. 24,822
Marcelo 65		

2002, Division 1 Play Off Semi Final, 1st leg.

Blues 1	Millwall 1	Att. 28,282
Hughes 56	Dublin 80	

April 29

Playing record for this day
Playing record for this day is...16 games, Won 4, Drawn 7, Lost 5, GF 19, GA 24.
Today's success rate.....46.88% Year ranking....192nd

Match of the Day
FROM 1972
HILLSBOROUGH LIVE WITH THE SOUND OF BLUES

Blues secure two precious promotion points at Sheffield

Thousands of Blues fans made the trip to Hillsborough today for this crucial clash against Sheffield Wednesday. At kick-off the crowd was 28,132 and the noise created when the teams came out was deafening.

Trevor Francis started eagerly with an attack on goal from a solo run deep from midfield. He was eventually stopped by the Wednesday defence, but the move was typical of the energetic flair with which Birmingham were playing. They missed a chance from Hatton when the ball bounced away from the post. This was a close call but just two minutes later at the other end Wednesday almost snatched a goal of their own, when a shot from Craig curled round the post after beating Cooper.

The rest of the first half produced ample goal opportunities, but they all proved to be fruitless. The second half, was only minutes old when Thompson blocked another goalbound shot from Francis.

Blues encouraged by this, stepped up the pressure and won a corner soon after. The kick was taken by Taylor and arrived at Hatton via Latchford's cross. Hatton in a perfect position steered his header past Springett to give Blues a 1-0 lead. The joy lasted just four minutes before the Owls were back, Sunley heading in a neatly worked free kick and to add to Birmingham's problems Cooper was injured in trying to save the effort and needed treatment before he continued. The visitors heads didn't drop and they fought on admirably in an action packed game. It wasn't long before their hard work paid off with a second goal. a fantastic strike from Francis on 65 minutes which proved to be the winner. Up until this point he had been kept reasonably quiet until he collected a loose ball inside the Wednesday penalty area. Avoiding the tackle of Prophett he unleashed a cracking right-foot drive which zipped across the turf into the bottom far corner of the net. With time almost up there was nearly a devastating blow for Birmingham when out of nothing Whitehead and Hynd got into a muddle and the ball almost crept past Cooper off Whitehead for a freak own goal. However, things were going Birmingham's way and they held out to claim an important victory in their quest for promotion.

SHEFFIELD WEDNESDAY
Springett, Thompson, Clements, Prophett, Mullen, Pugh, Sinclair, Craig, Joicey, Sunley, Sissons.

BIRMINGHAM CITY
Cooper, Carroll, Pendrey, Smith, Hynd, Whitehead, Campbell, Francis, Latchford, Hatton, Taylor.

REFEREE
Mr B Matthewson (Bolton)

Garry Pendrey

Blues news extra   1903...Fund raiser for Warwickshire CCC.
Blues 2 West Bromwich Albion 3

Blues news extra   1978...£10,000 for 30-goal Latchford
Former Blues striker Bob Latchford's two goals for Everton against Chelsea brought his season's total to 30. He becomes the first Division One striker to hit 30 league goals in one season for six years earning him a cheque for £10,000 from a national newspaper.

Blues news extra   1981...Cap number 6 for Langan
Blues full back Dave Langan helped the Republic of Ireland to a 3-1 win over Czechoslovakia in Dublin, winning his sixth International cap.

Birthdays
James Dyson born today in 1979   Barry Bridges born today in 1941

Playing record for this day
Playing record for this day is...14 games, Won 6, Drawn 4, Lost 4, GF 20, GA 18.
Today's success rate.....57.14% Year ranking....85th

Match of the Day
FROM 1973
WEAKENED LEEDS ARE
NO MATCH FOR STRONG BLUES

FA Cup finalists go down 2-1 in a Freddie Goodwin tribute game

A crowd of 34,449 turned out at St Andrews to see Blues take on the FA Cup finalists in the last league game of the 1972-73 season. They got to see a Leeds side, but nowhere near the side which would play at Wembley the following Saturday. The visitors manager Don Revie was again prepared to risk a £5,000 League fine by fielding a reserve side. The crowd let their feelings known when the the list of 'unknowns' was read out before the kick off. Shouts of "WHO!"(yes even back in 1973 the famous 'WHO' chant was heard at St Andrews) greeted ten names, only Peter Lorimer was spared as he was the only player likely to make the FA Cup final line-up.

Yet the substance of the Leeds team did not devalue Birmingham's fine and deserved victory, they would have given the very best in the league a run for their money such was the standard manager Goodwin had installed around St Andrews during the season. Despite a neat display of football by the home side it was the novices from Leeds who stunned Blues by taking the lead in the ninth minute. Lorimer's long cross to the far post aimed at Jordan was won by Hynd. His header only managed to loop over the stranded Dave Latchford and under the bar. This slip-up only inspired Blues to press forward and in doing so the game became littered with some niggly fouls. Mann of Leeds was the first of five players cautioned when he sent Pendrey flying with a sliding challenge. Blues levelled the score on 29 minutes when Latchford then Burns headed on Hynd's deep free kick to Francis. His run and shot from eight yards deflected off Terry Yorath before beating Gary Sprake in the Leeds goal.

The second half started with Blues receiving their first booking, John Roberts being the guilty man foir a foul on Joe Jordan. Then shortly after Ellam was replaced by McGinley on 49 minutes, Blues took the lead with a little help from the substitute's first touch. From a great cross from Malcolm Page it was McGinley who sliced his clearance to Burns, he controlled well, side stepped Galvin and swept the ball past a helpless Sprake for a 2-1 lead to Blues. As the game entered the closing stages Pendrey became the fifth and final name added to referee Wallace's notebook, and Lorimer hit the bar with a thunderbolt from 25 yards. Blues held on and at the end then the fans sang the praises of manager Goodwin and his team. They refused to move until the Blues boss had acknowledged the crowd and eventually he appeared on the muddy St Andrews pitch with chairman Keith Coombes. It was an emotional and fitting tribute to the man who had put together a strong side, and restored credibility at St Andrews.

BIRMINGHAM CITY
Dave Latchford, Martin, Pendrey, Page, Hynd, Roberts, Campbell, Francis, Bob Latchford, Burns, Hope (Hendrie 73).
LEEDS UNITED
Sprake, Galvin, Hampton, Yorath, Ellam (McGinley 49), Frank Gray, Liddell, Lorimer, Jordan, Mann, Bates.

REFEREE
Mr E Wallace (Crewe)

John Roberts

Blues news extra   1903...Fund raiser for Ibrox tragedy.
Bob McRoberts scored Blues equaliser against Villa in a charity game for the victims of the Ibrox disaster. The game finished all square at 1-1.

Birthdays
George Hicks born today in 1902

May 1

Playing record for this day
Playing record for this day is...14 games, Won 5, Drawn 6, Lost 3, GF 23, GA 21.
Today's success rate.....57.14% Year ranking....84th

The Matches played on this day

1920, Division 2.
Blues 0	Tottenham Hotspur 1	Att. 39,000

1922, Division 1.
Preston North End 2	Blues 2	Att. 20,000
	Crosbie(2)	

1926, Division 1.
Arsenal 3	Blues 0	Att. 22,240

1937, Division 1.
Blues 2	Manchester City 2	Att. 25,000
Morris, Clarke		

1940, Wartime.
Blues 3	Northampton Town 1	
Gardner, Bodle, Trigg.		

1943, Wartime.
Chesterfield 1	Blues 1	
	Acquaroff	

1948, Division 2.
Blues 0	Tottenham Hotspur 0	Att. 35,569

Blues won their 59th point of the season to reach their best ever total under the two points for a win rule in the Football League.

1953, Division 2.
Brentford 1	Blues 2	Att. 9,000
Dare 90	Lane 34	
	Murphy 65	

1963, Division 1.
Blues 3	West Ham United 2	Att. 14,392
Auld 43	Scott 9	
Hennessey 65	Hurst 27	
Harris 75		

Blues first home win since October 27 (11 matches without a home league win).
Bertie Auld struck again in the second half but this effort was disallowed for offside.

1971, Division 2.
Charlton Athletic 1	Blues 1	Att. 10,723
Curtis 5	B.Latchford 60	

1979, Division 1.
Manchester City 3	Blues 1	Att. 27,366
Power 15	Lynex 42	
Deyna 72, 83		

Blues 19th away defeat of the season, a club record to date. It was also Blues 18th consecutive away league defeat which is not only a club record to date but a Football League record.
Malcolm Briggs an 87th minute substitute for Alan Buckley made his debut and only appearance for the Blues. He thus became the Blues player with the shortest senior career at the club.

1982, Division 1.
Notts County 1	Blues 4	Att. 10,710
McCullough 12	Phillips 1	
	Evans 49, 81	
	Harford 68	

1989, Division 2.
Blues 1	Bradford City 0	Att. 4,735
Frain 39		

1993, Division 1.
Bristol Rovers 3	Blues 3	Att. 5,150
Taylor 40, 45	Saville 62	
Saunders 64	Mardon 68	
	Smith 90	

Match of the Day
FROM 1982
GOOD EVANS, BLUES WIN AWAY
A long time coming, but Blues win away in emphatic style

It took 31 attempts stretching back to November 1980 but at last the sequence was over and Blues recorded a victory on their travels. It was a superb performance from the visitors who brushed aside Notts County in sensational style after a fantastic start when Les Phillips put them ahead earlt on. Despite an equaliser on 12 minutes, Blues, under the leadership of acting skipper Dave Langan came storming back to win convincingly by 4-1.

Blues hopes of avoiding the dreaded drop from Division One were given a tremendous boost when they took the lead after just 70 seconds. Mick Harford holding the ball up extremely well in attack, supplied Van Mierlo who hit a first-time shot at goal. From the rebound Phillips reacted quickly to steer it in for the simplest of goals from close in. Within a minute Blues almost made it two when the ball ran across the face of the County goal and Harford came tantalisingly close to tapping in, but it just evaded his outstretched leg and ran harmlessly out of play. Notts eventually found their feet and mounted a few promising moves of their own, culminating in a deserved equaliser ten minutes later. From Christie's quickly taken throw in McCullough sprinted away, weaving through the Blues defence relatively unchallenged. When Coton came out to confront him, he produced the most delightful chip to cap a wonderfully worked and superbly executed goal. Blues responded well and their best reposte was a 30-yard thunderbolt from Curbishley which took two attempts by 'keeper Avramovic to save. With both defences now aware of the striking capabilities of their opponents, the game drifted into a dour midfield struggle as play became overcautious.

The second half started with Notts County doing most of the pressing. Then the sequence was broken by a touch of inspiration from Van Mierlo, beating O'Brien he chased down the flank but before he could deliver his centre the full back got back, but could only stop him illegally with a trip. The free kick came to nothing but the move seemed to galvanise the Blues team and now they were in the ascendancy. Blues were soon on the attack again and a superb pass from Dillon found Langan on the right in space. Taking the ball on, he shot from distance but the effort was well blocked. The loose ball eventually made its way out to Phillips lurking on the left hand side of the penalty area, and from his chipped pass Evans smacked a ferocious volley which Avramovic could only palm into the roof of the net. It was now a constant flow of Blues pressure and three minutes later the County 'keeper saved well from Langan after he was nicely set up from another wonderful ball by Dillon. Harford then put Blues into a thoroughly deserved 3-1 lead after 68 minutes, and a relaxed team could now play some exibition and entertaining football at their leisure. From the best move of the game, Tony Evans finished off with a simple side-footed shot in the 81st minute. Blues then put together a sequnce of 18 passes to the cheers of the many travelling fans amonst the 10,710 crowd at Meadow Lane. It was a very impressive display and Blues were good value for their fully deserved and emphatic 4-1 win.

BIRMINGHAM CITY
Coton, Langan, Hawker, Stevenson, Van Den Hauwe, Curbishley, Van Mierlo, Dillon, Harford, Phillips, Evans,
NOTTS COUNTY
Avramovic, Benjamin, O'Brien, Goodwin, Kilcline, Richards, Chiedozie, Harkouk, McCullough, Christie, Mair.

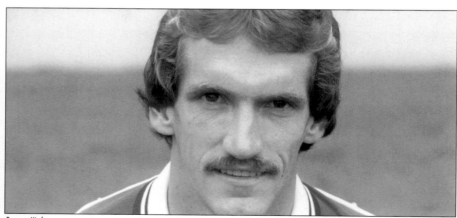

Tony van Mierlo

Blues news extra

1996...John Frain's Testimonial, Blues 0 Aston Villa 6
Attendance at St Andrews was 8,000 raising £45,000 for the Blues full back who had given the club 12 years service.

Playing record for this day

Playing record for this day is...13 games, Won 7, Drawn 3, Lost 3, GF 14, GA 9.

Today's success rate.....65.38% Year ranking....23rd

Match of the Day

FROM 1972

BLUES ARE PROMOTED

Latchford goal ends seven-year wilderness in Division Two

The equation was simple, one game left, one point required to gain promotion to Division One after seven years in the Second Division wilderness. Birmingham's travelling army of 18,000 were up for this one, and in a confident mood. They swelled the Brisbane Road crowd to 33,383 for the evening kick off. Many were locals who were full-time supporters of the club next in line to benefit from any Blues slip-up on the night, Millwall, and they were clearly intent on causing havoc should things start to go right for Birmingham. Orient, the other side in this huge game, had nothing but professional pride to play for and the result, no matter what, would not affect their position in the table at all.

Blues got the game under way and within minutes it was clear how much they were under pressure, their play dominated by the fear of a single error. It was no surprise then that the opening exchanges were almost entirely made in midfield, Blues were content to sit back and earn their draw by rigid defending even from deep in the Orient half of the playing field. One of the few chances that did come Birmingham's way was snatched at by Latchford and the ball sailed over the bar. At the other end Pendrey bravely blocked a goalbound strike from Lazarus, and striker Mickey Bullock almost broke Blues' hearts when he was stopped by a fine save from Paul Cooper. Blues' best chance came just before the half-time break when Goddard acrobatically tipped over a shot from Hatton.

Blues started the second period with much more confidence, obviously Freddie Goodwin's team talk had done the trick. They showed no sign of fear and were prepared to chase the game now, as if they had been told only a win, not a draw, was required. Straight away it was noticeable that Francis, who had hardly been involved in the first half, was now seeking possession and when he received the ball for the first time after the restart, he struck a beauty from outside the area which Goddard saved brilliantly. Then minutes later he sent a spectacular volley from Taylor's cross just inches wide. Blues looked increasingly likely to score and on 58 minutes they put one foot firmly into Division One, with a goal from Bob Latchford. A corner from Taylor was headed in by the Blues centre forward who was being pulled back by the 'keeper. The goal sparked chaos all around, Orient's players surrounded the referee complaining about Latchford's foul on Goddard, Blues fans invaded the pitch and then the Millwall fans decided to introduce themselves. Chaos prevailed for some time as police tried to shepherd fans back to their place. Play eventually resumed in full swing and it was Blues again dominating. Taylor broke through and almost made the game well and truly safe, but he was denied again by a superb diving save from Goddard.

This brought about another pitch invasion, only this time it was the Millwall fans. Play was halted again and when it restarted Blues were soon attacking the Orient goal. A lob by Hatton just cleared the bar in the closing minutes, this led to loud whistling from the crowd as well as 'Keep Right On to the End of the Road' which was even louder. The referee finally signalled the end of the game after almost 100 minutes play, including stoppage time, and the players charged off.

Blues fans stormed the pitch and the promotion party started, even the announcement of a bomb in the ground didn't stop the celebrations, but after a time the police did and everyone was evacuated. Everyone it seems apart from the Birmingham team and chairman Keith Coombes who were still in their dressing room, choosing not to leave. Coombes summed up the mood of the club by saying after the game, "I didn't care even if it was a real bomb, I can go happy now I know we are back in Division One"... WHAT A NIGHT!!!

BIRMINGHAM CITY

Cooper, Carroll, Pendrey, Smith, Hynd, Whitehead, Campbell, Francis, Latchford, Hatton, Taylor.

ORIENT

Goddard, Arber, Rose, Hoadley, Harris, Allen, Lazarus, Brisley, Bullock, Walley, Bowyer,

REFEREE

Mr M Lowe (Sheffield)

The Matches played on this day

1921, Division 2.		
Blues 4	Port Vale 0	Att. 28,000
Hampton,		
Davies(2,1 pen), Barton		
1925, Division 1.		
Notts County 0	Blues 1	Att. 8,000
	Islip	
1931, Division 1.		
Blues 2	Leicester City 1	Att. 10,365
Curtis, Bradford		
1936, Division 1.		
Blues 1	WBA 3	Att. 28,124
Barkas(pen)		
1972, Division 1.		
Orient 0	Blues 1	Att. 33,383
	B.Latchford 58	
1981, Division 1.		
Blues 1	Everton 1	Att. 12,863
Evans 34	Eastoe 38	
1983, Division 1.		
Blues 1	Brighton & HA 1	Att. 15,977
Handysides 3	Smith 59	
1987, Division 2.		
Blues 1	Grimsby Town 0	Att. 4,457
Whitton 75		

St Andrew's lowest attendance for 74 years and ironically it was against the same team, Grimsby in April 1913.

1988, Division 2.		
Ipswich Town 1	Blues 0	Att. 11,067
Atkinson 68		
1992, Division 3.		
Stockport County 2	Blues 0	Att. 7,840
Gannon 8		
Preece 12		
1995, Division 2.		
Blues 0	Bradford City 0	Att. 25,139
1999, Division 1.		
Blues 1	Ipswich Town 0	Att. 27,685
Furlong 60		

2002, Division 1 Play Off Semi Final, 2nd leg.

Millwall 0	Blues 1	Att. 16,391
	John 90	

After missing two glorious chances Stern John tapped in from three yards to win the game and the tie 2-1.

Blues news extra

1942...Friendly Blues 0 Leicester City 3 Played at Villa Park.

Birthdays

Mark Dennis born today in 1961

The Matches played on this day

1924, Division 1.
Blues 0   Cardiff City 0   Att. 33,000
Blues keeper Dan Tremelling broke the hearts of Cardiff fans saving Len Davies's penalty. Cardiff needed to win to claim the championship but lost out by 0.024 of a goal to Huddersfield on goal average.

1930, Division 1.
Blues 3   Leicester City 0   Att. 9,340
Bradford(3)

1947, Division 2.
Blues 4   Bradford Park Ave 0   Att. 23,083
Dougall, Bodle(2),
Mitchell(pen)

1961, Inter Cities Fairs Cup Semi Final, 2nd leg.
Blues 2   Inter Milan 1   Att. 29,530
Harris 4, 64   Lindskog 66

1966, Division 2.
Blues 4   Ipswich Town 1   Att. 9,115
Jackson 5   Brogan 9
Fenton 15, 86
Vowden 65
Herriott saved Baxter's penalty in the second half

1980, Division 2.
Blues 3   Notts County 3   Att. 33,863
Bertschin 18   Mair 36
Curbishley 22   Christie 40
Dillon 43   Kilcline 73
This match was screened by ATV's Star Soccer

1986, Division 1.
Blues 0   Arsenal 1   Att. 6,234
          Woodcock 84

1998, Division 1.
Blues 0   Charlton Athletic 0   Att. 25,877
Blues needing a win to make the top six and a play off place, came desperately close hitting both bar and post.
Blues eventually finished level with Sheffield United on points and goal difference, losing out on goals scored.

Playing record for this day
Playing record for this day is...8 games, Won 4, Drawn 3, Lost 1, GF 16, GA 6.
Today's success rate.....68.75% Year ranking....13th

Match of the Day
FROM 1980
RELIABLE BLUES AT THEIR TYPICAL BEST
Another emotional roller coaster ride for the fans in six goal thriller

Birmingham, with one of the best home records in the division went into this crucial game against mid-table opposition, needing just a draw to ensure promotion. So, although not taking anything for granted, the crowd which swelled to 33,863 arrived at St Andrews confident the Blues would sweep aside the Magpies and make sure of a promotion spot with a victory, after all you can always rely on Birmingham, can't you?

Blues as you would expect started in dominant mood against a County side playing only for professional pride. A goal for the Blues was imminent and it duly arrived well before anyone suffered an anxiety attack within the crowd, scored by Bertschin after 18 minutes. A neat move saw, Dillon beat his full back on the right put in a chipped cross to Givens who rather than shoot from the acute angle, screwed the ball across the face of the County goal for Bertschin to nod in at the far post. It was all going suspiciously to plan and when Blues added a second four minutes later even the most pessimistic of Blues fans was convinced. The goal came direct from a Curbishley free kick 25 yards out, after Givens had been fouled by Kilcline. Moments later the Blues further teased the crowd with the help of Avramovic who brilliantly saved a Gemmill free kick from almost the same spot as Curbishley's strike two minutes before. Then just at the point when the fans started to believe this promotion game was a doddle a lapse in the Blues defence allowed County back in the game at 2-1. A great cross from Hunt on the right was met by the alert Mair who nipped in to poke the ball past Wealands at the near post. Just four minutes later Mair turned from goal scorer to goal provider when putting Christie clean through after Broadhurst slipped. Taking the ball on the County striker made the one-on-one with the 'keeper look easy with a crisp low shot past the oncoming Wealands. That was it, the reality stick had given everyone a huge smack in the face and we all stood on the terraces trying to convince ourselves, we knew all along, and they hadn't really fooled us. Within minutes Blues were back in the lead through Dillon. Bertschin's cross from the right was too long for Dillon and Givens in the centre, however, the latter after chasing the loose ball centred from the left, this fell to Bertschin who laid the ball off for Dillon to sweep a low left-foot drive into the corner of the net.

The tension resumed early in the second half when Masson's fierce volley was brilliantly saved by Wealands, an early indication that County were not going to easily surrender. With just 27 minutes of the game remaining Brian Kilcline got forward for a set piece and prodded home a close range equaliser to ensure a heart stopping finale to the game that had already left most people emotionally drained. Time after time innocuous looking forward passes by County had the crowd wincing at the potential danger. However the Blues defence of Broadhurst, Lees, Gallagher and Todd held firm right up to the long awaited final whistle. A mass, but good humoured, pitch invasion ensued and the promotion party got into full swing when the players arrived in the main stand directors enclosure to thank the crowd who in turn thanked them for the season's achievement, and for that unforgettable 90 minutes of football.

BIRMINGHAM CITY
Wealands, Broadhurst, Lees, Curbishley, Gallagher, Todd, Ainscow, Givens, Bertschin, Gemmill, Dillon.
NOTTS COUNTY
Avramovic, Richards, O'Brien, Benjamin, Stubbs, Kilcline, McCulloch, Masson, Christie, Hunt, Mair.

REFEREE
Mr KG Salmon (Barnet)

Birthdays
Malcolm Beard born today in 1942

Playing record for this day

Playing record for this day is...14 games, Won 5, Drawn 3, Lost 6, GF 22, GA 19.

Today's success rate.....46.43% Year ranking....195th

May 4

Match of the Day

FROM 1955

BLUES TAKE TITLE IN STYLE

Doncaster brushed aside in Blues five goal rampage

Blues finally did it! Promotion at last to the First Division where they have not been since they were relegated in 1950. In a double bonus they also secured the second Division championship, pipping Luton. A crowd of 21,305 watched the match, including many travelling Blues fans, and also followers of Rotherham, who would have benefited from a slip-up by Blues. Birmingham had to win this game, and they did so with an emphatic four goal burst in a one-sided second half, which eventually ended with a 5-1 scoreline.

The opening minutes were a typical tense clash of biting tackles and goalmouth excitement, Blues taking advantage of a strong wind by loading high crosses which Hardwick often had difficulty with. However he kept them out with an array of improvised goalkeeping manoeuvres.

The importance of the first goal was such that Blues allowed gaps in defence to appeal. Doncaster took advantage of these, and Schofield did well to keep out a Jimmy Walker attempt. Moments later the keeper again pulled out a spectacular save from Geoff Walker which had been deflected on its way towards him.

On 38 minutes however, the pressure from Blues paid off when Astall scored. Latching onto a pass from Murphy he outclassed the Rovers' defence, and although his shot was blocked by Hardwick, Astall followed up to hammer in the rebound.

This brought about more pressure from Blues as they pushed for another to wrap up the game. However, despite forcing three quick corners, it was Doncaster on a breakaway who got the game's second goal just a minute before half time. Jimmy Walker rose to plant his header past Schofield from only the second corner of the game. So, typically Blues, after dominating and needing to win, were now level at the break and needing another goal. Again they would have to do it the difficult way.

The second half started much in the same manner as the first, only this time Blues put their chances away. The first came on 55 minutes. Hardwick again only half saving a shot by Murphy, who picked up the rebound to score via the inside of the post. Just ten minutes later Brown controlled a cross from Hall skilfully enough to turn and fire past Hardwick. There was no restraining Blues now, and after 73 minutes Brown went through on a weaving run which opened up the Rovers' defence again. He then waited at the edge of the area and lobbed a pass to Astall, to volley in Blues' fourth. A memorable night ended perfectly when, right on the final whistle, Govan scored a simple fifth goal, and the championship celebrations started in earnest.

BIRMINGHAM CITY
Schofield, Hall, Badham, Boyd, Smith, Warhurst, Astall, Kinsey, Brown, Murphy, Govan.

DONCASTER ROVERS
Hardwick, Makepeace, Gavin, Hunt, Williams, Herbert, Mooney, Jeffrey, Jimmy Walker, McMorran, Geoff Walker.

(R-L) Charlton Athletic goalkeeper Sam Bartram punches clear from teammate Ken Chamberlain and Birmingham City's Eddie Brown, watched by teammate Cyril Hammond

Birthdays

Paul Hart born today in 1953

May 5

The Matches played on this day

1923, Division 1.
Burnley 0 | Blues 2 | Att. 8,000
| Bradford, Rawson |

1928, Division 1.
Blues 2 | Derby County 1 | Att. 20,000
Curtis, Carr(og) |

1934, Division 1.
Blues 1 | Huddersfield Town 3 | Att. 19,442
Barkas(pen) |

1945, Wartime.
Blues 4 | WBA 1
Massart(3), Lewis |

1956, FA Cup Final.
Blues 1 | Manchester City 3 | Att. 98,982
Kinsey 13 | Hayes 2
| Dyson 64
| Johnstone 66

This is the biggest attendance the Blues have played in front of. The first game covered live by TV involving the Blues. Gate receipts £49,886

1979, Division 1.
Blues 0 | Arsenal 0 | Att. 14,015
This was the 100th league meeting against Arsenal

1984, Division 1.
Blues 0 | Liverpool 0 | Att. 18,809
This match screened by Central's The Big Match

1987, Division 2.
Blackburn Rovers 1 | Blues 0 | Att. 5,624
Garner 90 |

1990, Division 3.
Blues 0 | Reading 1 | Att. 14,278
| Gilkes 82

1996, Division 1.
Blues 1 | Reading 2 | Att. 16,233
P.Barnes 4 | Nogan 10
| Quinn 23

Playing record for this day

Playing record for this day is...10 games, Won 3, Drawn 2, Lost 5, GF 11, GA 12.
Today's success rate.....40% Year ranking....233rd

Match of the Day
FROM 1956
CUP FINAL BLUES
Cup goes to City of Manchester after brave Brum fight

On Saturday evening commemorative banquets were held for the players of FA Cup finalists Manchester City and Birmingham City in two London night spots no more than a stone's throw apart. Disappointingly this was as near to the trophy as Blues got all day. Blues lost their fighting spirit, an early goal, the battle in the Wembley cauldron, and most importantly, they lost their chance of a major trophy.

The day seemed so promising, with the teams coming out to a huge roar from the 100,000 fans crammed into the home of English football - Wembley Stadium. On a lovely hot day, after the introduction to the Queen, the game kicked off, and everything seemed perfect until the third minute. Revie, starting the move ten yards from his penalty area, swung over a long pass which cleared the head of Hall. Clarke raced in from behind to deliver a return ball to Revie who had made ground quickly. The ball was back-heeled square to Hayes inside the area, and he hit a crisp first-time shot past Merrick. Even then this was viewed as a stimulant - something to get Blues quickly into top gear. Unfortunately it simply did not, and this was the day's biggest disappointment. Although Blues hit back with a Kinsey shot which went in off the post to equalise 11 minutes later, there was still something lacking in their overall performance. Their spirit, prominent in other rounds, simply wasn't there when needed. When the Blues' famous battle cry "Keep Right On" failed to raise the tempo after the goal, things began to look ominous. Blues held on until half time with the scores remaining level, but they were clearly frustrated by the astute offside trap employed by Revie's men.

Manchester City started off the better team in the second half, and were 2-1 up after 65 minutes. Johnstone, running at Green on the right, was presented with an opportunity to feed Dyson, who had run diagonally across the field to the edge of the area. A perfectly timed pass allowed Dyson to take the ball in his stride, and fire past Merrick as he came out to narrow the angle. The winning team then put the game well beyond Blues' reach with a sucker-punch goal three minutes later. It came from a Blues attack, Trautmann dived bravely at the feet of Brown, took the ball from him and kicked long upfield. It was flicked on by Hayes into the path of Johnstone, who had sprinted clear of the static defence. He finished with a lovely strike into the bottom corner.

Moments later Trautmann received treatment, after a collision with Murphy whilst saving Brown's header at goal. The goalkeeper played on, despite holding his head in agony for the final 20 minutes. Any shot on target would have made a save impossible in his condition, but Blues failed to trouble him further. The game, and Blues' FA Cup dream withered for another year.

BIRMINGHAM CITY
Merrick, Hall, Green, Newman, Smith, Boyd, Astall, Kinsey, Brown, Murphy, Govan
MANCHESTER CITY
Trautmann, Leivers, Little, Barnes, Ewing, Paul, Johnstone, Hayes, Revie, Dyson, Clarke

REFEREE
Mr A Bond (Middlesex)

Fulham goalkeeper Ian Black (l) claims the ball, watched by Birmingham City's Noel Kinsey (r)

Blues news extra   1883...Friendly Blues 1 West Bromwich Albion 5
This is the first game played against the Albion

1981...Joe Gallagher's Testimonial
Blues centre half Joe Gallagher was rewarded for his 11 year service with a testimonial played at St Andrews against Aston Villa who won 6-3.

Birthdays
Ian Muir born today in 1963

Playing record for this day

Playing record for this day is...11 games, Won 5, Drawn 3, Lost 3, GF 13, GA 14.

Today's success rate.....59.09% Year ranking....62nd

Match of the Day

FROM 1995
CHAMPIONS!!!

Blues take Division Two title in the McAlpine Stadium

Blues arrived at their last game of the season needing a point to ensure promotion and with it the Second Division championship.

Blues started in an unfamilar cautious approach and clearly looked shaky. However after Ian Bennett had saved brilliantly from Jepson in the opening ten minutes, they settled well. Hunt had Blues best chance of the half on 13 minutes. A corner evaded everyone in the middle and ran to Hunt on the far post he stubbed his shot from an acute angle and the ball rolled agonisingly wide. Claridge, but was unlucky when a glorious lob looked a goal all the way as it cleared the head of 'keeper Francis, but the ball dropped onto the crossbar. Blues had to settle for an evenly balanced 0-0 draw at the interval which meant one firm hand at least was on the trophy.

Huddersfield playing only for pride, started the brighter in the second half, and a header from Booth went narrowly wide just five minutes after the restart. An evenly fought battle lasted for almost 22 minutes, then Blues grabbed the lead to mass jubilation amongst the 4,000 travelling fans behind the goal. The scorer was Claridge. From a great run and pass by full back Cooper, the striker collected and spun round to smack a low drive past Francis from within the penalty area. Birmingham were now firmly in pole position and they grew more confident. With just eight minutes remaining Paul Tait who had come on as a substitute, scored the decisive goal to make it 2-0. It was the result of a fine strike from Gary Cooper which Francis couldn't hold, when the ball dropped from his grip Tait prodded it over the line from barely a yard out. Huddersfield scored a late 88th minute goal when Bullock nodded in Jepsons' cross. The final whistle went and the party began for the Blues fans who refused to move untill the team had come out to receive their due congratulations.

BIRMINGHAM CITY

Bennett, Poole, Frain, Ward, Whyte, Daish, Hunt (Donowa), Claridge, Hendon, Williams (Tait), Cooper.

HUDDERSFIELD TOWN

Francis, Trevitt, Cowan, Bullock, Scully, Sinnott, Collins (Moulden 74), Duxbury, Booth, Jepson, Dunn (Billy).

REFEREE

Mr J Winter (Middlesbrough)

Paul Tait in action against Millwall

The Matches played on this day

1922, Division 1.
Blues 0   Preston NE 2   Att. 19,000
1933, Division 1.
Portsmouth 1   Blues 1   Att. 10,000
                   Grosvenor
1944, Wartime.
Northampton Town 0 Blues 5
                   Roberts(2), Mulraney(2), Faulkener
1950, Division 1.
Wolverhampton W. 6 Blues 1   Att. 42,935
Pye 2, 85   Trigg 70
Mullen 9, 24
Walker 31
Swinbourne 36
Blues left back Dennis Jennings became the oldest player to play in a competitive first team game for the club to date, aged 39 years, 9 months, and 17 days. Blues were already relegated when they arrived for the game at Molineux
1959, Inter Cities Fairs Cup Round 2, 1st leg.
Blues 1   Dinamo Zagreb 0   Att. 21,411
Larkin 41
1967, Division 2.
Cardiff City 3   Blues 0   Att. 12,872
Brown 4, 7
Jones 85
1985, Division 2.
Middlesbrough 0   Blues 0   Att. 7,840
1988, Division 2.
Blues 0   Leeds United 0   Att. 6,024
1989, Division 2.
Blues 1   Hull City 0   Att. 4,686
Yates 86
Blues last home game of the season. Attendances averaged just 6,289 the lowest seasonal total in the club's history.
1995, Division 2.
Huddersfield Town 1 Blues 2   Att. 18,775
Bullock 87   Claridge 73
                   Tait 85
The opening of the McAlpine Stadium. Blues won the championship with 89 points, a seasonal record points total to date.
2001, Division 1.
Huddersfield Town 1 Blues 2   Att. 19,290
Booth 44   Woodhouse 21, 45

May 7

The Matches played on this day

1921, Division 2.		
Portsmouth 0	Blues 2	Att. 10,000
	Hampton, Davies	
1927, Division 1.		
Blues 2	Sheffield United 3	Att. 14,226
Bradford, Briggs		
1932, Division 1.		
Newcastle United 0	Blues 3	Att. 10,000
	Bradford(2), Smith	
1938, Division 1.		
Leicester City 1	Blues 4	Att. 15,000
	Dearson, Clarke, White(2)	
1949, Division 1.		
Sunderland 1	Blues 1	Att. 28,007
	Roberts	
1951, Festival Of Britain.		
Blues 3	Airdrie 5	Att. 7,985
Berry(2), Kelly(og)		
1966, Division 2.		
Blues 3	Rotherham United 0	Att. 11,473
Hockey 22		
Vowden 50		
Barber 75		
1968, Division 2.		
Blues 4	Charlton Athletic 0	Att. 19,916
Bridges 25, 82		
Pickering 80		
Vincent 89		
1977, Division 1.		
Sunderland 1	Blues 0	Att. 34,193
Holden 83		
1979, Division 1.		
QPR 1	Blues 3	Att. 9,600
Roeder 45	Buckley 7, 80	
	Dark 83	

Better late than never! Blues' last game of the 1978-79 season and they finally register an away league win.

1983, Division 1.		
Blues 2	Tottenham Hotspur 0	Att. 18,947
Halsall 17		
Harford 78		

This game screened by ITV's The Big Match.

1984, Division 1.		
Norwich City 1	Blues 1	Att. 13,601
Watson 64	Gayle 87	
2000, Division 1.		
Blues 0	Grimsby Town 0	Att. 25,263

Playing record for this day

Playing record for this day is...13 games, Won 7, Drawn 3, Lost 3, GF 28, GA 13.

Today's success rate.....65.38% Year ranking....22nd

Match of the Day
FROM 1968
BRIDGES BRACE WINS IT
Charlton look anything but Athletic at St Andrews

Blues' final home match ended in a comfortable victory in front of the smallest crowd of the season. Just 19,916 saw two goals from Barry Bridges take his season total to 28, and further strikes from Fred Pickering and Johnny Vincent.

Three of the goals were supplied by left back Ray Martin, the first one for Bridges on 25 minutes. Charlton goalkeeper Charlie Wright blocked a shot from Vowden, who had collected Martin's cross, and Bridges picked up the loose ball and rammed it into the net.

There were plenty of chances for both sides, but no further score for a long while. Peacock's attempt at goal went wide, and Charlton's finishing was poor. The second half began, and both teams then brought on their substitutes. Holland replaced Hince for Charlton and young Darrell was brought on in place of Wylie for Blues. Darrell played with enthusiasm and liveliness in midfield, and showed plenty of initiative in attack. A bungle for Blues was typical of the match when Vincent shot for goal and Wright bent to collect it. It hit him on the head and rebounded for Bridges. His attempt again bounced off Wright, and Bridges finally sent the ball wide.

It was ten minutes before the end when Blues' second goal came. Pickering took advantage of a mistake by Keirs and volleyed the ball into the roof of the net. Just two minutes later Martin pushed down the left, supplying the ball for Bridges to tap over the line. With the score now 3-0 and just eight minutes to go Blues fans were expecting no more action. They were proved wrong when, on 89 minutes, Martin centred the ball, and Vincent hurled himself forward to head straight past Wright. It was an easy win for Blues, despite the missed chances for both sides.

BIRMINGHAM CITY

Herriot, Murray, Martin, Wylie (Darrell), Foster, Beard, Bridges, Vowden, Pickering, Page, Vincent.

CHARLTON ATHLETIC

Wright, Keirs, Kinsey, Campbell, Went, Reeves, Hince (Holland), Tees, Treacy, Gregory, Peacock.

England's Barry Bridges dashes in to charge Scotland goalkeeper Bill Brown

May 8th

Blues news extra 1996...Eight man Blues beat Villa to take the cup: Blues 2 Aston Villa 0

In an incident packed Birmingham Senior Cup final at St Andrews Blues beat Villa 2-0 and had three men sent off. Villa themselves were reduced to ten men in a hectic last 15 minutes. Ricky Otto and Jasen Bowen scored the goals whilst the red carded Blues men were John Cornforth, Ian Jones and Paul Peschisolido. Villa's early bath victim was Ben Petty.

May 9th

Blues news extra 1929...France 1 England 4, friendly played in Paris

Blues centre forward Joe Bradford won his sixth cap for England

1942...Friendly
Blues 2 Leicester City 4

1956...England spurn two penalties against the Brazilians
England won their first international against Brazil at Wembley by 4-2 thanks to Colin Grainger's brace on his England debut. However Atyeo and Byrne both had penalty kicks saved by the brilliant Gylmar in goal for the South Americans. Blues full back Jeff Hall won his sixth cap for England.

May 10th

Sadly Missed...Leslie Knighton died on this day in 1959, aged 75
Leslie Knighton became the Blues fifth manager in June 1928. He took the Blues to their first FA Cup final in 1931, when they were beaten 2-1 by WBA. In the season after that he took Blues to ninth in the First Division. He left the club in August 1933 to take over Chelsea where he stayed for five and a half years. After a term as Shrewsbury manager he retired from football to become a golf club secretary in Bournemouth, where he died after a short illness.

Blues news extra 1923...France 1 England 4, friendly played in Paris

England's first international against the French. Blues full back Percy Barton wins his third cap for England.

1930...Germany 3 England 3, friendly played in Berlin
England's first International against the Germans. Blues centre forward Joe Bradford won his tenth cap and 'keeper Harry Hibbs his third cap for England.

May 11th

Blues news extra 1999...Another Birmingham Senior Cup

Blues 4 Wolverhampton Wanderers 0
Blues scorers: A.Johnson, Dyson, Rea, Holland

The Matches played on this day

May 12th
1945, Wartime.
WBA 2   Blues 3
                  Massart(3)
1951, Festival Of Britain.
Blues 0   NK Dinamo Zagreb 2   Att. 12,058
                  Dvornic 65
                  Cajkovski 80
1967, Division 2.
Charlton Athletic 1   Blues 0   Att. 10,102
Firmani 82
1982, Division 1.
Leeds United 3   Blues 3   Att. 18,583
Worthington   Harford 20, 33
19, 85 (pen)   Evans 82
Connor 35
1984, Division 1.
Southampton 0   Blues 0   Att. 16,455
Blues were relegated to Division Two, on the last day of the
season. This match screened by Central TV's The Big Match.
2002, Division 1 Play-Off Final.
Blues 1   Norwich City 1   Att. 71,597
Horsfield 102   Roberts 91
Played at the Millennium Stadium, Cardiff
After extra time Blues won 4-2 on penalties

Playing record for this day (12th)
Playing record for this day....6 games, Won 1, Drawn 3, Lost 2, GF 7, GA 9
Success rate...41.67% Year ranking....223rd

Match of the Day
FROM 2002
BLUES ARE BACK IN FOOTBALL'S ELITE!!!
Darren Carter's penalty books place in Premiership for first time

It took 16 years, four failed attempts in the play-off semi finals, 120 minutes, and six penalty kicks, but Birmingham were finally back in top flight football. When Darren Carter smashed in the winning spot-kick the noise in the Millennium Stadium reached record levels. Blues fans were left wallowing in the glory of the club's biggest win for years, a memorable day that will be celebrated for years to come. Blues started the game clear favourites, having beaten Norwich twice in the regular season 4-0 at St Andrews, and 1-0 at Carrow Road. Birmingham were also the team with the best current form, unbeaten in their last 12 games. Norwich scraped into the play-off places on the last day of the season, on goal difference over Burnley, but showed in the two-legged semi-final win over Wolves that they were not to be taken lightly.

Blues got off to a great start and on 15 minutes Stern John was given a glorious chance after a ball from Hughes sent him clean through on goal. However, with just the keeper to beat he made a hash of trying to bend the ball round Green with the outside of his boot, and it drifted well wide of the target. Still Blues went forward and were denied another chance of a goal via the penalty spot when Horsfield was apparently tripped by Mackay but, referee Barber ignored the incident. Norwich, who had yet to trouble the Blues goal suddenly became a threat and finished the half looking the better side, but still couldn't force a save of any note from Vaesen in the Blues goal. Not so at the other end, and right on the stroke of half time Green produced a magnificent reflex save to stop a volley from Horsfield, who had been put clear just four yards out from Mooney's headed knock down.

Chances soon dried up in the second half as both sides sensed the pressure mounting. The best chances however both fell to Blues and Tebilly. Two minutes into the half his header was cleared off the the line by Drury, and four minutes from the end his snap shot from eight yards just cleared the crossbar. At the other end a timely interception from Jeff Kenna stopped the ball running to Norwich substitute Iwan Roberts, who would have a simple chance.

Roberts soon got his opportunity to hit the target and Norwich took the lead just 43 seconds into extra time. Grainger badly misjudged a pass to Notman on the right and from his beautifully flighted cross Roberts rose unmarked in the area to steer his header into the bottom corner of the net. Blues battled back and Norwich frantically defended for 12 minutes before they finaly succumbed to a deserved equaliser from Horsfield's header after a great knock down by Stern John. Blues continued to stream forward looking for a winner, and with three minutes of extra time remaining Michael Johnson almost snatched a dramatic headed goal, but the ball struck the bottom of the post.

So, the game now hinged on the outcome of a penalty shoot-out, Blues were given an early boost by winning the toss. They would now take their penalties in front of the end housing their own 33,000 fans, but also they would avoid the goal where the shoot-out in the Worthington Cup final had taken place. This left Norwich with the first kick, and up stepped Roberts to cap a fine individual performance by slotting his penalty into the bottom left hand corner. Next it was Stern John for Blues. Again it went into the corner with Green guessing correctly but failing to make any contact with the ball. Norwich then sent Phil Mulryne up to take the first blasted penalty, and for the jubilant Blues fans behind the goal, the first save. Vaesen diving to his left managed to block the shot with his trailing arm. Paul Devlin was next for Birmingham making no mistake with the best penalty so far, despite Green again guessing correctly with the dive. Now the pressure was really on for Norwich and Daryl Sutch in particular as he was next up. His kick produced the loudest roar from the Blues fans since the Horsfield goal as it rolled wide of the left post. This left Stan Lazaridis to send Green the wrong way for the first time and Blues were now on the brink of glory. Clint Easton stepped up knowing he simply had to score his penalty or the game was over for Norwich, his kick was well hit and just beat Vaesen, who got a hand to the ball but could only push it into the side netting to his left. Blues needed one more successful penalty and the task fell to 18-year-old Darren Carter. His penalty whizzed past the oustretched arm of Green who again guessed correctly but failed to make any contact, and Birmingham City were now a Premiership club.

BIRMINGHAM CITY
Vaesen, Kenna, Grainger, Tebilly, Michael Johnson, Vickers (Carter 71), Devlin, John, Horsfield (Andrew Johnson 113), Hughes, Mooney (Lazaridis 69).
NORWICH CITY
Green, Kenton, Drury, Mackay, Fleming, Rivers (Notman 90), Holt, Mulryne, Nielsen (Roberts 83), McVeigh (Sutch 102), Easton.

REFEREE
Mr Graham Barber (Tring)

Darren Carter (c) is mobbed by his teammates after scoring the clinching penalty against Norwich City in Cardiff

Blues news extra   May 13th 1933...Italy 1 England 1, friendly played in Rome

England's first international against the Italians. Blues 'keeper Harry Hibbs won his 15th cap for England.

May 13
1989, Division 2.

Crystal Palace 4	Blues 1	Att. 17,581
Wright 12, 20, 29	Sturridge 77	
Clarkson(og) 13		

2000, Division 1 Play-Off Semi Final, 1st leg.

Blues 0	Barnsley 4	Att. 26,492
	Shipperley 11	
	Dyer 48, 60	
	Hignett 84	

2001, Division 1 Play-Off Semi Final, 1st leg.

Blues 1	Preston North End 0	Att. 29,072
Eaden 55		

May 14-17

The Matches played on this day

May 14
1963, Division 1.
| Burnley 3 | Blues 1 | Att. 14,340 |
| Irvine 14, 58, 75 | Bloomfield 74 | |

1977, Division 1.
| Blues 1 | Everton 1 | Att. 22,436 |
| Kendall 55 | Latchford 76 | |

Bob Latchford sent off in the 82nd minute

1983, Division 1.
| Southampton 0 | Blues 1 | Att. 20,327 |
| | Harford 87 | |

Blues avoid relegation in their last game of the season

May 15
1956, Inter Cities Fairs Cup, Qualifying Group.
| Inter Milan 0 | Blues 0 | Att. 8,000 |

Blues first game in this European competition. They finished top of their qualifying group with 7 points from 4 games, and move on to meet Barcelona in the semi finals.

1982, Division 1.
| Coventry City 0 | Blues 1 | Att. 15,905 |
| | Harford 85 | |

Blues finally avoided relegation in their last game of the season. This match screened by Cental TV's, The Big Match.

May 16
1999, Division 1 Play-Off Semi Final, 1st leg.
| Watford 1 | Blues 0 | Att. 18,535 |
| Ngonge 4 | | |

Blues hit the post through Holland, whilst Mooney hits the post for Watford. Adebola had the best chance but missed a sitter on 67 minutes
Watford's Paul Robinson was sent off 14 minutes from the end.

May 17
1947, Division 2.
Millwall 0	Blues 2	Att. 15,000
	McIntosh	
	Dougall	

2001, Division 1 Play Off Semi Final, 2nd leg
Preston North End 2	Blues 1	Att. 16,928
Healey 24	Horsfield 58	
Rankine 90		

After extra time 2-2 on aggregate, Preston won 4-2 on penalties.
Jon McCarthy broke his leg for the third time at Blues.
Preston's Graham Alexander hit the bar with a penalty during normal time.

May 14th
Blues news extra   1930...Austria 0 England 0, friendly played in Vienna

Blues forward Joe Bradford won his 11th cap, and keeper Harry Hibbs his fourth cap for England

Birthdays
Christopher Wreh born today in 1975   Clinton Morrison born today in 1979

Clinton Morrison

May 15th
Blues news extra   1929...first defeat for England.

Spain became the first overseas opposition to beat England in an international. The friendly in Madrid was a seven goal thriller and won by the Spanish 4-3. Blues forward Joe Bradford won his seventh cap for England.

1957...Denmark 1 England 4, WC qualifier
England won comfortably in Copenhagen and should have done so by a bigger margin. They dominated the Danes and Manchester United's Tommy Taylor hit the bar twice in the second half. Blues full back Jeff Hall won his sixth cap for England.

Birthdays
Colin Robinson born today in 1960   Vince Overson born today in 1952

May 16th
Blues news extra   1888...Friendly Blues 15 Long Eaton Rangers 0
The Long Eaton team arrived with only eight players. Officials quickly asked among the crowd to help out and three spectators were found to make up the numbers.

1956...Sweden 0 England 0, friendly in Stockholm
Blues full back Jeff Hall won his seventh cap for England.

Birthdays
Roy Martin born today in 1929

Neil Whatmore

May 17th
Blues news extra   1961...Defeat by the Scots in the USA.
Blues first game in an international tournament in America and Canada ended with a 4-1 defeat by Scottish club Third Lanark. The game took place in New York City.

1967...FA Youth Cup final, 1st leg
Sunderland 1 Blues 0. This Blues youth side included Dave and Bob Latchford, Garry Pendrey, and Keith Bowker all of whom went on to have successful careers as senior players at St Andrews.

1995...Blues receive the championship trophy
Although Blues were comprehensively beaten by Nottingham Forest the 10,742 crowd at least got to see Liam Daish lift the Second Division championship trophy. The game was won 4-1 by the visitors. The Blues goalscorer was Paul Harding.

Birthdays
Neil Whatmore born today in 1955   Steve Castle born today in 1966

May 18-22

The Matches played on this day

May 18
1940, Wartime.
Arsenal 1   Blues 2
           Trigg, Turner
Played at White Hart Lane, Tottenham
1951, Festival Of Britain.
Home Farm 1   Blues 2   Att. 3,000
           Stewart, Berry

1963, Division 1.
Blues 3   Leicester City 2   Att. 23,931
Harris 27   Heath 58
Auld 63   McLintock 76
Lynn(pen) 65
Blues avoided relegation with this win.
2000, Division 1 Play-Off Semi Final, 2nd leg
Barnsley 1   Blues 2   Att. 19,050
Dyer 54   Rowett 33
           Marcelo 75
Blues lost 5-2 on aggregate.

May 19
1945, Wartime.
Blues 4   Nottingham Forest 1
Mulraney, Massart,
Dearson, Matthews

May 20
1940, Wartime.
Blues 0   Leicester City 0
1951, Festival Of Britain.
Cork Athletic 2 Blues 5   Att. 2,750
         Trigg(2), Higgins, Stewart, Dailey
1999, Division 1 Play-Off Semi Final, 2nd leg.
Blues 1   Watford 0   Att. 29,100
Adebola 2
After extra time. 1-1 on aggregate, Watford won 7-6 on penalties
Blues centre back David Holdsworth sent off after 53 mins.
May 21
1956, Inter Cities Fairs Cup, Qualifying Group.
Zagreb XI 0   Blues 1   Att. 12,000
         Brown 62
Eddie Brown scored Blues first goal in European competition.

May 18th

Blues news extra 1935...Holland 0 England 1,

Blues 'keeper Harry Hibbs won his 23rd cap for England. England's winner was scored by Fred Worrall (Portsmouth) on his international debut.

Birthdays

Howard Gayle born today in 1958   Barry Horne born today in 1962

May 19th

Blues news extra 1957...17th cap for Jeff Hall

Blues full back Jeff Hall helped England to a 1-1 draw against the Republic of Ireland in Dublin. The point earned England qualification for the 1958 World Cup finals in Sweden. Sadly however this proved to be Jeff Hall's last international before his untimely death from polio in 1959

Birthdays

Tony Coton born today in 1961

Tony Coton

May 20th

Blues news extra 1956...First cap for Blues star Astall

Blues winger Gordon Astall's international debut was marked with a goal. Deputising for the injured Stanley Matthews he scored England's third goal in an emphatic 5-1 win against Finland in Helsinki. This after Nat Lofthouse had become the first England substitute to come on and score twice. Blues were also represented by Jeff Hall the full back winning his eighth cap.

1933...Switzerland 0 England 4, friendly

England won convincingly in Berne against the Swiss with Cliff Bastin(Arsenal) scoring two and having another disallowed and James Richardson(Newcastle) also adding a brace. Blues 'keeper Harry Hibbs won his 17th cap for England.

Birthdays

Graham Potter born today in 1975   John Sissons born today in 1934

May 21st
Blues news extra   1921...First for Barton and England

Blues full back Percy Barton made a good start to his international career helping England beat Belguim 2-0 in Brussels, in the first international between these countries.

1981....West Germany 3 Republic of Ireland 0, Friendly International

Irish full back Dave Langan won his eighth cap as a Blues player.

1961...Blues in Canada

Blues lost again on their USA and Canada tour, going down 1-0 against Montreal Canatalia in Montreal.

Howard Kendall

May 22nd
Blues news extra   1967...FA Youth Cup final, 2nd leg

Sunderland 1 Blues 0.... lost 2-0 on aggregate Blues lost their first FA Youth Cup final at Roker Park by the same score they had done at St Andrews five days before. Blues kept the same team as in the first leg on the 17 May.

Birthdays
Howard Kendall born today in 1946

May
23-25

Match of the Day
FROM May 23 1963
BIG STEP TOWARD CUP WIN
First leg puts Blues on their way to lifting the cup at Villa Park

This was Birmingham's first domestic final in seven years and one they simply had to win, as the opposition were their neighbours and rivals Aston Villa. Blues went into the match as the underdogs having been beaten by Villa just two months previously in a league match by 4-0. Both sides started at full strength in front of a St Andrews crowd of 31,580.

Blues started well with close efforts from Harris and Leek, both well saved by Simms in goal for Villa. Blues best chance came soon after when another shot from Harris was pushed onto the crossbar by Simms. Meanwhile Thomson clattered Blues 'keeper Schofield in a rash challenge for the ball and in another incident, Leek sent Crowe flying with a late tackle, both fouls coming in the early stages of a typically keenly fought local derby. Then the first goal came, and to the joy of the home fans it was scored by Ken Leek on 14 minutes. A ball from midfield by Harris released Auld and his left wing cross was hammered in by Leek, this time Simms had no chance of saving. Bloomfield became the first casualty, leaving to have a thigh wound bandaged up and he returned to spend time hobbling on the wing in order to try run the knock off, he did so successfully much to the relief of the Blues fans, and management. However, Villa got back into the game and equalised through Thomson. Lee started the move and after advancing deep into Blues territory he sent in a hard, low cross which Thomson hit first time and it sped past Schofield as he was coming out to close the Villa man down.

The second half started badly for Villa. Defender Sleeuwenhoek collided with his 'keeper and ended up with an injury which he had to leave the field to have treated. Soon after that Blues had a man off too when Smith was hurt in a hefty challenge by Thomson. The first real opportunity at goal was converted and it put Blues back in front on 52 minutes. Again Harris and Auld were the instigators, and Leek the goal scorer, with a low drive within the area from Auld's inch-perfect cross. The game became ill-tempered and referee Crawford was starting to lose patience with the persistent fouling. Crowe became the latest victim, he was elbowed in the face after a midfield tussle with Auld. Aitken was then given a stern lecture when he was seen to shove Hellawell away in the chest in yet another confrontation. Then Fraser and Harris came close to exchanging punches as they squared up to one another and team mates had to drag them apart. They were also given a warning by the Doncaster official. Blues then got a killer third goal after 66 minutes. From a Harris right wing cross, Bloomfield nipped in unchecked by the static defence to squeeze the ball past Simms and in off the post. Blues were now 3-1 up and they confidently strolled through the remainder of the game, content to take their lead to Villa Park for the second leg. In the closing stages Simms saved Villa keeping out two glorious strikes at goal from Leek then Auld. The final whistle went with Blues still holding a two goal advantage at 3-1.

BIRMINGHAM CITY
Schofield, Lynn, Green, Hennessey, Smith, Beard, Hellawell, Bloomfield, Harris, Leek, Auld.

ASTON VILLA
Simms, Fraser, Aitken, Crowe, Sleeuwenhoek, Lee, Baker, Graham, Thomson, Wylie, Burrows.

REFEREE
Mr E Crawford (Doncaster)

Colin Green

Birthdays
Hymie Kloner born today in 1929

May 24th

Blues news extra   1980...Scotland 0 England 2, Home International

Midfielder Archie Gemmill wins his fifth cap as a Blues player.

1981...Poland 3 Republic of Ireland 0

Full back Dave Langan wins his ninth cap as a Blues player.

Birthdays

Cammie Fraser born today in 1941   Kevin Langley born today in 1964

Archie Gemmill

May 25th

Blues news extra   1942...Friendly

Coventry City 4 Blues 2

1961...Blues register first win in Canada

Blues won for the first time on their tour of USA and Canada. They beat Hamilton Steelers 4-2 in Hamilton, Ontains.

Birthdays

Paul Peschisolido born today in 1971

The Matches played on this day

May 26
1945, Wartime.
Nottingham Forest 0 Blues 0
1947, Division 2.
Newport County 0 Blues 3   Att. 14,000
                   Bodle(2), Dougall
Last league meeting v Newport
1991, Leyland Daf Cup Final.
Blues 3   Tranmere Rovers 2 Att. 58,756
Sturridge 21   Cooper 61
Gayle 41, 86   Steel 66
Played at Wembley Stadium

May 27
1963, League Cup Final, 2nd leg.
Aston Villa 0   Blues 0   Att. 37,921
Blues won 3-1 on aggregate and the League Cup is lifted in
front of almost 38,000 fans at Villa Park.

Match of the Day
FROM May 26 1991
GAYLE BLOWS AWAY ROVERS
Wembley cup win at last for Blues

Never before, and probably never again would Wembley see scenes like these. 48,000 Blues fans in a crowd of 58,576 converged on the twin towers in the hope of seeing their team lift their first cup there.

The Blues team didn't disappoint. Led by Lou Macari, and inspired by big Brummie John Gayle they dominated as much on the field as the Bluenoses did in the stands.

After a bright start Blues swept ahead on 21 minutes when a long clearance was headed on by Gayle to the nippy Simon Sturridge, who raced on to beat Nixon with a neatly placed shot just inside the penalty area. Blues settled on the lead, and were happy to keep Tranmere at bay. The tactic worked well and Tranmere hardly troubled Martin Thomas at all.

As half time approached, a pass out of defence came to Gayle who stepped over the ball, throwing his marker. He smashed a rising shot which beat Nixon from just inside the penalty area to put Blues 2-0 up on 41 minutes. Blues still had time to almost score a third, when Peer had a volley brilliantly saved by Nixon.

This was the sort of game where you didn't want a half time break as, sure enough, Blues, never a team to do anything the easy way, lost their momentum. Tranmere rallied after the break and gave themselves real hope on 61 minutes when Cooper halved the deficit. Blues wobbled, and five minutes later Tranmere were now level through Jim Steel. The game then ebbed from end to end as if the next goal was the winner. As the game entered the final few minutes it now certainly would be.

With one moment of magic required, up stepped John Gayle. A free kick to Blues near the halfway line, and Clarkson floated the ball into the Tranmere box. Overson beat Higgins in the air, looping his header to a waiting Gayle. With his back to goal he sprung an amazing scissors kick, and the ball smashed into the corner of a bemused Nixon's net in the 86th minute. The goal was indeed the winner. What a goal, and what a winner it was!!!

BIRMINGHAM CITY

Thomas, Clarkson, Frain, Peer, Overson, Matthewson, Peer, Gayle, Robinson, Gleghorn, Sturridge (Bailey).

TRANMERE ROVERS

Nixon, Higgins, Brannan, McNab (Martindale) Hughes, Vickers (Malkin), Morrissey, Irons, Steel, Cooper, Thomas.

REFEREE

Mr JE Martin (Alton, Hants)

Ian Clarkson

May 26th
Blues news extra   1956...Caps for Astall and Hall

Blues winger Gordon Astall deputising for the injured Stanley Matthews made his second appearance and full back Jeff Hall his ninth for England in another win against the world champions West Germany. England won 3-1 in Berlin making it four wins in succession against the Germans.

Birthdays
Richard Sbragia born today in 1956

May 27th

Blues news extra 1961...Revenge for Blues in Canada

Blues won for a second time on their USA/Canada tour avenging the opening defeat by Third Lanark in New York. Blues won this one 3-2 in Toronto, Canada.

Birthdays

Jimmy Haarhoff born today in 1981

Sadly Missed

John Gordon died today in 2001, aged 69

May 28th

Birthdays

David Preece born today in 1963

May 29th

Birthdays

Alec Jackson born today in 1937   Marc North born today in 1966

Nigel Gleghorn

May 30th

Blues news extra 1942...Friendly

WBA 4 Blues 1

1961...Blues hit double figures

The fifth game of Blues tour of USA and Canada produced their biggest win. Blues beat the Canadian side Calgary All Stars 11-2 in Calgary.

Birthdays

Lyndon Hooper born today in 1966

May 31st

Birthdays

Tresor Luntala born today in 1982   Frank Carrodus born today in 1949

The Matches played on this day

June 1st
1972, Anglo Italian Cup.
Lanerossi Vicenza 0   Blues 0   Att. 3,000

June 4th
1972, Anglo Italian Cup.
Sampdoria 2   Blues 1   Att. 15,000
                      Campbell(pen)

June 5th
1940, Wartime.
Blues 0   Coventry City 0
The 1939-40 season came to a close. This was the latest a
season has finished ever in Football League history.

June 7th
1972, Anglo Italian Cup.
Blues 5   Lanerossi Vicenza 3   Att. 23,642
B.Latchford(2), Francis,
Hatton, Taylor

June 8th
1940, Wartime
Blues 8   Walsall 1
Bodle(2), Duckworth(2),
Jones(2), Brown, Godfrey(og)

June 10th
1972, Anglo Italian Cup
Blues 2   Sampdoria 0   Att. 19,510
B.Latchford, Hatton

June 2nd
Birthdays
John Metcalfe born today in 1935.

June 3rd
Birthdays
John Trewick born today in 1957   Kevan Broadhurst born today in 1959

Blues news extra   1961...Blues tour of USA and Canada, played in Vancouver, Canada
Third Lanark 1 Blues 1

June 4th
Blues news extra   1977...England 1 Scotland 2
Played at Wembley. Blues striker Trevor Francis won his third cap for England. It was Scotland's first win at Wembley in ten years.

June 6th
Blues news extra   1908...Austria 1 England 6, friendly played in Vienna
Blues full back Walter Corbett won his first cap in England's first international against Austria.

Birthdays
Colin Brazier born today in 1957

John Berry

June 7th

Birthdays

Lou Macari born today in 1949

Blues news extra   1961...Blues tour of USA and Canada, played in Victoria, Canada

Victoria All Stars 1 Blues 5

June 10th

Birthdays

Nicky Platnauer born today in 1961

Blues news extra   1961...Blues tour of USA and Canada, played in Vancouver.

British Columbia 2 Blues 5

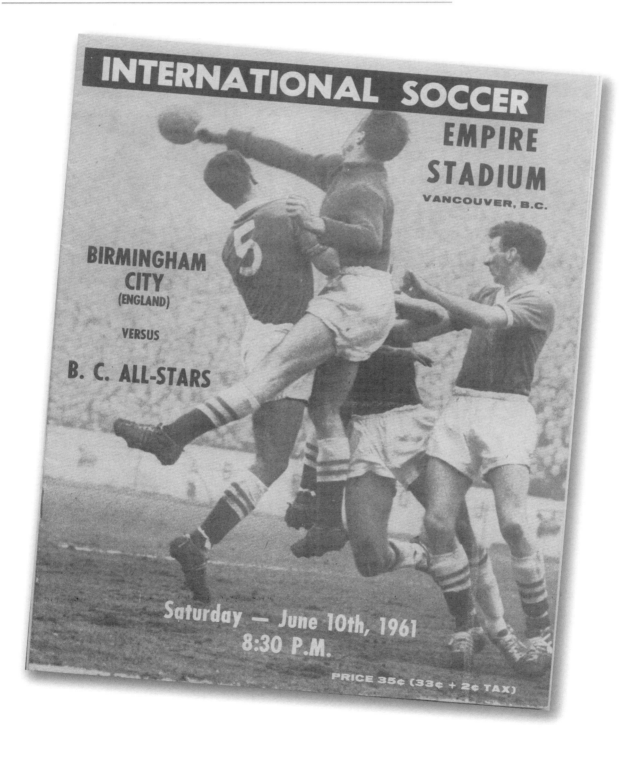

June 11th
Birthdays
Walter Aveyard born today in 1918

Blues news extra   1908...Hungary 0 England 7, friendly played in Budapest
Blues full back Walter Corbett won his second cap in England's first international against Hungary.

June 12th
Birthdays
Ray Ranson born today in 1960   Steve Smith born today 1957   Gary Bull born today 1966

June 13th
Birthdays
John Connolly born today in 1950   Tony Hateley born today in 1941

Blues news extra 1908...Bohemia 0 England 4,
friendly played in Prague Blues full back Walter Corbett won his third and final cap for England in this first and only international against Bohemia.

June 14th
Birthdays
Richard Dryden born today in 1969   Harry Hooper born today in 1933

June 16th
Birthdays
Alex Govan born today in 1929

June 17th
Birthdays
Roger 'Harry' Willis born today in 1967

June 18th
Birthdays
Matthew Regan born today in 1944   Kevin Drinkell born today in 1960

Season 54-55

June 19th

Birthdays

Doug Pimbley born today in 1917   Jimmy Greenhoff born today in 1946   Bryan Hughes born today in 1976

Cecil Russell born today in 1904

June 20th

Birthdays

Graham Leggat born today in 1934

Bryan Hughes

June 21-30

June 22nd
Birthdays
Bob Catlin born today in 1965

June 23rd
Birthdays
Dele Adebola born today in 1975

June 27th
Birthdays
Darren Wassall born today in 1968   Tommy Capel born today in 1922

Blues news extra   1998..Sir Alf suffers a stroke

Sir Alf Ramsey committed to hospital after suffering a stroke whilst at home.

June 28th
Birthdays
Freddie Goodwin born today in 1933   Kenny Cunningham born today in 1971

June 30th
Birthdays
Mike Hellawell born today in 1938   Terry Lees born today in 1952

Dele Adebola

Blues news extra 1/7/1923...Blues tour of Spain; Real Madrid 0 Blues 3

Blues beat the Spanish giants by three goals despite playing with ten men towards the end of the game. Alec McClure was sent off for gamesmanship just after Real had been awarded a controversial penalty. Full back Jack Jones was penalised for handball whilst protecting his false teeth from a pile driver of a shot coming straight at him. The ball smashed his dentures in two. Alec McClure then advised his 'keeper Tremelling to stand at a post and make no attempt to save the spot kick in a defiant protest against the penalty being awarded.

2/7/1998...Bruce leaves to manage Sheffield.

Steve Bruce's two years as a player with Blues came to an end. He left to take over as manager at Sheffield United.

5/7/1910... McRoberts makes Blues history

Former Blues centre forward Bob McRoberts was appointed as Birmingham's first ever manager of team affairs.

10/7/2000...The 'Horse' Breaks Blues transfer record.

Blues smashed their transfer record by signing Fulham centre forward Geoff Horsfield. He cost £2,225,000 a fee that easily surpassed the previous record held by Peter Ndlovu who was signed for £1.6 million.

Birthdays

July 3rd
Lee Bradbury born today in 1975

July 4th
Michael Johnson born today in 1973

July 8th
Adrian Bird born today in 1969

Tommy Williams born today in 1980

July 10th
John Hughes born today in 1921

Lee Bradbury

Birthdays

July 11th..... Kenny Brown born today in 1967

July 12th..... Terry Cooper born today in 1944

July 13th..... Jack Wheeler born today in 1919

        Matthew Fox born today in 1971

July 14th..... Dave Robinson today in 1948

July 15th..... Alan Ainscow born today in 1953

Terry Cooper

Birthdays

July 21st.....
Kevin Poole born today in 1963
Mick Halsall born today in 1961

July 23rd.....
Keith Downing born today in 1965

July 25th.....
Jack Coxford born this day 1904

July 26th.....
Ken Leek born today in 1935
Bob Meacock born today in 1910

July 28th.....
Andy Legg born today in 1966
Fred Hawley born this day 1890

July 29th.....
Brian Farmer born today in 1933
Barry Squires born today in 1931

July 30th.....
John Gayle born today in 1964

July 31st.....
Paul Tait born today in 1971

Season 50-51

July 21-31

Blues news extra 22/7/1998...Friendly Birmingham 4 Tottenham 2

Blues scorer: Furlong, McCarthy, Adebola(2)

24/7/1888...Blues name change

Blues today became a limited company and elected a board and chairman. He was Walter Hart and his first business was to announce the unanimous decision of the clubs' name change. Small Heath Alliance would now be known as simply Small Heath.

26/7/1994...Friendly Walsall 1 Blues 2

Manager Barry Fry used 21 players in this pre-season game. Blues come from behind to win with goals from Shutt(73) and Harding(82)

25/7/1998...Friendly Birmingham 4 Manchester United 3

Peter Ndlovu bagged a hat trick.

29/7/1983...Tour of Sweden Gallivare 2 Blues 1

Blues scorer: Hopkins

31/7/1983...Tour of Sweden Ranea 0 Blues 5

Blues scorers: Handysides(2), Harford(2), Van Den Hauwe

30/7/69...Friendly Reading 0 Blues 2

This game marked the opening of Elm Park's floodlights. Both goals came from Geoff Vowden

General view of St Andrews, home of Birmingham City, where the pitch was scorched due to the undersoil heating

Terry Hibbitt

Blues news extra
3/8/1983...Tour of Sweden Alvsbyn 0 Blues 1

Blues scorer: Handysides

7/8/1983...Tour of Sweden Haparanda 0 Blues 5

Blues scorer: Blake(2), Hopkins, Phillips, Wright, Handysides

Birthdays

August 1st
Tony Rees born today in 1964   Sean Francis born today in 1972

August 2nd
Tony Godden born today in 1955

August 3rd
Richard Knight born today in 1979

August 4th
Dave Howitt born today in 1952   Steve Phillips born today in 1954

August 5th
Terry Cooke born today in 1976.

Sadly Missed
Terry Hibbitt died today in 1994, aged 46

August 6th
Paul Gorman born today in 1963   Ron Wylie born today in 1933

August 8th
Joe Devine born today in 1905   Julian Dicks born today in 1968   Dean Peer born today in 1969

The Matches played on this day

August 3rd
1974, Texaco Cup.

| WBA 0 | Blues 0 | Att. 3,000 |

August 4th
1979, Anglo Scottish Tournament

Blues 0	Bristol City 4	Att. 7,631
	Mabbutt 6, 12	
	Ritchie 28, 75	

August 5th
1972, FA Cup 3rd/4th play off

| Blues 0 | Stoke City 0 | Att. 25,841 |

Played at St Andrews
Blues won 4-3 on penalties, scorers:
Campbell, Francis, Hope, Harland
1977, Anglo Scottish Tournament

| Plymouth Argyle 1 | Blues 1 | Att. 5,176 |
| Austin 27 | Craven(og) 57 | |

August 6th
1979, Anglo Scottish Tournament

| Plymouth Argyle 1 | Blues 1 | Att. 3,137 |
| Johnson 43(pen) | Bertschin 70 | |

August 7th
1974, Texaco Cup

| Peterborough United 1 | Blues 1 | Att. 8,915 |
| Cozens 48 | Taylor 62 | |

1999, Division 1

Blues 2	Fulham 2	Att. 24,042
Hughes(og) 62	Horsfield 36, 58	
Lazaridis 84		

Future Blues forward Geoff Horsfield scored both goals for Fulham, and was then sent off.

August 8th
1979, Anglo Scottish Tournament

Fulham 0	Blues 5	Att. 2,899
	Bertschin 16, 28	
	Evans 29	
	Ainscow 50	
	Dillon 65	

1999, Division 1

Port Vale 0	Blues 2	Att. 10,465
	Furlong 21	
	Adebola 68	

August
9-15

The Matches played on this day

August 9th
1969, Division 2.

Leicester City 3	Blues 1	Att. 35,168
Fern 26	Summerill 89	
Manley 51		
Lochead 82		

Garry Pendrey became Blues youngest ever captain at just 20 years 6 months.
The opening game of the season was shown on ATV's Star Soccer programme.

1977, Anglo Scottish Tournament.

Bristol Rovers 1	Blues 1	Att. 2,317
Hamilton 40	Francis 72	

1997, Division 1.

Blues 2	Stoke City 0	Att. 20,608
Devlin 33		
Ndlovu 87		

August 10th
1968, Division 2.

Blues 1	Norwich City 2	Att. 27,515
Pickering 30	Manning 73	
	Curran 90	

1974, Texaco Cup.

Blues 3	Norwich City 1	Att. 14,847
Campbell 32	Boyer 65	
Hatton 42		
Francis 57		

Match screened by ATV's Star Soccer

1999, League Cup 1st Round, 1st leg

Blues 3	Exeter City 0	Att. 18,978
A.Johnson 17		
Wilkinson(og) 42		
Adebola 75		

August 11th
1998, League Cup 1st Round, 1st leg.

Blues 2	Millwall 0	Att. 14,133
Adebola 70		
M.Johnson 87		

2001, Division 1.

Wimbledon 3	Blues 1	Att. 9,142
Shipperley 45	Hughes 88	
Connolly 50		
Purse(og) 76		

Tommy Mooney has his header cleared by Millwall's Stuart Nethercote, Tim Cahill and David Livermore

Blues news extra August 10th 1968...New social club at St Andrews

Blues opened a new bar and social club at St Andrews, the D Club was open to the public for the first time before and after home games as well as during the weekday evenings.

August 10th 1980...Royal Blues

Amongst the thousands who turned up at the club's annual open day at St Andrews was a VIP guest ,HRH the Prince of Wales. Prince Charles was given a tour of the ground by manager Jim Smith.

Birthdays

August 9th
Don Givens born today in 1949

August 10th
Jim Hagan born today in 1956

August 11th

Carl Tiler born today in 1970	Alan Kelly born today in 1968	Tommy Mooney born today in 1971

The Matches played on this day

August 12th
1972, Division 1
Blues 1	Sheffield United 2	Att. 37,045
B.Latchford 6	Hockey 7	
	Woodward 57	

Season opener shown on ATV's Star Soccer show.
1977, Anglo Scottish Tornament.
Blues 1	Bristol City 0	Att. 9,512
Francis 18		

1995, Division 1
Blues 3	Ipswich Town 1	Att. 18,910
Tait 64	Marshall 47	
Otto 73		
Bowen 85		

Three players made their debuts-Andy Edwards,Richard Forsyth and goalscorer Jason Bowen. Ian Muir also played his first game in his second spell at the club.
1997, League Cup 1st round, 1st leg.
Gillingham 0	Blues 1	Att. 5,246
	Francis 85	

2000, Division 1
QPR 0	Blues 0	Att. 13,926

Blues record signing Geoff Horsfield made his debut. The centre forward was bought from Fulham for £2.23 million in the summer.

August 13th
1994, Division 2
Leyton Orient 2	Blues 1	Att. 7,578
Purse 6	Claridge 17	
Bogie 66		

Future Blues centre half Darren Purse netted the first goal of Blues double winning season 1994-95

August 14th
1971, Division 2
Sunderland 1	Blues 1	Att. 9,749
Watson 77	Bowker 18	

1993, Division 1
Charlton Athletic 1	Blues 0	Att. 7,708
Chapple 39		

1999, Division 1
Norwich City 0	Blues 1	Att. 15,261
	McCarthy 12	

August 15th
1970, Division 2
Blues 2	QPR 1	Att. 30,785
Summerill 9	Bridges 48	
Vowden 36		

1972, Division 1
Blues 3	Newcastle United 2.	Att. 35,831
McFaul(og) 14	Barrowclough 36	
Hope 27	Macdonald 39	
B.Latchford 82		

Bob Latchford had three second half goals disallowed.
1987, Division 2
Blues 2	Stoke City 0	Att. 13,137
Rees 1, 51		

Tony Rees scored after just 45 seconds.
Stoke hit the crossbar four times in the game.
1995, League Cup 1st round, 1st leg.
Blues 1	Plymouth Argyle 0	Att. 7,964
Cooper 45		

Blues news extra August 13th 1983...Another cup win against Villa

Blues 1 Aston Villa 0....Att. 11,763
Blues won the Birmingham Senior Cup against their arch rivals with a goal from Ian Handysides two minutes into the second half. Both sides fielded full strength line-ups.

August 13th 1980...Friendly

Blues 10 FC Lucerne(Switzerland) 0
Blues scorers; Evans(3) Gemmill(3)
Bertschin, Worthington, Towers, and one own goal.

August 13th 1983...Friendly

Blues 1 Ajax 0
Blues scorer; Steve Fox

Birthdays

August 12th
Nigel Gleghorn born today in 1962

August 16

The Matches played on this day

1969, Division 2
Blues 1   Oxford United 3   Att. 27,067
Summerill 39   G.Atkinson 13, 26
           Skeen 50

1975, Division 1
Leicester City 3   Blues 3   Att. 25,547
Samuels 30(pen)   Hatton 44
Alderson 67   Kendall 61, 76(pen)
Roberts(og) 86
Garland(Leicester City) sent off after 26 minutes.

1980, Division 1
Blues 3   Coventry City 1   Att. 21,907
Curbishley 19, 53   Blair 76
Dillon 26
Coventry's Ray Gooding sent off

1992, Division 1
Blues 1   Notts County 0   Att. 10,614
Donowa 9
This game televised by Central's The Big Match

1994, League Cup 1st round, 1st leg
Shrewsbury Town 2   Blues 1   Att. 5,049
Clarke 16   Daish 85
Spink 79
Former Blues forward Wayne Clarke scores the opening goal.

1998, Division 1
Blues 3   Crystal Palace 1   Att. 16,699
Adebola 12   Mullins 73
O'Connor 29(pen)
Forster 90
Blues conceded their first goal in 10 hours and 45 minutes of football

---

Playing record for this day
Playing record for this day is...6 games, Won 3, Drawn 1, Lost 2, GF 12, GA 10.
Today's success rate.....58.33% Year ranking....74th

Match of the Day
FROM 1998

FIT FOR THE PALACE
Royal Blues hit the top after super show

Blues got their season off to a great start the week before at Port Vale, in this their first game at St Andrews they were even more clinical, and their ability to score at will put them at the summit of Division One on goal difference above Wolves, Norwich, and Watford who all had a six point maximum total.

Blues started in irresistible form, their passing and movement the best seen in years. It took just 12 minutes for the move which led to Adebola continuing his goal-a-game start to the season. A cross from Charlton was deflected by Ndlovu for the big striker to pounce and fire into the roof of the net from six yards. There was no let up and Blues second chance to score came soon afterwards. Again Adebola and Charlton were involved in the move which led to a penalty, a neat interchange of passing between the two left Charlton surging into the box only to be dragged back by his shirt, a clear cut decision for referee Lynch. O'Connor placed his kick low into the left-hand corner, Miller having gone the right way made no contact with the ball. Blues continued to dominate in the St Andrews sunshine and the 16,699 crowd rose to appreciate their efforts when the half-time whistle sounded.

If anything Blues got a little over confident in the second half and their casual approach almost bought Palace an unlikely comeback. With just 17 minutes to play an innocuous looking cross from Austin caused mayhem as Bennett rushed out to punch a ball Johnson looked to be clearing easily, the pair both missed it and Mullins nipped in to flick into the unguarded goal. To their credit Blues didn't panic and were soon back to their early first half dominance, the composure that was so impressive in the opening 30 minutes making a welcome return. In the last minute Grainger advanced down the left and his hard low cross was nudged in by substitute Nicky Forster at the near post.

BIRMINGHAM CITY

Bennett, Gill, Charlton, Marsden, Ablett, Michael Johnson, McCarthy (Purse 90), O'Connor, Adebola, Hughes (Grainger 66), Ndlovu (Forster 87).

CRYSTAL PALACE;

Miller, Edworthy, Smith, Curcic (Austin 61), Hreidarsson, Linighan, Lombardo, Warhurst, Dyer (Bent 60), Jansen, Mullins.

REFEREE
Mr K Lynch (Kirk Hammerton)

Blues news extra   1982...Friendly Forest Green 1 Blues 2

Blues scorer Neil Whatmore(2)

Birthdays

Dennis Hill born today in 1929   Stan Lazaridis born today in 1972   Bill Hunter born today in 1900

Playing record for this day
Playing record for this day is...5 games, Won 3, Drawn 0, Lost 2, GF 9, GA 8.
Today's success rate.....60% Year ranking....56th

August 17

Match of the Day
FROM 1993
BLUES TASTE SWEET
COCA COLA CUP TIE WIN

Stunning performance puts Blues 3-0 up in the first leg

What a difference a year makes. At this stage in the 1991-92 Coca-Cola-Cup Blues had been humiliated by Exeter by a 4-1 defeat. 12 months on and another Devon club arrived at St Andrews in the first round, this time however Blues coasted to a convincing 3-0 win. Blues boss Terry Cooper was quick to highlight the difference, he said after the game, "A year ago, they would have given us some trouble, but not now." It was the overall performance from the Blues team which was pleasing not just the result. Although from a lower Division Plymouth were never going to be push overs. There was no casualness though from Blues as they started off at great pace, putting the visitors under immediate pressure. A great start was only soured by the injury to Keith Downing who limped off with a twisted ankle after just nine minutes. Despite the Blues onslaught it was 21 minutes before they opened the scoring through a wonderful strike from George Parris. A neat lay off from Peschisolido put him in the clear but still 25 yards from goal, taking one look up he unleashed a tremendous drive which sailed over the advancing Plymouth 'keeper Newland and cracked the underside of the crossbar before dropping over the line. John Frain then hit a second goal to make the game safe just eight minutes later. It was a fine individual goal, weaving his way through the green-and-white defensive wall to chip his shot across the 'keeper and into the corner. Plymouth's only chance of the half came on 40 minutes and was well saved by Miller who up to then had had little to do.

Within three minutes of the restart Plymouth's Steve Castle forced Miller into another fine save, and moments later Marshall blazed wide a shot from within ten yards, this was the last chance the Deven club had in the game. Blues suddenly recaptured their first half form and quickly added a third on 58 minutes. A great diagonol run from Peschisolido finished with him playing a clever wall pass with Dave Smith, the return allowed the Canadian striker to smash it first time into the top corner with the 'keeper left motionless on the edge of the six yard box.

BIRMINGHAM CITY
Miller, Hiley, Frain, Parris, Dryden, Saville, McMinn (Donowa 80), Smith, Peschisolido, Whyte, Downing (Mardon 9).

PLYMOUTH ARGYLE
Newland, Patterson, Naylor, Hill, Comyn, McCall, Garner, Castle, Evans, Marshall, Dalton (Edworthy h/t).

REFEREE
Mr EJ Parker (Preston)

George Parris (L)

Birthdays
Ray Barlow born today in 1926

Sadly Missed
Ian Handysides died today in 1990, aged 27

August 18

Playing record for this day

Playing record for this day is...9 games, Won 2, Drawn 4, Lost 3, GF 14, GA 18.
Today's success rate.....44.44% Year ranking....207th

The Matches played on this day

1951, Division 2.
Blues 2	Bury 1	Att. 24,000
Trigg 48	Daniel 19	
Higgins 64		

1956, Division 1.
Manchester United 2	Blues 2	Att. 30,752
Viollet 28, 81	Jones(og) 66	
	Govan 69	

1962, Division 1.
Tottenham Hotspur 3	Blues 0	Att. 51,140
Blanchflower (pen) 20		
Greaves 58		
Jones 88		

1970, League Cup 1st round.
Blues 3	Wrexham 3	Att. 21,623
Murray 50	Griffiths 33(pen)	
Hateley 60	May 51	
Vincent 65	Provan 77	

1979, Division 2.
Blues 3	Fulham 4	Att. 19,179
Evans 28	Davies 51, 81	
Dillon 33	Guthrie 60	
Bertschin 35	Dennis(og) 75	

1987, League Cup 1st round, 1st leg.
Mansfield Town 2	Blues 2	Att. 4,425
Stringfellow 32	Whitton 42	
Overson(og) 70	Handysides 83	

1992, League Cup 1st round, 1st leg.
Exeter City 0	Blues 0	Att. 3,030

1996, Division 1.
Blues 1	Crystal Palace 0	Att. 18,765
Devlin 24		

Blues first game under new manager Trevor Francis
This game shown live on Sky Sports TV

2000, Division 1.
Blues 1	Fulham 3	Att. 21,659
Sonner 38	Collins 1	
	Saha 31	
	Davies 45	

Summer signing Danny Sonner scored on his St Andrews debut.
Record signing Geoff Horsfield was stretchered off after clashing with a suspected broken leg. A scan revealed nothing more than severe bruising.

Match of the Day

FROM 1970
SUB HATELEY SAVES BLUES BLUSHES
Blues down twice but earn replay against Wrexham

Blues came from behind twice in this League Cup tie at St Andrews to level the scores and force a replay at the Racecourse Ground, Wrexham. The player responsible for keeping them in the competition was Tony Hateley who despite having just 45 minutes proved a match saver. He was the provider of two goals and his mere presence earned Blues a third later in the game. Blues manager Freddie Goodwin placed Hateley on the subs' bench, stating that his style of play was too similar to that of Bob Latchford for the two to play together.

Birmingham, however, started well, and almost scored after seven minutes when Vincent put in a left wing cross which Murray hit from ten yards out, the ball struck the crossbar before being cleared away out of danger. On 33 minutes Wrexham went ahead after Murray brought down Mason in the penalty area, and Griffiths calmly placed his spot kick wide of Kelly into the bottom left-hand corner. Blues then had a lucky escape on the stroke of half time when a great save from Kelly prevented the visitors going 2-0 up. Robinson's hesitation in challenging Provan was responsible, and the shot had Kelly scrambling across his goal line to palm the ball away for a corner.

The second half began with the crowd's first-half calls for Hateley positively answered and he took the field for the restart in place of Johnston. He received a huge ovation from the 21,623 in attendance and much was expected of him as he lined up to try and salvage the game. The difference He made became evident in the 50th minute when he provided the ball for Murray to score. The sloppy Blues defence then contrived to hand the lead back to Wrexham within 60 seconds, when Griffiths made it 2-1. The inspirational Hateley then got involved in another comeback on the hour mark, when his deft header found Vowden who volleyed in Birmingham's second equalising goal.

Blues gained an advantage for the first time in the game on 65 minutes when Vincent struck. From a three man break away the Wrexham defence was caught out by a brilliant decoy run from Hateley which left a gap in which Vincent came through to rifle in a wonderfully worked goal, finishing with a precisely placed right foot shot inside the area. More dubious Blues defending allowed Wrexham to level the scores with 13 minutes remaining, after a close-range shot from Davis rebounded off Martin, and Provan was left with plenty of time to tap in from within the six yard box. In the dying minutes super sub Hateley almost capped a wonderful individual performance when he came close to scoring a dramatic winner with a header from Hockey's cross. The Wrexham 'keeper was well positioned to save with a two-handed push round the post. At the end the scores remained level and Blues faced an awkward trip to north Wales for the replay.

BIRMINGHAM CITY
Kelly, Martin, Thomson, Hockey, Hynd, Robinson, Murray, Vowden, Latchford, Vincent, Johnston (Hateley h/t)
WREXHAM
Gaskell, Ingle, Mason, Davis, May, Vansittart, Provan, Park, Moir, Kinsey, Griffiths.

Bert Murray

Blues news extra   2002...Blues Premiership kick off
Blues played their first ever Premiership game, going down 2-0 to champions Arsenal at Highbury.

Birthdays
Jon McCarthy born today in 1970   Tommy Carroll born today in 1942   Jimmy Harris born today in 1933

Playing record for this day

Playing record for this day is...13 games, Won 6, Drawn 2, Lost 5, GF 21, GA 14.

Today's success rate.....53.85% Year ranking....117th

August 19

Match of the Day

FROM 1989

DIVISION THREE LIFE STARTS WITH A 3-0 WIN

Crewe derailed at St Andrews as Blues take first Division Three points

Blues got their Division Three campaign off to a flying start after dropping to the level for the first time in their history.

Dave Mackay, appointed the Blues manager in the close season after Garry Pendrey's departure, brought new hope to the club.

His team set a devastating pace in their opening game, their first league encounter for 95 years against Crewe who themselves had been encouraged by a pre-season win against Blues local rivals Villa. A good crowd of 10,447 turned out. Blues went into the game with new signings Phil Sproson a £50,000 buy from Port Vale, and Trevor Matthewson, a £45,000 bargain from Lincoln, forming their central defence, with Dennis Bailey from Crystal Palace partnering Mark Yates and Simon Sturridge in attack. The Crewe side included ex-Villa full back Kenny Swain making his debut for the Railwaymen.

Blues dominated the first half in bright sunshine at St Andrews and were always looking dangerous, Sturridge's pace stood out against Swain, who was now in the twilight of his career. The Blues pressure eventually paid off and they went a goal up when Mark Yates rose unmarked to head past Edwards from 12 yards. Blues were 2-0 up soon after when Sturridge again broke free to race clear and hit a rising shot on the run which flew past the helpless 'keeper. With half time approaching Blues wrapped up the game when Bailey converted a cross with a diving header a minute before the interval.

Blues surprisingly eased off in the second half and although this brought a slight improvement to Crewe's attacking play they hardly managed an effort of note to trouble 'keeper Martin Thomas all afternoon. At the final whistle the score remained 3-0 and Blues had registered their biggest league win since the 4-1 victory over Crystal Palace in October 1986.

BIRMINGHAM CITY

Thomas, Clarkson, Frain, Atkins, Sproson, Matthewson, Peer, Bailey, Yates, Langley, Sturridge.

CREWE ALEXANDRA

Edwards, Swain, Edwards, Callaghan, Dyson, Walters, Jasper, Murphy, Fishenden, Gardiner, Sussex.

REFEREE

Mr H King

Mark Yates

August 20

Playing record for this day
Playing record for this day is...11 games, Won 2, Drawn 2, Lost 7, GF 13, GA 26.
Today's success rate.....27.27% Year ranking....264th

The Matches played on this day

1938, Football League Jubilee.
Coventry City 2   Blues 0   Att. 12,133
Blues first game with numbered shirts on their backs.
1949, Division 1.
Blues 0   Chelsea 3   Att. 45,000
1955, Division 1.
Blues 2   Manchester United 2   Att. 37,994
Kinsey 62   Viollet 34, 82
Astall 85
1960, Division 1.
Bolton Wanderers 2   Blues 2   Att. 20,543
Parry 39   Gordon 16
Birch 65   Hooper 67
1966, Division 2.
Wolverhampton W. 1   Blues 2   Att. 23,537
McIlmoyle 77   Murray 52, 68
Blues first win at Molineux for 26 years.
Bert Murray and Barry Bridges made their debuts for Blues.
1968, Division 2.
Charlton Athletic 3   Blues 1   Att. 14,220
Keirs 34   Vincent 86
Curtis 50
Gregory 61(pen)
Blues skipper Ron Wylie sent off after 68 minutes.
1974, Division 1.
Blues 3   Leicester City 4   Att. 27,961
Burns 20   Weller 7
Francis 40, 85(pen)   Worthington 27, 35
    Rofe 89
1977, Division 1.
Blues 1   Manchester United 4   Att. 28,005
Hibbitt 53   Macari 5, 23, 83
    Hill 75
This match screened by ATV's Star Soccer
1980, Division 1.
Nottingham Forest 2   Blues 1   Att. 26,561
Birtles 38   Worthington 46
Ponte 62
Blues Mark Dennis and Martin O'Neil of Forest sent off in the 90th minute.
1985, Division 1.
Watford 3   Blues 0   Att. 14,278
Barnes 17, 90
West 15
1994, Division 2.
Blues 1   Chester City 0   Att. 12,188
Donowa 20
The redeveloped Tilton Road stand was opened to the public for the first time. Fans in the 7,000 seated stand brought a banner which simply read "Thankyou, David Sullivan"

Match of the Day
FROM 1966
13th TIME LUCKY
At last 26 years of Molineux hurt is over after Murray double

A glorious summer day saw 23,537 crowd into Molineux for this local derby. Blues fielded their new signings Bridges and Murray from Chelsea. Wolves included 19-year-old John Farrington in their team after he showed great promise in a midweek practice game. Wolves started the game kicking off towards the South Bank with Ron Flowers leading the attack into the Blues half. The heat was already beginning to take its toll on the players and the constant attempts at pushing forward were tiring for both teams.

Farrington justified his place in the squad on just six minutes when he hurried down the right wing and sent a powerful shot which buried itself in the side netting.

For Blues, Bridges received the ball from Green and took a shot which forced MacLaren to make a hasty save. Knowles and Hunt stretched the Blues defence to the limit, and then Foster got a round of applause from the crowd when he stole the ball off McIlmoyle near the Blues goal and cleared to safety. On 38 minutes Wagstaffe was brought down by Martin who was booked for the offence, then two minutes later Blues almost managed to fight their way into the lead. Hockey took a brilliant shot from 20 yards out but it was well saved by MacLaren. The second half began with a close call from Wolves. McIlmoyle posed the threat as he sent his close range shot goalwards, but it was saved by Herriot. MacLaren had to make the next save when Hockey produced a great solo effort which forced the Wolves goalkeeper to come off his line, but the final shot lacked the vital ingredient needed to force it over the line. However, it was Hockey's cross which lead to Blues taking the lead on 52 minutes. The ball popped up all over the penalty area before finally falling to Murray. The ex-Chelsea striker proved his worth when he slammed the ball past MacLaren in the Wolves goal.

Just two minutes later there was another chance when Bobby Thomson sent a cross to Murray but he failed to get his head to the ball. Then a cross from Wagstaffe found McIlmoyle's head, and was headed goalwards with plenty of force. Herriot just about managed to flick the ball over the bar, and the resulting corner was no threat at all. Blues were beginning to increase their attacks on goal and so were Wolves, who were worried now that they may lose this clash. Their fears were doubled when Murray again scored in the 68th minute. Hockey sent the ball into the middle where Vowden carefully headed it down. Murray ran through from midfield and slammed it into the net to put Blues two goals up. Wolves did not give up the fight and a shot on target from Knowles was saved by Herriot. This renewed faith was enough to increase optimism in the Wolves side and Blues' winning margin was reduced in the 77th minute when Farrington crossed the ball to McIlmoyle who headed it into the net.

WOLVERHAMPTON WANDERERS
MacLaren, Knighton, Thomson, Bailey, Flowers, Holsgrove, Farrington, Knowles, McIlmoyle, Hunt, Wagstaffe.
BIRMINGHAM CITY
Herriot, Martin, Green, Wylie, Foster, Beard, Hockey, Thomson, Bridges, Vowden, Murray.

REFEREE
Mr J Finney (Knighton, Rads)

Blues news extra
1881...Blues stopped for being too good
Blues friendly with Darlaston All Saints ended early when the referee abandoned the game after an hour because he said it had become a 'no contest'. This came just after Blues had scored their 16th goal against their demoralised opponents. The referee had no hesitation in making up his mind and the players left before kicking off again. Blues scored eight goals in the 15 minutes that were played after half time.

Playing record for this day
Playing record for this day is...8 games, Won 5, Drawn 1, Lost 2, GF 14, GA 11.
Today's success rate.....68.75% Year ranking....15th

Match of the Day

FROM 1999

GOOD START CONTINUES

Braces from Hughes and Furlong sink ten man Vale

Blues continued their unbeaten start to the 1999-2000 season with their first home win of the campaign against Port Vale who played almost the entire game with ten men.

The match got off to a controversial start when Furlong was the victim of a bad tackle by Tommy Widdrington who received a straight red card from referee Wilkes after just two minutes play. Blues made the advantage pay just seven minutes later when a superb piece of skill from Bryan Hughes brought them the lead. Collecting the ball wide just outside the Vale penalty area he turned and nutmegged Rougier before rushing into the area. As the visitors converged to cover he curled a chip from 15 yards which drifted into the top corner to complete a fantastic opening goal. The lead was doubled ten minutes later, a clearance out was won by Hyde who played Furlong in with a pass straight through the middle of the Vale defence. The Blues striker held off his marker before hitting the ball past Musselwhite from almost the penalty spot. The 18,089 crowd sensed a huge Blues win at this stage were but were stunned by a defensive lapse at the other end that allowed Vale back in the game on 31 minutes. Rowett's short pass to Hyde had him under pressure and the ball broke to Naylor in space, he intelligently squared to Rougier who hit a first time shot which beat Poole from 25 yards, despite the keeper getting a hand to it. Blues regained their two goal advantage just three minutes later when a corner from Lazaridis was knocked down by Rowett fortunately fell to Furlong on the edge of the six yard box. His low drive through a crowd of players gave Musselwhite no chance. Blues defence was then guilty of another lapse of concentration, just four minutes from half time. Naylor escaped the defensive attention to collect a pass inside the penalty area and as Michael Johnson came to cover he lost his balance. The Vale forward wriggled his way through the four defenders to place a shot past the helpless Kevin Poole.

The second half was quickly brought to life by a wonderfully worked Blues free kick. With Lazaridis in attendance, Rowett rolled the ball to Holdsworth who backheeled straight into Hughes' path into the area, and with a first time shot he tucked it away from seven yards. Blues were content to register their first home win of the season in style by a 4-2 margin.

BIRMINGHAM CITY

Poole, Rowett, Grainger, Hyde, Holdsworth, Michael Johnson, McCarthy, Andrew Johnson (Adebola 59), Furlong (Ndlovu 82), Hughes, Lazaridis (Holland 67).

PORT VALE

Musselwhite, Carragher, Walsh, Gardner, Tankard, Rougier, Minton, Brammer, Widdrington, Bent, Naylor (Foyle 57).

REFEREE

Mr C Wilkes (Gloucester)

Bryan Hughes

Blues news extra   1982..Friendly Walsall 0 Blues 3

Blues scorers; Harford(2), McKay

Birthdays

Carl Francis born today in 1962

August 22

The Matches played on this day

1948, Division 1.
Wolverhampton W. 2 | Blues 2 | Att. 54,361
| | Bodle, Trigg |

1951, Division 2.
Blues 1 | Leeds United 1 | Att. 17,081
Ferris 16(pen) | Stevenson 55 |

1953, Division 2.
Blues 6 | Swansea Town 0 | Att. 27,000
Purdon 5, 73
Murphy 18, 57, 67
Kinsey 36
Swansea played the second half with ten men after midfielder Lucas went off injured.

1956, Division 1.
Blues 3 | Portsmouth 1 | Att. 33,307
Astall 9 | Henderson 79 |
Govan 40, 77
Unlucky Alex Govan hit the bar with one effort and had a goal disallowed with another moments later.

1959, Division 1.
Blues 0 | Wolverhampton W. 1 | Att. 41,260
| Mason 27 |

1961, Division 1.
Nottingham Forest 2 | Blues 1 | Att. 19,436
Le Flem 55, 72 | Harris 77 |

1964, Division 1.
Nottingham Forest 4 | Blues 3 | Att. 26,019
Barnwell 15 | Hellawell 8
Addison 68, 82 | Harley 25
Hinton 72 | Lynn 33(pen)

1970, Division 1.
Carlisle United 0 | Blues 3 | Att. 9,244
| Vincent 42
| B.Latchford 54, 69
Carlisle's Stan Ternent sent off after 36 minutes

1978, Division 1.
Blues 1 | Middlesbrough 3 | Att. 24,182
Bertschin 26 | Armstrong 3
| Ashcroft 25
| Mills 34

1979, Division 2.
Sunderland 2 | Blues 0 | Att. 25,877
Robson 30
Brown 66

1987, Division 2.
Aston Villa 0 | Blues 2 | Att. 30,870
| Rees 50
| Handysides 57

1989, League Cup 1st round, 1st leg.
Blues 2 | Chesterfield 1 | Att. 6,722
Atkins 12 | Waller 68
Bailey 77

1992, Division 1.
Cambridge United 0 | Blues 3 | Att. 5,015
| Rennie 3, 14
| Donowa 78

1993, Division 1.
Blues 2 | Wolverhampton W. 2 | Att. 15,117
Peschisolido 50 | Venus 35
Saville 52 | Thomas 36
This match shown live on Central TV's The Big Match

1995, League Cup 1st round, 2nd leg.
Plymouth Argyle 1 | Blues 2 | Att. 6,529
Heathcote 45 | Edwards 52
| Hunt 54
Blues won 3-1 on aggregate

1998, Division 1.
Sheffield United 0 | Blues 2 | Att. 17,458
| Adebola 55
| Forster 80
Sheff Utd defender Ian Hamilton sent off

2000, League Cup 1st round, 1st leg.
Southend United 0 | Blues 5 | Att. 3,694
| Eaden 5
| Marcelo 10
| M.Johnson 29
| Adebola 75
| Hughes 86

2001, League Cup 1st round, 1st leg.
Blues 3 | Southend United 0 | Att. 12,015
Mooney 7, 90(pen)
Whelan(og) 16
Southend reduced to nine men within a minute of stoppage time after Rawle and Cort were both dismissed.

Playing record for this day
Playing record for this day is...18 games, Won 10, Drawn 3, Lost 5, GF 41, GA 20.
Today's success rate.....63.89% Year ranking....29th

Match of the Day
FROM 1953

BLUES FIND SWANS EASY
Murphy hat-trick inspires biggest post-war win

A torrential downpour threatened to keep the St Andrews crowd down to a minimum but the 27,000 who braved the early afternoon rain, were treated to a magnificent attacking display by the Blues, who reached their biggest post-war winning margin. it was a great overall team performance by Blues who managed to subdue the threat of Allchurch in place of the injured Len Boyd.

Blues kicked off and immediately went on an all-out assault on the visitors goal. Their adventurous play was quickly rewarded when Purdon put them ahead after just five minutes. Good understanding betwen Murphy and Purdon helped them exchange some several quick passes before Murphy's final telling flick inside was coolly converted with a well placed side-footed shot from eight yards by Purdon.

Swansea tried desperately to get back into the game but the impressive Blues defence kept them well away from goal and Merrick finished by having one of the quietest games of his career. Blues added a second goal on 18 minutes, Murphy tapping in a simple chance after Stewart's cross proved a fraction of an inch too high for the challenging Purdon and 'keeper Groves. An inevitable third came Blues' way on 36 minutes. Stewart sent over a trademark inswinging corner which Purdon headed against Groves and Charles on the goal line, before either could clear the danger, Kinsey stooped to bravely head in his first goal for the club.

There was further misery for the visitors when just before half time skipper Lucas hurt his ankle in a clash with Murphy and had to go off, leaving Swansea to play the remaining 46 minutes with ten men.

Blues played some great football after the break and in a confident, relaxed mood the crowd were kept well entertained. They added a fourth goal on 57 minutes when Murphy produced a high class piece of individual skill, controlling a long clearance from his own half he set off on a fine run ending with a shot inside the area which Groves could only help into the roof of the net when trying to save. It was 5-0 ten minutes later with Murphy completing his hat-trick. Again it was from a Stewart cross, this time chipped into the box, Govan cleverly jumped over the ball aware of Murphy's presence behind him and the acting skipper swept the ball past Groves with a fine first-time shot. Stewart handicapped by a cut over his left eye sine the 40th minute had blood now covering his entire face and with great reluctance he eventually went off to receive treatment. He was by far the most effective player on the pitch and received a resounding ovation from the crowd when he returned. He responded by setting up Blues final goal in the 73rd minute for Purdon. A great ball from Warhurst gave him the opportunity to send over another delightful cross, inch perfect in length and strength, Purdon showed his admiration of the precise pass by crashing the ball first time past Groves who had absolutely no chance of stopping the thunderbolt from ten yards. Blues almost added a terrific seventh goal in the last minute when Govan had a snap shot from close in cleared off the line by Keane, with 'keeper Groves still on the ground after saving the initial effort from Purdon.

BIRMINGHAM CITY
Merrick, Hall, Martin, Bannister, Badham, Warhurst, Stewart, Kinsey, Purdon, Murphy, Govan.
SWANSEA TOWN
Groves, Thomas, Keane, Pearson, Charles, Lucas, Cyril Beech, Allchurch, Medwin, Cliff Jones, Griffiths.

REFEREE
Mr RJ Burgess (Reading)

Birmingham City's Peter Murphy (r) is foiled by Tottenham Hotspur's Mel Hopkins (c) and goalkeeper Ron Reynolds (l)

Playing record for this day

Playing record for this day is...11 games, Won 4, Drawn 3, Lost 4, GF 13, GA 10.
Today's success rate.....50% Year ranking....154th

Match of the Day

FROM 1997

BLUES RECORD MAKES GOOD READING

Blues continue bright start to the season with emphatic win

Trevor Francis' Birmingham side had been doing well of late with three wins, six goals, and three clean sheets. Reading by contrast were dull and predictable, the sort of side Blues struggled to break down only a year ago, now it was almost taken for granted that dogged defensive tactics would be swept aside at St Andrews.

The game began slowly with wayward passes which frustrated both teams in the heat of a glorious sunny afternoon better suited to cricket than football. The first chance in the opening stages was a shot from Devlin which struck the side netting. Blues finally broke down the Reading rearguard in the 37th minute through the persistence of Paul Devlin. Martin O'Connor's speculative overhead kick dropped between two Reading defenders who were a tad slow clearing the danger, Devlin quickly seized on the opportunity and drove the ball forcefully past 'keeper Mautone. The second half went the way of the first but the heat was starting to take its toll on the pace of the game, this led to Blues making a double substitution just before the hour mark. Kevin Francis replaced Furlong, and Michael Johnson took over from Hey. This made an immediate difference with two pairs of fresh legs now on the field there was a sudden surge of enthusiasm throughout the the whole side. However, Blues urgency to get forward with speed, skill and trickery was being punished by some desperately late and clumsy challenges by the visitors. The referee's patience broke when Ndlovu was sent flying by a late lunge from Andy Bernal and he received a straight red card. With ten men Blues sensed a bigger margin of victory was there for the taking and this added yet more fresh impetous from Birmingham.

However, despite continuous pressure, the score looked increasingly likely to remain 1-0 until two late goals improved the winning margin. In fact, on the day Blues were probably more than three goals better than Reading, but a one goal margin would have not done the home side justice at all.

Steve Bruce justified his place in the starting line up by netting the second goal for Blues after 81 minutes, heading in Martin Grainger's long and perfectly measured cross from the left wing. Then with just two minutes of the game remaining Bryan Hughes sent over another great cross to rival that of Grainger's, and Peter Ndlovu steered in a rare headed goal to complete the scoring. There was still time for Devlin to go close but he was denied twice by last-ditch blocks from two goal bound strikes which might have earned him a hat-trick. At the other end Ian Bennett soaked up the sun with the rest of the spectators and he had no save of any note to make at all during the 90 minutes Such was Blues dominance, and Reading's inability to modify their intial defensive ploy once they went a goal behind.

BIRMINGHAM CITY

Bennett, Wassall, Grainger, O'Connor, Bruce, Ablett,
Hey (Johnson), Devlin (Holland), Furlong (Francis), Hughes, Ndlovu.

READING

Mautone, McPherson, Wdowczyk (Roach), Primus, Booty, Bernal,
Houghton, Lambert, Swailes (Bodin), Asaba, Hodges.

REFEREE

Mr E. Lomas (Manchester)

Peter Ndlovu

Birthdays

Martin Grainger born today in 1972   **William Beel born today in 1945**

August 24

Playing record for this day
Playing record for this day is...16 games, Won 8, Drawn 4, Lost 4, GF 30, GA 25.
Today's success rate.....62.50% Year ranking....38th

The Matches played on this day

1949, Division 1.		
Blues 2	WBA 0	Att. 50,000
Dailey(2)		
1953, Division 2.		
Plymouth Argyle 2	Blues 2	Att. 20,800
Davis 8	Kinsey 68	
Tadman 73	Govan 85	
1955, Division 1.		
Newcastle United 2	Blues 2	Att. 34,390
Keeble 39	Murphy 17	
Davies 24	Astall 62	
1957, Division 1.		
Blues 3	Aston Villa 1	Att. 50,807
Kinsey 9	McParland 24	
Murphy 40		
Brown 71		
1960, Division 1.		
WBA 1	Blues 2	Att. 22,102
Jackson 32	Rudd 51	
	Hooper 67	
1963, Division 1.		
Blues 2	Bolton Wanderers 1	Att. 24,817
Lynn 29(pen)	Davies 40	
Hellawell 30		
1966, Division 2.		
Portsmouth 4	Blues 5	Att. 16,934
Lewis 59	Vowden 19, 81	
Hiron 74	Bridges 40	
McCann 87	Beard 73(pen)	
Barton 88	Murray 86	
1968, Division 2.		
Blues 5	Portsmouth 2	Att. 23,915
Pickering 1, 87	Pointer 36	
Vowden 5	Trebilcock 44	
Summerill 23		
Vincent 66		

Fred Pickering's first goal timed at 13 seconds

1974, Division 1.		
Leeds United 1	Blues 0	Att. 30,820
Clarke 59		

This game screened by BBC's Match of the Day

1976, Division 1.		
Blues 0	Leeds United 0	Att. 35,399
1977, Division 1.		
Chelsea 2	Blues 0	Att. 18,008
Stanley 15		
Lewington 81		

Blues keeper Jim Montgomery saved a penalty in the 65th minute

1985, Division 1.		
Chelsea 2	Blues 0	Att. 16,634
Rougvie 17		
Jones 73		
1991, Division 3.		
Fulham 0	Blues 1	Att. 4,762
	Rodgerson 36	
1993, League Cup 1st round, 2nd leg.		
Plymouth Argyle 2	Blues 0	Att. 3,659
Barlow 66		
Marshall 90		
1996, Division 1.		
Sheffield United 4	Blues 4	Att. 16,332
Taylor 45, 70	Furlong 9	
Walker 67, 72	Newell 22	
	Devlin 75(pen)	
	Hunt 83	

Blues were 2-0 up, then 4-2 down in this eight goal thriller at Bramall Lane.

1999, League Cup 1st round, 2nd leg.		
Exeter City 1	Blues 2	Att. 2,338
McConnell 75(pen)	Richardson(og) 22	
	O'Connor 50	

Blues won 5-1 on aggregate.
Exeter substitute Smith was sent off in the 90th minute.

Match of the Day
FROM 1966
NINE GOAL THRILLER AT FRATTON
It's two wins from two for the free-scoring Blues

Blues got their promotion campaign off to a flying start with another win against Portsmouth at Fratton Park. Just four days after beating local rivals Wolves at Molineux, they finished this latest game for the most part far superior. Blues went into the game making no changes to the 2-1 winning team from Wolves. Portsmouth on the other hand made three. They had started the season with a dull 0-0 draw with Norwich and out of the side went Tindall, McClelland, and Portwood, making way for Roy Pack, ex-Blues man Johnny Gordon and Tony Barton (a future Villa boss). The game quickly became a midfield tussle with few goal chances. Possession favoured the home side for the opening 15 minutes. Blues did get their chance though, and the difference between the two sides was the ability to finish chances. Blues' first chance came on 19 minutes and they opened the scoring. A miskick by Harris fell to Vowden inside the area, who tucked the ball away easily. The balance of play swung dramatically after the goal and it was Blues who now passed the ball around with confidence. From such a move they doubled their lead just before half time when Thompson threaded a fine ball through for Bridges, who raced forward beating the offside trap and clipping the ball past Milkins as he came out to cover. At half time Blues led 2-0 in an average but non-spectacular game which gave little indication to the 16,934 crowd of what drama was to come.

Indeed the second half quickly followed that of the first with the home side having most of the possession, but a solid looking Blues defence was more than capable of keeping the Pompey attack at bay. Portsmouth did manage to break through on 59 minutes, however, when a defensive lapse let Lewis in to bring the score to 2-1. Then after 73 minutes all hell was let loose as the game suddenly became a goal riot with six shared between the two sides in just 15 minutes play. A penalty was awarded for a Wilson handball and Malcolm Beard put Blues 3-1 up from the spot kick. Within a minute Pompey were back in the game at 3-2 when Hiron was gifted an opportunity in the Blues penalty area. Blues then scored two in five minutes through Vowden and Murray, and it was 5-2 and game over. However their solid looking defence suddenly became nervously leaky as McCann, then Barton, scored in the 87th and 88th minutes to put Portsmouth right back in the game at 5-4 and still two minutes to play. However both sides held out for the final 120 seconds without conceding any further goals, and Blues had won their second game of the season.

PORTSMOUTH
Milkins, Pack, Wilson, Gordon, Haydock, Harris, Barton, McCann, Hiron, Lewis, Kellard.
BIRMINGHAM CITY
Herriott, Martin, Green, Wylie, Foster, Beard, Hockey, Thomson, Bridges, Vowden, Murray.

Fratton Park, home of Portsmouth

Birthdays
Jason Bowen born today in 1972   **Tony Van Mierlo born today in 1957**

Playing record for this day
Playing record for this day is...19 games, Won 11, Drawn 3, Lost 4, GF 29, GA 24.
Today's success rate.....65.79% Year ranking....20th

August 25

Match of the Day
FROM 1956
NEVER SAY DIE BLUES
Three goals in seven minutes brings victory

Blues fighting spirit was highlighted as they came back from a disastrous first half, when they trailed 2-0, with a six-minute blast in the second period to lead Arsenal 3-2. They eventually got a fourth goal to claim victory and maintain their unbeaten start to the 1956-57 league campaign. Blues went into the game making their first team selection change, bringing Johnny Watts in for Albert Linnecor in midfield. Arsenal were forced to make one change with Don Roper coming in for injured skipper Peter Goring.

Arsenal made the better start, although their finishing was as inefficient troublesome as Blues' passing. This meant that the game really lacked excitement for the 37,200 crowd for the first 20 minutes. Up to 28 minutes the game was summed up by the opening goal. A real messy affair from yet another free kick. Holton took the kick just 10 yards into the Blues half. A long ball sailed over everyone's heads, but Tapscott had run around the back. As the ball bounced, it appeared to just fail to make contact, but his presence was enough to keep Merrick occupied and the ball slipped past and straight into the net, the goal awarded to Holton. Still Blues struggled to make any in-roads to mount any serious assault on the Arsenal goal, wayward passing and a solid defence the most obvious reasons. No surprises then when Arsenal extended their lead after 36 minutes. It was a more conventional goal, but another one that the Blues defence should have dealt with. Tapscott easily beat Green on the left flank and crossed for Roper, who was unmarked by Smith, and he had ample time to bring the ball down and slot it comfortably past Merrick. Finally, five minutes before half time, Blues got a break, and Govan brought Kelsey into the game for the first time with a shot that the 'keeper had to dive full length to tip round the post. Manager Arthur Turner said at half time worked. Within minutes of the restart Blues looked a completely different side. They forced three corners in succession and Kinsey and Brown came within a whisker of a goal. The better side in the second period, Murphy got a goal back on 69 minutes, beating Dodgin in the air to head in Astall's centre. The crowd, sensing Blues could get back in to level the game, expected even more when Brown equalised just five minutes later. A great run from Govan finished with a through ball to Brown who, for once, was completely free of the defence. Although Kelsey got his hand to the shot, the ball made its way into the bottom left hand corner of the net. Just two minutes later Blues completed a remarkable comeback to the total delight of St Andrews, when man-of-the-match Alex Govan headed in Astall's corner kick. They were on fire, and soon afterwards Astall hit the crossbar with a rasping 20-yard drive. Hall then cleared a Roper shot off the line with a diving header at the other end, but with four minutes remaining Murphy headed in a fourth Blues goal from another glorious cross by Astall.

BIRMINGHAM CITY

Merrick, Hall, Green, Watts, Smith, Warhurst, Astall, Kinsey, Brown, Murphy, Govan

ARSENAL

Kelsey, Charlton, Evans, Wills, Dodgin, Holton, Clapton, Tapscott, Roper, Bloomfield, Tiddy

REFEREE

Mr A R Burnhair (Leicestershire)

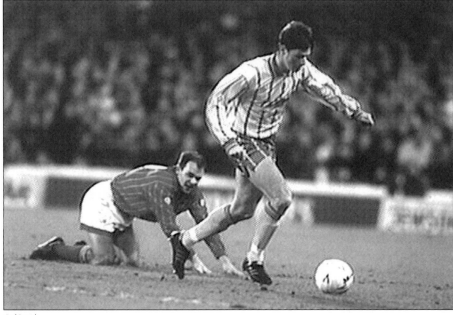

Paul Fenwick

Birthdays

Paul Fenwick born today in 1969   **Keith Bertschin born today in 1956**

August 26

Playing record for this day
Playing record for this day is...19 games, Won 8, Drawn 7, Lost 4, GF 32, GA 30.
Today's success rate.....60.53% Year ranking....49th

Match of the Day
FROM 1959
THE ONE THAT ALMOST GOT AWAY
Blues win by odd goal in seven, after leading by three

Manager Pat Beasley stuck loyally with the team that lost their opening game of the 1959-60 season to Wolves at St Andrews. After an encouraging start it was Blues who were 3-0 up against Newcastle's 5 man attack and this despite an injury to Astall, which in effect put him out of the game bar taking the occasional throw in. However from a position of comfort Blues managed to concede two penalties either side of a goal from White in the second half, which to keep the crowd of 26,981 on edge right to the very last kick.

As early as the second minute Stubbs was left all alone in the Newcastle penalty area with the ball at his feet needing a simple shot anywhere on target to record Blues first goal of the season. Maybe the occasion got to him, as his hesitancy allowed Harvey to dive and smother the ball, to his and the Newcastle defence's relief. Stubbs soon made amends with a well worked goal just five minutes later. Hooper beat his full back raced clear to centre, Astall ran towards the ball in the area and at the last second jumped over it, this fooled not one, but two defenders and once again Stubbs was left with a simple chance, which he didn't miss. Blues were in total command, mainly due to the play of their wingers Astall and Hooper who were running Newcastle's ageing defenders Scoular and McMichael ragged. It was a bitter blow, when Astall, after treading on the ball in the 17th minute was left limping and eventually had to leave the field for treatment.

Astall returned after 14 minutes during which Blues had played some of their best football, Harvey had already saved well from Gordon, and a shot from Stubbs was blocked on the line by McMichael after it had beaten the 'keeper. However, with a full complement of players, albeit one nowhere near fully fit, Blues scored a second after 34 minutes. The goal was Orritt's from the time he collected the loose ball on the half way line to charge forward straight through the middle to the time he smashed the ball past Harvey from the edge of the penalty area. It was a fantastic individual effort well appreciated by the St Andrews crowd. Two minutes later they were celebrating a third Birmingham goal, another lofted cross from Hooper evaded the 'keeper's dive forward and Gordon headed into the unguarded net at the far post. With a minute to the half-time interval Scoular denied Blues a near certain fourth goal when preventing a through ball for Stubbs with his outstretched arm, an offence which earned him a booking by the referee.

The second half started with a mini-revival for Newcastle, and Schofield was involved as much in the first five minutes of the restart, as he had been in the entire first half. Then after just seven minutes of the half Neal impeded Allchurch wide on the right of the penalty area, it was nothing more than obstruction. However the referee rather than give an indirect free kick he harshly pointed to the penalty spot, and Eastham strode up to give Newcastle some hope. Blues were suddenly on the rack and just three minutes later White intercepted a defender's pass and charged forward to beat Schofield for the second time in the game. Thankfully Blues were handed a stroke of luck when a minute later, Keith handled needlessly inside his own penalty area and Hooper restored their two goal advantage with the penalty. This seemed to kill Newcastle off for a time, but the next goal scoring chance fell to the visitors, Bell shooting over the bar from close in, after Allchurch's fine run and cross. Blues too, had their moments, Franks cleared off the goal line from Hooper's shot. Likewise Blues centre half Smith prevented Allchurch from scoring in the same manner moments later. It was end to end attack right to the final kick and Blues were given a nervy last few seconds when Eastham converted a second penalty right on full time. Newcastle managed to launch one more attack and Schofield was given the game's second loudest cheer when he caught Taylor's cross. The loudest cheer came when the final whistle sounded straight from his kick out.

BIRMINGHAM CITY
Schofield, Farmer, Allen, Watts, Smith, Neal, Astall, Gordon, Stubbs, Orritt, Hooper.
NEWCASTLE UNITED
Harvey, Keith, McMichael, Franks, Scoular, Bell, Taylor, Eastham, White, Allchurch, Scott.

Birthdays
Jeff Wealands born today in 1951   Dean Williams born in 1972.

The Matches played on this day

1978, Division 1.
| Blues 1 | Derby County 1 | Att. 21,963 |
| Givens 42 | Daly 24 | |

1980, League Cup 2nd round, 1st leg.
Blues 2	Bristol City 1	Att. 12,163
Ainscow 24	Ritchie 69	
Gemmill 47(pen)		

1985, Division 1.
Blues 3	Oxford United 1	Att. 10,568
Kennedy 23	Aldridge 14	
Briggs(og) 40		
Hopkins 67		

1989, Division 3.
| Bristol City 1 | Blues 0 | Att. 8,938 |
| Taylor 74 | | |

1995, Division 1.
| Blues 3 | Norwich City 1 | Att. 19,267 |
| Hunt 23, 49(pen), 71 | Sheron 86 | |

1997, League Cup 1st round, 2nd leg.
Blues 3	Gillingham 0	Att. 7,921
Furlong 68		
Devlin 75		
Ndlovu 78		

Blues won 4-0 on aggregate

2000, Division 1.
Nottingham Forest 1	Blues 2	Att. 18,820
Bart Williams 52	Marcelo 16	
	Eaden 45	

After 11 successive defeats Blues finally gained a victory over Notts Forest.

Bryan Orritt

Blues news extra   1882...Abandoned due to heat!

Blues friendly against Walsall Town was
halted then abandoned due to the players suffering from heat
exhaustion. Blues were leading 4-3 when the game was
stopped after 70 minutes. Several of the players had left the field
already and many more were feeling ill with the effects of a
very hot day where temperatures reached almost 100 degrees Fahrenheit.

August 27

Playing record for this day
Playing record for this day is...19 games, Won 6, Drawn 3, Lost 10, GF 24, GA 28.
Today's success rate.....39.47% Year ranking....235th

The Matches played on this day

1921, Division 1.

Blues 2	Burnley 3	Att. 40,000
Elkes(2)		

1927, Division 1.

Tottenham Hotspur 1	Blues 0	Att. 37,408

1928, Division 1.

Leicester City 5	Blues 3	Att. 20,000
	Briggs, Crosbie, Ellis	

1932, Division 1.

Blues 0	Arsenal 1	Att. 31,952

1938, Division 1.

Blues 1	Sunderland 2	Att. 25,000
Jennings(pen)		

1949, Division 1.

Stoke City 3	Blues 1	Att. 30,000
	Capel	

1952, Division 2.

Luton Town 0	Blues 1	Att. 20,893
	Briggs 30	

1955, Division 1.

Sheffield United 0	Blues 3	Att. 27,000
	Kinsey 33	
	Brown 64	
	Murphy 87	

1958, Division 1.

WBA 2	Blues 2	Att. 46,800
Hogg 69	Houghton 64	
Allen 84(pen)	Brown 89	

1960, Division 1.

Blues 1	Sheffield Wed. 1	Att. 27,180
Hooper 63	Fantham 61	

1966, Division 2.

Blues 2	Norwich City 1	Att. 25,516
Vowden 6	Curran 81	
Murray 39		

1969, Division 2.

Hull City 0	Blues 0	Att. 12,242

1977, Division 1.

Leeds United 1	Blues 0	Att. 24,551
Hankin 49		

This match screened by BBC's Match of the Day

1983, Division 1.

West Ham United 4	Blues 0	Att. 19,729
Cottee 24, 27		
Martin 37		
Swindlehurst 52		

1988, Division 2.

Watford 1	Blues 0	Att. 12,656
Bamber 36		

1991, League Cup 1st round, 2nd leg.

Blues 4	Exeter City 0	Att. 6,179
Hicks 9		
Yates 31		
Peer 52		
Gleghorn 67		

Blues won 5-0 on aggregate

1994, Division 2.

Swansea City 0	Blues 2	Att. 5,797
	Claridge 76, 80	

1999, Division 1.

Stockport County 2	Blues 0	Att. 6,115
Wilbraham 77		
D'Jaffo 85		

2001, Division 1.

Blues 2	Stockport County 1	Att. 18,478
Grainger 2	Kuqi 86(pen)	
Mooney 21(pen)		

Match of the Day
FROM 1991
A NEW DAWN FOR COOPER?
Rodgerson - worth every penny!

Strikes from midfielders Nigel Gleghorn, Mark Yates and Dean Peer, and a fourth from defender Martin Hicks put Blues into the second round draw of the Rumbelows League Cup with their fourth successive win for new manager Terry Cooper. Ian Rodgerson, Birmingham's man-of-the-match was instrumental in all of his team's best moves. On ten minutes Sturridge's diagonal run towards the right corner flag opened up a huge gap in front of Rodgerson. His shot from just inside the area was palmed away by Kevin Miller into the path of a crowd of players, the ball encountering centre half Hicks, commendably far forward, who was able to turn it in at the back post. With a 2-0 aggregate advantage, Blues were now able to relax and take full control. Ian Clarkson and Richardson worked a neat triangle with Sturridge, whose shot went just wide of Miller's right-hand post. This was followed by a Richardson cross over the bar, and from the subsequent corner, Sturridge missed an excellent opportunity from only six yards. On 31 minutes, Rodgerson's perfect cross to Mark Yates, enabled the midfielder to pick his spot inside of Miller's right-hand post. Birmingham were now two goals up, 3-0 on aggregate. Birmingham goalkeeper, Martin Thomas only needed to make one save in the first half, a routine one, when Mark Cooper shot straight at him. Miller, in contrast was continuously under fire, finishing the first half with a Sturridge shot directed at his left hand side, which required some quick work to get his hands safely around the ball.

The second half began in like manner. Only six minutes in Sturridge exquisitely dummied David Cole without laying a foot on a through ball from Clarkson, but his shot was directly at Miller. On 52 minutes, Miller was cruelly exposed by his defence as Blues claimed their third goal of the match. Gleghorn fed to the overlapping Frain who picked out a late arriving Dean Peer with a deep cross enabling the midfielder to plant the ball across Miller into the left-hand corner. After 67 minutes, Blues broke again against a now frantic Exeter defence, with substitute Trevor Aylott picking out Gleghorn with an enormous pass. He ghosted into the area and round Scott Daniels to fire an acutely angled shot across Miller and in off the far post. Exeter briefly came back into the game when awarded a free kick and Cooper's shot rattled an upright. Okenla came on for Sturridge at 72 minutes, and could well have had a fifth. He laid the ball off for Gleghorn whose cross was met by Aylott, but he was unable to get quite enough head on the ball to send it home.

BIRMINGHAM CITY
Thomas, Clarkson, Hicks, Mardon, Frain, Rodgerson, Peer, Yates, Gleghorn, Dolan (Aylott 50), Sturridge (Okenla 72)

EXETER CITY
Miller, Daniels, Brown, Cole, Kelly, Hiley, Cooper, Williams, O'Shaughnessy (Marshall 54), Rowbotham, Moran

REFEREE
Mr PS Danson (Blaby, Leics)

Ian Rodgerson

Birthdays

Alan O'Neill born today in 1973   Jeff Kenna born today in 1970

Playing record for this day

Playing record for this day is...21 games, Won 8, Drawn 5, Lost 8, GF 29, GA 34.

Today's success rate.....50% Year ranking....170th

Match of the Day
FROM 1976
LEAGUE CHAMPS LOSE OUT TO BLUES

Blues beat Liverpool in revived second half drama

Blues faced one of their toughest opponents in the form of champions Liverpool, who included new signing David Johnson. The first half had little real action, chances being few and far between. None of the players stood out, and the match lacked interest for those fans expecting to see a top-class battle.

However the half-time team talk seemed to work, and it took just seven minutes to come into effect when Blues' first on-target shot of the match resulted in a goal. A long clearance from Dave Latchford was nodded on by Burns and Withe for Francis to send to the left-hand side of the goal, England goalkeeper Ray Clemence being well beaten. In reply Liverpool mounted a tough counter-attack, having been quite lax in defence. The crowd enjoyed this new-found vigour, and it went some way to making up for the poor first half. Despite the fact that it was high summer, the weather was awful. Heavy rain and cool temperatures made for a slippery pitch, but it also increased the crowd's pleasure as the players found themselves skidding around the field on more than a few occasions. Liverpool came back with an equaliser on 75 minutes. Ray Kennedy sent a perfectly measured pass to David Johnson who headed in at the far post.

Blues were now looking for a win and they deservedly got it. Kendall's free kick seemed to be heading to safety, but Joe Gallagher was in the right place at the right time to head the ball past Clemence and put Blues ahead. Blues held out for the final quarter of an hour to seal a famous victory.

BIRMINGHAM CITY

Latchford, Page, Styles, Kendall, Gallagher, Want, Pendrey, Francis, Burns, Hibbitt, Withe.

LIVERPOOL

Clemence, Neal, Jones, Thompson, Kennedy, Hughes, Keegan, Johnson, Heighway, Toshack (Fairclough), Callaghan.

Kevin Keegan, holds off Kenny Burns

The Matches played on this day

1920, Division 2.			
South Shields 3	Blues 0		Att. 15,000
1922, Division 1.			
Blues 0	Newcastle United 2		Att. 35,000
1926, Division 1.			
Blues 3	Blackburn Rovers 1		Att. 30,000
Briggs, Bradford(2)			
1937, Division 1.			
Stoke City 2	Blues2		Att. 30,000
	Richards, Morris		
1943, Wartime.			
Coventry City 0	Blues 0		
1948, Division 1.			
Blues 1	Chelsea 0		Att. 48,000
Stewart			
1950, Division 2.			
Leicester City 1	Blues 3		Att. 31,000
Rowley 82	Trigg 27		
	Smith 71		
	Stewart 86		
1954, Division 2.			
Blues 3	Rotherham United 1		Att. 27,000
Govan 54, 57	Guest 4		
Warhurst 66			
1957, Division 1.			
Nottingham Forest 1	Blues 1		Att. 28,555
Wilson 69	Brown 44		
1963, Division 1.			
Leicester City 3	Blues 0		Att. 27,661
Riley 19			
Keyworth 83			
Stringfellow 88			
1965, Division 2.			
Preston North End 3	Blues 3		Att. 16,397
Dawson 15, 27	Vowden 23		
Godfrey 58	Beard 44, 60		

Brian Sharples replaced Ron Wylie, becoming the first substitute to be used by the Blues.

1968, Division 2.			
Cardiff City 4	Blues 0		Att. 15,008
Toshack 60, 64			
Bell 76			
Clark 86			
1971, Division 2.			
Portsmouth 1	Blues 0		Att. 14,729
Trebilcock 14			

Portsmouth had two goals disallowed

1973, Division 1.			
Blues 1	Tottenham Hotspur 2		Att. 37,754
Hatton 48	Peters 43, 69		
1974, Division 1.			
Leicester City 1	Blues 1		Att. 24,018
Worthington 36	Francis 65		

Trevor Francis had a goal disallowed after 63 mins

1976, Division 1.			
Blues 2	Liverpool 1		Att. 33,228
Francis 52	Johnson 75		
Gallagher 76			
1979, League Cup 2nd round, 1st leg.			
Blues 2	Preston North End 1		Att. 13,660
Ainscow 37	Potts 72		
Dillon 80			

Goalscorer Potts had a 54th minute penalty saved by Blues keeper Jeff Wealands

1982, Division 1.			
Manchester United 3	Blues 0		Att. 48,673
Moran 47			
Stapleton 50			
Coppell 70			
1990, League Cup 1st round, 1st leg.			
Blues 0	Bournemouth 1		Att. 5,110
	Blissett 6		
1993, Division 1.			
Barnsley 2	Blues 3		Att. 7,241
Redfearn 30	Smith 55, 75		
Anderson 77	Shutt 90		
2000, Division 1.			
Blues 4	Barnsley 1		Att. 17,160
Ndlovu 9	Appleby 71		
Grainger 35(pen)			
Holdsworth 51			
Hughes 90			

Barnsley had Morgan sent off after 86 mins.

August 29

The Matches played on this day

1921, Division 1.
Chelsea 1   Blues 2   Att. 30,000
           Elkes, Hampton

1923, Division 1.
Liverpool 6   Blues 2   Att. 16,000
           Bradford(2)

1925, Division 1.
Sunderland 3   Blues 1   Att. 25,000
           Bradford
Blues first game under the new offside rule.

1927, Division 1.
Blues 3   Huddersfield Town 1 Att. 20,000
Bradford(2), Harris

1931, Division 1.
Everton 3   Blues 2   Att. 30,000
           Briggs, Curtis

1934, Division 1.
WBA 1   Blues 2   Att. 22,025
           Sandford(og), Bradford

1936, Division 1.
Blues 2   Portsmouth 1   Att. 30,000
Dearson, Morris

1942, Wartime.
Leicester City 0 Blues 1
           McCormick

1951, Division 2.
Leeds United 1 Blues 1   Att. 15,008
Iggledden 35   Purdon 11
Ted Purdon scored on his Blues debut

1953, Division 2.
Rotherham United 1 Blues 0 Att. 14,000
Burke 29

1956, Division 1.
Portsmouth 3 Blues 4   Att. 25,685
Gordon 3   Govan 8, 54, 74
Merrick(og) 26 Astall 31
Harris 47

1959, Division 1.
Tottenham Hotspur 0 Blues 0 Att. 45,243

1962, Division 1.
Blues 2   Arsenal 2   Att. 27,135
Leek 30   Strong 7, 11
Lynn 55(pen)

1964, Division 1.
Blues 1   Stoke City 2   Att. 20,692
Lynn 57(pen) Ritchie 25
           Bebbington 35

1967, Division 2.
Middlesbrough 1 Blues 1   Att. 25,814
Rooks 54   Vincent 7

1970, Division 2.
Blues 1   Luton Town 1 Att. 30,141
Vowden 24   MacDonald 82(pen)

1978, League Cup 2nd round.
Blues 2   Southampton 5 Att. 18,464
Gallagher 44 Boyer 21, 63
Francis 80   MacDougall 45, 75
           Peach 53
Blues striker Keith Bertschin broke his leg

1981, Division 1.
Everton 3   Blues 1   Att. 33,045
Ainscow 11   Van Mierlo 4
Eastoe 49
Biley 87
Jeff Wealands saved Everton's Asa Hartford's 35th minute penalty, twice. After the first kick referee George Courtney ordered a retake because the Blues keeper had moved before the kick was taken. Tony Van Mierlo scored on his Blues debut. This game screened by ATV's Star Soccer

1987, Division 2.
Blues 1   Bournemouth 1 Att. 8,284
Kennedy 63   Armstrong 65
First meeting against Bournemouth

1989, League Cup 2nd round, 2nd leg.
Chesterfield 1 Blues 1   Att. 3,313
Hewitt 47   Bailey 88
Blues won 3-2 on aggregate

1997, Division 1.
Stockport County 2 Blues 2 Att. 6,260
Armstrong 7   Devlin 69
Angell 50   Francis 73

1998, Division 1.
Blues 0   Barnsley 0   Att. 19,825

Playing record for this day
Playing record for this day is...22 games, Won 6, Drawn 9, Lost 7, GF 32, GA 39.
Today's success rate.....47.62% Year ranking....181st

Match of the Day

FROM 1956

GOVAN TRIO SEALS IT

Blues win seven goal thriller at Fratton Park

A crowd of 25,685 were treated to a fine seven goal thriller at Fratton Park as Blues showed their true spirit in an exciting game. Three times they found themselves in arrears, and three times they were able to fight themselves back into contention. It was a fantastic team effort from the visitors and all played their part well. Brown provided the opening for the first goal, Kinsey played his part as provider also, Murphy delivered the cross for the winner. In defence Watts at right back and Green played soundly with Merrick the final barrier supplying a safe pair of hands. It was Portsmouth who took the lead after just three minutes when Gordon found space to head in from close range. Then just five minutes later Blues drew level when Brown's right wing breakthrough provided Govan with the equaliser. Portsmouth then regained the lead on 26 minutes with a fortuitous goal when Pickett fired in a shot which cannoned off the post and the rebound struck the unfortunate Merrick on the back and rolled in. Blues equalised for a second time just five minutes later when Watts put Astall clear and the right winger sped through to beat Uprichard with a fierce swerving drive which the 'keeper could only watch the ball fly past him and into the net behind him. The second half started in controversy and Blues were unlucky again as the referee chose to overrule a linesman's flag, which was raised for an infringement against Dale the Pompey forward. He allowed the advantage as the Blues defence momentarily stopped, Harris didn't and went on to roll the ball over the line for a simple goal. Again Blues rallied and their notorious fighting spirit brought them an equaliser again when Govan scored in the 54th minute. Then he completed his hat-trick to put Blues ahead for the first time 16 minutes from the end as Portsmouth began to tire.

PORTSMOUTH

Uprichard, McGhee, Gunter, Pickett, Rutter, Dickinson,
Harris, Gordon, Henderson, Barnard, Dale.

BIRMINGHAM CITY

Merrick, Hall, Green, Watts, Smith, Warhurst,
Astall, Kinsey, Brown, Murphy, Govan.

Alex Govan

Birthdays

David Rennie born today in 1964   **Ken Rowley born today in 1926**

Playing record for this day

Playing record for this day is...24 games, Won 8, Drawn 5, Lost 11, GF 43, GA 41.

Today's success rate.....43.75% Year ranking....211th

Match of the Day

FROM 1999

BLUES TURN ON FIVE STAR SHOW

Early blushes before Crewe buried in goal avalanche

The St Andrews crowd of 24,085 were treated to a rare Blues goal bonanza after seeing the visitors take the lead shortly after the kick off. Blues started the game eager to avenge the previous week's defeat at Stockport, facing an unbeaten Crewe side. It was the visitors who took the early advantage when Cramb found space in the Blues penalty area to turn defender Michael Johnson inside out before curling a right-foot shot from 15 yards which went in off the post. The lead lasted just eight minutes and it was Johnson who levelled with a close range header from Rowett's free kick to the far post. Blues completed their comeback just eight minutes later with a neat move and cross from the left wing. Grainger's throw in to Furlong was touched into the path of Lazaridis who outpaced his marker to send in a great outswinging cross which McCarthy headed in at the near post. Blues further increased the lead on the half-hour mark through Furlong, another fast flowing move ending with a high cross from Rowett and Hughes climbed well to head back to the Blues striker who hooked the ball in from six yards. Blues continued to press but at half time they went in without further adding to the 3-1 scoreline.

There was no let up from the home side as the second half got under way. Barely two minutes had gone before Crewe's Macauley somehow managed to scoop McCarthy's shot off the line. Blues had to wait until the 51st minute for their fourth goal, the simplest one of the game. Andy Johnson running into the area sent over a beautifully flighted cross which found Furlong onside and on his own barely eight yards out. Kearton pulled off an amazing stop to deny him, only to see the ball rebound to Holdsworth who tapped into the empty net. Although Crewe hit the post through Little two minutes later, Blues were in total command and but for two superb saves from Kearton could have got close to double figures. However they had to settle for five and the last goal came with just six minutes remaining. Hyde's cross was poorly headed away by Wright and Ndlovu nipped in, controlled well, side-stepped the defender and slipped the ball wide of Kearton's reach. Blues had thus recorded their biggest league win at St Andrews since the demolition of Blackpool in 1994.

BIRMINGHAM CITY

Poole, Rowett, Grainger, O'Connor (Hyde 74), Michael Johnson, Holdsworth, McCarthy, Andrew Johnson (Ndlovu 74), Furlong (Adebola 78), Hughes, Lazaridis.

CREWE ALEXANDRA

Kearton, David Wright, Shaun Smith, Steve Wright, Foran (Macauley 33), Charnock, Lunt (Bignot 86), Sorvel, Little (Peter Smith 74), Rivers, Cramb.

REFEREE

Mr G Laws (Whitley Bay)

Garry Rowett

The Matches played on this day

1919, Division 2.
Blues 4   Hull City 1   Att. 16,000
Gibson, Walker, Godfrey, Whitehouse
Blues produced their first matchday programme, replacing the single page team sheet.

1924, Division 1.
Blues 2   Everton 2   Att. 30,000
Linley, Crosbie

1926, Division 1.
Leicester City 5   Blues 2   Att. 25,000
    Bradford, Harris

1930, Division 1.
Blues 3   Sheffield United 1   Att. 27,576
Morrall, Briggs, Bradford

1933, Division 1.
Blues 0   Manchester City 1   Att. 30,000

1939, Division 2.
Blues 2   Leicester City 0   Att. 15,000
Farrage, Sharman(og)

1947, Division 2.
Plymouth Argyle 0   Blues 3   Att. 20,000
    Dougall, Bodle, Aveyard

1952, Division 2.
Blues 1   Fulham 4   Att. 30,000
Briggs 56   Robson 34, 63
    Brennan 52
    Stevens 66

1954, Division 2.
Bristol Rovers 1   Blues 1   Att. 26,191
Bradford 23   Warhurst 3

1958, Division 1.
Blues 0   Luton Town 1   Att. 32,129
    Groves 88

1961, Division 1.
Blues 1   Nottingham Forest 1   Att. 21,079
Harris 53   Booth 29

1966, Division 2.
Blues 3   Portsmouth 0   Att. 23,493
Pack (og) 43
Thomson 60
Vowden 64

1969, Division 2.
Blues 3   QPR 0   Att. 32,660
Murray 3, 5, 15

1972, Division 1.
WBA 2   Blues 2   Att. 37,252
Gould 39   Hatton 53
Suggett 80   B.Latchford 89

Blues unveiled their new away kit a red yellow and black coloured penguin shirt.

All three Latchford brothers were in action for the first time at senior level, in the same game. Peter Latchford kept goal for West Brom, whilst Dave was the Blues keeper. Bob Latchford scored past his brother to earn Blues a share of the points.

August
30

The Matches played on this day *

1975, Division 1.
Ipswich Town 4   Blues 2   Att. 22,649
Johnson 11, 41   Hatton 64, 65
Hamilton 17
Wymark 29

1977, League Cup 2nd round.
Blues 0   Notts County 2   Att. 14,993
   Carter 19(pen)
   Sims 49

1980, Division 1.
Southampton 3   Blues 1   Att. 21,683
Baker 5   Worthington 52
Channon 33
Keegan 38

1983, Division 1.
Notts County 2   Blues 1   Att. 11,031
Harkouk 43, 72   Harford 23
Tony Rees made his Blues debut.
Blues had Robert Hopkins sent off after 53 minutes.

1986, Division 2.
Blues 1   Derby County 1   Att. 12,209
Clarke 1   Gregory 20
Wayne Clarke's goal timed at 44 seconds.

1988, League Cup 1st round, 1st leg.
Wolverhampton W. 3   Blues 2   Att. 11,007
Bull 52, 82   Thompson(og) 35
Dennison 66   Bird 64

1992, Division 1.
Blues 2   Grimsby Town 1   Att. 6,807
Gleghorn 12   Mendonca 4
Rowbotham 88

1994, Division 2.
Blues 0   Wycombe Wanderers 1   Att. 14,305
   Regis 67
The Regis brothers Dave and Cyrille appeared on opposite sides in this game with Cyrille coming out on top, scoring the winner.

1995, Division 1.
Huddersfield Town 4   Blues 2   Att. 12,305
Dalton 7, 51   Ward 11, 72
Jepson 63
Bullock 70

1999, Division 1.
Blues 5   Crewe Alexandra 1   Att. 24,085
M.Johnson 12   Cramb 4
McCarthy 20
Furlong 30
Holdsworth 52
Ndlovu 77

Peter Ndlovu

Birthdays
Dennis Singer born today in 1937   **Peter Withe born today in 1951**

Playing record for this day

Playing record for this day is...22 games, Won 7, Drawn 4, Lost 11, GF 30, GA 40.

Today's success rate.....40.91% Year ranking....231st

Match of the Day

FROM 1960

QUICK, AT THE DOUBLE

Home and Away wins over the Albion completed within a week

Blues' great start to the 1960-61 season continued as they Blues erased the recent defeat by Albion and completed the double over them. In the previous three seasons Blues had fallen to their neighbours by 5-3, 6-0, and 7-1 at St Andrews. A new look Blues, although retaining many of the same side were now under the control of newly appointed manager Gil Merrick, and the difference was alreadt noticeable. Blues remained unbeaten, taking six points from their four games, whilst Albion remained pointless. It was the visitors who started the better in a scrappy opening, but they deserved their early lead on 12 minutes. A quick move left the Blues defence lost as first Burnside, then Jackson, combined well to set the latter free on the right wing. The ball into the centre was slightly overhit, but Kevan, who had rushed from the halfway line, managed to beat Schofield and his defence in the race for the loose ball, and toe poked it into the net. The goal seemed to be of more benefit to Blues than Albion as it brought on the home side's best period of play, resulting in an equaliser just five minutes later. Before the goal came, Wallace had to save well from Astall's header after Blues' third corner kick in quick succession. On Blues' next raid Rudd, charged down the right flank and his fierce ball was diverted into the net by Albion's Williams trying to cut out the pass. The match became a fine end to end attacking game after this, with Albion creating the better chances. Schofield pulled off a great full length diving stop to keep out Hope. Then, after blocking an effort from Burnside, the ball fell invitingly for Kevan with the 'keeper helplessly prostrate on the deck and out of his goal. Unbelievably Kevan put his shot wide when it seemed easier to score.

The second half started where it had left off, with Albion again looking likely to regain the lead. Within three minutes of the restart they had another great scoring opportunity and Burnside almost took it, only the upright kept it out as the shot flew past a well beaten Schofield. At the other end Astall again got a header in on target, but this time a well positioned Wallace made the save look easy. The chance for Astall was a rare break for the Blues defence, who were being constantly kept in the game by the Albion forwards. Blues then rubbed salt into the wounds of the Baggies by taking the lead with just 16 minutes of the game left. It was a simple but effective move. Astall threw the ball to Weston on the right and went on the overlap for the return. From his cross Gordon, at the near post, headed backwards over the head of Wallace and into the far corner of the net. With Albion still in a state of shock from conceding the goal, and so late on, they fell to another after 85 minutes. A shot by Hooper was blocked by Robson, and Astall pounced to smash the loose ball into the roof of the net. It was hit with such power Wallace had to prise it from between the iron stanchion and net in the top corner angle of the goal.

BIRMINGHAM CITY

Schofield, Farmer, Allen, Watts, Smith, Neal, Astall, Gordon, Weston, Rudd, Hooper.

WEST BROMWICH ALBION

Wallace, Howe, Graham Williams, Billington, Jones, Robson, Jackson, Burnside, Kevan, Hope, Hogg.

Bryan Robson

1920, Division 2.		
Blues 5	Hull City 1	Att. 30,000
Crosbie(2), Barton,		
Lane(2)		
1925, Division 1.		
Blues 1	Manchester City 0	Att. 20,000
Bradford		
1929, Division 1.		
Aston Villa 2	Blues 1	Att. 38,000
	Bradford	
1932, Division 1.		
Manchester City 1	Blues 0	Att. 26,000
1935, Division 1.		
Wolverhampton W. 1	Blues 1	Att. 35,000
	Harris	
1938, Division 1.		
Leeds United 2	Blues 0	Att. 13,578
1940, Wartime.		
Nottingham Forest 2	Blues 3	
	Jones, Bodle, Godden	
1946, Division 2.		
Tottenham Hotspur 1	Blues 2	Att. 51,256
	Jones(2)	
1949, Division 1.		
WBA 3	Blues 0	Att. 50,299
1955, Division 1.		
Blues 3	Newcastle United 1	Att. 38,690
Brown 47	White 48	
Warhurst 69		
Murphy 78		
1957, Division 1.		
Chelsea 5	Blues 1	Att. 43,806
Brabrook 14	Brown 61	
Allen 24		
Greaves 25, 44		
Lewis 45		

A fourth minute collision between Blues 'keeper Gil Merrick and Chelsea striker Jimmy Greaves forced Merrick off the field for 13 minutes and he required stitches to a cheek wound.

August 31

The Matches played on this day

1960, Division 1.
Blues 3   WBA 1   Att. 37,740
Williams(og) 17   Kevan 12
Gordon 74
Astall 85

1963, Division 1.
Fulham 2   Blues 1   Att. 21,260
Chamberlain 20,   Lynn(pen) 57
54 (pen)

1965, Division 2.
Middlesbrough 1   Blues 1   Att. 17,300
Orritt 25   Vowden 21

1968, Division 2.
Preston North End 4 Blues 1   Att. 13,112
Spavin 44   Greenhoff 52
Lee 49
Irvine 59
Knighton 80
Jimmy Greenhoff's Blues debut.
Spavin opened the scoring by knocking in the rebound after
Jim Herriott had saved Ritchie's penalty.

1974, Division 1.
Blues 1   Wolverhampton W. 1 Att. 33,785
Burns 62   Richards 78

1976, League Cup 2nd round.
Blackpool 2   Blues 1   Att. 12,203
Ronson 5   Pendrey 65
Hatton 30

1982, Division 1.
Blues 0   Liverpool 0   Att. 20,176

1985, Division 1.
Everton 4   Blues 1   Att. 28,066
Lineker 12, 22, 85   Kennedy 26
Steven 78(pen)
Blues had Ken Armstrong sent off after 68 minutes

1991, Division 3.
Blues 1   Darlington 0   Att. 8,768
Sturridge 39
First league meeting v Darlington

1993, Division 3.
Blues 2   Crystal Palace 4   Att. 13,856
Peschisolido 41, 81 Williams 17
                 Armstrong 31, 85
                 Shaw 48

1998, Division 1.
Bradford City 2   Blues 1   Att. 13,910
Mills 59   Ndlovu 56
Moore 73
Andrew Johnson at 17 years old became the third
youngest Blues player to make his league debut.

Gordon Astall

Blues news extra   1889...Friendly v Aston Villa

Blues, of the Football Alliance,
claimed the scalp of local rivals, and Football
League side, Aston Villa, winning 4-0. Villa
finished 1888-89 as runners up in the
Football League.

Blues news extra   1942...RAF at St Andrews

Blues drew 1-1 with an RAF XI in
this home friendly game.

Playing record for this day

Playing record for this day is...25 games, Won 5, Drawn 7, Lost 13, GF 25, GA 37

Today's success rate.....34% Year ranking....256th

Match of the Day
FROM 1984
WOMBLES WALLOPED

Clarke double blasts Wimbledon at St Andrews

Blues 100% start to the season was still intact after their first home game, and indeed first ever league match against the Wimbledon. The 10,445 crowd also had a new goal scoring hero in Wayne Clark, manager Ron Saunders' £80,000 buy from Wolves in the close season. The Wimbledon line up included ex-Blues trainee player Nigel Winterburn in defence.

Blues were the brighter starters without causing visiting keeper Dave Beasant too much concern and the only save of note within the first 15 minutes came from Tony Coton in the home goal. This early warning stung Blues into a quick retaliation and they opened the scoring on 18 minutes. Brian Roberts created the goal with an angled shot from the right was only partially pushed away by Beasant straight to Mick Ferguson who slammed in from close range. Although Wimbledon countered well soon after the Blues defence remained in control. At the other end Clarke was unfortunate not to open his goal account when a deft header struck the bar toward the end of the first half. The score remained 1-0 at the break.

Blues started the second period with an all-out attack looking to put the game safe, but for all their endeavour Wimbledon kept them out with some frustrating but effective defensive play. However, Blues doubled their lead after 59 minutes through Robert Hopkins who struck a fine volley from just inside the penalty area following a miscued clearance. The Dons however got themselves back in the game just four minutes later when Cork headed in from a free kick. It was new boy Wayne Clarke who put Blues into a strong 3-1 lead in the 75th minute. Receiving a Van Den Hauwe pass he turned to sprint clear of Smith and finished with a low cross shot past Beasant. Blues then inexplicably let Wimbledon back in the game again just six minutes later. Cork was again left unmarked to beat Coton this time with a close-range right-foot shot. A Wimbledon comeback was finally thwarted when Clarke added a fourth on 86 minutes. Substitute Martin Kuhl started the move which allowed Van Den Hauwe to cross for Clarke to nip in at the near post to poke the ball and complete the 4-2 final victory.

BIRMINGHAM CITY

Coton, Roberts, Van Den Hauwe, Wright, Hagan, Daly, Stevenson(Kuhl), Gorman, Ferguson, Clarke, Hopkins.

WIMBLEDON;

Beasant, Kay, Winterburn, Galliers (Gage), Smith, Hatter, Evans, Ketteridge, Cork, O'Berg, Hodges.

Byron Stevenson

Birthdays

Gary Jones born 1951

Terry Hennessey born today in 1942

Derek Carr born today in 1927

Sadly Missed

Harry Storer died today in 1930, aged 69

The Matches played on this day

1894, Division 1.		
Aston Villa 2	Blues 1	Att. 20,000
	Hands	

This was the first ever Football League fixture between Blues and Villa.

1900, Division 2.		
Burslem Port Vale 2	Blues 2	Att. 3,000
	Aston, Main	
1903, Division 1.		
Derby County 4	Blues 1	Att. 7,000
	Leonard	
1906, Division 1.		
Preston North End 2	Blues 0	Att. 10,000
1917, Wartime.		
Blues 2	Hull City 1	
Montgomery, Whitehouse		
1919, Division 2.		
South Shields 1	Blues 0	Att. 12,000
1923, Division 1.		
Aston Villa 0	Blues 0	Att. 59,147
1928, Division 1.		
Huddersfield Town 0	Blues 0	Att. 25,000
1930, Division 1.		
Leicester City 2	Blues 1	Att. 15,000
	Briggs	
1934, Division 1.		
Stoke City 2	Blues 0	Att. 25,000
1937, Division 1.		
Blues 3	Middlesbrough 1	Att. 30,000
Beattie(3)		
1945, Wartime.		
West Ham United 3	Blues 2	
	Massart, Edwards	
1948, Division 1.		
Middlesbrough 1	Blues 1	Att. 37,000
	Garrett	
1951, Division 2.		
Blues 0	Nottingham Forest 2	Att. 24,000
	Collindridge 11	
	Ardron 80	
1956, Division 1.		
Burnley 2	Blues 0	Att. 25,531
McKay 35, 59		
1962, Division 1.		
Manchester United 2	Blues 0	Att. 39,847
Giles 7		
Herd 50		
1970, Division 2.		
Blues 0	Middlesbrough 1	Att. 27,769
	Hickton 72	
1971, Division 2.		
Hull City 1	Blues 0	Att. 16,746
Pearson 78		
1973, Division 1.		
Blues 0	Derby County 0	Att. 34,596

Game screened by ATV's Star Soccer

1979, Division 2.		
Blues 1	Bristol Rovers 1	Att. 15,330
Dillon 40	Barrowclough 27(pen)	
1981, Division 1.		
Blues 1	Ipswich Town 1	Att. 17,328
Evans 45	Brazil 63	

Neil Whatmore made his Blues debut

1984, Division 1.		
Blues 4	Wimbledon 2	Att. 10,445
Ferguson 18	Cork 62, 84	
Hopkins 58		
Clarke 75, 87		
1987, Division 2.		
Millwall 3	Blues 1	Att. 6,758
Lawrence 32	Rees 3	
Walker 79		
Stevens 89		
1990, Division 3.		
Blues 3	Leyton Orient 1	Att. 5,847
Bailey 29	Sayer 50	
Hopkins 43		
Moran 88		

Richie Moran scores on his Blues debut

1992, Division 1.		
Blues 2	Southend United 0	Att. 8,234
Tait 14		
Beckford 52		

September 2

The Matches played on this day

1893, Division 2.
Walsall Town Swifts 1	Blues 3	Att. 5,000
	Lee(2), Wheldon	

1895, Division 1.
Sheffield United 2	Blues 0	Att. 6,000

1899, Division 2.
Blues 3	Walsall 2	Att. 8,000
Wigmore(2), Wharton		

1901, Division 1.
Blues 0	Liverpool 0	Att. 10,000

1905, Division 1.
Blues 1	Preston North End 1	Att. 18,000
Jones		

1908, Division 2.
Blues 2	Bolton Wanderers 0	Att. 8,000
Eyre(2)		

1911, Division 2.
Blues 2	Bradford Park Avenue 3	Att. 20,000
Kidd(2, 1pen)		

1914, Division 2.
Nottingham Forest 1	Blues 1	Att. 4,000
	W.Smith	

1916, Wartime.
Blues 2	Huddersfield Town 1	
Roulson(pen), Whitehouse		

1922, Division 1.
Blues 0	Chelsea 1	Att. 35,000

1931, Division 1.
Blues 4	Newcastle United 1	Att. 20,000
Briggs(2), Curtis, Bradford		

1933, Division 1.
Blues 2	Everton 2	Att. 34,029
Haywood, Grosvenor		

1936, Division 1.
WBA 3	Blues 2	Att. 26,013
	Morris, Jones	

1939, Division 2
Blues 2	Burnley 0	Att.20,000
Dearson, Duckhouse		

1944, Wartime.
Blues 4	Port Vale 0	
Trigg(4)		

1950, Division 2.
Notts County 0	Blues 1	Att. 34,648
	Smith 1	

1953, Division 2.
Blues 3	Plymouth Argyle 0	Att. 22,000
Purdon 1		
Stewart 51		
Kinsey 59		
Ted Purdon's goal timed at 15 seconds		

1959, Division 1.
Newcastle United 1	Blues 0	Att. 35,395
White 70		

1961, Division 1.
Blues 1	Leicester City 5	Att. 21,950
Bloomfield 89	Keyworth 1, 78	
	Wills 58, 60	
	Walsh 69	

1964, Division 1.
Fulham 3	Blues 1	Att. 13,100
Metchick 37, 54, 85	Beard 90	

1967, Division 2.
Blues 0	Ipswich Town 0	Att. 25,463

1972, Division 1.
Wolverhampton W. 3	Blues 2	Att. 32,529
Munro 5	Hope 67	
McCalliog 11, 24(pen)	Burns 77	

1978, Division 1.
Bolton Wanderers 2	Blues 2	Att. 20,284
Worthington 49, 70(p)	Francis 50, 87	

1980, League Cup 2nd round, 2nd leg.
Bristol City 0	Blues 0	Att. 6,955
Blues won 2-1 on aggregate		

1989, Division 3.
Blues 2	Swansea City 0	Att. 8,071
Bailey 59		
Hopkins 74		

1995, Division 1.
Barnsley 0	Blues 5	Att. 11,129
	Hunt 54(pen)	
	Claridge 60	
	Charlery 67	
	Forsyth 76	
	Doherty 84	

Blues equalled their best win over Barnsley, and their best away win for 36 years Steve Claridge misses a penalty Barnslys' Keeper David Watson and defender Charlie Bishop both sent off.

1997, Division 1.
Tranmere Rovers 0	Blues 3	Att. 6,602
	Hughes 11	
	Furlong 44	
	Ndlovu 45	

Playing record for this day

Playing record for this day is...27 games, Won 12, Drawn 7, Lost 8, GF 48, GA 32.

Today's success rate.....57.41% Year ranking....82nd

Match of the Day

FROM 1995

A GAME OF ONE HALF

Five star Blues too much for nine man Barnsley

The Blues fans who travelled to Barnsley enjoyed a terrific day in the sun watching a super second half goal avalanche, this in contrast to the many who instead chose to visit Lords to see the rain affected Nat West Final, which Warwickshire eventually won the following day. Blues made two changes to the team that lost at Huddersfield. Out went Hiley and Donowa and Barry Fry handed debuts to defender Michael Johnson and striker Ken Charlery. The Barnsley team was unchanged after a good start winning both their previous home games, and included future Blues full back Nicky Eaden.

After an entertaining first half in which Blues created no less than ten goal-scoring opportunities the score remained goalless. Blues got their first goal on 54 minutes when Claridge was tripped by Watson as he faced an open net, Hunt scored from the spot past ex-Villa keeper Butler after Watson was red carded for the foul. Just six minutes later Blues wrapped the game up when doubling their lead against the ten men. Whyte sent a long ball forward from defence which put Claridge free and this time he shot first time past the keeper. Blues were now playing with great confidence and put together a superb third goal. After several quick one-touch passes Charlery was left to fire in from just outside the penalty area. Then another five man move led to substitute Forsyth shooting Blues into a 4-0 lead with 14 minutes still to play. The visitors piled forward and could have scored twice more either side of a disallowed goal from Claridge . It was Claridge who set up the final goal however, when he swapped passes with Doherty to send the sub clear and coolly place a low shot into the corner. In the very last minute Blues were handed another prime scoring chance when a goalbound shot by Forsyth was knocked away by Bishop on the goal-line and he too was red carded. Penalty taker Hunt had already been substituted by Louie Donowa so the kick was given to Claridge who shot weakly enabling Butler to block with his outstretched leg.

BARNSLEY

Watson, Eaden, Shirtliff, Archdeacon, Viveash (Butler), Bishop, Bullock, Redfearn, Payton, Liddell, Sheridan.

BIRMINGHAM CITY

Bennett, Poole, Whyte, Ward, Edwards, Johnson, Hunt (Donowa), Claridge, Bowen (Forsyth), Charlery, Cooper (Doherty).

REFEREE

Mr T Heilbron (County Durham)

Jonathan Hunt

Blues news extra 1925...Spanish giants beaten

Blues beat top Spanish side Real Madrid in a friendly at St Andrews by 3-0.

Birthdays

Chris Whyte born today in 1961

Sadly Missed

Stan Harland died today in 2001, aged 61

Playing record for this day
Playing record for this day is...31 games, Won 8, Drawn 6, Lost 17, GF 41, GA 63.
Today's success rate.....35.48% Year ranking....247th

September 3

Match of the Day
FROM 1892
OFF TO A FLYING START

Patient wait for home crowd but all worth it a Blues win 5-1

A crowd of 2,500 waited patiently in the rain at the Muntz Street ground before the Burslem Port Vale team eventually arrived at 4pm, precisely 30 minutes late. One of their players had missed his train to the ground, so the visitors finally kicked of this first Football League game for both sides with ten men.

Blues won the toss and had a strong wind behind them as the first ball was kicked. They were soon on top and Wheldon and Hands came very close to scoring but for the alert Frail in goal for Vale. The best chance fell to Short but although the Blues forward hit his shot well, it cannoned off the crossbar. With Blues laying siege to the Vale goal something had to give and just five minutes into the game they registered their first goal in the Football League. A deep cross from the right saw three forwards charge down Frail and both he and the ball went over the goal line, Wheldon was credited with this historical landmark goal for Small Heath and Blues were 1-0 up.

Vale responded well and Charsley pulled off a smart save to deny striker Scarratt. At the other end Frail, keen not to be pushed into another error, was warned by the referee after sending goal scorer Wheldon, flying with a strong challenge which was adjudged a foul. Blues had to wait until the 37th minute to increase their lead and it came following a goalkeeping howler from Frail who spilled a straightforward catch which allowed Short to tap into an empty net. The goal disrupted the Vale defence and during another hectic scramble in the penalty area Wheldon again managed to poke the ball over the line. Blues went into the half time interval well in control and leading 3-0.

Vale to their credit never gave in and started the second half determined to get a goal at least for their efforts, but Blues countered and Hallam belted in a 20-yard shot which flew in after just five minutes of the restart. Then a nice move between Walker and Bliss ended with the latter shooting past Charsley for a well deserved consolation goal for the visitors and it was now 4-1 after 55 minutes. Blues were stung into a quick response and soon Edwards had an effort which struck the post. Within minutes Wheldon missed an open goal from inside six yards. Vale encouraged by these missed opportunities attacked with more confidence and Scarratt again had a good effort well saved by Charsley. With the referee about to end the game Blues broke away through Edwards who hit a shot on the run which gave Frail no chance and wrapped the game up at 5-1.

BIRMINGHAM CITY
Charsley, Bayley, Speller, Ollis, Jenkyns, Ted.Devey, Hallam, Edwards, Short, Wheldon, Hands.
BURSLEM PORT VALE
Frail, Clutton, Elson, Farrington, McCrindle, Delves, Walker, Scarratt, Bliss, Jones.

REFEREE
Mr E Aitchinson (Long Eaton)

Alan Whitehead

Birthdays
Archie Styles born today in 1949
Willie Bell born today in 1937.

Alan Whitehead born today in 1951

Sadly Missed
Bob Brocklebank died today in 1981, aged 73

The Matches played on this day		
1892, Division 2.		
Blues 5	Burslem Port Vale 1	Att. 2,500
Wheldon(2), Short, Hallam, Edwards		
1894, Division 1.		
Everton 5	Blues 0	Att. 8,000
First league meeting v Everton		
1898, Division 2.		
Burton Swifts 2	Blues 6	Att. 3,000
	Abbott(2), McRoberts(2), Dunlop, Leake	
1904, Division 1.		
Manchester City 2	Blues 1	Att. 30,000
	Green(pen)	
1906, Division 1.		
Blues 2	Bristol City 2	Att. 10,000
Green, Mounteney		
1910, Division 2.		
Fulham 3	Blues 0	Att. 25,000
1913, Division 2.		
Blues 3	Stockport County 2	Att. 15,000
Reed(2), Hastings		
1921, Division 1.		
Burnley 3	Blues 1	Att. 30,000
	Elkes	
1924, Division 1.		
Blues 0	Tottenham Hotspur 2	Att. 20,000
1927, Division 1.		
Blues 0	Manchester United 0	Att. 25,863
1932, Division 1.		
Everton 4	Blues 1	Att. 30,000
	Grosvenor(pen)	
1934, Division 1.		
Blues 1	WBA 2	Att. 25,000
White		
1938, Division 1.		
Manchester United 4	Blues 1	Att. 22,228
	Harris	
1945, Wartime.		
Blues 3	Luton Town 2	
Dougall(2), Bodle		
1947, Division 2.		
Blues 1	Coventry City 1	Att. 30,000
Bodle		
1949, Division 1.		
Blues 0	Burnley 1	Att. 37,000
1951, Division 2.		
Sheffield Wed. 1	Blues 1	Att. 32,490
	Higgins	
1952, Division 2.		
Blues 2	Luton Town 2	Att. 17,500
Briggs, Murphy		
1955, Division 1.		
Blues 0	Preston North End 3	Att. 48,000
1958, Division 1.		
Blues 0	WBA 6	Att. 35,915
1960, Division 1.		
Fulham 2	Blues 1	Att. 19,297
	Rudd	
1966, Division 2.		
Coventry City 1	Blues 1	Att. 36,339
	Vowden	
1968, League Cup 2nd round.		
Blues 0	Chelsea 1	Att. 31,560
1969, League Cup 2nd round.		
Brighton & Hove A. 2	Blues 0	Att. 24,232
1977, Division 1.		
Blues 0	Liverpool 1	Att. 26,239
1983, Division 1.		
Blues 2	Watford 0	Att. 11,931
Hopkins, Halsall		
1985, Division 1.		
Blues 1	Manchester City 0	Att. 11,706
Geddis		
1986, Division 2.		
Brighton & Hove A. 2	Blues 0	Att. 9,750
1988, Division 2.		
Blues 2	Leicester City 3	Att. 7,932
Walsh(og), Robinson		
1991, Division 3.		
Hull City 1	Blues 2	Att. 4,801
	Sturridge, Robinson	
1994, Division 2.		
Blues 4	Plymouth Argyle 2	Att. 13,202
Regis(2), Wallace, Tait		
Plymouth had Andy Comyn sent off.		
Future Blues player Steve Castle scores for Argyle.		

September 4

Playing record for this day
Playing record for this day is...25 games, Won 13, Drawn 6, Lost 6, GF 51, GA 28.
Today's success rate.....64% Year ranking....28th

The Matches played on this day

1893, Division 2.		
Blues 4	Rotherham 3	Att. 3,000
Wheldon, Hands, Mobley, Hallam		
1897, Division 1.		
Blues 3	Burton Swifts 1	Att. 1,500
Inglis(2), Abbott		
1907, Division 1.		
Middlesbrough 1	Blues 0	Att. 10,000
1909, Division 2.		
Blues 2	Oldham Athletic 2	Att. 20,000
Millington, Beer		
1920, Division 2.		
Blues 1	South Shields 1	Att. 30,000
Whitehouse		
Last league meeting against South Shields.		
1926, Division 1.		
Huddersfield Town 0	Blues 2	Att. 20,000
	Bradford(2)	
1929, Division 1.		
Blues 4	West Ham United 2	Att. 20,000
Bradford(3), Barkas		
Joe Bradford's 9th hat-trick for Blues		
1935, Division 1.		
Leeds United 0	Blues 0	Att. 14,298
1937, Division 1.		
Blues 2	Portsmouth 2	Att. 40,000
Morris, White		
1943, Wartime.		
Blues 1	Coventry City 2	
Revell		

Match of the Day

FROM 1967
SIX OF THE BEST FOR BLUES
Blues climb to victory with five different scorers

Blues leapt into second place in the Second Division with a resounding win over Hull. Fred Pickering, their £55,000 signing from Everton, scored his first goal for the club during a battering of the visitors defence in the second half. Bridges played with skill and enthusiasm, and his central position meant that he had little attention paid to him. This allowed him to score his two goals, and turn provider for Vincent. After a pretty dull opening, the first goal came on nine minutes. Wylie bustled through and tried a shot which hit the underside of the bar and bounced out for Bridges to head into the net.

Next Vincent almost scored, then Hull's attempt was cleared by Murray after Herriot totally misread a long free kick from Beardsley. Three minutes before half time Pickering shot on target, but the ball rebounded. It was tidied up by Murray with a ferocious shot into the net. Just two minutes later Bridges scored his second, and Blues' third. He latched on to an overhead pass from Hockey and hammered the ball past Hull goalkeeper Swan. Blues entered the second half confident of a win, but in the 50th minute the defenders stood still and watched Wagstaff centre the ball from the left for Chilton to run it into the net. Then the same two players again took advantage of the defensive lapses. Chilton passed the ball to Wagstaff who took his time and beat Herriot with ease. Blues had gone from three up to being just one goal ahead, and they needed to pull themselves together. This they did in the 58th minute when Pickering headed in Hockey's left wing centre. An attempt from Vincent just missed, skimming over the bar, but the 71st minute saw another goal added thanks to Vowden. He rose to accept a free kick from Murray and nodded the ball past Swan. Ray Martin was brought on in place of Wylie, and with minutes to go Vincent completed the scoring with Blues' sixth goal, giving the home team eight points from a possible ten.

BIRMINGHAM CITY

Herriot, Murray, Green, Wylie (Martin), Sharples, Beard, Bridges, Vincent, Pickering, Vowden, Hockey.

HULL CITY

Swan, Greenwood, Dennis Butler, Jarvis, Banks, Simpkin, Beardsley, Wagstaff, Chilton, Houghton, Ian Butler.

Birmingham City team group - 1967

Birthdays

Richard Cooke born today in 1965   Jackie Stewart born today in 1921   John Beresford born today in 1966.

Fred Pickering

The Matches played on this day

1946, Division 2.

Blues 4	Leicester City 0	Att. 35,000

Jones(2), Mulraney, Dougall

Blues 3-0 up within 23 minutes

1948, Division 1.

Everton 0	Blues 5	Att. 49,199

Trigg(2), Stewart(2), Garrett

Jackie Stewart scored twice on his 27th birthday

1954, Division 2.

Luton Town 1	Blues 0	Att. 16,347

Adam 82

1957, Division 1.

Blues 0	Nottingham Forest 2	Att. 26,772

Barrett 80
Wilson 85

1963, Division 1.

Blues 2	Leicester City 0	Att. 23,851

Leek 35
Hellawell 74

1965, Division 2.

Blues 2	Charlton Athletic 2	.Att. 15,331

Jackson 36(pen) Campbell 20
Beard 65 Bailey 74

1967, Division 2.

Blues 6	Hull City 2	Att. 25,913

Bridges 9, 44 Chilton 50
Murray 42 Wagstaff 51
Pickering 58
Vowden 71
Vincent 80

1971, Division 2.

Blues 4	Charlton Athletic 1	Att. 25,231

Francis 63 Peacock 15
B.Latchford 65, 69, 90

1976, Division 1.

Norwich City 1	Blues 0	Att. 19,271

Boyer 11

1979, League Cup 2nd round, 2nd leg.

Preston North End 0	Blues 1	Att. 11,043

Lynex 54

Blues won 3-1 on aggregate

1982, Division 1.

Blues 1	Stoke City 4	Att. 14,412

Curbishley 75 Hawker(og) 20
Chamberlain 35, 38
Griffiths 44

Blues had Kevin Dillon sent off after 39 minutes

1984, Division 2

Fulham 0	Blues 1	Att. 6,031

Clarke 70

1990, League Cup 2nd round, 2nd leg.

Bournemouth 1	Blues 1	Att. 4,490

Blissett 40 Downs 85(pen)

Blues lost 2-1 on aggregate

1993, Division 1.

Blues 3	Derby County 0	Att. 14,582

Saville 28, 41
Frain 36

1996, League Cup 2nd round, 2nd leg.

Blues 2	Brighton & Hove A. 0	Att. 20,060

Newell 40, 86

Playing record for this day

Playing record for this day is...27 games, Won 12, Drawn 6, Lost 9, GF 51, GA 47.

Today's success rate.....55.56% Year ranking....97th

Match of the Day
FROM 1956
GEORDIE BOYS ARE CANED
Six of the best from rampant Birmingham at St Andrews

Super Scot Alex Govan did it again, just six days after his hat-trick against Portsmouth he hit another trio against Newcastle, helping Blues to a super 6-1 win. The Blues winger now had ten goals for the season, in just six games.

Blues completely destroyed Newcastle from the first to the last minute in a scintillating display of attacking football. They could have been one up as early as the second minute, when Murphy headed straight at the keeper from Brown's cross. He soon made amends, however, as that was the only chance Blues missed all evening. They took the lead in the 12th minute when a delightful touch from Kinsey enabled Murphy to grab a chance in the area.

Kinsey lobbed a pass over his marker and, between the covering defenders for Murphy to nip in and smash the ball in on the half-volley. Blues were quicker to everything, and pace was the key to their second goal eight minutes later. Brown outpaced the entire defence, creating his own shooting chance, which Simpson saved well.

However the loose ball fell to Govan, who reacted quickest to follow up and place his shot into the unguarded net. Although Milburn tried to exact a Newcastle revival, Blues' defence was in as equally good form as their forwards, and when they were beaten Merrick was as alert as ever, twice pouncing at the Newcastle man's feet to thwart any danger. It was Milburn again who brought about the best save of the evening when Merrick dived full stretch to beat out his 15-yard shot on the half hour mark. Blues then scored a third goal eight minutes before half time when Murphy converted Govan's cross from inside the area.

Blues started the second half too relaxed, but were stung into action by a goal from the visitors on 56 minutes. They failed to clear Davies' corner cleanly, and after a scramble in the goalmouth Keeble poked the ball over the line from just a yard out. Blues roared back, but a fourth goal evaded them until 19 minutes from time. From a cross by Brown, Kinsey controlled the ball, and with the Newcastle defence expecting a piledriver he elected instead to chip the ball into the top corner. It was one of the best goals seen at St Andrews, and one that will never be forgotten by any of the 32,506 strong crowd. This started another goal rush and four minutes later Govan raced through the weary United defence to net Blues' fifth. Just four minutes after that he completed his hat-trick when finishing off another run and pass from Brown. Eddie Brown, who had a great game, almost added a seventh late on when his header struck the crossbar.

BIRMINGHAM CITY
Merrick, Hall, Green, Watts, Smith, Warhurst, Astall, Kinsey, Brown, Murphy, Govan

NEWCASTLE UNITED
Simpson, Batty, McMichael, Scoular, Stokoe, Casey, Davies, Milburn, Keeble, Hannah, Prior

Birthdays

Bill Finney born today in 1931

David Linney born today in 1961

Doug Bell born today in 1959

Steve Bryant born today in 1953

Alex Govan (R)

The Matches played on this day

1970, Division 2.
Cardiff City 2   Blues 0   Att. 22,081
Toshack 24, 34
Aged just 16 years, 4 months, and 16 days, Trevor Francis became the Blues youngest debutant when he replaced Bob Latchford as a second half substitute.

1972, League Cup 2nd round.
Blues 1   Luton Town 1   Att. 20,962
B.Latchford 54   Anderson 9

1973, Division 1.
Chelsea 3   Blues 1   Att. 25,660
Hutchinson 26   Page 11
Hollins 75
Kember 82

1981, Division 1.
Blues 4   Nottingham Forest 3   Att. 19,035
Broadhust 31   Wallace 1, 45, 75
Evans 38
Whatmore 73, 85
Peter Shilton saved Archie Gemmill's twice taken penalty in the 50th minute.

1987, Division 2
Crystal Palace 6   Blues 0   Att. 7,011
Bright 14
Redfearn 56
Thomas 73
Gray 82, 87(pen)
Cannon 89

1992, Division 2.
Blues 0   Portsmouth 4   Attt. 12,152
    Daniel 21
    Walsh 46
    Kuhl 62
    Whittingham 65

1995, Anglo Italian Cup, Qualifying Group stage
Blues 2   Genoa 3   Att. 20,430
Bowen 5, 9   Nappi 86
This was the highest attendance apart from the final since the competition's reintroduced in the 1990s.

1998, Division 1.
Blues 1   Bury 0   Att. 15,935
Adebola 20
Former Liverpool keeper Bruce Grobelaar aged 40 played for Bury. They conceeded their first goal in over 7 hours of league football

1999, Division 1.
Bolton Wanderers 3   Blues 3   Att. 11,668
Frandsen 14, 53   Holdsworth 27
Holdsworth 90(pen)   Furlong 38, 45
Frandsen had a goal disallowed for Bolton on 63 minutes. Graham Hyde was sent off in the last minute.

2000, League Cup 1st round, 2nd leg.
Blues 0   Southend United 0   Att. 3,694
Blues won 5-0 on aggregate

September 6

Playing record for this day

Playing record for this day is...21 games, Won 5, Drawn 8, Lost 8, GF 16, GA 26.

Today's success rate.....42.86% Year ranking....217th

The Matches played on this day

1890, Football Alliance.
| Walsall Town Swifts 5 | Blues 2 | Att. 5,000 |
| | W.Devey, Reynolds(og) | |

1902, Division 2.
| Leicester Fosse 1 | Blues 3 | Att. 5,000 |
| | Field(2), McRoberts | |

1913, Division 2.
| Blues 1 | Bradford Park Ave 2 | Att. 25,000 |
| W.H. Jones | | |

1919, Division 2.
| Hull City 0 | Blues 0 | Att. 10,000 |

1920, Division 2.
| Hull City 1 | Blues 0 | Att. 14,000 |

1922, Division 1.
| Blues 0 | Newcastle United 0 | Att. 20,000 |

1924, Division 1.
| Sunderland 4 | Blues 0 | Att. 30,000 |

1930, Division 1.
| Derby County 0 | Blues 0 | Att. 15,000 |

1933, Division 1.
| Manchester City 1 | Blues 0 | Att. 20,000 |

1947, Division 2.
| Blues 2 | Luton Town 1 | Att. 25,000 |
| Bodle, Aveyard | | |

1950, Division 2.
| Blues 1 | Coventry City 1 | Att. 25,000 |
| Higgins 51 | Simpson 29 | |

1952, Division 2.
West Ham United 1	Blues 2	Att. 25,000
Moroney 25	Higgins 57	
	Murphy 60	

1958, Division 1.
Bolton Wanderers 2	Blues 0	Att. 24,707
Lofthouse 43		
Edwards 50		

1960, Division 1.
Arsenal 2	Blues 0	Att. 20,541
Herd 46		
Kane 68		

1961, Division 1.
| WBA 0 | Blues 0 | Att. 20,541 |

1969, Division 2.
Bolton Wanderers 2	Blues 0	Att. 10,998
Taylor 70		
Byrom 89		

1975, Division 1.
| Blues 1 | QPR 1 | Att. 27,305 |
| Kendall 28 | Thomas 39 | |

1980, Division 1.
| Blues 1 | Liverpool 1 | Att. 27,042 |
| Worthington 53 | Dalglish 49 | |

1983, Division 1.
| Blues 1 | Stoke City 0 | Att. 13,728 |
| Blake 35(pen) | | |

1986, Division 2.
| Sheffield United 1 | Blues 1 | Att. 10,297 |
| Foley 61 | Bremner 48 | |

Blues had Steve Whitton sent off after 65 minutes

1988, League Cup 1st round, 2nd leg.
| Blues 1 | Wolverhampton W. 0 | Att. 19,035 |
| Whitton 61 | | |

Blues won on the away goal rule after the tie finished 3-3 on aggregate

Match of the Day

FROM 1952
BLUES STILL UNBEATEN ON TRAVELS

Blues maintained their unbeaten away record at Upton Park, a ground they had not lost at since the war. They went into the game with five team changes from the side that drew with Luton a week earlier at St Andrews. In defence the injured Jack Badham was replaced by Ray Ferris. Roy Warhurst was back from injury, meaning Watts returned to his reserve duties. There were two positional changes, and the other alteration was Ken Rowley in place of Jackie Stewart on the wing. West Ham included former Albion left back John Kinsell.

It was Blues who had the first chance at goal. After good approach work from Warhurst, Rowley shot high and wide. The next chance fell to Cox, and it was a much closer effort. From Murphy's pass, centre forward Briggs, crossed for his winger who drove a shot over the bar from ten yards out. West Ham's opening assault on the Blues goal produced the game's first excitement. Tucker, a young winger on his debut for the Hammers, hit a shot dangerously across the goal. Merrick parried away to Roy Martin who, under pressure, sliced his clearance back toward goal where the keeper had to divert it away, this time out for a corner. After 25 minutes of end-to-end football it was West Ham who broke the deadlock with a goal from Moroney. A scramble in the Blues' penalty area was eventually ended with Woodgate's chipped cross from the byline, and Moroney, unmarked, headed powerfully past Merrick. The goal was against the run of play and Blues continued to attack, but the closest they got to a goal, for all their endeavours, came from a Hammers defender. On the stroke of half time Allison, in trying to head out Rowley's swerving cross, misjudged the flight horribly and the ball went just wide of the post.

Immediately after the break Blues had a lucky escape when an unmarked Petchey blazed his shot over the bar from no more than ten yards out. This piece of luck inspired Blues, and eight minutes later they created their best chance yet. Briggs back-heeled the ball to Rowley inside the area who hit it first time, producing a fine save by Gregory. The ball dropped to Higgins who struck the post. Blues, still pressing, equalised on 57 minutes when Higgins converted from Cox's corner kick.

In a dramatic turnaround, Murphy put Blues ahead just three minutes later. Taking a pass from Green he raced forward to curl a superb shot past Gregory who, even from that distance had no chance.

Straight from the kick-off Blues almost got a third. Warhurst, collecting a loose ball, sent it in for Rowley to hit. Gregory beat his shot away and also scrambled away a second effort on the rebound. Boyd picked it up, and his piledriver from 25 yards was pushed round the post by the busy West Ham 'keeper. In an end-to-end finish Blues held on, and should have wrapped the game up ten minutes from time when Rowley missed a sitter from four yards his effort rolling wide. The last chance of the game fell to West Ham three minutes from time, but Merrick saved well and Blues held out to deserve their win.

WEST HAM

Gregory, Wright, Kinsell, Carter, Allison, O'Farrell, Woodgate, Barrett, Moroney, Petchey, Tucker.

BIRMINGHAM

Merrick, Green, Martin, Boyd, Ferris, Warhurst, Cox, Higgins, Briggs, Rowley, Murphy

REFEREE

Mr W Ling (Cambridgeshire)

Tommy Briggs

Blues news extra   1941...Friendly
Blues 3 Czechoslovakian Army XI 2

Birthdays
Brian Sharples born today in 1944

Paul Moulden born today in 1967

Bruce Rioch born today in 1947

Sadly Missed
Joe Bradford died today in 1980, aged 79

Playing record for this day

Playing record for this day is...25 games, Won 10, Drawn 7, Lost 8, GF 40, GA 37

Today's success rate.....54% Year ranking....115th

Match of the Day
FROM 1968
THE ORIGINAL SUPER SUB

Vowden comes on to make Football League history at St Andrews

Geoff Vowden created soccer history as the first Football League substitute to score a hat-trick. This was his first experience as a substitute in fouryears at the club, having never before been dropped from the starting line-up before this match.

In front of a crowd of 25,001 at St Andrews the scoring began on 26 minutes with a superb shot from Jimmy Greenhoff. He then turned provider for the second goal, supplying the cross for Fred Pickering to volley Blues into a 2-0 lead on 40 minutes.

The teams emerged from the players tunnel with a notable change to the home sides' personnel, Geoff Vowden lined up for the restart and skipper Ron Wylie was missing due to a muscle strain he had picked up towards the end of the first period.

Huddersfield also made a substitution with Frank Worthington on for Lawson. This paid dividends for them and 18 minutes into the second half Worthington nicked a goal to put the visitors right back in the game at 2-1.

There was still high drama to come in the last 20 minutes. The first of Vowden's goals came after 71 minutes with a header and another header just three minutes later increased Blues lead to 4-1. The record-breaking goal came a minute before time with an excellent shot from another assist by Johnny Vincent, giving Huddersfield' keeper Oldfield no chance as the ball sped past him with great power. The sub duly grabbed the match ball at the end of the game and now had the distinction of being Birmingham's leading scorer, his trio bringing his season to five.

BIRMINGHAM CITY
Herriott, Murray, Green, Wylie(Vowden), Foster, Beard, Vincent, Greenhoff, Pickering, Page, Summerill.

HUDDERSFIELD TOWN
Oldfield, Smith, Legg, Nicholson, Ellam, Cherry, Dobson, Lawson (Worthington), Ainson, McGill, Hill.

St Andrews - 1999

Birthdays

Des Bremner born today in 1952
Billy Smith born today in 1926

Sam Smith born today in 1909

Byron Stevenson born today in 1956.

The Matches played on this day

1889, Football Alliance.

Blues 3	B'ham St Georges 2	Att. 2,000
Short, Stanley, W.Devey		

Blues first game in the Football Alliance

1895, Division 1.

Aston Villa 7	Blues 3	Att. 13,000
	Walton, Mobley, Hands	

1901, Division 1.

Blues 2	Bolton Wanderers 0	Att. 12,000
Aston, McRoberts		

1903, Division 1.

Blues 3	Nottingham Forest 3	Att. 10,000
Leonard, Wilcox, Athersmith		

1907, Division 1.

Blues 2	Preston North End 0	Att. 10,000
Mounteney, Wigmore		

1908, Division 1.

Blues 3	Bradford Park Ave. 1	Att. 5,000
Eyre(2), W.H. Jones		

1912, Division 2.

Bradford Park Ave. 0	Blues 0	Att. 12,000

1918, Wartime.

Nottingham Forest 1	Blues 0	

1927, Division 1.

Sunderland 4	Blues 2	Att. 15,000
	Bond, Bradford	

1929, Division 1.

Blues 4	Huddersfield Town 1	Att. 25,000
Bradford(2), Curtis, Liddell		

1932, Division 1.

Blues 3	Manchester City 0	Att. 20,000
Briggs, Bradford(2)		

1935, Division 1.

Blues 1	Arsenal 1	Att. 42,804
Devine		

1938, Division 1.

Blues 2	Leicester City 1	Att. 25,000
Kelly, Jones		

1940, Wartime.

Blues 2	Nottingham Forest 1	
Trigg, Bye		

1946, Division 2.

Blues 0	Burnley 2	Att. 53,000

1957, Division 1.

Blues 1	Newcastle United 4	Att. 29,784
Hellawell 61	Curry 51, 74	
	Hill 52	
	Mitchell 87(pen)	

Mike Hellawell marked his Blues debut with a goal.

1963, Division 1.

Blues 1	Manchester United 1	Att. 36,874
Harley 76	Chisma 11	

1966, Division 2.

Plymouth Argyle 1	Blues 1	Att. 18,920
Bickle 78	Murray 54	

1968, Division 2.

Blues 5	Huddersfield Town 1	Att. 25,001
Greenhoff 26	Worthington 63	
Pickering 40		
Vowden 71, 74, 89		

Geoff Vowden became the first sub in Football League history to score a hat-trick.

1971, League Cup 2nd round.

QPR 2	Blues 0	Att. 15,032
Francis 48		
Marsh 60		

1974, Division 1.

QPR 0	Blues 1	Att. 16,058
	Gallagher 41	

1985, Division 1.

Blues 0	Aston Villa 0	Att. 24,971

1991, Division 3.

Reading 1	Blues 1	Att. 6,649
Byrne 16	Sturridge 30	

1993, Anglo Italian Cup, Preliminary round.

Stoke City 2	Blues 0	Att. 8,633
Cranson 4		
Stein 51(pen)		

1996, Division 1.

Tranmere Rovers 1	Blues 0	Att. 8,548
Aldridge 61		

The Matches played on this day

1894, Division 1.
Blues 2   Bolton Wanderers 0   Att. 5,000
Wheldon(2)
Blues first game in the First Division
George Wheldon also missed a penalty in the second minute.
Joe Cassidy of Bolton had a goal disallowed for offside

1900, Division 1.
Blues 0   Leicester Fosse 0   Att. 7,000

1906, Division 1.
Blues 2   Newcastle United 4   Att. 17,000
Jones, Beer

1917, Wartime.
Hull City 1   Blues 2
               Montgomery, Boxley

1923, Division 1.
Blues 0   Sunderland 2   Att. 25,000

1924, Division 1.
Blues 1   Bolton Wanderers 0   Att. 15,000
Howarth(og)

1928, Division 1.
Blues 1   Everton 3   Att. 30,000
Briggs

1934, Division 1.
Blues 1   Manchester City 3   Att. 20,000
Mangnall

1937, Division 1.
Middlesbrough 1   Blues 1   Att. 15,000
               Jones

1945, Wartime.
Blues 4   WBA 0
Edwards, Mulraney,
Duckhouse, Jones

1948, Division 1.
Manchester City 1   Blues 0   Att. 26,841

1951, Division 2.
Brentford 1   Blues 0   Att. 25,000
Monk 83

1954, Division 2.
Blues 4   Ipswich Town 0   Att. 21,238
Kinsey 8, 60
Warmington 45
Astall 88
Peter Warmington scored on his Blues debut.

1956, Division 1.
Blues 3   Preston North End 0   Att. 44,500
Govan 30, 50, 83
Alex Govan's third hat trick in nine days

1962, Division 1.
Blues 5   Burnley 1   Att. 24,423
Leek 6   Pointer 89
Hellawell 8, 20
Bloomfield 60
Bullock 88

1965, Division 2.
Blues 2   Leyton Orient 2   Att. 7,598
Vowden 26   Scott 57, 75
Thomson 50

1973, Division 1.
Leeds United 3   Blues 0   Att. 39,736
Lorimer 17, 44(pen), 47
Match screened by ATV's Star Soccer

1979, Division 2.
Blues 2   Chelsea 1   Att. 17,182
Lynex 51   Walker 54
Curbishley 62

1982, Division 1.
Norwich City 5   Blues 1   Att. 13,860
Bertschin 4, 80   Broadhurst 38
O'Neil 26, 29
Barham 57

1984, Division 2.
Crystal Palace 0   Blues 2   Att. 6,519
               Hopkins 9
               Clarke 48

1990, Division 3.
Stoke City 0   Blues 1   Att. 16,009
               Gleghorn 57

1998, Division 1.
Blues 2   Stockport County 0   Att. 16,429
Marsden 15
Hughes 67
Blues went top of Division One.

Playing record for this day

Playing record for this day is...23 games, Won 12, Drawn 3, Lost 8, GF 38, GA 28.

Today's success rate.....58.70% Year ranking....68th

Match of the Day
FROM 1962

JOY AT LAST FOR BLUES

First win of the season is a real five goal tonic for the home fans

After patiently waiting five league games a crowd of 24,423 left St Andrews happy after witnessing Blues first win of the season, and a super five goal show too. Blues came out attacking right from the first whistle, barely a minute had elapsed when a pass from Beard sent Hellawell clear on the wing. From his cross Bullock flicked the ball on to Leek who headed just inches over the top. Then the home fans erupted after six minutes when Blues deservedly got the game's first goal. Thwaites simple pass to Bloomfield started the move but there was nothing simple about the next pass, Bloomfield threaded a superb ball to pick out Leek's run through the middle leaving him clear without a defender in sight. He ran on to round the keeper and slide the ball into the empty net, a glorious goal for the Blues. It was 2-0 just two minutes later after another fabulous move, Bullock this time sending Hellawell in on goal with another dream pass. The winger raced forward and as Blacklaw advanced to narrow the angle, Hellawell hit a low shot which zipped off the turf passing the keeper and hit the back of the net via the base of the far post. A shell-shocked Burnley surely couldn't have imagined they would find Blues in such superb form. The home team swept into a 3-0 lead on 20 minutes with a second from Hellawell. This time from Thwaites' corner he belted the ball in with a fantastic acute-angled volley. Blues continued to threaten the Burnley goal in a relentless assault right up until half time, but without futher addition to the score.

The same pattern emerged in the second half and the crowd were by now waiting to celebrate the inevitable fourth goal. This came on the stroke of the hour when a long ball from Hellawell found Bloomfield in space and he calmly dribbled the ball round the helpless keeper to net with ease. With Blues now coasting to a win they rewarded the St Andrews' faithful with a fifth goal two minutes from the final whistle. Fittingly it was Bullock who had worked tirelessly all afternoon who scored what should have been the game's last goal. Burnley had not looked like finding the net until ball sped from Pointer's boot, but as this happened in the 89th minute it was no more than a consolation.

BIRMINGHAM CITY
Schofield, Lynn, Sissons, Hennessey, Smith, Beard, Hellawell, Bloomfield, Leek, Bullock, Thwaites.
BURNLEY
Blacklaw, Angus, Elder, Joyce, Talbot, Miller, Connelly, McIlroy, Pointer, Robson, Harris.

REFEREE
Mr GD Roper (Swaffham Prior)

George Smith

Blues news extra   1982...Football Combination win: Blues 1 Oxford Utd 0

Nigel Winterburn who never made a first team appearance for the Blues got the winner in this reserve game at St Andrews against Oxford. Winterburn later went on to have a successful career at Arsenal

Birthdays

Jerry Gill born today in 1970   Jim Dailey born today in 1927   Nicky Forster born today in 1973

Playing record for this day

Playing record for this day is...25 games, Won 11, Drawn 8, Lost 6, GF 42, GA 30.

Today's success rate.....60% Year ranking....52nd

Match of the Day

FROM 1972
BLUES BLAST MAN CITY

Latchford destroys City with super hat-trick, as Blues hit four

Dave Latchford made his long-awaited comeback to the senior side taking the place of the injured Mike Kelly. Birmingham's other team changes from the disappointing defeat at Molineux were Tommy Carroll in for Howitt, and Trevor Francis returning in place of Taylor.

It was Francis who made the first notable move when he skipped past Jeffries on the left, but his intended through ball to Latchford was charged down at the last second. Then it was Francis again in the thick of the action when he forced Corrigan into the first save of the game.

Collecting a pass from Bobby Hope, he sent in a fierce low drive which zipped off the turf before the 'keeper brilliantly turned it round the post. Then in the fifth minute came the game's first foul when Want was badly injured in a clumsy challenge by Summerbee. Want was forced to leave the field on a stretcher and Kenny Burns was sent on as substitute.

Further troubles were bestowed on Blues when they fell behind to the game's first goal on 25 minutes. From a free kick Towers blasted directly at a crowd of players and the ball rebounded for him to have another go, this time the ball sped low into the corner past an unsighted Latchford. Blues fought back and an equaliser was found just two minutes later with the first of Latchford's three goals. It was a typical poacher's classic after Corrigan could only parry a snap shot from Hatton and the striker calmly stroked in the loose ball from close in.

Birmingham then completed a full turnaround in the score by going into the lead, with a perfectly-timed second goal from Latchford, just four minutes before the interval. Corrigan who was having a super game up until this point, completely misjudged a corner from Hope, leaving him hopelessly stranded as Latchford fired in a cracking shot into the unguarded goal. Blues continued their momentum immediately after the restart and were soon well on top. It took them just seven minutes to increase their lead to 3-1 when Campbell rounded off a fantastic move involving four players. Blues were on fire and playing some fantastic football, another goal was imminent and duly arrived on 55 minutes when Bob Latchford scored to complete a magnificent hat-trick. With so much pressure on the visitor's goal, Corrigan and Jeffries got into a mix up. Latchford arrived and accepted a simple chance to score Blues fourth.

Man City, to their credit, never gave up but soon tired, they were given slight hope when Marsh hit a super shot which unfortunately came back off the bar, but a full recovery was never possible.

With 16 minutes of the game remaining Davies was brought off with a badly bleeding nose and the visitors sent on Oakes as a substitute.

BIRMINGHAM CITY

Dave Latchford, Carroll, Pendrey, Want (Burns 5), Hynd, Harland, Campbell, Francis, Bob Latchford, Hope, Hatton.

MANCHESTER CITY

Corrigan, Jefferies, Donachie, Doyle, Booth, Bell, Summerbee, Marsh, Davies (Oakes 74), Lee, Towers.

REFEREE

Mr K Styles (Barnsley)

Dave Latchford

Birthdays

Richie Moran born today in 1963

September 10

Playing record for this day

Playing record for this day is...24 games, Won 7, Drawn 7, Lost 10, GF 28, GA 36.

Today's success rate.....43.75% Year ranking....213th

The Matches played on this day

1892, Division 2.
Walsall Town Swifts 1 Blues 3   Att. 2,500
Wheldon, Jenkyns, Pinches(og)
First league meeting v Walsall, and the first at Walsall's new home the Chuckery Blues first away win in the Football League Walsall defender Alf Pinches became the first to score an own goal.

1898, Division 2.
Blues 1   Bursten Port Vale 2   Att. 10,000
Abbott

1904, Division 1.
Blues 1   Notts County 2   Att. 12,500
Beer(pen)

1910, Division 2.
Blues 1   Bradford Park Ave. 0   Att. 18,000
McKay

1919, Division 2.
Blues 4   South Shields 0   Att. 12,000
Millard(2), Morgan(2)

1921, Division 1.
Everton 2   Blues 1   Att. 30,000
   Crosbie

1923, Division 1.
Blues 0   Bolton Wanderers 3   Att. 15,000

1927, Division 1.
Everton 5   Blues 2   Att. 35,000
   Bradford, Briggs

1928, Division 1.
Blues 1   Leicester City 0   Att. 20,000
Briggs

1930, Division 1.
Blues 1   Newcastle United 1   Att. 19,862
Bradford

1932, Division 1.
Blues 2   Blackpool 1   Att. 19,148
Curtis(pen), Bradford

1938, Division 1.
Blues 1   Stoke City 2   Att. 30,000
Harris

1947, Division 1.
Blues 0   Newcastle United 0   Att. 35,000

1949, Division 1.
Sunderland 1   Blues 1   Att. 48,552
   Dailey

1952, Division 2.
Leeds United 0   Blues 1   Att. 14,133
   Rowley 55

1955, Division 1.
Burnley 3   Blues 2   Att. 22,549
Pilkington 13   Kinsey 59
Cheesebrough 20   Astall 69
McKay 41

1958, Division 1.
Leeds United 0   Blues 0   Att. 25,228

1960, Division 1.
Blues 1   Preston North End 3   Att. 24,410
Gordon 28   Smith 44
   Alston 45, 69

1966, Division 2.
Blues 1   Bury 3   Att. 22,345
Thomson 12   Claxton 34
   Owen 60
   Aimson 68

1977, Division 1.
Middlesbrough 1   Blues 2   Att. 19,242
Ashcroft 58   Francis 38, 77

1983, Division 1.
Wolverhampton W. 1   Blues 1   Att. 15,933
Eves 9   Wright 28(pen)
This match screened by BBC's Match of the Day.

1988, Division 2.
Oldham Athletic 4   Blues 0   Att. 5,796
Cecere 5, 84
Bunn 80
Marshall 90

1994, Division 2.
Oxford United 1   Blues 1   Att. 8,077
Moody 47(pen)   Claridge 79

1996, Division 1.
Blues 0   Oldham Athletic 0   Att. 17,228

Match of the Day

FROM 1977

DAYLIGHT ROBBERY AT BORO

Francis double nicks the points in awayday smash and grab raid

Poor finishing and bad luck robbed Middlesbrough of a victory they should have wrapped up by half time. Blues were almost entirely under the cosh defending resolutely and at times desperately. On the two occasions their defenders grabbed a respite, Trevor Francis put away break away goals to steal an unlikely victory.

An early sign of what was to curse the Middlesbrough forwards came after just four minutes. A great through ball by Souness split the Blues defence wide apart and sent Mills away with just Montgomery to beat, but he screwed his shot wide.

McAndrew was the next culprit when presented with a chance from a free kick floated in by Souness. The ball fell to the Boro' defender just two yards out, but he failed to make contact. When Middlesbrough eventually did put the ball in the net after 33 minutes they found luck as well as their finishing had deserted them, a corner headed in by Ashcroft looked a legitimate goal and it was initially given. After protests by the Blues defence however, the ref consulted his linesman and disallowed the effort and restarted the game with a drop ball just two yards from the goal line. After an almighty scramble Montgomery eventually dropped onto the bobbling ball to keep his goal intact. Further grief was then bestowed on the hosts when from a rare break away Francis put Blues ahead with a fine individual goal. From Sbragia's desperate tackle on Mills the ball eventually came to Bertschin on the half way line and he played a short pass to Francis to take in his stride, racing clear of the entire Boro' defence. He got within touching distance of the penalty area before unleashing a well placed shot which flew across Platt and crept into the corner of the net. Moments before half time Francis was about to repeat the move when he was sent flying by a clumsy trip by Boam who was booked for his efforts.

Middlesbrough's luck changed soon after half time when they deservedly equalised with a strike from new signing Ashcroft. He found space in the Blues area to head home Cragg's far post cross past Montgomery for a goal on his Ayresome Park debut. Blues then lost the services of their man-of-the-match Francis when he went off to have his injured ankle treated, but he returned three minutes later with it heavily strapped. Middlesbrough continued to dominate play looking for the winner but time after time their finishing let them down. Blues then snatched an unlikely victory with another goal for Francis midway through the second period.

MIDDLESBROUGH

Platt, Craggs, Cooper, Souness, Boam, McAndrews, Mahoney, Mills, Ashcroft, Brine, Armstrong.

BIRMINGHAM CITY

Montgomery, Rathbone, Pendrey, Towers, Sbragia, Want, Broadhurst, Francis, Bertschin, Hibbitt, Emmanuel.

REFEREE
Mr M Lowe (Sheffield)

Gary Emmanuel

Blues news extra   1980...Gemmill goal helps the Scots Sweden 0 Scotland 1

Blues midfielder Archie Gemmill got another priceless goal for Scotland gaining valuable points in their World Cup qualifier in Stockholm. It was Gemmill's seventh cap for the Scots as a Blues player.

Birthdays

Ken Faulkner born today in 1923

Playing record for this day

Playing record for this day is...20 games, Won 5, Drawn 4, Lost 11, GF 19, GA 36.

Today's success rate.....35% Year ranking....250th

Match of the Day

FROM 2001

BLUES AT THE MEMORIAL GROUND

Solid and professional performance on day of world tragedy

The tragic events in New York almost caused the cancellation of this League Cup tie the game going ahead at the last minute as many fans had travelled to Bristol whilst the full horrific story thousands of miles away were still unfolding. The game at the Memorial Ground kicked off on time and when an announcement was made to hold the statutory minute's silence you could not hear a pin drop.

Blues went into the game handing Joey Hutchinson, a product of their youth scheme, his senior debut. It was certainly a day he'll never forget and he made an impressive start. Blues weathered a gritty early display from their Third Division opponents and were quick to force two corners in the first ten minutes. They slowly took control and when they snatched the lead on the stroke of half time the feeling was that it was effectively the winner. A free kick played to Grainger was swung over to Andy Johnson who headed into the roof of the net from close range.

Blues increased their lead after stepping up another gear 15 minutes into the second half. From Eaden's corner, Sonner helped the ball on into the area where Michael Johnson lunged forward and forced it over the line. Just six minutes later Blues were 3-0 up after good work from Sonner and Woodhouse, their quick interchange of passing ending with a through ball to Hughes who went free on goal. As he approached Howie, he fainted to go right and with the keeper committed, side footed home. Blues played out the remainder of the game almost at exhibition pace and for the main looked comfortable despite a couple of late half-chances for the home side. As the game drew to a close Gill went close with a rasping shot from distance and Grainger went even closer with an effort which skimmed the bar. Blues were through to the next round where they would meet Manchester City at Maine Road.

BRISTOL ROVERS

Howie, Wilson, Thomson, Foran, Jones, Gall, Mauge, Hillier (Hammond 60), Ellington, Weare (Cameron h/t).

BIRMINGHAM CITY

Poole, Gill, Grainger, Sonner, Michael Johnson, Hutchinson, Eaden, Andrew Johnson (Furlong 75), Horsfield (Marcelo 68), Hughes (Burrows 80), Woodhouse.

REFEREE

Mr R Harris (Oxford)

Danny Sonner

Blues news extra 1877...Blues open new ground

Blues officially opened the Muntz Street ground with a friendly against Saltley College. Blues won the game easily by 5-0 and the new ground was well received by the club's fans. The gate receipts were 6s/8d (34p) which went towards the £5 annual rent on the site in Bordesley Green.

Birthdays

John Roberts born today in 1946

Gary Poole born today in 1967

Ian Brown born today in 1965.

George Parris born today in 1964.

Chris Holland born today in 1975.

The Matches played on this day

1897, Division 2.

Blues 2	Leicester Fosse 1	Att. 3,000

Abbott, Gadsby

1909, Division 2.

Blues 1	Burnley 5	Att. 3,000

Chapple

1911, Division 2.

Blues 1	Barnsley 3	Att. 5,000

Millington

Blues trainer Billy George made his debut in goal due to an injury crisis. This was his 400th league game.

1920, Division 2.

Cardiff City 2	Blues 1	Att. 30,000
	Crosbie	

1926, Division 1.

Blues 2	Sunderland 0	Att. 40,000

Briggs(2)

1935, Division 1.

Blues 2	Leeds United 0	Att. 14,298

Jones, White

1937, Division 1.

Chelsea 2	Blues 0	Att. 35,000

1948, Division 1.

Blues 1	Preston North End 0	Att. 44,000

Garrett

1950, Division 2.

Coventry City 3	Blues 1	Att. 30,453
Roberts 40, 50	Berry 20	
Chisholm 66		

1954, Division 2.

Blues 0	Hull City 0	Att. 25,000

1957, Division 1.

Blues 0	Tottenham Hotspur 0	Att. 26,484

1963, Division 1.

Blues 0	WBA 1	Att. 34,666
	Foggo 59	

1965, Division 2.

Plymouth Argyle 6	Blues 1	Att. 10,606
Trebilcock 44, 75, 86	Vowden 69	
Williams 50		
Lord 60		
Jennings 88		

Blues fell to their heaviest defeat by Plymouth, Mike Trebilcock was the hero for the Pilgrims with a hat-trick.

1971, Division 2.

Luton Town 0	Blues 0	Att. 14,678

1973, Division 1.

Blues 2	Chelsea 4	Att. 30,252
Hatton 41	Pendrey(og) 15	
Taylor 65	Osgood 37	
	Webb 70	
	Baldwin 84	

Blues Malcolm Page broke his leg, and Ray Martin broke a nose during the game.

1974, League Cup 2nd round.

Crewe Alexandra 2	Blues 1	Att. 7,194
Riley 3	Gallagher 80	
Nicholls 85		

1976, Division 1.

Blues 0	WBA 1	Att. 38,448
	T.Brown 60	

1982, Division 1.

West Ham United 5	Blues 0	Att. 18,754
Van Der Elst 23		
Goddard 29		
Stewart 59(pen), 75		
Clark 85		

1999, Division 1.

Blues 1	WBA 1	Att. 25,495
A.Johnson 42	Hughes 53	

Blues left back Martin Grainger broke his leg

2001, League Cup 2nd round.

Bristol Rovers 0	Blues 3	Att. 5,582
	A.Johnson 45	
	M.Johnson 61	
	Hughes 67	

Blues biggest win over Bristol Rovers.

September 12

Playing record for this day

Playing record for this day is...24 games, Won 5, Drawn 7, Lost 12, GF 33, GA 43.

Today's success rate.....35.42% Year ranking....248th

Match of the Day

FROM 2000

BLUES SUBS STORM BACK

Down early but not out as substitutions turn the game round in second half

Blues impressive start to the new season continued after a mild first half blip against Preston.

The visitors set out early to weather the storm only to find not even a breeze forthcoming. It wasn't long before they found the confidence to push forward against a side involved in two successive play-off semi-finals. On 34 minutes the visitors snatched a deserved lead when Macken skipped clear of a desperate Grainger lunge to pull a cross back for Cartwright. Although he missed the ball completely with an air shot he was fortunate to have Rankine follow up behind him to place a low shot into the corner from 12 yards. Blues continued to create little in the way of danger for Preston and they went in one down at the half-time break.

Enter the decisive and inspired substitutes, Andy Johnson replacing Marcelo, and Steve Robinson, on for Jacques Williams, and Blues suddenly rose a standard or two in the second half. They waisted little time in getting level. An Eaden pass was controlled on the chest by Johnson and the forward then turned neatly to slip past Murdock and tee up Ndlovu who was overlapping on the left hand side of the penalty area. The winger took the ball in his stride to beat Lucas with a low cross shot. Within eight minutes Blues were in front and the turnaround was complete. Grainger's free kick from wide on the right was curled in with pace forcing Lucas to parry and as the ball dropped Andy Johnson nodded in from under the cross-bar, barely a yard out. Blues were now dominating and with 13 minutes of the game remaining a long ball down the line from Grainger would have been easily picked up by Johnson but for a push and trip by Gregan just inside the penalty area. Martin O'Connor stepped up to send the keeper the wrong way and Blues were now 3-1 up, which is how the match finished.

BIRMINGHAM CITY

Bennett, Eaden, Grainger, O'Connor, Michael Johnson (Purse 30 mins), Holdsworth, Williams (Robinson h/t), O'Connor, Marcelo (Andrew Johnson h/t), Hughes, Ndlovu.

PRESTON NORTH END

Lucas, Alexander, Edwards, Murdock, Gregan, Cartwright(Jackson 70 mins), Appleton, McKenna (Gunnlaugsson 70), Basham (Robinson 79), Macken, Rankine.

REFEREE

Mr J Robinson

Darren Purse

Birthdays

Bud Brocken born today in 1957

Playing record for this day

Playing record for this day is...22 games, Won 10, Drawn 8, Lost 4, GF 37, GA 29.

Today's success rate.....63.64% Year ranking....31st

Match of the Day
FROM 1930
AWAY DAY BLUES FOR MAN CITY
Blunder by Blues' keeper doesn't stop the win

A crowd of 17,705 piled into St Andrews despite the miserable weather to see this clash against Manchester City. Fillingham was in the side at centre half in place of Morrall who was injured. For the visitors, Tilson was also out of the game and his place was filled by Race.

The pitch was affected by the weather and this made comfortable play difficult. The first action of the game came from the visitors when Toseland sent a lovely ball goalwards, but the header from Tait just went wide. Then a shot from Ridley curled its way over the bar for Blues, but it was not long before the home side took the lead. The opening goal came on six minutes when Crosbie took a ball from Hicks and followed it through to Briggs who nudged it over the line. This boosted play from Blues, and a shot on target from Bradford was saved by Barber, who then had to punch the ball to safety when Horsman took a corner kick and almost scored.

Manchester City tried to equal the score, but their first threatening attack was deflated when the flag went up for offside. Then striker Brook evaded a challenge from Firth to send the ball to his attacking line, but no-one managed to get onto it and it ran loose. For Blues a superb corner from Cringan resulted in a spectacular save by Barber.

The equaliser for the visitors came in the 38th minute and was well earned. Brook hit a low strike towards goal which deflected off the leg of Fillingham before crossing the line.

The second half action began early with a mix up from Blues, which led to the falling behind just two minutes in. Hibbs fell to the ground diving for a shot, and as he clambered up he kicked the ball to clear it from danger. Unfortunately it struck Tait and rebounded off him to trickle into the unguarded goal. Tait tried to increase the score just a minute later, but this time Hibbs denied him. The Blues goalkeeper then managed to get on to a powerful shot from Marshall and edged it round the post.

It was Blues turn to come back on 58 minutes. It was quite a surprise however, as the visitors were in control at this stage. Briggs saw an opening and decided to go for goal. He shot lamely, but nevertheless it had enough pace to trickle over the line.

This goal was enough to wake up the visitors, and they stepped up their attack on the home goal. It all proved to be too much for them though, as they failed in their quest to restore their lead. Blues, however, were determined to win, and win they did. On 74 minutes Barber misread a pass and lost his hold of the ball. Bradford was on hand, and the merest of knocks was enough to send the ball into the goal giving them the win they were seeking.

BIRMINGHAM CITY

Hibbs, Liddell, Barkas, Firth, Fillingham, Cringan, Horsman, Crosbie, Briggs, Bradford, Hicks.

MANCHESTER CITY

Barber, Ridley, Robertson, Barrass, Cowan, McMullen, Toseland, Marshall, Tait, Race, Brook.

REFEREE

Mr AH Adams (Nottingham)

Gary Bull

Blues news extra 1941...Wartime friendly Blues 4 Wolves 0

Birthdays

Andy Needham born today in 1955

The Matches played on this day

1890, Football Alliance.

Blues 0	Sunderland Albion 3	Att. 5,000

1902, Division 2.

Blues 4	Manchester City 0	Att. 12,000
Jones, McMillan, Leonard(2)		

1909, Division 2.

Blues 2	Glossop 2	Att. 3,000
Lowe, Millington		

1913, Division 2.

Notts County 5	Blues 1	Att. 12,000
	A.W.Smith	

1919, Division 2.

Blues 4	Coventry City 1	Att. 18,000
Morgan, Whitehouse, Millard(2)		

First league meeting v Coventry

1922, Division 1.

Blues 2	Stoke City 0	Att. 20,000
Bradford(2)		

1924, Division 1.

Blues 2	Cardiff City 1	Att. 18,500
Bradford(2)		

1926, Division 1.

Sheffield Wed. 0	Blues 0	Att. 13,376

1930, Division 1.

Blues 3	Manchester City 2	Att. 17,705
Briggs(2), Bradford		

1947, Division 2.

Brentford 1	Blues 2	Att. 10,000
	Trigg, Edwards	

1952, Division 2.

Blues 3	Leicester City 1	Att. 30,000
K.Rowley 53	A.Rowley 7	
Murphy 63		
Briggs 84		

1958, Division 1.

Blues 2	Burnley 1	Att. 24,004
Brown 53	Robson 32	
Murphy 59		

1961, League Cup 1st round.

Blues 1	Swindon Town 1	Att. 11,584
Neal 54	Smith 21	

1965, Division 2.

Leyton Orient 2	Blues 1	Att. 7,114
Flatt 46, 49	Thomson 43	

1966, League Cup 2nd round.

Nottingham Forest 1	Blues 1	Att. 19,271
Newton 34	Vowden 57	

1967, League Cup 2nd round.

Plymouth Argyle 0	Blues 2	Att. 10,038
	Hockey 18	
	Vowden 72	

Despite a floodlight failure after seven minutes the game went on until the 63rd minute when it became too dark, then the ref called a halt, so that engineers could repair the lights.

1969, Division 2.

Blues 2	Sheffield United 1	Att. 27,201
Vincent 40	Tudor 16	
Murray 49		

1972, League Cup 2nd round, replay.

Luton Town 1	Blues 1	Att. 13,806
Aston 65	Campbell 88	

After extra time

1975, Division 1.

Wolverhampton W. 2	Blues 0	Att. 25,142
Carr 51, 71		

Wolves Ken Hibbitt missed his 26th minute penalty This game screened by ATV's, Star Soccer

1980, Division 1.

Brighton & Hove A. 2	Blues 2	Att. 15,788
McNab 20	Curbishley 10	
Lawrenson 48	Bertschin 71	

First league meeting v Brighton

1986, Division 2.

Blues 1	Huddersfield Town 1	Att. 6,934
Clarke 13	Dicks(og) 85	

1994, Division 2.

Rotherham 1	Blues 1	Att. 3,799
Hazel 37	Bull 54	

Gary Bull scored on his Blues debut.

Playing record for this day

Playing record for this day is...**23 games, Won 7, Drawn 5, Lost 11, GF 38, GA 41.**
Today's success rate.....41.30% Year ranking....226th

The Matches played on this day
1889, Football Alliance.

Blues 2	Bootle 2	Att. 2,000

W.Devey, Stanley
1895, Division 1.

Blues 1	Stoke 2	Att. 7,500

Hallam
1896, Division 2.

Blues 5	Darwen 1	Att. 800

Inglis, Walton,
Robertson(2), Nixon(og)
1901, Division 1.

Manchester City 1	Blues 4	Att. 18,000
	Aston(2), McRoberts, McMillan	

Blues went top of the First Division with five points from three games.
1907, Division 1.

Bury 1	Blues 0	Att. 12,000

1912, Division 2.

Blues 0	Wolverhampton W. 0	Att. 3,000

1918, Wartime.

Blues 2	Nottingham Forest 3	

Whitehouse, Walker
1929, Division 1.

Sheffield United 4	Blues 2	Att. 15,000
	Curtis, Barkas(pen)	

1935, Division 1.

Manchester City 3	Blues 1	Att. 30,000
	Guest	

1940, Wartime.

Cardiff City 5	Blues 2	
	Trigg(2)	

1946, Division 2.

Barnsley 3	Blues 1	Att. 28,000
	Mulraney	

1949, Division 1.

Blues 1	Wolverhampton W. 1	Att. 47,000

Dailey
1957, Division 1.

Burnley 3	Blues 1	Att. 20,422
Pilkington 6	Neal 80	

Cheesebrough 34
Shackleton 38
1960, Division 1.

Blues 2	Arsenal 0	Att. 22,904

Stubbs 9, 68
1963, Division 1.

Burnley 2	Blues 1	Att. 20,550
Bellamy 53	Harris 81	

Harris 88
1968, Division 2.

Middlesbrough 3	Blues 1	Att. 17,398
Hickton 23	Vincent 40	

Gates 43, 67
1974, Division 1.

Blues 3	Derby County 2	Att. 27,795
Hatton 27	Rioch 84	
Francis 63, 79	Davies 87	

(both pens)
This match screened by ATV's Star Soccer.
1985, Division 1.

Ipswich Town 0	Blues 1	Att. 11,616
	Geddis 73	

1991, Division 3.

Blues 1	Peterborough United 1	Att. 9,408
Cooper 90	Hicks(og) 76	

1st league meeting v Peterborough
1993, Anglo Italian Cup preliminary round.

Blues 2	Wolverhampton W. 2	Att. 2,710
Wratten 68, 76	Burke 65	
	Mills 85	

Adam Wratten replaced Paul Tait as a second half substitute and this made his debut and only appearance for the Blues with two goals, not bad for a defender!! The 2,710 crowd was the lowest St Andrews attendance for a competitive senior game since 1910.
1996, Division 1.

Blues 3	Stoke City 1	Att. 18,612
Furlong 2, 65	Forsyth 66	

Legg 32
1997, Division 1.

Blues 0	Sunderland 1	Att. 17,478
	Gray 72	

1999, League Cup 1st round, 1st leg.

Blues 2	Bristol Rovers 0	Att. 17,457

O'Connor 51(pen)
Holdsworth 67

Match of the Day

FROM 1974

FRANCIS IS SPOT ON

Two penalties nick two points against Derby

Both sides came out attacking at St Andrews with the Blues defence under heavy pressure from the Derby forwards. Rioch made the first attacking move, a left-footed shot which sailed high over the bar. Blues responded with Francis cleverly gaining control of the ball in midfield to lob through for Hatton to chase, only to see Webster beat off the challenge.But it was Blues who got the vital first goal in the 27th minute, when Francis, beating Nish on the right, funnelled a low centre to Hatton, who flicked in his first goal of the season. Birmingham continued to pile on the pressure and just before the half-time whistle almost made it two. Following a dummy from Taylor down the left, Burns moved inside to unleash a fierce rising drive from just inside the penalty area which Boulton only just managed to save with a magnificent backwards dive.

Blues resumed the second half with Hynd on for Page who had apparently sustained a strain. Francis, who had caused so much trouble for Derby in the first period was soon in action again. He was bundled over by Gemmill for the first free kick of the second half. Although Derby mounted few attacks during the early minutes, Blues almost lost their advantage by playing far too close at the back. Forced to concede a free kick on the right, the ball was knocked on to Davies, who headed against the post. This seemed to wake up the home defence, although all they had to contend with during the next few minutes play were a couple of off-target long-range shots by Gemmill. Gemmill's third attempt was a little more serious, but, following a right-wing corner he was off target. In the 63rd minute a left-wing corner kick by Taylor found Gallagher, who nodded the ball down and then challenged Davies. Davies used his hand to control the ball within the penalty area, and the referee had no choice other than to award the penalty. Francis took it and the Blues were up, two goals to nil. In the 65th minute, Kendall went off with a badly bruised thigh. Unable to provide a substitute, the visitors were forced to play on with only ten men, against a Derby team who were desperately trying to regain some advantage. Blues had to face increasing attacks, particularly from Davies. First Newton and then Rioch provided long balls to the centre forward, necessitating action from Latchford in the first instance, but, in spite of this, it was Blues who added to the scoreline in the 79th minute. Francis was seemingly legitimately dispossessed of a long through ball by Daniel in the penalty area but as he went down the referee pointed to the spot. The same player then stepped up to make it three goals for Blues. The last ten minutes went Derby's way, as a Birmingham side sorely missing Kendall were unable to defend against first Rioch, despite Latchford's attempt to half block the pass from Hector, and then Davies, despite a strong challenge from Gallagher. The game finished Blues 3, Derby 2 and the homw team had achieved a well-deserved victory.

BIRMINGHAM CITY

Latchford, Martin, Styles, Kendall, Gallagher, Page,(Hynd) Campbell, Francis, Burns, Hatton, Taylor,

DERBY COUNTY

Boulton, Webster, Nish, Rioch,Daniel, Todd, Powell, Gemmill, Davies, Hector, Lee (Newton)

REFEREE

Mr Nippard

Colin Todd, Derby County

Birthdays

Malcolm Briggs born today in 1961   Paul Mardon born today in 1969   Mick Bodley born today in 1967

Playing record for this day

Playing record for this day is...23 games, Won 12, Drawn 6, Lost 5, GF 29, GA 23.

Today's success rate.....65.22% Year ranking....24th

Match of the Day

FROM 1948

STEWART QUARTET WINS THE BATTLE OF THE CITIES

Jackie Stewart, Blues' acquisition from Raith, showed why he was so eagerly sought after. He single-handedly destroyed a strong Manchester City defence, which up until now had been one of the toughest defences to crack.

Since arriving Stewart had now netted 14 goals for the Blues. He finished the 1947-48 season with seven goals from 17 appearances, and had now matched that number of goals already just eight games into the 1948-49 campaign. All that despite the fact that he was primarily a winger. On this occasion however, he switched to a more central forward position for Trigg, who was injured late in the first half and only managed to continue by limping around near the right-hand touch line.

Blues were already in front by this time thanks to a Stewart goal midway through the half. However it was when the forced tactical switch took place that they excelled, despite having just the ten fit players. Stewart was on fire in the second half, claiming a hat-trick, with Blues third goal coming 15 minutes from time. He then scored a fourth before the mancunians added a very late consolation goal. Blues, therefore, remained unbeaten at St Andrews after a fine start to their First Division campaign.

BIRMINGHAM CITY

Merrick, Green, Jennings, Harris, Duckhouse, McKee, Stewart, Dougall, Trigg, Garrett, Laing

MANCHESTER CITY

Swift, Sproston, Westwood, Fagan, McDowell, Walsh, Oakes, Black, Godwin, Linacre, Clarke

John Stewart

Blues news extra 1908...Dorrington heroics help Blues to cup win

Blues beat Villa to win the Lord Mayor's of Birmingham Cup after a superb double save from the penalty spot by 'keeper Jack Dorrington. Villa were awarded a spot kick in the second half after a hand ball. Harry Hampton took the kick and his firmly struck shot was blocked by a diving Dorrington, the ball rebounded back out to Hampton who was about to tap into the empty net when he was tripped by Frank Womack resulting in another penalty. Harry strode up again to take the kick, choosing this time to place his shot into the opposite corner. Dorrington saved once more and this time clung onto the ball to the delight of Womack and his team mates.

The Matches played on this day

1894, Division 1.		
Wolverhampton W. 2	Blues 1	Att. 4,000
	Wheldon	
First league meeting v Wolves		
1900, Division 2.		
New Brighton Tower 0	Blues 0	Att. 4,000
1906, Division 1.		
Aston Villa 4	Blues 1	Att. 45,000
	Mounteney	
1923, Division 1.		
Sunderland 1	Blues 1	Att. 25,000
	Rawson	
1924, Division 1.		
Blues 1	Notts County 0	Att. 20,000
Bradford		
1928, Division 1.		
Arsenal 0	Blues 0	Att. 30,118
1934, Division 1.		
Middlesbrough 0	Blues 1	Att. 15,000
	Bradford	
1937, Division 1.		
Blues 4	Leicester City 1	Att. 25,000
Jones(3), White		
1945, Wartime.		
WBA 0	Blues 0	
1948, Division 1.		
Blues 4	Manchester City 1	Att. 40,000
Stewart(4)		
1951, Division 2.		
Blues 2	Doncaster Rovers 2	Att. 17,000
Dorman 31	Green(og) 3	
Badham 70	Martin 27	
1954, Division 2.		
Ipswich Town 1	Blues 2	Att. 16,783
Crowe 12	Murphy 29	
	Warmington 55	
1956, Division 1.		
Chelsea 1	Blues 0	Att. 40,530
Parsons 15		
1962, Division 1.		
Sheffield Wed. 5	Blues 0	Att. 22,255
Dobson 10		
Holiday 61, 87		
Layne 75, 80		
1970, League Cup 2nd round, replay.		
Blues 2	Colchester United 1	Att. 17,606
Vowden 83	Jones 13	
Summerill 87		
1973, Division 1.		
Blues 1	Liverpool 1	Att. 35,719
B.Latchford 65	Hall 85	
1979, Division 2.		
Blues 1	Charlton Athletic 0	Att. 16,156
Lynex 78		
1984, Division 2.		
Blues 2	Carlisle United 0	Att. 11,740
Clarke 11		
Harford 12		
Blues Tony Coton saved Tommy Craig's 35th minute penalty.		
1987, Division 2.		
Blues 1	Blackburn Rovers 0	Att. 6,052
Whitton 52		
Blues had Vince Overson sent off after 88 minutes.		
1990, Division 3.		
Blues 1	Bury 0	Att. 7,344
Peer 67		
1992, Anglo Italian Cup preliminary round		
Sunderland 0	Blues 1	Att. 5,871
Sale 24		
1998, League Cup 2nd round, 1st leg.		
Macclesfield Town 0	Blues 3	Att. 2,275
	Forster 66	
	Marsden 71	
	Rowett 89	
Former Blues keeper Ryan Price appeared for Macclesfield		
2001, Division 1.		
Manchester City 3	Blues 0	Att. 31,714
Goater 23, 42		
Dunne 24		

Playing record for this day
Playing record for this day is...23 games, Won 11, Drawn 2, Lost 10, GF 37, GA 40.
Today's success rate....52.17% Year ranking....137th

Match of the Day
FROM 1964
BLUES INFLICT ALBION'S FIRST DEFEAT OF SEASON

In front of a larger than average Hawthorns crowd, Blues inflicted the first home defeat of the season on the Baggies. They snatched an early first-half goal when Auld received a pass from Leek, giving him a clear run on goal. Taking the ball in his stride, the winger shot firmly past Potter. It was another 15 minutes before Blues had any cause for alarm. Lynn cleared the ball from the goal line with two attackers geared up for action. Albion could not get their wings moving, whereas Blues made excellent progress near the touch lines. Albion supporters were angered by some fierce tackles on Clark and Foggo, and by an off side decision which resulted in them being denied a goal after Kaye had shot past Schofield. The rest of the first half alternated from one end to the other, but despite several scrimmages near the City goal and a Jones header to the crossbar, Albion could not find an equaliser.

Albion came out in the second half determined to retrieve the situation. City's goal was constantly under fire, and the area around the goal began to resemble a mud bath. Cram mounted attack after attack and the Baggies laid siege to the visitors goal. Then when Auld kicked the ball up field to find Williams awkwardly placed in front of his own goal. The Albion captain could not avoid turning the ball in. There was no way back for the home team and the score remained 2-0 at full time.

WEST BROMWICH ALBION:
Potter, Cram, Graham Williams, Fraser, Jones, Simpson, Foggo, Brown, Kaye, Hope, Clark.
BIRMINGHAM CITY:
Schofield, Martin, Hennessey, Foster, Beard, Hellawell, Lynn, Jackson, Thomson, Leek, Auld.

REFEREE
Mr R Tinkler (Boston)

The Matches played on this day
1893, Division 2.
Blues 4   Walsall Town Swifts 0   Att. 2,000
Jenkyns, Izon(3)
Blues 13th succesive league win, a club record to date Charlie Izon became the first Blues player to score a hat-trick on his debut, the only other player to achieve this was Peter Murphy in 1952.
1899, Division 2.
Blues 5   Chesterfield 3   Att. 8,000
McRoberts, Bennett(2), Main, Wilcox
1st league meeting v Chesterfield
1905, Division 1.
Blues 2   Aston Villa 0   Att. 30,000
Jones, Mounteney
The 11th league match between the local rivals and Blues finally recorded their first win against Villa.
1907, Division 1.
Blues 0   Bury 1   Att. 10,000
Blues first ever defeat at St Andrews.
1911, Division 2.
Blues 0   Derby County 4   Att. 12,000
1916, Wartime.
Blues 4   Sheffield Wed. 1
Whitehouse(2), Freeman, Wallace
1922, Division 1.
Blues 0   Manchester City 1   Att. 30,000
1925, Division 1.
Blues 1   Huddersfield Town 3   Att. 25,000
Scriven
1929, Division 1.
West Ham United 0   Blues 1   Att. 16,000
   Bradford
1931, Division 1.
Sunderland 2   Blues 3   Att. 20,000
   Crosbie, Bradford, Briggs
1933, Division 1.
Blues 2   Blackburn Rovers 0   Att. 20,000
S.J.Smith, Curtis(pen)
1936, Division 1.
Manchester City 1   Blues 1   Att. 20,000
   Morris
1944, Wartime.
Coventry City 0   Blues 1
   Faulkner
1950, Division 2.
Bury 4   Blues 1   Att. 16,809
Plant 27, 43, 73   Dorman 44
Hartlett 33
1953, Division 2.
Luton Town 2   Blues 0   Att. 12,227
Downie 80(pen)
Cummins 84
1959, Division 1.
Chelsea 4   Blues 2   Att. 31,651
Greaves 4, 6, 90   Scott(og) 12
Blunstone 33   Hooper 35(pen)
1961, Division 1.
Blues 2   Burnley 6   Att. 18,742
Hellawell 79   Pointer 13, 29, 70
Bloomfield 80   Robson 15
   McIlroy 44
   Harris 63
1964, Division 1.
WBA 0   Blues 2   Att. 26,018
   Auld 8
   Williams 71(og)
1967, Division 2.
Blues 1   Blackburn Rovers 1   Att. 28,972
Bridges 60   Newton 90
1969, Division 2.
Blues 3   Norwich City 1   Att. 26,408
Summerill 45, 70   Forbes 50
Murray 46
Tony Hateley goal disallowed for Blues
1972, Division 1.
Derby County 1   Blues 0   Att. 23,753
Hector 80
1978, Division 1.
Norwich City 4   Blues 0   Attt. 16,407
Robson 3
Ryan 47(pen)
Chivers 60
Reeves 86
Jimmy Calderwood was involved in a freak accident in the dressing room when he slipped and injured his head, requiring eight stitches. Fortunately this occured just before the team sheet was handed over to the referee and Blues were able to call up young Mark Dennis for his debut.
1989, Division 3.
Blues 2   Tranmere Rovers 1   Att. 8,604
Gordon 60   Muir 84
Bailey 82
First league meeting v Tranmere

Ken Leek

Playing record for this day

Playing record for this day is...26 games, Won 9, Drawn 8, Lost 9, GF 45, GA 41.

Today's success rate....51.92% Year ranking....140th

Match of the Day

FROM 1958

BROWN THE FOUR GOAL HERO

Leeds battered by super Eddie Brown quartet

Blues registered their second win of the season just four days after the first against Burnley, also at St Andrews. This was a much more convincing result, although they had to come back from a 19th minute goal. The match was also a personal triumph for centre forward Eddie Brown who bagged all four goals, becoming the first Blues striker to hit four in a game since Jackie Stewart did against Manchester City almost ten years ago to the day.

Leeds nearly gifted Blues the ideal start when Hair, trying to block a shot by Hooper, forced his 'keeper Wood into a fantastic reflex save. A keenly contested game was brought to life when Leeds took the lead on 19 minutes with their first real goal threat. Overfield put in a deep cross and Forrest ran in unchecked to head past the helpless Merrick. This goal produced Blues best spell of the game and within five minutes they had levelled the score. Taylor beat two men and cut in from the left wing but over ran the ball as he was about to cross, However Ashall's mishit clearance sent it back to him. This time he was able to pass to the unmarked Brown who couldn't miss from close in. Blues continued to press forward and Wood saved well from both Murphy and Taylor. Blues deservedly went in front on 32 minutes when Brown collected a perfectly weighted through ball from Neal to run on and place a low shot past the advancing Wood and into the bottom corner of the net. Leeds almost equalised moments later when Forrest rattled the cross-bar with a fierce shot from the edge of the penalty area.

The second half started with Blues launching an all-out assault on the Leeds goal and it took just four minutes for Brown to complete his hat-trick. After receiving the ball within the area he turned sharply and hit a rising shot which cannoned of the top corner stanchion and back into play. After consulting a linesman the referee confirmed that it had gone in and pointed to the centre circle. Ten minutes later Brown put the ball in the net again but this time the effort was disallowed as he was offside when accepting Taylor's pass. His fourth goal was only delayed another ten minutes and in the 69th minute he beat Hair on the right wing, cut in and shot past Wood inside the near post. Blues were dominating in every area of the pitch and really should have scored a fifth when Hooper centred the ball for Murphy, he steadied himself nicely only to hit the bar from just eight yards out. In the dying minutes of the game Leeds brought about a fabulous save from Merrick when he dived full stretch in the air to turn the strikers effort round the post. But this was the only effort on target produced by the Yorkshire team in the entire second half.

BIRMINGHAM CITY
Merrick, Hall, Green, Watts, Sissons, Neal, Hooper, Jones, Brown, Murphy, Taylor.
LEEDS UNITED
Wood, Ashall, Hair, Gibson, Marsden, Cush, Meek, Crowe, Forrest, O'Brien, Overfield.

Eddie Brown

Birthdays

Andy Edwards born today in 1971

September 18

1897, Division 2.

| Loughborough Tn 0 | Blues 2 Walton(2) | Att. 2,000 |

Blues ninth succesive away league win, a club record to date.

1909, Division 2.

| Blues 1 Chapple | Fulham 1 | Att. 12,000 |

1920, Division 2.

| Blues 1 Whitehouse | Cardiff City 1 | Att. 35,000 |

1926, Division 1.

| WBA 1 | Blues 2 Briggs(2) | Att. 26,803 |

1935, Division 1.

| WBA 0 | Blues 0 | Att. 18,083 |

1937, Division 1.

| Blues 1 Jones | Charlton Athletic 1 | Att. 35,000 |

1943, Wartime.

| Leicester City 2 | Blues 2 Hinsley, Bright | |

1946, Division 2.

| WBA 3 | Blues 0 | Att. 42,031 |

1948, Division 1.

| Burnley 2 | Blues 2 Trigg, Bodle | Att. 40,000 |

1954, Division 2.

| Lincoln City 1 Finch 31 | Blues 1 Kinsey 66 | Att. 14,537 |

Finch missed a penalty for Lincoln on 26 minutes

1957, Division 1.

| Tottenham Hotspur 7 Stokes 22, 25, 31, 41, 90 Dyson 35 Harmer 78(pen) | Blues 1 Brown 29 | Att. 35,192 |

Blues 'keeper Gil Merrick was injured on 31 minutes and spent the second half playing at left back.

1963, Division 1.

| WBA 3 Foggo 71 Clark 89 Jackson 90 | Blues 1 Harris 37 | Att. 29,662 |

1965, Division 2.

| Blues 1 Beard 27 | Portsmouth 3 Lewis 34, 35(pen) Barton 44 | Att. 11,793 |

1971, Division 2.

| Blues 1 B.Latchford 40 | Bristol City 0 | Att. 28,745 |

1976, Division 1.

| Aston Villa 1 Gray 13 | Blues 2 Burns 29 Connolly 43 | Att. 50,084 |

This match screened by ATV's Star Soccer.

1982, Division 1.

| Blues 1 Evans 45 | Coventry City 0 | Att. 11,681 |

Noel Blake made his Blues debut

1984, Division 2.

| Blues 0 | Portsmouth 1 Webb 80 | Att. 18,012 |

Blues had Robert Hopkins sent off after 73 minutes

1990, Division 3.

| Blues 1 Bailey 42 | Exeter City 1 Dryden 75 | Att. 7,703 |

1st league meeting v Exeter

1993, Division 1.

| Blues 1 Donowa 1 | Grimsby Town 1 Gilbert 39 | Att. 11,302 |

Louie Donowa's goal timed at 58 seconds

1994, Division 2.

| Blues 4 Bull 18, 33 Tait 21 Dominguez 67 | Peterborough United 0 | Att. 10,800 |

Steve Claridge missed a penalty with the score 3-0.

1996, League Cup 2nd round, 1st leg.

| Coventry City 1 Daish 88 | Blues 1 Furlong 38 | Att. 11,828 |

1999, Division 1.

| Ipswich Town 0 | Blues 1 Furlong 10(pen) | Att. 19,758 |

2001, Division 1.

| Blues 2 A.Johnson 19, 40 | Burnley 3 Little 10, 72 I.Moore 34 | Att. 18,246 |

Playing record for this day

Playing record for this day is...23 games, Won 7, Drawn 10, Lost 6, GF 29, GA 33.

Today's success rate....52.17% Year ranking....138th

Match of the Day

FROM 1994

BLUES SHINE IN TV WIN

Posh hammered by new look Blues team

Blues made four changes for this match, which was televised live. Barry Fry had been out and exchanged Dave Regis and Roger Willis for Southend's Jonathon Hunt and Gary Poole. Both made their debuts as Poole replaced Richard Scott and Hunt pushing Paul Harding onto the bench. Other alterations saw the return of Ward for Regis, while John Frain made way for Bryan Small at left back. Peterborough who had future Blues players Gary Breen and Ken Charlery in their side, gave 17-year-old 'keeper Mark Tyler his debut. Posh also had former Blues defender Kevin Ashley in their line-up.

The new-look Blues team gelled quickly and dominated the early stages without creating any clear cut openings. When they did strike on 18 minutes through Gary Bull it effectively killed the game. The second, three minutes later was a dreadful mistake from Ashley, who was caught between heading clear and heading back to his 'keeper, but succeeded only in managing to knock the ball straight into Tait's path and the Blues skipper easily beat Tyler. This goal threatened to open the floodgates for the Blues but they managed just one more before the break when Bull got his second on 33 minutes. Again it was a simply executed goal, Claridge fired in a hard low cross and Bull turning his man in the penalty area and swept the ball in from ten yards.

Peterborough started the second half the better and could have been back within reach of the Blues but for poor finishing against a very shaky looking defence. Barry Fry then replaced Wallace with the tricky Dominguez to give the Posh defence something to worry about. Within minutes the decision had paid off when he was brought down in the area. Claridge stepped up but could only smash his penalty against the foot of the post. Dominguez then weaved his way through again with a magical run and registered a superb solo goal to put the game beyond Peterborough on 67 minutes. The 4-0 win saw Blues rise to sixth place in the Division Two table.

BIRMINGHAM CITY

Bennett, Poole, Small, Ward (Harding 82), Dryden, Whyte, Hunt, Claridge, Bull, Tait, Wallace (Dominguez 56)

PETERBOROUGH UNITED

Tyler, Ashley, Clark, McGorry, Heald, Welsh, Morrison (Brissett 69), Breen, Farrell (Williams 69), Charlery, Henry.,

REFEREE

Mr R Poulain (Huddersfield)

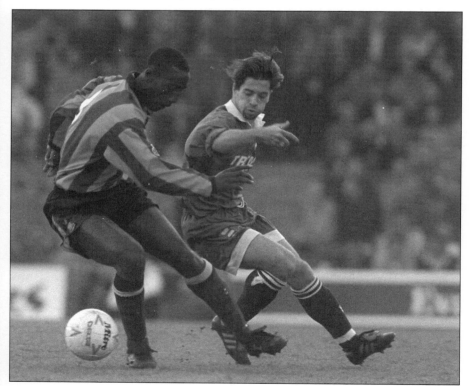

Jose Dominguez

Birthdays

Howard Forinton born today in 1975   **Roy Warhurst born today in 1926**

Playing record for this day

Playing record for this day is...22 games, Won 3, Drawn 9, Lost 10, GF 30, GA 40.

Today's success rate....34.09% Year ranking....254th

Match of the Day

FROM 1981
UNSETTLED EVANS
IS BLUES HAT-TRICK HERO

Man City sunk by Super Blues

Blues striker Tony Evans sent a clear message to Jim Smith with a scintillating performance in front of 20,109 fans at St Andrews. With Frank Worthington returning fresh from a summer in the USA, Evans could not have timed his hat-trick better. Blues started the game without skipper Archie Gemmill who was suffering from a knee strain so his place was given to teenager Ian Handysides. Manchester City manager John Bond dropped both his full backs which allowed Kevin Bond, his son, a debut for the club.

The visitors also had brought back England striker Dennis Tueart and he lined up alongside Trevor Francis who was making only his second return to St Andrews since his £1 million move in February 1979.

There was a sensational start for the Blues as they took the lead after just two minutes. The long ball out of defence fell to Whatmore who turned sharply to break away with Evans making a fine run down the middle in space. Whatmore found him with a fine right-wing cross and the striker took the ball in his stride, coolly side-footing his shot past Corrigan as the 'keeper came out towards him. Manchester City responded well and Wealands saved from Francis, then Tueart.

The second half began just as spectacularly for Blues, with a goal this time coming inside the opening minute. Whatmore held the ball up well and waited patiently for Dennis to race forward on the overlap. From his surging run and whipped in cross, Evans nipped in at the near post to steer a close range header past Corrigan for his second goal of the game. Blues were soon running riot and another snap shot from Evans was only prevented from going in by a lunge from defender Reid who managed to deflect the ball wide for a corner. Then a shot by Dillon from distance struck Caton and the ball ballooned up in the air over Corrigan's head but dropped agonisingly the wrong side of the cross bar. A measure of Blues dominance came in the 75th minute when John Bond decided to withdraw forward Reeves for Phil Boyer. Still Blues pressed forward and a chance fell to Brocken who went clean through. However with just Corrigan to beat he completely miskicked and the ball ran out of play. Evans collected a deserved third goal soon after the introduction of Worthington on as sub for Van Mierlo. Worthington collected a loose ball in midfield and proceeded to wriggle his way through the visitors defence until within striking range, from 30 yards his shot was struck so sweetly Corrigan could only parry the effort. The ball rolled into the path of Evans who accepted the gift to complete a fine hat-trick.

In the last few minutes a rare break from Francis produced a magnificent save from Wealands and at the other end in stoppage time Corrigan pulled off an equally brilliant save to deny Handysides.

BIRMINGHAM CITY

Wealands, Langan, Dennis, Dillon, Broadhurst, Todd,
Brocken, Whatmore, Evans, Handysides, Van Mierlo (Worthington 74 mins).

MANCHESTER CITY

Corrigan, Bond, Caton, Reid, Booth, Tueart,
O'Neill, Gow, Francis, Hutchinson, Reeves (Boyer 75 mins)

REFEREE

Mr PJ Richardson (Lincoln)

Tony Evans

Birthdays

Tony Hey born today in 1970   **David Seaman born today in 1963**   **Ron Fenton born today in 1940**

The Matches played on this day

1891, Football Alliance.

Burton Swifts 6	Blues 3	Att. 2,000
	E.Devey, Wheldon(2)	

1896, Division 2.

Blues 1	Lincoln City 2	Att. 6,500
Edwards		

1903, Division 1.

Blues 2	Aston Villa 2	Att. 25,000
Wilcox, Robertson		

1908, Division 2.

Fulham 1	Blues 1	Att. 38,000
	Green	

First league meeting v Fulham

1914, Division 2.

Glossop 3	Blues 3	Att. 500
	Tinkler, A.W.Smith(pen), Gibson	

1925, Division 1.

Blues 0	Notts County 1	Att. 5,000

1931, Division 1.

Blues 1	Sheffield United 3	Att. 30,000
Crosbie		

1936, Division 1.

Charlton Athletic 2	Blues 2	Att. 35,000
	Jones, Morris	

First league meeting v Charlton
Blues led 2-0 at half time

1942, Wartime.

Derby County 3	Blues 1	
	Ottewell	

1953, Division 2.

Blues 2	Fulham 2	Att. 22,000
Purdon 13, 28	Jezzard 1, 16	

Fulham's first goal timed at 14 seconds after kick off

1959, Division 1.

Blues 3	Leicester City 4	Att. 25,003
Hooper 10(pen), 17	Riley 30	
Smith 87	Keyworth 59, 70	
	Cheesebrough 61	

1962, Division 1.

Blues 0	WBA 0	Att. 28,625

1964, Division 1.

Sheffield United 3	Blues 1	Att. 16,390
Birchenall 42, 73	Thomson 88	
Jones 55		

1970, Division 2.

Portsmouth 1	Blues 0	Att. 18,037
Hiron 39		

1972, League Cup 2nd round, 2nd replay.

Blues 1	Luton Town 0	Att. 11,451
Francis 72		

Played at the County Ground, Northampton.

1973, Texaco Cup 1st round, 1st leg.

Stoke City 0	Blues 0	Att. 9,530

Blues first tie in the newly established Texaco Cup
19-year-old central defender Joe Gallagher made his debut.

1981, Division 1.

Blues 3	Manchester City 0	Att. 20,109
Evans 2, 46, 77		

1987, Division 2.

Blues 0	Shrewsbury Town 0	Att. 7,183

1989, League Cup 2nd round, 1st leg.

Blues 1	West Ham United 2	Att. 10,987
Sproson 86	Allen 39	
	Slater 87	

1992, Division 2.

Luton Town 1	Blues 1	Att. 8,481
Claridge 90(pen)	Rowbotham 50	

1998, Division 1.

Blues 0	Grimsby Town 1	Att. 17,563
	D.Smith 50	

Grimsby's first win at St Andrews since 1936.
Former Blues player David Smith netted the only goal.

2000, League Cup 2nd round, 1st leg.

Wycombe Wan.3	Blues 4	Att. 2,537
Rammell 45	Horsfield 2, 22	
Baird 71	A.Johnson 24, 87	
Bates 86		

September 20

Playing record for this day
Playing record for this day is...19 games, Won 8, Drawn 2, Lost 9, GF 24, GA 29.
Today's success rate....47.37% Year ranking....179th

The Matches played on this day

1902, Division 2.

| Burnley 2 | Blues 1 | Att. 3,000 |
| | McMillan | |

1913, Division 2.

| Blues 1 | Leicester Fosse | Att. 20,000 |
| Ballantyne | | |

1919, Division 2.

| Coventry City 1 | Blues 3 | Att. 15,000 |
| | Millard(2), Whitehouse | |

1924, Division 1.

| Preston North End 1 | Blues 0 | Att. 15,000 |

1926, Division 1.

| Blues 1 | Everton 0 | Att. 15,000 |
| Briggs | | |

1930, Division 1.

| Portsmouth 2 | Blues 2 | Att. 15,000 |
| | Hicks, Briggs | |

1947, Division 2.

| Blues 1 | Leicester City 0 | Att. 30,000 |
| Dougall | | |

1952, Division 2.

Notts County 2	Blues 0	Att. 24,538
Crookes 1		
Wylies 24		

1958, Division 1.

Preston North End 3	Blues 0	Att. 20,000
Hatsell 17		
Thompson 40		
Mayers 47		

1961, Division 1.

Blues 1	WBA 2	Att. 22,902
Hellawell 89	Burnside 17	
	Kevan 84	

Blues finished with ten men after Stubbs was carried off early in the first half with a dislocated shoulder.

1966, League Cup 2nd round, replay.

Blues 2	Nottingham Forest 1	Att. 21,510
Vowden 20	Crowe 28 (pen)	
Bridges 52		

1969, Division 2.

| Charlton Athletic 0 | Blues 1 | Att. 13,988 |
| | Hateley 68 | |

Charlton 'keeper Burns saved Dave Robinson's penalty after 35 minute.

1975, Division 1.

Blues 4	Burnley 0	Att. 25,830
Campbell 51		
Withe 54		
Kendall 66		
Francis 75		

1980, Division 1.

| Blues 1 | WBA 1 | Att. 22,016 |
| Givens 88 | A.Brown 70 | |

1986, Division 2.

Hull City 3	Blues 2	Att. 6,851
Roberts 46, 50	Clarke 55, 81	
Skipper 47		

1988, Division 2.

Walsall 5	Blues 0	Att. 8,780
Forbes 67		
Shakespeare 70		
A.Taylor 78		
Naughton 84		
Rees 86		

First league meeting with Walsall for 87 years, and by far Blues heaviest defeat by the Saddlers.

1994, League Cup 2nd round, 1st leg.

Blackburn Rovers 2	Blues 0	Att. 14,517
Wilcox 55		
Sutton 60		

1995, League Cup 2nd round, 1st leg.

Blues 3	Grimsby Town 1	Att. 7,446
Claridge 23	Woods 34	
Hunt 43		
Daish 75		

1997, Division 1.

Middlesbrough 3	Blues 1	Att. 30,125
Kinder 23	Furlong 51	
Back 41		
Emerson 43		

Match of the Day

FROM 1975

BELL'S BLUE BOYS BATTER BRAVE BURNLEY

Post-Goodwin era starts with encouraging 4-0 win

Newly appointed Blues boss Willie Bell got off to a flying start as a rejuvenated Blues thrashed visitors Burnley.

Blues had slightly the better of a keenly fought first half, creating four good chances which were well stopped by the disciplined Burnley defence. Jimmy Adamson was well aware of the transformation a team can have shortly after a manager's departure he said afterwards, "The dismissal of Freddie Goodwin was bound to affect their players and the crowd. It was a game of emotion with the players fighting to justify themselves." Blues did indeed thoroughly justify themselves, proving they were a better side than their poor league position suggested. However, the transformation was not apparent until the second half.

Blues exerted their authority on the game immediately after the restart and were a goal ahead just six minutes later. A neat pass from striker Peter Withe setting up an unmissable chance for Alan Campbell who swept it into the net. Withe then scored a second goal just three minutes later to put the result beyond any doubt. Once Francis started to weave his magic Burnley crumbled completely and Blues then ran riot. An inch perfect cross was headed in by Withe within minutes of the second goal but this was mysteriously disallowed. Further misfortune fell upon Burnley's team when from an innocuous challenge with Kenny Burns, Collins was stretchered off with a broken leg. Burnley gambled by throwing centre half Waldron into attack to replace the striker and substitute Ingham filled the vacancy in defence. Blues then added a third goal through Kendall, who met Dave Latchford's free kick from what seemed to be an offside position to blast his shot on the half volley wide of Stevenson in the Burnley goal and into the top corner of the net. With Blues now in total command Francis added a fourth 15 minutes from time to send the fans home victorious for the first time this season. Everything seemed as bright as the glorious Birmingham sunshine and what a time to hit top form. Burnley's defeated but gracious manager summed it up very nicely, "Their first goal was beautifully taken, and their fans lifted them with their tremendous chanting."... Now bring on the Villa!!!

BIRMINGHAM CITY

Latchford, Martin, Bryant, Kendall, Gallagher, Burns, Campbell, Francis, Withe, Hatton, Hibbitt.

BURNLEY

Stevenson, Brennan, Newton, Noble, Waldron, Thomson, Flynn, Hankin, Summerbee, Collins(Ingham), James.

Joe Gallagher

Birthdays

Eamonn Dolan born today in 1967   Simon Rea born today in 1976

Playing record for this day

Playing record for this day is...21 games, Won 9, Drawn 3, Lost 9, GF 32, GA 31.

Today's success rate....50% Year ranking....156th

Match of the Day

FROM 1968

BLUES TOO HOT FOR VILLA

Vital victory, as Vowden, Vincent & co sink Villa

A re-shaped defence handed Blues their first clean sheet of the season and four blistering goals brought them an oustanding victory over rivals Villa in a dramatic Second City derby at St Andrews. Villa who started well, paid the price for an uncoordinated final 30 minutes, when they conceded four goals. Their opponents in contrast looked classy and enthusiastic throughout and fully deserved their emphatic victory.

Birmingham were put under some pressure early on and centre half Dave Robinson was forced to make two vital clearances from off his own goaline. Robinson was just one of a seven players in the Blues line-up, who were products of the clubs' youth policy.

For an hour both sides seemed content on battling it out in midfield with neither prepared to take a risk and push men forward.

This all changed when Birmingham suddenly sprang into action with two goals in three minutes. The first by Summerill after 63 minutes came from an assist by Greenhoff's headed knockdown, and the second three minutes later from Jimmy Greenhoff who headed home Vowden's cross. This deflated Villa who looked a despondent outfit in the closing 15 minutes.

Blues were in total control and on 83 minutes scored a third when Vincent headed in from another exquisite cross by Vowden. Blues were making a mockery of the expensively assembled Villa side.

Greenhoff then set up Vowden with an unmissable chance a minute from full time to make the score a resounding 4-0. There was no doubt at all who had won and the 40,527 crowd vociferously let it be known as they left St Andrews on a terrific afternoon for any Blues fan.

BIRMINGHAM CITY

Herriott, Martin, Green, Wylie, Robinson, Beard,
Hockey, Greenhoff, Vowden, Vincent, Summerill.

ASTON VILLA

Wright, Aitken, Edwards, Turnbull, Hole, Ferguson,
Greenhaigh, Woodward, Godfrey, Anderson.

Johnny Vincent

September 22

The Matches played on this day

1894, Division 1.
Preston North End 0   Blues 1   Att. 5,000
  Hands
1st league meeting v Preston

1900, Division 2.
Blues 6   Gainsborough Trinity 0 Att. 2,000
Leake(2), McRoberts(2),
Walton, Thornley(og)

1906, Division 1.
Blues 2   Liverpool 1   Att. 10,000
Jones, Mounteney

1923, Division 1.
Blues 0   Arsenal 2   Att. 20,000

1928, Division 1.
Blues 4   Blackburn Rovers 0 Att. 30,000
Bradford(2), Briggs(2)

1934, Division 1.
Blues 1   Blackburn Rovers 0 Att. 15,000
White

1945, Wartime.
Swansea Town 2   Blues 4
  Mulraney, Dougall, Massart(2)

1951, Division 2.
Everton 1   Blues 3   Att. 27,138
Buckle 71   Purdon 3
  Wardle 70(pen)
  Briggs 81

1956, Division 1.
Blues 2   Cardiff City 1   Att. 39,931
Kinsey 13   O'Halloran 11
Govan 79

1962, Division 1.
Blues 4   Fulham 1   Att. 20,477
Leek 25   Langley (pen) 70
Harris 38
Lynn(pen) 44
Auld 81

1965, League Cup 2nd round.
Mansfield Town 2   Blues 1   Att. 9,344
Middleton 16   Beard 48
Scanlon 54

1973, Division 1.
QPR 2   Blues 2   Att. 18,701
Hynd(og) 23   B.Latchford 32
Bowles 24   Burns 86

1979, Division 2.
Orient 2   Blues 2   Att. 5,550
Mayo 49, 90   Lynex 19
  Curbishley 21
Colin Todd made his Blues debut.

1981, Division 1.
Arsenal 1   Blues 0   Att. 19,504
Talbott 20

1984, Division 2.
Wolverhampton W. 0 Blues 2   Att. 12,698
  Kuhl 79
  Hopkins 84

1990, Division 3.
Wigan Athletic 1   Blues 1   Att. 3,907
Page 46   Tait 82

1998, League Cup 2nd round, 2nd leg.
Blues 6   Macclesfield Town 0 Att. 3,443
Ndlovu 6, 19
Askey(og) 37
Marsden 57
Rowett 66
M.Johnson 90
Blues won 9-0 on aggregate, their biggest ever aggregate
win in any competition Lowest crowd at St Andrews for
65 years.

Playing record for this day

Playing record for this day is...17 games, Won 11, Drawn 3, Lost 3, GF 41, GA 16.

Today's success rate....73.53% Year ranking....6th

Match of the Day

FROM 1962

BLUES FOUR-CE A WIN

Hard work brings the points at St Andrews

The 20,477 St Andrews crowd were treated to an exciting game as Blues swept aside Fulham 4-1. A depleted home side which included young reserves Winston Foster and Brian Sharples faced a Fulham side without the expertise of Johnny Haynes. Both sides came out attacking, with plenty of good, fast, open approach work marred only by some wild finishing during the opening 20 minutes. Then on 25 minutes Leek seized on a short through pass by Harris and ran through a gap in the Fulham defence before accurately placing his shot in the corner of the net as Macedo came to block it. A goal at last for Birmingham, after 298 minutes play - the previous one being against Burnley four games ago. Fulham responded immediately. Cook hit a thunderbolt shot from outside the area which required a spectacular save from Withers, then he had to move smartly to punch a shot from Key over the bar. Blues kept up the pressure with Mullery and Macedo both busy.

During this period Leek sustained a cut above the left eye from a heading duel with Mealand, and required treatment off the pitch. On his return, Blues again went into the attack, and on 38 minutes, Harris was able to nod the ball into the net off a finely judged centre to the far post by Auld. Blues were demonstrating their superiority by finding the gaps in the Fulham defence, and although the visitors were opening up attacks, they couldn't find the strength or skill to punch through the Blues defence. In the 44th minute, following an almighty scramble in the Fulham goalmouth, several shots were charged down before Auld's effort was pushed around the post by Mullery. However from the resultant corner kick the ball was centred and Lynn converted, Blues were now coasting, three goals up at the half-time whistle.

An injury sustained by Withers just after the resumption resulted in a free kick to Blues and Withers absence for eight minutes treatment. Unfortunately the home team were unable to take advantage from the set piece, and although they continued to press, it was the visitors who scored in the 70th minute. Key, had already crashed the ball home, only to be denied as the referee awarded a penalty for a foul commited by Foster on Brown. Langley took the penalty kick and sent Withers the wrong way. Blues, who had been easing off the pressure a little, came back into the fray and there were some heated exchanges between Cook and Auld, ending with a booking for Auld. But in the 81st minute Auld, picking up from a great centre from Hellawell, made it four goals for Blues. All the steam went out of Fulham after that, and Blues finished the game well on top looking to increase their lead still further.

BIRMINGHAM CITY

Withers, Lynn, Sharples, Hennessey, Foster,Beard,
Hellawell, Bloomfield, Harris, Leek and Auld

FULHAM

Macedo, Mealand, Langley, Mullery, Dodgin, Robson,
Key, Cook, Stan Brown, Henderson and Chamberlain

REFEREE

Mr LV Faulkner (Liverpool)

Colin Withers

Blues news extra   1980...Blues open new club shop Birmingham City FC have

Birmingham City FC officially opened their new club shop which is siuated on Cattell Road. This was further redeveloped 13 years later to the new superstore which is now in its place.

Birthdays

Gordon Astall born today in 1927   **Ray Ferris born today in 1920**   **Bert Murray born today in 1942**

Playing record for this day

Playing record for this day is...23 games, Won 8, Drawn 7, Lost 8, GF 25, GA 29.
Today's success rate....50% Year ranking....169th

Match of the Day

FROM 1975

BLUES WITHE THE WINNER

Blues new-found winning streak under acting manager Willie Bell continued with a determined victory over Newcastle at St Andrews. The opening 16 minutes were packed with action, four goals being shared between the two teams. Peter Withe, Blues' £40,000 bargain buy from Wolves scored two for the home team, with the other one being a penalty from Trevor Francis.

The 31,166 strong crowd had barely had time to settle themselves before Blues took the lead on just 41 seconds. A free kick from Howard Kendall on the right seemed to be going straight towards Newcastle goalkeeper Mike Mahoney. Withe collided with him in mid-air and Mahoney dropped the ball. The Blues striker curled it over the line, and the linesman raised his flag for a foul. He quickly dropped it,however, when he noticed that the referee was pointing to the centre spot, and the goal stood.

The second goal came on 12 minutes, scored again by Withe. He stuck to a superb 50 yard pass from ex-Newcastle midfielder Terry Hibbitt, and as Mahoney moved out from his line Withe took the shot. His first effort hit the goalkeeper on the leg and rebounded back to him but he made sure at the second attempt.

Two minutes later and Newcastle drew back a goal thanks to skipper Geoff Nulty, but their hopes didn't last long and Blues increased their lead on 16 minutes. John Bird handled a corner from Hibbitt and a penalty was awarded. Francis duly stepped up to take the spot kick and made no mistake in slamming the ball home past Mahoney.

A pass from Alan Gowling was converted into a 75th minute goal by Tommy Craig from 30 yards but that was the end of the scoring.

BIRMINGHAM CITY

Latchford, Martin (Pendrey), Bryant, Kendall, Gallagher, Kenny Burns, Campbell, Francis, Withe, Hatton, Hibbitt.

NEWCASTLE UNITED

Mahoney, Nattrass, Kennedy, Nulty, Bird, Howard, Micky Burns, Cassidy, Tudor, Gowling, Craig.

REFEREE

Mr Reg Matthewson (Bolton)

Alan Campbell

Birthdays

Kenny Burns born today in 1953   **Kevin Rogers born today in 1963**   **Liam Daish born today in 1968**
Richard Edghill born today in 1974

The Matches played on this day
1893, Division 2.
Liverpool 3   Blues 1   Att. 8,000
                     Jenkyns
First league meeting v Liverpool
1899, Division 2.
Gainsborough T. 1   Blues 4   Att. 2,000
                     McRoberts, Wharton, Bennett(2)
1905, Division 1.
Liverpool 2   Blues 0   Att. 15,000
1911, Division 2.
Stockport County 2   Blues 0   Att. 5,000
1916, Wartime.
Bradford Pk Ave. 2   Blues 3
                     Montgomery, Whitehouse, Jephcott
1922, Division 1.
Bolton Wanderers 3   Blues 0   Att. 15,000
1931, Division 1.
Blues 0   Sunderland 0   Att. 15,000
1933, Division 1.
Newcastle United 0   Blues 0   Att. 22,000
1944, Wartime.
Leicester City 0   Blues 1
                     Shaw
1950, Division 2.
Blues 1   QPR 1   Att. 27,000
Heath(og) 9   Addinall 14
1st league meeting v QPR
1961, Division 1.
Arsenal 1   Blues 1   Att. 31,749
Skirton 34   Harris 60(pen)
Johnny Schofield saved George Eastham's 37th
minute penalty.
1964, League Cup 2nd round.
Blues 0   Chelsea 3   Att. 15,300
                     Graham 32
                     Tambling 70, 90
1967, Division 2.
Blackpool 1   Blues 0   Att. 25,572
Ingram 80
1972, Division 1.
Blues 2   Everton 1   Att. 37,133
B.Latchford 7   Newton 10
Francis 66
1975, Division 1.
Blues 3   Newcastle United 2 Att. 31,166
Withe 1, 12   Nulty 14
Francis 16(pen)   Craig 75
Peter Withe's goal timed at 41 seconds.
1978, Division 1.
Blues 1   Chelsea 1   Att. 18,458
Givens 73   McKenzie 59
1980, League Cup 3rd round.
Blues 1   Blackburn Rovers 0 Att. 14,805
Gallagher 58
1986, League Cup 2nd round, 1st leg.
Middlesbrough 2   Blues 2   Att. 9,412
Stephens 9   Whitton 6
Ripley 86   Clarke 65
1989, Division 3.
Brentford 0   Blues 1   Att. 5,386
                     Sturridge 85
1995, Division 1.
Watford 1   Blues 1   Att. 9,422
Moralee 7   Finnan 11
1997, League Cup 2nd round, 2nd leg.
Stockport County 2   Blues 1   Att. 2,074
Armstrong 37   Furlong 70(pen)
Mutch 87
Blues won 5-3 on aggregate
2000, Division 1.
Blues 2   Tranmere Rovers 0 Att. 17,640
Grainger 73
Horsfield 90
Mark Burchill on loan from Celtic made his Blues debut
2001, Division 1.
Blues 0   Preston North End 1 Att. 23,004
                     Alexandder 57
Blues 4000th league game

September 24

The Matches played on this day

1892, Division 2.
Blues 4 — Lincoln City 1 — Att. 2,500
Wheldon(2), Jenkyns, Mobley
First league meeting v Lincoln

1898, Division 2.
Loughborough Town 1 Blues 1 — Att. 2,000
McRoberts

1904, Division 1.
Blues 2 — Newcastle United 1 — Att. 15,000
Jones(2)

1910, Division 2.
Blues 1 — Gainsborough Trinity 1 Att. 12,000
Jones

1921, Division 1.
Sunderland 2 — Blues 1 — Att. 30,000
Whitehouse

1927, Division 1.
Blackburn Rovers 4 Blues 4 — Att. 10,000
Bradford(4)

1932, Division 1.
Blues 3 — Blackburn Rovers 1 — Att. 25,000
Grosvenor, Curtis, Gregg

1938, Division 1.
Blues 1 — Preston North End 3 — Att. 20,000
Farrage

1949, Division 1.
Arsenal 4 — Blues 2 — Att. 53,000
Berry(2)

1955, Division 1.
Charlton Athletic 2 Blues 0 — Att. 21,913
Kiernan 23
Gauld 87

1960, Division 1.
Blues 3 — Nottingham Forest 1 Att. 26,615
Astall 14 — Vowden 1
Singer 57
Gordon 80

1966, Division 2.
Blues 2 — Rotherham United 3 Att. 19,515
Bridges 8 — Casper 62
Thomson 34 — Chappell 77
Lyons 78

1977, Division 1.
WBA 3 — Blues 1 — Att. 29,160
T.Brown 2, 76(pen) Connolly 7
Regis 12
This match screened by BBC's Match of the Day.

1983, Division 1.
Everton 1 — Blues 1 — Att. 15,253
Sharp 49(pen) Gayle 42

1985, League Cup 2nd round, 1st leg.
Bristol Rovers 2 Blues 3 — Att. 4,332
O'Connor 8 — Wright 37(pen), 57
Randall 26 — Geddis 81

1988, Division 2.
Blackburn Rovers 3 Blues 0 — Att. 7,562
Bird(og) 1
Hendry 22
Garner 45

1994, Division 2.
Blues 2 — Hull City 2 — Att. 12,192
Claridge 30(pen) Windass 42(pen)
Dominguez 53 Peacock 54
Hull's captain Gregg Abbott sent off in the second half.

1996, League Cup 2nd round, 2nd leg.
Blues 0 — Coventry City 1 — Att. 15,218
McAllister 63
Coventry centre half and former Blues star, Liam Daish sent off after 75 minutes.
Blues lost 2-1 on aggregate.

Playing record for this day

Playing record for this day is...18 games, Won 5, Drawn 5, Lost 8, GF 32, GA 36.

Playing record for this day is...18 games, Won 5, Drawn 5, Lost 8, GF 32, GA 36.

Match of the Day

FROM 1960

BLUES ON SONG AT FOREST THANKS TO SINGER

New boy Singer inspires Blues recovery to win 3-1

Gil Merrick's faith in Newport County forward Jimmy Singer paid off immediately as he produced an inspired performance on his debut. His fine display was instrumental in helping Blues lead the fight back after being a goal down in the first minute.

Blues shortcomings in recent games had mainly centred on the attack but with Singer available this was about remedied. The whole side was rejuvenated. Trevor Smith played his best game of the season and kept 19-year-old Geoff Vowden (a future Blues player) out of the game, once he had put the visitors ahead in the first minute. Forest's other teenager,18-year-old Dick Le Flem, was also well marshalled by Farmer in a solid looking Blues defence.

Forest made a sensational start to the game when Vowden headed them in front after a minute's play. Trevor Smith had needlessly impeded Billy Younger just inside the Blues half, the centre forward then soared through the air to convert Joe McDonald's free kick. The equaliser came in the 14th minute when a Gordon cross was headed on by Singer to Astall, whose sharp volley on the turn left Thomson helpless.

In the second half Blues started the better and soon took total control of the game. Singer's goal came in the 57th minute after Thomson had failed to hold an overhead kick from Stubbs. The new man was well placed to plant his header over the goal line. Blues increased their lead to 3-1 with ten minutes of the game remaining, a goal from Gordon puting the result beyond any doubt. After some good approach work by Astall his cross found Gordon in the box, after the 'keeper had fumbled the ball again this left a simple shot from six yards which Gordon blasted into the roof of the net.

BIRMINGHAM CITY
Schofield, Farmer, Allen, Watts, Smith, Beard, Hooper, Gordon, Stubbs, Singer, Astall.
NOTTINGHAM FOREST
Thomson, Patrick, McDonald, Whitefoot, McKinley, Iley, Gray, Booth, Vowden, Younger, Le Flem.

George Allen

Birthdays

Louie Donowa born today in 1964

Playing record for this day

Playing record for this day is...21 games, Won 6, Drawn 4, Lost 11, GF 23, GA 38.

Today's success rate....38.10% Year ranking....243rd

Match of the Day

FROM 1984

NO JOY FOR PILGRIMS AT THE SHRINE

Blues set up handsome advantage over Plymouth in cup tie

Blues gained a victory in this Milk Cup tie, despite a constant battle from Plymouth who did not give up without a fight. The scoreline suggests that this was an easy win, but it certainly was not. Blues fielded 20-year-old former Sunderland reserve Mark Prudhoe in goal, and despite some poor cover he managed to more than hold his own.

The struggle began at kick-off, and the first goal could have come for either team. It eventually arrived for Plymouth on 37 minutes, with a strong shot from Gordon Staniforth. The goal shook Blues into action, so much so that it took only two minutes for the equaliser to come with a spectacular goal from Wayne Clarke.

On 52 minutes an attempt from Robert Hopkins was saved by Plymouth 'keeper David Philp. Hopkins, frustrated by this, ran straight into the keeper as he lay on the ground, and was promptly booked for the offence. This was his third booking of the season.

The home team took the lead after 61 minutes with a Hopkins volley, and Mick Harford headed Blues' third five minutes later. On 75 minutes Tony Rees was brought on as a substitute for Daly, and it proved to be a wise move as he finished the scoring just three minutes from time with a fourth goal.

This was Blues best start to the season since World War Two, and even though the side were playing well below their potential, they now had a secure lead to take to Home Park for the second leg.

BIRMINGHAM CITY

Prudhoe, Roberts, Hagan, Wright, Armstrong, Daly (Rees), Kuhl, Clarke, Harford, Halsall, Hopkins.

PLYMOUTH ARGYLE

Philp, Nisbet, Rowe, Harrison, Goodyear (Uzzell), Burrows, Hodges, Rogers, Tynan, Staniforth, Coughlin.

REFEREE

Mr John Hough (Macclesfield)

Mick Harford

Birthdays

Ronnie Morris born today in 1970   Fred Slater born today in 1925

The Matches played on this day

1893, Division 2.		
Burslem Port Vale 5	Blues 0	Att. 1,000
1897, Division 2.		
Blues 2	Burton Swifts 1	Att. 7,500
Hare(2)		
1909, Division 2.		
Burnley 2	Blues 0	Att. 5,000
1920, Division 2.		
Leicester City 3	Blues 0	Att. 17,000
1926, Division 1.		
Blues 2	Bury 2	Att. 23,984
Briggs(2)		
1937, Division 1.		
Preston North End 2	Blues 1	Att. 25,000
	White	
1943, Wartime.		
Blues 1	Northampton Town 3	
Gee		
1946, Division 2.		
Blues 1	WBA 0	Att. 50,535
Dearson		
1948, Division 1.		
Blues 2	Stoke City 1	Att. 49,800
Harris, Dougall		
1954, Division 2.		
Blues 1	Bury 3	Att. 22,000
Lane 32	Clarke 9, 54	
	Fletcher 86	
1961, League Cup 1st round.		
Swindon Town 2	Blues 0	Att. 13,063
Morgan 25		
Hunt 48		

Swindon play the second half with ten men when Smith, their centre forward is injured.

1963, League Cup 2nd round.		
Norwich City 2	Blues 0	Att. 16,714
Mannion 28		
Allcock 85		

Blues played the whole game with virtually ten men due to Leek's injury after 15 seconds.

1965, Division 2.		
Bolton Wanderers 1	Blues 2	Att. 11,925
Hill 75	Thomson 1	
	Vowden 42	
1971, Division 2.		
Blackpool 1	Blues 1	Att. 22,160
Suddick 41	Francis 17	
1974, Division 1.		
West Ham United 3	Blues 0	Att. 29,495
Paddon 44		
Jennings 64		
Robson 80		

Bob Hatton had a 63rd minute goal disallowed for Blues.

1976, Division 1.		
Coventry City 2	Blues 1	Att. 25,989
Green 23	Burns 32	
Yorath 86		
1982, Division 1.		
Brighton & Hove A. 1	Blues 0	Att. 9,845
Gatting 69		
1984, League Cup 2nd round, 1st leg.		
Blues 4	Plymouth Argyle 1	Att. 7,964
Clarke 39	Staniforth 37	
Hopkins 61		
Harford 66		
Rees 86		
1991, League Cup 2nd round, 1st leg.		
Luton Town 2	Blues 2	Att. 6,315
Gray 48	Rodgerson 3	
Nogan 83	Gleghorn 59	

Blues 100th League Cup tie

1993, Division 1.		
Blues 1	Luton Town 1	Att. 11,081
Shutt 32	Telfer 77	
1999, Division 1.		
Blues 2	QPR 0	Att. 18,748
Furlong 45, 63(2 pens)		

September 26

The Matches played on this day
1891, Football Alliance.
Blues 4   Lincoln City 0   Att. 2,000
Wheldon(3), Brown
1896, Division 2.
Burton Swifts 1   Blues 1   Att. 2,000
                       Inglis
1903, Division 1.
Middlesbrough 3   Blues 1   .Att. 20,000
                       Howard
1908, Division 2.
Blues 2   Burnley 0   Att. 20,000
Fairman, W.H.Jones
1914, Division 2.
Blues 1   Wolverhampton W. 2   Att. 20,000
Gibson
1925, Division 1.
Blues 3   WBA 0   Att. 34,850
Islip(2), Briggs
1931, Division 1.
Blackburn Rovers 1   Blues 2   Att. 10,000
                       Bradford, Jones(og)
1936, Division 1.
Blues 2   Grimsby Town 3   Att. 20,000
Jones, Harris
1942, Wartime.
Northampton Town 4   Blues 1
                       Ottewell
1953, Division 2.
West Ham United 1   Blues 2   Att. 30,000
Newman(og) 28   Purdon 65
                       Kinsey 72
1959, Division 1.
Burnley 3   Blues 1   Att. 23,471
Pointer 10   Orritt 60
McIlroy 73
Connelly 89
1962, League Cup 2nd round.
Blues 5   Doncaster Rovers 0   Att. 11,361
Harris 44
Leek 46, 75
Bloomfield 70
Auld 81
1964, Division 1.
Blues 3   Everton 5   Att. 21,240
Leek 49   Scott 27, 52
Hellawell 55   Pickering 35, 44
Hennessey 71   Morrissey 47
1967, Division 2.
Blues 6   Middlesbrough 1   Att. 28,885
Pickering 7, 76   Crossan 56
Vowden 32
Beard 43(pen)
Bridges 52
Vincent 75
For the second time this season Blues hit six goals in a game
under floodlights.
1970, Division 2.
Blues 1   Charlton Athletic 1   Att. 20,767
Summerill 71   Plumb 52
1972, Division 1.
Arsenal 2   Blues 0   Att. 30,003
Storey 10
George 70
1979, League Cup 3rd round.
Blues 1   Exeter City 2   Att. 13,669
Ainscow 65   Neville 47, 59
1981, Division 1.
Aston Villa 0   Blues 0   Att. 40,763
1987, Division 2.
Plymouth Argyle 1   Blues 1   Att. 8,912
Tynan 10   McElhinney(og) 43
1989, Division 3.
Blues 2   Walsall 0   Att. 10,834
Bailey 28(pen)
Tait 90
1998, Division 1.
Norwich City 2   Blues 0   Att. 16,584
Bellamy 79
Roberts 88
2000, League Cup 2nd round, 2nd leg.
Blues 1   Wycombe Wanderers 0   Att. 8,960
Ndlovu 66
Blues won 5-3 on aggregate
2001, Division 1.
Watford 3   Blues 3   Att. 13,099
Smith 9   Hughes 4
Cox 30   Horsfield 47
Glass 73   Grainger 85

Playing record for this day

Playing record for this day is...23 games, Won 9, Drawn 5, Lost 9, GF 43, GA 35.
Today's success rate....50% Year ranking....145th

Match of the Day
FROM 1967

BLUES BURY BORO'
Super exhibition from the Blues in goal rampage

A crowd of 28,885, Blues' second largest of the season, saw this resounding win over Middlesbrough. Ray Martin was in the side, replacing the injured Colin Green, while Bert Murray, Johnny Vincent and Trevor Hockey dominated the midfield supply area in a team superbly led by Ron Wylie.
The first goal for Blues came in the seventh minute, the result of a lovely move between Wylie and Murray. Murray came pushing down the touchline, interpassed with Wylie, and sent the ball waist-high into the middle. Pickering did not connect properly, but his touch was sufficient enough to beat McPartland.
Vowden had an attempt saved in the 24th minute, and Herriot then cleared a Middlesbrough try with a header that almost reached the halfway line. Another two attempts from Vowden were saved, until he finally beat McPartland after 32 minutes, connecting with a cross from Hockey.
Two minutes before half time Blues won a penalty, after Hockey had raced onto a long goal kick from Herriot. Hockey was tackled and, although the offence was unclear, the penalty was given and taken by Beard who netted with ease.
Middlesbrough almost pulled a goal back a minute later, but O'Rourke's header hit the post. Blues got their fourth goal on 52 minutes when Bridges picked up Wylie's free kick and hammered the ball under the Middlesbrough goalkeeper from 30 yards.
Blues kept up the pressure and it was a surprise when Crossan drove past Herriot on 56 minutes to score for MIddlesbrough.
Just 15 minutes before the end Vincent took full advantage of a mistake by Worthington and smashed the ball past McPartland into the net.
The final goal came just one minute later from Pickering, slipping in a cross from Hockey and rounding off a match in which, there was only ever going to be one team in it.

BIRMINGHAM CITY
Herriot, Murray, Martin, Wylie, Page, Beard, Bridges, Vincent, Pickering, Vowden, Hockey.
MIDDLESBROUGH;
McPartland, Hickton, Gates, Crossan, Worthington, Horner, Kear, McMordie, O'Rourke, Horsfield, Lawson.

REFEREE
Mr Maurice Fussey

1904

Playing record for this day

Playing record for this day is...19 games, Won 7, Drawn 6, Lost 6, GF 31, GA 31.

Today's success rate....52.63% Year ranking....133rd

Match of the Day

FROM 1961

ALL TO PLAY FOR IN ROME

European final ends all square at St Andrews

21,005 fans filed into St Andrews to see the first leg of the Inter Cities Fairs Cup against Roma. Blues started on the attack early in the first half, with attempts from Bloomfield and Hennessey just a little off target. The Roma 'keeper, standing at over six feet, was a great presence in the goalmouth and it was his skill and agility which kept Blues' scoring down to a bare minimum. Auld in the Blues attack was on particularly good form for this game. Hellawell put in a fine shot across the goal, but it posed no real threat and went to safety. The Italian side had a tough job on their hands, and found it hard to break through the strong Blues midfield consisting of Beard, Foster and Hennessey. Blues stood strong, but their efforts could not hold Roma forever. Orlando was fouled but he evaded Sissons in defence to send the ball across goal to Manfredini, who put the ball into the back of the net in the 30th minute.

The second half started with Blues attacking with the same enthusiasm which began the first period. Second attempts were sent across the goalmouth before being swept away out of danger. The Italians seemed to have slowed down in attack, so it was a wake-up call for Blues when they managed to slip through to score a second goal. Menichelli made an attempt at goal, but it was cleared by Beard, only to bounce to Manfredini who again sent the ball over the line with ease.

Blues were determined not to give in easily and put up a gallant fight, giving Cudicini in the Roma goal a heavy workout. Blues spent a good 15 minutes raining attempts on the keeper, and some of the saves he pulled off were outstanding. The scoreline showed Blues the cold hard fact that they were two goals down, with just ten more minutes of play remaining. Hellawell then had a go at goal himself and this time Cudicini was well beaten by his shot. Blues took advantage and stepped up their attacks. Harris watched his shot bounce off the crossbar, and rebound to Orritt who won back possession. He sent the ball goalwards from close range and it went over the line for the equaliser.

BIRMINGHAM CITY

Schofield, Farmer, Sissons, Hennessey, Foster, Beard, Hellawell, Bloomfield, Harris, Orritt, Auld.

AS ROMA

Cudicini, Fontana, Corsini, Giuliano, Losi, Carpanesi, Orlando, Da Costa, Manfredini, Angelillo, Menichelli.

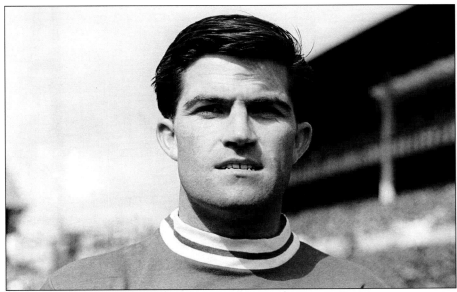

Bertie Auld

Blues news extra   1879...First game against the Villa

Billed a 'friendly' these two rivals met at Blues' Muntz Street ground for their first game together. Blues won the game by a hotly disputed goal to nil. The Villa players and officials complained bitterly about the pitch after describing the surface as only fit for pot holing.

1941...Friendly Blues 2 RAF XI Oling.

Birthdays

Scott Hiley born today in 1968

The Matches played on this day

1890, Football Alliance.

Grimsby Town 3	Blues 1	Att. 2,000
	Jenkyns	

1902, Division 2.

Blues 3	Preston North End 1	Att. 10,000
Leonard, McMillan, Wigmore		

1913, Division 2.

Wolverhampton W. 1	Blues 0	Att. 16,000

1919, Division 2.

Blues 4	Huddersfield Town 2	Att. 16,000
Elkes(2), Whitehouse, Burkinshaw		

Jack Elkes scored twice on his league debut.

1924, Division 1.

Blues 1	Burnley 0	Att. 20,000
Cringan		

1930, Division 1.

Blues 2	Arsenal 4	Att. 31,693
Briggs, Roberts(og)		

1947, Division 2.

Leeds United 0	Blues 1	Att. 37,135
	Trigg	

1952, Division 2.

Blues 2	Southampton 0	Att. 22,000
Rowley 27, 85		

1958, Division 1.

Blues 4	Leicester City 2	Att. 33,291
Gordon 13	Kelly 35, 42	
Murphy 56(pen) 78		
Hooper 89		

Johnny Gordon scored just 13 minutes into his debut with his first shot on goal.

1961, Inter Cities Fairs Cup Final, 1st leg.

Blues 2	AS Roma 2	Att. 21,005
Hellawell 80	Manfredini 30, 62	
Orritt 87		

1966, Division 2.

Blues 0	Plymouth Argyle 0	Att. 18,313

1969, Division 2.

Blues 1	Carlisle United 1	Att. 28,765
Summerill 37	Balderstone 77(pen)	

1975, Division 1.

Aston Villa 2	Blues 1	Att. 53,782
Hamilton 51	Francis 12	
Little 70		

This game screened by ATV's Star Soccer

1980, Division 1.

Norwich City 2	Blues 2	Att. 13,801
Padden 17	Ainscow 25	
Fashanu 41	Worthington 70	

1986, Division 2.

Blues 2	Ipswich Town 2	Att. 7,227
Clarke 55, 81	Brennan 45	
	Wilson 58	

Ipswich's Chris O'Donnell sent off after 20 minutes

1988, League Cup 2nd round, 1st leg.

Blues 0	Aston Villa 2	Att. 21,177
	Gage 6	
	A.Gray 45	

1992, Division 1.

Blues 0	Wolverhampton W. 4	Att. 14,391
	Roberts 14, 39, 45	
	Downing 42	

1994, Auto Windscreens Shield 1st round.

Peterborough Utd 3	Blues 5	Att. 2,044
Henry 1	Bull 10	
Brissett 28	Dominguez 30	
Charlery 70	Hunt 44, 65, 72	

Jonathon Hunt became the first Blues player to score a hat-trick since David Geddis, nine years ago. Blues keeper Ryan Price conceded a goal one minute into his debut. Future Blues forward Ken Charlery scored for the Posh

1997, Division 1.

Sheffield United 0	Blues 0	Att. 20,553

Blues defender Darren Wassall sent off.

Blues 'keeper Ian Bennett saved the 85th minute spot kick.

September 28

Playing record for this day
Playing record for this day is...17 games, Won 8, Drawn 2, Lost 7, GF 38, GA 36.
Today's success rate....52.94% Year ranking....127th

The Matches played on this day

1895, Division 1.

Blues 1	Bolton Wanderers 2	Att. 4,500
Mobley		

1901, Division 1.

Liverpool 3	Blues 1	Att. 20,000
	McMillan	

1907, Division 1.

Liverpool 3	Blues 4	Att. 20,000
	Green, Mounteney(2), Eyre	

1912, Division 2.

Blues 1	Stockport County 1	Att. 20,000
Hall		

1918, Wartime.

Blues 4	Leeds City 2	
J.Godfrey(2),		
Davies, Whitehouse		

1929, Division 1.

Blackburn Rovers 7	Blues 5	Att. 25,000
	Bradford(3), Crosbie(2)	

Syd Puddefoot scored four for Blackburn
Joe Bradford's hat trick was his second in successive games.

1935, Division 1.

Blackburn Rovers 1	Blues 2	Att. 12,000
	Jones, Harris	

1940, Wartime.

WBA 1	Blues 2	
	Dearson, Eastham	

1946, Division 2.

Southampton 1	Blues 0	Att. 24,920

First league meeting v Southampton.

1957, Division 1.

Sheffield Wed. 5	Blues 3	Att. 20,311
Smith(og) 10	Orritt 21, 55	
Quixall 63, 66	Murphy 89	
Ellis 84, 86		

1963, Division 1.

Sheffield Wed. 2	Blues 1	Att. 18,903
Fantham 59	Thomson 89	
Holliday 82		

Blues' Alex Harvey sent off on 62 minutes.
Bobby Thompson scored on his debut for Blues.

1968, Division 2.

Carlisle United 2	Blues 3	Att. 7,632
McVitie 57	Greenhoff 53	
Murray 73	Summerill 68	
	Green 85	

1971, Division 2.

Blues 4	Watford 1	Att. 28,095
B.Latchford 23,	McGettigan 38	
24, 48		
Francis 62		

Bob Latchford's hat-trick was the 100th scored by a Blues player in the club's history.

1974, Division 1.

Blues 3	Arsenal 1	Att. 25,584
Burns 21	George 70	
Hatton 44, 71		

1985, Division 1.

QPR 3	Blues 1	Att. 10,911
Rosenior 7	Armstrong 17	
Bannister 18		
Dawes 56		

1991, Division 3.

Blues 3	Preston North End 1	Att. 8,760
Matthewson 34	Shaw 44	
Gleghorn 71		
Rodgerson 79		

1996, Division 1.

Blues 0	QPR 0	Att. 17,430

Match of the Day

FROM 1974

BLUES SLIP IN TO WIN
Poor conditions at St Andrews don't stop goals

Very heavy rain preceded this game, and the quality of the playong surface was affected by this. Indeed it was stil raining as the match kicked off, with the conditions lowering the attendance somewhat.

Early in the game Blues had a couple of attacks on goal, whilst Arsenal seemed to favour midfield. However this didn't stop Kidd, gaining possession after five minutes, trying to take advantage of Latchford's absence from his line. Luckily for Blues, Gallagher was on hand to tackle the striker and clear the ball. Also for Arsenal, George had a shot on target from 19 yards which curled just around the upright.

After ten minutes, the home team were able to mount a more serious attack on goal with Hatton making a good attempt, but just failing to break through. Campbell then tried to fire in a right-footed shot, but Rimmer managed to force it away with a dive which brought about a corner. The kick was taken and Burns got his head to the ball, but it was collected by Rimmer at the far post.

The play was now beginning to become predictable. On 21 minutes Pendrey supplied the ball to Campbell, who knocked it on for Styles. He then pushed it forwards to Francis who evaded the Arsenal defence to put in a lovely cross for Burns, who in turn headed it into the net, just inside the left-hand post. Arsenal goalkeeper Rimmer tried too hard to stop the shot, and as a result he smashed into the upright and needed a lengthy spell of attention before he was fit to carry on.

Ball almost equalised for Arsenal after 29 minutes, and then again a few minutes later when his header struck the crossbar and bounced to safety. Francis took his turn at trying for a goal, but it was saved by Rimmer, then at the opposite end it was George who tried next, but he shot too high and the ball went out. Then Matthews was booked on 32 minutes for a tackle on Taylor which left him flat out on the ground. Rimmer was getting a real work-out, having to make diving saves from a 25-yard shot by Francis, and a first-time shot by Taylor who had now fully recovered.

Injury time in the first half saw Blues finally getting the all-important second goal. Hatton ran through and passed to Taylor, who shot towards goal before Hatton slipped in to ensure its journey over the line.

The second half began with Kendall needing treatment for an injury to his leg, and straight after a knock to his ankle meant that he continued to limp. On 65 minutes Radford was booked for dissent, and it was beginning to look like Blues would settle for their 2-0 score. Then after 75 minutes they were punished for complacency. Martin made a mistake in his own half allowing Brady to gain possession and nudge it forward for George to slide into the net past Latchford who had come off his line. The goal spurred Blues into action, and they regained their two-goal advantage within a minute. A poor back-pass to Rimmer enabled Blues' number 10 Hatton to grab hold of the ball, evade the defence and roll it over the line.

BIRMINGHAM CITY
Latchford, Martin, Styles, Kendall, Gallagher, Pendrey, Campbell, Francis, Burns, Hatton, Taylor.
ARSENAL
Rimmer, Storey, Simpson, Kelly, Blockley, Matthews, George, Ball, Radford, Kidd, Brady.

REFEREE
Mr E Jolley (Manchester)

Bob Hatton

Birthdays

Bobby Hope born today in 1943   Ted McMinn born today in 1962   Guy Russell born today in 1967
Nico Vaesen born today in 1969.

Playing record for this day

Playing record for this day is...19 games, Won 5, Drawn 9, Lost 5, GF 27, GA 29.

Today's success rate....50% Year ranking....165th

Match of the Day

FROM 1992

ITALIAN JOB WELL DONE

Blues Sale to a draw and go into next round

3,102 trooped into St Andrews to watch this preliminary round tie in the Anglo-Italian Cup against Cambridge United. The last time Blues were in the same competition was back in 1971.

Terry Cooper had strengthened his back four with 6ft 3in defender Martin Hicks, while goalkeeper Martin Thomas was back in the squad after 11 months on the sidelines, and was thrown in at the deep end.

The Blues defence failed to stop a header from Lee Philpott after he connected with a pass by Devon White on the right. A surprised Thomas was left to pick the ball up from the back of the net after just 19 seconds.

Pride was restored for Blues when the equaliser arrived after 15 minutes, beginning with Ian Rodgerson who was starting his first match in five weeks. He picked up a loose ball and crossed to Nigel Gleghorn, who knocked it down for Louie Donowa to ram into the back of the net.

With ten minutes to go before the half-time break, Cambridge again pulled into the lead. A super volley from Paul Raynor went straight into the goal, and the game looked to be going their way. The second half didn't alter things and on 60 minutes, Raynor took another free kick from the left touchline and crossed the ball to Tony Dennis who threw himself at the ball and headed it into the net to put Cambridge two goals ahead. With 19 minutes to go Frain beat the offside trap and got onto a long clearance by Thomas. He chipped a shot which, although parried by the visitors 'keeper, had enough life to roll over the line.

A header from Donowa went just wide of the post, but Blues' remained determined. They kept heart, and when Mark Sale came on as substitute for Tait on 85 minutes it gave the team fresh hope.

It took Sale just three minutes to make his mark on the match. Donowa sent a low cross to Frain, who made an attempt at goal. Sheffield got a hand to it, but could only parry it. The ball flew to Sale who made sure that he did not miss. The draw gave Blues the vital point they needed to move into the international stages of the competition.

BIRMINGHAM CITY

Thomas, Clarkson, Frain, Matthewson, Hicks, Rogers, Rodgerson, Tait (Sale), Donowa, Gleghorn, Sturridge (Rowbotham).

CAMBRIDGE UNITED

Sheffield, Fensome, Kimble, Dennis, Chapple, Daish, Raynor, Leadbitter, White, Cheetham, Philpott.

REFEREE

Mr R Groves (Weston-Super-Mare)

John Frain

Birthdays

Richard Scott born today in 1974   **John Deakin born today in 1966**

The Matches played on this day

1893, Division 2.		
Ardwick 0	Blues 1	Att. 5,000
	Wheldon	

1899, Division 2.		
Blues 0	Bolton Wanderers 0	Att. 12,000

1905, Division 1.		
Blues 2	Sheffield United 0	Att. 15,000
Wilcox, Mounteney		

1911, Division 2.		
Blues 4	Leeds City 3	Att. 10,000
Hall(4)		

1916, Wartime.		
Chesterfield 0	Blues 3	
	Montgomery, Mercer, Roulson(pen)	

1922, Division 1.		
Blues 2	Bolton Wanderers 0	Att. 25,000
Bradford(2)		

1933, Division 1.		
Blues 4	Leeds United 0	Att. 21,566
Bradford, Grosvenor,		
S.J.Smith, Cutis		

1944, Wartime.		
Blues 3	Leicester City 3	
Mulraney(2), Trigg		

1950, Division 2.		
Chesterfield 1	Blues 1	Att. 12,309
Marriott 68	Trigg 25	

1961, Division 1.		
Blues 2	Bolton Wanderers 1	Att. 17,192
Auld 28	Stevens 88	
Bloomfield 34		

1964, Division 1.		
Wolverhampton W. 0	Blues 2	Att. 22,000
	Lynn 25	
	Leek 40	

1967, Division 2.		
Blues 2	Millwall 3	Att. 30,576
Pickering 15	Weller 70, 90	
Vincent 52	Wilson 89	

The half-time entertainment consisted of models in mini skirts promoting the new High Street fashion boutique by the name of "Fannys"!!

1972, Division 1.		
West Ham United 2	Blues 0	Att. 26,482
Bonds 3		
Best 67		

Alan Campbell's 24th minute penalty was saved by West Ham 'keeper Grotier.

1978, Division 1.		
Leeds United 3	Blues 0	Att. 23,331
Flynn 38		
Gray 53(pen)		
Hankin 76		

Blues 'keeper Jim Montgomery played his 600th professional game.

1987, Division 2.		
WBA 3	Blues 1	Att. 15,399
Palmer 15	Kennedy 73	
Gray 49		
Singleton 86		

1989, Division 3.		
Blackpool 3	Blues 2	Att. 5,737
Overson(og) 23	Sturridge 9	
Garner 31	Gleghorn 85	
Gabbiadini 83		

1995, Division 1.		
Blues 0	Oldham Athletic 0	Att. 17,264

Playing record for this day

Playing record for this day is...17 games, Won 8, Drawn 4, Lost 5, GF 29, GA 22.

Today's success rate....58.82% Year ranking....65th

Match of the Day
FROM 1964
BAD SHOW FROM WOLVES
Supporters angry at Directors for another loss

Wolves started out quite well, almost looking like they would get the first goal, but Blues soon made up for lost time, mounting a counter-attack to beat them all. Schofield suffered a kick in the face from one of his team-mates, and Lynn earned himself a telling off from the referee. The Wolves supporters took a distinct dislike to Lynn after he gave Buckley, in his first senior game, a hard time. Each time Lynn touched the ball boos and catcalls were heard from the home crowd, but it didn't stop the determination of the Blues right back. In the 25th minute he scored the first goal for Blues, and his fifth of the season. Jackson was felled in the penalty area and Blues appealed for a spot kick. However the referee awarded an indirect free kick. The Wolves defence took their place in the area, but it wasn't enough to prevent the shot from Leek making its way to Lynn, who nudged it into the net.

This threw Wolves into disarray. The next action came in the 40th minute when a corner kick from Broadbent fell to Leek who took a long-distance shot which was perfectly aimed and beat Wolves goalkeeper Davies with no problem at all. This was the last real chance that Blues had on goal, and it was not long before Wolves started to respond. After early clashes, which Foster had not been involved in, the Blues centre half was sent off when he crossed paths with Knowles.

With the Blues team depleted Wolves decided now was the time to come in for the attack. It was too late, however, and Schofield had only one good save to make to keep the ball out.

The home team had now lost nine games out of 11, and the Wolves supporters vented their feelings at the management and directors.

WOLVERHAMPTON WANDERERS

Davies, Showell, Thomson, Goodwin, Flowers, Woodruff, Wharton, Broadbent, Galley, Knowles, Buckley.

BIRMINGHAM CITY;

Schofield, Lynn, Martin, Hennessey, Foster, Beard, Hellawell, Jackson, Thomson, Leek, Auld.

REFEREE

Mr K Dagnall (Bolton)

Stan Lynn

Birthdays

Trevor Morgan born today in 1956

Playing record for this day

Playing record for this day.... 18 games, Won 5, Drawn 8, Lost 5, GF 27, GA 26.
Success rate...50% Year ranking....157th

Match of the Day

FROM 1955

BROWN MAKES AMENDS FOR MISSED CHANCES

Spurs hammered but escape with a 3-0 defeat

Blues made one change from their 2-0 defeat at Charlton, with Ken Green coming in at right back in place of the injured Jeff Hall. Struggling Tottenham were also forced to make a change when Baily reported unfit and Harmer was given his debut in midfield to cover. Meanwhile captaining the Spurs side for this game was former Villa defender Danny Blanchflower. A crowd of 31,320 were at St Andrews expecting a home victory despite Blues record of just two wins in their opening ten league games.

Blues took the lead in the 18th minute when Govan managed to outpace Blanchflower and cross from the byline and the unfortunate Clarke trying desperately to clear only managed to head into his own net. Shortly afterwards Spurs broke through Stokes who had Robb on his left unmarked in the Blues penalty area, but he overhit his pass and the simple chance went begging. In a scrappy first half these were the only two highlights. Straight after the break Brown wasted an excellent chance to double Blues lead when blazing over from Lane's header inside the area. Moments later Lane was guilty of missing when presented with a great chance. When Tottenham countered they found Merrick in great form, a move started by Harmer and finished by Robb, producing a superhuman stop by the 'keeper. Blues were unlucky not to get a second goal after 69 minutes when a shot from Lane on the edge of the area struck the crossbar. A minute later Govan provided Brown with the simplest chance of the game but somehow he shot straight at Ditchburn. The rebound went out to Lane 20 yards out who sliced his kick across the area and out for a throw in. Brown made amends for his earlier misses when heading in from Govan with 15 minutes of the game left, and Blues wrapped up the points with a third from Murphy just a minute from time after good work again by the Scottish winger.

BIRMINGHAM CITY

Merrick, Green, Badham, Boyd, Smith, Warhurst, Astall, Lane, Brown, Murphy, Govan.

TOTTENHAM HOTSPUR

Ditchburn, Hopkins, Withers, Marchi, Clarke, Blanchflower, Robb, Harmer, Stokes, Brooks, Walters.

REFEREE

Mr RP Hartley (Burnley)

Trevor Smith

Blues news extra   1980...Friendly. Blues 0 Tampa Bay Rowdies 0

Birthdays

Paul Furlong born today 1968.   **Danny Hill born today 1974.**   **John Sheridan born today 1964.**

The Matches played on this day

1892, Division 2.

Blues 2	Grimsby Town 3	Att. 3,000

Wheldon(2)

First league meeting v Grimsby.

1904, Division 1.

Preston North End 2	Blues 2	Att. 8,000
	Wilcox, McRoberts.	

1910, Division 2.

Leeds City 1	Blues 1	Att. 8,000
	Bonthron(pen)	

1921, Division 1.

Blues 1	Sunderland 0	Att. 30,000

Whitehouse

1927, Division 1.

Blues 1	Bolton Wanderers 1	Att. 12,000

Harris

1932, Division 1.

Leeds United 1	Blues 1	Att. 14,193
	Thorogood.	

1938, Division 1.

Charlton Athletic 4	Blues 4	Att 20,000
	Harris(2), Duckhouse, White	

The game was attended by guest of honour Prime Minister Neville Chamberlain a day after his meeting with German Chancellor Adolf Hitler where he made the "Peace in our time" speech.

Blues staged a remarkable come back after going 3-0 down to a Jonathon Wilkinson hat-trick within 30 minutes, to level at 3-3 by half time.

1949, Division 1.

Blues 0	Bolton Wanderers 0	Att. 25,000

1955, Division 1.

Blues 3	Tottenham Hotspur 0	Att. 31,320

Clarke(og) 16
Brown 75
Murphy 90

1957, Division 1.

WBA 0	Blues 0	Att. 39,909

1960, Division 1.

Manchester City 2	Blues 1	Att. 27,665
Law 9	Singer 73	
Barlow 55		

1966, Division 2.

Millwall 3	Blues 1	Att. 15,776
Julians 14	Vowden 77	
Neil 15		
Broadfoot 48		

1977. Division 1.

Aston Villa 0	Blues 1	Att. 45,436
	Bertschin 33	

This match screened by ATV's Star Soccer.

1983, Division 1.

Blues 2	Leicester City 1	Att. 15,212
Rees 41	Lineker 48	
Harford 45		

1986, Full Members Cup 1st round.

Brighton & Hove A. 0	Blues 3	Att. 3,794
	O'Regan(og) 2	
	Clarke 63	
	Kuhl 75	

Blues biggest win over Brighton.

1988, Division 2.

Blues 3	Barnsley 5	Att. 4,892
Langley 56	Beresford 24	
Robinson 59	Broddle 26	
Atkins 89	Currie 58	
	Rees 70	
	Lowndes 89	

1994, Division 2.

Wrexham 1	Blues 1	Att. 6,002
Connolly 39	Claridge 88	

2000, Division 1.

Watford 2	Blues 0	Att. 12,335
Nielsen 57		
Cox 76		

October 2

Playing record for this day

Playing record for this day.... 18 games, Won 3, Drawn 9, Lost 6, GF 27, GA 23.

Success rate...41.67% Year ranking....221th

Match of the Day
FROM 1976
DERBY SCALDED BY BURNS
King Kenny hits four as Blues run riot aginst the Rams

In the week running up to the game a local sports shop owner and Blues fan offered a reward of a £3,000 TR7 sports car to the player netting a sixth goal during any Blues fixture. The feat had not been achieved since January 1972 when Portsmouth were beaten 6-3 at St Andrews in a Division Two fixture. Little did the 29,190 crowd expect the car to be claimed within days of being offered, but it came mighty close.

Derby's weakened team helped. Both Roy McFarland and Kevin Hector failed fitness tests, while influential sweeper Colin Todd had rocked the club by handing in a transfer request. Blues had one injury problem in midfielder Howard Kendall, so Calderwood was called up to cover for the second successive game.

Heavy rain had left a difficult pitch and Blues soon took advantage on eight minutes when Burns headed in a deep centre from Gary Jones. Moments later a deft back-heel by Francis sent Calderwood clear and his cross-shot came back off the post to Burns, who slipped when following in and as a result the ball cleared the bar. He made amends on 22 minutes after Francis and Hibbitt had linked well. Burns burst through, taking out a defender and the 'keeper as he chased across the area. He turned the ball in and, despite a sliding lunge from Thomas, the ball rolled into the corner.

Burns completed his hat-trick just nine minutes later, stabbing home a Francis cross from close range. The crowd responded with "We want six", acknowledging the car was within reach. However the only addition to the score was for the visitors. A Leighton James effort was deflected by Page and it spun under Latchford's despairing dive two minutes before the break.

It was Derby who started stronger in the second half with two great chances. Page this time blocked Nish's shot which went over the bar. Then Nish again found a good position in the Blues area, only to have his effort cleared off the line by Styles. Blues weathered the storm and on 70 minutes got a fourth, again from Burns. He took advantage of hesitancy betwen keeper Moseley and Daniel to nip in and slide the ball into an unguarded net. With three minutes remaining Connolly beat off three Derby defenders to curl in a left-foot shot. Unfortunately Blues were beaten for time to go for the sixth and car-winning goal.

BIRMINGHAM CITY
Latchford, Page, Styles, Calderwood, Gallagher (Pendrey), Want, Jones, Francis, Burns, Hibbitt, Connolly.
DERBY COUNTY
Moseley, Thomas, Nish, Rioch, Daniel, Todd (King), Newton, Gemmill, George, Macken, James.

Blues news extra   1955...First cap for Jeff Hall. Denmark 1 England 5
Blues full back Jeff Hall made his England debut in Copenhagen. This was England's first win against the Danes. Bristol Rover's Geoff Bradford, also on his debut, got England's fifth in the 82nd minute.

Blues news extra   1965...Blues pair in Welsh line up Wales 0 England 0
Colin Green won his third cap as a Blues player, and Terry Hennessey his 15th cap. They helped Wales to a keenly fought draw at Ninian Park, Cardiff.

Birthdays
Micky Bullock born today 1946.

Playing record for this day

Playing record for this day.... 19 games, Won 8, Drawn 5, Lost 6, GF 33, GA 30.
Success rate....55.26% Year ranking....102nd

Match of the Day
FROM 1972
CUP JOY FOR ROYAL BLUES

Barry error proves the winner as Blues through to round four

Coventry suffered from their decision not to include transfer-listed Blockley in the team as Blues took full advantage of his absence and strode to victory in this League Cup tie. In front of a relatively small crowd of 27,803, Coventry played less confidently without the defensive strongman and had little potential for scoring throughout the game.

Blues took the lead on just two minutes when Francis slipped through an opening in front of goal and pushed in a superb goal. Coventry were already beginning to regret leaving out Blockley, and this increased when his replacement Barry got on to a centre from Burns and headed the ball into his own net on 34 minutes.

With just over a third of the game gone, Blues were two goals up and confident of the win. However at the start of the second half the game took a turnaround. Alderson began shooting at goal, and his efforts paid off when a shot eventually beat Dave Latchford, bringing the score to 2-1. Machin almost brought the scores level when his long-range effort hit the woodwork, and Alderson's attempt also failed to hit the target. Summerill for Blues, appearing in his first senior game since January, tried hard to increase the lead and almost succeeded towards the end of the match.

BIRMINGHAM CITY
Dave Latchford, Martin, Want, Campbell, Hynd, Page, Burns, Francis, Bob Latchford, Pendrey, Summerill.
COVENTRY CITY
Glazier, Coop, Cattlin, Machin, Barry, Parker, Mortimer, Smith, Rafferty, Carr, Anderson.

Ray Martin

Blues news extra   1962...First cap for Mike Hellawell. England 1 France 1
Birmingham City winger Mike Hellawell got England's European Championship qualifiers off to a good start with a well earned point against the French at Bramall Lane, Sheffield.

Birthdays
Mick Ferguson born today 1954.   Richard Forsyth born today 1970.

October 4

Playing record for this day
Playing record for this day.... 19 games, Won 6, Drawn 6, Lost 7, GF 26, GA 22.
Success rate...47.37% Year ranking....178th

The Matches played on this day

1890, FA Cup 1st qualifying round.		
Blues 8	Hednesford Town 0	Att. 1,500
Wheldon(3), Hallam,		
W.Devy(2), Jenkyns,		
Webster(og)		
1902, Division 2.		
Burslem Port Vale 2	Blues 2	Att. 3,000
	McMillan, Athersmith	
1913, Division 2.		
Blues 1	Hull City 1	Att. 14,000
Hastings		
1919, Division 2.		
Huddersfield Town 0	Blues 0	Att. 5,000
1924, Division 1.		
Leeds United 0	Blues 1	Att. 24,000
	Islip	
1930, Division 1.		
Blackburn Rovers 2	Blues 1	Att. 15,000
	Horsman	
1947, Division 2.		
Blues 3	Fulham 1	Att. 40,000
Bodle, Trigg(2)		
Harold Bodle scored on his 27th birthday.		
1952, Division 2.		
Bury 3	Blues 0	Att. 16,069
Plant 41, 42		
Dale 78		
1958, Division 1.		
Everton 3	Blues 1	Att. 38,408
J.Harris 49	Murphy 59	
Hickson 55, 72		
1966, League Cup 3rd round.		
Blues 2	Ipswich Town 1	Att. 15,116
Beard(pen) 32	Crawford 80	
Hockey 45		
1969, Division 2.		
Bristol City 2	Blues 0	Att. 18,706
Garland 85		
Galley 87		
1975, Division 1.		
Blues 2	Sheffield United 0	Att. 26,121
Hatton 16		
Francis 76		
1977, Division 1.		
Blues 2	QPR 1	Att. 21,304
Francis 41, 43	Masson 13	
1980, Division 1.		
Wolverhampton W. 1	Blues 0	Att. 22,777
Richards 42		
1986, Division 2.		
Blues 1	Barnsley 1	Att. 6,427
Kennedy 59	Foreman 45	
1988, Division 2.		
Blues 0	Plymouth Argyle 1	Att. 4,921
	Tynan 76	
1989, League Cup 2nd round, 2nd leg.		
West Ham United 1	Blues 1	Att. 12,187
Dicks 53	Atkins 71	
Blues lost 2-1 on aggregate		
1994, League Cup 2nd round, 2nd leg.		
Blues 1	Blackburn Rovers 1	Att. 16,275
McGavin 10	Sutton 71	
Blues lost 3-1 on aggregate		
1997, Division 1.		
Blues 0	Crewe Alexandra 1	Att. 16,648
	Rivers 58	

Match of the Day

FROM 1977

WHAT A KNIGHT, SIR ALF'S FINE RUN CONTINUES

Fourth win in five now for caretaker boss, after super Francis double

Two goals by Trevor Francis within 90 seconds transformed this game after QPR had taken an early lead. The goals, one poached from a dreadful 'keeping error, the other a sweetly hit shot from 25 yards, continued Blues fine run under new caretaker boss Sir Alf Ramsay. They had now taken eight points from ten since he took temporary charge in September after the departure of Willie Bell. A clearly delighted Sir Alf was however remaining coy on taking on the manager's job at St Andrews permanently, he said after the game, "I thought the team played exceptionally well particularly in the first half, and I am looking forward to the clash against Coventry on Saturday - if I am still in charge."

Blues didn't quite have things all their own way, indeed if it was not for some fine goalkeeping from Jim Montgomery they might have been well out of the game within the first quarter of an hour. The Blues 'keeper saved brilliantly from QPR centre half David Needham and then stopped Don Givens moments later with a superb point blank save. It was no surprise when the visitors took the lead with a goal from Don Masson. The ball was well worked from midfield through Busby and Eastoe, the latter finding Masson free inside the box with a fine chipped pass. He finished with a crisp low volley which gave Montgomery no chance. At this point Blues looked out of the contest completely, it was going to take a mistake or a moment of magic to get them back in the game. Who, in the 21,304 crowd would have believed Blues would get both within two minutes? That's exactly what happened. First an innocuous header by defender Shanks should have been picked up easily by Parkes without any trouble at all. The 'keeper somehow spilled the ball and it rolled out to Francis, who scored from five yards out.

The crowd hadn't yet quietened before they erupted again two minutes later after another wonder strike from their idol. Collecting a loose ball on the half way line Francis carried it forward another 20 yards, out sprinting the entire QPR defence. When he got within range he pulled back his right leg and struck the ball hard and low and it zipped off the turf and crashed into the bottom corner of Parkes goal. This time he was entirely blamless, no goalkeeper could have stopped that shot.

In the second half Francis had chances to complete his hat-trick but missed with one effort and had another brilliantly saved by Parkes, who made amends for his first half error. Blues controlled the game through their midfield led by the impressive Terry Hibbitt. The best chance of the half fell to Bertschin whose fierce left-foot drive struck a post 18 minutes from time. Rangers had chances too and they will rue the misses from Bowles and Busby in the dying minutes of the game.

BIRMINGHAM CITY
Montgomery, Calderwood, Pendrey, Page, Howard, Want, Connolly, Francis, Bertschin, Hibbitt, Emmanuel.
QUEEN'S PARK RANGERS
Parkes, Clement, Shanks, Leach, Needham, Abbott, Eastoe (Williams 73), Busby, Masson, Bowles, Givens.

Sir Alf Ransay with Brian Clough

Blues news extra 1941...Friendly. Blues 2 Aldershot Army XI 4

Birthdays
Harold Bodle born today 1920.

Playing record for this day

Playing record for this day.... 17 games, Won 7, Drawn 3, Lost 7, GF 32, GA 27.
Success rate...50% Year ranking....148th

Match of the Day
FROM 1968
GREENHOFF SUPER SHOW
Four goals and a penalty which could have been five

St Andrews was once again the setting for an amazing goal fest as the 27,318 spectators were entertained with nine goals. This was the third occasion Blues had hit five goals at home in 12 outings.

Fulham however should have scored themselves after just 45 seconds when 'keeper Jim Herriott saved well from a Frank Large header. Blues immediately broke and had the ball in the net just a minute later. Ron Wylie won it in midfield, put Vowden away and when he rolled a pass into Vincent's path the striker made no mistake with a firmly hit shot from inside the penalty area. Wylie was dominating the midfield and with 16 minutes gone he sent Greenhoff a fantastic ball to run through the Fulham defence and fire past McClelland before the 'keeper had time to move. With Blues well on top it was only a matter of time before the home crowd were celebrating again and when Dempsey gave away a corner, Vincent swung in the perfect cross for Greenhoff to thump home with a powerful header on 25 minutes. Blues went into the break comfortably on top at 3-0 with no one expecting the second half drama which was just round the corner.

It took just three minutes of the second half for Fulham to start their incredible comeback. First a cross from Barrett was headed in by Large, then a minute later a hard low cross from Kerrigan was deflected past his own 'keeper by the unfortunate Dave Robinson and the score was now 3-2. Just four minutes later, a move involving Malcom Macdonald allowed Barrett to skip past Martin and his teasing cross was met by Large who slid just in front of Herriot to squeeze the ball over the line, Fulham had levelled the score with three in a five minute burst. Blues could have panicked but they settled well and began to regain control. After 65 minutes Greenhoff sprinted clear of Matthewson only for the defender to trip him inside the box, Greenhoff took responsibility for the penalty himself but his kick rolled wide.

Greenhoff made amends just a minute later when a much firmer shot from further out went through several covering players and into the corner of the unsighted McCelland's net to regain the lead at 4-3. Fulham hit back again and on 68 minutes a cross from their tricky winger Barrett was headed in by Macdonald to level again at 4-4. The game was settled on 71 minutes when a terrible blunder handed Greenhoff an easy winner. A long ball by Vincent was dropped by the Fulham 'keeper under no pressure and the ball rolled invitingly to Greenhoff who tapped in for his fourth, Blues fifth, and the games ninth and winning goal.

BIRMINGHAM CITY
Herriot, Martin, Page, Wylie, Robinson, Beard,
Hockey, Greenhoff, Vowden, Vincent, Summerill.
FULHAM
McClelland, Pentecost, Dempsey, Matthewson, Ryan, Brown,
Callaghan, Kerrigan, Large, Macdonald, Barrett.

REFEREE
Mr J Finney (Hereford)

Blues news extra   1955...Friendly. Coventry City 2 Blues 2

Birthdays

Tim Carter born today 1967.   Paul Fitzpatrick born today 1965.

The Matches played on this day

1895, Division 1.

| Preston North End 3 | Blues 2 | Att. 2,000 |
| | Mobley(2) | |

1901, Division 1.

| Blues 3 | Newcastle United 1 | Att. 12,000 |
| Aston, McMillan, McRoberts | | |

1907, Division 1.

| Blues 1 | Middlesbrough 4 | Att. 20,000 |
| Green | | |

1912, Division 2.

| Preston North End 1 | Blues 0 | Att. 8,000 |

1918, Wartime.

| Sheffield United 1 | Blues 3 | |
| | Godfrey(3) | |

1929, Division 1.

| Blues 1 | Middlesbrough 1 | Att. 15,000 |
| Bradford | | |

1935, Division 1.

| Blues 2 | Chelsea 1 | Att. 20,000 |
| Harris, Craig(og) | | |

1940, Wartime.

| Blues 1 | WBA 3 | |
| Jones | | |

1946, Division 2.

| Blues 4 | Nottingham Forest 0 | Att. 35,000 |
| Bodle, Trigg, Edwards(2) | | |

1957, Division 1.

Blues 4	Manchester City 0	Att. 28,500
Murphy 3, 5, 53		
Brown 49		

1963, Division 1.

Blues 0	Everton 2	Att. 23,593
	Temple 22	
	Kay 69	

1968, Division 2.

Blues 5	Fulham 4	Att. 27,318
Vincent 2	Large 48, 53	
Greenhoff 16, 25,	Robinson(og) 49	
65, 71	Macdonald 68	

Jimmy Greenhoff scored four times and missed a penalty.

1974, Division 1.

Blues 1	Coventry City 2	Att. 30,282
Francis 48(pen)	Lloyd 20	
	Holmes 74	

1982, League Cup 2nd round, 1st leg.

| Shrewsbury Town 1 | Blues 1 | Att. 5,003 |
| Cross 19 | Handysides 5 | |

1983, League Cup 2nd round, 1st leg.

Derby County 0	Blues 3	Att. 13,114
	Watson(og) 17	
	Rees 38	
	Gayle 85	

1985, Division 1.

Blues 0	Sheffield Wed. 2	Att. 11,708
	Sterland 40	
	Armstrong(og) 46	

1991, Division 3.

| Shrewsbury Town 1 | Blues 1 | Att. 7,035 |
| Henry 57 | Gleghorn 34 | |

October 6

1875

Playing record for this day

Playing record for this day.... 19 games, Won 7, Drawn 6, Lost 6, GF 32, GA 29.
Success rate....52.63% Year ranking....132nd

Match of the Day
FROM 1970
3rd ROUND LEAGUE CUP
NAIL BITER

Both teams began this third round League Cup encounter at St Andrews with aggression and fervour determined to avoid a replay. But after 15 minutes of attacking moves, that all important first goal seemed as elusive as ever. Then, in the 15th minute, Forest's Cormack sent a cross in, but Hockey dived to block it, and inadvertently headed the cross firmly past Kelly into his own goal. This error of judgment spurred Blues into further attacking. Barron managed a frantic save at Summerill's feet which resulted in a corner, from which Lyons gave away a penalty by palming the ball over the bar. Summerill took the penalty kick and netted off the inside of the goalkeeper's left hand post. Despite several more attacking moves from both sides - Winfield going close for Forest with a 25 yard shot that just swerved over the bar; Vincent following this with a similar attempt at the other end and Vowden hitting wide from just ten yards - the first half ended with the same scoreline.

Blues came out at the beginning of the second half and attacked straight away, but it was Hindley's free kick that created Forest's first real danger. Hynd was knocked cold in a clash in Forest's goalmouth, and within seconds of the game resuming Thomson managed to head Hindley's rising header off the line after Kelly had been beaten. Following this with a long kick, the Forest right back contributed to Blues second goal, just seven minutes from full-time.

Summerill, catching the rebound from Hindley, managed to volley the ball home. Latchford almost managed to make it three when his last-minute header was just tipped away by the Forest goalie.

BIRMINGHAM CITY

Kelly, Thomson, Pendrey, Hockey, Hynd, Robinson Murray, Vowden, Latchford, Vincent, Summerill (Beard)

NOTTINGHAM FOREST

Barron, Hindley, Winfield, Chapman, O'Kane, Newton, Lyons, Richardson, Ingram, Cormack, Rees (Cottam)

Mike Kelly

Birthdays

Paul Sansome born today 1961.   Seamus McDonagh born today 1962.

Playing record for this day

Playing record for this day.... 18 games, Won 9, Drawn 3, Lost 6, GF 38, GA 37.
Success rate...58.33% Year ranking....75th

Match of the Day

FROM 1967
VILLAINS ARE CAUGHT

Blues hammer rivals in their own backyard in goal blitz

From the outset it looked like Blues were more likely to finish this clash the victors, and they did it with style. Villa's two new signings from Preston, Greenhalgh and Godfrey, made their presence tell and scored their two goals. Barry Stobart, a mighty presence in the side was out of the team, replaced by teenager David Rudge who was playing only his fourth senior game this season.

The crowd of 49, 984 saw the Holte End play host to its own mini battle, with both sets of fans struggling to be heard over each other.

Villa started early on the attack, but there was no successful outcome for some fine play between Godfrey and Broadbent. Then after just four minutes Villa took the lead. Wylie misjudged his kick, and sent it directly to Anderson who crossed the ball. Greenhalgh leapt unchallenged and his header crept over the line just inside the left hand post.

Herriot dropped the ball minutes later and almost gave away another goal to Villa. However, it wasn't long before Blues managed to equalise in the 21st minute. Vincent's throw in on the left went to the near post, where Vowden got his head to it and raised it for Bridges to perform the move of the game. With his back to the goal he leapt into the air and opted for a scissor-kick. He pulled it off with ease, and the ball went sailing into the net past a surprised Withers.

In the 24th minute things got very heated and resulted in a tangle between Vincent and Tindall. The referee managed to part them, and Beard came over to make sure they stayed apart while they listened to their telling off.

On the half-hour mark Villa's second goal came from their other new signing. Godfrey brought the ball through the Blues defence after a superb cross from Rudge and coolly slotted under Herriot.

Villa's joy only lasted as long as it took for Blues to be awarded a penalty on 37 minutes. Pickering's ball went to Bridges who fed it into the centre where it hit Chatterley's boot and bounced up onto his hand. He protested furiously that it was an accident, but his pleas fell on deaf ears. Beard casually stepped up to the spot and fired the shot straight into the back of the net.

At the start of the second period Pickering's attempt was saved, and Greenhalgh also missed his chance. Then Blues took the lead when Vowden got onto a ball from Vincent and shot past Withers on 59 minutes. Just two minutes later the final goal came from Bridges who slotted in a superb cross from Wylie which had sailed over the entire Villa defence. Villa almost got one back but it wasn't to be. The only other action was a booking for Tindall in the 83rd minute for a foul on Vincent.

ASTON VILLA

Withers, Bradley, Aitken, Chatterley, Sleeuwenhoek, Tindall, Rudge, Broadbent, Greenhalgh, Godfrey, Anderson (Park)

BIRMINGHAM CITY

Herriot, Murray, Green, Wylie, Page, Beard, Vincent, Pickering, Vowden, Hockey.

REFEREE

Mr BJ Homewood
(Sunbury-on-Thames)

1946

Birthdays

Pat Howard born today 1947.   John Cornforth born today 1967.   Kevin Bremner born today 1957.
George Smith born today 1945.

October 8

The Matches played on this day

1891, Football Alliance.
Nottingham Forest 2   Blues 0   Att. 2,000
1892, Division 2.
Blues 6   Crewe Alexandra 0   Att. 2,500
Walton, Wheldon,
Hallam, Devey,
Mobley, Hands
First league meeting v Crewe.
1898, Division 2.
Grimsby Town 2   Blues 0   Att. 2,000
1904, Division 1.
Blues 2   Middlesbrough 1   Att. 14,000
Field, Beer(pen)
1910, Division 2.
Blues 1   Stockport County 3   Att. 14,000
Jones
1921, Division 1.
Blues 0   Huddersfield Town 2   Att. 40,000
1927, Division 1.
Sheffield Wed. 2   Blues 3   Att. 19,974
   Briggs(2), Bradford
1932, Division 1.
Blues 2   Sheffield Wed. 1   Att. 14,999
Thorogood, Grosvenor
1938, Division 1.
Blues 0   Bolton Wanderers 2   Att. 25,000
1949, Division 1.
Blues 0   Portsmouth 3   Att. 38,000
1955, Division 1.
Blues 1   Sunderland 2   Att. 38,000
Hudgell(og) 14   Fleming 40, 69
1960, Division 1.
West Ham United 4   Blues 3   Att. 16,000
Grice 15, 52   Hellawell 30, 84
Musgrove 25   Rudd 77
Dunmore 60
1966, Division 2.
Ipswich Town 3   Blues 2   Att. 15,120
Crawford 15, 58   Vowden 80
Green(og) 26   Thomson 84
1968, Division 2.
Blues 2   Cardiff City 0   Att. 28,238
Vincent 56
Greenhoff 79
1969, Division 2.
Oxford United 2   Blues 0   Att. 12,476
Shuker 9, 31
1977, Division 1.
Blues 1   Coventry City 1   Att. 27,414
Francis 44(pen)   Ferguson 59
1985, League Cup 2nd round, 2nd leg.
Blues 2   Bristol Rovers 1   Att. 3,686
Kennedy 75   Randall 5
Tanner(og) 85
Blues won 5-3 on aggregate.
1988, Division 2.
Bournemouth 0   Blues 1   Att. 6,186
   Frain 39
Blues 'keeper Martin Thomas saved Dave Puckett's
50th minute penalty.
1991, League Cup 2nd round, 2nd leg.
Blues 3   Luton Town 2   Att. 13,252
Peer 29   Gray 60, 63
Gleghorn 59, 89
Blues won 5-4 on aggregate
1994, Division 2.
Blues 1   Huddersfield Town 1   Att. 15,265
Bull 42   Bullock 13
1995, Division 1.
Blues 2   Southend United 0   Att. 17,341
Claridge 42, 75
1996, Division 1.
Huddersfield Town 3   Blues 0   Att. 10,904
Edwards 17
Stewart 23
Dalton 45
1999, Division 1.
Walsall 1   Blues 0   Att. 7,126
Rammell 74
2000, Division 1.
Crewe Alexandra 0   Blues 2   Att. 6,829
   Hughes 54
   Marcelo 81

Playing record for this day

Playing record for this day.... 24 games, Won 10, Drawn 2, Lost 12, GF 34, GA 38.
Success rate...45.83% Year ranking....197th

Match of the Day
FROM 1991
GLEGHORN PLAYS THE BLUES
Last-minute header leads to Blues glory!

In front of 13,252, Blues started the second leg of this Rumbelow Cup tie with a 2-2 draw behind them, and everything to play for. After 59 minutes they were cruising home to a 4-2 aggregate win, and yet on 63 minutes they were staring defeat in the face as Luton clawed back two goals in rapid succession. Not until the eleventh hour did Ian Rodgerson and Gleghorn pull it all back to give Birmingham the victory that they so desperately desired.

On 29 minutes Gleghorn found Trevor Matthewson in support, and his cross was perfectly placed by midfielder Dean Peer past Chamberlain's left hand. On 59 minutes John Frain whipped over a left footed free kick. Gleghorn, arriving late and beyond the defence, planted his header firmly, before slithering over the grass and on to the track beyond.

A minute later Phil Gray, unmarked, converted Richard Harvey's cross from the left, and after 63 minutes a stunned St Andrews crowd watched him race onto Matthew Jackson's long ball to side-foot past a helpless Martin Thomas from 12 yards.

Blues just about managed to hold it together until the 89th minute when a free kick was blocked to Rodgerson on the right. He beat his man and picked out Gleghorn, who put a diving header in at the far post, an almost carbon copy of his previous goal. Richardson and Gleghorn had led Blues to a famous victory at St Andrews which was richly deserved.

BIRMINGHAM CITY

Thomas, Clarkson, Hicks, Mardon, Matthewson, Rodgerson Peer, Frain, Gleghorn, Donowa, Sturridge

LUTON TOWN

Chamberlain, Jackson, Beaumont, Peake, Harvey, Telfer, Thompson (Nogan h/t), Preece, Pembridge, Gray, Harford (Stein)

REFEREE

Mr K Burge (Tonypandy)

Nigel Gleghorn

Birthdays

Andy Kennedy born today 1964.   John Frain born today 1968.   Curtis Fleming born today 1968.

Playing record for this day
Playing record for this day.... 15 games, Won 4, Drawn 2, Lost 9, GF 17, GA 30.
Success rate...33.33% Year ranking....259th

Match of the Day

FROM 1979

LYNEX NICKS THE POINTS, BUT JOHNSON STEALS THE SHOW

Steve Lynex continued to prove that he was the bargain buy of the season for manager Jim Smith with another goal, a crucial late winner against Sunderland. He had now scored five goals in just seven full appearances. None of his goals was more crucial to the Blues cause than this 82nd minute strike against fellow promotion hopefuls Sunderland. Although not spectacular in its execution the strike ended the hopes of a valuable point for the visitors and a 260 minute goal drought for Birmingham City, their last league goal being scored at Orient 17 days previously.

Although Lynex grabbed the glory by scoring the winner his overall performance was bettered by that of another Albion reject, Willie Johnston, whose trickery mesmerised the Sunderland defence all night in a wonderful display. Fresh from his spell in the NASL Johnston kept the 19,260 crowd thoroughly entertained with a performance earning him the man-of-the-match award. Within the first few minutes he embarrased Sunderland full back Steve Whitworth when his turn and shimmy landed the defender on his backside when trying to time his challenge for the ball. Whitworth wasn't the only defender to be totally confused by the the wizardry of the Blues winger who displayed his entire repertoire of tricks during the course of the evening. Blues should have sewn the game up well before Lynex's strike, but although the midfield moved the ball well through Curbishley and Towers, Givens up front lacked the sharpness required to turn good approach play into goals.

With Joe Gallagher leading a strong back four alongside the ever reliable Colin Todd, Blues never looked like conceding a goal during the game. The trouble was for 82 minutes they never looked like scoring one either. So with the stage set for a match winning hero, up stepped Lynex with a typical but important poachers' special. From another well worked move out of defence by Todd the ball landed at the feet of Curbishley, without a moments hesitation he sprayed it out wide for Ainscow. In space, the winger sent over a low cross which Lynex side-footed in at the near post from barely three yards out. At half time it always looked like a game which was going to be won by the one goal, if it got one, and so it was. The crowd realised it too and they erupted when the ball bulged the back of the net.

Blues had been many observers promotion favourites and the two points gained put them in a great position for a quick return to top flight football.

BIRMINGHAM CITY
Wealands, Todd, Dennis, Curbishley, Gallagher, Towers, Ainscow, Lynex, Givens (Bertschin 58), Gemmill, Johnston.
SUNDERLAND
Farmer, Whitworth, Gilbert, Clarke, Elliott, Hindmarsh, Chisholm, Lee, Hawley, Robson, Dunn.

The Matches played on this day
1897, Division 2.
Blues 4   Gainsborough Trinity 3 Att. 4,500
Abbott(2), Robertson, Hare
1909, Division 2.
Wolverhampton W. 4 Blues 2   Att. 10,000
                    Buckley, Chapple
1920, Division 2.
Blackpool 3   Blues 0   Att. 10,000
1926, Division 1.
Tottenham Hotspur 6 Blues 1   Att. 29,392
                    Bradford
1937, Division 1.
Leeds United 1   Blues 0   Att. 20,698
1943, Wartime.
Derby County 5   Blues 3
                    Mulraney, Trigg(2)
1948, Division 1.
Bolton Wanderers 0 Blues 0   Att. 43,376
1954, Division 2.
Fulham 2   Blues 1   Att. 31,500
Stevens 4   Astall 56
Robson 44
1965, Division 2.
Blues 1   Norwich City 0   Att. 11,622
Jackson 17
First league meeting v Norwich.
1971, Division 2.
QPR 1   Blues 0   Att. 16,039
Marsh 5
1973, League Cup 2nd round.
Blackpool 1   Blues 1   Att. 7,943
Burns 57   Burns 72
1979, Division 2.
Blues 1   Sunderland 0   Att. 18,960
Lynex 81
Willie Johnston made his Blues debut.
1982, Division 1.
Blues 2   Luton Town 3   Att. 13,772
Langan 66(pen)   Stein 59
Brazier 85   Walsh 61
                    Moss 80
Kevin Dillon's intial penalty was saved by the Luton 'keeper who had moved, the re-taken kick was converted by Dave Langan.
1984, League Cup 2nd round, 2nd leg.
Plymouth Argyle 0   Blues 1   Att. 4,650
                    Clarke 26
Blues won 5-1 on aggregate.
Blues had Mick Halsall sent off after 31 minutes.
1993, Division 1.
Sunderland 1   Blues 0   Att. 19,265
Howey 31
Sunderland full back John Kay stretchered off after 44 mins with a double fracture to his right leg.
Blues had Paul Marden sent off after 80 minutes.

Jeff Wealands

Birthdays

Jim Montgomery born today 1943.   **Foley Okenla born today 1967.**

October 10

Playing record for this day

Playing record for this day.... 18 games, Won 5, Drawn 7, Lost 6, GF 18, GA 22.
Success rate...47.22% Year ranking....182nd

Match of the Day

FROM 1981

SAINTS SENT PACKING

Worthington, Whatmore share the goals in four goal hammering

Blues manager Jim Smith, hoping to improve a defence which had conceded five goals in the last two games, considered dropping Jeff Wealands in goal and giving the position to 20-year-old Tony Coton, but in the end decided to field an unchanged squad. Southampton boss Lawrie McMenemy also chose an unchanged team, opting not to select defender Reuben Agboola in a side which boasted England skipper Kevin Keegan who had scored nine goals already this season.

The first half began with plenty of action from Blues. Brocken stole the ball from Holmes and knocked it over to Whatmore, who then sent Gemmill chasing forward. The ball went to Worthington, who passed to Van Mierlo. He went past Golac and crossed to the far post, but there was no-one there to take advantage of the chance and the ball was wasted. The pace of the early play was calm, and Blues were the team doing most of the attacking with chances at goal occurring frequently. Keegan had Southampton's first goal attempt, but Wealands collected the ball with little effort.

A great chance for Blues in the 15th minute ended in disappointment when Worthington passed the ball to Gemmill, whose shot rebounded off Golac into the path of Whatmore. His confident strike bent around Wells, but hit the post and went out to safety.

Channon was booked in the 17th minute for a foul on Dennis, and the excitement continued when Worthington won a free kick for after a foul by Watson. The shot appeared to be going in, but was saved by Wells. Channon later had an appeal for penalty turned down after he was apparently brought down by Broadhurst, who was later booked for felling Keegan.

The second half began, and it wasn't long before the first goal arrived. David Langan made a superb 30-yard pass to Whatmore, who crossed for Worthington. He was brought down in the penalty area and a penalty was given. The Southampton players protested, and Ball was booked for dissent. Worthington took his place for the spot kick, but Wells went the right way. However the ball rebounded straight back to the Blues striker who made no mistake this time, ramming the ball into the net.

A second goal for Blues came in the 58th minute, again thanks to Worthington. Dillon pushed the ball forward for Worthington, who surprised the crowd by not passing. Instead he flipped the ball into the air and hit a forceful volley straight into the bottom corner of the net.

Southampton, in a bid to save face, tried to up the tempo of the game, and a good attempt from Keegan was just off target. In the 66th minute they brought on Puckett in place of Holmes. All their efforts were in vain, and after 73 minutes Blues increased their lead. Brocken delivered a perfectly measured pass to Whatmore, who finished off the move with a quick-fire shot into the net.

An attempt from substitute Puckett ran just wide of the post, and it proved to be their last real try at goal. The game was wrapped up after 78 minutes when a loose ball fell to Worthington. He seemed certain to but it rebounded again, this time off the post. Whatmore was there to clear up headed home his second goal of the game.

BIRMINGHAM CITY

Wealands, Langan, Dennis, Dillon, Broadhurst, Todd, Brocken, Whatmore, Worthington, Gemmill, Van Mierlo.

SOUTHAMPTON

Wells, Golac, Holmes (Puckett), Baker, Watson, Waldron, Keegan, Channon, Moran, Armstrong, Ball.

REFEREE

Mr Brian Martin (Nottingham)

Franc Worthington

Blues news extra 1955...Merrick's 14th cap Wales 1 England 4

Whilst his team mates were beating Lincoln at St Andrews, the Blues 'keeper was at Ninian Park. He helped win this World Cup qualifier for England as Wolves' Dennis Wilshaw scored twice on his England debut.

Birthdays

Carl Shutt born today 1961.
Mark Ward born today 1962.

Dave Howell born today 1956.

Ian Bennett born today 1971.

Playing record for this day
Playing record for this day.... 16 games, Won 6, Drawn 5, Lost 5, GF 22, GA 22.
Success rate...53.13% Year ranking....126th

Match of the Day
FROM 1969
BLUES BURN THE ROVERS
Promotion dreams increased with 3-0 win

In front of 25,602 Blues gave third placed Blackburn a decisive 3-0 mauling, using the direct long ball methods employed so successfully by manager Stan Cullis at Wolves in the 1950s. Blues were at full strength and were expecting few problems from a team that had suffered two defeats in the last two away games.

Only minutes into the game the Blackburn defence was threatened. Murray took the ball from Wilson's toe, forcing Hunter into hooking away for a corner. A few minutes later Vowden connected but could only head over the bar from just seven yards out.

During the first 15 minutes the only threat to Blues' goal came from a header by Mulvaney from a corner which scraped the bar. On 16 minutes a Beard free kick soared into the goalmouth where Vowden, beating the Blackburn defenders, back-headed it into the net past Blacklaw.

On 25 minutes Summerill created for Hateley, whose low drive was only kept out by Blacklaw's full-length save. Then on 42 minutes Summerill's persistence paid off when his tackle on Knighton enabled Vowden to pounce on the ball and fire it home.

Within ten seconds of the second half starting Murray hit a cross shot which only narrowly missed the upright. Blackburn seemed to rally themselves after this and in the next couple of minutes Herriot was compelled to save twice from Fryatt before the game was paused for treatment to Sleeuwenhoek. Closer marking from Blackburn slowed down the flow of long balls and it wasn't until the 58th minute that Hateley had another header just off target following a cross from Beard.

Blackburn continued to push through Fryatt, but Blues' defence held. Hockey broke through giving Hateley another great chance, but he was off balance and hooked his shot almost over the Cattell Road roof from only ten yards. On 80 minutes a Murray pass to Beard was chipped to Summerill and headed just over the top. This was followed by another near miss from Murray when he hit an upright with an angled shot from the right. Then on 84 minutes a Hockey chip from inside left enabled Summerill to steer the ball inside Blacklaw's left hand post which saw Blues win 3-0.

BIRMINGHAM CITY
Herriot, Martin, Thomson, Beard, Sleeuwenhoek, Pendrey, Murray, Vowden, Hately, Hockey, Summerill
BLACKBURN ROVERS
Blacklaw, Newton, Wilson, Hunter, Mulrooney, Knighton, Connelly, Fryatt, Martin, Rogers, Hill

REFEREE
Mr AP Oliver (Leigh-on-Sea)

Glenn Hoddle, Tottenham Hotspur and Gary Pendrey, Birmingham City

Blues news extra   1941...Friendly. Blues 4 Northampton Town 1

Birthdays
Mike O'Grady born today 1942.   Marcelo born today 1969.

The Matches played on this day
1890, Football Alliance.
Sheffield Wed. 3	Blues 3	Att. 7,000
	Walton, W.Devey, Hallam	
1902, Division 2.		
Blues 2	Barnsley 1	Att. 7,000
Athersmith, Leonard		
1913, Division 2.		
Barnsley 1	Blues 1	Att. 8,800
	Gibson	
1919, Division 2.		
Blues 4	Blackpool 2	Att. 16,000
Walker, Whitehouse, Jones(og), Elkes		
1924, Division 1.		
Blues 1	Aston Villa 0	Att. 48,000
Islip		
1930, Division 1.		
Blues 1	Blackpool 1	Att. 29,650
Curtis		
1947, Division 2.		
Blues 0	Chesterfield 0	Att. 30,000
1952, Division 2.		
Swansea Town 1	Blues 1	Att. 24,827
Medwin 67	Purdon 31	
1958, Division 1.		
West Ham United 1	Blues 2	Att. 29,500
Musgrove 15	Neal 49	
	Hooper 75	
1961, Inter Cities Fairs Cup Final, 2nd leg.		
Roma 2	Blues 0	Att. 50,000
Lojacono 56		
Pestrin 90		
Blues lost 4-2 on aggregate.		
1967, League Cup 3rd round.		
Derby County 3	Blues 1	Att. 24,827
Hector 22	Bridges 2	
Hokinson 56		
O'Hare 57		
1969, Division 2.		
Blues 3	Blackburn Rovers 0	Att. 25,602
Vowden 16, 48		
Summerill 84		
1975, Division 1.		
Liverpool 3	Blues 1	Att. 36,532
Toshack 14, 58, 85	Hatton 80	
1980, Division 1.		
Blues 1	Aston Villa 2	Att. 33,879
Worthington 49(pen)	Cowans 35(pen)	
	Evans 84	
This match screened by ATV's Star Soccer in its new time slot of Saturday evening.		
1986, Division 2.		
Portsmouth 2	Blues 0	Att. 11,252
Quinn 72, 76		
1995, Anglo Italian Cup, Qualifying Group stage		
Perugia 0	Blues 1	Att. 1,500
	Castle 62	

October 12

The Matches played on this day

1889, Football Alliance.
Sunderland Albion 6	Blues 1	Att. 1,000
	Davenport	

1895, Division 1.
Bury 4	Blues 5	Att. 6,000
	Wheldon(2), Mobley, Jones(2)	

First league meeting v Bury.
1901, Division 1.
Blues 0	Aston Villa 2	Att. 23,000

1907, Division 1.
Sheffield United 1	Blues 0	Att. 12,000

1912, Division 2.
Blues 3	Burnley 0	Att. 15,000
Jones, Hastings, Hall		

1918, Wartime.
Blues 4	Sheffield United 1	
Brown(3), Walker		

1929, Division 1.
Liverpool 1	Blues 1	Att. 28,000
	Curtis	

1935, Division 1.
Liverpool 1	Blues 2	Att. 30,000
	Harris, Jones	

1940, Wartime.
Mansfield Town 4	Blues 1	
	Jennings	

1946, Division 2.
Coventry City 0	Blues 0	

1957, Division 1.
Blues 1	Wolverhampton W. 5	Att. 43,005
Astall 13	Wilshaw 10	
	Murray 20	
	Deeley 30	
	Clamp 52(pen), 80(pen)	

1968, Division 2.
Bristol City 0	Blues 0	Att. 19,478

1974, Division 1.
Luton Town 1	Blues 3	Att. 15,097
Hindson 10	Francis 2, 5, 70	

Trevor Francis hit his first hat-trick in top flight football.
1988, League Cup 2nd round, 2nd leg.
Aston Villa 5	Blues 0	Att. 19,753
Mountfield 1		
Gage 11, 17		
Olney 18		
Daley 68		

Derek Mountfield's goal timed at just 45 seconds
Blues lost 7-0 on aggregate
1991, Division 3.
Blues 3	Stockport County 0	Att. 12,634
Cooper 31		
Drinkell 42		
Donowa 90		

Andy Kilner missed a penalty for Stockport after 66 minutes and was sent off two minutes later.
1996, Division 1.
Blues 3	Bradford City 0	Att. 25,157
Devlin 1, 50		
Hunt 88		

1997, Division 1.
Blues 1	Wolverhampton W. 0	Att. 17,832
Marsden 8		

Former Wolves player Chris Marsden scored just eight minutes into his debut for Blues.
1999, League Cup 3rd round.
Blues 2	Newcastle United 0	Att. 19,795
O'Connor 45(pen)		
Purse 59		

Ian Bennett saved Alan Shearer's penalty after just three minutes. In conceding the penalty Newcastle 'keeper Steve Harper was sent off for the trip, denying a goalscoring chance to Andy Johnson.

Playing record for this day

Playing record for this day.... 18 games, Won 9, Drawn 3, Lost 6, GF 30, GA 31.
Success rate....58.33% Year ranking....77th

Match of the Day
FROM 1996
DEVLIN TAKES LEADING ROLE IN THE 39 SECONDS
Early strike sets up resounding win in front of a packed St Andrews

A bumper St Andrews crowd of 25,157, many taking advantage of the generous ticket price offer, were treated to a quick strike from Paul Devlin, the goal coming before many of them had taken up their seats.

After a frustrating 90 minutes in their last game at St Andrews, Blues could not have wished for a better start in this one. A great through ball from Barry Horne sent Devlin away. The Blues striker calmy swept it under Nixon's despairing dive to ease the tension in a packed crowd at St Andrews. Now with the pressure off, Blues could really turn it on. In an almost non stop bombardment they raided the Bradford goal which Nixon did exceptionally well to keep them out.

Devlin's goal ended a Blues famine of 7 hours 52 minutes without a goal but their play thereafter suggested the wait for the next goal wouldn't be as long, despite Nixon, the goal frame, and some poor finishing.

It was Devlin who pepped up the Blues fans with a second goal after the break. Again it was from a superb through ball this time courtesy of Jonathon Hunt who skilfully controlled a huge defensive header from Steve Bruce, turned quickly and without the need to look up threaded the ball into space to put Devlin clean through and he finished in almost identical style as his first goal. With Blues now in total control, Devlin contrived to set up his own chance with a breathtaking run from the halfway line. He left the entire defence in his wake and but for a tired looking finish would have capped one of the greatest goals ever scored at St Andrews. Blues had to wait until two minutes from time to add their third and last goal, and what a bizarre effort it was to. A corner bobbled around the Bradford area and Hunt tried his luck with an overhead kick which he miscued, the ball then took an almighty deflection and rolled past the unsighted Nixon into the net. For Nixon who had saved his side so bravely throughout the game it was rough justice. He summed it up by dropping backwards in mock passing out, laying fully stretched out in his six yard area during the entire goal celebration. However he would have to concede Blues thoroughly deserved their 3-0 win.

BIRMINGHAM CITY
Bennett, Finnan (Bowen 86), Ablett, Horne, Breen, Bruce, Hunt, Devlin, Furlong, Holland, Legg.
BRADFORD CITY
Nixon, Mohan, Sas, Jacobs, Liburd, Cowans (Hamilton 53) Waddle, Duxbury, Kiwomya, Moore (Pinto 67), Shutt (Stallard 53)

REFEREE
Mr NS Barry (Scunthorpe)

Paul Devlin

Birthdays
Dennis Harper born today 1936.

Playing record for this day

Playing record for this day.... 16 games, Won 4, Drawn 4, Lost 8, GF 19, GA 29.

Success rate....37.50% Year ranking....244th

Match of the Day
FROM 1973
LATCHFORD SAVES THE BLUES

Striker Bob is goalkeeping hero in super win over local rivals

Stiker Bob Latchford, so often the star of Blues victories with his prolific scoring, today became the hero in the unfamiliar position of goalkeeper. His performance between the posts would have impressed either of his brothers both of whom were 'keepers. Bob Latchford took over the green jersey after an injury to Gary Sprake in the 38th minute when the score was 1-1 and kept a clean sheet to ensure victory.

Blues were soon on the rack as Wolves started in brilliant form. From their very first attack they scored when Richards took advantage of a bobbling ball within the penalty area to hit low past Sprake and into the corner. Wolves continued to dominate and really should have been three up in the first 20 minutes. They then paid the penalty when Francis equalised via a 22nd minute spot kick after Jefferson had been penalised for hand ball. With Blues slowly getting back into the game it came as a bitter blow when the injury to Sprake occured. They delayed bringing on their substitute until half time, when it became clear Sprake would take no further part. Hynd then joined the defence which allowed Kenny Burns the freedom to roam up front with Francis. Before then however the Blues goal had a lucky escape when the referee disallowed Dougan's shot from a quickly taken free kick.

The substitution dramatically changed the second half as Wolves came under threat from Burns in his new role. With Blues well on top it came as no surprise when he latched onto a Taylor cross sending his acrobatic diving header wide of Pierce and into the top corner of the net, this after 61 minutes. Francis was then denied a third goal by a crucial last-minute tackle from McCalle who repeated the challenge when denying Burns moments later. It was all Blues pressure in the closing stages and another superb header from Burns struck the bar. In the last minute another stunning piece of magic from Francis set himself up for a strike at goal but this also came back off the bar and the desperate Wolves defence scrambled clear before Burns made anything of the rebound.

BIRMINGHAM CITY

Sprake (Hynd h/t), Clarke, Want, Pendrey, Burns, Roberts, Campbell, Francis, Bob Latchford, Hatton, Taylor.

WOLVERHAMPTON WANDERERS

Pierce, Palmer, Gerry Taylor, Jefferson, Munro, McCalle, McCalliog, Hibbitt, Richards, Dougan, Daley.

REFEREE

Mr W Gow

Bob Latchford

Birthdays

Steve Vickers born today 1967.　　**Phil Sproson born today 1959.**

October 14
-1875-

Playing record for this day

Playing record for this day.... 18 games, Won 9, Drawn 4, Lost 5, GF 32, GA 18.
Success rate...61.11% Year ranking....44th

Match of the Day
FROM 1989

TOWN ARE COBBLERS
Blues cruise to 4-0 win, a thrashing for sorry Northampton

In a game packed with long stoppages Blues climbed to victory in front of a home crowd of 8,731. The threats from Northampton were never far away, however, and the first attempt arrived just 20 seconds into the game. Berry collected a header from Roberts and volleyed in a shot which Blues 'keeper Thomas succeeded in flicking away from the left-hand corner of the goal.

After that display, Blues were determined not to let the game get away, and opened the scoring in three minutes. A not so successful one-two from Bailey and Sturridge allowed the ball to run to Gleghorn who, unmarked, made sure he knocked the ball home from ten yards.

Barnes' 20 yard shot on seven minutes flew narrowly over the bar, and Sproson was booked for timewasting after 12 minutes. Northampton were experts at setting the offside trap for a frustrated Blues side, and the referee's whistle could be heard frequently. There were plenty more chances at goal, Berry's shot curled over the heads of two players and landed in front of goal where Thomas dived to his right to make the save. Sturridge fed the ball to Atkins, but his low drive was not enough to give Northampton goalkeeper Gleasure anything to worry about.

Eight minutes before half time Sturridge had to be replaced after injuring an ankle. John Deakin came on in his place. Despite seven minutes being added in stoppage time, the final action in the first half was another miss from Atkins, going narrowly to the right of the goal.

The second half began with yet another long stoppage after Bailey was felled, but thenGleghorn scored another early goal after the Northampton offside trap was finally beaten. He ran on to a long header from Matthewson and slotted the ball into the net. Atkins was booked for dissent, and Northampton tried to score in response, but a shot from Donald was brilliantly saved by Thomas.

Blues' third goal came after 56 minutes when the offside trap was beaten yet again. Deakin ran onto a long ball from Roberts, only to be brought down in the penalty area by Wilcox. Bailey stepped up to do the honours, and made no mistake in slotting the ball home from the spot, netting his seventh of the season.

Northampton's first booking came when Wilson made a late tackle on Bell, who had just relieved him of the ball. The visitors then nearly pulled back a consolation goal but Brown's touch failed, and almost immediately they found themselves the receiving end. Gordon slammed a 50-yard volley to Gleghorn, whose perfectly measured cross was popped into the net by Bailey, waiting at the far post.

BIRMINGHAM CITY

Thomas, Roberts, Frain, Atkins, Sproson, Matthewson, Bell, Bailey, Gordon, Gleghorn, Sturridge (Deakin).

NORTHAMPTON TOWN

Gleasure, Quow, Wilson, Thomas, Wilcox, McPherson, Berry, Collins, Donald, Barnes, Brown.

REFEREE

Mr Harrison (Oldham).

Arthur Grosvenor

Blues news extra   1933..First cap for Arthur Grosvenor. Northern Ireland 0 England 3

Blues midfielder Arthur Grosvenor celebrated winning his first full England cap by scoring for his country in
this convincing 3-0 win over Ireland in Belfast. Derby County's John Bowers also scored on his England debut.

Playing record for this day

Playing record for this day.... 19 games, Won 11, Drawn 1, Lost 7, GF 34, GA 19.
Success rate...60.53% Year ranking....47th

Match of the Day

FROM 1966

HARD WORK FOR WIN

Blues struggle for bid win at St Andrews

Blues were hoping to break the spell which had left them without a win in a league game since the final Saturday in August. Hockey was left out of the team due to suspension, and Stan Cullis also decided to separate Murray and Bridges.

Blues started the action on three minutes when Murray's header bounced off the crossbar. Bridges had a good try within the first five minutes also, but he ran out of steam and the ball went to safety. On six minutes Blues had their nerves frayed when Peters scored for the Robins. Luckily for the home side the referee judged him to be offside and the goal was disallowed.

Then on ten minutes Vowden pushed Blues into the lead when he side-footed into an empty net after Gibson had lost his hold on the ball. Straight away a fired up Blues had another chance, but Bridges sent the ball too high and it sailed over the crossbar. Fenton's try was saved well by Gibson, and lovely play resulted in a move which presented the ball to Thomson who shot just wide of the post. Further chances from Murray and Bridges were to no avail, and Blues were beginning to become disheartened.

The visitiors came close to equalising when Sharpe put in a shot which he nudged just an inch or two wide of the post. The 15,000 crowd were starting to lose patience with Blues, and jeers and whistles could soon be heard. Bush made a good try and another shot from him brought about a great save from Blues goalkeeper Herriot.

The second half started with further goal attempts from Bridges and Murray, but both the team and the crowd were getting frustrated. On the hour mark Vowden, who had been suffering since a tackle at the goalmouth early on in the game, came off to be replaced by Thwaites.

On 65 minutes Blues increased their lead when Thwaites made his presence felt in the visitors defence and sent the ball to Murray who shot home. Three minutes later the third goal for Blues was a welcome gift from Bristol defender Ford. Wylie lost possession, but as Ford turned to flick the ball back to his 'keeper he sent it straight over Gibson's head into the goal.

A fourth goal arrived for the home side when Thwaites latched onto a free kick from Wylie and evaded two defenders to slip the ball into the net.

BIRMINGHAM CITY
Herriot, Martin, Green, Wylie, Foster, Beard, Bridges, Thomson, Fenton, Vowden (Thwaites), Murray.
BRISTOL CITY
Gibson, Ford, Briggs, Parr, Connor, Low, Peters, Derrick, Bush, Sharpe, Bartley.

REFEREE
Mr G C Kew (Leeds)

Stan Cullis

Blues news extra   1979..Friendly. Blues 1 Los Angeles Aztecs 0

The Aztecs including Dutch super star Johan Cruyff were well beaten by
a good performance from the Blues. Terry Lees got the winner from the penalty spot.

Birthdays

Steve Wigley born today 1961.

The Matches played on this day
1887, FA Cup 1st round.

Blues 6	Aston Unity 1	Att. 2,000

Smith(2), Figures,
W.Dixon(2), Stanley.
1898, Division 2.

Blues 4	Newton Heath 1	Att. 5,000

Abbott, Walton,
Robertson, Inglis
1904, Division 1.

Wolverhampton W. 0	Blues 1	Att. 8,000
	Wilcox	

1910, Division 2.

Derby County 1	Blues 0	Att. 10,000

1921, Division 1.

Huddersfield Town 1	Blues 0	Att. 15,000

1927, Division 1.

Blues 3	Middlesbrough 2	Att. 20,000

Bradford, Bloxham,
Briggs
1932, Division 1.

WBA 1	Blues 0	Att. 29,145

1938, Division 1.

Blues 3	Derby County 0	Att. 27,858

White(2), Brown
1949, Division 1.

Huddersfield Town 1	Blues 0	Att. 22,872

1955, Division 1.

Portsmouth 0	Blues 5	Att. 29,357
	Kinsey 1	
	Brown 9, 38, 70	
	Govan 44	

Noel Kinsey's goal timed at 35 seconds after kick off.
The attendance was boosted by 200 visiting naval officers
from Soviet Union who joined the Blues support when seeing
they were the side in a change strip of red.
Eddie Brown had a goal disallowed after 25 minutes.
1960, Division 1.

Blues 1	Chelsea 0	Att. 23,337

Hellawell 54
1962, League Cup 3rd round.

Barrow 1	Blues 1	Att. 6,289
Howard 67	Wolstenholme 69	

Trevor Wolstenholme scored on his Blues debut
This was Birmingham's first goal in 699 competitive minutes
play.
1966, Division 2.

Blues 4	Bristol City 0	Att. 15,358

Vowden 10
Murray 65
Ford 68(og)
Thwaites 75
Blues biggest win over Bristol City.
1974, Division 1.

Blues 1	Leeds United 0	Att. 36,513

Francis 88
1977, Division 1.

Ipswich Town 5	Blues 2	Att. 21,250
Mariner 3	Francis 2, 65	
Mills 42		
Woods 46		

Whymark 75(pen), 88
1983, Division 1.

Aston Villa 1	Blues 0	Att. 39,318

Withe 29
Villa had Gibson sent off after 61 minutes.
Villa's, Nigel Spink saved Noel Blake's 75th minute
penalty.
1988, Division 2.

Blues 1	WBA 4	Att. 10,453
Bremner 16	Hopkins 35, 37	
	Phillips 65	
	Robson 87	

Blues Vince Overson sent off after 27 minutes.
1994, Division 2.

Brighton & Hove A. 0	Blues 1	Att. 11,004
	Donowa 86	

Blues inflict Brighton's first home defeat of the season.
1996, Division 1.

Blues 1	Ipswich Town 0	Att. 15,664

Bowen 50

October 16

Playing record for this day

Playing record for this day.... 15 games, Won 8, Drawn 3, Lost 4, GF 28, GA 19.
Success rate...63.33% Year ranking....33rd

Match of the Day

FROM 1976

BATTLING BLUES BEAT BORO

Charlton's table toppers are no match for Bell's Blues

The early leaders Middlesbrough arrived at St Andrews in confident mood, they left well beaten, and having conceded more goals in this game than their previous nine. Jack Charlton's men had recorded seven clean sheets in their opening nine matches of the 1976-77 season. Blues on the other hand had just discovered their attacking flair and were playing their first game since their remarkable 5-1 demolition over Derby County at St Andrews.

It was no surprise then that boss Willie Bell stuck with the same side from that Derby win a fortnight before, Blues aiming to maintain their excellent recent form.

It was Birmingham who got off to a cracking start, needing an early goal to open up play as Boro' maintained a tactic of frustrating the opposition with stout defending and tough tackling. In the eighth minute Blues were a goal up through a Joe Gallagher header and never looked back, despite conceding a break away goal from Phil Boersma. Gallagher's goal came after a tremendous leap and full body twist in the air, as he rose to head in Jones' corner after evading the close attention of McAndrew in the penalty area. Blues defence however was left cut open by a swift counter attack in the 26th minute. The lapse allowed Souness space to thread a pass to Boersma who raced clear of the back four to finish easily past a stranded Dave Latchford.

The second half developed into a tight game of midfield scrapping, the tough tackling however transgressed the laws of the game just once, when Souness was booked after a clumsy challenge on Hibbitt. Blues refusing to get bogged down or frustrated, were then rewarded with a goal to put them back into the lead courtesy of Burns. He latched onto a Connolly corner to the far post, and his shot found the back of the net via 'keeper Platt and former England full back Terry Cooper (a future Blues manager). This brought about the game's best period of play as Middlesbrough had to come forward, leaving gaps for Blues to manoeuvre more positively in midfield. The inevitable third goal came after 73 minutes, and fittingly it was man-of-the-match Trevor Francis who converted his own piece of individual magic. A fantastic left-wing run left the Boro' defence wide open and when Francis cut inside and into the area, Platt could only stop him by a trip. After receiving treatment, Francis picked himself up to smash the penalty into the roof of the net. Blues had stuck to the task of breaking down the Middlesbrough defence and their patience was deservedly rewarded with a fine 3-1 win.

27,740 left St Andrews well satisfied with the display, if only they could now find the consistency needed to climb the First Division table.

BIRMINGHAM CITY
Latchford, Page, Styles, Calderwood, Gallagher, Want (Pendrey), Jones, Francis, Burns, Hibbitt, Connolly.
MIDDLESBROUGH
Platt, Craggs, Cooper, Souness, Boam, Madden, McAndrew, Mills, Brine, Boersma, Armstrong,

Thomas Myhre

Birthdays

Roy McDonough born today 1958.   Thomas Myhre born today 1973.

Playing record for this day

Playing record for this day.... 22 games, Won 9, Drawn 6, Lost 7, GF 40, GA 41.
Success rate...54.55% Year ranking....113th

Match of the Day

FROM 2000
"SIGN HIM UP!!!"

Delighted fans call for Burchill signing after super show

A great performance from on loan Mark Burchill left the 15,579 crowd in no doubt as to his potential and demanding that the board "Sign him up." Blues dominated against a Stockport side with just one win in 12 league games. This one was effectively decided from the 14th minute when Geoff Horsfield got the opening goal. This after Nash had pulled off a wonderful save from Johnson's header. When the ball was played back into the box via Sonner and Hughes, Horsfield found enough space to place his shot low into the corner. Stockport briefly rallied taking advantage of some dubious defending, only to produce some poor finishing, highlighted by Tod's double miskick from six yards out. With the 1-0 lead Blues had this game won without any doubt.

The turning point came however, on the hour. Burchill was introduced for the struggling Horsfield who had taken a knock when scoring earlier. When joined by fellow striker Marcelo five minutes later, the game suddenly changed dramatically. It took four minutes before a loose ball was pounced on by Marcelo just inside the Stockport half and he slipped it into space for Burchill. The advancing keeper could only trip him as he skipped past and Grainger drove in the penalty for 2-0. There was no denying the Scot a goal and in the final ten minutes he got two. After a clash between Sonner and Tod the ball broke for O'Connor who played in Burchill again. This time he managed to round the 'keeper on two feet and turn the ball into the empty net. With three minutes remaining Eaden ran into the box, pulled the ball back for Burchill to smash in Blues fourth and his second of the game. In the last minute Burchill chased through again looking for the hat-trick only to be pulled down again by Nash who received a second yellow card and left to get the team bath ready.

Mark Burchill's inspired 30 minutes was bettered by his performance at Tottenham later in the month but after making 17 appearaces(ten as a sub) and scoring five goals, he returned to Celtic when his loan period expired.

BIRMINGHAM CITY
Bennett, Gill, Grainger, Sonner, M.Johnson, Holdsworth, Eaden, O'Connor, Horsfield, Hughes, Adebola
STOCKPORT COUNTY
Nash, Connelly (Clare 11), Nicholson, Flynn, Clark, Moore, Wiss, (Bailey 58), Tod, Wilbraham (Lawson 74), Smith, Brebner,

REFEREE
Mr W.Jordon (Tring)

The Matches played on this day

1881, FA Cup 1st round.

Blues 4	Derby Town 1	Att. 1,000

Slater(2), Hards, A.James.
Blues first senior competitive game.
1891, Football Alliance.

Blues 4	Walsall Town Swifts 1	Att. 2,000

Hands(2), Morris, Wheldon
1896, Division 2.

Blues 2	Gainsborough Trinity 2	Att. 6,000

Inglis, Leake
1903, Division 1.

Blues 2	Blackburn Rovers 1	Att. 11,000

Windridge(2)
1908, Division 2.

Oldham Athletic 2	Blues 0	Att. 20,000

1st league meeting v Oldham
1914, Division 2.

Blues 0	Hull City 0	Att. 7,000

1925, Division 1.

Aston Villa 3	Blues 3	Att. 55,000
	Bradford(2), Spiers(og)	

Blues, 3-0 down staged a super fight back in the last 11 minutes. The equaliser came in the last minute.
1929, Division 1.

Leicester City 2	Blues 1	Att. 20,000
	Curtis	

1931, Division 1.

Blues 2	Grimsby Town 1	Att. 18,000

Gregg, Bradford
1936, Division 1.

Blues 4	Huddersfield Town 2	Att. 26,172

Fillingham, Jones, White(2, 1pen)
1942, Wartime.

Stoke City 1	Blues 3	
	Bate, Craven, Gill	

1953, Division 2.

Bristol Rovers 1	Blues 1	Att. 35,164
Bradford 58	Purdon 34	

First league meeting v Bristol Rovers.
Gordon Astall made his Blues debut.
1959, Division 1.

Nottingham Forest 0	Blues 2	Att. 24,754
	Gordon 21	
	O'Connor 43(pen)	

2000, Division 1.

Blues 4	Stockport County 0	Att. 15,579

Horsfield 12
Grainger 69(pen)
Burchill 79, 87
2001, Division 1.

Nottingham Forest 0	Blues 0	Att. 18,210

Blues news extra 1955...Friendly. Torquay Utd 2 Blues 3

1959...Trevor Smith wins first cap for England in the 1-1 draw with Wales at Cardiff

1980...Langan for Eire   Republic Of Ireland 2 Holland 1

Blues full back Dave Langan played a starring role in an inspirational Irish victory in this World Cup qualifier in Dublin. This was Langan's first cap for Ireland since his transfer to St Andrews in July 1980.

October
17

The Matches played on this day
1964, Division 1.

Sheffield Wed. 5	Blues 2	Att. 16,161
Wilkinson 10, 77	Auld 22	
Quinn 30	Hennessey 70	
Fantham 44, 88		

1970, Division 2.

QPR 5	Blues 2	Att. 13,074
Marsh 5, 14, 67	B.Latchford 15, 20	
Venables 17		
McCulloch 65		

1981, Division 1.

| Manchester United 1 | Blues 1 | Att. 48,514 |
| Coppell 64 | Worthington 34(pen) | |

Blues forced to play the last 15 minutes with ten men.
1987, Division 2.

Bradford City 4	Blues 0	Att. 12,256
Leonard 52, 81		
Palin 55		
McCall 89		

Blues heaviest defeat by Bradford City.
1989, Division 3.

Chester City 4	Blues 0	Att. 1,882
Croft 57		
Pugh 62		
Painter 68		
Butler 74		

First league meeting v Chester.
The lowest attendance for any Blues senior fixture since 1914
1992, Division 1.

Tranmere Rovers 4	Blues 0	Att. 7,901
Aldridge 44(pen), 77		
Mungall 51		
Irons 69		

Tranmere 'keeper Eric Nixon saved John Frain's 79th minute penalty.
1998, Division 1.

Blues 3	Crewe Alexandra 1	Att. 20,087
Ndlovu 8	Johnson 29	
O'Connor 43(pen)		
Furlong 53		

2000, Division 1.

Blues 4	Stockport County 0	Att. 15,579
Horsfield 12		
Grainger 69(pen)		
Burchill 79, 87		

2001, Division 1.

| Nottingham Forest 0 | Blues 0 | Att. 18,210 |

Mark Burchill

Birthdays

Jim Smith born today 1940.

Playing record for this day

Playing record for this day.... 16 games, Won 4, Drawn 6, Lost 6, GF 14, GA 17.
Success rate....43.75% Year ranking....212th

Match of the Day

FROM 1986
NOT ALL DOOM AND GLOOM

Blues produce a rare win in tough times

Blues ended their eight game run without a league win in emphatic style against Crystal Palace. Having won the two opening games of the 1986-87 season they had failed to record another victory to date. Still manager John Bond kept faith with his stumbling side and they went into this game unchanged from their last outing at Portsmouth which ended in a 2-0 defeat.

Blues gave the St Andrews crowd something to celebrate on 20 minutes when they took the lead. On-loan winger Richard Cooke from Tottenham was clearly looking to impress and his weaving run down the touch line ended with an intelligent pass to Clarke who cut the ball back to leave Des Bremner clear, his shot giving Wood in the Palace goal no chance. Then on 27 minutes Blues fans were further treated when a Kuhl cross from the left was met by Overson who glanced his header wide of Wood to register his first goal for club. For once the Blues players could almost relax as they went into the interval with cheers not silence greeting them.

Normal service seemed to have been resumed early in the second half after a terrible mix up between Kuhl and Hagan, their hesitancy left Taylor time to nip in, rob the ball, round a stranded Hansbury and tap into an open net, Palace were back in the game with 62 minutes gone. Blues looking so comfortable just moments before were now under the cosh and Palace piled on the pressure with the home defence desperately trying to keep them out. However, St Andrews almost erupted with relief when a spectacular effort from Whitton restored the two goal lead on 65 minutes. Centre back Cannon gave away a free kick for a push on Kennedy, Bremner tapped the kick to Whitton who belted the ball from fully 30 yards out and it whistled past Wood like a bullet. The goal eased the tension and Blues took control of the last 20 minutes with some confident passing football. In the last minute of the game a defensive lapse allowed Wayne Clarke to nip and and net his ninth goal of the season to complete a rare 4-1 win.

BIRMINGHAM CITY

Hansbury, Ranson, Williams (Storer), Hagan, Overson, Bremner, Kuhl, Clarke, Whitton, Kennedy, Cooke.

CRYSTAL PALACE

Wood, Stebbing, Brush (Higginbottom), Taylor, Droy, Cannon, Finnigan, Ketteridge, Barber, Wright, Otulakowski.

REFEREE

Mr D Hedges (Oxford)

Robbie Savage

Birthdays

Mike Kelly born today 1942.   Robbie Savage born today 1974.

October 19

Playing record for this day
Playing record for this day.... 20 games, Won 9, Drawn 4, Lost 7, GF 36, GA 32.
Success rate...55% Year ranking....107th

Match of the Day
FROM 1957
A GREAT DAY AT HIGHBURY

Blues ended their London jinx with a thrilling win against Arsenal coming from a goal behind to record a 3-1 victory. Twice before this season they had left London with heavy defeats losing 7-1 at Spurs and 5-1 at Chelsea. This result was even more impressive, as manager Arthur Turner had been forced to reshuffle his line-up. Hall was out through injury and Brian Farmer came in as a straight replacement, but the other changes were not so simple. Newman was moved into midfield as Blues welcomed back Trevor Smith at centre half, this meant Watts switched to the back four. Dick Neal took over at inside left and Murphy at left wing.

Within a minute Arsenal took the lead and Blues fans in the 39,006 crowd must have been wondering if they were again going to witness another London capitulation from their team. It was a goal Merrick will want to forget. He seemed to be well behind a 30-yard shot from Holton but the ball bounced off his chest which presented Swallow with a simple chance. Blues were suddenly under the cosh as Arsenal, boosted by the early success, confidently strode forward. Merrick redeemed his early error by saving well at the feet of Herd as he chased forward to meet a long ball from Holton. Having weathered a ten minute storm Blues began to put some passes together themselves and were soon competing for territorial advantage with their hosts. Sullivan pulled off a great save to deny Astall a spectacular goal from 25 yards. Blues' next attack brought them a well deserved equaliser on 25 minutes scored by Orritt. After Farmer and Newman had worked well, Astall was given the ball wide on the right and from his curling cross Evans, could only clear as far as Orritt who seized on the loose ball to smash it past Sullivan. Blues then almost turned the whole game round seconds later when Sullivan again parried an Astall long-range shot, this time onto the post before gratefully dropping on the ball. At the other end Merrick pulled off a fantastic save from Herd from close range.

Blues continued to go on the attack in the second half despite leaving Arsenal with openings to counter, and this made for a thrilling end-to-end battle of open attacking football. Despite both teams mounting non-stop raids, the goals that eventually won the game didn't arrive until eight minutes from time. Brown, who was at the heart of all Blues forward moves, was again involved in assisting the winner, running straight down the middle of the Arsenal defence he beat Dodgin but then slipped over. Recovering quickly he simply chipped the ball over for Neal who nodded in at the far post after he had sprinted almost two thirds of the field. Blues sealed a fine win just four minutes later before Arsenal could mount any retaliatory threat. Again Brown was prominent when he slipped the ball to Neal from Newman's knock down. From the edge of the penalty area Neal cracked a superb right-foot shot which arrowed into the top corner of the net and Blues had clinched a sound 3-1 victory over the Gunners.

ARSENAL
Sullivan, Charlton, Evans, Holton, Dodgin, Goring, Nuttt, Swallow, Herd, Bloomfield, Tiddy.
BIRMINGHAM CITY
Merrick, Farmer, Green, Newman, Smith, Watts, Astall, Orritt, Brown, Neal, Murphy.

REFEREE
Mr AE Buckle (Peterborough)

Brian Farmer

Birthdays
Mathew Jackson born today 1971.

The Matches played on this day
1899, Football Alliance.

Blues 2	Sheffield Wed. 2	Att. 3,000
W.Devey(2)		

1895, Division 1.

Stoke 6	Blues 1	Att. 8,000
	Jones	

Stoke forward Schofield hit a hat-trick.
1901, Division 1.

Blues 5	Sheffield United 1	Att. 15,000
McMillan(2), Athersmith,		
Jones, McRoberts		

1907, Division 1.

Blues 1	Chelsea 1	Att. 20,000
Green		

First league meeting v Chelsea
1912, Division 2.

Hull City 1	Blues 2	Att. 10,000
	Jones, Robertson	

1918, Wartime.

Blues 2	Bradford Park Ave. 0	
Hawley, Walker.		

1929, Division 1.

Leeds United 1	Blues 0	Att 20,067

1935, Division 1.

Sheffield Wed. 3	Blues 1	Att. 13,479
	White	

1940, Wartime.

Blues 4	Mansfield Town 1	
Trigg(2), Jones, Harris		

1946, Division 2.

Chesterfield 0	Blues 1	Att. 15,000
	Jones	

1957, Division 1.

Arsenal 1	Blues 3	Att. 39,006
Swallow 1	Orritt 25	
	R.Neal 72, 78	

1960, Inter-Cities Fairs Cup 1st round, 1st leg.

Blues 3	Ujpesti Dozsa 2	Att. 23,381
Gordon 30, 83	Gorocs 15, 49	
Astall 62		

1963. League Div 1

Sheffield United 3	Blues 0	Att. 18,974
Pace 38, 64, 72		

1968, Division 2.

Blues 1	Millwall 2	Att. 29,770
Greenhoff 13(pen)	Possee 8	
	Gilchrist 49	

1971, Division 2.

Swindon Town 1	Blues 1	Att. 14,024
Horsfield 28	R.Latchford 61	

1974, Division 1.

Blues 3	Newcastle United 0	Att. 33,339
Burns 8		
Styles 35		
Hatton 79		

1985, Division 1.

WBA 2	Blues 1	Att. 14,747
Varadi 20	Kennedy 3	
Valentine 30		

Lee Jenkins suffered a broken ankle on his debut for Blues and never played another game for the club.
1991, Division 3.

Blues 3	Wigan Athletic 3	Att. 9,662
Sturridge 13	Jones 5	
Gleghorn 52	Daley 40, 63	
Rodgerson 90		

1993, Division 1.

Blues 2	Bolton Wanderers 1	Att. 12,071
Shutt 53	Thompson 87	
Phillips 77(og)		

1999, Division 1.

Blues 0	Manchester City 1	Att.. 22,126
	Jobson 47	

Playing record for this day

Playing record for this day.... 20 games, Won 9, Drawn 5, Lost 6, GF 29, GA 16.

Success rate...57.50% Year ranking...80th

Match of the Day

FROM 2001

THE BLUES ARE BACK

Marcelo hat-trick puts Blues back in the top six

The goings on at St Andrews just lately had the First Division rubbing their hands for a time, lying in 14th place just a month ago, thrashed at Manchester City 6-0, and rendered managerless just five days before.

This game basically centred around a period either side of half time when Blues battered the the visitors. The release of tension had a positive effect. Gerry Gill played probably his best game for the club while Tresor Luntala was insprirational in midfield. Elsewhere Grainger seemed assured once again and Nico Vaesen's huge smile at the end of the game spoke volumes about his fast returning confidence, this being his second clean sheet in succession. From the moment Blues took the lead on 36 minutes there was no turning back.

It was from Gill's high cross that Marcelo rose at the far post to score with a looping header and this set the Blues on their way to the first league win at St Andrews since 8 September. Within three minutes a deflected shot from Sonner on the edge of the penalty area doubled the lead, and on the stroke of half time they settled the game when Marcelo flicked a third goal in at the near post following a corner.

Blues came out for the second half with the instruction to have fun and play, it took just three minutes to see the effects of releasing the shackles from the team. From a running cross from Lazaridis Marcelo twisted in the air to time his header perfectly and thump it past Walsh, to gain his first hat-trick for the Blues and seal a 4-0 victory.

BIRMINGHAM CITY

Vaesen, Gill, Grainger, Sonner, Purse, Michael Johnson, Luntala,

Marcelo(Ferrari 90), Furlong, O'Connor (Woodhouse 72), Lazaridis (Burrows 90).

BRADFORD CITY

Walsh, Locke, Myers, McCall, Tod, Weatherall,

Molenaar (Halle h/t), Whalley (Makel 78), Jess (Grant 78), Ward, Blake.

REFEREE

Mr E.Wolstenholme (Blackburn)

Marcelo

Blues news extra 1923... First cap and goal for Joe Bradford. Northern Ireland 2 England 1

England lost to Ireland for only the third time in 38 Internationals and only the second time in Belfast, despite Blues centre forward Joe Bradford marking his international debut with a goal.

Blues news extra 1962..Hellawell's 2nd cap for England. Northern Ireland 1 England 3

Another good performance from Blues winger Mike Hellawell, two goals from Huddersfield's Mike O'Grady making his international debut, and onefrom Jimmy Greaves helped England to a comfortable win over Northern Ireland in Belfast.

Blues news extra Hennessey wins fourth cap. Wales 2 Scotland 3.

Terry Hennessey won his fourth cap for Wales whilst at Birmingham in this defeat by the Scots at Cardiff, Dennis Law netting the winner for Scotland.

Birthdays

David Foy born today 1972.

The Matches played on this day
1883, FA Cup 1st round.
Blues 1   Birmingham Excelsior 1 Att. 1,500
A.James
1894, Division 1.
Blues 2   Aston Villa 2   Att. 14,000
Hallam, Wheldon(pen)
Blues took a 2-1 lead with their first ever penalty, having waited three years since the penalty rule was introduced. Fred Wheldon made no mistake with the spot kick. Later in the game Blues conceded a penalty and Hodgetts equalised for Villa.
1900, Division 2.
Blues 2   Woolwich Arsenal 1   Att. 8,000
Aston, Higginson
1906, Division 1.
Blues 4   Bolton Wanderers 2   Att. 12,000
Jones(2), Beer(pen), Anderson
1917, Wartime.
Blues 2   Bradford Park Ave. 0
Wootton, Whitehouse
1923, Division 1.
Blues 0   Huddersfield Town 1   Att. 18,000
1928, Division 1.
Manchester United 1 Blues 0   Att. 17,522
1934, Division 1.
Blues 0   Chelsea 1   Att. 20,000
1945, Wartime.
Brentford 2   Blues 1
                    White
1951, Division 2.
Blues 2   West Ham United 1   Att. 21,000
Briggs 36   Woodgate 39
Stewart 80
1956, Division 1.
Blues 3   Luton Town 0   Att. 32,000
Brown 12, 51
Orritt 20
1970, Division 2.
Blues 0   Leicester City 0   Att. 25,381
1973, Division 1.
Manchester United 1 Blues 0   Att. 48,937
Stepney 66(pen)
United 'keeper Alex Stepney scored the winner.
1976, Division 1.
Tottenham Hotspur 1 Blues 0   Att. 20,193
Osgood 49(pen)
1979, Division 2.
Blues 2   Swansea City 0   Att. 18,624
Lynex 70
Gemmill 90
Blues central defender Colin Todd made the 500th league appearance of his professional career.
1984, Division 2.
Notts County 1   Blues 3   Att. 5,790
Goodwin 67   Clarke 44, 48
                    Harford 56
1987, Division 2.
Sheffield United 0   Blues 2   Att. 9,287
                    Withe 7, 85
1990, Division 3.
Blues 0   Grimsby Town 0   Att. 10,123
1998, Division 1.
Blues 1   Swindon Town 1   Att. 19,485
Marsden 58   Gooden 74
Blues full back Simon Charlton sent off.
2001, Division 1.
Blues 4   Bradford City 0   Att. 25,011
Marcelo 36, 45, 48
Sonner 39

October 21

Playing record for this day

Playing record for this day.... 16 games, Won 6, Drawn 4, Lost 6, GF 21, GA 21.
Success rate...50% Year ranking....162nd

The Matches played on this day

1893, Division 2.
Blues 4   Woolwich Arsenal 1   Att. 3,000
Wheldon(2),
Hallam, Hands
First league meeting v Arsenal.
1899, Division 2.
Sheffield Wed. 4   Blues 0   Att. 9,000
1905, Division 1.
Bolton Wanderers 0 Blues 1   Att. 18,000
                 Jones
1911, Division 2.
Gainsborough Trinity 0 Blues 0   Att. 2,000
1916, Wartime.
Blues 2   Barnsley 0
Morgan, Rounds(og)
1922, Division 1.
Middlesbrough 2   Blues 1   Att. 15,000
                 Whitehouse
1933, Division 1.
Blues 0   Wolverhampton W. 0   Att. 33,166
1939, Wartime.
Wolverhampton W. 2 Blues 3
                 Broome, Edwards, Dearson
1944, Wartime.
Stoke City 0   Blues 0
1950, Division 2.
Brentford 2   Blues 1   Att. 19,207
Sinclair 1   Trigg 60
Goodwin 81
1961, Division 1.
Blues 3   Chelsea 2   Att. 20,079
Bloomfield 23, 44   Tambling 51(pen)
Harris 28   Bridges 59
Stan Lynn signed from Villa made his Blues debut.
1967, Division 1.
Norwich City 4   Blues 2   Att. 16,963
Curran 24, 29, 40   Bridges 50
Foggo 42   Vowden 70
1972, Division 1.
Blues 1   Southampton 1   Att. 30,757
Roberts 75   Bennett 80
New £140,000 signing from Arsenal, John Roberts scored on
his St Andrews debut.
1978, Division 1.
Blues 0   Aston Villa 1   Att. 36,145
                 Gray 8
This match screened by ATV's Star Soccer.
1989, Division 3.
Blues 0   Huddersfield Town 1 Att. 7,951
                 Smith 54
1995, Division 1.
Blues 3   Grimsby Town 1   Att. 16,445
Claridge 52, 89   Woods 77
Charlery 72

Match of the Day

FROM 1961
CHELSEA COMEBACK NOT ENOUGH

Three goal lead is whittled away but Blues hang on to win

Both teams started positively at St Andrews in front of a 20,079 crowd who witnessed plenty of thrilling attacking football and a victory for the Blues, although only after a nervy fightback in the first quarter of an hour in the second half.

In the opening minutes Schofield was alert to a fine shot from Brabrook which he saved superbly at full-stretch, moments later a half-cleared header from Foster fell to Bradbury which was on its way in until a last second deflection sent the ball wide for a corner. Blues first chance fell to winger Hellawell who brought an equally magnificent save out of Bonetti with a powerful drive from within the penalty area. Then after 13 minutes a right wing corner flashed across the Chelsea goalmouth to find an unmarked Jimmy Harris. His first time shot was somehow instinctively pushed into the air, there followed a tremendous scramble for the loose ball which Orritt won but his header flashed wide of the upright. The match between the division's bottom clubs was proving to be a vastly entertaining encounter. It was the home crowd who were rewarded with the first goal to celebrate after 23 minutes. The move was started by debutant Stan Lynn. He collected the ball just yards from his own byline and with one almighty kick sent Jimmy Harris away on the left wing. From his centre into the middle Bloomfield found the net with a sweetly hit side-footed shot from close in. Blues were now in top gear and soon after Orritt came close to putting Blues 2-0 up when his inswinging corner kick hit the side netting. Blues did however get a second moments later, Hellawell setting up Harris with a simple header from his inch-perfect cross. The Chelsea goal was having a charmed life and Orritt came desperately close again to scoring from another great pass from Hellawell. With half time approaching Blues put themselves in a commanding position through another goal by Bloomfield. Lynn got forward to within shooting range and let fly with one of his renowned blockbuster shots. This was charged down by a Chelsea defender but the ball fell nicely to Bloomfield who placed the rebound into the top corner of the net well wide of Bonetti.

Blues started the second half as they had ended the first, dominating the game. But it was from a rare Chelsea break that Blunstone got forward and raced into the penalty area. The nearest defender to him was Hennessey but he could only stop the Chelsea skipper by an illegal challenge and referee Haynes had no doubt in awarding the visitors a penalty. Tambling strode forward to send Schofield the wrong way and give Chelsea some consolation. The goal had little immediate effect on the overall play and Blues carried on attacking and indeed came close to netting a fourth through Lynn on another surge forward from defence. Things however changed after Chelsea stunned the Blues on 59 minutes by scoring a second. A cross from Murray seemed to be well covered by Lynn but the speed of Bridges enabled him to just nick his header in first and the ball flew past a motionless Schofield. Chelsea, who had looked dead and buried at half time. Then as the game entered the final minutes, near disaster for Blues when Sissons gave the ball straight to Bridges when attempting a simple back pass to his 'keeper. Fortunately a combination of Schofield and Sissons who hurried back to cover his error, got the ball out to safety. This was Chelsea's last chance to draw level and it was Blues who finished the stonger.

BIRMINGHAM CITY

Schofield, Lynn, Sissons, Hennessey, Foster, Beard, Hellawell, Bloomfield, Harris, Orritt, Auld.
CHELSEA
Bonetti, Shellito, Harris, Brabury, Scott, Anderton, Murray, Tambling, Brabrook, Bridges, Blunstone.

REFEREE
Mr W Haynes (Newburgh)

Jimmy Harris

Birthdays
Brian Rushton born today 1943.

Playing record for this day

Playing record for this day.... 19 games, Won 5, Drawn 7, Lost 7, GF 24, GA 28.

Success rate...44.74% Year ranking....203rd

Match of the Day

FROM 1955

BOYD WITH A LATE WINNER

Len Boyd's goal clinches seven goal thriller at St Andrews

The St Andrews crowd of 28,500 were treated to a classic seven goal thriller. Len Boyd sent most of them home happy when he swept in the winner with just two minutes of the game left.

Play started with the visitors missing a great chance in the opening minute. After Blues full back Green fluffed his clearance allowing Hayes a chance from 12 yards out, but he stubbed his shot and the ball trickled wide of the post. Blues fresh from a 5-0 win at Portsmouth couldn't seem to get going at all, pegged back by a lively Manchester City forward line who were well on top in the early stages. However they defended well and against the run of play opened the scoring on 24 minutes. A long throw in by Lane evaded everyone and Murphy standing at the near post hooked the ball in from a yard out. In another Blues raid Lane collided with 'keeper Trautmann which left him shaken but able to carry on after a short stoppage for treatment. The effects of the knock however were still evident when Blues almost scored a minute later. He dropped a simple catch and his defenders scrambled the ball away. Seconds later he flapped at a cross which put Murphy in the clear and from his lob over the stranded 'keeper, Ewing chased back to head clear from off the goal line. Now it was the visitors turn to score whilst under pressure, Barnes put a long ball through the middle which Hayes chased after, as Merrick rushed out Hayes nodded the ball over his head into the empty net. With four minutes of the half remaining Blues got back into the lead. A great run by Brown ended with a hard, low centre, Lane collected and veered out to his right then suddenly turned to whip the ball into the top left-corner with Trautmann left flat footed. However in scoring the goal Lane fell awkwardly and was sidelined whilst he received attention to the injury.

Just two minutes into the second half Blues got what most thought a match winning third goal. The move was started by Green who played an accurate long ball down the line for Brown who ran on to cross from the byline. The ball sailed over the waitong forwards, but Govan arrived just in time at the far post to side-foot low into the corner. Manchester City came back stronger after the goal and on 63 minutes they reduced the score to 3-2 with a well deserved goal. The goal was scored by Roy Faulkner making his league debut, a close range shot from Cunliffe's cross. Just six minutes later they levelled the score at 3-3, Badham bringing down Cunliffe in the area and Dyson smashing in from the penalty spot. This led to a sensational final six minutes in which Blues scored once but missed two chances either side of the winning goal. The first fell to Brown who miskicked from 12 yards when faced with an open goal. Then four minutes later Boyd netted from a free kick awarded for handball just outside the area. Trautmann diving backwards got both hands to the ball but the power took it over the line when he landed. Lane still had time to put himself in the clear when racing round Phoenix but Trautmann saved well in the one-on-one confrontation.

BIRMINGHAM CITY

Merrick, Green, Badham, Boyd, Smith, Warmington, Astall, Lane, Brown, Murphy, Govan.

MANCHESTER CITY

Trautmann, Little, Branagan, Phoenix, Ewing, Barnes, Cunliffe, Faulkner, Dyson, Hayes, Fagan.

REFEREE

Mr FU Stringer (Nantwich)

Len Boyd (R)

Blues news extra 1924..Barton wins seventh English cap. England 3 Northern Ireland 1

Blues full back Percy Barton helped England beat Ireland again at Goodison Park in the last of his seven caps.

Blues news extra 1955.. Kinsey and Hall oppose each other. Wales 2 England 1

Noel Kinsey and Jeff Hall won their second international caps whilst at St Andrews, and were opponents for the day at Cardiff. Kinsey had the better time, his side winning 2-1.

Birthdays

Mark Jones born today 1966.   **Darren Rowbotham born today 1966.**

The Matches played on this day

1892, Division 2.		
Ardwick 2	Blues 2	Att. 6,000
	Wheldon(2)	

1st league meeting v Ardwick (Now known as Manchester City)

1898, Division 2.		
New Brighton Tower 4	Blues 0	Att. 3,000
1904, Division 1.		
Blues 5	Bury 0	Att. 12,000
Wilcox, Field,		
Green(2), McRoberts		

Blues biggest win over Bury

1910, Division 2.		
Blues 1	Barnsley 0	Att. 10,000
Freeman		
1921, Division 1.		
Blues 1	Bolton Wanderers 1	Att. 20,000
Crosbie		
1927, Division 1.		
Blues 2	Bury 2	Att. 15,000
Harris, Bradford		
1932, Division 1.		
Aston Villa 1	Blues 0	Att. 54,000
1938, Division 1.		
Grimsby Town 1	Blues 0	Att. 12,000
1949, Division 1.		
Blues 0	Everton 0	Att. 30,000
1955, Division 1.		
Blues 4	Manchester City 3	Att. 28,500
Murphy 24	Haynes 35	
Lane 41	Faulkner 63	
Govan 47	Dyson 69(pen)	
Boyd 88		
1960, Division 1.		
Aston Villa 6	Blues 2	Att. 46,306
O'Neill 1, 67	Hellawell 66	
Hitchens 31, 84, 87	Thompson 86(og)	
McParland 49		

Alan O'Neill scored on his debut after 25 seconds.

1966, Division 2.		
Carlisle United 2	Blues 0	Att. 10,900
Wilson 10		
Carlin 80		
1973, Texaco Cup 2nd round, 1st leg.		
Blues 1	Newcastle United 1	Att. 12,422
B.Latchford 33	Macdonald 48(pen)	
1977, Division 1.		
Blues 3	Derby County 1	Att. 23,108
Hibbitt 35, 54	O'Rierdan 88	
Towers 87		
1983, Division 1.		
Blues 0	Tottenham Hotspur 1	Att. 19,016
	Archibald 78	

Game kicked off five mins late as the Spurs team bus was delayed in traffic.

1988, Division 2.		
Manchester City 0	Blues 0	Att. 20,205
1994, Division 2.		
Brentford 1	Blues 2	Att. 7,779
Ward(og) 83	Shearer 38	
	Ward 70	

Blues midfielder Mark Ward scord at both ends!

1997, Division 1.		
Charlton Athletic 1	Blues 1	Att. 10,072
Mendonca 62	Devlin 83	
2000, Division 1.		
Sheffield Wed. 1	Blues 0	Att. 14,695
Harkness 58		

October 23

Playing record for this day

Playing record for this day.... 17 games, Won 7, Drawn 6, Lost 4, GF 22, GA 18.
Success rate...58.82% Year ranking....66th

The Matches played on this day

1897, Division 2.
Blues 2   Newton Heath 1   Att. 3,000
Lewis(2).
1909, Division 2.
Grimsby Town 0   Blues 2   Att. 5,000
     Freeman, Wilcox
Blues registered their only away win of the 1909-10 season.
1920, Division 2.
Sheffield Wed. 1   Blues 2   Att. 30,000
     Whitehouse(2)
1926, Division 1.
Manchester United 0   Blues 1   Att. 32,010
     Harris
1937, Division 1.
Blues 1   Derby County 0   Att. 23,992
Brunskill
1943, Wartime.
Stoke City 1   Blues 1
Dearson
1948, Division 1.
Blackpool 1   Blues 0   Att. 30,000
1957, Inter Cities Fairs Cup Semi Final, 1st leg.
Blues 4   Barcelona 3   Att. 30,791
Brown 2   Tejada 3
Orritt 32   Evaristo 18
Murphy 36, 62   Villaverde 34
1965, Division 2.
Blues 0   Southampton 1   Att. 11,861
     Chivers 83
1971, Division 2.
Blues 2   Preston North End 2   Att. 28,956
B.Latchford 19   Ingram 22
Francis 37   Tarbuck 89
1974, Texaco Cup Semi Final, 1st leg.
Newcastle United 1   Blues 1   Att. 19,866
Macdonald 59   Hatton 43
Kenny Burns had a goal disallowed after 71 minutes.
1976, Division 1.
Newcastle United 3   Blues 2   Att. 30,898
Burns 1, 72   Gallagher 10
Craig 58   Francis 52(pen)
Tommy Burns goal timed at 56 seconds.
Mick Rathbone made his Blues debut.
1982, Division 1.
Blues 0   Ipswich Town 0   Att. 12,051
Ipswich striker Paul Mariner sent off after 79 minutes.
1990, Division 3.
Crewe Alexandra 1   Blues 1   Att. 4,449
Sussex 73   Gleghorn 11
Blues eigth consecutive league draw, a club record.
1993, Division 1.
Peterborough United 1 Blues 0   Att. 7,575
Philliskirk 26(pen)
Peterborough's Dave McDonald sent off after 70 minutes.
1999, Division 1.
Grimsby Town 1   Blues 1   Att. 6,266
Allen 34   Wreh 37
2001, Division 1.
Blues 2   Gillingham 1   Att. 27,101
Horsfield 35, 47   Ipoua 52

Match of the Day

FROM 1957

BLUES BEAT BARCA

After a shaky start it's first blood to the Blues in semi-final clash

Blues gave themselves a real chance of European glory after a thrilling seven goal game at St Andrews against the Barcelona. They now travelled to the Nou Camp Stadium needing a draw to qualify for the final where they would meet the London FA victors of the other semi final. Despite being without Ken Green and John Newman in defence Blues held out against a Spanish side.

Blues could not have dreamed of a better start and they went in front within two minutes with little effort. A speculative shot from Larkin was being shepherded out by the Spanish 'keeper when Brown nipped in to turn his shot just inside the post. The celebrating 30,791 were soon brought down to earth when immediately after the restart Barcelona went up the other end to equalise.

The goal came from left winger Tejada who got free on the flank and as the Blues defence lined up for the cross the Spaniard swung a curling shot over Merrick and into the top corner of the net. Blues were now being outplayed by the visitors and to level things up they reverted to some hard graft. This however took effect later and it was Barcelona who went ahead for the first time on 18 minutes. In a lightning-quick move their centre forward Martinez raced away on the left wing and sent over a low centre, Evaristo nipped in to beat the challenge of the defenders and Merrick by toe-poking the ball in with his outstretched leg. It was all Barcelona now and Merrick kept Blues in the game with two fantastic saves from Martinez and Villaverde. Blues got back into the game right on time as Barcelona were threatening to race away from them. It was Larkin again who put the ball into the box. His cross was weakly cleared away by a defender and Orritt pounced to slam the ball in from seven yards. Barcelona stormed back to hit the goal of the game when Villaverde controlled a long ball on his chest, turned and volleyed into the top of the net, Merrick still hadn't moved for it by the time it had bounced out and rolled beyond the six yard box. This goal on 34 minutes was followed by another Blues equaliser just two minutes later. From Astall's corner Brown picked up the ball beyond the far post to cross back into the box, Murphy rose highest to thump his header past Ramallets from close range.

In the second half Blues tough tackling started to take effect much to the relief of the fans. The game became less fluent, even scrappy but at least they were in the tie. Blues took the lead for the second time in the game just after an hour's play after Ramallets had saved a fierce volley from Murphy. Murphy then netted the match winner with another rasping long-range shot that gave Ramallets no chance. In the last few minutes Barcelona wasted a great chance of an equaliser when Villaverde somehow managed to clear the bar with his effort. Blues held on to take the all important advantage to Spain in three weeks time.

BIRMINGHAM CITY
Merrick, Farmer, Allen, Larkin, Smith, Watts, Astall, Orritt, Brown, Neal, Murphy.
BARCELONA
Ramallets, Segarra, Gracia, Fltats, Olivella, Boach, Basora, Villaverde, Martinez, Evaristo, Tejada.

REFEREE
Mr S Pazza

Peter Murphy (c)

Blues news extra   1888..Friendly.
Blues 6 Long Eaton Rangers 2
1954..Doncaster raced off
Blues away fixture with Doncaster was victim of an early cancellation due to a clash with Donaster races.

Birthdays
Sid Ottewell born today 1919.

Playing record for this day

Playing record for this day.... 18 games, Won 8, Drawn 6, Lost 4, GF 37, GA 23.

Success rate...61.11% Year ranking....43rd

Match of the Day

FROM 1953

BLUES STING THE BEES

30 minute first half swarm produces five goal pot

A breathtaking 30-minute display by the Blues had the 24,000 St Andrews crowd buzzing as new boy Astall and his Birmingham team mates swarmed to sting the Bees of Brentford by five at half time. Blues at full strength welcomed back Gil Merrick to the side fresh from international duty with England. The crowd were introduced to new £14,000 signing from Plymouth, Gordon Astall who was making his St Andrews debut. The Brentford team included 19-year-old future Blues star Jimmy Bloomfield.

It took just seven minutes for Astall to impress his new fans with a scintillating run which left his full back Latimer for dead. He sent over a perfect cross for centre forward Purdon, but before the Blues striker could get a head to it, Bragg chasing back deflected the ball past his 'keeper Newton. With Blues in total command they pressed forward again and were two up after 17 minutes. Peter Murphy ran the ball to within striking range before letting loose with a 25-yard shot which zipped off the turf before ending up in the net behind Newton. Kinsey then created and finished his own move when he went straight through the heart of the flimsy looking Brentford defence to score a third on 27 minutes. A shell shocked Brentford then conceded a fourth when Purdon thumped in a header from Govan's inch-perfect cross just after the half hour mark. Just six minutes later the crowd were celebrating again as Blues rattled in a fifth to complete an astonishing 30-minute period of attacking play which had annihilated their opponents. Govan himself scored the fifth heading in a cross from Jeff Hall the Scot would have been proud of himself. Blues were given a resounding ovation when leaving the field at half-time 5-0 up.

Uncharacteristically for a team under Bob Brocklebank's charge Blues cruised in the second half at training session pace and although they dominated with possession, they failed to add to their five first-half tally. They conceded a consolation goal for Brentford late on, this after some good work and finishing from Bloomfield. At full time Blues had equalled their best win over Brentford. The match proved to be Jack Badham's last game for the club a great servant at centre half for 19 years. He was replaced the following week by another future Blues international defender Trevor Smith.

BIRMINGHAM CITY

Merrick, Hall, Green, Boyd, Badham, Warhurst, Astall, Kinsey, Purdon, Murphy, Govan.

BRENTFORD

Newton, Monk, Latimer, Harper, Bragg, Coote, Goodwin, Rainford, Dare, Bloomfield, Robertson.

Ted Purdon

October 25

Playing record for this day
Playing record for this day.... 17 games, Won 7, Drawn 4, Lost 6, GF 22, GA 21.
Success rate....52.94% Year ranking....128th

The Matches played on this day
1902, Division 2.
Blues 2   Burton United 0   Att. 7,000
Field, Athersmith.
1913, Division 2.
Huddersfield Town 7 Blues 0   Att. 10,000
1919, Division 2.
Blues 0   West Ham United 1   Att. 25,000
First league meeting v West Ham.
1924, Division 1.
Huddersfield Town 0 Blues 1   Att. 15,000
                 Bradford
Blues without a goal in their six previous games at Leeds
Road, shocked the champions-elect by snatching a 40th
minute winner by Joe Bradford.
The win took Blues to the top of the First Division with 16
points from 12 games.
1930, Division 1.
Blues 6   Chelsea 2   Att. 18,000
Bradford(2), Curtis,
Briggs(2), Crosbie
1947, Division 2.
Blues 2   Bury 0   Att. 35,000
Bodle, Dougall
1952, Division 2.
Sheffield United 2 Blues 2   Att. 30,000
Browning 6   Murphy 56
Hagan 53   Wardle 80
1958, Division 1.
Wolverhampton W. 3 Blues 1   Att. 36,156
Showell 31   Astall 40
Mullen 51, 76
1969, Division 2.
Blues 1   Cardiff City 1   Att. 28,385
Hateley 9   Clark 16
1975, Division 1.
Norwich City 1   Blues 0   Att. 20,178
Boyer 21
1980, Division 1.
Blues 1   Stoke City 1   Att. 16,535
Bertschin 56   Doyle 75
1983, League Cup 2nd round, 2nd leg.
Blues 4   Derby County 0   Att. 7,786
Harford 35, 72, 87
Gayle 38
Blues won 7-0 on aggregate.
1986, Division 2.
Sunderland 2   Blues 0   Att. 15,553
Gray 40
Buchanan 46
1988, Division 2.
Blues 0   Stoke City 1   Att. 6,262
Stainrod 73
1997, Division 1.
Blues 0   Oxford United 0   Att. 16,352.
1998, Division 1.
QPR 0   Blues 1   Att. 10,272
                 Adebola 6
2000, Division 1.
Blues 1   Gillingham 0   Att. 26,044
Marcelo 90
First league meeting v Gillingham

Match of the Day
FROM 1983
DEMOLITION DERBY
Harford causes havoc as Blues cruise into round three

Already 3-0 up from the first leg, Birmingham coasted through, and entertained a 7,786 crowd, with another mouthwatering feast at St Andrews.
Mick Harford ended his goal famine of just two in 11 games with a finely timed hat-trick as Blues finished 4-0 winners on the night, and emphatic 7-0 victors over the two legs.
Blues dominated this game throughout, but it took 35 minutes to produce the first goal. Stevenson breaking away on the right wing drilled in a low shot across goal which deflected wide. Hopkins chased in and just beat 'keeper Cherry to the ball to chip it back across goal. This time it left Harford with a simple header.
The goal opened up Derby and within three minutes Birmingham netted a second. The move started with Blake inside his own half, and finished with Gayle hitting a rasping shot which swerved viciously in the air deceiving Cherry and curling inside the post.
Blues were quoted at 80-1 to win the competition outright, but playing like they did, the odds looked generous indeed.
Blues played the entire second half at exhibition pace but still managed further goals, the first from Harford, his second of the game on the hour mark. Then with 15 minutes remaining he completed his hat-trick, Phillips and Hopkins combined well on the half-way line which allowed Hopkins to race clear, and from his cross Harford charged in to place a firm but well directed header wide of Cherry's reach.
This was the first time Blues had hit four goals in a competitive game since the same stage of this competition 12 months previously when they beat Shrewsbury 4-1. It was easily their most accomplished performance of the season so far and the fans were hopeful it would act as a fillip to their league campaign.

BIRMINGHAM CITY
Coton, Hagan, Van Den Hauwe, Blake, Wright, Stevenson, Gayle, Phillips, Harford, Halsall, Hopkins,
DERBY COUNTY
Cherry, Hooks, Harvey, McFarland, Watson, Futcher, Plummer, Davison, Campbell, Wilson, Robertson.

REFEREE
Mr R Milford (Bristol)

Mick Harford

Blues news extra 1879..Birmingham Senior Cup kicks off. Blues 2 Wednesbury Old Athletic 1
Blues won their first game in the Birmingham Senior Cup, defeating one of the region's better clubs by a 2-1 margin.

Blues news extra 1941.. St Andrews stages International England 2 Wales 1
St Andrews staged its second international this time between England and Wales. England won 2-1 in front of 25,145 fans.

Birthdays
Simon Charlton born today 1971.   David Burrows born today 1968.   Robert Hopkins born today 1961.

Playing record for this day

Playing record for this day.... 22 games, Won 10, Drawn 5, Lost 7, GF 41, GA 28.
Success rate....56.82% Year ranking....86th

Match of the Day

FROM 1982

BLUES TAME SHREWS
WITH EASY WIN

A stroll for Blues into the next round of the Milk Cup

Blues cruised into the third round of the Milk Cup with a scintillating second half against Shrewsbury Town after the tie had been evenly poised at 1-1 following the first leg at Gay Meadow. It was 1-1 at the end of the first half as Blues treated the meagre 7,861 crowd three further goals. There was nothing unlucky about the Blues 13th game of the season and the win set up tie against Derby County at St Andrews in the next round.

A cold wet night greeted the loyal band of supporters who turned up and they witnessed a mistake-riddled opening 28 minutes football from both sides. Following the first controlled piece of play, Curbishley in midfield sent Dillon away down the right wing with a glorious pass. Dillon ran to the byline and threaded a super low cross to the near post where Evans nipped in to tuck the chance away. A fantastic goal worthy of a bigger audience.

The goal should have galvanised the Blues performance, instead it spurred on Shrewsbury who looked the better side afterwards. With ten minutes of the half left their efforts were rewarded when they earned an equaliser. A hopeful long ball from defence by Griffin fell between Blake and Stevenson, as they stood waiting for the other to take charge and clear, Brown nipped in gratefully to accept the gift and struck a first time shot which went in off the post.

There was a startling difference to the Blues in the second half and it took just 15 minutes for the goal which proved to be the winner. A simple but effective pass from Brazier gave Handysides a shooting chance, his effort was deflected to Curbishley on the edge of the area. After taking one touch to bring the ball under control, his next sent the ball hurtling past Ogrizovic with a crisply hit shot.

Within two minutes Blues netted their best goal of the night and ended any hope of a Shrewsbury fightback. Brazier chased a long ball out towards the corner flag just beating MacLaren to the ball, he cut it back from the line and centred to the far post where man-of-the-match Curbishley came powering in to smash a superb volley into the net.

As the game entered the final ten minutes Blyth was surprisingly cautioned for time wasting. They eventually added a fourth goal when Brazier collected a long ball from Broadhurst and set up Dillon to crack home a wonderful strike from just outside the penalty area.

BIRMINGHAM CITY
Blyth, Mumford, Van Den Hauwe, Stevenson, Blake, Broadhurst, Dillon, Evans, Brazier, Curbishley, Handysides.

SHREWSBURY TOWN
Ogrizovic, Williams, Johnson, Petts, Pearson, Griffin, Cross, MacLaren, Brown, McNally, Bates.

Tony Evans

Birthdays

Jimmy Cochrane born today 1935.

The Matches played on this day

1889, FA Cup 2nd qualifying round.			
Oldbury Town 1	Blues 3		Att. 1,000
	W.Devey(2), Davenport.		
1895, Division 1.			
Blues 1	Aston Villa 4		Att. 10,000
Jones			
1901, Division 1.			
Nottingham Forest 1	Blues 1		Att. 11,000
	Jones		
1907, Division 1.			
Nottingham Forest 1	Blues 1		Att. 10,000
	Green		
1912, Division 2.			
Blues 0	Glossop 0		Att. 5,000
1918, Wartime.			
Bradford Park Ave. 1	Blues 1		
	J.Godfrey		
1929, Division 1.			
Blues 1	Sheffield Wed. 0		Att. 27,221
Hicks			
1935, Division 1.			
Blues 4	Portsmouth 0		Att. 30,000
White, Harris(2), Jones			
1940, Wartime.			
Leicester City 2	Blues 1		
	Gardner		
1946, Division 2.			
Blues 4	Millwall 0		Att. 25,000
Bodle, Trigg(2), Dougall			
1st league meeting v Millwall			
1957, Division 1.			
Blues 5	Bolton Wanderers 1		Att. 26,225
Orritt 5	Parry 1		
Watts 30			
Brown 34, 46			
Murphy 44(pen)			
Blues a goal down to Parry in 30 seconds.			
1960, Inter Cities Fairs Cup 1st round, 2nd leg.			
Ujpesti Dozsa 1	Blues 2		Att. 25,000
Szusza 63	Rudd 88		
	Singer 90		
Blues won 5-3 on aggregate			
Blues midfielder Johnny Gordon sent off after 83 minutes			
1963, Division 1.			
Blues 2	Wolverhampton W. 2		Att. 24,804
Woodfield(og) 6	Wharton 32		
Harley 16	Hinton 75		
1966, League Cup 4th round.			
Grimsby Town 2	Blues 4		Att. 11,298
Tees 21	Bridges 2, 88		
Cockerill 33(pen)	Fenton 67		
	Vowden 77		
1968, Division 2.			
Derby County 1	Blues 0		Att. 34,218
Carlin 75			
1974, Division 1.			
Sheffield United 3	Blues 2		Att. 21,639
Dearden 31	Hatton 58		
Woodward 44	Styles 88		
Eddy 62(pen)			
1976, Division 1.			
Bristol City 0	Blues 1		Att. 21,927
	Burns 71		
1982, League Cup 2nd round, 2nd leg.			
Blues 4	Shrewsbury Town 1		Att. 7,861
Evans 29	Brown 35		
Curbishley 60, 62			
Dillon 83			
Blues won 5-2 on aggregate			
1985, Division 1.			
Blues 0	Coventry City 1		Att. 9,267
	Gibson 16		
The sprinkler system at St Andrews went haywire, soaking players and both dugouts in a hilarious incident during the game.			
1991, Division 3.			
WBA 0	Blues 1		Att. 26,168
	Drinkell 48		
1996, Division 1.			
Blues 2	Norwich City 3		Att. 18,869
Devlin 40, 86	Johnson 19		
	Adams 49(pen)		
	Scott 54		
2001, Division 1.			
Grimsby Town 3	Blues 1		Att. 5,419
Boulding 28, 57	Marcelo 49		
Jevons 35			

October 27

Playing record for this day
Playing record for this day.... 18 games, Won 4, Drawn 4, Lost 10, GF 21, GA 37.
Success rate...33.33% Year ranking....260th

Match of the Day
FROM 1962
LEEK INSPIRES BLUES FIGHTBACK
Second City derby won by second half Blues superiority

A crowd of 42,207, the largest gate of the season, watched this nail-biting duel as Birmingham City met Aston Villa in their 17th post-war league game. Villa made the early running and Withers did well to cut out a Ewing centre.

The first Blues pressure came after Hellawell was impeded, but Leek just failed to get his head to the cross. Then Blues won three right-wing corners in as many minutes, but Villa were able to cut out the threat in the penalty area. In the 11th minute a back-pass from Watts was intercepted by O'Neill. The inside right chipped it across to Thomson, but Lynn raced back to clear from the line. After 15 minutes, Villa had the slight edge, although neither team had yet settled down.

Hennessey worked well for Blues, doing a lot of fetching and carrying. In the 18th minute a Wylie pass cleared the way for O'Neill, but he failed to control the ball properly, and the opportunity was lost. This was followed by a free kick to Blues on the edge of the penalty area. Auld screwed the ball across, but Sidebottom lunged to flip it clear, and Aitken completed the clearance to thwart the on-rushing Hellawell. Burrows had shown little of his form so far, but in the 25th minute he outpaced Lynn and hooked the ball into the centre where Hennessey was able to intercept an O'Neill challenge. Then Auld showed Lee a fine pair of heels to find the head of Harris with a perfect cross, but the centre forward failed to collect cleanly and the ball went past the right-hand post. In the 32nd minute Auld again centred along the face of the goal from the byline. But Harris, only a couple of yards out, missed a chance when the ball skidded off the side of his feet for a goal kick. Villa were the better side as the half progressed. Ewing had a shot rebound off the far post, but Thomson spoiled the chance by moving off side. Then Ewing again flashed through to Wylie, but the inside left overran the ball. The first half ended Birmingham City 0, Aston Villa 0.

The first chance of the second half fell to Blues when Auld forced an opening and Leek headed his centre down to Stubbs, who had plenty of time to turn and shoot, but put it wide. It was Villa who broke the deadlock in the 55th minute. Aitken robbed Harris and sent the ball to Thomson in midfield. Spotting O'Neill, Thomson passed immediately, and O'Neill moved in to fire past Withers. Only four minutes later, Auld, who had just beaten three Villa defenders, was brought down in the penalty area by Sleeuwenhoek. Lynn took the penalty kick and equalised. Then Villa regained the lead when Burrows also scored from the penalty spot, the result of Smith holding off Thomson. With the tension almost at breaking point, Auld then took a free kick on the left and floated the ball across to Leek, and the Blues man out jumped everyone to head the ball in via the near post. Four goals in six minutes. Sidebottom was injured in the process, and four minutes stoppage time was incurred as he received treatment. He eventually resumed and moments later was able to clear a header from Stubbs. Then Villa broke clear to win a corner, but Burrows inswinger was saved by Withers on the near post. In the 73rd minute Leek put Blues ahead for the first time. Auld chipped over a left wing corner, and while several Villa players hesitated, Leek moved in to steer the ball into the far corner with his left foot. Villa almost equalised when Burrows went through, but again he was dispossessed at the vital moment. Towards the end, Villa began to flag and Blues were able to hold on for a victory which was well deserved for their second half superiority.

BIRMINGHAM CITY
Withers, Lynn, Sissons, Wats, Smith, Hennessey, Hellawell, Stubbs, Harris, Leek, Auld
ASTON VILLA
Sidebottom, Lee, Aitken, Crowe, Sleeuwenhoek, Deakin, Ewing, O'Neill, Thomson, Wylie, Burrows

REFEREE
Mr LJ Tirebuck (Halifax)

The Matches played on this day

1888, FA Cup 2nd qualifying round.
Blues 3 — Burslem Port Vale 2 — Att. 2,000
Watson(2), Hill

1894, Division 1.
Stoke City 2 — Blues 2 — Att. 1,500
Mobley, Hands
First league meeting v Stoke.

1900, Division 2.
Blackpool 0 — Blues 0 — Att. 3,000

1906, Division 1.
Manchester United 2 — Blues 1 — Att. 14,000
Jones

1917, Wartime.
Sheffield United 3 — Blues 1
Bowser

1923, Division 1.
Huddersfield Town 1 — Blues 0 — Att. 10,000

1928, Division 1.
Blues 2 — Aston Villa 4 — Att. 40,000
Cringan, Bradford

1934, Division 1.
Wolverhampton W. 3 — Blues 1 — Att. 30,000
Mangnall

1945, Wartime.
Blues 1 — Brentford 0
Massart

1951, Division 2.
Sheffield United 4 — Blues 2 — Att. 31,528
Ringstead 6 — Stewart 5
Smith 23 — Rowley 89
Brook 36
Hagan 44

1956, Division 1.
Aston Villa 3 — Blues 1 — Att. 54,862
Lynn 2 — Kinsey 83
Roberts 25
Sewell 44

1962, Division 1.
Blues 3 — Aston Villa 2 — Att. 42,207
Lynn(pen) 59 — O'Neill 55
Leek 61, 73 — Burrows (pen) 60

1970, League Cup 4th round.
Bristol Rovers 3 — Blues 0 — Att. 21,426
Hynd (og) 14
Gilbert 65
Stubbs 84
Blues heaviest defeat by Bristol Rovers

1973, Division 1.
Blues 0 — Everton 2 — Att. 31,181
Harper 39
Connolly 51

1979, Division 2.
Blues 1 — Shrewsbury Town 0 — Att. 17,869
Ainscow 55

1984, Division 2.
Blues 0 — Oxford United 0 — Att. 20,416

1990, Division 3.
Shrewsbury Town 4 — Blues 1 — Att. 6,050
Clarke 20, 24, 49 — Bailey 83
Wimbleton 82
Former Blues striker Wayne Clarke destroyed the Blues with a 29 minute hat-trick either side of half time. Blues first league defeat of the season, their 13th league game. This was Blues best start to a league season for 91 years.

1999, Division 1.
QPR 2 — Blues 2 — Att. 11,196
Steiner 40 — Marcelo 74, 76
Kiwomya 52
Blues striker Marcelo marked his debut for the club with two goals.

Playing record for this day

Playing record for this day.... 20 games, Won 9, Drawn 8, Lost 3, GF 40, GA 22.
Success rate...65% Year ranking....25th

Match of the Day
FROM 2000
BLUES FANS 'RAIN' SUPREME

1500 Bluenoses are a perfect 10/10 in atrocious conditions

This match will best be remembered by those present for the atrocious weather conditions. The rain started at precisely 2.55pm and continued in varying degrees of strength from torrential to downpour, for the whole afternoon. Added to the swirling wind, the tail end of a tornado which destoyed parts of the south coast, football would have been difficult for the very best, let alone two gutsy teams from the Nationwide League. This 'Match of the Day' is dedicated to the travelling army of fans who were present at Fratton Park on that afternoon.

It's long been considered by author that the fans of Birmingham City are amongst the best in the world. How many other clubs command a bigger following of die-hard fanatics having achieved less on the field of play? Blues supporters have had to endure the constant reminders of the club's achievements at virtually every ground they visit, yet still they turn out in huge numbers.

Trevor Francis acknowledged the fans plight with empathy, his son James had spent the afternoon watching from the Milton Road end also, the manager described him as, "looking like he'd just got out of a swimming pool" when they met up at the end of the game. In the final ten minutes the rain fell so heavily it made visibility almost impossible. Portsmouth's Lee Bradbury summing up the final ten minutes said, "You couldn't see a thing. The rain was torrential and it stung your eyes when you looked up for a goalkick, I'm sure the ref would have called it off had it been like that from the start. As it was, he said we may as well finish the game as there was only a few minutes left." But the last word has to go to Leon Hickman of the Birmingham Evening Mail. In his 500 word tribute entitled 'My Shout' he said, "Many comments have been made about Blues fans in the past, I've made a few myself. But this, truly, was their finest, gloriously mad ten minutes."

For the record former on loan Blues striker Lee Bradbury headed Portsmouth into the lead from a corner four minutes before half time. Blues equalised through an Adebola header which skidded of the turf and into the corner just three minutes into the second half. This after Martin Grainger had struck the bar with a penalty moments earlier. The game finished 1-1, and although the author didn't catch pneumonia, he was there to see it to a finish.

PORTSMOUTH
Hoult, Hiley, Edinburgh (Waterman 71), Primus (Miglioranzi 66), Moore, Panopolous, Derry, Thogerson, Hughes, Bradbury, Claridge.

BIRMINGHAM CITY
Bennett, Gill(Burchill h/t), Michael Johnson, Sonner, Purse, Holdsworth, Eaden, Andrew Johnson(Hughes 61), Marcelo(Adebola h/t), O'Connor, Grainger.

REFEREE
Mr M Halsey (Welling)

Trevor Francis

Birthdays
Ian Osborne born today 1952.

The Matches played on this day

1893, Division 2.		
Newcastle United 0	Blues 2	Att. 3,000
	Mobley, Wheldon	
First league meeting v Newcastle		
1899, FA Cup 3rd qualifying round.		
Blues 10	Oswestry United 2	Att. 1,000
Sanivens(2), Wharton(2),		
Main(2), Wigmore,		
McRoberts(2), Adey.		
1905, Division 2.		
Blues 2	Arsenal 1	Att. 16,000
Beer, Jones		
1911, Division 2.		
Blues 2	Grimsby Town 2	Att. 15,000
Hall(pen), Gildea		
1916, Wartime.		
Leeds City 1	Blues 1	
	Hopkins	
1922, Division 1.		
Blues 2	Middlesbrough 0	Att. 28,000
Bradford, Foxall		
1933, Division 1.		
Stoke City 1	Blues 1	Att. 20,000
	Roberts	
1939, Wartime.		
Walsall 1	Blues 2	
	Jennings, Dearson	
1944, Wartime.		
Blues 1	Stoke City 1	
Bright		
1950, Division 2.		
Blues 3	Blackburn Rovers 2	Att. 25,000
Stewart 55	Charlton 49	
Trigg 62	Graham 83	
Smith 75		
1961, Division 1.		
Aston Villa 1	Blues 3	Att. 39,790
McParland 50	Harris 1, 55	
	Orritt 40	
Jimmy Harris's goal timed at 39 seconds		
1967, Division 2.		
Blues 4	Rotherham United 1	Att. 21,478
Vowden 22	Galley 44	
Bridges 57, 70, 73		
1972, Division 1.		
Coventry City 0	Blues 0	Att. 35,161
1978, Division 1.		
Coventry City 2	Blues 1	Att. 25,446
Hutchinson 30, 48	Givens 80	
Alan Buckley made his Blues debut.		
Blues had Garry Pendrey sent off after 67 minutes		
1980, League Cup 4th round.		
Blues 2	Ipswich Town 1	Att. 18,968
Worthington 30(pen)	Wark 25(pen)	
Ainscow 51		
1981, League Cup 2nd round, 2nd leg.		
Nottingham Forest 2	Blues 1	Att. 16,316
Needham 7	Evans 88	
Robertson 74		
Blues lost 5-3 on aggregate.		
Blues Kevan Broadhurst and Forest's Ian Wallace were		
both sent off in the 46th minute		
1989, Division 3.		
Bury 0	Blues 0	Att. 3,383
1997, Division 1.		
Blues 1	Ipswich Town 1	Att. 16,786
Bruce 81	Holland 35	
1998, League Cup 3rd round.		
Blues 1	Wimbledon 2	Att. 11,845
Marsden 34	Ardley 35, 46	
2000, Division 1.		
Portsmouth 1	Blues 1	Att. 15,218
Bradbury 41	Adebola 48	

October 29

The Matches played on this day

1892, Division 2.
Darwen 2   Blues 3   Att. 2,000
Mobley, Hallam, Hands
Blues left back Fred Speller suffered a broken leg and Blues played out the last 15 minutes with ten men.
1898, FA Cup 3rd qualifying round.
Blues 8   Chirk 0   Att. 3,000
Walton(3), Inglis(2),
Abbott(2), Leake.
1904, Division 1.
Aston Villa 2   Blues 1   Att. 40,000
Wilcox
1910, Division 1.
Leicester Fosse 2   Blues 0   Att. 10,000
1921, Division 1.
Bolton Wanderers 1   Blues 2   Att. 19,140
Bradford(2)
1927, Division 1.
Sheffield United 3   Blues 1   Att. 15,000
Bond
1932, Division 1.
Blues 1   Middlesbrough 4   Att. 7,588
Bradford
1938, Division 1.
Blues 3   Aston Villa 0   Att. 55,301
Harris(2), Brown
1949, Division 1.
Middlesbrough 1   Blues 0   Att. 35,000
1955, Division 1.
Wolverhampton W.1   Blues 0   Att. 47,006
Wilshaw 5
1960, Division 1.
Blues 1   Wolverhampton W. 2   Att.32,273
Showell 81(og)   Mason 31
Murray 60
1962, League Cup 3rd round, replay.
Blues 5   Barrow 1   Att. 11,765
Leek 6   Kemp 80
Stubbs 58
Arrowsmith(og) 61
Harris 67, 90
1966, Division 2.
Blues 1   Blackburn Rovers 1   Att. 17,626
Beard 88   Connelly 85
1977, Division 1.
Arsenal 1   Blues 1   Att. 31,355
Rice 85   Bertschin 16
This match screened by ATV's Star Soccer.
1983, Division 1.
WBA 1   Blues 2   Att. 20,224
Perry 75   Gayle 7
Harford 73
1985, League Cup 3rd round.
Blues 1   Southampton 1   Att. 4,832
Kennedy 33   Puckett 20
1986, League Cup 3rd round.
Tottenham Hotspur 5   Blues 0   Att. 15,542
Waddle 24
C.Allen 44, 58
Roberts 63
Hoddle 87
1988, Division 2.
Swindon Town 2   Blues 1   Att. 6,937
Atkins(og) 22   Atkins 79(pen)
White 68
1991, League Cup 3rd round.
Blues 1   Crystal Palace 1   Att. 17,270
Sturridge 84   Gray 87
1994, Division 2.
Blues 2   Bristol Rovers 0   Att. 15,886
Bull 28
Claridge 43
1995, Division 1.
Port Vale 1   Blues 2   Att. 8,875
Porter 80(pen)   Tait 7
Claridge 71
1996, Division 1.
Portsmouth 1   Blues 1   Att. 6,334
Bradbury 71   Furlong 22

Playing record for this day

Playing record for this day.... 22 games, Won 8, Drawn 5, Lost 9, GF 37, GA 33.
Success rate...47.73% Year ranking....174th

Match of the Day
FROM 1962
BARROW JUST NO MATCH
Five star Blues cruise into round four

In this League Cup replay at St Andrews Blues saw off Fourth Division Barrow without any difficulty. It was their third win in seven days after beating Wolves and Villa in First Division fixtures. Beard and Smith were both absent for Blues, making way for Watts and Wolstenholme. The first goal came in the sixth minute, scored by Leek after a struggle in the Barrow goal area. This was about the only real action in the first half. The second period was brighter, and looked more promising. The second goal came on 58 minutes when Stubbs took a pass from Leek. He ran at goal and slotted in straight past the Barrow goalkeeper. The third goal was actually put into the back of the net by Arrowsmith who fired in an own goal just three minutes later. Then a centre from Sissons came to Harris who headed the ball home with ease to get the fourth on 67 minutes. This was the first of two for Harris, but before his second Barrow saved face a little by pulling one back. Dixon passed the ball to Kemp, who shot straight past Withers on 80 minutes.
Harris got Blues fifth goal in the final minute of the match, rounding off another easy win for the home side.

BIRMINGHAM CITY
Withres, Lynn, Sissons, Hennessey, Watts, Wolstenholme, Hellawell, Stubbs, Harris, Leek, Auld.
BARROW
Caine, Arrowsmith, Richardson, Hale, Robinson, Clarke, Armstrong, Darwin, Howard, Dixon, Kemp.

1938

Birthdays

Terry Goode born today 1961.
Roy Morton born today 1955.

Beau Brummie born today 1966.
(Club Mascot)

Stewart Barrowclough born today 1951.

Playing record for this day

Playing record for this day.... 16 games, Won 4, Drawn 7, Lost 5, GF 20, GA 20.

Success rate...46.88% Year ranking....190th

Match of the Day

FROM 1976

FRANCIS FOR ENGLAND

Another supreme performance

Blues went into the game making two changes to the side that beat Bristol City in midweek. They welcomed back Archie Styles after a two game absence through injury, Mick Rathbone being relegated to the bench. The other change was in midfield where Jimmy Calderwood took over number 4 spot from Gary Emmanuel. Blues lined up hoping to stretch their St Andrews winning run to a third game, just one behind their best since rejoining the top flight four years ago.

The inspirational Trevor Francis took just 90 seconds to weave his magic and set up a sensational opening goal for Kenny Burns. From a throw in by Jones, Francis with his back to goal, collected and swung round in one movement, totally bemusing Gillard. As the defender slipped Francis got away and sent over a crisp low cross into the box where Kenny Burns raced in to hammer it past Parkes.

QPR were soon back in the game and it took them just nine minutes to level the score. A momentary lapse in the Blues defence was all it took for Stan Bowles to punish them with a deft through ball to Peter Eastoe. He took the ball on his own and with Latchford coming off his line to cover, he coolly chipped the 'keeper for a deserved equaliser.

However, Blues, and Trevor Francis in this form were a match for anyone, and with half time approaching, the most memorable moment of the game came. It had international class stamped all over it, and of course it was produced by the Blues number 8. Archie Styles took a quick throw in to Francis on the right, he evaded the challenge from McLintock with breath-taking ease. McLintock recovered and closed in on the Blues striker again, this time with the help of Clement. Francis merely dropped his right shoulder, rushed to the left and left the Scot beaten for dead. The pace beat Clement leaving Francis with a clear chance to centre the ball, pulling back his right foot he instead unleashed a crisp low shot which whistled past Parkes and smashed into the bottom corner.

The Blues defence led by Joe Gallagher, whose performance was exceptional. He kept Bowles out of harm's way for the entire second half and when the England striker got away, big Joe was there again to clear the effort of the goal line. As the game entered the final five minutes it was left again to Francis to produce another last moment of magic. He set off on a run which saw him nutmeg two QPR defenders before reaching the byline, he then chipped over a cross to Connolly. The winger desperately tried to gain control but couldn't get a finishing touch to the ball the created chance deserved by Parkes. At the final whistle the crowd acclaimed the Francis display with the chant "Francis for England" a sentiment now echoed by many elsewhere.

BIRMINGHAM CITY

Latchford, Page, Styles, Calderwood, Gallagher, Pendrey, Jones, Francis, Burns, Hibbitt, Connolly.

QUEENS PARK RANGERS

Parkes, Clement, Gillard, Hollins, McLintock, Webb, Eastoe, Leach, Masson, Bowles, Givens.

Birmingham City's goal scorer Stern John celebrates on the final whistle as Millwall stand dejected

Birthdays

Stern John born today 1976.

October 31

The Matches played on this day

1885, FA Cup 1st round.

| Blues 9 | Burton Wanderers 2 | Att. 1,000 |

Stanley(4), Davenport(2),
Evetts, A.James, Morris

Eddie Stanley scored Blues first hat-trick in the FA Cup.

1891, FA Cup 2nd qualifying round, replay.

| Blues 2 | Burton Wanderers 1 | Att. 2,000 |

Taylor, Wheldon.

1896, Division 2.

| Blues 0 | Grimsby Town 1 | Att. 7,500 |

1903, Division 1.

| Blues 0 | Sheffield Wed. 0 | Att. 13,000 |

1908, Division 2.

| Leeds City 2 | Blues 0 | Att. 15,000 |

1914, Division 2.

| Clapton Orient 1 | Blues 1 | Att. 8,000 |
| | Gibson | |

1925, Division 1.

| Newcastle United 2 | Blues 3 | Att. 30,000 |
| | Islip(2), Crosbie | |

1931, Division 1.

| Blues 2 | Bolton Wanderers 2 | Att. 20,000 |

Bradford(2)

1936, Division 1.

| Blues 1 | Bolton Wanderers 1 | Att. 25,000 |

Morris

1942, Wartime.

| Blues 1 | Coventry City 0 | |

Harris

1953, Division 2.

Derby County 2	Blues 4	Att. 18,278
Smith 59(og)	Astall 11	
McLaren 85	Purdon 20	
	Murphy 22	
	Stewart 60	

Blues centre half Trevor Smith scored an own goal on his Blues debut.

1959, Division 1.

Arsenal 3	Blues 0	Att. 34,605
Barnwell 3		
Herd 29		
Henderson 67		

1960, League Cup 2nd round.

| Bradford Park Ave. 0 | Blues 1 | Att. 4,736 |
| | Hellawell 20 | |

Blues first League Cup tie

1964, Division 1.

Blackburn Rovers 3	Blues 1	Att. 13,721
Byrom 22	Harley 36	
England 63		
Newton 83		

1970, Division 2.

Blues 2	Swindon Town 1	Att. 18,502
Vincent 48	Noble 70	
Robinson 90		

1972, League Cup 4th round.

| Blackpool 2 | Blues 0 | Att. 13,332 |
| Burns 38, 85 | | |

Dave Latchford saved Alan Suddick's 25th minute penalty

Playing record for this day

Playing record for this day.... 22 games, Won 10, Drawn 7, Lost 5, GF 38, GA 30.
Success rate....61.36% Year ranking....42nd

Match of the Day
FROM 2000
WHITE HOT BLUES
Premiership Spurs stunned by sensational Blues battering

Having accounted for Premiership giants Newcastle from the competion in 1999-2000 Blues saw this as a surprise rather than a giantkilling, the real shock being the manner in which they totally dominated the first 45 minutes converting three of their four efforts on target in devastating style. Blues silenced the White Hart Lane crowd of 27,096 when taking a 15th minute lead through Adebola. Lazaridis after beating his full back for pace sent over a low pass to Adebola lurking at the far edge of the six yard box. Unmarked he had time to control with his right foot and coolly place a left-foot shot which went in via the side netting. Adebola's second goal was as spectacular as his first goal was simple. Collecting the ball wide on the right and some 35 yards out from goal, he turned and cut inside the Spurs defence to unleash a swirling left-foot screamer which hit the roof of Sullivan's net despite the keeper's despairing dive. The destruction of Spurs continued in the last minute of the half with another stunning counter attack. A rare Tottenham move almost entered the Blues penalty area but was intercepted by Grainger who then sprinted virtually the whole length of the pitch before sending over a precise curling cross for Burchill to nip round the back of Vega and side-foot the ball home from five yards. Blues fans gave their team a standing ovation as they made their way off at half time having witnessed a clinical performance. The second half was bound to be something of an anti-climax and Tottenham seemed resigned to going out of the competition. However they were given the chance of a consolation goal on the hour when Clemence caught Lazardis's trailing leg and fell inside the area. Darren Anderton stepped up to send Bennett the wrong way and Spurs made the score more respectable. One of the biggest roars of the second half from the travelling Blue Army was reserved for the introduction of former kop hero Jose Dominguez who replaced Willem Korsten after 68 minutes, the other was the sound of the final whistle.

TOTTENHAM HOTSPUR

Sullivan, Carr, Thatcher, Freund(Davies 10 mins, Young h/t), Perry, Vega, Sherwood, Clemence, Ferdinand, Korsten(Dominguez 68), Anderton.

BIRMINGHAM CITY

Bennett, Gill, Grainger, O'Connor, Purse, M.Johnson, Eaden, Adebola, Burchill (Ndlovu 73), Hughes, Lazaridis(Robinson 78).

REFEREE

Mr D Pugh (Wirral)

Blues news extra 1957..Lights go on at St Andrews. Blues 3 Borussia Dortmund 3

Two goals from Bryan Orritt and one from Alex Govan saw Blues draw with top German side Borussia Dortmund 3-3 in a friendly to mark the openning of the newly erected floodlights at St Andrews. 45,000 turned out to witness the match.

Stan Lazaridis

Birthdays

Geoff Scott born today 1956.

The Matches played on this day
1981, Division 1.

Blues 3	WBA 3	Att. 21, 301
Gemmill 32	Regis 38, 39, 73	
Evans 75		
Worthington 78(pen)		

1987, Division 2.

Oldham Athletic 1	Blues 2	Att. 5,486
Williams 89	Frain 6	
	Whitton 75(pen)	

Blues first and only win on artificial surface.
1989, Division 3.

Blues 1	Cardiff City 1	Att. 7,468
Sturridge 50	Morgan 9	

1993, Division 1.

Blues 1	Millwall 0	Att. 9,377
Shutt 39		

This game screened live by Central TV's The Big Match.
1998, Division 1.

Blues 1	Huddersfield Town 1	Att. 19,170
Ndlovu 52	Stewart 60	

Goalscorer Peter Ndlovu was later sent off by referee Rob Styles.
2000, League Cup 3rd round.

Tottenham Hotspur 1	Blues 3	Att. 27,096
Anderton 60(pen)	Adebola 15, 28	
	Burchill 45	

November 1

Playing record for this day
Playing record for this day.... 16 games, Won 7, Drawn 5, Lost 4, GF 30, GA 23.
Success rate...59.38% Year ranking....57th

The Matches played on this day

1890, Football Alliance.

Blues 5	Stoke 1	Att. 2,500

Short(3), Wheldon, W.Devey

1902, Division 2.

Bristol City 1	Blues 1	Att. 12,000

McRoberts

First league meeting v Bristol City.

1913, Division 2.

Blues 2	Lincoln City 0	Att. 20,000

A.W.Smith, Hodges

1919, Division 2.

West Ham United 1	Blues 2	Att. 20,000

Short, Millard

1924, Division 1.

Blues 1	Blackburn Rovers 1	Att. 15,000

Bradford

1930, Division 1.

Manchester City 2	Blues 0	Att. 11,479

1947, Division 2.

Southampton 2	Blues 0	Att. 27,000

Saints second goal was scored by future Blues manager Alf Ramsey from the penalty spot after 80 minutes.

1952, Division 2.

Blues 3	Barnsley 1	Att. 20,000

Rowley 20(pen)   Chapple 38
Stewart 41
Murphy 53

1958, Division 1.

Blues 2	Portsmouth 2	Att. 23,695

Brown 33   Cutler 9
Taylor 46   Saunders 14

1969, Division 2.

Watford 2	Blues 3	Att. 17,440

Walley 30   Vowden 17
Eddy 33(pen)   Murray 25
   Vincent 57

First league meeting v Watford

1975, Division 1.

Blues 1	West Ham United 5	Att. 28,474

Francis 5   Brooking 15
   Pendrey(og) 38
   Lampard 67
   Taylor 68, 72

1980, Division 1.

Middlesbrough 1	Blues 2	Att. 14,061

Jankovic 43   Worthington 62, 89

1986, Division 2.

WBA 3	Blues 2	Att. 15,029

Williamson 8, 33   Lynex 68
Crooks 24   Clarke 69

Wayne Clarke has a goal disallowed for Blues in the 89th minute

1992, Division 1.

Charlton Athletic 0	Blues 0	Att. 4,445

1994, Division 2.

Blues 5	Crewe Alexandra 0	Att. 14,212

Hunt 24, 31, 90
Donowa 40
Claridge 84

1997, Division 1.

QPR 1	Blues 1	Att. 12,715

Barker 36   Furlong 42

Match of the Day

FROM 1994

BLUES BACK IN THE HUNT

Crewe derailed by Hunt and Co, as Blues move in on leaders

Blues were back in the top five and moving in on the leaders after another relentless attacking blitz at St Andrews with Crewe the latest victims. Crewe were into the game on the back of a 7-1 hammering by Hull in their last fixture and had now conceded 12 in two games. Both sides went into the game unchanged, which was something of a novelty for the Blues under Barry Fry. Ironically Fry had made it known he was desperate to keep a settled line-up.

In a game almost entirely dominated by the home side the visitors should have taken an early lead when a cross was headed wide by Walters with the goal wide open, Bennett having missed the ball in its flight. The let off was all Blues needed to exert their authority, and apart from a long range efort from Ashley Ward which Bennett was grateful to hold on to, Crewe offered very little after the 20 minute mark. Blues got their first goal on 24 minutes after a surging run by Donowa he nipped inside squaring the ball to Hunt who whipped his shot past Gayle. Just seven minutes later Bull headed down for Hunt to lash a shot into the other corner of Gayle's goal and the 14,212 crowd were now contemplating a huge Birmingham win. Five minutes before the break Donowa got free again with his superior pace and finished his solo run off with a fine left-foot shot.

Blues coasted through the second half almost too casually and after Crewe tired they added two late goals to complete the rout. Claridge who seemed to be struggling finished off Dominguez's run and pass from close in. Then in the last minute Hunt completed his hat-trick, the first by a Birmingham player since David Geddis over nine years before. The promised goal avalanche had materialised in style and Blues finished 5-0 winners.

BIRMINGHAM CITY

Bennett, Poole, Whyte, Ward, Barnett, Daish, Hunt, Claridge, Bull (McGavin 68), Donowa (Dominguez 68), Shearer.

CREWE ALEXANDRA

Gayle, Booty, Wilson, MacAuley, Lennon (Collins 79), Smith, Whalley, Murphy, Walters, Ward (Tierney 75), Rowbotham.

REFEREE

Mr G Kain (Bootle)

Mark Ward

Blues news extra   1941..Wartime friendly Blues 7 Birmingham Works AFA 0

Birthdays

Geoff Horsfield born today 1973.   Winston Foster born today 1941.

Playing record for this day

Playing record for this day.... 17 games, Won 6, Drawn 1, Lost 10, GF 22, GA 29.
Success rate...38.24% Year ranking....241st

Match of the Day
FROM 1963
THE AULD ONES ARE BEST
Blues take the points after cool Bertie Auld strike

Blues long awaited first away win of the season was gained at Chelsea after an inspirational 50-second goal by Harley. Chelsea fought back, Beard foiling a Moore attempt, and Smith intercepting more than one move. For Blues, Hennessey tried hard to find openings for Bullock and Hellawell, but quick tackling foiled all attempts. Chelsea's pressure paid off and in the ninth minute Brown's corner kick found Moore, who headed the equaliser over a pack of defenders. Blues fight back lacked confidence, with a shot from Bullock from the edge of the box soaring into the terraces, while Bullock's shot at goal was an easy save for Bonetti. Then a pass forward from Harley to Bloomfield allowed him to deliver a superb ball out to Auld. Auld cut in past Harris and crashed it into the net. Blues confidence now restored, they began to give Chelsea defenders a hard time whilst their half-back line remained firm. Both sides were guilty of erratic play with plenty of misdirected shots. Venables had a chance, but drove over the bar after Withers had pushed out a high centre from Brown. Harley's shot at goal from Hennessey's pass was blown offside, and Withers was again called to defend a high cross from Blunstone, which he successfully caught. Frustration began to cause scrappy play and there were one or two minor clashes, including a warning from the referee after Blunstone threw the ball against Harley.

In the second half, Chelsea came out attacking, and Withers had to defend once or twice, then Murray hit the bar following a superb dribble by Blunstone. Venables had another chance to equalise, but Withers flung himself on the ball just as he was about to shoot.

Chelsea finally equalised in the 78th minute with Moore's second goal from a cross by McCreadie. But less than two minutes later a Bloomfield cross to Bullock was netted from almost point blank range. The victory was Birmingham's and it was well deserved.

CHELSEA
Bonetti, Ron Harris , McCreadie, Hinton, Mortimore, Sorrell Brown, Venables, Murray, Graham Moore, Blunstone

REFEREE
Mr JR Osborne (Ipswich)

BIRMINGHAM CITY
Withers, Lynn, Green, Hennessey, Smith, Beard, Hellawell, Bloomfield, Harley, Bullock, Auld

Colin Green

Birthdays
Jonathan Hunt born today 1971.   David Massart born today 1919.

The Matches played on this day		
1889, Football Alliance.		
Nottingham Forest 0	Blues 0	Att. 1,000
1901, Division 1.		
Blues 1	Bury 0	Att. 15,000
Wigmore		
1907, Division 1.		
Blues 3	Manchester United 4	Att. 20,000
Jones, Eyre(2)		
1912, Division 2.		
Clapton Orient 0	Blues 2	Att. 10,000
	Bumphrey, Jones	
1918, Wartime.		
Blues 5	Hull City 1	
J.Godfrey(2), Whitehouse,		
Walker(2)		
1929, Division 1.		
Burnley 3	Blues 1	Att. 15,000
	Crosbie	
1935, Division 1.		
Preston North End 3	Blues 1	Att. 10,000
	Harris	
1940, Wartime.		
Blues 1	Leicester City 2	
Trigg		
1946, Division 2.		
Bradford Park Ave 2	Blues 0	Att. 21,638
1957, Division 1.		
Luton Town 3	Blues 0	Att. 17,000
Turner 38, 46		
McLeod 50		
1963, Division 1.		
Chelsea 2	Blues 3	Att. 22,974
Moore 9, 78	Harley 1	
	Auld 17	
	P.Bullock 80	
1968, Division 2.		
Blues 0	Oxford United 1	Att. 23,466
	G.Atkinson 80	
1st league meeting v Oxford		
1974, Division 1.		
Blues 2	Chelsea 0	Att. 30,364
Hatton 28		
Kendall 56		
Blues reduced to ten men for 20 minutes when Styles left the field with a leg wound, that required eight stitches.		
1985, Division 1.		
Luton Town 2	Blues 0	Att. 8,550
Stein 47		
Harford 70		
1991, Division 3.		
Blues 3	Torquay United 0	Att. 9,478
Gleghorn 33(pen)		
Sturridge 51		
Donowa 72		
1st league meeting v Torquay		
1993, Division 1.		
Bristol City 3	Blues 0	Att. 9,192
Allison 30, 53, 89		
1996, Division 1.		
Port Vale 3	Blues 0	Att. 8,388
Naylor 22, 41		
Guppy 68		

November 3

-1875

Playing record for this day
Playing record for this day.... 15 games, Won 8, Drawn 4, Lost 3, GF 33, GA 24..
Success rate...66.67% Year ranking....19th

Match of the Day

FROM 1979

ANOTHER STEP NEARER PROMOTION

Blues too strong for Fulham in comfortable Craven Cottage win

Blues were far stronger than their hosts and exerted their authority in every position on the field. They made just one error in defence, no surprise with the enforced experiment of striker Keith Bertschin playing left back, and dominated the midfield through Towers' strength, while Don Givens who led the attack was in inspirational form. It was a foul on the Irish centre forward which led to Blues taking the lead from the penalty spot after just 26 minutes, Archie Gemmill making no mistake with the 12-yard spot kick. The defensive error, which marred an otherwise perfect display from the championship seeking Blues, came just eight minutes later. A lapse on the right wing and slowness to cover the resultant centre allowed Davies to knock in an equaliser for Fulham. After this Blues took total control, and Givens restored their advantage two minutes before the half time interval.

Blues settled the game with a third goal just four minutes after the restart, again man-of-the-match Givens, was responsible. Lock, under pressure, could only head past his own 'keeper as the Blues men moved in menacingly. The scoreline now represented sweet revenge for an opening day defeat by the Londoners. However referee Mr Letts gave the travelling Blues fans an edgy 17 minutes when he awarded the home side a penalty minutes later. An innocuous ball lobbed into the penalty area bounced harmlessly away from danger but struck Gallagher on the arm as he tried to let it run out of play. From the spot kick Lock made amends for his earlier own goal. The game's last goal came on 68 minutes and it was Givens who rounded off a fine move and great performance to put Blues 4-2 up. A result which put them a step nearer to a quick return to top flight football.

FULHAM
Digweed, Peters, Strong, Bullivant, Money, Gale, Marinello, Beck, Guthrie, Lock, Davies.
BIRMINGHAM CITY
Wealands, Todd, Bertschin, Curbishley, Gallagher, Towers, Ainscow, Evans, Givens, Gemmill, Johnston.

Keith Bertschin

Birthdays

Wayne Mumford born today 1964.

Playing record for this day

Playing record for this day.... 20 games, Won 6, Drawn 8, Lost 6, GF 30, GA 26.
Success rate...50% Year ranking....150th

Match of the Day
FROM 1916
WHITEHOUSE A HAT-TRICK HERO

Blues claim best win of the season with five goal rout of Sheffield United

Blues maintained their unbeaten home record for the season with a resounding 5-0 win over Sheffield United who before the game were just a place behind them in the league table. An estimated crowd of 20,000 turned out in splendid weather to see if Blues could topple Leeds City at the top of the division with another home win, and they duly delivered with an emphatic scoreline.

From the first kick Blues were on top in a game almost exclusively played within the Blades half of the field. Indeed it took Blues just a minute to open the scoring, Edwards winning the ball in midfield put Brook away on the wing with a great pass and from the wingers deep cross Montgomery scored with a downward header. Moments later a cross from Montgomery caused confusion in the United area after Sturgess miskicked his clearance completely, this forced Gough to scramble the ball away before the Blues forwards converged in numbers. The 'keeper then pulled off a great save to deny McClure, and on the next attack Jephcott's lob was just too high, landing on top ot the net. Blues attack was relentless with the visitors unable to do anything but defend an area 30 yards from goal. On 24 minutes Whitehouse finished a good run with a terrific ball to Jephcott. He flicked it over the head of Sturgess into the path of Mercer who ran on to score. Just five minutes later Blues went 3-0 up with their best goal of the game. Whitehouse collected the ball after a defensive clearance and turned to beat off two United defenders before firing in from 25 yards, the ball hitting the roof of the net like a rocket. Poor Gough in the visitors goal was playing well but had conceded three goals whilst his opposite number Pearson was a mere spectator for the entire first half. With a minute remaining until half time Blues added a fourth, Whitehouse who, was clearly being held back by Pantling, somehow shrugged off the challenge to run on and collect another long clearance and with just the 'keeper to beat he placed his shot coolly into the corner.

The second half was no different and soon Blues were pressing again, Mercer with the 'keeper to beat snatched at his shot putting it wide when it seemed easier to score. Then on 53 minutes Blues added a fifth goal and it was Whitehouse again, claiming his hat-trick. Jephcott this time took on the flimsy United defence to cross from the byline and Whitehouse after, swept it in with his right foot. In the last 20 minutes Blues went close again when Montgomery was fouled just outside the area, McClure took the kick which thumped against the crossbar. In the end Blues had to settle for a 5-0 scoreline.

BIRMINGHAM CITY

Pearson, Ball, Womack, Gardner, McClure, Edwards, Jephcott, Mercer, Montgomery, Whitehouse, Morgan.

SHEFFIELD UNITED

Gough, Sturgess, Pantling, Tummon, Poole, Brelsford, Shearman, Masterman, Gillespie, Brown, Simmons.

REFEREE

Mr DH Asson (West Bromwich)

Alex McClure

The Matches played on this day

1899, Division 2.

Burton Swifts 0	Blues 3	Att. 1,500
	Archer(pen), Wharton, McRoberts	

1905, Division 1.

Blackburn Rovers 5	Blues 1	Att. 10,000
	Cornan	

1911, Division 2.

Nottingham Forest 0	Blues 1	Att. 7,000
	Graham	

1916, Wartime.

Blues 5	Sheffield United 0	
Whitehouse(3),		
Montgomery, Mercer		

1922, Division 1.

Blues 0	Cardiff City 0	Att. 25,000

1933, Division 1.

Blues 1	Liverpool 2	Att. 18,000
Roberts		

1939, Wartime.

Luton Town 1	Blues 2	
	Duckhouse, Dearson	

1944, Wartime.

Blues 1	Wolverhampton W. 0	
Small		

1950, Division 2.

Hull City 3	Blues 2	Att. 30,000
Carter 15	Trigg 42, 58	
Harrison 32, 86		

1961, Division 1.

Blues 1	Blackpool 1	Att. 21,450
Orritt 34	Charnley 38	

1967, Division 2.

Derby County 2	Blues 2	Att. 25,484
Baker 50	Vincent 75	
Durban 58	Bridges 80	

1972, Division 1.

Blues 0	Tottenham Hotspur 0	Att. 38,504

1978, Division 1.

WBA 1	Blues 0	Att. 31,988
Trewick 24		

This game screened by BBC's Match of the Day.

1986, Full Members Cup 2nd round.

Charlton Athletic 3	Blues 2	Att. 821
Gritt 11	Geddis 47	
Beggs 18	Shirtliff(og) 65	
Stewart 55		

The lowest attendance for a senior Blues fixture for 72 years.

1989, Division 3.

Reading 0	Blues 2	Att. 3,527
	Sturridge 34	
	Hicks(og) 82	

Blues first win at Elm Park.

1992, Division 1.

Blues 2	Newcastle United 3	Att. 14,376
Speedie 9	Peacock 7	
Potter 33	Scott 31	
	Matthewson (og) 38	

1995, Division 1.

Blues 2	Millwall 2	Att. 23,016
Castle 24	Dixon 58	
Charlery 88	Rae 85	

1997, Division 1.

Blues 0	Bradford City 0	Att. 14,532

2000, Division 1.

Blues 1	Bolton Wanderers 1	Att. 20,043
Grainger 50(pen)	Ricketts 66	

2001, Division 1.

Blues 2	Rotherham United 2	Att. 28,436
Branston(og) 45	Lee 16	
Horsfield 51	Swailes 54	

November 5

The Matches played on this day

1887, FA Cup 2nd round.
Blues 0	Aston Villa 4	Att. 12,000

1892, Division 2.
Bootle 1	Blues 4	Att. 1,500
	Walton, Mobley,	
	Wheldon, Hands	

1898, Division 2.
Woolwich Arsenal 2	Blues 0	Att. 7,000

1904, Division 1.
Blues 2	Blackburn Rovers 0	Att. 12,000
Wigmore, Green		

1910, Division 2.
Blues 1	Wolverhampton W. 3	Att. 20,000
Foxall		

1921, Division 1.
Blues 0	Arsenal 1	Att. 28,620

1927, Division 1.
Blues 1	Aston Villa 1	Att. 50,000
Crosbie		

1932, Division 1.
Chelsea 4	Blues 2	Att. 30,000
	Grosvenor, Curtis(pen)	

1938, Division 1.
Wolverhampton W 2	Blues 1	Att. 25,000
	Phillips	

1949, Division 1.
Blues 0	Blackpool 2	Att. 35,000

1955, Division 1.
Blues 3	Chelsea 0	Att. 30,499
Astall 2, 42		
Boyd 46		

1960, Division 1.
Blackburn Rovers 2	Blues 0	Att. 13,400
Macleod 40		
Thomas 87		

Blackburn played with ten men after Derek Dougan was forced out with a pulled thigh muscle.

1963, Division 1.
Arsenal 4	Blues 1	Att. 33,908
Baker 10, 34, 64	Bloomfield 8	
Strong 86		

1966, Division 2.
Bolton Wanderers 3	Blues 1	Att. 9,875
Rimmer 40	Hockey 88	
Byron 53		
Lee 67		

1977, Division 1.
Blues 2	Wolverhampton W. 1	Att. 28,103
Francis 31	Patching 75	
Hibbitt 79		

Jim Montgomery saved a penalty from Wolves Kenny Hibbitt in the 23rd minute. This was Sir Alf Ramsay's first game in charge as permanent Blues manager.

1983, Division 1.
Blues 1	Coventry City 2	Att. 16,169
Blake 17	Gibson 30	
	Bennett 60	

Blues striker Mick Harford required 40 stitches to a badly cut mouth and face.

1988, Division 2.
Blues 0	Portsmouth 0	Att. 5,866

1994, Division 2.
Shrewsbury Town 0	Blues 2	Att. 5,942
	Bull 4	
	Hunt 64	

Blues first win at 'bogey' ground Gay Meadow on their 11th visit.

Playing record for this day

Playing record for this day.... 18 games, Won 5, Drawn 2, Lost 11, GF 21, GA 32.
Success rate....33.33% Year ranking....258th

Match of the Day
FROM 1955
CHELSEA BURNT BY EARLY BLUES FIREWORKS
Astall stunner timed at 65 seconds

A pre-match firework display entertained the 30,499 crowd but it was two early rockets from the Blues team that lit up St Andrews in a sparkling 3-0 win over Chelsea. The visitors in their change strip of red were hoping to extend their unbeaten run to six games and were that keen to get started they were out well before their hosts for the kick off.

Blues got the game off to perfect start from the first set piece within the opening minute. Brown was bundled over by Wicks just outside the area and Govan floated the ball to Astall who cracked in a super shot on the volley from ten yards. The early goal unnerved the visitors and Blues almost capitalised on a sloppy error from Sillett. A cross by Kinsey fell to the defender who without looking back heeled it straight into the path of Govan but his first time shot sailed wide. Chelsea were then unlucky not to equalise midway through the half when a free kick taken by Blunstone rebounded out to Armstng his shot smashing off the post onto Merrick's shoulder and out for a corner. With three first half minutes remaining Blues got an all important second from a corner delivered by Govan. The kick landed at Brown's feet and his shot cannoned off the crossbar onto the goal line, as he appealed for the goal Kinsey collected the ball squared it to Astall who drove his shot in from the edge of the penalty area and it hit the roof of the net.

The second half started in equally dramatic fashion with another quickfire goal from the Blues. From Hall's long ball Sillett headed clear only as far as Boyd who struck a first time shot from 20 yards into the top corner past Robertson's outstretched arm. Chelsea to their credit never gave up and gamely fought their way back into the game, but could never find that elusive goal. This despite Merrick's uncharacteristic error 20 minutes from time, dropping a corner to cause chaos in the six-yard box before Badham and Hall scrambled it away between them. As the game entered the last few minutes Blues almost rounded off a fine performance with a lovely goal from Peter Murphy. Warhust hit a long ball down the middle to Astall who controlled well turned and slipped a clever back heel pass to Murphy, his shot on the run was brilliantly pushed round the post by Robertson.

BIRMINGHAM CITY

Merrick, Hall, Badham, Boyd, Smith, Warhurst, Astall, Kinsey, Brown, Murphy, Govan.

CHELSEA

Robertson, Williams, Sillett, Saunders, Wicks, Armstrong, Blunstone, Smith, Bentley, McNichol, Parsons.

REFEREE
Mr K Dagnall (Bolton)

Gordon Astall

Birthdays

Mick Burton born today 1969.   Jim Barrett born today 1930.

Playing record for this day

Playing record for this day.... 18 games, Won 7, Drawn 4, Lost 7, GF 27, GA 33.

Success rate...50% Year ranking....171st

Match of the Day

FROM 1965

FAB FOUR FROM BLUES

Blues break deadlock to bring goal flurry

Blues were missing six regular first team players, all because of injury, and for the same reason Cardiff were short of their star man John Charles. Johnson passed a fitness test just before the match and was included in the squad at the expense of young Toshack who had been hoping for his first game. Cardiff's Andrews posed the first real threat of the game, but his shot was saved by Herriot. For Blues Thwaites had a good attempt, but it was blocked on the line by Coldrick. A five-minute attack on the Cardiff goal proved fruitless, and so followed a long, barren spell of half-efforts and disappointments.

Thomson had an opportunity presented to him by Jackson and it was a fine save by Wilson that prevented the goal from being scored. Free kicks awarded for fouls by Lynn and Foster allowed Cardiff to encroach further into Blues' territory. The third of these saw King's shot carry high over the bar, and then Blues lost a chance when Page miskicked and. Then after 33 minutes a penalty for Blues broke the deadlock. Coldrick brought down Darrell in the area, and Lynn stepped up to take the spot kick which went straight into the net. Jackson's header two minutes later almost increased the score, but instead hit the bar. Then his quick-fire shot slipped through Wilson's arms and went wide. Darrell's shot was cleared by Rodrigues and Thomson's attempt also went wide. Just a minute before the half-time break came Blues' second goal. A lovely pass between Wylie and Thomson set the ball up for Bullock who headed into the net.

The half-time interval barely gave the players enough time to catch their breath. It was reduced to just five minutes in order for Cardiff to be able to catch their train back home. Back on the pitch they decided to speed up the game and attacked the Blues goal from the outset. However, it was Blues who scored again in the 48th minute. Darrell's effort went over, but Jackson made amends for that one when his fierce shot went into the net, hitting Coldrick on the head as it whizzed past. Cardiff scored on 53 minutes through George Andrews, and then Thomson cancelled it out with another Blues goal a minute later. The final action came with a Cardiff goal on 62 minutes, again from Andrews.

BIRMINGHAM CITY

Herriot, Fraser, Lynn, Wylie, Foster, Page, Jackson, Thomson, Bullock, Darrell, Thwaites.

CARDIFF CITY

Wilson, Harrington, Rodrigues, Hole, Coldrick, Houston, Farrell, Johnson, Andrews, Harkin, King.

REFEREE

Mr RV Spittle (Great Yarmouth)

Ron Saunders

Birthdays

Kenny Lowe born today 1961.   Brian Roberts born today 1955.   William Havenga born today 1924.
Mick Rathbone born today 1958.   Ron Saunders born today 1932.

The Matches played on this day

1897, Division 2.
Blues 1   Loughborough Town 0   Att. 5,000
Abbott

1909, Division 2.
Leicester Fosse 3   Blues 1   Att. 10,000
Freeman

1920, Division 2.
Wolverhampton W. 0   Blues 3   Att. 30,000
Burkinshaw, Crosbie, McClure

1926, Division 1.
Cardiff City 1   Blues 0   Att. 10,000

1937, Division 1.
Blues 2   Huddersfield Town 2   Att. 25,000
Dearson(2)

1943, Wartime.
Walsall 2   Blues 4
Trigg(2), Bright, Dearson

1948, Division 1.
Arsenal 2   Blues 0   Att. 62,000

1954, Division 2.
West Ham United 2   Blues 2   Att. 25,500
Hooper 46   Murphy 45, 55
Dick 70

1965, Division 2.
Blues 4   Cardiff City 2   Att. 10,743
Lynn 33(pen)   Andrews 53, 62
Bullock 44
Jackson 48
Thomson 54

1971, Division 2.
Blues 2   Orient 0   Att. 27,349
Hatton 19
B.Latchford 66
Bob Hatton scored on his St Andrews debut.

1974, Texaco Cup Semi Final, 2nd leg.
Newcastle United 4   Blues 1   Att. 17,754
Kennedy 10   Burns 67
Natrass 21
Pendrey(og) 62
Cannell 85
Blues lost 5-2 on aggregate.

1976, Division 1.
Arsenal 4   Blues 0   Att. 23,063
Stapleton 7
Nelson 50
Macdonald 50(pen)
Ross 60
Gary Jones was sent off.

1982, Division 1.
Blues 2   WBA 1   Att. 18,520
Dillon 74(pen)   Eastoe 37
Blake 78
This match screened by ITV's The Big Match

1985, League Cup 3rd round, replay.
Southampton 3   Blues 0   Att. 9,085
Armstrong 30, 35(pen)
Wallace 72
Southampton's David Armstrong missed a 59th minute penalty.

1991, Division 3.
Brentford 2   Blues 2   Att. 8,798
Smillie 29   Sturridge 24
Blissett 72   Cooper 56

1990, Leyland Daf Cup preliminary round.
Walsall 0   Blues 1   Att. 5,053
Skipper(og) 60

1993, Division 1.
Nottingham Forest 3   Blues 0   Att. 16,996
Collymore 13
Glover 70, 75

1999, Division 1.
Portsmouth 2   Blues 2   Att. 12,756
McLoughlin   Lazaridis 59
35, 88(pens)   M.Johnson 62
Blues defender Darren Purse sent off in the 88th minute.

November 7

The matches played on this day

1903, Division 1.
Sunderland 3 — Blues 1 — Att. 12,000
Wigmore

1908, Division 2.
Blues 2 — Barnsley 1 — Att. 10,000
Green, W.H.Jones

1914, Division 2.
Blues 3 — Arsenal 0 — Att. 15,000
A.W.Smith(2), Gibson

1925, Division 1.
Blues 0 — Bolton Wanderers 1 — Att. 25,000

1931, Division 1.
Sheffield Wed. 5 — Blues 1 — Att. 17,438
Bradford

1936, Division 1.
Brentford 2 — Blues 1 — Att. 25,000
Dearson

1942, Wartime.
Blues 4 — Walsall 3
Walton, Dearson(3)

1953, Division 2.
Blues 0 — Blackburn Rovers 0 — Att. 25,000

1959, Division 1.
Blues 1 — Luton Town 1 — Att. 19,007
Barrett 53 — Bingham 8

1964, Division 1.
Blues 2 — Arsenal 3 — Att. 20,219
Leek 83 — Baker 6
Vowden 85 — Eastham 37
Samuels 65

1970, Division 2.
Sunderland 2 — Blues 1 — Att. 15,994
Hughes 70 — Summerill 25
Porterfield 88

1973, League Cup 3rd round, replay.
Newcastle United 0 — Blues 1 — Att. 19,276
Francis 98(pen)
After extra time

1981, Division 1.
Brighton & HA 1 — Blues 1 — Att. 18,292
Robinson 68 — Evans 22

1984, League Cup 3rd round, replay.
WBA 3 — Blues 1 — Att. 16,717
Thompson 64 — Shearer 49
Robertson 75
Cross 90
Ian Brown made his Blues debut and only appearance for the club. Blues had Tony Rees sent off after 54 minutes.

1987, Division 2.
Hull City 2 — Blues 0 — Att. 7,901
G.Williams 42
Overson(og) 66

1992, Division 2.
Bristol City 3 — Blues 0 — Att. 10,008
Rosenior 45
Shelton 47
Cole 85

1998, Division 1.
WBA 1 — Blues 3 — Att. 19,472
Carbon 79 — Ndlovu 5, 33
Adebola 11

2000, Division 1.
Norwich City 1 — Blues 0 — Att. 13,900
Forbes 45
Blues reduced to ten men after 80 mins after David Holdsworth's sending off.

2001, Division 1.
Blues 0 — WBA 1 — Att. 23,554
Johnson 36
Danny Sonner sent off in the 75th minute.

Playing record for this day
Playing record for this day.... 19 games, Won 5, Drawn 3, Lost 11, GF 22, GA 33.
Success rate...34.21% Year ranking....253rd

Match of the Day
FROM 1998

NUDDY MARVELOUS
Albion destroyed by early Ndlovu blast

Blues enjoyed their first win at the Hawthorns for four-and-a-half years and ironically it was just as convincing this time as it was back in April 1994 when the Blues crushed the Albion 4-2.

Often guilty of spurning their chances Blues set off taking two out of two in the first 11 blistering minutes. First a long ball from Rowett was left to run by Adebola for McCarthy to cross from the edge of the 18-yard box. The ball was met by a leap from Ndlovu and his header smacked into the top corner. With Albion still reeling McDermott slipped when about to clear a loose ball from just inside the his own half and by the time he had picked himself up Adebola was running clear on goal. As Miller came out to present the one-on-one the striker merely slid the ball under the 'keeper's lunge and it rolled into the net as the 3,000 travelling Blue Army celebrated right behind it. With Blues in control they were happy to play some wonderful exhibition football as all Albion were now playing for was professional pride. A Holland header then bounced towards Ndlovu, but the Albion defence failed to recognised the potential danger even from 45 yards out. The Zimbabwean international swivelled away from Murphy's challenge and then beat Carbon wrong footing the defender to leave a right-foot shot which flew past Miller's despairing dive. Blues were 3-0 up and announced their declaration at half time by bringing off Adebola for Nicky Forster.

The second half started with Rowett almost forgetting the half-time plan and he should have scored when left unmarked from a McCarthy corner, but headed wide. This apart, Blues were content to get some exta light training work done. The 19,472 crowd briefly raised an eybrow when Carbon headed in Bortolazzi's corner 11 minutes from the end, but it only proved that the Brummie Road hadn't actually fallen asleep.

This win was the start of a period when Blues looked forward to the rich pickings that an Albion fixture bought, they won the return at St Andrews 4-0 then on their next match at the Hawthorns the following season handed them another thrashing 3-0.

WEST BROMWICH ALBION
Miller, McDermott (Mardon 62), Murphy, Carbon, Van Blerk, Quinn (Maresca 80), Flynn, Bortolazzi, Kilbane, Hughes, Evans (De Freitas).

BIRMINGHAM CITY
Poole, Rowett, Grainger, Marsden (Ablett 90), Purse, Johnson, McCarthy, Adebola (Forster h/t), Furlong (Robinson 82), Holland, Ndlovu.

REFEREE
Mr K.Leach (Eton)

Peter Ndlovu

Birthdays
Neil Dougall born today 1921.

Playing record for this day

Playing record for this day.... 17 games, Won 7, Drawn 4, Lost 6, GF 25, GA 22.
Success rate...50% Year ranking....152nd

Match of the Day
FROM 1995
BLUES EARN EXTRA BONUS
Rushfeldt and Charlery star in late cup win

The draw for the Coca Cola Cup bought these two sides together for the first time in a cup encounter since they met at Wembley in the Leyland Daf Cup final in May 1991. That game ended in late drama with a Blues win, this game at Prenton Park was no different. Blues went into the game with two changes from the side that had dramatically snatched a draw at St Andrews against Millwall. Liam Daish returned and Michael Johnson moved to left back for the suspended Gary Cooper. The other change was in midfield where Ward was back with Otto moving to the bench. The game started in complete contrast to the first tie with neither side creating anything for the first half an hour. The first opportunity fell to Blues and Rushfeldt who anticipated a back pass from McGreel and nipped in to put himself in a one-on-one with Coyne, but his hesitancy on the ball saw his shot blocked. With just the one chance during the first 45 minutes the teams went in at half time level at 0-0. Rushfeldt quickly made amends in the second half when he got on the end of a deep cross from Poole to head in his first goal for the club on 51 minutes. It was his last contribution to the game as he was substituted soon afterwards by Charlery. Blues had defended well allowing Tranmere nothing at all in the way of clear goal scoring chances right up to the last minute, when Aldridge netted a controversial equaliser. Extra time was almost exclusively Blues and Charlery in particular. With just six minutes gone good work by Otto and a neatly chipped cross from Claridge allowed him to beat Teale and score from an acute angle. After a nervy five minute spell when Nevin skimmed the bar with a   long-range shot, then Bennett pulled off an incredible point-blank save from close in, Blues regained control and made the game safe two minutes before the first period of extra time. A simple but decisive goal by Charlery gave Coyne no chance.

TRANMERE ROVERS

Coyne, Stevens, Thomas, McGreel, Teale, Jones, Brannan, Aldridge, Bennett (Branch 74), Moore Nevin.

BIRMINGHAM CITY

Bennett, Poole, Johnson, Ward, Edwards, Daish, Hunt (Finnan 90), Claridge, Rushfeldt (Charlery 69), Castle, Tait.

REFEREE

Mr K Lynch (Knaresborough)

Paul Tait (L) Steven Claridge (R)

Blues news extra   1885..Blues now a professional outfit

Blues decided to become a professional organisation, shortly after the FA allowed clubs to pay players.

Blues news extra   1941..Wartime friendly Blues 2 All Welsh XI 3

Birthdays

Andy Gosney born today 1963.   **David Holdsworth born today 1968.**   **Mark Prudhoe born today 1963.**
Johnny Jordan born today 1921.   **Alan Curbishley born today 1957.**
Jackie Brown born today 1914.

The Matches played on this day
1884, FA Cup 1st round.

B'ham Excelsior 2	Blues 0	Att. 2,000
1890, Football Alliance.		
Bootle 1	Blues 1	Att. 1,000
	W.Devey	
1902, Division 2.		
Blues 3	Glossop 1	Att. 5,000
McRoberts(2), Beer		
1913, Division 2.		
Blackpool 2	Blues 2	Att. 5,000
	A.W.Smith, Walker	
1919, Division 2.		
Blues 2	Wolverhampton W. 0	Att. 30,000
Short(2)		
1924, Division 1.		
West Ham United 0	Blues 1	Att. 28,000
	Bradford(pen)	
1930, Division 1.		
Blues 0	West Ham United 2	Att. 25,000
1947, Division 2.		
Blues 3	Doncaster Rovers 0	Att. 25,000
Goodwin(2), Bodle		
1952, Division 2.		
Lincoln City 1	Blues 1	Att. 16,220
Johnson 75	Trigg 24	
1958, Division 1.		
Blackburn Rovers 3	Blues 2	Att. 28,800
Dobing 44, 85	Brown 9	
Vernon 76	Larkin 78	
1969, Division 2.		
Blues 2	Swindon Town 0	Att. 28,167
Murray 7		
Vowden 20		

Due to an error by the referee,Swindon kicked off both halves of the game.
1975, Division 1.

Manchester City 2	Blues 0	Att. 28,329
Bell 22, 30		
1980, Division 1.		
Blues 1	Crystal Palace 0	Att. 16,910
Bertschin 17		
1983, League Cup 3rd round.		
Blues 2	Notts County 2	Att. 10,484
Handysides 8	Harkouk 54	
Phillips 64	Chiedozie 66	
1986, Division 2.		
Blues 1	Oldham Athletic 3	Att. 6,082
Clarke 65(pen)	Henry 1	
	Williams 42	
	Palmer 70	

Tony Henry's goal for Olham was timed at 38 seconds. Blues keeper Roger Hansbury saved a 10th minute penalty from Ron Futcher.
1995, League Cup 3rd round, replay.

Tranmere Rovers 1	Blues 3	Att. 9,151
Aldridge 90	Rushfeldt 51	
	Charlery 96, 103	

After extra time..... 90 minutes score 1-1
1997, Division 1.

Blues 1	Norwich City 2	Att. 16,464
Devlin 27(pen)	Forbes 23, 36	

The Matches played on this day
1889, Football Alliance.
Blues 0   Walsall Town Swifts 2   Att. 3,000
1895, Division 1.
Blues 1   Nottingham Forest 0   Att. 5,000
Mobley
1901, Division 1.
Blackburn Rovers 3   Blues 1   Att. 6,000
                 Archer(pen)
1907, Division 1.
Blackburn Rovers 1   Blues 0   Att. 14,000
1912, Division 2.
Blues 4   Lincoln City 1   Att. 35,000
Hall(2), Jones, Bumphrey
1918, Wartime.
Hull City 0   Blues 3
                 Brown(2), Whitehouse
1929, Division 1.
Blues 2   Arsenal 3   Att. 33,904
Bradford, Crosbie
1935, Division 1.
Blues 2   Brentford 1   Att. 25,000
Jones, Stoker
First league meeting v Brentford
1940, Wartime.
Stoke City 5   Blues 0
1946, Division 2.
Blues 3   Manchester City 1   Att. 30,000
Dougall, Mulraney, Trigg
1957, Division 1.
Blues 2   Sunderland 3   Att. 25,800
Murphy 7   Revie 2, 20
Govan 54   Bingham 67
1963, Division 1.
Blues 3   Blackpool 2   Att. 17,516
Lynn 29   Crawford 50
Auld 57   Ball 55
Bloomfield 73
1968, Division 2.
Blackburn Rovers 3   Blues 2   Att. 11,721
Fryatt 54, 88   Pickering 64, 80
Darling 60
Fred Pickering was made captain for the day, against his former club.
1974, Division 1.
Burnley 2   Blues 2   Att. 15,835
Hankin 20, 72   Rodaway(og) 19
                 Taylor 55
1982, League Cup 3rd round.
Blues 3   Derby County 1   Att. 12,475
Handysides 33
Dillon 69(pen)
Curbishley 88
1985, Division 1.
Blues 0   Newcastle United 1   Att. 8,162
                 Reilly 13
Blues had Wayne Clarke sent off after 79 minutes.
1988, Simod Cup 1st round.
Aston Villa 6   Blues 0   Att. 8,324
Platt 3
Gallacher 34
McInally 38, 75
Mountfield 37
Evans 42
Blues heaviest defeat by Villa.
1991, Division 3.
Huddersfield Town 3   Blues 2   Att. 11,688
Roberts 8, 49   Gleghorn 59
Onoura 77   Matthewson 80

Playing record for this day
Playing record for this day.... 18 games, Won 7, Drawn 1, Lost 10, GF 30, GA 38.
Success rate...41.67% Year ranking....225th

Match of the Day
FROM 1982
BLUES SHOW BOTTLE
TO EARN MILK CUP WIN
Derby swept aside by fabulous Birmingham display

Blues progressed to round four of the Milk Cup brushing aside a poor Derby side who finished the game with just nine men.

Blues were the slightly better starters in a scrappy first half, their advantage only recognised by the fact that they made fewer errors. Their first chance fell to striker Mick Ferguson, back in the side in place of Tony Evans. Another misguided pass in defence was seized upon by him and from a great position he hit a weak shot straight at Cherry. However it was Ferguson, with help from Van Den Hauwe and Handysides, who enabled Blues to take the lead with a goal on 33 minutes. He guided a header on to the left wing which gave Van Den Hauwe space in which to race clear, he squared the ball to Handysides, who struck it first time and after a considerable deflection off the unfortunate Foster, it flew past Cherry.

Blues were gifted a great chance in the 69th minute when Barton underhit a back pass to Cherry. Handysides was quickly on to it and was in the process of rounding the 'keeper to score when he was pulled down. Referee Salmon awarded the penalty but then ignored the new directive to punish offences such as this with a sending off. Dillon smashed in the spot kick, to make it 2-0.

Just eight minutes later Salmon produced a red card after Broadhust was heavily challenged by a late tackle by Powell. This brought about Derby's best period of play and although it only lasted five minutes they managed to reduce the score to 2-1. Blues keeper Coton was caught out of position off his line in no man's land from a Hill centre, Swindlehurst headed in comfortably needing only to get the effort on target for the ball to hit the back of the exposed net. Blues retaliated and a surging run by man-of-the-match Handysides was crudely stopped by former Wolves centre half McCalle, leading to another red card. With Derby's frail defence now laid bare, Curbishley strolled through two minutes from time to add a third goal for Blues.

BIRMINGHAM CITY
Coton, Hagan, Van Den Hauwe, Stevenson, Blake, Broadhurst, Dillon, Brazier, Ferguson, Curbishley, Handysides,
DERBY COUNTY
Cherry, Barton, Buckley, Powell, Foster, McAlle, Brolly, Mills (Wilson 67), Hill, Swindlehurst, Dalziel.

REFEREE
Mr Ken Salmon (Barnet)

Ian Handysides

Birthdays
Ricky Otto born today 1967.   **Simon Black born today 1975.**

Playing record for this day

Playing record for this day.... 15 games, Won 5, Drawn 5, Lost 5, GF 16, GA 18.

Success rate...50% Year ranking....166th

Match of the Day

FROM 1945

BLUES WIN FIVE GOAL THRILLER

New £14,000 signing Lawton not enough to stop Brum victory

In front of the season's highest crowd of 52,959 Birmingham, in their change strip of red-and-white stripes, continued their impressive start to the season with a thrilling 3-2 win over Chelsea at Stamford Bridge. Blues went into this game without the services of Edwards and Dearson - both selected to play for Wales. Chelsea were boosted by new signing Tommy Lawton, a £14,000 capture from Everton.

Blues made a great start and were 1-0 up after just six minutes when Wilson Jones converted Mulraney's centre via a clever flick on by Harris. With Blues still continuing to dominate, Chelsea, equalised on 15 minutes against the run of play. The goal was a breakaway by Williams, who intercepted a pass from Mitchell in midfield and ran on, slipping the ball to his right for Lawton who easily rounded Merrick to score his first goal for Chelsea. The goal, however, steadied the Blues, and although they attacked less, they still held the territorial advantage against their hosts. With four minutes to the break, Blues' dominance was rewarded by going into the lead again from the penalty spot - a shot which Arthur Turner hammered past Woodley in the Chelsea goal.

The second half started with Chelsea in the ascendancy, searching for a second equaliser. This eventually came on the hour, through Lawton again, repaying some of the huge fee paid for him. However, with 11 minutes remaining, Blues hit the game's best goal to effectively win the contest. Turner, who was by far the best player on the field, won yet another decisive tackle in his own half. Getting up from the challenge immediately, he advanced with the ball. As Chelsea's midfield closed in he sent an exquisite long ball down the middle for Wilson Jones, who took the pass on the run, beat his marker with a nutmeg, and chipped the ball. It sailed over the advancing Woodley, who could only watch as it went straight over his head and dropped into the net behind him.

CHELSEA

Woodley, White, Tennant, Russell, Harris, Ross, Goulding, Williams, Lawton, Goulden, Bain.

BIRMINGHAM CITY

Merrick, Duckhouse, Jennings, Harris, Turner, Mitchell, Mulraney, Dougall, Wilson Jones, Bodle, White.

REFEREE

Mr E.Flinstone (Newmarket)

Gil Merrick

Birthdays

Graham Hyde born today 1970.   Jackie Lane born today 1931.

The Matches played on this day

1894, Division 1.

| WBA 4 | Blues 1 | Att. 4,523 |
| | Hands | |

First league meeting v WBA.

1900, Division 2.

| Blues 0 | Chesterfield 0 | Att. 6,000 |

1906, Division 1.

| Blackburn Rovers 1 | Blues 0 | Att. 10,000 |

1917, Wartime.

| Leeds City 1 | Blues 0 | |

1923, Division 1.

| Blues 2 | West Ham United 0 | Att. 20,000 |
| Bradford, Islip | | |

1928, Division 1.

| Blues 2 | West Ham United 2 | Att. 25,000 |
| Bradford, Hicks | | |

1934, Division 1.

| Derby County 1 | Blues 1 | Att. 20,077 |
| | Guest | |

1945, Wartime.

| Chelsea 2 | Blues 3 | |
| | Jones(2), Turner(pen) | |

1951, Division 2.

| Hull City 0 | Blues 1 | Att. 27,482 |
| | Briggs 40 | |

1956, Division 1.

Manchester City 3	Blues 1	Att. 21,005
Johnstone 54, 60	Kinsey 34	
Hayes 59		

1962, Division 1.

Blues 2	Nottingham Forest 2	Att. 22,024
Harris 51	Julians 7	
Leek 59	Palmer 33	

Harris goal disallowed on 32 minutes.

1973, Division 1.

| Southampton 1 | Blues 1 | Att. 25,297 |
| Fisher 68 | Hatton 46 | |

1979, Division 2.

| Blues 1 | Cambridge United 0 | Att. 17,120 |
| Lynex 52 | | |

First league meeting v Cambridge

1984, Division 2.

| Manchester City 1 | Blues 0 | Att. 25,369 |
| Phillips 25 | | |

1990, Division 3.

| Chester City 0 | Blues 1 | Att. 2,273 |
| | Hopkins 88 | |

Nigel Gleghorn took over from injured 'keeper Martin Thomas who was stretchered off in the 57th minute.

November 11

The Matches played on this day

1882, FA Cup 1st round.
Blues 3   Stafford Road Works 3   Att. 2,000
Slater(2), T.James

1883, FA Cup 1st round, replay.
B'ham Excelsior 3   Blues 2   Att. 2,000
   A.James, Stanley
Played at Aston Lower Grounds

1893, Division 2.
Lincoln City 2   Blues 5   Att. 1,000
   Wheldon, Mobley(3), Walton

1899, Division 2.
New Brighton Tower 2   Blues 2   Att. 1,500
   Scrivens, Leake

1905, Division 1.
Blues 3   Sunderland 0   Att. 11,000
Anderson, Jones, Tickle

1911, Division 2.
Blues 1   Chelsea 4   Att. 25,000
Gibson

1916, Wartime.
Bradford City 1   Blues 1
   Whitehouse

1922, Division 1.
Cardiff City 1   Blues 1   Att. 20,000
   Watkins

1933, Division 1.
Portsmouth 0   Blues 2   Att. 15,000
   White, Fillingham

1939, Wartime.
Coventry City 3   Blues 1
   Brown

1944, Wartime.
Wolverhampton W. 0   Blues 4
   Trigg(3), Faulkner

1950, Division 2.
Blues 0   Doncaster Rovers 2   Att. 27,000
   Doherty 53, 80

1958, Inter Cities Fairs Cup 1st round, 1st leg.
Blues 2   Cologne XI 0   Att. 20,266
Larkin 59
Taylor 67

1959, Inter Cities Fairs Cup Semi Final, 2nd leg.
Blues 4   Union St Gilloise 2   Att. 14,152
Gordon 10, 62   Jansen 61
Larkin 32   Diricx 88(pen)
Hooper 90(pen)
Blues won 8-4 on aggregate
Blues winger Brian Taylor broke his leg in the 12th minute and was stretchered off, later Barrett has to leave the field through injury and Blues finished the game with nine men.

Playing record for this day
Playing record for this day.... 22 games, Won 11, Drawn 5, Lost 6, GF 43, GA 29.
Success rate...61.36% Year ranking....41th

Match of the Day
FROM 1978

UNITED HUMBLED BY FIVE GOAL THRASHING

Blues were again stuggling when this fixture arrived, they had lost eight of their last nine games and they remained rooted to the bottom of the table. They started well with two great chances, Givens had a shot scrambled away by Greenhoff and Houston cleared another effort from Dillon of his goal line both within the opening ten minutes. Even so not many would have predicted what was about to happen in this extraordinary performance.

A mistake by Page allowed Macari to feed Jordan and United were 1-0 up on 13 minutes. On 23 minutes Birmingham's luck changed when they gained an equaliser from Dillon. Good work by Givens set up the chance, and when the striker won a chase for a loose ball he slipped a fine pass to Dillon who crashed in a low right-foot shot from eight yards which left Roche in the United goal no chance. Then came a bizarre incident involving Blues Argentinian international Alberto Tarantini. Just after United had made a substitution, Tarantini went over to restart the game with a throw in, as he approached the visitors' coach Tommy Cavanagh to retrieve the ball it was thrown to him but, the ball hit him on the head accidently. Tarantini fell as if hit by a sniper, and remained sprawled out on the floor until Blues boss Jim Smith emerged to have a word in the defender's ear. Suddenly the Argentinian got up and resumed the game. However Jim Smith can take credit for the second Blues goal, Tarantini, sent over a wonderful free kick to Givens who headed across United's goal for Buckley to nod in from close range.

Within two minutes Blues went further ahead, the inspirational Givens again involved. The Irish international won the ball from Greenhoff and delivered a pefectly weighted pass to Buckley, who ran on to chip the ball over the advancing Roche.

The Blues received a tremendous welcome when the teams emerged for the second half. They quickly got back into their stride and added a third goal just six minutes after the restart. Fittingly this was scored by Givens. Blues were now unbelievably 4-1 up. In the last minute they grabbed a fifth goal to cap an amazing afternoon. Again it was Givens, who knocked down the ball from another free kick taken by Tarantini and Calderwood charged in to thump the ball past Roche. Blues were jubilant and celebrated their first five goal haul since back in December 1976. This was the first time United had conceded five in a league game for six years.

BIRMINGHAM CITY
Freeman, Tarantini, Dennis, Towers, Gallagher, Page,
Dillon, Buckley, Givens, Calderwood, Fox.

MANCHESTER UNITED
Roche, Nicholl, Houston, McCreery, Brian Greenhoff, Buchan,
Coppell, Jimmy Greenhoff, Jordan, Macari, McIlroy

REFEREE
Mr T. Spencer (Swindon)

Birmingham City's Len Boyd (r) runs out, followed by goalkeeper Gil Merrick (c) - 1956

Blues news extra   1886 ... A record breaking 13!!! Blues 13 Coseley 0

Blues set their all time record goal tally in any competitive senior game by hitting 13 against Coseley in this amazing second round Birmingham Senior Cup tie.

Birthdays
Len Boyd born today 1923.

Jim Smith

The Matches played on this day
1961, Division 1.

Blackburn Rovers 2	Blues 0	Att. 12,080

Lawther 10
Pickering 71

1967, Division 2.

Blues 3	Preston North End 0	Att. 27,664

Vincent 38, 70
Hockey 78

1972, Division 1.

Newcastle United 3	Blues 0	Att. 26,010

Gibb 2
Howard 45
MacDonald 80

1978, Division 1.

Blues 5	Manchester United 1	Att. 23,550

Dillon 23   Jordan 13
Buckley 32, 34
Givens 51
Calderwood 90

1980, Division 1.

Blues 2	Nottingham Forest 0	Att. 22,433

Worthington 4, 61
Phil Hawker made his Blues debut.

1989, Division 3.

Blues 0	Leyton Orient 0	Att. 7,491

1992, Anglo Italian Cup International stage, Group A.

Blues 1	A.S.Bari 0	Att. 4,970

Cooper 48
Game was held up for 55 minutes due to a floodlight failure
which occured just after half time, the game finally finished
at 9.55pm.
Four players were sent off in the last five minutes. For Blues
David Speedie and Louie Donowa, while the Italians had
Marcell Montanari and Massimo Brambati dismissed.

1995, Division 1.

Reading 0	Blues 1	Att. 10,203
	Charlery 75	

November 12

The Matches played on this day

1892, Division 2.
Blues 3   Burton Swifts 2   Att. 3,000
Mobley, Walton, Jenkyns

1898, Division 2.
Blues 9   Luton Town 0   Att. 4,000
Gardner(2), McRoberts,
Wharton, Inglis,
Robertson(3), Abbott
Blues best win over Luton
This is still Luton's heaviest defeat in the Football League

1904, Division 1.
Nottingham Forest 0   Blues 2   Att. 10,000
          McRoberts, Jones

1910, Division 2.
Chelsea 2   Blues 2   Att. 17,000
         Jones, Wigmore

1921, Division 1.
Arsenal 5   Blues 2   Att. 30,000
       Whitehouse, Bradford

1927, Division 1.
Burnley 2   Blues 1   Att. 12,000
         Bradford

1932, Division 1.
Blues 0   Huddersfield Town 2   Att. 10,000

1938, Division 1.
Blues 1   Everton 0   Att. 27,548
Phillips

1949, Division 1.
Newcastle United 3   Blues 1   Att. 30,113
         Slater

1955, Division 1.
Blackpool 2   Blues 0   Att. 22,967
Taylor 30
Mudie 50

1960, Division 1.
Blues 3   Manchester United 1   Att. 31,549
Neal 21   Charlton 81
Gordon 72
Taylor 76
Blues 'keeper Johnny Schofield sustained a fractured skull and later has a metal plate inserted in his head to support him. Bryan Orritt took over in goal whilst Schofield was off the field receiving treatment, however the 'keeper incredibly returned later on to finish the game. Giles of Manchester United was also carried off following a separate incident which reduced the visitors to ten men also.

1966, Division 2.
Blues 4   Charlton Athletic 0   Att. 14,023
Vowden 19, 50
Bullock 44
Vincent 65

1969, Division 2.
Portsmouth 1   Blues 1   Att. 16,508
Munks 25   Murray 55
Tony Hateley goal disallowed for Blues

1977, Division 1.
Everton 2   Blues 1   Att. 37,793
Latchford 32, 51   Bertschin 13

1983, Division 1.
Luton Town 1   Blues 1   Att. 11,111
Stein 16   Hopkins 9

1988, Division 2.
Oxford United 3   Blues 0   Att. 5,589
Foyle 11, 89
Bardsley 55(pen)

1994, FA Cup 1st round.
Slough Town 0   Blues 4   Att. 13,394
         Shearer 9, 36
         McGavin 33, 40
Blues were drawn away in this first round tie, however after a request from Slough the game was switched to St Andrews.

Playing record for this day
Playing record for this day.... 17 games, Won 7, Drawn 3, Lost 7, GF 35, GA 26.
Success rate...50% Year ranking....144th

Match of the Day

FROM 1966

NEW BOYS SCORE!

Blues get four in well deserved win

New signings Vincent and Bullock were in the side fielded against Charlton at St Andrews today. They were to make their presence felt, with both of them hitting the back of the net in front of a crowd of 14,034. Ex-Villa man Kenning was the first Charlton player to pose a threat to Blues, but his shot was stopped by Herriot. Shortly after that Bridges almost scored, but despite avoiding Kinsey and Charlton goalkeeper Wright he shot wide of the post. Bullock was brought down by King and this gave Blues a free kick, and the former Leicester player a ticking off. Blues deservedly took the lead after 19 minutes when Beard took a free kick which he slammed into the centre. It came to Vowden who evaded the defence and shot in past Wright.

Vincent and Bullock were giving their all to the game. Chances were plenty at both ends, but none were destined for the back of the net. A corner by Hockey was sent to Bridges who shot over the bar, and then Herriot made a save when Glover sent a quick volley goalwards. Vowden put the ball into the net on 37 minutes, but it was disallowed and a free kick was awarded to Charlton. King brought down Bullock once again, and he was cautioned by the referee.

Just before the half time break Bullock scored a great goal for Blues. The 20-year-old centre forward got onto a low cross from Beard and his shot banged against the crossbar before going into the net.

In the second half Johnny Vincent produced a fine solo effort which saw him beat three Charlton men but then send his shot high over the bar. Bullock got possession of the ball on 50 minutes and sent it on to Bridges who crossed it for Vowden to side foot into the net. Wright then had to make two good saves from Martin and Bullock. Herriot stopped Charlton from scoring at the other end, being agile enough to save a shot and then get up to stop the rebound coming his way from Halom. On 65 minutes Vowden turned provider for Vincent to score his first. He ran for the ball and, against the odds, got possession. It went to Vincent who hit it into the goal. King tried to stop its passage into the net, but an effort only succeeded in helping it across the line. More chances for both teams followed, and an effort from Vowden on 80 minutes really should have gone in, but he sent it wide.

BIRMINGHAM CITY
Herriot, Martin, Green, Thomson, Sharples, Beard,
Bridges, Vincent, Bullock, Vowden, Hockey.
CHARLTON ATHLETIC
Wright, Bonds, Kinsey, Reeves, King, Appleton,
Kenning, Gregory, Saunders, Halom, Glover.

REFEREE
Dr DWG Brady (Rotherham)

Peter Bullock

Playing record for this day
Playing record for this day.... 13 games, Won 8, Drawn 2, Lost 3, GF 24, GA 11.
Success rate...69.23% Year ranking....12th

November
13

Match of the Day
FROM 1937
AWAYDAY WIN, AT LAST!
Blues hit Blackpool with three goal second half burst

After twice coming close in seven away attemps Blues finally achieved their first success of the season on their travels. Blues had made two changes to the side which had fought to a creditable 2-2 draw with Huddersfield in their previous game. Clarke came in for White who was suffering from a sprained ankle, and Trigg pulled a thigh muscle in training allowing Samuel Bellamy, a 24-year-old amateur from Small Heath, his senior debut at right back.

Blues, in their new away strip of white shirts and black shorts, were soon under pressure from the home side. In the early stages Bellamy in particular was unsettled on more than a few occasions as Watmough and Hampson chose almost exclusively to attack the left flank. Fortunately man-of-the-match Fillingham at centre half for Blues covered well for the debutant. Blackpool missed several good opportunities and their best came after 15 minutes when Hampson blasted wide from barely five yards out. However Blues came the closest to opening the scoring when, on a rare breakaway, Dearson's trickery led to Blackpool centre back Watson slipping, this allowed the through ball to Kendrick, but his shot struck the base of the post. With half time approaching Watmough at the other end forced an error out of England 'keeper Harry Hibbs. His shot seemed comfortable enough for the 'keeper to stop but a late bobble caused the ball to bounce awkwardly off his arm. It rolled agonisingly close to the goal line before Hibbs recovered to scramble it away to safety. Blues started a little better in the second half, this time with the aid of the breeze which Blackpool had failed to take advantage of in the first period. It took just five minutes for Blues to punish the Seasiders with a simple but effective goal. Brunskill sent a long ball towards Kendrick, with his back to goal he allowed the ball to bounce then flicked it over defender Watson's head for Clarke to run on behind them and hit a crisp first time shot into the corner. Just six minutes later Blues struck again. Having had his first corner cleared back out Morris' second attempt evaded everyone before curling into the top corner. With 20 minutes of the game remaining Blackpool's keeper Wallace gifted Blues a simple third goal with a dreadful error. His poorly hit goal kick struck Kendrick and the ball cannoned off the Blues striker to Clarke who couldn't have believed his luck as he calmly tapped into the unguarded goal. The goal deflated Blackpool and Blues were allowed to coast through the final stages of the game with a winning score of 3-0.

BLACKPOOL
Wallace, Daniel Blair, Witham, Hall, Watson, Samuel Jones, Watmough, Hampson, Jimmy Blair, Thomas Jones, Munro.

BIRMINGHAM CITY
Hibbs, Bellamy, Hughes, Brunskill, Fillingham, Richards, Clarke, Beattie, Kendrick, Dearson, Morris.

REFEREE
Mr H Berry (Huddersfield)

Harry Hibbs

Birthdays
Keith Bannister born today 1930.   Dennis Bailey born today 1965.

The Matches played on this day

1897, Division 2.

Grimsby Town 3	Blues 1	Att. 2,000
	Wallace	

1909, Division 2.

Blues 1	Lincoln City 0	Att. 5,000
Needham		

1920, Division 2.

Blues 4	Wolverhampton W. 1	Att. 40,000
Hampton(2), Barton, Lane		

Blues fans witnessed one of the most spectacular goals seen at St Andrews, when Percy Barton scored with a header from fully 30 yards out.

1926, Division 1.

Blues 1	Burnley 0	Att. 10,000
Bradford		

1937, Division 1.

Blackpool 0	Blues 3	Att. 12,000
	Clarke(2), Morris	

1943, Wartime.

Blues 5	Walsall 1
Trigg(2, 1pen), Mulraney(2), Bright	

1948, Division 1.

Blues 1	Huddersfield Town 0	Att. 35,000
Hepplewhite(og)		

Blues centre forward Fred Slater broke his leg just 10 minutes into his debut for the club, the team therefore played 80 minutes with ten men but still won the points.

1954, Division 2.

Blues 3	Blackburn Rovers 1	Att. 24,129
Brown 37	Langton 87	
Astall 73		
Govan 77		

Top of the table Blackburn were fresh from a 9-0 win over Middlesbrough the previous week. Blues at this stage of the season were 13th place in the table.

1957, Inter Cities Fairs Cup Semi Final, 2nd leg.

Barcelona 1	Blues 0	Att. 60,000
Kubala 86		

Tie finished 4-4 on aggregate.

1965, Division 2.

Carlisle United 1	Blues 0	Att. 10,243
Welsh 32		

1st league meeting v Carlisle

1971, Division 2.

Norwich City 2	Blues 2	Att. 24,262
Govier 23	Campbell(pen) 30	
Stringer 63	B.Latchford 38	

1982, Division 1.

Notts County 0	Blues 0	Att. 9,118

1996, Division 1.

Blues 3	Bolton Wanderers 1	Att. 17,033
Furlong55	Sheridan 75	
Bowen 56		
Todd(og) 81		

Bolton's Jimmy Phillips sent off on 29 minutes, and captain Gerry Taggart sent off on 85 minutes. Blues' Paul Devlin sent off on 29 minutes.

November 14

Playing record for this day
Playing record for this day.... 18 games, Won 6, Drawn 2, Lost 10, GF 24, GA 34.
Success rate...38.89% Year ranking....239th

The Matches played on this day

1885, FA Cup 1st round.			
Blues 3	Darwen 1	Att. 2,000	
Felton, Morris, Stanley			
1891, FA Cup 3rd qualifying round.			
Blues 4	Burton Swifts 2	Att. 3,000	
Hands, Walton(2), Wheldon			
1896, Division 2.			
Blues 5	Woolwich Arsenal 2	Att. 2,000	
Hodgetts, Farnall,			
Walton, Hare, Robertson			
1903, Division 1.			
Blues 0	WBA 1	Att. 12,563	
1908, Division 2.			
Tottenham Hotspur 4	Blues 0	Att. 25,000	
First league meeting v Spurs.			
1914, Division 2.			
Derby County 1	Blues 0	Att. 4,000	
1925, Division 1.			
Manchester United 3	Blues 1	Att. 23,559	
	Crosbie		
1931, Division 1.			
Blues 2	Leicester City 0	Att. 16,000	
Grosvenor, Bradford			
1936, Division 1.			
Blues 1	Arsenal 3	Att. 39,940	
Devine			
1942, Wartime.			
Walsall 1	Blues 0		
1953, Division 2.			
Doncaster Rovers 3	Blues 1	Att. 16,000	
Tindill 36	Kinsey 34		
Harrison 56			
Lawlor 88			
Lawley missed a penalty for Doncaster after 31 minutes.			
1959, Division 1.			
Everton 4	Blues 0	Att. 19,172	
Shackleton 5, 9, 68			
J.Harris 55			
Blues had Johnny Watts sent off after 50 minutes.			
1960, League Cup 3rd round.			
Blues 0	Plymouth Argyle 0	Att. 15,300	
1962, League Cup 4th round.			
Blues 3	Notts County 2	Att. 13,187	
Auld 17	Sheridan 35		
Lynn 25(pen)	Moore 67		
Harris 90			
1964, Division 1.			
Leeds United 4	Blues 1	Att. 32,030	
Storrie 3	Thompson 18		
Giles 30(pen)			
Charlton 58			
Collins 61			
1970, Division 2.			
Blues 1	Orient 0	Att. 14,137	
Page 83			
1987, Division 2.			
Blues 2	Leicester City 2	Att. 8,666	
Whitton 29, 69	Walsh 6		
	Cusack 68		
1998, Division 1.			
Blues 0	Oxford United 1	Att. 18,216	
	Murphy 27		

Match of the Day

FROM 1962

STILL IN THE CUP

Blues manage to hold on for win in cup clash

Scoring twice in the first 25 minutes, Blues thought they had this League Cup match against Notts County sewn up. They were wrong, and in the end had to battle hard to gain the victory. Blues had two justified calls for penalties early on in the game, but neither was awarded. Firstly Auld, and then Stubbs were brought down in the area as they were about to shoot, but the appeals fell on deaf ears.

In the 17th minute Auld took a pass from Leek and shot straight past County's goalkeeper Smith to score the first goal of the game. The second came just eight minutes later thanks to a penalty from Lynn, awarded for handball. Notts County fought back and Sheridan's shot hit a Blues defender and sailed towards Withers. The Birmingham City goalkeeper failed to keep hold of the ball and it went straight between his legs into the net.

The second half began with Blues recognising the very real threat of losing the game and promptly set about sealing the win. Auld had a couple of good attempts at goal, but each time he was denied by skilful goalkeeping. County were able to add another goal thanks to a second blunder by Withers. He failed to catch a high centre put over by right winger Moore. As a result the ball slipped into the net to bring the scores level. Fortunately for the Blues a last-minute goal saved the game. Harris hit a shot from close range with such force that even the energetic County goalkeeper Smith had no chance of saving it.

BIRMINGHAM CITY
Withers, Lynn, Sissons, Watts, Smith, Hennessey, Hellawell, Stubbs, Harris, Leek, Auld.
NOTTS COUNTY
Smith, Hampton, Bircumshaw ,Loxley, Gibson, Carver, Moore, Sheridan, Jones, Edwards, Withers.

REFEREE
Mr Smith (Newport)

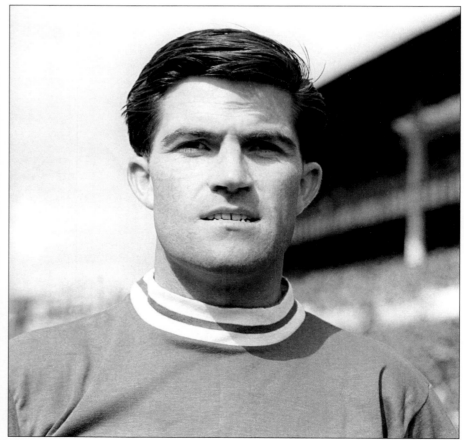

Bertie Auld

Birthdays
Dave Mackay born today 1934.

Playing record for this day

Playing record for this day.... 17 games, Won 9, Drawn 3, Lost 5, GF 25, GA 20.
Success rate...61.76% Year ranking....40th

Match of the Day

FROM 1952

ONE HULL OF A GAME

Ten man Hull fight all the way but Cox grabs late Blues winner

A cracking game at St Andrews was eventually won by Blues after late replacement Geoff Cox hit the winner seven minutes from time. Blues who were leading 3-0 with 26 minutes to play were suddenly pegged back to 3-3 in the space of ten minutes. Blues started the game with Johnny Schofield in goal for the injured Gil Merrick out with an achilles tendon problem. The other change from the team which earned a draw at Lincoln was the introduction of winger Geoff Cox in place of Wardle, A crowd of 18,000 were at St Andrews for this Second Division game in which Hull won the toss and kicked off.

Blues made the brighter start and and were rewarded with a goal after ten minutes. Good play on the left by Cox and Warhurst created an opening for the former to cut inside and cross, Trigg just couldn't reach it at the near post but Stewart following up behind him managed to turn the ball in just inside the far post. Hull replied soon after with a 35-yard effort from Harris which Schofield did well to tip over the bar. Before the corner could be taken referee Ellis called for a white ball as fog was begining to fall on a gloomy afternoon at St Andrews. There then followed a scrappy period of play as Hull defended in numbers and their attacks produced little more than harmless long range efforts. However as the half-time break loomed Blues broke again to increase their lead.

Cox crossed for Murphy in the area, allowing the ball to bounce the Blues forward lifted the ball over Bly's dive and it dropped into the net despite a desperate lunge from Neal on the goal line. The restart was delayed as the Hull full back was helped off the field.

The second half started with Hull now down to ten men, a half-time inspection to Neal's injury found he'd displaced a cartilage which meant Jensen dropping back to cover in defence. Hull now faced being handicapped for the remainder of the game. Blues quickly took advantage of their plight and just five minutes into the half they went 3-0 up. It started with a brilliant solo run from Murphy who sprinted from the half-way line only to be tripped from behind in the box. Trigg sent Bly the wrong way with his penalty kick. Hull seemed doomed at this stage but continued to fight on and deservedly got a goal back on 64 minutes. From Horton's cross Green headed clear to the edge of the penalty area but Durham intercepted and hit a first-time shot which cannoned off the underside of the crossbar into the net. Hull then further reduced the deficit after 72 minutes when an accurate pass from Durham got Bursell in behing the Blues defence. The striker scored with an acute-angled shot which Schofield got a hand to but could not keep out. Just two minutes later Blues were stunned by a third and equalising goal, again it was the Durham-Bursell combination that did the damage. Durham this time found his 17-year-old strike partner in an even better position, and from ten yards Bursell's shot beat Schofield again to complete an amazing fight back from 3-0 down. This stung Blues into action and suddenly Bly's goal came under siege after wave upon wave of pressure. As time went on the entire Hull team dropped back in an effort to hold on to the point. However with seven minutes remaining Blues own 17-year-old winger Cox shot through a crowd of players and the ball went in off the post to secure a dramatic face-saving win at 4-3. What a game!

BIRMINGHAM CITY
Schofield, Green, Martin, Boyd, Badham, Warhurst, Stewart, Briggs, Trigg, Murphy, Cox.
HULL CITY
Bly, Phillips, Neal, Harris, Berry, Durham, Harrison, Bursell, Jensen, Todd, Horton.

REFEREE
Mr AE Ellis (Halifax)

The Matches played on this day

1969, Division 2.

Preston North End 4	Blues 1	Att. 22,564
Hockey(og) 4	Hateley 81	
Lee 8		
Irvine 23, 86		

1975, Division 1.

Blues 3	Arsenal 1	Att. 21,652
Francis(pen) 46	Ball 77	
Withe 60		
Hatton 76		

1980, Division 1.

Coventry City 2	Blues 1	Att. 18,758
Blair 40	Curbishley 36	
Hunt 80		

This match screened by ATV's Star Soccer on Saturday night

1986, Division 2.

Millwall 0	Blues 2	Att. 4,795
	Clarke 5	
	Rees 48	

1992, FA Cup 1st round.

Reading 1	Blues 0	Att. 7,667
Quinn 5		

Blues keeper Martin Thomas was sent off when conceding a penalty. Trevor Matthewson took over in goal and saved Quinn's spot kick

1995, Anglo Italian Cup Qualifying group stage.

Ancona 1	Blues 2	Att. 1,500
Sesia 51	Edwards 29	
	Tenoni(og) 33	

1997, Division 1.

Nottingham Forest 1	Blues 0	Att. 19,610
Campbell 16		

Tommy Briggs

Blues news extra
1941..Wartime friendly Aston Villa 7 Blues 0

1995..New look St Andrews opened Blues 1 Aston Villa 1

The new all-seater £7.4 million Tilton Road and Kop stands were opened in front of a 19,766 crowd. Before the game a commemorative plaque was unveiled by a representative of the National Heritage, Baroness Trumpington. Jack Wiseman on behalf of the Blues board also received a cheque for £2.3 million towards the cost of the development. In the game it was Villa took the lead through Lamptey on ten minutes and they held that advantage at half time. 13 minutes into the second half Blues forward Steve McGavin beat Mark Bosnich in the Villa goal to level the scores.

Birthdays
Bryan Small born today 1971.

Playing record for this day

Playing record for this day.... 15 games, Won 8, Drawn 2, Lost 5, GF 31, GA 20.
Success rate...60% Year ranking....53rd

Match of the Day

FROM 1974
LEAGUE LEADERS TOPPLED

Life without Francis no problem as Blues chase top spot

Early Division One pace setters Manchester City came crashing down at St Andrews beaten by a Blues side looking very sharp despite the long term loss of their leading striker Trevor Francis. Francis with ten goals from 15 league games so far was likely to be out for sometime with an achilles injury, but Blues had Gordon Taylor as a more than adequate replacement. Apart from Francis, Blues went into this game making three other changes. In defence they welcomed back Joe Gallagher at centre half for Roger Hynd and Archie Styles took over from Garry Pendrey at left back, whilst up front Bob Hatton was back again in place of Paul Hendrie. Manchester City with a side brimming full of star players remained at full stength and unchanged. The game started with Blues having to defend well to weather the early City onslaught. An early mix up between Page and Gallagher allowed the visitors a chance but the shot from Marsh failed to trouble Latchford in the Blues goal. The deadlock was broken on 11 minutes and it was Blues who took the advantage.

Page taking the ball from defence fed Styles on the left flank who ran on to slip it inside for Kendall who finished with a crisp right-foot shot into the corner. Styles was also involved in Blues next goal when he floated in a wonderful free kick which found Burns whose downward header was turned in from close range by Hatton. The 35,143 crowd were in total ecstasy when just ten minutes later Blues went further ahead with a devastating route one goal. From Latchford's goal kick Burns again outjumped the City defence to knock it into Hatton's path. Running free he rounded the stranded MacRae to slot in the 100th league goal of his career. Blues were worthy of their 3-0 half-time lead.

The second half saw the visitors try an unlikely comeback and they controlled possession for long periods but generally the Blues defence remained untroubled by anything City threw at them. Blues then added a late fourth goal and fittingly it went to man-of-the-match Kenny Burns. City were unable to cope with his aerial ability all afternoon and when Campbell crossed from the right in the 83rd minute Burns rose again to plant a firm header past MacRae and wrap up a sensational 4-0 win.

BIRMINGHAM CITY

Latchford, Martin, Styles (Pendrey), Kendall, Gallagher, Page, Campbell, Taylor, Burns, Hatton, Calderwood.

MANCHESTER CITY

MacRae, Hammond, Donachie, Doyle, Barrett, Oakes, Summerbee, Bell, Marsh, Henson, Tueart.

Malcolm Page (No. 2), Gordon Taylor (No. 11), Kenny Burns, challenge Allan Clarke of Leeds.

Blues news extra   1981..Friendly Blues 1 FC Groningen 1

Blues earned a good draw in a tough friendly at St Andrews against a decent Dutch side. Ian Handysides got the equaliser five minutes from time.

Birthdays

Paul Barnes born today 1967.

The Matches played on this day
1889, FA Cup 3rd qualifying round.

Wednesbury Old A. 1	Blues 5	Att. 2,000
	Walton (2),	
	W.Devey (2), Heath	

1907, Division 1.

Blues 2	Bolton Wanderers 1	Att. 10,000
Green, Eyre		

1912, Division 2.

Nottingham Forest 3	Blues 1	Att. 10,000
	Jones	

1918, Wartime.

Blues 3	Coventry City 1	
Walker(2), J.Godfrey		

1929, Division 1.

Bolton Wanderers 0	Blues 0	Att. 15,000

1935, Division 1.

Derby County 2	Blues 2	Att. 23,893
	Calladine, Harris	

1940, Wartime.

Blues 6	Stoke City 2	
Trigg(5), Craven		

1946, Division 2.

West Ham United 0	Blues 4	Att. 30,000
	Bodle, Edwards(2), Trigg	

1957, Division 1.

Everton 0	Blues 2	Att. 34,875
	Murphy 38, 83	

1960, League Cup 3rd round, replay.

Plymouth Argyle 3	Blues 1	Att. 14,132
Carter 34	Wyatt 31(og)	
Kirby 56		
Jackson 80		

Brian Farmer was forced out of the game with a shoulder injury after 55 minutes, Blues finished with ten men.
1963, Division 1.

Blackburn Rovers 3	Blues 0	Att. 14,800
Harrison 44		
McEvoy 76		
Douglas 83		

1968, Division 2.

Blues 1	Blackpool 0	Att. 22,206
Summerill 61		

1974, Division 1.

Blues 4	Manchester City 0	Att. 35,143
Kendall 11		
Hatton 20, 30		
Burns 83		

Bob Hatton's second goal was the 100th League goal of his career.
1985, Division 1.

Southampton 1	Blues 0	Att. 13,167
Wallace 67		

1991, FA Cup 1st round.

Torquay 3	Blues 0	Att. 4,123
Loram 39		
Hall 40, 55		

Blues had Mark Cooper sent off after 81 minutes

Playing record for this day
Playing record for this day.... 18 games, Won 9, Drawn 2, Lost 7, GF 33, GA 29.
Success rate....55.56% Year ranking....98th

Match of the Day
FROM 1962

ALF GETS A GOING AWAY GIFT
Ipswich hit for five as Ramsey leaves for England post

Blues travelled to Portman Road, on an impressive eight match unbeaten league run. Ipswich in contrast were struggling after their championship win the previous season and were in the relegation zone. Their manager Alf Ramsey was about to leave and take up the position of England boss and this in particular inspired Blues winger Mike Hellawell who had recently been left out of the national side. Blues were unchanged and at full strength for the game, Ipswich had Reg Pickett replacing the injured John Elsworthy, this apart it was their title-winning side that lined up.

The game was sensationally brought to life in the 16th minute when Blues struck twice in a minute to leave Ipswich doomed to another home defeat. Blues attacked through Stubbs whose cross was helped on by Auld to Harris who placed his shot wide of the diving Bailey. Then on the other flank Hellawell outpaced Compton to cut in and shoot on the run. Although Bailey somehow saved the effort the ball fell to Leek who miskicked leaving Auld to convert the simple tap in from close range. Ipswich could have folded but to their credit came back and only a fine finger tip save from Withers denied a spectacular effort from Crawford from 25 yards out. Ipswich got back into the game on 36 minutes when good work again from Crawford put Phillips clear to race in and hit past Withers. With Ipswich fans still celebrating Pickett underhit a back pass and Harris nipped in to take the ball round the stranded 'keeper and knock it in the unguarded net. There was no further addition to the score and Blues went into the break with a deserved 3-1 lead.

Ipswich started the second half eager to get back into the game and Withers saved well from Leadbetter. The Blues defence were holding the home side at bay as they surged forward in the opening ten minutes of the half. With Ipswich overcommitted Blues hit them on the break and on 55 minutes Blues netted a fourth and killer goal. Auld broke away and his cross was steered into the path of Leek from Hennessey's precise header. Leek this time made no mistake with his shot from just inside the penalty area which smashed into the roof of the net. This brought an end to the Ipswich sting and Blues took almost total control. With just a minute of the game left Auld's corner kick was volley in by Leek to give the Blues an amazing 5-1 lead, Ipswich's heaviest defeat at home in their short First Division life.

IPSWICH TOWN
Bailey, Carberry, Compton, Baxter, Nelson, Pickett, Stephenson, Moran, Crawford, Phillips, Leadbetter.
BIRMINGHAM CITY
Withers, Lynn, Sissons, Watts, Smith, Hennessey, Hellawell, Stubbs, Harris, Leek, Auld.

Mike Hellawell

Blues news extra 1980..Gallagher assists England win England 'B' 1 Australia 'B' 0

Blues centre half Joe Gallagher got his international career off to a cracking start when he nodded
the ball down for Arsenal's Alan Sunderland to sweep home the only goal in this 'B' international.

Birthdays

Andrew Harris born today 1970.　　　Pat Wright born today 1940.　　　Peter Bullock born today 1941.

The Matches played on this day

1888, FA Cup 3rd qualifying round.

Blues 4	Leek 0	Att. 2,000

Hill, Jenkyns,
Devey, Stanley

1894, Division 1.

Blues 4	Stoke 2	Att. 3,000

Walton, Hallam,
Mobley, Wheldon

1900, Division 2.

Grimsby Town 1	Blues 1	Att. 4,000
	Higginson	

1906, Division 1.

Blues 2	Sunderland 0	Att. 10,000

Jones, Tickle

1917, Wartime.

Blues 3	Leeds City 1

Mercer, Stevens(2)

1923, Division 1.

Blues 0	Notts County 0	Att. 12,000

1928, Division 1.

Newcastle United 1	Blues 0	Att. 30,000

1934, Division 1.

Blues 3	Grimsby Town 2	Att. 20,000

Jones(2), Guest

Blues 2-0 down after 20 minutes, they fought back to 2-2 by half time After having a goal disallowed Charles Wilson Jones headed Blues winner on 63 minutes.

1945, Wartime.

Millwall 5	Blues 1
	Jones

1951, Division 2.

Blues 0	Blackburn Rovers 1	Att. 22,000
	Quigley 4	

1956, Division 1.

Blues 4	Charlton Athletic 2	Att. 29,000
Astall 32	Ayre 10	
Kinsey 53	Hurst 73	
Brown 60		
Murphy 73		

1962, Division 1.

Ipswich Town 1	Blues 5	Att. 16,775
Phillips 35	Harris 16, 43	
	Auld 17	
	Leek 55, 89	

1973, Division 1.

Stoke City 5	Blues 2	Att. 19,179
Ritchie 9, 78	Hynd 50	
Robertson 25	B.Latchford 56	
Hurst 62		
Mahoney 70		

1979, Division 2.

Watford 1	Blues 0	Att. 14,378
Ward 15		

1984, Division 2.

Charlton Athletic 2	Blues 1	Att. 4,841
Aizlewood 26	Morley 82	
Lee 72		

Tony Morley scored on his Blues debut.

1990, FA Cup 1st round.

Blues 1	Cheltenham Town 0	Att. 7,942
Sturridge 57		

1996, Division 1.

Wolverhampton W. 1	Blues 2	Att. 22,627
Bull 9	Breen 7	
	Legg 58	

2001, Division 1.

Sheffield United 4	Blues 0	Att. 15,686
Montgomery 15		
Brown 65		
Peschisolido 78, 81		

Playing record for this day

Playing record for this day.... 15 games, Won 7, Drawn 3, Lost 5, GF 25, GA 24.

Success rate...56.67% Year ranking....88th

Match of the Day

FROM 1961

BLUES PUT HAMMERS UNDER THE COSH

Outstanding win in super Blues show

Before a crowd of 20,645 at St Andrews, Birmingham City were slow startersone minute, and dashing heroes the next. West Ham appeared to dominate the first half, with all play being in the area approaching Blues' goal. However, the Hammers despite some pretty midfield play, attacking moves made little headway. Smith and Lynn kept Summerill well protected, and there was always the feeling that should Blues mount a full-blooded attack, West Ham would be left floundering.

And so it proved to be true. After a half-time talking to, Blues came out on the attack. Within the first minute Hennessey had made a brisk raid, followed up with a shot against the goalpost, and after this initial foray Bloomfield and Hellawell mounted a constant bombardment on the hapless Leslie. Together they produced two identical goal-scoring chances within two minutes of each other, and both were capitalised upon. The first by Auld who headed Hellawell's centre past Leslie, and the second by Orritt with a superb header.

A third goal was added by Harris from a penalty kick after he had been impeded in his attempts to reach a bouncing ball heading goalwards. Right at the end Hellawell again broke loose, and it was Bloomfield himself who was there on the goal-line to flick the ball in for a climax. The crowd and players were jubilant - Blues had achieved an outstanding 4-0 success.

BIRMINGHAM CITY

Schofield, Lynn, Sissons, Hennessey, Smith, Beard, Hellawell, Bloomfield, Harris, Orritt, Auld.

WEST HAM

Leslie, Kirkup, Bond, Moore, Brown, Hurst, Crawford, Woodman, Sealey, Dick, Musgrove.

Bryan Orritt

Birthdays

Damien Johnson born today 1978.

November 19

-187-

The Matches played on this day

1898, FA Cup 4th qualifying round.
Blues 10   Druids 0   Att. 4,000
Abbott(2), McRoberts(3),
Gardner, Inglis(2),
Leake, Hughes(og)

1904, Division 1.
Blues 2   Sheffield Wed. 1   Att. 10,000
Jones, Green

1910, Division 2.
Blues 0   Clapton Orient 1   Att. 12,000

1921, Division 1.
Blackburn Rovers 1   Blues 1   Att. 15,000
                      Bradford

1927, Division 1.
Blues 1   Arsenal 1   Att. 10,030
Crosbie

1932, Division 1.
Sheffield United 2   Blues 1   Att. 10,000
                      Briggs

1938, Division 1.
Huddersfield Town 3   Blues 1   Att. 12,000
                       Morris

1949, Division 1.
Blues 1   Fulham 1   Att. 20,995
Brennan

1955, Division 1.
Blues 5   Huddersfield Town 0   Att. 24,900
Astall 1
Warhurst 15
Murphy 20
Brown 81, 85

1960, Division 2.
Tottenham Hotspur 6   Blues 0   Att. 46,010
White 2
Dyson 7, 70
Jones 14, 86
B.Smith 83(pen)
Blues keeper Colin Withers made his debut for the club.

1966, Division 2.
Derby County 1   Blues 2   Att. 17,382
Hector 18(pen)   Thomson 16
                  Beard 36

1977, Division 1.
Blues 1   Leicester City 1   Att. 21,208
Francis 26   Waddle 58
Kevin Dillon made his debut for Blues.

1983, Division 1.
QPR 2   Blues 1   Att. 10,824
Stainrod 58   Harford 46
Fenwick 76
Blues first experience of playing a full competitive fixture on an artificial surface.

1988, Division 2.
Hull City 1   Blues 1   Att. 5,134
Edwards 89   Langley 16

1991, League Cup 3rd round, replay
Crystal Palace 1   Blues 1   Att. 10,698
Thomas 117   Gleghorn 108
After extra time

1994, Division 2.
Blues 0   Bournemouth 0   Att. 15,477

Playing record for this day
Playing record for this day.... 16 games, Won 4, Drawn 7, Lost 5, GF 28, GA 22.
Success rate...46.88% Year ranking....187th

Match of the Day
FROM 1955
THE TERRIERS TERRORISED
Blues take just 40 seconds to hammer Huddersfield

Blues got off to a fantastic start against Huddersfield and dominated the game winning 5-0. The afternoon started with a minute's silence in memory of Blues former captain and member of the 1931 FA Cup final team, George Morrall who died during the week.

From the first throw in of the game taken by Kinsey, Govan went clear to send over a hard low cross, and after steadying himself, Astall shot from an acute angle into the bottom corner of the net. Five minutes later a cross from Brown just evaded Murphy in the centre but ran to Govan who smashed a fierce shot which Fearnley blocked. Huddersfield's first attempt on goal came on the quarter hour when Merrick saved from Simpson's 15-yard strike. Moments later Blues had doubled their lead when Astall this time got clear to centre, Boyd controlled well and flicked it into an opening for Warhurst to charge in and hit a left-foot shot into the the corner. On 20 minutes Blues got a third goal through Murphy, side-footing in Astall's cross with cool precision. When Huddersfield broke they found the Blues defence in equally confident mood, Glazzard collecting Metcalfe's pass in the area and shaped to shoot on goal but had the ball nicked away by Smith's well-timed tackle. However, this was not as classy as Warhurst's cheeky overhead kick to Merrick which completed the clearing up job. A Blues attack after 31 minutes again ended in a Fearnley save from Kinsey, somersaulting to the top corner to tip over the bar, He could do nothing about Kinsey's next effort just before half time. Latching onto a pass from Badham his cross-come-shot struck the bar and Wilson hurriedly cleared the danger.

Blues dominance continued in the second half with more heroics from Fearnley who did well to keep the score down. He was involved in the second half's turning point when chasing out to thwart Kinsey on 67 minutes, the forward just won the race but his shot hit the side netting. The two men collided with Fearnley coming off worse. After prolonged treatment, the battered 'keeper continued but was clearly injured. With this additional advantage Brown added two late goals in the last nine minutes to hand Blues an emphatic five goal win.

BIRMINGHAM CITY
Merrick, Hall, Badham, Boyd, Smith, Warhurst, Astall, Kinsey, Brown, Murphy, Govan.
HUDDERSFIELD TOWN
Fearnley, Wilson, Conwell, Watson, Quested, McGarry, Metcalfe, Simpson, Glazzard, Frear, Hobson.

REFEREE
Mr W Hickson (Wigan)

Alex Govan

Birthdays
Gary Ablett born today 1965.

Playing record for this day

Playing record for this day.... 14 games, Won 3, Drawn 1, Lost 10, GF 9, GA 24.
Success rate...25% Year ranking....266th

Match of the Day

FROM 1937

A REAL KNOCKOUT DERBY!

Ten Man Wolves struggle after Gardiner head injury

In front of the biggest attendance of the season at St Andrews Blues welcomed local rivals Wolves, who were in the running for the First Division championship. They were forced into one change with Ashall swapping wings to deputise for the injured Maguire, leaving a place open for Kirkham to make his debut for the club. Blues, who gained their first victory in 12 matches against Wolves the previous season, were without England international goalkeeper Harry Hibbs, and Frank Clack was brought into the team. However, they were boosted by the return of Cyril Trigg, back after injury.

In a sensational start to the game Birmingham almost scored within the opening few seconds. After good work from Clarke and Beattie, the former crossed the ball from close in and Morris almost put through his own goal. From the resulting corner, Wolves broke away to the other end, where the Birmingham goal had a narrow escape. Kirkham centred for Galley, but with the goal at his mercy he made an awful mess of his shot and the ball rolled harmlessly wide.

As the half wore on it was Birmingham who were taking control, with Clarke on the right wing causing most of the problems, and from one of his crosses Kendrick headed narrowly wide with Wolves 'keeper Scott beaten. Birmingham continued their relentless pressure on the Wolves goal and Scott again saved well from Beattie's free kick. Beattie then dribbled through the Wolves defence and from 25 yards wide on the right tested Scott with a majestic lob, which dropped onto the crossbar and rolled down the back of the net out for a goalkick. Wolves countered through Ashall who rounded Hughes to centre for Galley. His header slipped from the grasp of Clack but fortunately for the 'keeper, Fillingham saved the day with an acrobatic overhead kick. This became a turning point in the game for Wolves as from this moment they dominated the game territorially. However as half time approached it was Blues who snatched a dramatic lead. Beattie collecting a loose ball in midfield cleverly skipped through the challenge of the converging Cullis and Gardiner who collided with each other knocking both men out. He ran on to chip the ball over to Morris who knocked it back for Dearson to smash the ball first time into the roof of the net. As Blues celebrated, Gardiner was carried off with a head wound whilst Cullis got to his feet albeit groggily and played out the remaining seconds of the half.

The second half started without the injured Gardiner and ten man Wolves struggled throughout as Cullis was effectively a passenger. Blues soon took advantage and just after the hour mark went 2-0 up through a goal by centre forward Kendrick. Although Gardiner reappeared shortly after with a bandaged head the game was already lost and Blues saw out the remaining 20 minutes with no further addition to the score.

BIRMINGHAM CITY

Clack, Trigg, Hughes, Brunskill, Fillingham, Richards, Clarke, Beattie, Kendrick, Dearson, Morris.

WOLVERHAMPTON WANDERERS

Scott, Morris, Jach Taylor, Smalley, Cullis, Gardiner, Ashall, McIntosh, Galley, Bryan Jones, Kirkham.

REFEREE

Mr WE Ross-Gower (London)

Stan Cullis, Wolverhampton Wanderers

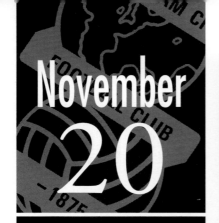

November
20

Don Dearson

Blues news extra   1929..Hibbs for England England 6 Wales 0

Birmingham's keeper Harry Hibbs became England's number 1 for the first time at Stamford Bridge on this day in 1929. He didn't disappoint, keeping
a clean sheet as England swept aside the Welsh easily. George Camsell of Middlesbrough scored twice, and Leicester City's Ernie Hine got one from the
penalty spot. England also got a goal through Hugh Adcock of Leicester City who was the cousin of Birmingham's Joe Bradford.

Birthdays

Neil Sproston born today 1970.   **Phil Summerill born today 1947.**   **Ivor Linton born today 1959.**
Gary Cooper born today 1965.

Playing record for this day

Playing record for this day.... 20 games, Won 7, Drawn 2, Lost 11, GF 23, GA 35.
Success rate...40% Year ranking....234th

Match of the Day

FROM 1978

BLUES WANDER TO VICTORY

Blues climb table with 3-0 hammering of Bolton

Blues needed to raise themselves off the bottom of the First Division with a much sought after win. A windswept St Andrews was the venue for this clash against a poor Bolton side, and although Blues won with ease, they failed to do it with style. Bolton's run of six successive away defeats continued, whereas Blues had now scored nine times in their last three games.

The first goal arrived on just 80 seconds when Steve Fox delivered a perfectly measured ball to Kevin Dillon, positioned just inside the Bolton penalty area. Dillon evaded the advances of Peter Nicholson and flicked the ball over the Bolton player's head. He then turned and slammed it into the net.

It was a great start for the home team, and Bolton didn't seem to have touched the ball yet. Then a mistake by Joe Gallagher in the ninth minute allowed Frank Worthington to have a shot at goal, but he hit the post. Just three minutes later Blues almost scored again. Dillon's 20-yard shot hit the crossbar, and the rebound went to Alan Buckley, but the Blues striker was surrounded by defenders and the chance went begging. In the second half play became disjointed. A back pass from Tarantini in the 48th minute lacked power and fell short of its intended target. It landed for Frank Worthington, who rushed the job and shot wide. Tarantini made up for the error five minutes later when he passed to Fox on the right. Fox tried to cross the ball for Givens at the far post but Paul Jones intercepted for Bolton and headed it straight into the net for an own goal. Bolton were still reeling from that surprise when, on 59 minutes, Fox made a solo run through the defence and shot for goal. The ball bounced off McDonagh, and trickled back for Buckley to nudge over the line. Calderwood scored another goal in the 81st minute, but it was disallowed for offside. It didn't matter however, as Blues had more than showed they were capable of moving themselves up the table.

BIRMINGHAM CITY

Freeman, Tarantini, Dennis, Towers, Gallagher, Page, Dillon, Buckley, Givens, Calderwood, Fox.

BOLTON WANDERERS

McDonagh, Nicholson, Burke, Greaves, Jones, Walsh, Morgan, Reid, Gowling, Worthington, McNab.

1925

November 22

Playing record for this day

Playing record for this day.... 15 games, Won 8, Drawn 3, Lost 4, GF 29, GA 20.
Success rate...63.33% Year ranking....32nd

Match of the Day
FROM 1958
BUNNY HAS SPURS HOPPING
Two from Larkin as Tottenham swept aside by lethal Blues

White Hart Lane is never an easy ground to visit at any time but this one was always going to be difficult. Blues made three changes from their last game, a 1-0 win over Newcastle. England internationals Merrick and Hall were out injured and replaced by Schofield and Farmer, but the team was boosted by the return of Eddie Brown.

As early as the 15th minute Bunny Larkin was on target, beating the in form Hollowbread with a fierce right-foot shot. The move was started by the impressive Brian Farmer who won a tackle in the centre circle before threading a super pass for Larkin to run on to and finish. Blues were constantly a threat and Hollowbread was playing the game of his life to keep the score down. He'd already kept out an effort from Johnny Gordon and within the first 30 minutes he'd superbly saved from Taylor, Gordon again and Larkin twice. Blues 'keeper Schofield at the other end was relatively untroubled.

Blues deservedly went 2-0 up on 31 minutes when Larkin and Taylor set up Hooper whose initial effort was blocked again by Hollowbread's knee, the rebound came back to Hooper who slammed it in from eight yards. Before half time the Spurs 'keeper managed to deny Brown and Larkin again with two sensational saves and the home side went in at the interval very grateful to have conceded just two. Tottenham came out for the second period a totally different side and for the first 10 minutes had Blues under pressure with Blanchflower now becoming influential. Blues however weathered the storm and a break on 58 minutes killed any Spurs revival stone dead. Trevor Smith played a long ball from defence to Larkin who outpaced the home defence to latch onto the pass and blast it past Hollowbread on the run. Just two minutes later Hooper collected the ball in midfield and set off on a mazy run. As he aproached the penalty area he cut the ball back for Taylor who swept it past Hollowbread from six yards. Blues had further chances to improve the 4-0 scoreline including efforts from Brown, Larkin and Taylor which all went close but at the end left the field to a huge roar. The 28,708 had seen one of the best displays by a visiting team all season, while Blues fans had witnessed their teams' best performance in months.

TOTTENHAM HOTSPUR

Hollowbread, Baker, Hopkins, Blanchflower, Norman, Iley, Brookes, Harmer, Dunmore, Smith, Medwin.

BIRMINGHAM CITY

Schofield, Farmer, Allen, Watts, Smith, Neal, Hooper, Gordon, Brown, Larkin, Taylor

REFEREE
Mr G McCabe (Sheffield)

White Hart Lane, home of Tottenham Hotspur

Blues news extra 1930..Blues duo help England victory Wales 0 England 4

Blues centre forward Joe Bradford was again on the mark for England as they beat Wales convincingly 4-0 in Wrexham. It was Bradford's seventh goal in 12 internationals and proved to be his last. Blues 'keeper Harry Hibbs winning his sixth cap also helped out in the win by saving Fred Keenor's penalty kick.

Blues news extra 1941..Wartime friendly Blues 4 Czechoslovakian Army 0

Birthdays

Mick Farmer born today 1944.

Sadly Missed

David Wiseman died today in 1978, aged 93

Playing record for this day

Playing record for this day.... 19 games, Won 8, Drawn 6, Lost 5, GF 28, GA 27.
Success rate...57.89% Year ranking....79th

Match of the Day
FROM 1999
BLUES WIN THE BATTLE

McCarthy breaks a leg as Blues limp through costly victory

Blues were left counting the cost to their promotion campaign after an ill tempered game at St Andrews against visiting Tranmere Rovers. Already beset with injury problems which had recently forced them to buy one striker and loan another, they now faced the prospect of having wingers McCarthy and Lazaridis out for some time after the former broke his leg and the latter pulled out suffering from knee ligament injuries. New signing Marcelo also limped of the pitch with an ankle injury.

The game itself started in controversy and barely a minute had gone when referee Jeff Winter awarded a penalty, having adjudged Challinor to have pushed Marcelo as he waited for McCarthy's cross. Grainger stepped up to smack in his first goal of the season with a rising kick into the corner. Tempers flared to boiling point when a hefty challenge by Hyde on Taylor brought about a mass brawl involving virtually all outfield players. Referee Winter took action by yellow carding Marcelo for his initial push on Clint Hill and giving a red card to Hill for his retaliation. Hyde whose clumsy challenge caused the incident escaped unpunished. The football continued with Blues taking a 2-0 lead on 26 minutes when Marcelo headed in Rowett's perfectly flighted corner. Tragedy then struck when McCarthy was fouled as he made a run down the right wing which led to him being stretchered off with a broken leg. From the free kick Blues went 3-0 up, Lazaridis simply knocking the ball square for Hyde to belt a 25-yard shot into the corner giving Rovers keeper Achterberg no chance.

The 22,132 who had taken advantage of a the special £5 admission price had had full value for their money so few could complain about the less lively second half. Blues content to hold on to their advantage without further casulties, Tranmere seemingly resigned to defeat and looking for any offer of consolation. With 13 minutes remaining they got one when Grainger under pressure from Koumas headed past Poole from David Kelly's outswinging cross. There was still time for Lazaridis to pick up an injury which effectively ended his game as he spent the remaining 11 minutes hugging the touchline without receiving the ball, and Blues were grateful when the final whistle went.

BIRMINGHAM CITY
Poole, Rowett, Grainger, Hyde, Purse, Holdsworth, McCarthy (Johnston h/t),
Wreh (Adebola 59), Marcelo, Hughes (O'Connor h/t), Lazaridis.

TRANMERE ROVERS
Achterberg, Morgan, Challinor, Hill, Allen, Parkinson,
Murphy, Mahon (Koumas 61), Jones, Taylor (Hazel 15), Allison (Kelly 75)

REFEREE
Mr J Winter (Cleveland)

Jon McCarthy

Blues news extra   1979..No joke as Jasper joins the board
Life-long Blues fan and comedian Jasper Carrott joined the Blues board of directors, fulfilling a life long ambition for the Brummie celebrity.

Birthdays
Frank Worthington born today 1948.

The Matches played on this day
1889, Football Alliance.

Blues 3	Grimsby Town 1	Att. 3,000

W.Devey(2), Heath
1895, Division 1.

Blues 5	Preston North End 2	Att. 5,000

Wheldon(2), Jones(2), Mobley
1901, Division 1.

Everton 1	Blues 0	Att. 20,000

1907, Division 1.

Newcastle United 8	Blues 0	Att. 16,000

1912, Division 2.

Blues 3	Bristol City 0	Att. 20,000

Hastings, Robertson, A.R.Smith
1918, Wartime.

Coventry City 1	Blues 3	

Whitehouse, J.Godfrey, Davies
1929, Division 1.

Blues 0	Everton 0	Att. 20,000

1935, Division 1.

Blues 2	Aston Villa 2	Att. 60,250

Jones(2)
The biggest league attendance ever at St Andrews
1946, Division 2.

Blues 3	Sheffield Wed. 1	Att. 32,425

Trigg(2), Dougall
1957, Division 1.

Blues 0	Blackpool 0	Att. 32,168

1960, Inter Cities Fairs Cup 2nd round, 1st leg.

KB Copenhagen 4	Blues 4	Att. 2,500
Ravn 34	Gordon 35, 66	
Clausen 65, 79	Singer 49, 61	
Torstensen 73		

1963, Division 1.

Blues 3	Nottingham Forest 3	Att. 18,158
Auld 24, 57	Julians 22	
Smith 43	Winfield 27	
	Leflem 34	

Two minutes silence was held out of respect for President Kennedy.
1968, Division 2.

Bolton Wanderers 0	Blues 0	Att. 7,005

1974, Division 1.

Tottenham Hotspur 0	Blues 0	Att. 27,761

1985, Division 1.

Blues 0	Liverpool 2	Att. 15,062
	Rush 9	
	Walsh 26	

Blues eight consecutive league defeat their joint worst sequence of league results.
1991, Division 3.

Blues 1	Exeter City 0	Att. 11,319

Gleghorn 78
1996, Division 1.

Blues 1	Swindon Town 0	Att. 16,559

Furlong 29
1997, Division 1.

WBA 1	Blues 0	Att. 18,444

Sneekes 84
1999, Division 1.

Blues 3	Tranmere Rovers 1	Att. 22,132
Grainger 1(pen)	Grainger(og) 77	
Marcelo 26		
Hyde 45		

Jon McCarthy was stretchered off with a broken leg. Tranmere's Clint Hill sent off after 16 minutes.

November 24

Playing record for this day
Playing record for this day.... 15 games, Won 9, Drawn 3, Lost 3, GF 25, GA 15.
Success rate...70% Year ranking....10th

Match of the Day
FROM 1979
BERTSCHIN TRIO DECISIVE
Striker keeps up the Blues promotion push

A smashing hat-trick from 23-year-old Keith Bertschin at Kenilworth Road brought Luton Town down from the top of the Second Division. The former Ipswich Town player took hardly any time at all to begin the action, despite having scored just one goal previous to this match. The lead was taken in the sixth minute when Bertschin ran on to Joe Gallagher's pass to volley the ball past former Villa 'keeper Jake Findlay.

For a brief period from 26 minutes Luton's goal was under serious threat. Blues showed their abilities to the full, and solo attempts from Lynex and Dillon stood out as high-class play. Blues were by far the best team and goals should have been easier to come by.

Four minutes before half time Blues' battle began. For no apparent reason, Terry Lees put out a hand to stop the ball. A penalty was awarded, and Luton winger Moss took the kick. It was his sixth penalty, and his 13th goal of the season. In the 70th minute the ex-Blues striker Bob Hatton outpaced Mark Dennis and crossed the ball for Brian Stein, who placed it into the net to put Luton into the lead.

The equaliser for Blues came from a great solo effort by Bertschin. He tackled Grealish on the edge of the area, and relieved him of the ball, then beat Findlay to bring the score to 2-2.

Just as it seemed the game would finish with a draw, Bertschin secured victory with the best goal of the game. Willie Johnston sent an inch-perfect cross to the centre, which landed for the young striker to nudge into the net from almost the same spot as his second goal.

LUTON TOWN
Findlay, Stephens, Donaghy, Grealish, Saxby, Price, Hill, West, Stein, Hatton, Moss.
BIRMINGHAM CITY
Wealands, Lees, Dennis, Curbishley, Gallagher, Todd, Lynex, Towers, Bertschin, Dillon, Johnston.

REFEREE
Mr NC Taylor (Wiltshire)

Keith Bertschin

Birthdays
Phil Starbuck born today 1968.   Fred Hall born today 1924.

Playing record for this day
Playing record for this day.... 18 games, Won 8, Drawn 5, Lost 5, GF 25, GA 24.
Success rate...58.33% Year ranking....76th

November 25

Match of the Day
FROM 1972
GAZZA INSPIRES BLUES WIN
Rare Pendrey goal treat as Blues clip Canaries' wings

Blues were slowly finding their feet in the top division after registering their second successive league win against Norwich. They were showing signs of being able to live more comfortably in the higher division and they proved it with an emphatic four goal performance thanks to a fine individual display from Garry Pendrey. Blues now had 16 points from 20 games and lay a respectable 17th place in the table.

It was Norwich City who who stunned the 32,890 crowd when they took the lead on 22 minutes, Black taking advantage of hesitancy in the Blues defence to head in from a corner. However this was cancelled by a rare piece of goal-scoring by one of Birmingham's most popular players. Before today full back Pendrey had only scored once for Blues netting against Cardiff in a 3-0 win in Christmas 1971. This effort was an important equaliser, and his first in the top flight. The goal came on 36 minutes following a corner from Gordon Taylor. Keelan in the Norwich goal pushed it out to the edge of the penalty area where Pendrey was waiting. Without hesitation he drew his left leg back and hit the ball firmly and it dipped in under the crossbar to send the crowd into hysteria. Blues went in at half time grateful to be level with a full 45 minutes to make something of what had been a disappointing affair so far.

The game was much more keenly contested in the second half especially when Blues finally went into the lead on 74 minutes. Again the inspirational Pendrey was involved, setting up Hope with a clever pass inside from the left-hand flank, Hope copied Pendrey's finishing technique, hitting the ball first time in his stride from just inside the penalty area, again Keelan had no chance. With Blues now playing with great confidence they pushed men forward from all over the park. Just two minutes after Hope's goal Want increased the lead with a sweetly hit left-footer which flew across Keelan's despairing dive into the corner. As the game entered the final five minutes Blues wrapped up the scoring with another goal, albeit a scrappy one, to make it 4-1. Another Taylor corner caused mayhem in the Norwich penalty area and in the ensuing scramble Hatton managed to prod the ball over the line to complete a fabulous afternoon for the Blues fans.

BIRMINGHAM CITY
Dave Latchford, Martin, Pendrey, Harland, Hynd, Want Hope, Calderwood, Bob Latchford, Hatton, Taylor.
NORWICH CITY
Keelan, Butler, Black, Stringer, Govier, Briggs, Livermore, Bone, Cross, Paddon, Anderson.

Roger Hynd

Blues news extra 1975..Blues Celebrate Centenary: Blues 1 Celtic 0

Blues 100th birthday was celebrated in style with a win over Celtic at St Andrews. Peter Withe got the important winning goal in front of a 14,670 crowd.

The Matches played on this day

1893, Division 2.		
Middlesbrough 3	Blues 0	Att. 200
(Ironopolis)		
1899, Division 2.		
Woolwich Arsenal 3	Blues 0	Att. 4,000
1905, Division 1.		
Everton 1	Blues 2	Att. 15,000
	Jones, Anderson	
1911, Division 2.		
Blues 0	Bristol City 0	Att. 12,000
1916, Wartime.		
Grimsby Town 3	Blues 0	
1922, Division 1.		
Nottingham Forest 1	Blues 1	Att. 12,000
	Bradford	
1933, Division 1.		
Chelsea 1	Blues 1	Att. 18,000
	White	
1939, Wartime.		
Leicester City 1	Blues 3	
	Jones, Bye, Edwards	
1944, Wartime.		
Blues 2	Walsall 2	
Mulligan(og), Shelton(og)		
1950, Division 2.		
Blues 3	Luton Town 0	Att. 20,000
Higgins 8, 77		
Smith 24		
1961, Division 1.		
Sheffield United 3	Blues 1	Att. 16,838
Allchurch 15	Harris 84	
Simpson 62		
Hartle 76		
1967, Division 2.		
Blues 1	Crystal Palace 0	Att. 27,538
Vincent 60		
1972, Division 1.		
Blues 4	Norwich City 1	Att. 32,890
Pendrey 36	Black 22	
Hope 74		
Want 76		
Hatton 85		
1978, Division 1.		
Blues 1	Bristol City 1	Att. 21,552
Tarantini 70	Mabbutt 26	
1987, Simod Cup 1st round.		
Derby County 3	Blues 1	Att. 8,277
Trewick(og) 96	Whitton 110	
McCord 106		
Garner 114		
1989, Division 3.		
Blues 1	Bolton Wanderers 0	Att. 8,081
Bailey 74(pen)		
2000, Division 1.		
Blues 2	Huddersfield Town 1	Att. 22,120
Lazaridis 26	Armstrong 60	
Horsfield 44		
2001, Division 1.		
Blues 2	Coventry City 0	Att. 18,554
Marcelo 16, 54		

November 26

The Matches played on this day

1898, Division 2.
Blues 8   Darwen 0   Att. 2,000
Gardner(2),
Abbott 5(1 pen), Robertson
Blues had now scored 35 goals in four succesive home games without conceding a goal.

1904, Division 1.
Sunderland 1   Blues 4   Att. 12,000
   Wilcox, Jones(2), Green

1910, Division 2.
Blackpool 3   Blues 1   Att. 4,000
   Kidd

1921, Division 1.
Blues 1   Blackburn Rovers 0   Att. 20,000
Burkinshaw

1927, Division 1.
Portsmouth 2   Blues 2   Att. 18,862
   Crosbie(2)

1932, Division 1.
Blues 0   Wolverhampton W. 0   Att. 24,168

1938, Division 1.
Blues 2   Portsmouth 0   Att. 18,862
Jennings(pen), Dearson

1949, Division 1.
Manchester City 4   Blues 0   Att. 30,501

1955, Division 1.
Cardiff City 2   Blues 1   Att. 28,000
Kirtley 4   Brown 20
Dixon 50

1957, Inter Cities Fairs Cup Semi Final, replay.
Blues 1   Barcelona 2   Att. 20,000
Murphy 48   Evaristo 33
   Kubala 83
Played at the neutral St Jakob Stadium, Basle, Switzerland

1960, Division 1.
Blues 0   Leicester City 2   Att. 25,583
   Leek 11
   Wills 70

1966, Division 2.
Blues 3   Crystal Palace 1   Att. 16,820
Vowden 7   C.Jackson 27
Vincent 12
Bullock 22

1977, Division 1.
Norwich City 1   Blues 0   Att. 17,161
Gibbins 90

1983, Division 1.
Blues 0   Sunderland 1   Att. 11,948
   Bracewell 68
Before the kick off Blues fans were introduced to the newly crowned Miss World, Sarah Jane Hutt of Dorset
Sunderland's first win at St Andrews for 26 years.

1988, Division 2.
Blues 1   Ipswich Town 0   Att. 5,932
Whitton 25

1994, Division 2.
Stockport County 0   Blues 1   Att. 5,577
   Hunt 83

1995, Division 1.
Blues 2   Leicester City 2   Att. 17,350
Hunt 30, 49(pen)   Roberts 9
   Grayson 20
Dan Sahlin replaced another debutant Danny Hill, to make his only appearance for the Blues.

1996, Division 1.
Reading 0   Blues 0   Att. 8,407

Playing record for this day
Playing record for this day.... 18 games, Won 7, Drawn 4, Lost 7, GF 27, GA 21.
Success rate...50% Year ranking....147th

Match of the Day
FROM 1904

A SLIP UP FOR SUNDERLAND
Footwear the key as Blues hold their feet for victory

On a freezing bone-hard surface Blues decision not to copy their opponents and wear long metal studs on their boots proved decisive as they held their feet and duly recorded a great 4-1 win. Sunderland appeared the better side but at crucial times during the game they were on the brink of falling over when attacking and slipped when needing to defend, and this ultimately cost them the game. Blues made two changes Hartwell came in for Glover at right back and Tickle replaced Green up front. A crowd of 5,000 had gathered for the kick-off however this had grown to 12,000 by half time, many waiting to see if the game would go ahead after the late pitch inspection.

Blues were quickly on top and took the lead on eight minutes when Wilcox found space in the penalty area to fire into the corner from 12 yards. Sunderland hit back as best they could on the slippery Muntz Street surface. Robinson saved well from a Watkins effort and moments later another shot, this time by Bridgett went inches wide. With Sunderland dominating it was no surprise when Common equalised, running through the Blues defence onto a loose ball and driving past Robinson as he came out to cover. Blues regained the lead just seven minutes later with their next attack. A long-range shot by Tickle was followed up by Jones who charged the visiting 'keeper into the net.

The second half started with some dangerous tackling, during a multi-player melee in the Blues goal play was stopped for a moment by the referee who issued a warning before the game was allowed to continue. Sunderland were soon on top again, but could not finish their neat play with a worthy effort on target and Robinson for the most part of the second half remained untroubled. Blues wrapped up the game with two late goals. The first on 80 minutes when Jones showed pushed the ball wide of his full back and chased round to collect in the clear, he then cut in from the right and finished with a fine shot. In the dying minutes the Sunderland keeper Rowlandson spilt a simple catch and Green followed up to tap in the fourth goal.

BIRMINGHAM CITY
Robinson, Hartwell, Stokes, Beer, Wigmore, Dougherty, Tickle, Green, Jones, Wilcox, Field.
SUNDERLAND
Rowlandson, Rhodes, Watkins, Jackson, Fullarton, Farquhar, Brown, Bridgett, Gemmell, Common, Watkins.

REFEREE
Mr Dirk Chesterman

Blues News, season 1949-50

Blues news extra   1979..Dave Latchford's Testimonial: Blues Present 8 Blues Past 3

Birthdays
Geoff Anderson born today 1944.   Trevor Aylott born today 1957.

Playing record for this day

Playing record for this day.... 15 games, Won 6, Drawn 3, Lost 6, GF 23, GA 22.

Success rate...50% Year ranking....158th

Match of the Day
FROM 1954
GOAL FORCE WIND HITS VALE
Murphy and Co hit seven in St Andrews super show

The atrocious weather conditions around Birmingham reduced the St Andrews attendance to 16,500 but failed to reduce the excitement in a thrilling game against Port Vale. On a wet pitch and in swirling wind Blues blitzed their opponents with seven goals, and despite being reduced to ten men for 55 minutes Vale played their part in a magnificent game. The Port Vale skipper Tom Cheadle was forced to leave the field after sustaining a fractured rib when slipping over on the muddy surface.

Blues were in front as early as the eighth minute when Govan sent Brown away down the left wing, he crossed hard and low into the area and although the ball was partially cleared it made its way through to Murphy who swept it in from four yards. Blues, who were dominating the game, then made it 2-0 with a terrific goal just seven minutes later. Brown again beat Potts for pace to send over his trademark hard and low centre from the byline, Murphy superbly converted with a full stretch dive to head in from six yards. Within minutes the ball was bobbling dangerously in the visitors' penalty area, but this time it was scrambled away by the relieved Vale defence. Then Brown missed a sitter from five yards, after slipping he only managed to scoop his effort up for King to punch clear. As the half wore on Cunliffe on the left wing, and by far the best player for Port Vale, started to receive the ball more often and he was the only threat to the Blues goal. From one raid he skipped over Hall's sliding tackle to send a lovely cross in for Smith but the alert Green intercepted with a well timed tackle. On the stroke of half-time Cunliffe beat three Blues defenders before being brought down by Smith on the edge of the area, but from the free kick Askey slipped as he was about to shoot and another Vale chance went begging.

Port Vale's predicament became worse when Blues scored a third just one minute into the second half. Kinsey latched onto a long clearance from defence to send a high looping cross over for Govan who headed in at the far post. However five minutes later the visitors were given hope with a contentious penalty awarded after a tussle for the ball between Merrick and Hayward. The Vale forward kicked the ball from the keeper's grip when Merrick dived at his feet but as he got free Hayward then fell, the referee adjudging Merrick to have tripped him. Former Walsall defender Mullard stepped up to blast in the penalty. Blues were not to be denied though and wrapped up the game with two goals in as many minutes, Kinsey got the first and then Murphy completed his hat-trick after 72 minutes. Although Vale pulled another goal back through Hayward's strike two minutes later further goals from Brown (79) and Kinsey (85 mins) completed a resounding 7-2 win for the Blues.

BIRMINGHAM CITY

Merrick, Hall, Green, Boyd, Smith, Warhurst, Astall, Kinsey, Brown, Murphy, Govan.

PORT VALE

King, Potts, Turner, Sproson, Cheadle, Mullard, Cunliffe, Smith, Hayward, Leake, Askey.

REFEREE

Mr NC Taylor (Wiltshire)

Jeff Hall

The Matches played on this day

1897, Division 2.		
Newcastle United 4	Blues 0	Att. 11,000
1909, Division 2.		
Blues 1	Blackpool 2	Att. 1,000
Chapple		

This is still the lowest crowd for a senior game at St Andrews.

1920, Division 2.		
Blues 3	Stoke 0	Att. 30,000
Lane, Burkinshaw, Crosbie		
1926, Division 1.		
Blues 2	Leeds United 0	Att. 19,707
Harris, Bradford		
1937, Division 1.		
Bolton Wanderers 1	Blues 1	Att. 20,000
	Clarke	
1943, Wartime.		
Aston Villa 3	Blues 0	
1948, Division 1.		
Blues 1	Sheffield United 2	Att. 25,000
Hall		
1954, Division 1.		
Blues 7	Port Vale 2	Att. 16,500
Murphy 8, 15, 72	Mullard 51(pen)	
Govan 46	Hayward 74	
Kinsey 71, 85		
Brown 79		
1965, Division 2.		
Bristol City 2	Blues 0	Att. 13,727
Low 52		
Peters 74		

Blues full back Colin Green stretchered off with a broken leg.

1971, Division 2.		
Blues 3	Fulham 1	Att. 25,545
B.Latchford 4	Conway 3	
Hatton 21, 89		
1976, Division 1.		
Blues 0	Manchester City 0	Att. 29,722

Blues winger John Connolly had a goal disallowed after 35 minutes.

1982, Division 1.		
Blues 2	Sunderland 1	Att. 12,375
Ferguson 35	Rowell 89	
Evans 52		
1990, Leyland Daf Cup preliminary round.		
Blues 2	Lincoln City 0	Att. 2,922
Clarke(og) 33		
Sturridge 35		
1993, Division 1.		
Blues 0	Tranmere Rovers 3	Att. 9,915
	Malkin 44	
	Aldridge 67, 88	
1999, Division 1.		
Blues 1	Swindon Town 1	Att. 22,620
Grainger 26	Onuora 90	

Blues striker Dele Adebola suffered a hairline fracture to his leg. Iffy Onuora's equaliser for Swindon came in the sixth minute of stoppage time.

November 28

Playing record for this day

Playing record for this day.... 17 games, Won 8, Drawn 3, Lost 6, GF 33, GA 28.
Success rate....55.88% Year ranking....93rd

Match of the Day

FROM 1931

SMITH A DOUBLE, DOUBLE HERO

Sam the wham hits two again as Blues top Town by five

An early start and gloomy wet weather conditions did little to help the St Andrews crowd of just 10,000 for what seemed an attractive fixture, Huddersfield having impressively beaten Derby the previous week.

Blues got off to a blistering start, their first attack almost earning a goal for Briggs. Exchanging passes with Grosvenor on the right wing his initial cross was blocked by Goodall, from the rebound Briggs floated the ball over for Turner in the Huddersfield goal to tip over via the crossbar for a corner. Huddersfield too showed dashes of attacking play in a real end-to-end start, however their forwards more often than not were thwarted by the linesman's flag. Mangnall (a future Blues player) forced a good save from Hibbs but he too had already been flagged offside. Blues deservedly took the lead on 16 minutes when the promising partnership of Smith and Bradford combined well from a corner. From Curtis's flag kick Bradford nodded back at the near post to Smith who buried his header firmly into the roof of the net at the back post. A slick three man move just two minutes later brought Blues a second goal when Grosvenor passed to Bradford who squared the ball over to Curtis who slipped his shot across Turner low into the corner. Shortly after this period of high quality football from Blues they were briefly reduced to ten men when Barkas accidentally clashed with Jennings and the Blues full back was forced to leave the field for treatment. Huddersfield failed to capitalise and Blues went on to dominate the game. A third goal came on the half-hour mark when Smith robbed a hesitant Stoker of possession on the half way line to sprint clear down the centre of the field, as Turner came out he delivered a delightful chip over the keeper's head from 25 yards.

Although Huddersfield fared a little better in the second period, fine defending from Morrall and Cringan and some excellent saves from Harry Hibbs kept the Terriers at bay. Hibbs pulled off a breathtaking save to deny Mangnall who had slipped unnoticed into the area. Blues wrapped up the game with two goals in the last quarter of an hour Briggs deservedly getting the first on 75 minutes and Bradford the other eight minutes later.

BIRMINGHAM CITY
Hibbs, Liddell, Barkas, Stoker, Morrall, Cringan, Briggs, Grosvenor, Smith, Bradford, Curtis.
HUDDERSFIELD TOWN
Turner, Goodall, Spence, Carr, Young, Campbell, Jennings, Kelly, Mangnall, McLean, Bott

REFEREE
Mr A Fogg (Bolton)

Leslie Knighton

Blues news extra   1973..Bad light stops play: Newcastle United 1 Blues 1

Despite the 2pm afternoon kick off this game was abandoned when the dim light made visibility impossible. On a freezing day at St James Park. For the record Tudor put the home side 1-0 up after 17 minutes. Blues equalised through Keith Bowker after 63 minutes. The attendance was 5,538.

Birthdays

Martin Thomas born today 1959.   Ken Charley born today 1964.   Alex Jackson born today 1935.

Playing record for this day

Playing record for this day.... 17 games, Won 7, Drawn 3, Lost 7, GF 25, GA 28.
Success rate...50% Year ranking....167th

Match of the Day

FROM 1994
SUPER SHOW REWARD FOR BUMPER CROWD

A double bonus from the Blues board further improved the party atmosphere around St Andrews and bought about another thrilling attacking display on the pitch. With admission prices slashed a huge crowd broke all previous records for the Auto Windscreens Shild competition, in fact the attendance of 17,028 exceeded the total of the other six Southern Section ties played around the country. On the pitch it was announced before the game that Barry Fry had a £1 million pound kitty to find a striker to add to his squad and already York's Paul Barnes and Swindon's Jan Fjortoft were on the short list. For this game Blues made two changes, Paul Tait replacing Hunt and Jose Dominguez coming in for Peter Shearer. Blues were on top from the first kick Gillingham totally overawed by the St Andrews atmosphere. Donowa after a mazy run from the wing cut in and came within a whisker of snatching the lead. Then Dominguez in a carbon copy of the move on the other flank was tripped as he was about to shoot. Claridge's spot kick however was little more powerfully hit than a defender's back pass and the 'keeper had time to scoop and hold onto the ball. Dominguez was then presented with an even simpler chance but he somehow scooped the ball over the bar. Then a cross by Donowa was anticipated well by McGavin who got in front of his marker only to glance his header inches wide of the post. Blues eventually went ahead after 39 minutes whena neat five man move through the middle set up McGavin who planted a fierce low from eight yards out. Blues then doubled their lead in their next attack four minutes later. Ward was bundled over as he looked to play Dominguez in and from the free kick 20 yards out Poole slammed his first goal for the Blues since his move from Southend in September. It should have been three it could have easily been six but Blues went in at half time just 2-0 up and with the game surely won.

They coasted in the second half almost in exhibition mode, the crowd entertained themselves with a `Mexican Wave' as the game for a moment was almost forgotten. Tait turned the attention to the action when he converted another teasing cross from the ever dangerous Dominguez on 68 minutes. The game was over and Blues had progressed to the quarter-finals where they would meet Hereford.

BIRMINGHAM CITY
Bennett, Poole, Whyte, Ward (Lowe 69), Barnett, Daish, Claridge, McGavin, Dominguez, Donowa (Cooper 74).
GILLINGHAM
Barrett, Lindsey, Palmer, Carpenter, Arnott, Bodley, Hutchinson, Foster (Ramage 74), Pike, Reinelt, Watson.

REFEREE
Mr AD'Urso (Wickford, Essex)

Steve McGavin

Blues news extra 1993..Cooper resigns as Blues boss

Blues were today rocked by the sudden resignation of Terry Cooper who took over as manager in August 1991. Blues had not had the best of starts to the 1993-94 season but despite this owner David Sullivan said he pleaded with the manager to reconsider. Blues, who lost 3-0 on Saturday to Tranmere at St Andrews, had not won a game since October.

The Matches played on this day
1890, Football Alliance.
B'ham St George's 5   Blues 4   Att. 2,000
                Hallam(2), W.Devey(2)

1902, Division 2.
Blackpool 0   Blues 1   Att. 3,000
                      Leonard

1913, Division 2.
Blues 1   Grimsby Town 2   Att. 18,000
Walker
Just before the game Blues full back Frank Womack was approached by a man who offed 55 guineas to throw the game and allow a draw to take place. Womack alerted officials immediately and arrests were made soon after. The guilty man received a six month prison sentence.
1919, Division 2.
Rotherham County 0   Blues 3   Att. 12,000
                      Short, Millard(2)
1924, Division 1.
Blues 5   Liverpool 2   Att. 25,000
Bradford(3, 1pen),
Barton, Islip
Joe Bradford finally earned himself a match ball for his first hat-trick for the club.
1930, Division 1.
Bolton Wanderers 2   Blues 0   Att. 12,000
1947, Division 2.
Cardiff City 2   Blues 0   Att. 35,000
1952, Division 2.
Blues 0   Nottingham Forest 5 Att. 17,000
                      Ardron 9, 13, 71
                      Collindridge 52
                      Moore 73
Blues five-match unbeaten run came to an end.
1958, Division 1.
Blues 0   Manchester United 4 Att. 28,618
                      Charlton 11, 62
                      Bradley 29
                      Scanlon 42
1975, Division 1.
Coventry City 3   Blues 2   Att. 21,687
Powell 12   Burns 34
Cross 29   Kendall 65(pen)
Murphy 31
Coventry had Donal Murphy sent off after 43 minutes
1980, Division 1.
Everton 1   Blues 1   Att. 22,258
O'Keefe 43   Ainscow 26
Blues striker Frank Worthington sent off after 71 minutes, just four minutes after having a second goal disallowed.
1983, League Cup 2nd round, 2nd replay.
Blues 0   Notts County 0   Att. 9,678
Ian Muir made his Blues debut.
1986, Division 2.
Grimsby Town 0   Blues 1   Att. 4,734
                      Whitton 17
Blues had two goals disallowed and hit the woodwork twice during the game.
1994, Auto Windscreens Shield 3rd round.
Blues 3   Gillingham 0   Att. 17,028
McGavin 39
Poole 43
Tait 68
Steve Claridge had a penalty saved by Scott Barrett with the score 0-0.
1995, League Cup 4th round.
Middlesbrough 0   Blues 0   Att. 28,031
1997, Division 1.
Blues 2   Portsmouth 1   Att. 17,387
Furlong 35, 73   Hall 34
2000, League Cup 4th round.
Blues 2   Newcastle United 1 Att. 18,520
Adebola 31   Dyer 13
M. Johnson 90

November 30

Playing record for this day

Playing record for this day.... 18 games, Won 6, Drawn 4, Lost 8, GF 33, GA 39.
Success rate...44.44% Year ranking....208th

Match of the Day
FROM 1968
SUMMERILL 1-2-3 SINKS HULL
Blues hit 5 in a St Andrews day celebration

In front of a crowd of 21,077 at St Andrews, 21-year-old Phil Summerill scored the first hat-trick of his career, taking just seven minutes to complete the task. In the first half goals from Greenhoff and then Pickering put Blues 2-0 up, but brave Hull City never gave up and battled right up until Summerill's heroics near the end before conceding defeat.

Already 2-0 down, Hull City reduced the lead just two minutes before half time, Greenwood playing in an unaccustomed midfield role stormed through the Blues defence to hit a beauty from just outside the area. It gave hope to Hull who had played good open attacking football from the first to last whistle in a cracking game. Hull continued to press forward clearly encouraged by the goal, but attempts proved fruitless until the 71st minute when Butler swept home a cross from Greenwood to gain a well earned equaliser. Now the pressure was on Birmingham having squandered a two-goal lead, they responded well by regaining the advantage just a minute later. It was the start of Summerill's fine individual show. Finding himself wide on the right he attempted a cross into the centre but the effort sailed over McKechnie's head and into the net. Inspired by this freak effort Summerill then netted a second just seven minutes later. The striker then completed a magnificent hat-trick after a shot by Pickering rattled off the cross bar and rebounded to him close in, and he blasted it in from barley four yards out.

This short burst of high quality play from Blues, put an end to a brave Hull display. No more goals came and so they ended up 5-2 winners, almost repeating the result in the corresponding fixture of 1967-68, which ended with a 6-2 victory.

BIRMINGHAM CITY
Herriott, Martin, Green, Wylie, Robinson, Page,
Hockey, Greenhoff, Pickering, Vincent, Summerill.
HULL CITY
McKechnie, Banks, Beardsley, Pettit, Wilson, Greenwood,
Jarvis, Wagstaff, Lill, Simpkin, Butler.

REFEREE
Mr FM Nicholson (Manchester)

Phil Summerill

Blues news extra   1875..The birth of the Blues

Blues played their first game in late November against Holte Wanderers on a bitterly cold afternoon at their Arthur Street ground. The game, a 12-a-side friendly, was drawn 1-1 and David Keys had the honour of netting Blues first goal. Small Heath Alliance as they were known they lined up as follows: W.Edden, Wright, F.James, T.James, G.Edden, Edmunds(captain) T.Edden, Keys, Barmore, Barr, Sparrow, Morris.

Birthdays

Geoff Cox born today 1934.   Adam Wratten born today 1974.

Playing record for this day

Playing record for this day.... 15 games, Won 6, Drawn 4, Lost 5, GF 19, GA 18.
Success rate...53.33% Year ranking....124th

Match of the Day
FROM 1984
LOAN STAR MORLEY
FIRES BLUES

On-loan Tony Morley became an instant hero when he scored two more goals for Birmingham, his second proving to be the winner at Ninian Park. Blues started the game making just one change from the disappointing 0-0 draw with Barnsley. Tony Rees joined the forward line with Martin Kuhl dropping to the subs' bench. Cardiff made one change themselves, giving a debut to on-loan Lincoln City 'keeper David Felgate, who replaced Lee Smelt. A paltry crowd of 5,057 were treated to a pretty undistinguished opening 15 minutes before the home fans were given some inspiration when Blues won a corner. From the kick Gibbons rose well to plant a firm header goalwards which Seaman tipped over from just underneath the cross bar. This brought the game to life, and from this point on they dominated play for the remainder of the half. Blues took the lead on 19 minutes after good work by Rees and Clarke who set up the chance for Morley. Cutting in from the left he took a stride forward into the penalty area before cracking in a well placed shot past Felgate. It was only the third Blues goal in seven games and they had little time to celebrate before Cardiff struck back. The goal came indirectly from a free kick given away by Ranson. The kick was floated into the box and Dwyer got up to head against the bar, this caused confusion in the Blues defence and when the ball came back in, Elsey was left unmarked to knock it in from close range. The visitors quickly regained their composure, and but for a fantastic save from Felgate moments later would have regained the lead on 26 minutes.

The second half started in torrential rain and it was Cardiff who adjusted to the conditions better. A worrying moment for Seaman and Blues defence came soon after, when Flynn got in a header which just cleared the cross bar by a fraction of an inch. Blues had a great chance to go 2-1 up on the hour when Morley screwed his shot horribly wide. Then five minutes later Morley made amends for his miss to net his second, and put Blues firmly back in control. It was a well worked goal too. A series of passes between Rees, Clarke, and Morley left the latter with another glorious shooting chance and this time he made no mistake, driving the ball into the bottom corner of the net. Cardiff tried hard for an equaliser and had two loud appeals for penalties turned down by the referee. But Blues held out and deserved their fine 2-1 victory.

CARDIFF CITY
Felgate, King, Mullen, Dwyer, Martin, Tong, Flynn, Gibbins, Vaughan, Summerfield, Elsey,

BIRMINGHAM CITY
Seaman, Ranson, Roberts, Wright, Armstrong, Hagan, Morley, Clarke, Rees, Bremner, Hopkins.

REFEREE
Mr RT Stevens (Stonehouse)

Tony Morley

Blues news extra 1883..Blues hit 11!!! Blues 11 Dudley 0
Blues won a slightly one-sided Birmingham Senior Cup tie, hitting poor Dudley for eleven in an amazing game of high quality finishing.

December 2

FOOTBALL

The Matches played on this day
1893, Division 2.
Blues 8   Northwich Victoria 0   Att. 1,500
Wheldon(4),
Mobley(3), Walton
1899, Division 2.
Blues 5   Barnsley 0   Att. 4,000
Main, McRoberts,
Wigmore(2), Leonard
1905, Division 1.
Blues 3   Derby County 1   Att. 12,000
Tickle, Mounteney, Wigmore
1911, Division 2.
Burnley 1   Blues 1   Att. 13,000
                 Jones
1916, Wartime.
Blues 4   Notts County 0
Whitehouse(2),
S.Brooks, Montgomery
1922, Division 1.
Blues 3   Arsenal 2   Att. 29,772
Foxall, Linley(2, 1pen)
1933, Division 1.
Blues 0   Aston Villa 0   Att. 35,000
1939, Wartime.
Northampton Town 1 Blues 1
                 Jones
1944, Wartime.
Blues 0   Northampton Town 0
1950, Division 2.
Leeds United 3   Blues 0   Att. 23,355
Milburn 16
Browning 35
Burden 75
1961, Division 1.
Blues 3   Cardiff City 0   Att. 20,939
Leek 1, 28
Hellawell 69
Ken Leek scored twice on his St Andrews debut
1967, Division 2.
Charlton Athletic 3 Blues 1   Att. 38,369
Gregory 38   Bridges 36
Tees 54, 62
1972, Division 1.
Liverpool 4   Blues 3   Att. 45,407
Lindsay 32, 54   Taylor 13
Cormack 44   Hope 20
Toshack 78   B.Latchford 42
This game screened by BBC's Match of the Day.
1978, Division 1.
Southampton 1   Blues 0   Att. 23,391
Boyer 47
1980, League Cup 2nd round.
Liverpool 3   Blues 1   Att. 30,236
Dalglish 24   Bertschin 38
McDermott 67
Johnson 85
1992, Anglo Italian Cup, International Stage.
AC Cesena 1   Blues 2   Att. 2,090
Hubner 77(pen)   Frain 49(pen)
                 Sturridge 69
1994, FA Cup 2nd round.
Blues 0   Scunthorpe United 0   Att. 13,832
First senior competitive meeting v Scunthorpe.
1995, Division 1.
Southend United 3 Blues 1   Att. 7,770
Bodley 44   Claridge 29
Regis 45
Byrne 71
2000, Division 1.
Gillingham 1   Blues 2   Att. 9,247
King 26   M.Johnson 70
                 Horsfield 90
Southall put his penalty over the bar after 72 minutes
Martin Grainger sent off after 74 minutes.

Playing record for this day
Playing record for this day.... 19 games, Won 8, Drawn 5, Lost 6, GF 38, GA 24.
Success rate....55.26% Year ranking....101st

Match of the Day
FROM 1972
BLUES ROBBED IN FRONT OF THE KOP
Blues stun league leaders with 3-1 lead, then denied by ref

Blues fans were left feeling robbed after this game at Anfield. A disallowed goal would have made all the difference to the score, giving the visitors the draw that they deserved. The match was shown on Match of the Day later, and the injustice could be seen by all. However, it was too late and Blues accepted defeat with their heads held high. The visitors started the scoring on 13 minutes when Bobby Hope put Taylor away and he sent a shot skidding off Storton's back and past England goalkeeper Ray Clemence.

Kelly made a super save from an attempt by Keegan, and then Blues added another goal on 20 minutes when Taylor sent a cross for Bob Latchford to head down. Hope was on hand to nudge it across the goal line. Kelly made a save on 27 minutes to keep Liverpool at bay. Pendrey then made a bad challenge which resulted in a free kick for Liverpool, and from this Emlyn Hughes sent through Lindsay who scored with ease.

However Blues then scored a third when Hatton passed to Bob Latchford whose low shot beat Clemence on its way in to the net on 42 minutes. The two-goal lead didn't last long and just two minutes later Peter Cormack netted to narrow the deficit.

On 54 minutes the equaliser was scored when a free kick was awarded to Liverpool from an 18 yard challenge. Hughes took the kick and sent it to Lindsay who took no time in scoring his second of the match. Hatton was booked for a set-to with Hughes, and then the unthinkable happened. With 15 minutes to go Trevor Storton picked up a ball from Garry Pendrey and, in trying to keep it away from Bob Hatton, he pushed it over his own goal line. Understandably the Blues fans went wild, but not for long. The referee decided that Hatton had committed a foul and disallowed the goal and gave Liverpool a free kick. The decision was gratefully received by Liverpool and the ball then came to Kevin Keegan who headed to John Toshack. He then had only Mike Kelly in the Blues goal to beat, and this he did.

To round off an unfortunate end to a brilliant performance, Want was cautioned in the players' tunnel at the end of the match for apparently making a comment to the referee.

LIVERPOOL
Clemence, Lawler, Lindsay, Storton, Lloyd, Hughes, Keegan, Cormack, Heighway, Toshack, Callaghan.
BIRMINGHAM CITY
Kelly, Martin, Want, Pendrey, Hynd, Harland, Hope, Calderwood, Bob Latchford, Hatton, Taylor.

REFEREE
Mr A Hart (Kent)

Bobby Hope

Birthdays
George Edwards born today 1920.

December 3

Playing record for this day

Playing record for this day.... 19 games, Won 6, Drawn 5, Lost 8, GF 24, GA 29.

Success rate...44.74% Year ranking....204th

Match of the Day
FROM 1955
BLUES ATTACK AT THEIR BRILLIANT BEST

Four great goals pepper a superb team performance

You don't have to dominate a game of football with territorial advantage and neat passing. Sometimes just producing three wonder goals will suffice and that's exactly how Blues managed to destroy Arsenal in the first half much to the delight of the 35,765 St Andrews crowd. Arsenal were quickly on top and forced two corners which Blues defended well. The Gunners progress was helped by some wayward passing, still it was the home side who came closest to scoring when Boyd's 25-yard shot skimmed the crossbar. Moments later a defensive error allowed Tapscott in with only Merrick to beat, his shot struck the 'keeper on the knee and rebounded to Clapton, this time Merrick pulled off an amazing reflex save with his outstretched left leg whilst on the goal line. Shortly after this Blues took the lead somewhat against the run of play. Astall after a surging run on the right wing knocked the ball across the face of the visitors' goal where first Brown then Murphy jumped over the ball leaving Kinsey at the far post to hit low into the corner. Some of the referee's decisions were controversial and after a dubious corner was awarded to Arsenal the linesman was pelted with several pieces of orange peel. A great goal then followed as Blues doubled their lead on 36 minutes. Boyd picked up a loose ball in midfield and went through man after man on a sizzling run before crossing to Murphy. His shot on the run was blocked by a defender's leg but the ball ran to Kinsey who cracked in from just outside the penalty area. The goal was greeted with prolonged cheers by the crowd but a better one was to come Blues way just before half time. They were awarded a free kick on the halfway line after a foul on Kinsey. He took the kick quickly as Arsenal were getting men into position to defend, Warhust received and floated a fantastic ball into the penalty area where Astall, charged in and headed it on the first bounce over Kelsey who was left stranded just outside his six-yard box.

The second half was almost a repeat of the first as Arsenal again controlled but never looked like scoring. An amusing incident occured midway through the half when Kelsey charged out to meet a long ball from opposite number Merrick, however as he jumped to take the ball from Brown's head he realised he'd come beyond his penalty area and at the last minute he headed the ball clear. Impressed by the 'keeper's improvisation Brown applauded and when Kelsey then took a bow both players parted after a handshake. The Blues goal had a lucky escape towards the end of the game when a Bloomfield header struck the post and Boyd was on hand to kick clear. Blues rounded of a great win by notching a fourth through Brown, who tapped in a simple chance in the 89th minute to complete the 4-0 win.

BIRMINGHAM CITY

Merrick, Hall, Badham, Boyd, Smith, Warhurst, Astall, Kinsey, Brown, Murphy, Govan.

ARSENAL

Kelsey, Evans, Wills, Holton, Fotheringham, Goring, Tiddy, Bloomfield, Roper, Tapscott, Clapton.

REFEREE

Mr CG Porter (Taunton)

Gil Merrick

Birthdays

Alberto Tarantini born today 1955.   **Walter Quinton born today 1917.**

The Matches played on this day
1881, FA Cup 2nd round.

Wednesbury Old A. 6	Blues 0	Att. 3,000

1892, Division 2.

Blues 1	Sheffield United 1	Att. 2,000
Wheldon		

1898, Division 2.

Gainsborough Trinity 1	Blues 1	
	Gardner	

1904, Division 1.

Blues 2	Woolwich Arsenal 1	Att. 20,000
Dougherty, Jones		

1910, Division 2.

Blues 1	Glossop 2	Att. 2,000
Jones		

1921, Division 1.

Oldham Athletic 0	Blues 1	Att. 12,973
	Cameron	

1927, Division 1.

Blues 0	Leicester City 2	Att. 15,000

1932, Division 1.

Bolton Wanderers 2	Blues 2	Att. 8,000
	Bradford, Briggs	

1938, Division 1.

Arsenal 3	Blues 1	Att. 33,710
	Jennings(pen)	

1949, Division 1.

Blues 2	Charlton Athletic 0	Att. 29,000
Stewart, Berry		

1955, Division 1.

Blues 4	Arsenal 0	Att. 35,765
Kinsey 26, 36		
Astall 44		
Brown 89		

1956, Inter Cities Fairs Cup, Qualifying Group

Blues 3	Zagreb XI 0	Att. 40,144
Orritt 3		
Brown 60		
Murphy 67		

Blues first match in European competition at St Andrews. Substitutes were allowed and, Noel Kinsey replaced the injured Bryan Orritt.

1960, Division 1.

Blackpool 1	Blues 2	Att. 11,720
Charnley 86	Hellawell 11, 36	

1966, Division 2.

Huddersfield Town 3	Blues 1	Att. 14,930
Leighton 16	Bullock 70	
Dobson 44(pen)		
Nicholson 84		

1977, Division 1.

Blues 0	Nottingham Forest 2	Att. 29,925
	O'Neill 12	
	Woodcock 53	

1983, Division 1.

Liverpool 1	Blues 0	Att. 24,791
Rush 86		

1988, Division 2.

Bradford City 2	Blues 2	Att. 9,503
Leonard 31	Whitton 7	
Jewell 72	Richards 64	

1991, League Cup 2nd round, replay.

Crystal Palace 2	Blues 1	Att. 11,384
Gray 26(pen)	Peer 45	
Thorn 42		

1996, Division 1.

Blues 0	Barnsley 0	Att. 24,004

Barnsley 'keeper Dave Watson saved Steve Bruce's second half penalty.

December 4

Playing record for this day
Playing record for this day.... 14 games, Won 6, Drawn 3, Lost 5, GF 24, GA 29.
Success rate...53.57% Year ranking....122nd

The Matches played on this day
1897, Division 2.

Blues 6	Walsall 0	Att. 3,000

Hare, Oakes(2),
Abbott(2, 1pen), Kirton
1909, Division 2.

Hull City 7	Blues 0	Att. 6,000

Blues biggest ever defeat by Hull.
1920, Division 2.

Blues 3	Coventry City 2	Att. 30,000

Whitehouse(2), Lawrence(og)
1926, Division 1.

Liverpool 2	Blues 1	Att. 35,000
	Briggs	

1937, Division 1.

Blues 1	Arsenal 2	Att. 18,440

Morris
1943, Wartime.

Blues 3	WBA 0	

Mulraney(2), Trigg
1948, Division 1.

Aston Villa 0	Blues 3	Att. 61,632
	Stewart(2), Bodle	

1954, Division 2.

Notts County 3	Blues 2	Att. 14,000
Johnston 50	Govan 16	
Smith(og) 56	Murphy 87	

Broadbent 72
County 'keeper Bradley saved Noel Kinsey's 62nd
minute penalty.
1965, Division 2.

Blues 3	Manchester City 1	Att. 10,442
Thwaites 10	Summerbee 58	
Jackson 44		
Vowden 84		

1971, Division 2.

Middlesbrough 0	Blues 0	Att. 15,671

Defender Stan Harland made his debut for the
Blues. Bob Latchford sent off on 43 minutes.
1976, Division 1.

Leicester City 2	Blues 6	Att. 20,388
Kember 76	Emmanuel 12	
Worthington 83(pen)	Francis 14	
	Burns 33, 37, 64	
	Rofe(og) 53	

1982, Division 1.

Everton 0	Blues 0	Att. 13,703

1993, Division 1.

Nottingham Forest 1	Blues 0	Att. 22,061
Whyte(og) 32		

1999, Division 1.

Fulham 0	Blues 0	Att. 12,290

Match of the Day
FROM 1976
A SKATE TO VICTORY
Footwear the key to Blues 6-2 win on, Filbert Street ice rink

Should this game have been played? According to referee Ken Baker the pitch was playable, and as he noted after the game, "the quality of football bore out my decision." However according to both managers it should not have started. The pitch had received two inspections during the day, but it was only possible to play on if the right footwear was used and Blues certainly had the advantage there. They arrived at Filbert Street on the morning of the game and their players tried out three different types of boot. Using nylon studs, rubber studs, and a training shoe of flat suction soles. It was the latter which proved the perfect weapon in which to shoot down Leicester to such deadly effect.

Blues were simply quicker, more confident and above all much braver on the bone-hard surface. When the Leicester team realised they had the wrong footwear, they were already a beaten side. The home players led by Steve Kember, came over to the touchline to change their boots just after half an hours play, the game already beyond them at 3-0. Soon after Kenny Burns added a fourth.

When the second half started six Leicester players in all had changed into a training shoe similar to the visitors, but it was far too late. Blues struck a fifth through Rofe who couldn't help but turn the ball past his own 'keeper whilst under pressure from Burns. Just 55 minutes had elapsed and Blues now had a chance of claiming another prize. Just two months previously a local sports dealer, Blues fan Paul Banks, had offered a brand new sports car to the player who hit the sixth goal in any first-team game. Within a week Burns had almost claimed the TR7 car when scoring four against Derby in a 5-1 win. It took Blues, and Burns, a further ten minutes to notch the sixth, just reward for the Scottish striker who adapted to the conditions better than anyone else and missed nothing all afternoon. Burns said of his prize winning goal afterwards, "I'm going to sell the car and then share out the proceeds with my team mates. We agreed to do it this way when the prize was first donated." A nice gesture to a perfect team effort, as for Leicester they finally made an attacking contribution to the game late on, scoring twice through Kember on 76 minutes and Worthington from the penalty spot seven minutes later.

LEICESTER CITY
Wallington, Whitworth, Rofe, Kember, Blockley, Sims, Weller, Sammels,Worthington, Alderson, Earle
(Birchenall)

BIRMINGHAM CITY;
Latchford, Page, Styles, Pendrey, Gallagher, Want, Emmanuel, Francis, Burns, Hibbitt, Connolly.

REFEREE
Mr K Baker (Rugby)

Kenny Burns

Birthdays
Ian Clarkson born today 1970.   Steve Whitton born today 1960.

Playing record for this day
Playing record for this day.... 18 games, Won 10, Drawn 1, Lost 7, GF 41, GA 32.
Success rate....58.33% Year ranking....70th

December 5

Match of the Day
FROM 1964
SEESAW WITH SUNDERLAND
Goals for both sides in drama at St Andrews

In front of a crowd of 13,564 Blues were forced to keep Vowden out of the line-up due a thigh injury sustained in training. His place in the team was filled by Leek who had been absent for the two games. Sunderland's Harvey also failed a late fitness test and was replaced by Elliott on the right in midfield, while Parke was back in the side at right back after being declared fit following an ankle injury.

A close call came for Blues early on when Jackson's shot was moved along by Thomson, but Sunderland 'keeper Montgomery kept the ball out. Usher had the first chance for the visitors, but he eventually passed the ball to Sharkey who sent the ball way too high over the bar. Schofield had to leave his line to cover another shot from Sharkey, then Thwaites started an attack on the Sunderland goal. He provided the ball for Jackson who could only shoot straight into the arms of Montgomery.

Three corner kicks for Sunderland in the space of a minute put the Blues defence through their paces but they survived. Two minutes later it was a different story. Another corner for Sunderland was taken by Usher on 22 minutes, and Sharkey took advantage of his absent marker to send it flying past Schofield. Blues levelled the score just a minute later when a low pass from Thwaites found Thomson. He evaded two defenders to deliver his shot into the goal past Montgomery.

Three minutes into the second half Thwaites sent the Blues fans wild when he scored a great goal putting the home team into the lead. It took 20 minutes for Sunderland to get the equaliser. This came from another corner kick, this time taken by Mulhall who passed to McNab. He headed it down to Sharkey who sent it soaring into the net. The score didn't stay level for long as Blues were determined that the encounter would end up in their favour. Sharples headed them into the lead on 70 minutes, and then Sunderland drew level on 79 minutes with a goal from McNab. Just 30 seconds later the final goal of the game arrived, to give Blues a 4-3 win, volleyed into the net by Jackson.

BIRMINGHAM CITY
Schofield, Green, Martin, Hennessey, Foster, Beard, Jackson, Sharples, Thomson, Leek, Thwaites.
SUNDERLAND
Montgomery, Parke, Ashurst, Elliott, Rooks, McNab, Usher, Hood, Sharkey, Herd, Mulhall.

REFEREE
Mr KJ Sneddon (Southport)

Terry Hennessey

Blues news extra   1956..A lucky 13th for Hall England 5 Denmark 2
Jeff Hall made it a lucky 13 for England. His 13th cap helped them to a fine 5-2 win in this
World Cup qualifier at Molineux. Manchester United Tommy Taylor did the damage up front netting a hat-trick.

Birthdays
Bobby Thomson born today 1943.

December 6

The Matches played on this day
1890, FA Cup 2nd qualifying round.
Wednesbury Old A. 0 Blues 2   Att. 2,000
                      Short, Hallam
Blues were disqualified from the FA Cup when
investigations revealed Charlie Short was not a
registered player and therefore not allowed to take
part.
1893, Division 2.
Blues 6   Crewe Alexandra 1   Att. 500
Hallam, Mobley(2),
Hands, Walton, Jenkyns
1902, Division 2.
Blues 2   Woolwich Arsenal 0   Att. 10,000
Leonard, Wigmore
1913, Division 2.
Fulham 1   Blues 0   Att. 10,000
1919, Division 2.
Stoke 0   Blues 1   Att. 15,000
                       Short
1924, Division 1.
Nottingham Forest 1   Blues 1   Att. 10,000
                       Bradford(pen)
1930, Division 1.
Blues 2   Huddersfield Town 0 Att. 13,885
Bradford, Curtis
1947, Division 2.
Blues 1   Sheffield Wed. 0   Att. 31,217
Westlake(og)
1952, Division 2.
Everton 1   Blues 1   Att. 23,858
Potts 38   Murphy 52
1958, Division 1.
Chelsea 1   Blues 0   Att. 27,773
Greaves 55
1969, Division 2.
Blues 2   Huddersfield Town 2 Att. 24,956
Vowden 9   Worthington 60
Murray 89   Hoy 63
1975, Division 1.
Blues 2   Derby County 1   Att. 30,620
Burns 53   George 33
Page 59
Blues beat the league leaders and reigning champions.
1980, Division 1.
Blues 1   Leicester City 2   Att. 18,479
Scott(og) 71   Melrose 6, 11
1986, Division 2.
Blues 1   Blackburn Rovers 1   Att. 6,428
Clarke 53   Keeley 39
Blackburn skipper Glen Keeley sent off after 68
minutes
1997, Division 1.
Port Vale 0   Blues 1   Att. 7,509
                       Cottee 19

Playing record for this day

Playing record for this day.... 15 games, Won 8, Drawn 4, Lost 3, GF 23, GA 11.
Success rate...66.67% Year ranking....17th

Match of the Day
FROM 1975
PAGE BOOKS ANOTHER BLUES WIN
James debut overshadowed by fellow countryman's winner

This was an end-to-end game which provided great entertainment for the 30,620 crowd. It firstly turned turned in favour of the visitors after 33 minutes with a goal from Charlie George. Following a neat four man move the ball found its way to George who had little trouble sliding it past Latchford from within the penalty area. Try as they might Blues could not get back on terms before the half-time whistle, but they showed signs the equaliser was on its way.

The home team started the second period with the same momentum they finished the first half with, and it was all Blues pressure in the early stages. Then a sweeping move from Page sent Francis away down the left. From his inswinging cross, Kenny Burns flicked his header just inside the far post and beyond the reach of Boulton, for a fully deserved equaliser. This was a remarkable comeback as Burns had risen from his sick bed suffering from influenza the day before, but he declared himself fit just hours before kick off. Still Blues continued to drive forward making a total mockery of current league form as they looked like pinching yet another home victory. Their reward came via a Page special just before the hour mark. Latching on to a loose ball just outside the penalty area he got his whole body weight behind the ball to whack it straight in the direction of Boulton. Although it came within inches of the 'keeper's reach he could hardly move before the ball had screamed past him and hit the netting behind, it was a superb strike. A worried looking Dave Mackay couldn't quite get his sub's kit off quickly enough, eventually sending £800,000 buy Leighton James on four minutes later in a desperate attempt to rescue the game. It was all too late, and although Derby came back with a late surge, the Blues claimed victory. This was manager Willie Bell's 11th home point from seven games at St Andrews, good enough to win honours, the trouble was their away form was still rather dismal.

BIRMINGHAM CITY
Latchford, Osborne, Want, Kendall, Gallagher, Burns, Page, Francis, Withe, Hatton, Hibbitt.
DERBY COUNTY
Boulton, Thomas, Nish, Birch, McFarland, Todd, Newton (James 64), Gemmill, Lee, Hector, George.

Malcom Page

Blues news extra 1933..Grosvenor goal aids England victory: England 4 France 1
Tom Grosvenor Blues attacking midfielder scored his second goal in just his third game for England helping them to a fine 4-1 win over France at Tottenham's White Hart Lane ground. This friendly aslo proved to be the Blues player's last cap for his country.

1941..Wartime friendly Blues 3 British Army 6

Birthdays
Kevin Francis born today 1967.

Playing record for this day

Playing record for this day.... 21 games, Won 8, Drawn 3, Lost 10, GF 34, GA 31.
Success rate...45.24% Year ranking....199th

Match of the Day

FROM 1960

BOLD BLUES DISPLAY BEATS THE DANES

Blues stroll to the semi-final after fine win

Blues booked their place in the Inter Cities Fairs Cup semi-Final after a great performance in front of 22,486 fans at St Andrews winning the second leg 5-0. leg and so progressed 9-4 on aggregate. They now faced Italian giants Inter Milan.

Blues started the game with £48,000 worth of new talent on view in Jimmy Bloomfield and Jimmy Harris, the latter making his debut. The new attacking formation, with Singer omitted, and Stubbs and Bloomfield partnering Harris for the first time was successful as the final score shows. The win was never in doubt from the fourth minute onwards and a three goal burst in five minutes early in the second half, gave the result a solid look.

The first goal came from Robin Stubbs, who was given an opportunity to re-establish himself again after losing his place in October. He was picked out by an accurate long pass from Watts, controlled the ball with his first touch and burst through the Danish defence on the left to hammer past Jensen. The Bloomfield-Harris combination then struck its first blow, Harris running on to a fine through ball from his fellow newcomer, shot just wide of Jensen, but unfortunately just wide of the post too. Later the Danish 'keeper saved superbly from another Harris effort from the edge of the penalty area, leaping high, to turn the ball round the post. It was due to his abillity in goal that the team from Copenhagen got to half time still in the game just a goal down.

Goals started flowing early in the second half after a devastating three goal blitz within five minutes. The first came just three minutes into the half when Harris took advantage of a Helbrandt error to score his first goal for the Blues. The full back lost out in a 50-50 challenge, Harris was away finishing with a shot witch flew across the 'keeper and into the top corner. A minute later Hellawell took advantage of an error from Jensen who should have done better with Harris's 'daisy cutter' from 20 yards, Hellawell was quickly onto the ball as it slipped out of the 'keeper's grip, and knocked into the empty goal. Bloomfield added the Blues fourth goal after another slip up by the 'keeper. Despite a heartening rally from the Danes through their talented wingers Ravn and Clausen the Blues defence and their 'keeper Withers remained effectively untroubled. Blues completed the night's scoring in the 67th minute with a goal from Robin Stubbs. This time he cutt in from the right, and finished with another emphatic shot from 17 yards which gave the 'keeper no chance.

BIRMINGHAM CITY
Withers, Farmer, Allen, Watts, Smith, Neal, Hellawell, Stubbs, Harris, Bloomfield, Taylor.

KB COPENHAGEN
Jensen, Helbrandt, Poulsen, Krog, Kjoge, Petersen, Clausen, Ravn, Jorn Sorensen, Ole Sorenssen, Mortensen.

Jimmy Bloomfield

Blues news extra 1932..Hibbs wins his 13th cap for England: England 4 Austria 3

Blues 'keeper Harry Hibbs won his 13th cap in a fortunate England victory over Austria at Stamford Bridge.

Birthdays

Phil Hawker born today 1962.

The Matches played on this day
1889, FA Cup 4th qualifying round.

Blues 4	Walsall Town Swifts 0	Att. 2,000
W.Devey(3), Stanley		

1895, Division 1.

Blues 0	Everton 3	Att. 3,000

1901, Division 1.

Grimsby Town 1	Blues 0	Att. 6,000

1907, Division 1.

Blues 0	Sunderland 2	Att. 10,000

1912, Division 2.

Huddersfield Town 0	Blues 0	Att. 6,000

1918, Wartime.

Barnsley 2	Blues 1	
	Morgan	

1925, Division 1.

Burnley 3	Blues 1	Att. 15,000
	Briggs	

1929, Division 1.

Blues 3	Manchester City 0	Att. 18,000
Curtis, Haywood(2)		

1935, Division 1.

Blues 4	Huddersfield Town 1	Att. 15,000
Jones(2), White, Guest		

1940, Wartime.

Northampton Town 2	Blues 1	
	Trigg	

1946, Division 2.

Blues 3	Bury 0	Att. 20,000
Duckhouse, Dougall, Edwards		

1957, Division 1.

Blues 3	Manchester United 3	Att. 35,791
Murphy 15	Viollet 14, 46	
Astall 16	Taylor 18	
Kinsey 36		

The last visit of Sir Matt Busby's 'babes' before the tragic air crash in Munich just two months later.

1960, Inter Cities Fairs Cup 2nd round, 2nd leg.

Blues 5	KB Copenhagen.0	Att. 22,486
Stubbs 4, 67		
Harris 48		
Hellawell 49		
Bloomfield 53		

1961, Inter Cities Fairs Cup 2nd round, 2nd leg.

Blues 1	RCD Espanyol 0	Att. 16,874
Auld 59		

Blues lost 5-3 on aggregate
Four were sent off. Jimmy Harris and Bertie Auld for Blues, whilst Sanchez and Rivas went off for Espanyol.
Bertie Auld's goal was the last Blues have scored in European competitions, so far!!

1963, Division 1.

Blues 2	West Ham United 1	Att. 15,357
Auld 27	Britt 63	
Lynn(pen) 74		

1966, League Cup 5th round.

Sheffield United 2	Blues 3	Att. 15,023
Fenoughty 17	Bullock 31	
Mallender 32	Hockey 46	
	Vincent 72	

1968, Division 2.

Sheffield United 2	Blues 0	Att. 14,369
Hemsley 60		
Woodward 77		

1974, Division 1.

Stoke City 3	Blues 0	Att. 33,999
Greenhoff 15, 37		
Moores 28		

1976, Division 1.

Blues 2	Ipswich Town 4	Att. 31,161
Connolly 13	Mariner 10	
Burns 25	Wark 49	
	Talbot 75, 77	

1985, Division 1.

Blues 1	Watford 2	Att. 7,043
Wright 44(pen)	Blissett 49	
	Sterling 70	

1996, Division 1.

Blues 0	Grimsby Town 0	Att. 17,001

December 8

Playing record for this day
Playing record for this day.... 17 games, Won 8, Drawn 4, Lost 5, GF 40, GA 28.
Success rate....58.82% Year ranking....64th

The Matches played on this day
1888, FA Cup 4th preliminary round.
Blues 9   Burton Wanderers 0   Att. 2,000
E.Devey(4),
W.Devey(4), Short
Blues created a unique record in the FA Cup when brothers
Will and Ted Devey both hit four goals each in the same tie.
1894, Division 1.
Sunderland 7   Blues 1   Att. 6,000
              Hallam
First league meeting v Sunderland.
1900, Division 1.
Blues 1   Glossop 0   Att. 7,000
Aston(pen)
1906, Division 1.
Blues 5   Woolwich Arsenal 1   Att. 19,000
Green(2),
Jones(2), Beer
1917, Wartime.
Blues 0   Grimsby Town 1
1923, Division 1.
Blues 0   Everton 1   Att. 10,000
1928, Division 1.
Blues 2   Sheffield United 2   Att. 15,000
Bradford(2)
1934, Division 1.
Sunderland 5   Blues 1   Att. 20,000
              Barkas(pen)
1945, Wartime.
Blues 4   Southampton 0
Bodle, Jones, Edwards(2)
1951, Division 2.
Luton Town 2   Blues 4   Att. 17,000
Stobbart 38   Purdon 25
Taylor 86   Warhurst 42
              Stewart 48
              Smith 85
1956, Division 1.
Everton 2   Blues 0   Att. 29,529
Kirby 25
Jones 79(pen)
1962, Division 1.
Blues 3   Blackburn Rovers 3   Att. 16,089
Bloomfield 38   Ratcliffe 30
Leek 44, 84   Pickering 60
              Douglas 78
1973, Division 1.
Blues 1   Newcastle United 0   Att. 25,428
Burns 37
1979, Division 2.
Notts County 1   Blues 1   Att. 11,381
O'Brien 41(pen)   Lynex 30
1984, Division 2.
Blues 3   Middlesbrough 2   Att. 8,004
Wright 23(pen)   Currie 81(pen)
Saxby(og) 47   Mills 90
Rees 73
Billy Wright's penalty was the first Blues goal at St
Andrews for 510 minutes.
1992, Anglo Italian Cup International stage.
Blues 1   Ascoli Calcio 1   Att. 3,963
Sturridge 33   D'Ainsara 4
Ascoli had Rosario Pergoli sent off after 39 minutes
2001, Division 1.
Blues 4   Norwich City 0   Att. 17,310
Mooney 31, 45, 58(pen)
Marcelo 46

Match of the Day
FROM 2001
THE MOON SHINES FOR BLUES
Mooney trio clips the wings of high flying Canaries

Blues continued their slow rebuilding work after a convincing win over top six side Norwich, they were now within reach of the play-off places whilst the visitors held their position thanks mainly to results elsewhere. The hero of the hour Tommy Mooney almost didn't play, caretaker bosses Mills and Barron revealing later that they thought the partnership of the former Watford striker and Marcelo was too much of a likeness in style and only a late fitness failure from Geoff Horsfield allowed the pair to line up together.

The game was brought to life after 31 minutes when Blues took a 1-0 lead. Up to then a dull half an hour had seen only one incident of note, when Roberts and Purse clashed heads accidentally, leaving the Norwich forward to leave the field for prolonged treatment. Blues opener was courtesy of clever overlap and cross from Eaden, and Mooney glanced the faintest of near-post headers to leave 'keeper Green beaten. This brought little change to Norwich's lacklustre performance. Blues responded for the better not surprisingly buoyed by the lead and when Mooney added a spectacular second, the game was effectively won. He caught Green off his line to send a cracking volley sailing over the 'keeper's head. Norwich started the second half with more determination, Marcelo was the first to take advantage when he waltzed through the defence along and finished his own move by hitting a low shot across the turf into the corner. Blues continued to push forward eager to improve their goal difference over their play-off rivals. Mooney went close before adding the fourth goal from the penalty spot, Green this time blocking from close range after a good cross from Burrows, however referee Laws awarded the spot kick for a tug on the striker by Nedergaard.

BIRMINGHAM CITY
Bennett, Fleming, Burrows, O'Connor, Purse, Vickers,
Eaden, Mooney, Marcelo (Andrew Johnson 80), O'Connor, Lazaridis.

NORWICH CITY
Green, Nedergaard, Fleming, Mackay, Drury, McVeigh,
Holt, Russell (Kenton 69), Roberts (Libbra 25), Mulryne, Rivers (Notman 45).,

REFEREE
Mr G Laws (Whitley Bay)

Tommy Mooney

Blues news extra   1924..Double strike for Bradford in England win: England 4 Belgium 0

Birmingham was well represented in the national side at West Bromwich's Hawthorns ground today. Blues prolific scorer Joe Bradford hit two and fellow striker Billy Walker of Aston Villa got the other two in England's impressive win over Belgium. Walker should have completed his hat-trick but his poorly hit penalty was saved by the goalkeeper.

Playing record for this day

Playing record for this day.... 17 games, Won 5, Drawn 2, Lost 10, GF 23, GA 32.

Success rate...35.29% Year ranking....249th

Match of the Day
FROM 1950
SPARKLING TRIGG BRIGHTENS GLOOMY ST ANDREWS

The fog which engulfed Small Heath in the late afternoon made this game almost impossible for the 18,000 crowd to see, the cheers the only indication that goals had been scored as the Blues fans at the Tilton passed on information to other parts of the ground. The upshot of all this was a 3-1 win for Birmingham which was a good result in difficult playing conditions. Blues made two changes to the side which crashed 3-0 at Leeds the previous week, Green swapping to left back to cover the injured Jackie Badham which allowed Roy Martin to make his debut. Manager Bob Brocklebank also gave a debut to Ray Ferris who took over from the injured Roy Warhurst. On a wet and muddy surface Blues kicked off attacking the Railway End of the ground first. It was soon difficult to identify the players as the mud started to take its toll, a sliding tackle by Green on Hammers winger Woodgate left the full back's number completely obliterated. Referee Glendenning was also troubled by the surface, a slip caused him to drop his whistle and play was halted whilst the Sunderland official cleared the mud from it. After 11 minutes Blues took the lead through the persistence of first Trigg on the wing, then Higgins in the centre. Trigg after skipping over a challenge raced on but his first time cross was blocked, with the ball skidding away. Trigg accelerated again chipping into the area for Berry to hit. Gregory reacted superbly to parry but Higgins was on hand to net the rebound close in. West Ham hit back immediately but brave defending by Martin who threw himself at Barrett's fiercely hit free kick kept them out at the expense of the game's first corner.

Trigg again slipped his marker to create Blues second goal on 15 minutes, his cross this time was headed in crisply by Stewart and well out of Gregory's reach. With six minutes of the half remaining West Ham got back into the game through a classy piece of skill from their centre forward Robinson. Collecting the ball he ran at Atkins before pulling it back, leaving Atkins on his backside, Merrick was then left gazing as the ball flew past him from 20 yards out.

The light deteriorated in the second half as did the play and just before the fog fell Birmingham made the game safe scoring an important third goal on 70 minutes. Again the inspirational Trigg was involved when he was the cause of Forde conceding a corner, from Stewart's flag kick Smith rose to head in from eight yards. In the dying minutes Merrick saved brilliantly from Walker's header from a corner delivered by Gazzard, whilst at the other end Gregory slipped coming out to take a Higgins cross but with the goal at his mercy Stewart missed albeit by inches.

BIRMINGHAM CITY

Merrick, Green, Martin, Boyd, Atkins, Ferris, Stewart, Higgins, Trigg, Smith, Berry.

WEST HAM UNITED

Gregory, Yeomanson, Forde, Parker, Walker, O'Farrell, Southren, Barratt, Robinson, Gazzard, Woodgate.

REFEREE

Mr TW Glendenning (Sunderland)

Ray Ferris

Blues news extra 1931..Hibbs and England gain Spanish revenge England 7 Spain 1

England avenged that 4-3 defeat in Madrid back in May 1929 with an emphatic 7-1 win at Arsenal's Highbury ground. This was the second international between the two countries and England were happy to show their superiority in style, Blues keeper Harry Hibbs having little to do throughout most of the game.

Birthdays
Simon Sturridge born today 1969.

The Matches played on this day

1893, Division 2.

Burton Swifts 0	Blues 2	Att. 1,500
	Mobley, Hands	

1899, FA Cup 5th qualifying round.

Blues 0	Walsall 0	Att. 4,000

1905, Division 1.

Sheffield Wed. 4	Blues 2	Att. 12,000
	Tickle, Jones	

1911, Division 2.

Huddersfield Town 3	Blues 2	Att. 2,000
	Kidd, Millington	

1916, Wartime.

Huddersfield Town 2	Blues 1	
	Jephcott	

1922, Division 1.

Arsenal 1	Blues 0	Att. 30,000

1933, Division 1.

Tottenham Hotspur 3	Blues 2	Att. 18,000
	Roberts, White	

1939, Wartime.

Wolverhampton W. 6	Blues 2	
	Broome(2)	

1944, Wartime.

Northampton Town 2	Blues 1	
	Small	

1950, Division 1.

Blues 3	West Ham United 1	Att. 18,000
Higgins 11	Robinson 39	
Stewart 25		
Smith 70		

1961, Division 1.

Tottenham Hotspur 3	Blues 1	Att. 32,509
Allen 13, 21	Leek 82	
Mackay 59		

1967, Division 2.

Blues 2	QPR 0	Att. 25,281
Hazell(og) 2		
Pickering 74		

1972, Division 1.

Blues 1	Leicester City 1	Att. 32,481
Calderwood 58	Cross 33	

1978, Division 1.

Blues 1	Everton 3	Att. 23,391
Buckley 60	Ross 26	
	Todd 55	
	Latchford 74	

1989, FA Cup 2nd round.

Colchester United 0	Blues 2	Att. 3,858
	Gleghorn 4, 89	

1995, Division 1.

Blues 1	Watford 0	Att. 16,970
Francis 50		

2000, Division 1.

Blues 0	Wimbledon 3	Att. 16,778
	Francis 30, 81	
	Euell 44	

Wimbledon's John Hartson sent off after 66 minutes.

December 10

Playing record for this day

Playing record for this day.... 16 games, Won 7, Drawn 1, Lost 8, GF 33, GA 28.
Success rate...46.88% Year ranking....188th

Match of the Day

FROM 1994

TRUMPET PLAYING DAISH BLOWS AWAY CHESTER

Blues blow their own tune with a 4-0 thrashing of Chester

Blues bounced back from their dull FA Cup tie against Scunthorpe at St Andrews in sensational style with free scoring football making a welcome return. Blues left for the Deva Stadium still unable to complete the £1 million signing of Brummie forward Kevin Francis from Stockport who was expected to play in this game after having agreed a move. Barry Fry now expected to get his man within the next week. Blues therefore made just one change, Gary Cooper starting in place of the injured Mark Ward.

They were quickly into their stride and far quicker than their opponents, making scoring chances almost at will. Blues were a goal up on 24 minutes when a corner was flicked on by Whyte and thumped in by the head of Daish at the far post, warming up nicely before his international debut at Anfield for the Republic of Ireland 'B' side. Although Blues continued to dominate the game, their lead wasn't doubled until the last minute of the half. Steve Claridge scoring his first goal in six games with a close-range header after McGavin had knocked the ball down to him. Blues started the second half as they did the first, making plenty of clear cut chances but spurning them all with some dreadful finishing. Claridge had the best opportunates when shooting wide despite a gaping goal in front of him after 55 minutes. Fellow striker Steve McGavin put the game well beyond Chester's reach after 66 minutes when he capitalised on a misdirected clearance from Jenkins, and smashed it past Felgate with a first-time right foot shot. In the celebrations that followed Daish blew a child's trumpet from the touchline and recived a yellow card for time wasting. Blues replaced Paul Tait soon after with Kenny Lowe and with 14 minutes of the game remaining Lowe added a fourth goal. At the final whistle Blues settled for a 4-0 victory which took them from third to second in the Division Two.

CHESTER CITY
Felgate, Jenkins, Burnham, Alsford, Jackson, Shelton, Lightfoot, Flitcroft, Preece, Page (Murphy 74), Hackett (Chambers 52)
BIRMINGHAM CITY
Bennett, Poole, Whyte, Cooper, Barnett, Daish, Donowa, Claridge, McGavin, Dominguez (Doherty 74), Tait (Lowe 67)

REFEREE
Mr J Brandwood (Lichfield)

Liam Daish

Blues news extra   1993..Fry resigns and heads for Blues

Southend manager Barry Fry resigned ignoring pleas from his board
and Southend supporters. It was understood Blues wanted him to take over from Terry Cooper who quit only
days before Blues eventually appointed Fry Southend protest. After an investigation into
'poaching' Blues were punished, receiving a fine from the Football league.

Birthdays

Martin O'Connor born today 1967.   Mark Kendall born today 1961.

Playing record for this day
Playing record for this day.... 15 games, Won 8, Drawn 4, Lost 3, GF 33, GA 12.
Success rate...66.67% Year ranking....16th

December 11

Match of the Day

FROM 1954
LIVERPOOL GIVEN NINE GOAL HAMMERING

Brown leads the way with hat-trick, Astall and Murphy score twice

Blues went into the game missing the influential Welsh international Noel Kinsey out injured and his place went to Jackie Lane, Liverpool were at full strength. Blues got off to a blistering start and scored within a minute through Lane, his shot taking a wicked deflection off Lambert, which sent Liverpool's keeper Doug Rudham the wrong way. It was the perfect start on a difficult pitch which was just playable. The early goal meant Liverpool had to chase the game and Blues picked them off on the break almost every time they attacked.

Blues went 2-0 up after ten minutes when Brown latched onto Boyd's pass and his 18-yard first-time shot went in off the post. Rudham was unlucky with both goals, however the third was due to his error which was gratefully accepted by Brown. A corner by Astall was dropped by the keeper right onto Brown's toe and this chance was almost impossible to miss. Merrick at the other end was having a very fortunate afternoon. He knew nothing about an instinctive one-handed save from Payne and then watched the ball drop harmlessly wide for a corner, To their credit Liverpool always tried to attack rather than sit back in a damage limitation exercise. They managed to reduce the score on 19 minutes, Liddell hitting a thunderbolt which left Merrick motionless as the ball whistled past him into goal.

Blues scored again on 27 minutes when, Astall's pile driver flew in from the edge of the penalty area. This was the best goal of the game. Blues showed no let up in the second half and within four minutes scored when a long cross from Lane evaded everyone except Astall who stole in at the far post and put the ball in with his chest as it dropped on top of him. Then on 54 minutes Blues went 6-1 up, Liverpool failed to clear a corner from Astall and Murphy slammed the ball in from close range. Blues were so much in control the crowd began to wonder exactly how many Birmingham would score.

They eventually added a seventh through Govan in the 77th minute. Brown and Lane combined well to set him up and the Scotsman finished with a neat left-foot shot which flew across Rudham into the far corner. Then a magnificent run by Brown finished with him squaring the ball unselfishly to Murphy who placed his shot past Rudham for the eighth time in 84 minutes. Before the celebrations died down, Brown again went on a solo run, this time he went all the way taking the ball round Rudham to score in the empty net. This finished the scoring at   9-1 to Blues.

BIRMINGHAM CITY
Merrick, Hall, Green, Boyd, Smith, Warhurst, Astall, Lane, Brown, Murphy, Govan.
LIVERPOOL
Rudham, Lambert, Lock, Wilkinson, Hughes, Twentyman, Payne, Anderson, Liddell, Evans, A'Court.

REFEREE
Mr G McCabe (Sheffield)

Gordon Astall

The Matches played on this day
1909, Division 2.
Blues 1	Derby County 3	Att. 5,000
Freeman		

1920, Division 2.
Coventry City 0	Blues 4	Att. 22,000
	Burkinshaw, Lane, Hampton(2)	

1926, Division 1.
Blues 0	Arsenal 0	Att. 22,982

1937, Division 1.
Everton 1	Blues 1	Att. 17,018
	Morris	

1943, Wartime.
Blues 3	WBA 0	
Roberts, Trigg(2, 1pen)		

1948, Division 1.
Blues 0	Sunderland 0	Att. 29,000

1954, Division 2.
Blues 9	Liverpool 1	Att. 17,514
Lane 1	Liddell 19	
Brown 10, 15, 85		
Astall 27, 49		
Murphy 54, 84		
Govan 77		

Blues best win against Liverpool, and Liverpool's heaviest league defeat by any club.

1962, League Cup 5th round.
Blues 6	Manchester City 0	Att. 18,010
Leivers(og) 22		
Sear(og) 37		
Lynn 43, 81(pen)		
Leek 71		
Auld 85		

1965, Division 2.
Rotherham United 3	Blues 4	Att. 10,404
Chappell 7, 31	Vowden 55, 62, 85	
Hardy 21	Jackson 70	

1971, Division 2.
Blues 0	Sheffield Wed. 0	Att.29,272

1976, Division 1.
Blues 2	Sunderland 0	Att. 24,597
Jones 34		
Francis 60		

1982, Division 1.
Blues 0	Southampton 2	Att. 11,199
	Moran 67	
	Wallace 80	

1993, Division 1.
Crystal Palace 2	Blues 1	Att. 11,295
Southgate 19	Saville 44	
Salako 45		

First game in charge for new Blues boss Barry Fry
1999, FA Cup 3rd round.
Watford 0	Blues 1	Att. 8,144
	Rowett 66	

2001, Division 1.
Blues 1	Crystal Palace 0	Att. 20,119
Mooney 64(pen)		

Trevor Francis returned to St Andrews as manager of Crystal Palace just two months after being sacked by Blues. In a strange twist of fate after the match was finished Blues were allowed to appoint former Palace manager Steve Bruce who coincidently had resigned from Selhurst Park about two months before. Crystal Palace had Tommy Black sent off in the last minute.

December 12

Playing record for this day

Playing record for this day.... 20 games, Won 8, Drawn 3, Lost 9, GF 37, GA 35.

Success rate...47.50% Year ranking....175th

Match of the Day

FROM 1998

LORDS OF THE MANOR

Oxford hit for seven in Manor Ground downpour

For the second time in 11 months Blues stormed an opponents territory with a seven goal blast. In January the Blues baptised the new Britannia Stadium with their biggest away win for 104 years against Stoke by 7-0. In less scenic surroundings they almost matched that score with a 7-1 win over Oxford. Incredibly this result came a month after Oxford had lifted their relegation worries with a shock 1-0 win at St Andrews. Blues took the lead with their first corner, Grainger's kick was charged down only for the rebound to be struck by a stinging left foot shot which Salmon could only parry into Rowett who tapped in from underneath the crossbar at the far post. The 'keeper then did well to keep out a shot from Adebola a minute later but again the ball ran loose to present a chance for Furlong who slid in and knocked it into the empty net. The next goal coming on 31 minutes left Salmon no chance at all, an Ablett free kick floated over everyone to Rowett who smashed a volley into the roof of the net. With half-time approaching Adebola again bustled his way through the Oxford defence to square the ball for O'Connor to tap in, he miscued completely but the ball rolled on to Furlong who did the honours with his second goal. The onslaught by Blues restarted just ten minutes into the second half when Grainger almost burst the net with a fiercely hit shot from within the penalty area. There followed a 17-minute respite for the beleaguered Oxford defence before Ndlovu picked up a loose ball in midfield, weaved his way forward and hit a low angled shot which skidded into the net. Blues final goal was struck with a minute of the game left, substitute Bryan Hughes adding a smart volley after fellow sub Nicky Forster had returned his pass. As the soaked Blue Army celebrated Dean Windass popped up from nowhere to head past Kevin Poole in stoppage time, but most would have settled for a 7-1 win before the kick off anyway.

OXFORD UNITED;

Salmon, Robinson, Powell, Gray, Wilsterman, Gilchrist,
Remy (Rose 68), Smith, Thomson (Banger 68), Windass, Beachamp.

BIRMINGHAM CITY

Poole, Rowett, Grainger (Forster 86), O'Connor, Ablett, Johnson,
McCarthy (Marsh 69), Adebola (Hughes 69), Furlong, Robinson, Ndlovu.

REFEREE

Mr D Pugh (Wirral)

13 December 1998

Birthdays

Gary Ablett

The Matches played on this day
1964, Division 1.

| Blues 1 | Nottingham Forest 1 | Att. 14,396 |
| Thomson 25 | Barnwell 33 | |

1970, Division 2.

| Blues 1 | Sheffield Wed. 0 | Att. 14,239 |
| B.Latchford 58 | | |

1987, Division 2.

| Blues 1 | Aston Villa 2 | Att. 22,789 |
| Kennedy 18 | Thompson 13, 52 | |

1989, Leyland Daf Cup preliminary round.

| Blues 1 | Hereford United 0 | Att. 3,168 |
| Atkins 42 | | |

First meeting in any senior game against Hereford
This was St Andrews lowest post-World War One
attendance for a senior competitive game.
1990, FA Cup 2nd round.

Blues 1	Brentford 3	Att. 5,072
Aylott 61	Blissett 5	
	Godfrey 42	
	Jones 65	

Blues failed to reach the FA Cup 3rd round for the first
time in their modern history.
1992, Division 1.

Derby County 3	Blues 1	Att. 16,662
Johnson 50	Speedie 13	
Kitson 57		
Williams 70		

1998, Division 1.

Oxford United 1	Blues 7	Att. 7,189
Windass 90	Furlong 7, 43	
	Rowett 16, 31	
	Grainger 55	
	Ndlovu 72	
	Hughes 89	

Blues second seven goal haul in an away game this year,
after Stoke back in January.
2000, League Cup 5th round.

Blues 2	Sheffield Wed. 0	Att. 22,911
Sonner 27		
Adebola 56		

December 13

Playing record for this day

Playing record for this day.... 15 games, Won 7, Drawn 0, Lost 8, GF 22, GA 38.

Success rate...46.67% Year ranking....194th

Match of the Day

FROM 1997

WHAT A FINISH!

1-0 down, Blues storm back to win in the 97th minute

Blues hoped to continue their recent form and made four changes from their last game. Simon Charlton made his debut replacing Michael Johnson at left back. Martin O'Connor came in for the injured Chris Marsden, likewise Paul Devlin covered for Paul Furlong, and Peter Ndlovu made the side as Tony Cottee had returned following his loan period. A quiet first half of little incident was repeated for 35 second-half minutes with the only talking point being the number of bookings. Bruce, Devlin, Hughes, Symons, Van Blerk, Edghill, and Shelia were all yellow carded for various indiscretions. Only a substitution, on 80 minutes changed the course of the game. Kevin Francis had already been intoduced after an hour for Peter Ndlovu but when Nicky Forster came on for Devlin, Blues started to look like scoring. However, as is often the case, despite their pressure they were hit by the perfect sucker punch. From a late Manchester City corner Shelia got free at the near post and rose unchallenged to head in a soft goal.

As the disgruntled Blues fans started making for the exits the game went on and a hopeful snap shot from McCarthy moments later clipped a post right on what should have been the final whistle. A free kick awarded to Blues 35 yards out on the right made for another ideal opportunity to load the visitors area again and up came Ablett and Bruce. From the latter's header Margetson's reaction save sent the ball upwards, as it dropped Forster nipped in to nod over the line from a yard out. Blues had saved the game late on, how late, and in what minute? No one cared but the game went on , and on, and on!!! The stream of early leavers was halted and exits blocked as another chance put Forster through, his shot was parried by Margetson and the ball rolled away some 30 yards from goal. O'Connor latched onto the loose ball and surged forward. A neat cut back sent two converging defenders and the 'keeper the wrong way then chipped into the corner and St Andrews erupted.It was only when fans returned to radios or indeed the following days paper that they realised the winner was one of the latest scored in St Andrews history, officially timed after 97 minutes play.

BIRMINGHAM CITY

Bennett, Bass (Michael Johnson 51), Charlton, O'Connor, Bruce, Ablett, McCarthy, Robinson, Devlin (Forster 81), Hughes, Ndlovu (Francis 61).

MANCHESTER CITY

Margetson, Edghill, Symons, Wiekens, Shelia, Van Blerk, Brown, Brannan, Russell, Dickov, Rosler.

REFEREE

Mr A D'Urso (Billericay)

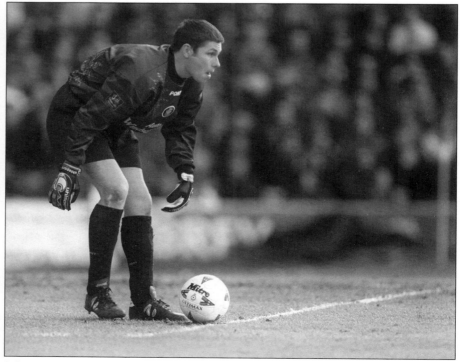

Ian Bennett

Birthdays

Billy Rudd born today 1941.   Eddie Newton born today 1971.   Tony Want born today 1948.

Playing record for this day
Playing record for this day.... 15 games, Won 6, Drawn 3, Lost 6, GF 21, GA 20.
Success rate...50% Year ranking....159th

December 14

Match of the Day
FROM 1994
BENNETT IN GOAL CONCEDED 'SCANDAL'

Record books consulted after late Scunthorpe consolation

On a night when records went tumbling, Blues became the first away team to win an FA Cup tie at Scunthorpe in 26 games going back 18 years. Home striker Wayne Bullimore countered this by becoming the first player to beat Blues 'keeper Ian Bennett in 14 hours and 58 minutes of football. Blues earned the reward of a glamorous third round tie at home to Liverpool by hitting two killer goals within three second-half minutes. On a difficult frozen surface both sides struggled early on to create anything likely to trouble the goalkeepers, however when opportunities came it was the home side who wasted them. Twice in the first half they were guilty of squandering guilt-edged chances to cause an upset, but on both occasions they missed the target completely. They were to pay dearly for these as Blues slowly got their game together but not until after the interval, the game being goalless after a generally uninspiring first half. The second period started much the same way as both sides continued to struggle in a scrappy opening 15 minutes. Then the tie burst into life with two goals in almost as many minutes. A surging run by Cooper, who had a great game all night, ended with him slipping a pass to McGavin who for once had lost his marker and he took the ball on to break the stalemate. As the celebrations continued goal maker and scorer swapped roles and Cooper blasted in from barely three yards out after Samways had only parried McGavin's shot into his path. With the game drawing to a close a silly free kick was given away which allowed Scunthorpe an unlikely looking comeback. Controversially Ian Bennett, who was in the process of amending his defensive wall, was beaten when the referee allowed Bullimore to chip the ball into the opposite corner. The last ten minutes were seen out comfortably and Blues deserved their 2-1 win.

SCUNTHORPE UNITED
Samways, Ford, Mudd (Sansam 87), Thornber, Knill, Bradley, Alexander, Bullimore, Juryeff, Thompstone (Carmichael 68), Smith.

BIRMINGHAM CITY
Bennett, Poole, Whyte, Cooper, Barnett, Daish, Donowa, Claridge, McGavin, Dominguez (Doherty 80).

REFEREE
Mr R Dilkes (Mossley)

Chris Whyte

Birthdays
Dennis Thwaites born today 1944.

The Matches played on this day

1895, Division 1.		
Sunderland 2	Blues 1	Att. 4,000
	Wheldon	
1899, FA Cup 5th qualifying round.		
Walsall 2	Blues 0	Att. 1,000
1907, Division 1.		
Woolwich Arsenal 1	Blues 1	Att. 3,000
	Green	
1912, Division 2.		
Blues 2	Leeds City 2	Att. 20,000
A.W.Smith, Tinkler		
1918, Wartime.		
Blues 2	Rotherham County 0	
J.Godfrey, Whitehouse		
1929, Division 1.		
Portsmouth 2	Blues 1	Att. 20,000
	Barkas(pen)	
1935, Division 1.		
Middlesbrough 0	Blues 2	Att. 10,000
	Jones(2)	
1946, Division 2.		
Luton Town 1	Blues 3	Att. 25,000
	Trigg(3)	
1957, Division 1.		
Leicester City 2	Blues 2	Att. 28,610
Rowley 31, 40	Astall 17	
	Kinsey 85	
Peter Murphy missed a 77th minute penalty.		
1963, Division 1.		
Bolton Wanderers 0	Blues 2	Att. 9,517
	Leek 9	
	Hellawell 58	
1968, Division 2.		
Blues 2	Bristol City 0	Att. 18,749
Pickering 1, 14		
Fred Pickering's goal was timed at 25 seconds.		
1974, Division 1.		
Middlesbrough 3	Blues 0	Att. 23,737
Foggon 44		
Hickton 68(pen)		
Page(og) 89		
1985, Division 1.		
West Ham United 2	Blues 0	Att. 17,481
McAvennie 36		
Stewart 40(pen)		
1991, Division 3.		
Bournemouth 2	Blues 1	Att. 6,048
Wood 44	Paskin 52	
Quinn 73		
1994, FA Cup 2nd round.		
Scunthorpe United 1	Blues 2	Att. 6,280
Bullimore 80	McGavin 63	
	Cooper 66	

December 15

Playing record for this day

Playing record for this day.... 14 games, Won 8, Drawn 2, Lost 4, GF 18, GA 17.
Success rate...64.29% Year ranking....27th

Match of the Day

FROM 1956
BUSBY BABES
BEATEN BY BLUES
30-minute onslaught has champs reeling in 3-1 victory

Despite the bitter wind and driving rain, 38,600 filed into St Andrews for the clash against champions-elect Manchester United, the dream team of the 1950s. Blues needed their strongest line up in defence, and were boosted by the return of Jeff Hall at right back for Brian Farmer. Trevor Smith, also recovered from injury, replaced Allen at centre half. In attack Brown returned as centre forward, allowing Murphy to regain his regular position, and Kinsey was the man left out from the side which lost at Everton a week ago. On a slippy, wet and muddy St Andrews surface the conditions were less favourable for the pacy United forwards. Blues, who had combined flair with tough, gritty performances so far this season, soon took hold of the slight advantage the weather gave them. Forcing an early corner, Astall's kick evaded all in the box. A Foulkes slip on the left side of the penalty area was seized by Govan, who chipped the ball back in for Brown to head on to Orritt. He placed his shot wide of Wood to put Blues 1-0 up after four minutes. United soon hit back with Pegg trying his luck from 20 yards, but Linnecor cleared the shot well at the expense of a corner. The flag kick found

Taylor, but his shot was again deflected wide by Green. Moments later Viollet was brilliantly stopped by a well-timed tackle by Smith as he looked to clear. Blues were pegged back, but coped reasonably well, and play eventually evened out with both sides contributing to an attacking game. After 24 minutes Blues were gifted a second goal when Jones completely misjudged Merrick's goal kick, allowing Brown to run clear with just Wood to beat. This he did, coolly lifting the ball over the 'keeper who dived forward.

Incredibly Blues went 3-0 up six minutes later. Linnecor intercepted a pass in his own half and looped the ball out to Murphy, who in turn threaded it on to Brown. He then went past Foulkes with a body swerve, before cracking his shot into the top right hand corner. With half time approaching, a superb sliding tackle from Warhurst took the ball away from two unmarked United players in front of goal. Blues continued to defend well after the break, but finally the inevitable happened when Whelan reduced the deficit to 3-1, finishing off Berry's cross with a close-range shot. This goal galvanised the visitors for the final 29 minutes. The ever dangerous Duncan Edwards was denied a certain goal by a Warhurst header off the line. Then Taylor and Viollet got in each other's way, preventing either of them from taking advantage of a simple strike from eight yards. In the closing minutes Merrick pulled off the save of the game, if not the season, to block Whelan's shot inside ten yards from a pass by Edwards. Blues had weathered two storms in the afternoon, but were worthy winners in the end. The final score being 3-1.

BIRMINGHAM CITY
Merrick, Hall, Green, Linnecor, Smith, Warhurst, Astall, Orritt, Brown, Murphy, Govan
MANCHESTER UNITED
Wood, Foulkes, Bent, Colman, Jones, Edwards, Berry, Whelan Taylor, Viollet, Pegg

REFEREE
Mr BM Griffiths (Newport)

Duncam Edwards - Manchester United

Birthdays
James Quinn born today 1974.

Sadly Missed
Sidney Wallington died today in 1989, aged 81

Playing record for this day

Playing record for this day.... 20 games, Won 8, Drawn 4, Lost 8, GF 32, GA 33.

Success rate...50% Year ranking....164th

Match of the Day
FROM 1989
BLUES STRIKE CHRISTMAS GOAL BONUS

Blues hit three to keep the pressure on title challengers

Christmas is a testing time for any title-challenging side and after this pre-holiday game Dave Mackay's Blues could be well satisfied after seeing the team move into seventh position. They were now within striking distance of the Division Three leaders and the win also answered some of the worries about their recent scoring record.

Blues were up against a poor Preston side who travelled badly, their record away from Deepdale reading just three wins all season, and after going behind in this game they never looked likely to come back, despite earning a late consolation penalty.

Blues were in a different class to their opponents, John Frain freed from his duties in defence used his excellent left foot in a more creative midfield role. His accurate balls forward, particularly to the brilliant Mark Yates, repeatedly opened up the Preston defence. It was one such exquisite left foot pass which set up Yates opening goal on 22 minutes. Frain then iced the cake on a fantastic team performance by conjuring up another piece of magic to finish himself in the 56th minute, and put Blues 3-0 up. In between the lively Dennis Bailey notched his tenth goal of the season just after half time to effectively wrap up the points. Bailey's goal-scoring had seemed to dry up of late but with a new look four man midfield, including Frain, he was his most dangerous for some time.

Preston's late revival never looked like changing the result and their goal would not have concerned anyone except Blues 'keeper Martin Thomas. The penalty, which was awarded four minutes from time, was converted by Preston substitute Mark Patterson, and this ended Thomas's chance of a seventh clean sheet in the Blues goal.

BIRMINGHAM CITY

Thomas, Roberts, Frain, Atkins, Overson, Matthewson, Bell, Bailey, Yates, Gleghorn, Langley.

PRESTON NORTH END

Kelly, Williams, Bennett, Atkins, Flynn, Hughes (Patterson 64) Rathbone, Ellis, Swan (Mooney 64), Shaw, Harper.

REFEREE

Mr RK Pawley (Cambridge)

Pat Van Den Hauwe

Blues news extra   1933..Blues thwarted by fog

Blues game against Sheffield Wednesday at St Andrews was abandoned when heavy fog fell after 70 minutes play making visibility impossible for the players and the referee. Blues were 2-1 up at the time.

Birthdays

Pat Van Den Hauwe born today 1960.

The Matches played on this day

1893, Division 2.

Blues 1	Newcastle United 4	Att. 2,500

Hallam

1899, Division 2.

Blues 3	Luton Town 0	Att. 2,000

Bennett(2), Scrivens

1903, FA Cup 1st round, 2nd replay.

Blues 1	Manchester United 1	Att. 4,000

Leonard

After extra time

1905, Division 1.

Blues 5	Nottingham Forest 0	Att. 10,000

Wilcox(3), Harper, Jones

1911, Division 1.

Blues 2	Blackpool 1	Att. 5,000

Hall, Kidd

1922, Division 1.

Blues 1	Everton 1	Att. 25,000

Foxall

1939, Wartime.

Walsall 1	Blues 2	
	Edwards, Broome	

1944, Wartime.

Blues 2	WBA 0	

Tranter(og), Trigg

1950, Division 2.

Blues 5	Swansea Town 0	Att. 16,000

Stewart 7
Trigg 20, 44, 82
Berry 54

1961, Division 1.

Fulham 0	Blues 1	Att. 12,630
	Leek 8	

1964, Division 1.

Manchester United 1	Blues 1	Att. 25,271
Charlton 39(pen)	Thwaites 74	

1967, Division 2.

Bolton Wanderers 1	Blues 1	Att. 10,258
Greaves 68	Farrimond(og) 22	

1969, Division 2.

Middlesbrough 4	Blues 2	Att. 17,020
Hickton 19, 41	Murray 47	
Laidlaw 26	Hateley 90	
Spraggon 70		

1972, Division 1.

Leeds United 4	Blues 0	Att. 25,285
Clarke 36, 56		
Lorimer 61		
Jones 71		

1978, Division 1.

Nottingham Forest 1	Blues 0	Att. 25,224
Gemmill 70		

1988, Division 2.

Blues 1	Chelsea 4	Att. 7,987
Whitton 54	Durie 38, 52	
	Dixon 48, 89	

1989, Division 3.

Blues 3	Preston North End 1	Att. 6,391
Yates 22	Patterson 86(pen)	
Bailey 48		
Frain 56		

1992, Anglo Italian Cup, Group A.

Lucchese 3	Blues 0	Att. 139
Bettari 6		
Paci 36		
Rastelli 60		

The lowest Blues attendance ever at a senior competitive game. Blues had John Gayle sent off after 70 minutes.

1995, Division 1.

Oldham Athletic 4	Blues 0	Att. 6,602
Poole(og) 26		
Francis(og) 56		
Barlow 58		
Halle 68		

Blues worst defeat by Oldham.

2001, Division 1.

Wolverhampton W. 2	Blues 1	Att. 21,482
Blake 39	Marcelo 40	
Rae 68		

First game in charge for new manager Steve Bruce.

December 17

Playing record for this day
Playing record for this day.... 17 games, Won 7, Drawn 3, Lost 7, GF 34, GA 24.
Success rate...50% Year ranking....142nd

The Matches played on this day

1892, Division 2.
Blues 12   Walsall Town Swifts 0   Att. 2,000
Wheldon(2), Walton(3),
Hallam(2), Mobley(3),
Hands(2)
Blues joint biggest win in any senior first team game to date.

1898, Division 2.
Glossop 1   Blues 2   Att. 1,000
             Abbott, Ingliss

1904, Division 1.
Blues 1   Everton 2   Att. 15,000
Jones

1910, Division 2.
Blues 2   Huddersfield Town 1   Att. 4,000
Gallimore, Hall

1921, Division 1.
Blues 2   Sheffield United 1   Att. 25,000
Elkes, Whitehouse

1927, Division 1.
Blues 1   West Ham United 2   Att. 30,000
Bradford

1932, Division 1.
Leicester City 2   Blues 2   Att. 10,000
                     Cringan, Gregg

1938, Division 1.
Blackpool 2   Blues 1   Att. 10,000
                White

1949, Division 1.
Chelsea 3   Blues 0   Att. 40,000

1955, Division 1.
Manchester United 2 Blues 1   Att. 27,704
Viollett 29   Brown 70
Jones 85

1960, Division 1.
Blues 2   Bolton Wanderers 2   Att. 19,050
Harris 8, 44   Stevens 31, 57

1966, Division 2.
Blues 3   Wolverhampton W. 2   Att. 27,527
Bridges 68   Wagstaffe 1
Bullock 76   Bailey 35
Vowden 88
Blues came back from 2-0 down with just 20 minutes remaining to win the game and thus complete a league double over Wolves for the first time in 46 years.

1977, Division 1.
Blues 0   Everton 0   Att. 22,177
This game was screened by BBC's Match of the Day.

1983, Division 1.
Southampton 2   Blues 1   Att. 15,248
Blake(og) 6   Stevenson 44
Hagan(og) 80
Ivor Linton made his Blues debut as a substitute for Howard Gayle.

1994, Division 2.
Blues 2   Leyton Orient 0   Att. 20,022
Donowa 2, 87

1999, Division 1.
Wolverhampton W. 2   Blues 1   Att. 19,724
Akinbiyi 40   Hughes 15
Pollet 63

2000, Division 1.
Wolverhampton W. 0   Blues 1....Att. 19,938
                     Adebola 31

Match of the Day
FROM 1966
BRIDGES OVER TROUBLED WATERS
Bridges makes breakthrough in dry game

Two successive league defeats meant that Blues were in fighting spirits against local rivals Wolves who, were eager to carry on their quest for promotion. Wolves captain Ron Flowers was brought back into the full back position, while Blues Hockey was on the right wing, with Bridges on the left.

The opening play saw Vowden caught in the offside trap, before Wolves pounced into attack taking the lead in the first minute. Bailey had possession, and he sent an inch-perfect cross to Wharton who headed against the post. The ball rebounded and Wagstaffe was in position to ensure the ball's passage across the line. This wasn't the start that Blues were hoping for, but it suited Wolves just fine. They continued on the attack and a super effort from Wharton was only just kept out of the net by Herriot. Blues also had a few good tries. Beard sent the ball to Hockey, and it was only the curling in mid-air of the ball which sent it straight into the arms of Wolves goalkeeper Davies. Flowers conceded a corner for Blues and the kick was taken by Hockey.

Unfortuantely it lacked aim and pace, and showed no signs of being a threat. Blues' determination showed through with a twin attack from Vincent and Vowden which was narrowly cleared by Bailey on the line. Wagstaffe was playing well, and a pass to Bailey saw him shoot wide of the post. Bullock's header didn't carry enough weight to cause worry for the Wolves 'keeper, and when Bridges slipped over the Blues fans were beginning to despair. Then 10 minutes before the half time interval Wolves increased their lead. Hawkins sent a free kick back into the midfield area where Bailey was on hand to ram in a 30-yard volley. Vowden hit back by putting the ball into the Wolves net, but the flag was already showing for offside.

The crowd of 27,527 witnessed one of the great comebacks in the second half, but not before the nerves were frayed a little more. Woodfield tried to clear the ball from the line, but Hockey smashed it back and Davies just managed to get a finger to it and flick the ball over the bar. The teams were both becoming desperate and tackles were beginning to show this. Wolves gave away two corners in the space of a minute, but neither of them brought anything for Blues. Thomson made an attempt which had the power but not the direction, and Bridges' shot on goal was saved by Davies. Murray's tackle on Knowles relieved the Wolves player of the ball, but also brought about strong appeals for a penalty. The referee decided against it, which was a lucky break for Blues. Maybe it was this luck which finally spurred them on to score. The first goal came on 68 minutes when Vowden sent the ball through to Bridges who beat Davies with a powerful shot. Wolves tried to restore their two goal lead to no avail when a volley from Knowles was saved by Herriot. On 75 minutes Beard was booked for a foul on Hunt, then just a minute later Bullock brought the scores level with a smashing shot striking the underside of the bar as it flew into the net. A few more chances from both sides came to nothing until the 88th minute when a super shot from Vowden raced into the net and put Blues into the lead for the first time.

BIRMINGHAM CITY
Herriot, Murray, Green, Thomson, Sharples, Beard, Hockey, Vincent, Bullock, Vowden, Bridges.
WOLVERHAMPTON WANDERERS
Davies, Flowers, Thomson, Bailey, Woodfield, Hawkins, Wharton, Hunt, Knowles, Burnside, Wagstaffe,

REFEREE
Mr K Dagnall (Bolton)

Birthdays
John Bond born today 1932.   Eric Hogan born today 1971.

Playing record for this day
Playing record for this day.... 14 games, Won 6, Drawn 4, Lost 4, GF 23, GA 17.
Success rate..57.14.% Year ranking....83rd

Match of the Day

FROM 1965

HISTORY MADE BY SUB FENTON

Blues excel in atrocious conditions to slam Bury for four

True fighting spirit and strength of character were as clear cut as the scoreline, as Blues battled through the torrential rain on a muddy St Andrews pitch. They were urged on by 10,811 die-hard supporters who braved the atrocious conditions to witness a thoroughly entertaining, performance. Only the wings offered any possibility of normal football, the middle being so boggy that moving the ball a few yards required a kick of Herculean proportions. Blues however coped adequately, with Trevor Hockey playing one of his most outstanding games for the club, he was simply everywhere on the park.

It was Hockey who created the games first goal-scoring chance, with a perfectly-flighted centre which put Dennis Thwaites free, but his shot from close range was saved by Chris Harker in goal for Bury. It took two men to mark Hockey such was his ability to manoeuvre on the quagmire of a pitch, but still he managed to get free to cause havoc. On 25 minutes from another of his crosses Blues took a well deserved lead, Bobby Thomson this time winning the ball with a glancing header which Thwaites tucked away easily from inside the six yard box. Within two minutes Thwaites returned the complement by heading Hockey's centre across goal for Thompson to smash in on the volley giving Harker no chance. Blues were now rampant and on the few occasions Bury managed to thwart the threat of Hockey, Foster took over in the middle and Wylie and Beard controlled the wings. With six minutes to go before half time Beard headed in a cracker from outside the penalty area, but the effort was disallowed due to Thomson being in an offside position.

Blues came out for the second half in equally dominant mood and there was no let up for the visitors. Moments after the restart Colquhoun kicked off the line after Hockey had rounded the 'keeper to shoot from a narrow angle. Despite the pressure, Blues had to wait until the hour mark before increasing their lead to 3-0. A great long ball pass from Jackson cleared the two central defenders and Thwaites was left in the clear to run on and beat the stranded Bury 'keeper. With the pitch taking its toll the pace from Blues slowed. With just six minutes remaining they were rocked by an injury to their 'keeper Jim Herriott after he dived at the feet of a Bury forward on a rare attack from the visitors. Thomson took over in goal allowing substitute Ronnie Fenton to join the attack. In the last minute he made history for the club when he headed in a cross from Cammie Fraser to become the first Blues substitute to score in a league game.

BIRMINGHAM CITY
Herriott (Fenton 84), Fraser, Martin, Wylie, Foster, Beard, Hockey, Jackson, Thomson, Vowden, Thwaites.
BURY
Harker, Turner, Leech, Bell, Colquhoun, Parry, Roberts, Owen, Pointer, Griffin, Bird.

Dennis Thwaites

Birthdays

Billy Hume born today 1935.   **Kevin Dillon born today 1959.**   **Tommy Williams born today 1957.**
Mark Cooper born today 1968.

December 19

Playing record for this day
Playing record for this day.... 17 games, Won 6, Drawn 3, Lost 8, GF 19, GA 25.
Success rate...44.12% Year ranking....209th

The Matches played on this day

1891, Football Alliance.		
Grimsby Town 1	Blues 2	Att. 1,000
	Lundie(og), Hallam	
1896, Division 2.		
Loughborough Town 2	Blues 0	Att. 1,000
1903, Division 1.		
Blues 0	Manchester City 3	Att. 12,000
1908, Division 2.		
Blues 1	Glossop 2	Att. 5,000
Smith		
1914, Division 2.		
Bristol City 2	Blues 3	Att. 4,000
	Barton, A.W.Smith, Gibson	
1925, Division 1.		
Blues 1	Arsenal 0	Att. 26,843
Briggs		
1931, Division 1.		
Chelsea 2	Blues 1	Att. 20,000
	Bradford	
1936, Division 1.		
Wolverhampton W. 2	Blues 1	Att. 15,000
	Clarke	
1942, Wartime.		
Wolverhampton W. 1	Blues 1	
	Jones	
1953, Division 2.		
Swansea Town 1	Blues 3	Att. 18,000
Medwin 6	Rowley 25, 75	
	Purdon 49	
1959, Division 1.		
Wolverhampton W. 2	Blues 0	Att. 22,363
Mason 19, 52		
1970, Division 2.		
Blues 1	Carlisle United 0	Att. 15,670
Francis 59		
1973, League Cup 5th round.		
Blues 1	Plymouth Argyle 2	Att. 15,273
Hatton 9	Welsh 36	
	Davey 37	
1986, Division 2.		
Blues 2	Sheffield United 1	Att. 5,007
Clarke 19(pen), 20	Foley 67	

Lowest attendance for a first team league fixture at St Andrews for 61 years. Blues 'keeper Roger Hansbury saved Morris's penalty after 33 minutes.

1987, Division 2.		
Blackburn Rovers 2	Blues 0	Att. 8,542
Hendry 46		
Sellars 48		
1992, Division 1.		
Blues 2	Watford 2	Att. 7,182
Peschisolido 25	Furlong 31, 81	
Frain 88		
1998, Division 1.		
Blues 0	Sunderland 0	Att. 22,095

Match of the Day
FROM 1953
A REAL SCRAP FOR POINTS WON IN SWANSEA
Happy scoring return for Rowley in an ill-tempered battle

Blues striker Ken Rowley marked his return to the side by hitting two goals, one in each half, including a beauty from 20 yards. In between Purdon netted another, this in reply to an early strike from Medwin. The game was then marred by niggly fouls and tempers came to a head in the closing minutes in a mass brawl, the teams leaving the field at the end of play under a police escort. Although Blues started well it was Swansea who broke away from the early onslaught to score after just six minutes. The move was started by Charles who cut in from the left wing, with the defence and Merrick expecting a cross, he decided to try his luck with a shot from the acute angle. Although not on target the ball eluded Merrick and fell perfectly for Medwin who had no trouble steering it into the empty net from close range. The goal inspired the home side and the pressure was now all on the Blues goal, Merrick saved brilliantly when coming out to snatch the ball away from the feet of Allchurch when he broke free moments after the goal.

Swansea were at this point by far the better side, and it took all of Blues resolve to keep their forwards at bay. Blues best goal attempt came from the boot of Swansea defender Hole, his back pass, being athletically turned round the post by King. This changed the course of the game with both sides now sharing the attacking in a great display of open football.

Blues got the equaliser after 25 minutes following a move started by Warhurst. His pass from midfield gave Purdon the space to chip a pass across the area to Rowley, who from 20 yards struck the ball first time and it flew past King and into the top corner of the net. It was a truly superb strike from a forward who last played for the club 13 months before. Blues had fought back well and a 1-1 scoreline was a fair reflection of both side's efforts when the half-time whistle sounded. The second half was a complete contrast, with Blues taking an early lead and dominating the game from that moment on. The change was inspired by the performance of Ted Purdon highlighted by the goal which proved to be the winner just four minutes after the restart. Following an exchange of passes with Govan he centred the ball to Astall at the far post, from his headed knock down both Purdon and Govan found themselves in the area and unmarked. The latter just missed the ball as he slid in, which left Purdon the chance to lash it into the open goal. From then on all Blues purposeful forward play involved Purdon who was easily the star of the second half. In frustration the Swansea defence reverted to illegal means to stop the inspired Blues forward and this led to some ugly scenes. Blues then further infuriated their hosts by netting a third goal with 15 minutes remaining, this effectively ended the game. A quick throw in by Govan found Rowley in space and able to run forward into the penalty area unchallenged and hammer the ball past a helpless King from 12 yards. With seven minutes remaining tempers boiled over in an extraordinary scene within the Swansea area, a scramble for the ball ended in a free-for-all fight involving everyone bar Merrick at the other end of the field. The referee blew furiously on his whistle to try to restore order and when peace eventually broke out he spoke to several players before play continued. The last remaining minutes took place in a terribly hostile atmosphere with the Blues players being booed by the crowd when any of them received the ball. When the final whistle sounded the teams were quickly sheperded away down the tunnel under a police escort.

SWANSEA TOWN
King, Leavey, Thomas, Beech, Hole, Williams, Medwin, Palmer, Mel Charles, Allchurch, Griffiths.
BIRMINGHAM CITY
Merrick, Hall, Green, Warhurst, Smith, Boyd, Astall, Kinsey, Purdon, Rowley, Govan.

REFEREE
Mr RJ Burges (Reading)

Ken Rowley

Birthdays
Willie Johnston born today 1946.   **Ray Devey born today 1917.**

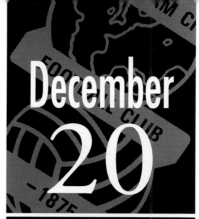
Playing record for this day

Playing record for this day.... 14 games, Won 8, Drawn 4, Lost 2, GF 27, GA 14.

Success rate...71.43% Year ranking....9th

Match of the Day

FROM 1995

BRUM'S MR BIG INSPIRES BLUES' HUGE WIN

Francis double sinks Boro's multi-million pound Premiership side

A big night, in front of a big St Andrews crowd, against Premiership big boys Boro', in Blues biggest game of the season, fittingly was won by Blues biggest local hero, Big Kevin Francis. Blues' 6ft 7in striker blasted Middlesbrough out with two monumental strikes within seven first half minutes.

Blues had threatened to claim a Premiership scalp in this competition for some time, they came desperately close to toppling both Blackburn and Liverpool, indeed it was a pretty close call when these met at the Riverside in the first match when Francis and Donowa near to breaking the stalemate in the closing minutes. Urged on by a vociferous 19,878 crowd, Blues started the better in this game too, their horror show 4-0 defeat at Oldham last time out a distant memory. Blues swept into the lead on 11 minutes after a fine period of intense pressure on the Boro' goal. Claridge who seemed to be everywhere on the pitch, picked off a pass intended for Hendrie from Pollock, and threaded the ball through for Francis to run on to. Collecting the ball and taking a couple of mighty strides forward to put himself clear, he then drove the ball past Walsh's right hand dive and it soared into the corner of the net. St Andrews erupted, but this was nothing compared to the decibel levels recorded after Francis' next goal seven minutes later. Again it was man-of-the-match Claridge who bustled his way through three hesitant defenders to claim a loose ball, taking it on to the byline he sent over a terrific cross to the back post, there was Francis on cue to thump a downward header which bounced and thudded into the roof of the net, Walsh this time left motionless such was the speed of the move and its execution. Blues then settled to a relaxed confident mood and played out the game with little trouble.

Blues 'keeper Ian Bennett was called on to save significant efforts twice in the game, the first from Pollock late in the first half which he made look easy. In the second half he waited patiently up until the 74th minute when he expertly arched backwards to flip Fjortoft's lob over the bar. The victory was expertly summed up by a jubilant Blues boss Barry Fry after the game who said, "I don't think anyone could deny that over 90 minutes we were the better team and deserved to win. I was proud of my lads, they were superb."

BIRMINGHAM CITY

Bennett, Poole, Edwards, Daish, Frain, Hunt, Forsyth (Barnes 87), Claridge, Francis (Donowa 73), Richardson, Hill.

MIDDLESBROUGH

Walsh, Pearson, Vickers, Whyte, Cox, Stamp, Pollock, Fleming (Moore h/t), Fjortoft, Juninho, Hendrie.

REFEREE

Mr M Pierce (Portsmouth)

Kevin Francis

Blues news extra   1941..Wartime friendly West Bromwich Albion 4 Blues 1

Birthdays

Jim Herriot born today 1939.

The Matches played on this day

1902, Division 2.			
Blues 3	Lincoln City 1	Att. 6,000	
Harrison(2), Leonard			
1913, Division 2.			
Blues 0	Leeds City 0	Att. 15,000	
1919, Division 2.			
Grimsby Town 1	Blues 3	Att. 4,000	
	Millard(2), Morgan		
1924, Division 1.			
Manchester City 2	Blues 2	Att. 40,000	
Bradford, Islip			
1930, Division 1.			
Blues 2	Liverpool 0	Att. 18,000	
Bradford, Curtis			
1947, Division 2.			
Barnsley 0	Blues 1	Att. 20,000	
	Bodle		
1952, Division 2.			
Blues 4	Rotherham United 0	Att. 12,000	
Purdon 10			
Murphy 49			
Trigg 70(pen)			
Wardle 79			
1958, Division 1.			
Blues 4	Aston Villa 1	Att. 31,827	
Astall 61(pen)	Hazelden 26		
Jackson 67, 77			
Neal 87			
1975, Division 1.			
Blues 2	Leicester City 1	Att. 21,890	
Francis 44(pen)	Lee 81		
Withe 75			
1980, Division 1.			
Blues 1	Ipswich Town 3	Att. 16,161	
Ainscow 88	Mariner 41		
	Wark 51		
	Brazil 82		
1983, League Cup 4th round.			
Blues 1	Liverpool 1	Att. 17,405	
Harford 74	Souness 30		
1995, League Cup 4th round, replay.			
Blues 2	Middlesbrough 0	Att. 19,878	
Francis 11, 17			
1996, Division 1.			
Southend United 1	Blues 1	Att. 5,100	
Williams 63	Devlin 88		
1997, Division 1.			
Swindon Town 1	Blues 1	Att. 10,334	
Finney 12	Forster 24		

Swindon midfielder Darren Bullock was sent off.

December 21

Playing record for this day
Playing record for this day.... 18 games, Won 9, Drawn 5, Lost 4, GF 36, GA 27.
Success rate....63.89% Year ranking....30th

The Matches played on this day

1889, Football Alliance.

Sheffield Wed. 9	Blues 1	Att. 1,500
	Brayshaw(og)	

Blues fielded just nine players due to sickness and injury succumbed to their joint equal heaviest defeat.
Blues 'keeper Francis Banks made his debut.

1895, Division 1.

Blues 2	WBA 2	Att. 6,000
Bruce, Adlington		

1901, Division 1.

Blues 1	Sheffield Wed. 1	Att. 8,000
Leonard		

1903, FA Cup 2nd round, 2nd replay.

Manchester United 1	Blues 1(n*)	Att. 8,000
	Field	
	After extra time	

Played at Bramall Lane, Sheffield

1907, Division 1.

Blues 2	Sheffield Wed. 1	Att. 5,000
Drake, Jones		

1912, Division 1.

Grimsby Town 2	Blues 2	Att. 5,000
	Robertson, Jones	

1918, Wartime.

Blues 2	Rotherham County 0
Whitehouse, Walker	

1929, Division 1.

Sunderland 1	Blues 3	Att. 14,223
	Hicks, Haywood, Briggs	

1935, Division 1.

Blues 4	Everton 2	Att. 16,994
Jones(og), Harris,		
White, Loughran		

1946, Division 2.

Blues 6	Plymouth 1	Att. 26,000
Bodle(3), Mulraney(2),		
Edwards		

First league meeting v Plymouth

1957, Division 1.

Aston Villa 0	Blues 2	Att. 39,889
	Brown 58	
	Kinsey 74	

Blues complete a league double over Villa, their first since 1905-06

1963, Division 1.

Blues 0	Fulham 0	Att. 13,092

1968, Division 2.

Millwall 1	Blues 3	Att. 11,921
Weller 84	Darrell 54	
	Vincent 66	
	Pickering 88	

Jimmy Greenhoff's 60th minute penalty was saved by Millwall 'keeper King.

1974, Division 1.

Blues 3	Liverpool 1	Att. 26,608
Taylor 30	Toshack 43	
Kendall 45(pen)		
Hatton 90		

1979, Division 2.

Oldham Athletic 1	Blues 0	Att. 6,652
Steel 25		

1985, Division 1.

Blues 1	Chelsea 2	Att. 10,594
Platnauer 80	Hagan(og) 36	
	Nevin 88	

Chelsea's Gerry Murphy sent off after 81 minutes.

1990, Division 3.

Tranmere Rovers 1	Blues 0	Att. 5,034
Irons 4		

1991, Division 3.

Blues 3	Fulham 1	Att. 8,877
Gleghorn 38	Brazil 73	
Rodgerson 72, 78		

Match of the Day

FROM 1974

MISERABLE RUN ENDS IN LAP OF HONOUR

Victory at last for Blues, and in some style too

Blues ended a disappointing run of three succesive defeats with a tremendous win over title hopefuls Liverpool in front of 26,608 jubilant fans at St Andrews.

Blues went into this game making two significant changes to their defensive line-up. Roger Hynd took over from Joe Gallagher in the centre, and he was joined by Garry Pendrey who was promoted from the subs' bench to cover for Malcolm Page, who in turn switched to right back for the absent Ray Martin. This new look defence was hoping to stop an in-form Liverpool side.

Blues made a fantastic start, Taylor shaving the post with his first effort at goal, Thompson almost put through his own net whilst under pressure from Burns, then Blues earned a golden opportunity to take a deserved lead via the penalty spot on 17 minutes. A great ball from midfield put Hatton away and as he burst into the area and shaped to shoot at goal, he was unceremoniously chopped down by a desperate lunge from Hughes. Alan Campbell confidently strode forward to take the kick, with a chance to put Blues ahead for the first time in five games, but it wasn't to be, Clemence guessed correctly, parried the ball, then scrambled it away with his left leg as Campbell raced in for the rebound.

This could have been the turning point of the game for the home team, heads might have dropped, and Liverpool, who so often take full advantage of any let off that goes their way, could have punished them. However, the incident inspired Blues to surge forward with greater intensity, and the crowd put the miss aside to roar them forward. On the half-hour mark their efforts were finally rewarded with a goal. Fittingly it was Campbell who started the move with a fine run which left two Liverpool defenders in his wake before slipping the ball to Taylor, he let fly with a low shot which skimmed along the turf and straight in the corner of Clemence's net.

Now Liverpool retaliated and Blues were soon on the back foot for the first time in the game. Latchford saved well from Toshack, then Cormack, before the latter then struck the post with a 20-yard thunderbolt, all three chances came within six minutes of the opening goal. Birmingham's defence were now hanging on for the half-time interval, and they got to within two minutes of the break before Liverpool finally cracked them open with a textbook move and finish. McDermott ran to the byline and centred a high cross to Toshack who thumped an unstoppable header past Latchford from within the six yard box. Blues responded with one last attack and on the stroke of half time were handed a second penalty. Again it was Hatton who darted into the box and as he took the ball round Clemence the 'keeper brought him down. This time the ball was passed to skipper Howard Kendall, Clemence dived the wrong way and Blues had snatched a dramatic 2-1 lead.

Liverpool again rallied and started the second half in search of a second equaliser. The Blues defence though held firm, led by the hard working Garry Pendrey and Roger Hynd they kept Keegan, Boersma, and Toshack out of harm's way and grew in confidence with each passing minute. Blues then wrapped up the points with a third goal on the stroke of full time, following a free kick conceded by a clumsy tackle on Campbell. Taylor floated the ball into the box where man-of-the-match Bob Hatton rose well to head down and over the dive of Clemence.

BIRMINGHAM CITY
Latchford, Page, Styles, Kendall, Hynd, Pendrey (Hendrie), Campbell, Taylor, Burns, Hatton, Calderwood.
LIVERPOOL
Clemence, Smith, Neal, Thompson, Cormack, Hughes, Keegan, McDermott, Boersma (Heighway), Toshack, Callaghan.

REFEREE
Mr R Crabb (Exeter)

Alan Campbell

Birthdays
Paul Cooper born today 1953.

Playing record for this day

Playing record for this day.... 15 games, Won 7, Drawn 2, Lost 6, GF 19, GA 21.
Success rate...53.33% Year ranking....125th

December 22

Match of the Day

FROM 1928
BRADFORD HAT-TRICK HELPS BEAT LEEDS

5-1 drumming of Leeds first home win in three months

Birmingham gained their first victory in exactly three months with their biggest score of the season in front of 16,057. The well deserved win was down to great play from the entire team, and particularly outstanding was Pike. Missing from the Leeds team was international player Edwards who was suffering from scarlet fever, and this enabled Hart to come back into the squad at centre half.

A brilliant start to the game saw Blues begin on the attack. Shots from Hicks and Briggs were knocked out for corners, and then Crosbie produced a shot from the middle which was destined to hit a Leeds defender. Bradford was in the right position, latched onto the rebound and shot into the net from close range to score the first for Blues.

Leeds tried to equal the score, but their attempts on the left were blocked by Cringan and the danger was averted. Blues took another shot from Bradford, but his aim was misjudged and the ball posed no threat to Leeds. Then Bradford's pass went to Briggs who sent a volley goalwards but it was knocked clear by Potts in the visitors goal. Both ends saw plenty of action and there were super moves between Leslie and Hicks, one of which led to a chance for Pike which was cleared by Potts.

Blues increased their lead on 19 minutes with a joint effort finally hitting the back of the net. A move between Briggs and Crosbie set the ball in motion, and Potts dived low to try and get on to Bradford's shot, but in vain and Blues were 2-0 up. The next effort came from Pike, but his 25-yard strike was wide of the target. Other attempts from both sides came before the break, but none of them proved good enough to hit the back of the net.

After half time the pressure remained from Blues and they were the first on the attack. Leeds soon made up for that by making the home defence work hard to stop the ball going in. Six minutes into the second half an attack on Keetley by Cringan and Smith resulted in a penalty being awarded to Leeds. Wainscoat took his position to take the spot kick which was spectacularly saved by Tremelling with a nifty left move. Then on 55 minutes the visitors pulled one goal back with a shot from Turnbull. Bradford had a shot saved on 62 minutes, but just a minute later Liddell got the ball into the net after a corner kick by Hicks. Hicks then missed a good chance when he shot across the face of the goal, but he made up for it shortly after when Briggs kept the Leeds defence occupied while Hicks sent the ball over the line. On 75 minutes Bradford got his hat-trick, and brought Blues score to five. There were still more efforts from both the teams, but no more goals were to follow.

BIRMINGHAM CITY
Tremelling, Smith, Randle, Liddell, Cringan, Leslie, Briggs, Crosbie, Bradford, Pike, Hicks.
LEEDS UNITED
Potts, Townsley, Menzies, Stacey, Hart, Reed, Turnbull, White Keetley, Wainscoat, Mitchell.

REFEREE
Mr A Josephs (South Shields)

Dan Tremelling

The Matches played on this day
1894, Division 1.
Blues 1   Nottingham Forest 2   Att. 3,000
Mobley
1st league meeting v Nottingham Forest.
1900, Division 2.
Blues 0   Burnley 1   Att. 10,000
1906, Division 1.
Blues 3   Bury 1   Att. 10,000
Mounteney(2), Wigmore
Blues last game at their Muntz Street ground,
they moved to St Andrews playing their first game there on Boxing Day.
Arthur Mounteney had the distinction of scoring Blues last goal at their old ground.
1917, Wartime.
Blues 2   Bradford City 1
McClure, Bowser
1923, Division 1.
Blues 0   WBA 0   Att. 32,000
1928, Division 1.
Blues 5   Leeds United 1   Att. 16,057
Bradford(3), Liddell, Hicks
1934, Division 1.
Everton 2   Blues 0   Att. 20,148
1945, Wartime.
Blues 1   Derby County 0
Bodle
1951, Division 2.
Blues 2   Leicester City 0   Att. 22,500
Briggs 37
Wardle 53
1956, Division 1.
Arsenal 4   Blues 0   Att. 28,644
Evans 10
Holton 15
Watts(og) 54
Smith(og) 72
1962, Division 1.
Leyton Orient 2   Blues 2   Att. 11,646
Musgrove 3   Bloomfield 57, 84
Bolland 25
1973, Division 1.
Ipswich Town 3   Blues 0   Att. 15,289
Lambert 35, 87
Hammond 68
1983, League Cup 4th round, replay.
Liverpool 3   Blues 0   Att. 11,638
Nicholl 36
Rush 62, 75(pen)
1984, Division 2.
Wimbledon 1   Blues 2   Att. 3,674
Fishenden 83   Geddis 15, 25
David Geddis scored twice on his Blues debut.
2001, Division 1.
Blues 1   Walsall 0   Att. 20,127
Purse 14(pen)
Matt Carbon sent off for Walsall in the 79th minute.

December 23

The Matches played on this day

1893, Division 2.
Blues 2   Middlesb. Ironopolis 1   Att. 2,000
Pumfrey, Walton

1899, Division 2.
Burslem Port Vale 3   Blues 0   Att. 1,500

1905, Division 1.
Manchester City 4   Blues 1   Att. 15,000
       Green

1911, Division 2.
Glossop 2   Blues 0   Att. 1,000

1916, Wartime
Sheffield Wed. 0   Blues 2
       Whitehouse, Edwards

1922, Division 1.
Everton 2   Blues 1   Att. 12,000
       Bradford

1933, Division 1.
Huddersfield Town 0   Blues 0   Att. 6,000
Blues Tom Grosvenor broke his leg and the ten men held on
to earn a point.

1944, Wartime.
WBA 1   Blues 4
       Trigg (2), White (2)

1950, Division 2.
Grimsby Town 1   Blues 1   Att. 14,000
Briggs 75   Smith 30

1961, Division 1.
Blues 1   Sheffield Wed. 1   Att. 19,078
Leek 30   Finney 27

1967, Division 2.
Blues 6   Huddersfield Town 1   Att. 26,163
Pickering 38, 67   Worthington 44
Vincent 56
Leggat 60
Vowden 65
Bridges 82

1972, Division 2.
Blues 1   Arsenal 1   Att. 32,721
Bowker 53   Kelly 6
This game shown on ATV's Sunday Star Soccer TV show.

1995, Division 1.
Blues 1   Tranmere Rovers 0   Att. 18,439
Hunt 75

2000, Division 1.
Blues 0   QPR 0   Att. 24,311

Playing record for this day
Playing record for this day.... 14 games, Won 5, Drawn 5, Lost 4, GF 20, GA 17.
Success rate....53.57% Year ranking....121st

Match of the Day

FROM 1967

MERRY CHRISTMAS FROM THE BLUES

With just two days to Christmas Blues delivered the perfect present to the 26,163 fans who braved torrential rain to cheer on their team at St Andrews. It was the third time this season they had rattled in six goals and all of their victims had been from the Yorkshire area, Hull and Middlesborough having both suffered back in September.

Blues went into the game at full strength keeping the same side which had drawn at Bolton the previous week, Huddersfield recalled Roy Ellam and Jimmy McGill to their side after injury and they too started at full strength and eager to gain revenge for the 3-2 loss to Blues in their first game of the season at their Leeds Road ground. The game started in awful conditions as the rain poured down and any attempt at flowing football was almost impossible. Goal chances were rare and when opportunities arose poor finishing by Vowden and Vincent gave the crowd little to cheer. The game however came to life in the 22nd minute when Hockey and Sleeuwenhoek clashed heads when trying to clear a corner, both men left the field for treatment and Blues continued with nine men. Pickering was called back as an emergency centre half before Hockey returned after a few minutes off the field. The reshuffle urged Huddersfield into a more attacking game and Herriott saved well from Hill, then somehow blocked another effort from McGill from close range in a frantic five minute spell. After eight minutes away Sleeuwenhoek returned to his position in defence but Hockey left the field to be replaced by Leggat. With Blues now back to a full complement of players they started to gain control of the game again and soon opened the scoring. A long ball from defence by Murray was neatly controlled then crossed by Vowden, it skidded of fthe wet surface evading keeper Oldfield and Pickering nipped in at the far post to toe poke it in. The lead lasted just six minutes however, Herriot misjudged a swirling cross by Hill and future Blues striker Frank Worthington was left with a simple header into an open goal. The teams went in at half time level at 1-1.

Blues started the second half much more the dominant side and after a few close calls they regained the lead on 55 minutes. Vincent's left-foot shot was deflected onto the bar by the 'keeper and then cleared into touch by the Town defence. From Wylie's quick throw in to Vincent the inside forward turned and struck another sweet left foot shot which this time left Oldfield no chance. During the goal celebrations Sleeuwenhoek still suffering from concussion collapsed again, but continued to play on after receiving more treatment before the restart. Blues now were in total control and five minutes later Vincent's cross was met in his stride by Leggat who almost burst the net. An effort by Bridges narrowly missed the target before a corner was only partially cleared to Vowden who smashed it into the roof of the net with a shot on the turn. Blues completed an amazing goal blitz when Pickering added another just two minutes later, the fourth in 12 minutes. With eight minutes of the game left Blues notched their sixth goal when Leggat's near post cross was nodded in by Bridges and the rout of Huddersfield was complete.

BIRMINGHAM CITY
Herriot, Murray, Green, Wylie, Sleeuwenhoek, Beard, Bridges, Vincent, Pickering, Vowden, Hockey (Leggat 30)
HUDDERSFIELD TOWN
Oldfield, Parkin, Cattlin (Harper 70), Nicholson, Ellam, Meagan, McHale, Dobson, Worthington, McGill, Hill

---

Blues news extra   1959..Friendly Dunfermline 5 Blues 2

Playing record for this day

Playing record for this day.... 10 games, Won 5, Drawn 1, Lost 4, GF 19, GA 16.
Success rate...55% Year ranking...109th.

Match of the Day

FROM 1932

BRADFORD HITS RECORD TALLY

Fifth minute strike beats Bloomer's Derby total, in super 4-0 win

Birmingham striker Joe Bradford became the most prolific goalscorer for one club in Football League history. His fifth minute goal, Birmingham's second brought up a record breaking 233 for the Blues and surpassed Bloomer's previous record of 232 for Derby County. Portsmouth started at full strength cheered on by a few hundred sailors on leave over Christmas who helped make up the 10,000 crowd at St Andrews. Birmingham were forced into one change owing to Cringan's injury, Calladine coming into the side as a replacement. The other changes was to the officials, match referee Mr Lewington of Croydon failed to arrive on time for kick off due to a delayed train and his senior linesman Mr Bourne of Bristol took over for the first five minutes of the game until he arrived at the ground.

Birmingham attacked the Railway End and started in sensational fashion. Just four minutes had passed when Blues were awarded a direct free kick almost on the line of the penalty area following Billy Smith's handball. Stoker took the kick which was charged down but a sliced clearance from Nichol allowed Grosvenor to fire the ball in from close range and give Blues a great start. Seconds later it was 2-0, right back Mackie made the the mistake for the visitors this time as he failed to control the ball properly after intercepting Briggs's pass to Bradford. The Blues striker pounced on the loose ball to smash it past Gilfillan who had advanced out of his goal to collect the back pass. Bradford was mobbed by his team mates as they celebrated his record breaking goal. Midway through the half Gregg, who had been limping for some time, went off for treatment leaving the home side with ten players but still Portsmouth could not find a way through. Gregg was off the field four minutes and with his first touch on resuming struck the bar. Blues next attack saw them increase the lead to 3-0 on 27 minutes, Grosvenor, who had twice had long-range shots blocked by defenders, made it third time lucky when his 20-yard drive flew into the top corner giving Gilfillan no chance.

Blues continued to dominate in the second half and but for some brilliant saves from the Portsmouth 'keeper they could easily have registered a double-figure score. He kept out another effort from Grosvenor early in the second half, and pulled off a quite brilliant piece of goalkeeping to deny Curtis's pile driver from 15 yards on the hour mark. Then on 80 minutes a cross from Briggs was headed powerfully at goal by Bradford only for the 'keeper to somehow fingertip it away. As the ball rolled towards goal Mackie raced back to clear off the line making up for his earlier mistake. However there was no stopping Gregg adding a fourth Birmingham goal with just two minutes of the game remaining to send the St Andrews crowd merrily home with a great Christmas holiday win to cheer.

BIRMINGHAM CITY
Hibbs, Booton, Barkas, Stoker, Morrall, Calladine, Briggs, Grosvenor, Bradford, Gregg, Curtis.
PORTSMOUTH
Gilfillan, Mackie, Billy Smith, Nichol, Allen, Thackeray, Worrall, Jack Smith, Weddle, Easson, Rutherford.

REFEREE
Mr WJ Lewington (Croydon)

Charlie Calladine

Birthdays

Noel Kinsey born today 1925.

Sadly Missed

Don Dorman died today in 1990, aged 76

The Matches played on this day			
1892, Division 2.			
Blues 6	Northwich Victoria 0	Att. 1,000	
Mobley(2), Wheldon(2), Walton, Hands			
1898, Division 2.			
Blues 2	Walsall 1	Att. 6,500	
Gardner, McRoberts			
1910, Division 2.			
Bolton Wanderers 5	Blues 1	Att. 6,000	
	Hall		
1921, Division 1.			
Blues 2	Sheffield United 1	Att. 15,000	
Whitehouse, Lane			
1927, Division 1.			
Derby County 4	Blues 1	Att. 8,000	
	Bradford		
1932, Division 1.			
Blues 4	Portsmouth 0	Att. 10,000	
Grosvenor(2), Bradford, Gregg			
1938, Division 1.			
Sunderland 1	Blues 0	Att. 12,000	
1949, Division 1.			
Blues 1	Stoke City 0	Att. 30,000	
Higgins			
1955, Division 1.			
Blues 0	Sheffield United 2	Att. 23,800	
	Grainger 51		
	Ringstead 89		
1960, Division 1.			
Newcastle United 2	Blues 2	Att. 14,950	
Scanlon 46	Neal 58		
Mitchell 69	Hellawell 75		

December 25

Playing record for this day
Playing record for this day.... 42 games, Won 18, Drawn 6, Lost 18, GF 70, GA 64.
Success rate...50% Year ranking....146th

The Matches played on this day
1889, Football Alliance.

B'ham St George's 4	Blues 1	Att. 5,000
	Heath	

1896, Division 2.

Blues 3	Walsall 3	Att. 7,500
Inglis, Hare, Izon		

1897, Division 2.

Blues 5	Darwen 1	Att. 6,500
Lewis, Abbott(3), Kirton		

1905, Division 1.

Middlesbrough 1	Blues 0	Att. 10,000

1906, Division 1.

Manchester City 1	Blues 0	Att. 24,000

1907, Division 1.

Blues 2	Manchester City 1	Att. 20,000
Eyre, Bluff		

1908, Division 2.

Blues 4	Stockport County 2	Att. 10,000
Chapple(4)		

1909, Division 2.

Glossop 4	Blues 1	Att. 3,000
	Chapple	

1911, Division 2.

Hull City 4	Blues 0	Att. 12,000

1912, Division 2.

Blues 3	Barnsley 1	Att. 35,000
Gardner, Robertson(2)		

1913, Division 2.

Blues 6	Glossop 0	Att. 25,000
Walker(2), Foster,		
Hall(2), Bumphrey		

1914, Division 2.

Blues 1	Bury 0	Att. 20,000
Gibson		

1916, Wartime.

Rotherham County 8	Blues 2	
	Turner(2)	

1917, Wartime.

Blues 0	Leicester Fosse 0	

1918, Wartime.

Blues 0	Leicester Fosse 2	

1919, Division 2.

Leicester City 1	Blues 0	Att. 20,000

1920, Division 2.

West Ham United 1	Blues 1	Att. 37,000
	Bradford	

Joe Bradford scored on his debut.
1922, Division 2.

Blues 0	Huddersfield Town 0	Att. 20,000

1924, Division 1.

Blues 2	Arsena 1	Att. 36,000
Crosbie, Islip		

1925, Division 1.

Blues 3	Tottenham Hotspur 1	Att. 29,568
Bradford(3)		

Match of the Day
FROM 1945
Blues stuff Foxes at Xmas

Blues went into this Football League South game at full strength looking to keep their unbeaten run going into a sixth game against their east midland rivals. Blues stormed into an early lead within minutes of the kick off through a Mulraney shot through a crowded penalty area. They were 2-0 through Jones who converted Dougall's cross, and moments later Jones got a third goal with just 20 minutes played. Leicester never gave up and a neat move allowed Dewis time to snatch a consolation goal on half an hour. Blues just came back stronger and a super passing move between Dougall, Harris and Bodle ended with a cracking shot from Dougall which gave keeper Calvert no chance. Just before the break Leicester pulled another back through Dewis after a mistake between Mitchell and Duckhouse. In a thrilling second half Blues scored two more from Bodle and Edwards to kill the game at 6-2. Indeed they could have had more, shots from Mulraney and Dougall hit the woodwork and at the other end Merrick did extremely well to prevent Dewis from completing a hat-trick with a superb save near the end.

BIRMINGHAM CITY
Merrick, Duckhouse, Jennings, Harris, Turner, Mitchell, Mulraney, Dougall, Jones, Bodle, Edwards.
LEICESTER CITY
Calvert, Frame, Howe, Smith, Grogan, Soo, Revie, Hernon Dewis, Pimbley, Liddle.

REFEREE
Mr W Wood (Bedford)

Birmingham City's Harold Bodle (c) fires in a shot

Blues news extra   1906..Muntz Street's last game and goal

The Birmingham League match between Blues and WBA reserves marked the end of Blues well loved home at Muntz Street. Blues who were two down early on fought back to win 5-2, with the honour of the last goal on the old ground going to Ernie Smith a player signed from Redditch who never made a first team appearance.

The Matches played on this day
1926, Division 1.

West Ham United 1	Blues 0	Att. 30,000

1928, Division 1.

Blues 0	Bolton Wanderers 2	Att. 40,000

1929, Division 1.

Manchester United 0	Blues 0	Att. 18,626

1930, Division 1.

Blues 0	Leeds United 1	Att. 24,991

1931, Division 1.

WBA 0	Blues 1	Att. 38,053
	Curtis	

1933, Division 1.

Sheffield United 2	Blues 1	Att. 20,000
	Roberts	

1934, Division 1.

Sheffield Wed. 2	Blues 1	Att. 23,496
	Mangnall	

1935, Division 1.

Grimsby Town 1	Blues 0	Att. 15,000

1936, Division 1.

Blues 2	Sunderland 0	Att. 15,000
Harris, Jones		

1940, Wartime.

Walsall 6	Blues 3	
	Trigg(3)	

Guest player Jack Rowley scored four times for Walsall
1942, Wartime.

Wolverhampton W. 0	Blues 1	
	Jones	

1943, Wartime.

Blues 0	Wolverhampton W. 3	

1945, Wartime.

Blues 6	Leicester City 2	
Jones(2), Dougall,		
Bodle, Edwards, Mulraney		

1946, Division 2.

Blues 3	Swansea Town 1	Att. 33,000
Dougall, Bodle, Feeney(og)		

1st league meeting v Swansea Town.
1947, Division 2.

Blues 0	Millwall 0	Att. 25,560

1948, Division 1.

Blues 2	Newcastle United 0	Att. 42,000
Trigg, Roberts		

1950, Division 2.

Blues 1	Manchester City 3	Att. 40,064
Trigg		

1951, Division 2.

Blues 4	Rotherham United 0	Att. 28,000
Smith(3), Purdon		

1952, Division 2.

Blues 4	Plymouth Argyle 0	Att. 31,703
Purdon, Murphy(2),		
Stewart		

Kick off delayed whilst a search was made for Plymouth captain John Porteus, eventually he was spotted by ground staff having celebrated the Christmas festivities a little early.
1953, Division 2.

Blues 3	Notts County 0	Att. 30,489
Rowley(2), Govan		

1954, Division 2.

Blues 0	Nottingham Forest 1	Att. 33,500

1956, Division 1.

Blues 4	Sheffield Wed. 0	Att. 24,380
Brown, Murphy,		
Astall, Govan		

December 26

-1875-

The Matches played on this day
1889, Football Alliance.

Grimsby Town 4	Blues 0	Att. 3,000

1891, Football Alliance.

Newton Heath 3	Blues 3	Att. 7,000
	Walton, Wheldon(2)	

1894, Division 1.

Sheffield Wed. 2	Blues 0	Att. 14,000

1895, Division 1.

Blues 1	Burnley 0	Att. 5,500
Adlington		

1898, Division 2.

Blues 5	Blackpool 0	Att. 4,000
Inglis, Walton,		
Abbott(2), McRoberts		

1900, Division 2.

Blues 2	Stockport County 0	Att. 7,000
Aston, McRoberts		

1st league meeting v Stockport.
1901, Division 1.

Aston Villa 1	Blues 0	Att. 40,000

1902, Division 2.

Blues 2	Chesterfield 1	Att. 11,000
Athersmith, Beer		

1903, Division 1.

Notts County 2	Blues 0	Att. 12,000

1904, Division 1.

Middlesbrough 0	Blues 1	Att. 10,000
	McRoberts	

1905, Division 1.

Blues 7	Middlesbrough 0	Att. 10,000
Green(5), Jones,		
Williamson(og)		

1906, Division 1.

Blues 0	Middlesbrough 0	Att. 32,000

The games marked the official opening of St Andrews.
1907, Division 1.

Blues 0	Notts County 0	Att. 28,000

1908, Division 2.

WBA 1	Blues 1	Att. 38,049
	King	

1910, Division 2.

Hull City 4	Blues 1	Att. 9,000
	Hall	

1911, Division 2.

Blues 5	Hull City 1	Att. 10,000
Kidd(2), Millington,		
Hall, Graham		

1912, Division 2.

Blues 1	Bury 2	Att. 8,000
A.W.Smith		

1913, Division 2.

Glossop 4	Blues 1	Att. 5,000
	Walker	

1914, Division 2.

Bury 1	Blues 3	Att. 9,000
	Roulson(2), Windridge	

1916, Wartime.

Blues 1	Rotherham County 3	
Turner		

1917, Wartime.

Leicester Fosse 3	Blues 0	

1918, Wartime.

Leicester Fosse 0	Blues 4	
	Whitehouse(2), J.Godfrey(2)	

1919, Division 2.

Blues 0	Leicester City 1	Att. 20,000

1921, Division 1.

WBA 1	Blues 0	.Att. 49,488

1922, Division 1.

Huddersfield Town 4	Blues 0	Att. 15,000

1923, Division 1.

Blues 3	Manchester City 0	Att. 30,000
Lane, Bradford, Harvey		

1924, Division 1.

Arsenal 0	Blues 1	Att. 40,000
	Islip	

1925, Division 1.

Tottenham Hotspur 2	Blues 1	Att. 44,429
	Bradford	

1927, Division 1.

Blues 1	Sunderland 1	Att. 20,000
Davies		

1928, Division 1.

Bolton Wanderers 6	Blues 2	Att. 20,000
	Pike, Bradford	

1929, Division 1.

Blues 0	Manchester United 1	Att. 35,682

1930, Division 1.

Leeds United 3	Blues 1	Att. 12,381
	Curtis	

Playing record for this day

Playing record for this day.... 84 games, Won 30, Drawn 19, Lost 35 GF 119, GA 119.
Success rate...47.02% Year ranking....186th

Match of the Day
FROM 1958
BOXING DAY BLUES
FOR MAN CITY
No hangover for Blues as they blast in six

Birmingham romped to their biggest win of the season in a scintillating display of attacking football against a very ragged Manchester City side. Following on from their previous big wins at St Andrews against Villa(4-1) and Blackpool(4-2) in succesive games, Blues had now scored 14 in three home games within the last six days. Manchester City in a change strip of gold and black similar to the shirts of Wolves were woefully short and they quickly sank in the St Andrews mud.

Blues made their intentions known as early as the first minute when Larkin's header crashed against the crossbar with the City defence and Trautmann well beaten. This was followed by the best shot of the game when Gordon turned and fired in from 20 yards wide on the right, Trautmann this time just tipping over at the last second at the expense of a corner. Finally Blues pressure was rewarded with a goal, It was Jackson who intercepted a risky pass and stuck a foot in to chip Trautmann, the ball hitting the underside of the bar and dropping over the line despite a last second lunge by full back Brannigan to keep it out. Blues should really have gone in at half time well in front but heroic goalkeeping kept the score down to just two as Birmingham added to their lead five minutes before the break. Neal drove a free kick hard and low into the penalty area and Larkin slid in to toe poke it past Trautmann inside the six yard box.

There was no change after the interval and Blues forced three quick corners in the opening five minutes after the restart. It was only a matter of time before Blues resumed their goal rush and the third came after 62 minutes. Taylor and Astall exchanged passes before Jackson intercepted another in the sequence to stab a foot out and divert the ball in from close range. The fourth goal came on 73 minutes when Gordon's shot bounced awkwardly in front of Trautmann and the ball went in via the keeper's arm. Then a stinging right foot shot from Larkin deflected off Ewing and sent Trautmann the wrong way to make the score 5-0.

For much of the game City had been pegged back in their own half but they broke away with five minutes of the game remaining and from this move they scored. Hannah, with one of his rare touches of the ball, strode forward to cross and the ball was headed in by Barlow. Blues added a sixth goal seconds later through another close range shot, this time from Taylor. The fog then descended and visibility in the last few minutes was very restricted. The 34,263 Blues fans weren't too worried however - they were more than happy with what they had seen and went away in a very happy Christmas holiday mood.

BIRMINGHAM CITY
Merrick, Hall, Allen, Watts, Smith, Neal, Astall, Gordon, Jackson, Larkin, Taylor.
MANCHESTER CITY
Trautmann, Brannigan, Sear, Cheetham, Ewing, Barnes, Fagan, Barlow, Hannah, Hayes, Sambrook.

Tony Want

Match of the Day

FROM 1975
BLUES SPURRED ON

Low crowd increases winter Blues

Blues' first away win of the season arrived today, a late Christmas present for manager Willie Bell and all the supporters who made the trip to White Hart Lane. The win was a result of good work by Blues players and poor play by Tottenham, and the lowest Boxing Day crowd since the war, 21,651, did little to help the home team.

In the 21st minute Blues took the lead when Terry Hibbitt supplied a long ball for Trevor Francis who evaded the Spurs defence to slip the ball into the net. The second goal came just nine minutes later, almost a replica of the first with Francis scoring again.

Francis played a part in the third goal which arrived after the half time break. On 49 minutes he received the ball from Howard Kendall and passed it on to Peter Withe. The Tottenham goalkeeper failed to move off his line in an attempt to block the shot, and Withe made no mistake as the ball went into the net.

Blues remained three goals ahead until the 76th minute when Spurs managed to pull one back with a penalty. The spot kick was awarded because of a handball by Joe Gallagher and Martin Chivers stepped up to do the honours. The goal went a little way towards raising Tottenham's spirits and increasing their efforts. Blues goalkeeper Dave Latchford had to make three terrific saves in the last ten minutes, but Spurs just couldn't break through. They gave up the fight in the end, and allowed Blues to enjoy their victory.

TOTTENHAM HOTSPUR

Jennings, Naylor, McAllister, Pratt, Young, Osgood, McGrath, Perryman, Chivers, Duncan, McNab.

BIRMINGHAM CITY

Latchford, Osborne, Want, Kendall, Gallagher, Burns, Bryant, Francis, Withe, Hatton, Hibbitt.

Trevor Francis

The Matches played on this day

1931, Division 1.		
Blues 1	WBA 0	Att. 57,806
Bradford		
1932, Division 1.		
Newcastle United 2	Blues 1	Att. 43,000
	Curtis	
1933, Division 1.		
Blues 4	Sheffield United 2	Att. 30,000
White, Robertson,		
Roberts, Bradford		
1934, Division 1.		
Sheffield Wed. 4	Blues 0	Att. 24,499
1935, Division 1.		
Blues 1	Grimsby Town 1	Att. 20,000
Guest		
1936, Division 1.		
Portsmouth 2	Blues 1	Att. 33,000
	Jones	
1938, Division 1.		
Blues 2	Middlesbrough 1	Att. 22,000
Morris, Trigg		
1942, Wartime.		
Northampton Town 5	Blues 1	
	McCormick	
1943, Wartime.		
WBA 1	Blues 1	
	Shaw	
1944, Wartime.		
Blues 0	Wolverhampton W. 0	
1945, Wartime.		
Leicester City 0	Blues 1	
	Mulraney	
1946, Division 2.		
Swansea Town 1	Blues 0	Att. 20,000
1949, Division 1.		
Blues 2	Derby County 2	Att. 45,477
Capel, Stewart		
1950, Division 2.		
Blues 1	Manchester City 0	Att. 32,000
Trigg		
1951, Division 2.		
Rotherham United 1	Blues 2	Att. 22,000
	Briggs, Badham	
1953, Division 2.		
Notts County 2	Blues 1	Att. 21,000
	Astall	
1955, Division 1.		
Blues 6	Everton 2	Att. 26,541
Brown(2), Kinsey(3),		
Govan		
1957, Division 1.		
Blues 3	WBA 5	Att. 48,396
Brown, Hooper(pen),		
R.Neal		
1958, Division 1.		
Blues 6	Manchester City 1	Att. 34,263
Jackson(2), Gordon,		
Larkin(2), Taylor		
1959, Division 1.		
Blues 2	West Ham United 0	Att. 29,745
Astall, Hooper		
1960, Division 1.		
Blues 2	Newcastle United 1	Att. 29,435
Bloomfield, Hellawell		
1961, Division 1.		
Blues 1	Manchester City 1	Att. 21,902
Leek		
1964, Division 1.		
Blues 2	West Ham United 1	Att. 23,324
Thwaites, Lynn		
1966, Division 2.		
Blues 3	Northampton Town 0	Att. 24,302
Vincent(2), Vowden		
1967, Division 2.		
Blues 4	Bristol City 1	Att. 40,429
Bridges, Vowden,		
Leggat, Briggs(og)		
1968, Division 2.		
Fulham 2	Blues 0	Att. 13,192
1969, Division 2.		
Blues 2	Blackpool 3	Att. 29,540
James(og), Hateley		
1970, Division 2.		
Blackburn Rovers 2	Blues 2	Att. 8,787
Bowker, Francis		
1972, Division 1.		
Everton 1	Blues 1	Att. 39,363
	B.Latchford	

Bob Latchford netted Blues 100th Boxing Day goal.

December 26

The Matches played on this day

1973, Division 1.
Blues 1   Coventry City 0   Att. 33,423
B.Latchford

1974, Division 1.
Derby County 2   Blues 1   Att. 26,121
                   Hatton

1975, Division 1.
Tottenham Hotspur 1   Blues 3   Att. 21,657
                   Francis(2), Withe

1977, Division 1.
West Ham United 1   Blues 0   Att. 25,572

1978, Division 1.
Wolverhampton W. 2   Blues 1   Att. 26,315
                   Buckley
Wolves first goal scored by Kenny Hibbitt was the 100th conceded by the Blues on Boxing Day Blues full back Mark Dennis was sent off at the end of the game.

1980, Division 1.
Leeds United 0   Blues 0   Att. 19,214

1983, Division 1.
Blues 1   Nottingham Forest 2   Att. 14,482
Rogers

1984, Division 2.
Blues 2   Grimsby Town 1   Att. 14,168
Geddis, Platenauer

1985, Division 1.
Blues 0   Nottingham Forest 1   Att. 10,378

1986, Division 2.
Reading 2   Blues 2   Att. 7,442
           Lynex, Clarke

1987, Division 2.
Blues 0   Plymouth Argyle 1   Att. 9,166

1988, Division 2.
Shrewsbury Town 0   Blues 0   Att. 7,347

1989, Division 3.
Bristol Rovers 0   Blues 0   Att. 6,573

1990, Division 3.
Blues 0   Brentford 2   Att. 6,612
Bretnford reduced to ten men when Kevin Godfrey was sent off.

1991, Division 3.
Darlington 1   Blues 1   Att. 4,421
           Rodgerson

1993, Division 1.
Stoke City 2   Blues 1   Att. 16,584
           Peschisolido

1994, Division 2.
Blues 1   Cambridge United 1   Att. 20,098
Otto
Ricky Otto scored on his Blues debut.

1995, Division 1.
Sheffield United 1   Blues 1   Att. 17,688
           Francis

1997, Division 1.
Ipswich Town 0   Blues 1   Att. 12,459
           McCarthy

1998, Division 1.
Sheffield United 0   Blues 1   Att. 22,005
           Furlong(pen)

1999, Division 1.
Blues 0   Sheffield United 2   Att. 22,874

2000, Division 1.
Blackburn Rovers 2   Blues 1   Att. 24,899
           Purse

2001, Division 1.
Sheffield Wed. 0   Blues 1   Att. 24,335
           Horsfield

The Birmingham City groundsman drives his tractor on to the St Andrews turf as fans work to clear the field from ice and snow

Blues Boxing Day record

At St Andrews;
Played 41, Won 21, Drawn 8, Lost 12, GF 76, GA 45.
Away from Home;
Played 43, Won 9, Drawn 11, Lost 23, GF 43, GA 74.

Playing record for this day

Playing record for this day.... 34 games, Won 9, Drawn 8, Lost 17, GF 46, GA 58.
Success rate...38.24% Year ranking....242nd

Match of the Day
FROM 1982
REJECTS REVENGE IS OH...SO...SWEET!!!

This was Blues biggest win of the season, and it moved them off the bottom of the table, the win was also their first over rivals Villa in two and-a-half years. This made for one of the merriest Christmas's at St Andrews for years. In contrast Villa conceded their 11th goal in four games, and created not one single chance of any note.

Man of the match Ian Handysides was everywhere, without doubt the sole reason why Blues had such an emphatic advantage for 90 minutes. It was his bustling determination which brought about Blake's opening goal on 23 minutes. His shot from inside the area came back off the post and Blake wasted no time in slamming in the rebound from six yards. This brought an almight roar from the kop but an equally deafening silence from the Tilton Road stand.

Handysides continued to terrorise Villa throughout the second half, it was from his work that Blues increased their lead after Walters had scythed him down just outside the area. The free kick was played into Handysides inside the area and he hit a snap shot on the turn. Rimmer parried but the midfielder rushed in to slam the rebound back into the net. Blues were pressing forward again soon after and a third goal came from a stroke of luck no one would have denied them. From a cross from Dave Langan, Jones' attempted clearance hit the sliding Ferguson and nestled nicely in the net. That was that, Villa had been truly beat by their hosts from across the city. A truly fabulous Christmas present.

BIRMINGHAM CITY

Coton, Langan, Van Den Hauwe, Stevenson, Blake, Broadhurst, Dillon, Ferguson, Harford, Curbishley, Handysides.

REFEREE

Mr R Lewis (Great Bookham)

ASTON VILLA

Rimmer, Jones, Williams, Evans, McNaught, Mortimer, Bremner, Shaw, Withe, Cowans, Walters.

Noel Blake

The Matches played on this day

1890, Football Alliance.		
Stoke 4	Blues 2	Att. 3,000
	Short(2)	
1897, Division 2.		
Blues 0	Manchester City 1	Att. 10,000
1898, Division 2.		
Blues 4	Manchester City 1	Att. 10,000
Abbott(2), Inglis, McRoberts		
1902, Division 2.		
Chesterfield 1	Blues 1	Att. 6,000
	McRoberts	
1907, Division 1.		
Notts County 0	Blues 0	Att. 5,000
1909, Division 2.		
WBA 3	Blues 1	Att. 12,104
	Millington	
1910, Division 2.		
Blues 1	WBA 1	Att. 37,520
Hall		
1913, Division 2.		
Bradford Park Ave 5	Blues 1	Att. 8,000
	Morgan	
1919, Division 2.		
Blues 4	Grimsby Town 0	Att. 25,000
Morgan, Elkes, Burkinshaw, Millard(og)		
1920, Division 2.		
Blues 2	West Ham United 0	Att. 60,000
Hampton(2)		
1921, Division 2.		
Blues 0	WBA 2	Att. 44,500
1924, Division 1.		
Everton 2	Blues 1	Att. 30,000
	Islip	
1926, Division 1.		
Blues 0	West Ham United 2	Att. 35,000
1930, Division 1.		
Sheffield United 3	Blues 1	Att. 20,000
	Cringan	
1932, Division 1.		
Blues 1	Newcastle United 2	Att. 40,000
Richardson(og)		
1937, Division 1.		
Blues 2	Liverpool 2	Att. 35,000
Morris, Kendrick		
1938, Division 1.		
Middlesbrough 2	Blues 2	Att. 33,000
	Harris, Phillips	
1939, Wartime.		
WBA 3	Blues 0	
1947, Division 2.		
Blues 1	Millwall 0	Att. 46,000
Goodwin		
1948, Division 1.		
Newcastle United 1	Blues 0	Att. 49,457
1949, Division 1.		
Derby County 4	Blues 1	Att. 37,459
	Brennan	
1952, Division 2.		
Plymouth Argyle 2	Blues 1	Att. 25,050
	Trigg(pen)	
1954, Division 2.		
Nottingham Forest 0	Blues 2	Att. 25,725
	Murphy, Burkitt(og)	
1955, Division 1.		
Everton 5	Blues 1	Att. 42,366
	Astall	
1958, Division 1.		
Manchester City 4	Blues 1	Att. 29,276
	Jackson	
1966, Division 2.		
Northampton Town 2	Blues 1	Att. 15,433
	Bridges	
1969, Division 2.		
QPR 2	Blues 1	Att. 15,688
	Page	
1971, Division 2.		
Blues 3	Cardiff City 0	Att. 40,793
Pendrey, Hatton, Francis		
1975, Division 1.		
Blues 1	Stoke City 1	Att. 37,166
Hatton		
1976, Division 1.		
Blues 0	West Ham United 0	Att. 39,978
1977, Division 1.		
Blues 3	Bristol City 0	Att. 24,110
Gallagher, Towers, Francis		
1980, Division 1.		
Blues 3	Sunderland 2	Att. 19,005
Gemmill, Bertschin, Worthington		

Blues debutant 'keeper Tony Coton saved John Hawley's penalty within seconds of the kick off.

1982, Division 1.		
Blues 3	Aston Villa 0	Att. 43,864
Blake, Handysides, Fergusson		
1983, Division 1.		
Arsenal 1	Blues 1	Att. 25,642
	Hopkins	

Blues full back Jim Hagan suffered a broken cheek bone.

December 28

Playing record for this day
Playing record for this day.... 27 games, Won 7, Drawn 9, Lost 11, GF 27, GA 40.
Success rate...42.59% Year ranking....218th

The Matches played on this day

1889, Football Alliance.

Blues 3	Long Eaton Rangers 1	Att. 2,000
Stanley(2), Pratt		

1901, Division 1.

Notts County 6	Blues 1	Att. 6,000
	Leonard	

1905, Division 1.

Sheffield United 3	Blues 0	Att. 15,000

1907, Division 1.

Bristol City 0	Blues 0	Att. 12,000

1908, Division 2.

Blues 0	WBA 0	Att. 30,035

1909, Division 2.

Blues 0	Bradford Park Ave 1	Att. 15,000

1912, Division 2.

Blues 1	Bradford Park Ave 1	Att. 20,000
Jones		

1914, Division 2.

Blues 3	Nottingham Forest 0	Att. 15,000
A.W.Smith(2, 1pen),		
Hodges		

1925, Division 1.

Huddersfield Town 4	Blues 1	Att. 25,000
	Bradford	

1929, Division 1.

Blues 1	Aston Villa 1	Att. 40,000
Crosbie		

1935, Division 1.

Blues 0	Wolverhampton W. 0	Att. 35,000

1936, Division 1.

Sunderland 4	Blues 0	Att. 15,000

1946, Division 2.

Blues 1	Tottenham Hotspur 0	Att. 44,171
Mulraney		

1957, Division 1.

Blues 3	Chelsea 3	Att. 37,976
Murphy 15, 41	Brabrook 56	
Brown 51	Greaves 73	
	Sillett 85	

1959, Division 1.

West Ham United 3	Blues 1	Att. 26,500
Musgrove 14, 82	Astall 11	
Brett 58		

Blues first defeat at Upton Park for 30 years.

1963, Division 1.

Blues 1	Arsenal 4	Att. 23,329
Harley 21	Baker 14	
	McLeod 20, 81	
	Armstrong 53	

Match of the Day

FROM 1998

ANOTHER COMMANDING WIN

Fortress Gigg Lane swept aside by Blues four goal blast

A tricky away fixture at Gigg Lane was made to look simple by another fine Blues performance. Bury's home record before this match was one of the best in the league. They had collected 24 out of a possible 28 league points at Gigg Lane and feared no one on their own patch. Blues countered this by recording two impressive seven goal hauls in the year and but for some spectacular goalkeeping from Dean Kiely this could well have been the third 'Magnificent 7.' The opening goal on 17 minutes had a familiar ring to it from both sides' point of view. A set piece was poorly defended allowing D'Jaffo to head in unmarked at the near post. On 32 minutes Blues converted a corner of their own, Marsh supplying Furlong to muscle in and head past Kiely for the equaliser. As the huge sigh of relief died down the emotion turned to joy as Blues went ahead two minutes later. A loose ball was picked up by O'Connor who burst forward to drive a low shot wide of Kiely and into the corner. Blues weathered the expected Bury retaliation albeit not convincingly at times until half time, leaving the 7,024 crowd to discuss the possibility of them becoming the third team to win at Bury in 13 attempts this season.

Any doubt was quickly wiped away when from 25 yards out Furlong unleashed a tremendous shot that swerved and whistled through the air before hitting the back of the net just 11 minutes after the restart. At 3-1 up the Blues then took total control of the game. Ndlovu broke free but narrowly missed from an acute angle, before Adebola nodded in Blues fourth to the chants of, 'We Want Seven' from the 2,568 Bluenose army behind the goal. Barring some acrobatic brilliance by Kiely Blues could have delivered even at this late stage. He saved a header from Furlong and somehow finger tipped McCarthy's left-foot screamer over the bar in a matter of moments. The only addition to the score came at the other end, and it was a fortunate one too. Furlong having gone back to defend a corner blocked a rasping shot from James with his arms protecting his face, and an unsympathetic Burns awarded a penalty. D'Jaffo was left to complete the scoring as he had opened it. But Blues had learnt their lesson from previous Gigg Lane visits and at the end had won commandingly by 4-2.

BURY
Kiely, Woodward, Williams, Daws, Lucketti, West, Swailes, Littlejohn, D'Jaffo, Billy, Barrick (James 71).

BIRMINGHAM CITY
Poole, Rowett, Marsh (Grainger 64), O'Connor, Ablett, Johnson, McCarthy (Hughes 73), Adebola, Furlong, Robinson, Ndlovu.

REFEREE
Mr W Burns (Scarborough)

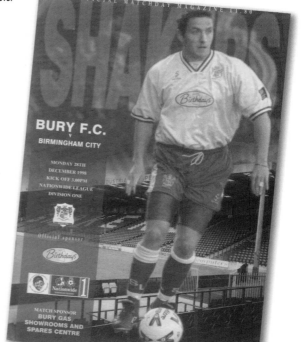

Birthdays
Gordon Taylor born today 1944.

Martin O'Connor

The Matches played on this day
1964, Division 1.

West Ham United 2	Blues 1	Att. 23,800
Byrne 30(pen)	Sharples 12	
Kirkup 73		

Blues first appearance on BBC's Match Of The Day TV show.
.1965, Division 2.

Blues 2	Huddersfield Town 1	Att. 19,750
Thwaites 37	Leighton 4	
Vowden 76		

1974, Division 1.

Blues 0	Ipswich Town 1	Att. 30,266
	Osbourne 1	

1985, Division 1.

Manchester City 1	Blues 1	Att. 24,055
McNab 89	Geddis 15	

1987, Division 2.

Shrewsbury Town 0	Blues 0	Att. 6,397

1991, Division 3.

Bury 1	Blues 0	Att. 4,254
Smith 82		

Bury keeper Kelly saved Nigel Gleghorn's 68th minute penalty.
1993, Division 3.

Blues 2	WBA 0	Att. 28,228
Saville 33(pen)		
Peschisolido 41		

Blues had Dave Barnett sent off after 69 minutes.
1994, Division 2.

Cardiff City 0	Blues 1	Att. 7,420
	Otto 59	

1997, Division 1.

Blues 0	Tranmere Rovers 0	Att. 19,533

1998, Division 1.

Bury 2	Blues 4	Att. 7,024
D'Jaffo 17, 86(pen)	Furlong 32, 56	
	O'Connor 34	
	Adebola 73	

1999, Division 1.

Nottingham Forest 1	Blues 0	
Harewood 81		

December 29

The Matches played on this day

1894, Division 1.
Blues 3   Liverpool 0   Att. 5,000
Mobley, Lewis, Walton

1900, Division 2.
Blues 2   Burslem Port Vale 1   Att. 4,000
McRoberts(2)

1906, Division 1.
Blues 3   Preston North End 0   Att. 20,000
Green(2), Jones
Benny Green sliding through the snow forced the ball in at the far post to score the first goal seen at the St Andrews. He was given a piano by a local business man for the landmark goal .

1917, Wartime.
Bradford City 0   Blues 3
   Morgan(2), Stevens

1918, Wartime.
Bradford City 2   Blues 3
   Whitehouse, Morgan, J.Godfrey

1923, Division 1.
Tottenham Hotspur 1   Blues 1   Att. 25,000
   Bradford(pen)

1928, Division 1.
Manchester City 2   Blues 3   Att. 35,000
   Pike(2), Bradford

1934, Division 1.
Aston Villa 2   Blues 2   Att. 42,000
   Mangnall(2)

1945, Wartime.
Blues 2   Coventry City 0
Edwards, Dougall

1951, Division 2.
Nottingham Forest 0   Blues 1   Att. 24,166
   Briggs 84
Briggs hit the bar twice with two first half shots at goal. Len Boyd was forced to leave the field just before half time with a suspected broken ankle, Blues played the whole of the second half with ten men.

1956, Division 1.
Blues 2   Burnley 0   Att. 32,000
Brown 35
Govan 72

1973, Division 1.
Blues 1   Leeds United 1   Att. 50,451
B.Latchford 21   Jordan 86
This was Leeds United's 23rd league game unbeaten, a record then for a Division One side.
This game screened on BBC's Match of the Day.

1979, Division 2.
Blues 2   Cardiff City 1   Att. 16,682
Worthington 10   Bishop 57
Bertschin 59

1982, Division 1.
Swansea City 0   Blues 0   Att. 11,840

1984, Division 2.
Blues 2   Fulham 2   Att. 11,827
Clarke 46   Hopkins 27
Hopkins 60   Wilson 89

1986, Division 2.
Blues 1   Millwall 1   Att. 8,008
Mortimer 30   Briley 43

1990, Division 3.
Blues 1   Bolton Wanderers 3   Att. 7,318
Bailey 70   Philliskirk 63
   Darby 80
   Reeves 87

2001, Division 1.
Stockport County 0   Blues 3   Att. 5,827
   Vickers 18
   Marcelo 49
   Mooney 76

Playing record for this day
Playing record for this day.... 18 games, Won 11, Drawn 6, Lost 1, GF 35, GA 16.
Success rate...77.78% Year ranking....2nd

Match of the Day
FROM 2001
EDGELEY PARK JINX OVER
Real holiday cheer as Blues bounce back into the top six

Not since Jonathon Hunt's solitary goal had Blues beaten Stockport on their travels and that was back in November 1994. They could, have won by more than the emphatic three goals they rattled in, and now had a nine point maximum haul over the Christmas holiday fortnight.

Blues didn't quite have it all their own way, it was Stockport who had the first chance and they should have opened the scoring within the first minute, McSheffrey missing with a header from barely five yards out with just 50 seconds gone on the clock. Blues got in front on 18 minutes. Steve Vickers fired in his first goal for the club from 15 yards with a low shot into the corner. McCarthy spurned Blues next chance when he created his own opening with a spendid run, the ball rolling wide of the post. At half time the visitors were well worth their slender one-goal advantage.

Blues hopes of an early goal to wrap the game up early in the second half became real on 49 minutes when Marcelo swept the ball in at the second attempt, the first having been blocked. Stockport to their credit responded well and never gave the game up. Flynn was unlucky with a shot which came back off the post with 20 minutes of the game remaining. Then Kenna saved Blues with an excellent defensive tackle having chased the width of the pitch to catch then nick the ball away from Daly. Blues made sure of the points with a peach of a goal from Mooney 14 minutes from time. His first time left-foot shot swerved into the top corner preventing any attempt of a save from Turner in the Stockport goal. A late appeal for a consolation penalty from Taylor, who appeared to be tripped by Woodhouse, was waved away by referee Cowburn, and Blues held on to win 3-0 at the final whistle.

STOCKPORT COUNTY
Turner, Lescott (Taylor 87), Clark (Woodthorpe h/t), Delaney, Flynn, Roger, Briggs, Gibb, McSheffrey (Williams 66), Daly, Welsh.

BIRMINGHAM CITY
Bennett, Kenna, Grainger, O'Connor (Bak 58), Purse, Vickers, McCarthy, Mooney, Horsfield (Hyde 80), Marcelo (Andrew Johnson 69), Woodhouse.

REFEREE
Mr G Cowburn (Blackpool)

Tommy Mooney

Blues news extra 1981..Friendly   Weymouth 1 Blues 3
The game was abandoned after 83 minutes due to a waterlogged pitch. Tony Van Mierlo (2) and Tony Evans got the Blues goals.

1962..Winter wipeout
The Big Freeze started with 42 matches postponed, including Blues' game at St Andrews.

Playing record for this day

Playing record for this day.... 14 games, Won 2, Drawn 1, Lost 11, GF 21, GA 34.

Success rate...17.86% Year ranking....267th

Match of the Day

FROM 1944

TRIGG FIRES BLUES TO COMFORTABLE CUP WIN

Walsall no match for hat-trick hero Cryril Trigg

Birmingham started their League Cup(North) campaign in fine style beating local neighbours Walsall thanks to a superb individual display from striker Cyril Trigg who netted his third hat-trick of the 1944-45 season. Blues started the game with Sidney King deputising in goal for Gil Merrick as the latter was off getting married on the morning of the game. They also welcomed back Trigg after two games out with injury and the fast improving Harold Bodle made a rare appearance in the starting line-up as his partner. Walsall had former Blues and Irish international winger Jackie Brown in their team as they kicked off towards the Tilton Road end.

It was the visitors who started the better and they could have taken the lead on several occasions but for some wayward finishing. The home side grateful of the let offs soon took control and had the lead midway through the first half with Trigg's first goal, never looking back after that. Trigg added two more in the second half completing his hat-trick with a thumping header from Bright's corner. Walsall gained some consolation with a late goal scored by Boonham but it was never likely to affect the result. Blues winning comfortably 3-1 at the finish.

BIRMINGHAM CITY

King, Jennings Hughes, Dearson, Turner, Shaw,
Mulraney, Small, Trigg, Bodle, Bright.

WALSALL

Billingsley, Shelton, Male, Lewis, Rist, Lowery,
Brown, Mulligan, Boonham, Lycett, Alsop.

REFEREE

Mr GS Blackhall (Wednesbury)

Cyril Trigg

The Matches played on this day

1893, Division 2.

Blues 6	Lincoln City 0	Att. 1,000

Devey, Wheldon(2), Mobley, Hands, Walton

1899, Division 2.

Walsall 1	Blues 0	Att. 3,000

1905, Division 1.

Preston North End 3	Blues 0	Att. 15,000

1911, Division 2.

Bradford Park Ave 3	Blues 0	Att. 14,000

1916, Wartime.

Blues 1	Bradford Park Ave 2

Bell

1922, Division 1.

Sunderland 5	Blues 3	Att. 10,000
	Bradford, Whitehouse(2)	

1933, Division 1.

Blues 0	Arsenal 0	Att. 34,771

1939, Wartime.

Coventry City 4	Blues 2
	Broome, Bodle

Played at Leamington

1944, Wartime.

Blues 3	Walsall 1

Trigg(3)

1950, Division 2.

Blues 1	Notts County 4	Att. 33,000
Stewart 20	Sewell 33, 73	
	Crooks 44, 87	

1967, Division 2.

Bristol City 3	Blues 1	Att. 23,493
Crowe 44	Vincent 62	
Galley 47, 84		

1972, Division 1.

Blues 1	Ipswich Town 2	Att. 32,705
Hatton 65	Johnson 6	
	Hamilton 19	

1978, Division 1.

Arsenal 3	Blues 1	Att. 27,877
Stapleton 15	Francis 44(pen)	
Rice 52		
Sunderland 71		

Trevor Francis's 133rd and last goal for the Blues.

1989, Division 3.

Notts County 3	Blues 2	Att. 7,786
Palmer 21	Atkins 13(pen)	
Johnson 27	Yates 74	
Lund 78		

December 31

Playing record for this day

Playing record for this day.... 16 games, Won 5, Drawn 5, Lost 6, GF 33, GA 31.
Success rate...46.88% Year ranking....189th

Match of the Day
FROM 1994
BLACKPOOL HIT FOR SEVEN
Blues see out the year in emphatic style

Blues made it 11 wins from 13 games the 18,025 St Andrews crowd wild with a magnificent 7-1 win over Blackpool, this after going a goal behind early on in the game.

Blues made three changes to the side that beat Cardiff last time out, bringing them back to full strength. Liam Daish returned to central defence in place of David Howell, and Louie Donowa took over from Neil Doherty. Barry Fry's third change took everyone by surprise when he recalled Kenny Lowe for his first start since the opening day defeat at Orient. Blackpool remained unchanged with their attack-minded side led by Sam Allardyce. It promised to be an open attacking game, and so it was. It was Blackpool who broke up the early Blues pressure and hit them on the break as early as the eighth minute, Bradshaw taking advantage of a rare defensive lapse to nip in and fire past a helpless Ian Bennett from close range. The shock however proved the perfect wake-up call for Blues as they roared back with an equaliser. It came from Bradshaw again just four minutes later when he was unlucky to deflect an innocuous looking cross past his own 'keeper, and for the second consecutive game at St Andrews a player had the dubious record of having scored, for both sides, equalling Ricky Otto's feat against Cambridge on Boxing Day.

The game became a frantic end-to-end thriller, and it was Blues who took the lead for the first time on 25 minutes, Donowa beating Brown on the wing to race clear and smash a rising shot from just inside the area, which flew past Capleton and into the roof of the net. Blues kept up their battering of the Blackpool goal and 12 minutes later they increased the lead to 3-1 when Claridge hit a superb shot from 30 yards. Despite the constant wave of non-stop Birmingham raids the score remained the same at the interval, and the players left to a fantastic reception from a genuinely appreciative crowd.

Nothing changed after the restart and soon Blues were peppering the Blackpool goal in search of more goals. It took just eight minutes to find the first, Otto crossed to the far post for Lowe who cleverly looped his header high and back across goal, and the ball dropped into the far corner of the net. Blues were now running riot, on 64 minutes Lowe turned to goal provider, when his cheeky back heeled pass rolled perfectly into the path of the unmarked Donowa, who tapped in number five. Now the Blues performance was exhibition like as they calmly knocked the ball about with everyone in the side looking to do a "Lowe" at almost every opportunity. On 73 minutes McGavin, who was on as substitute for Mark Ward, sent Claridge free with another well executed back-heeled pass, as Capleton rushed out at the striker's feet, the striker deftly chipped the ball over him for a 6-1 lead. Then with just four minutes remaining, Blues other substitute George Parris tapped in from close range after another free for all in the Blackpool penalty area, and Birmingham gained their biggest league win since back in 1959.

BIRMINGHAM CITY
Bennett, Poole, Whyte (Parris), Barnett, Daish, Lowe, Cooper, Ward (McGavin), Donowa, Claridge, Otto,
BLACKPOOL
Capleton, Brown (Horner), Burke, Gouck, Murphy, Bradshaw, Quinn, Mellon, Watson, Ellis, Mitchell,

REFEREE
Mr J Rushton (Stoke-on-Trent)

Ricky Otto

Birthdays

Steve Bruce born today 1960.   Kevin Ashley born today 1968.